# Benchmark Papers in Electrical Engineering and Computer Science

Series Editor: John B. Thomas
Princeton University

**Published Volumes**

SYSTEM SENSITIVITY ANALYSIS
J. B. Cruz, Jr.
RANDOM PROCESSES: Multiplicity Theory and Canonical Decompositions
Anthony Ephremides and John B. Thomas
ALGEBRAIC CODING THEORY: History and Development
Ian F. Blake
PATTERN RECOGNITION: Introduction and Foundations
Jack Sklansky
COMPUTER-AIDED CIRCUIT DESIGN: Simulation and Optimization
S. W. Director
ENVIRONMENTAL MODELING: Analysis and Management
Douglas Daetz and Richard H. Pantell
AUTOMATIC CONTROL: Classical Linear Theory
George J. Thaler
CIRCUIT THEORY: Foundations and Classical Contributions
M. E. Van Valkenburg
DATA COMMUNICATION: Fundamentals of Baseband Transmission
L. E. Franks
NONLINEAR SYSTEMS: Processing of Random Signals—Classical Analysis
A. H. Haddad
RANDOM PROCESSES, II: Poisson and Jump-Point Processes
Anthony Ephremides

Additional Volumes in Preparation

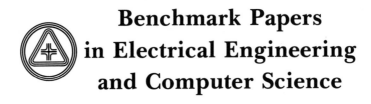

Benchmark Papers
in Electrical Engineering
and Computer Science / 11

A *BENCHMARK* ® Books Series

# RANDOM PROCESSES, II

## Poisson and Jump-Point Processes

Edited by
**ANTHONY EPHREMIDES**
*University of Maryland*

Dowden, Hutchinson & Ross, Inc.
Stroudsburg, Pennsylvania

Distributed by
**HALSTED PRESS** *A Division of John Wiley & Sons, Inc.*

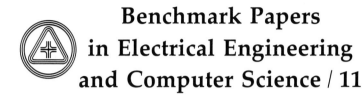

Benchmark Papers in Electrical Engineering and Computer Science, Volume 11
Library of Congress Catalog Card Number: 75-1287
ISBN: 0-470-24334-1



77 76 75 1 2 3 4 5

Manufactured in the United States of America.

LIBRARY OF CONGRESS CATALOGING IN PUBLICATION DATA

Ephremides, Anthony, comp.
Random processes, II: poisson and jump point processes.

(Benchmark papers in electrical engineering and computer science; v. 11)
Includes bibliographical references and indexes.
1. Point processes--Addresses, essays, lectures.
I. Title.
QA274.42.E63 519.2'3 75-1287
ISBN 0-470-24334-1

Exclusive Distributor: **Halsted Press**
A Division of John Wiley & Sons, Inc.

# Permissions

The following papers have been reprinted with the permission of the authors and copyright holders.

ACADEMIC PRESS, INC.—*Information and Control*
The Spectral Analysis of Impulse Processes
On the Statistics of Random Pulse Processes

INSTITUTE OF ELECTRICAL AND ELECTRONICS ENGINEERS, INC.—*IEEE Transactions of Information Theory*
Communication Under the Poisson Regime
Filtering and Detection for Doubly Stochastic Poisson Processes
Information Rates for Poisson Sequences
Level Crossings of Nondifferentiable Shot Processes
Regular Point Processes and Their Detection
Smoothing for Doubly Stochastic Poisson Processes

JOHN WILEY & SONS, INC.—*Stochastic Point Processes*
Point Processes Generated by Level Crossings

UNIVERSITY OF CALIFORNIA PRESS—*Proceedings of the Sixth Berkeley Symposium on Mathematical Statistics and Probability*
On Basic Results of Point Process Theory
Multivariate Point Processes
Nonhomogeneous Poisson Fields of Random Lines with Applications to Traffic Flow

# Series Editor's Preface

The Benchmark Series in Electrical Engineering and Computer Science is aimed at sifting, organizing, and making readily accessible to the reader the vast literature that has accumulated. Although the series is not intended as a complete substitute for a study of this literature, it will serve at least three major critical purposes. In the first place, it provides a practical point of entry into a given area of research. Each volume offers an expert's selection of the critical papers on a given topic as well as his views on its structure, development, and present status. In the second place, the series provides a convenient and time-saving means for study in areas related to but not contiguous with one's principal interests. Last, but by no means least, the series allows the collection, in a particularly compact and convenient form, of the major works on which present research activities and interests are based.

Each volume in the series has been collected, organized, and edited by an authority in the area to which it pertains. To present a unified view of the area, the volume editor has prepared an introduction to the subject, has included his comments on each article, and has provided a subject index to facilitate access to the papers.

We believe that this series will provide a manageable working library of the most important technical articles in electrical engineering and computer science. We hope that it will be equally valuable to students, teachers, and researchers.

This volume, *Random Processes: Poisson and Jump-Point Processes,* has been edited by Professor Anthony Ephremides of the University of Maryland. It contains fourteen papers developing the theory of point and jump processes with particular emphasis on the application of such processes to problems of estimation, detection, filtering, and control. The papers are all of recent date, the oldest having been published in 1968. In fact, the last two articles have appeared previously only as technical reports, reflecting the topicality of the area and its current importance in communications and control.

John B. Thomas

# Contents

# Contents by Author

# Introduction

Over the last few decades the theory of point processes has been developed, primarily as a result of investigations of queueing problems, inventory analysis, and population dynamics by operation researchers and statisticians. In these early stages of development the area of point processes was characterized by a strong emphasis on heuristic techniques centered around the Poisson model and was geared toward practical solutions to special problems. However, the applicability of the point-process model to a very large number of disciplines eventually triggered additional investigations by engineers and applied mathematicians.

In engineering the model became attractive in the analysis of telephone traffic. With the growth of biomedical engineering disciplines, point processes were used to model neural spike trains. In communications the analysis of impulsive noise and of photon detector systems for laser and optical transmission required the use of such processes.

The objective in these new engineering applications was the usual one of optimal design. Optimization in the environment of point processes proved to be a difficult, nonlinear problem, because, except for special cases of filtered Poisson processes that allowed use of the central limit theorem, these could not be approximated by processes of Gaussian or near-Gaussian statistics.

In recent years, in addition to continued investigations of practical and applied problems, a great deal of research has been done on the fundamental questions of the structure of point processes and their general properties. The convenient Poisson model, which has been used extensively due to its mathematical tractability, has been generalized and still remains an important special case. Efforts by theoretically oriented engineers have focused on optimization, which, depending on the context of the associated problem, may involve likelihood-ratio computations, rate-parameter estimation, information-theoretic considerations such as limits and bounds on coding capabilities, and a number of related questions. On the other hand, the approach of applied mathematicians and theoretical statisticians has been toward the derivation and analysis of the fundamental generating mechanisms of point processes, the implications of these mechanisms, and their generalization.

The area of point processes is, in a sense, still in its nascent stage. Although a number of practical techniques and basic theoretical results that are available today show the first signs of a solid basis for a coherent, unified theory, the lack of any monograph or textbook on the subject, and the continuation of diversified and often not closely related investigations in the various disciplines, show that the theory has not yet reached maturity. It is rather difficult for a scientist today to get acquainted with the "theory" of point processes. The available results are scattered widely in the literature, and the terminology used varies considerably, depending on the discipline, and is not even uniform within the same discipline. For example, in the rather specialized problem of detection in optical communications, a Poisson process whose photon intensity (number of photons per unit time) is a random process is called either a compound Poisson process or a doubly stochastic Poisson process.

This lack of cohesion is one of the reasons for assembling the present collection of papers. The selection process has probably been more difficult than it would have been in a more well-developed and more unified branch of random process theory. The size and number of research papers on point processes is formidable, particularly so in journals oriented toward operations research. An effort has been made to maintain a balance of representation of the different disciplines, as well as of both theoretical and applied results. By and large, though, the main criterion has been the significance of the results and the landmark nature of the paper. Unavoidably, the space constraint has made it necessary to omit some of the application disciplines, such as biomedical engineering and operations research. On the other hand, in these areas, one may argue that results concerning point processes have been generally applied directly or have been heuristically modified for use in specialized problems. Nevertheless, it should be noted that the papers included in this volume, although slightly biased toward electrical engineering applications, do bridge various disciplines and should convey the flavor and the significance of the general theory. There are only two other general introductions to this are [1, 2] available, to which the present collection should be a useful complement.

The general organization of this volume is as follows: In the first paper the basic model for communications at optical frequencies via Poisson photon arrivals is described. The next three papers generalize the model of the point process to that of a regular point process and then, by superposing a Markov transition chain on it, to that of a jump process. The mathematical sophistication rises considerably with these generalizations, but the central subject of the papers is still optimal detection, filtering, and smoothing. The fifth paper considers the information-carrying capabilities of Poisson sequences, thus completing the communications picture in the sense of formulating the questions and problems generated by the generalized Poisson models for the underlying observation processes but by no means completely solving them. These five papers have a natural unity and their landmark character lies in the fact that a solid foundation is provided for a rigorous derivation of optimal receivers in a non-Gaussian environment. Furthermore, these papers provide an inductive introduction to the mathematics necessary if one departs from the simple Poisson model.

The next three papers, although again oriented toward communications problems, do not consider explicitly the jump-process models; instead they use some of the models and tools most commonly encountered in the statistical rather than the probabilistic approach to randomness. In this sense they provide a smooth transition to the next few papers, which are drawn from the statistical literature. In particular, Paper 6 deals with the spectral analysis of impulse processes. Paper 7 is concerned more with the general statistics of random pulse processes. Paper 8 studies shot-noise processes generated by the model of level crossings of an ordinary random process. This model is the subject of the immediately following paper by Leadbetter. Although the mathematics used in Papers 6 through 8 is less complex than in the first five, the papers provide intuitively motivated new ideas for analyzing impulsive noise processes in some communications applications.

The next group of papers, numbered nine through twelve, represent landmark samples from the statistical literature on point processes. Although not directly concerned with engineering problems, they bear considerably on them by building an expanded theoretical framework for point processes. For example, Paper 9 studies the generation of point processes by level crossings of an ordinary process, an approach that is also used in Paper 8, but in the context of a specific application. Paper 10 provides a collection of fundamental results in the theory of point-process structure. Papers 11 and 12 develop the theory of multivariate point processes and line processes or Poisson random fields, respectively.

The last two papers represent, in a sense, the arrival at a summit. At the time of this writing they were available only in technical-report form. They do bring together under a unified model most of the kinds of point processes considered before and explain their basic nature as martingales or as stochastic integrals on martingales. They are essentially the two constituent parts of a single work that develops the martingale representation and then looks at its consequences and applications. Many questions are left unanswered and the solutions to some problems are not in suitably simple forms. However, they provide a set of rigorous, unified, and quite general representation results that can be used by engineers in communications, automatic control, and biomedical research, as well as by operations researchers and statisticians.

It should be noted that all the papers in this collection have been published in the last ten years, the majority in the last five. This is another indication of the recent development of point-process theory. It is often difficult to judge the significance of contemporary work and achievement. Therefore, it goes without saying that the personal bias of the editor is reflected in the selection and that other people may not agree entirely with the selection. Nevertheless, the collection should at least partially fill a gap and will prove useful as an introduction and state-of-the-art picture for the increasing number of investigators who engage in the study of the theory and application of random point processes.

The selected papers tend to revolve around engineering problems such as the filtering, detection, and estimation of point processes in the optical frequency environment (Papers 1 through 5, 13, 14) and the analysis and statistical description of shot processes in sampling, modulation, and photon-detector systems (Papers 6 through 8). In addition, a few papers from the statistical literature are included (Papers 9 through

12) which provide additional theoretical background for the understanding of the point-process model.

The chronological order of the papers has been slightly altered to provide conceptual continuity.

## References

1. P. A. W. Lewis (ed.), *Stochastic Point Processes* (Proceedings of a conference at IBM). Wiley, New York, 1972.
2. D. L. Snyder, *Stochastic Point Processes*. Wiley-Interscience, New York (in press).

# I

# Poisson Models in Communications

# Editor's Comments on Paper 1

1 **Bar-David:** *Communication Under the Poisson Regime*

At optical frequencies the classical approach to optimal detection and estimation of a signal in noise fails to work satisfactorily. The quantum nature of electromagnetic radiation has to be taken into account. In addition to the purely quantum theory of detection and estimation that is presently under development, a semiclassical theory has been developed that takes into account the photon energy packets of which the received field consists [1, 2]. The use of a point process as a model for the photon-arrival pattern at the counter is the basis for this paper. The process is assumed to be time-varying (nonstationary) Poisson. Maximum-likelihood signal amplitude estimation and detection probabilities are obtained. The development depends on the assumption of incoherent reception.

This paper, although assuming a somewhat restrictive model for the underlying Poisson process, is the first detailed mathematical treatment of the subject and one of the first that borrow and expand on the model of point processes in communications engineering.

## References


1. C. W. Helstrom, The detection and resolution of optical signals, *IEEE Trans. Inform. Theory,* **IT-10**, 275–287 (Oct. 1964).
2. Special issue of the *IEEE Proceedings on Optical Communications,* Oct. 1970.

# 1



Reprinted from *IEEE Trans. Inform. Theory,* **IT-15**(1), 31–37 (1969)

# Communication under the Poisson Regime

ISRAEL BAR-DAVID, MEMBER, IEEE

***Abstract*—By "Poisson regime" we mean a model in which intelligence is communicated by random discrete occurrences in time that obey Poisson statistics of arbitrarily time-varying mean, as for example when modulated electromagnetic radiation and background radiation at optical frequencies is incoherently detected by photon-sensitive surfaces.**

**The problems of optimal detection of signals of arbitrary shape and of the estimation of signal amplitude and delay are treated under a maximum-likelihood criterion. Detection probabilities, delay estimation errors, and the probability of "noise threshold" in delay estimation, are derived. Some results are basically different from those of parallel problems treating known signals in Gaussian noise.**

**The treatment is based on a representation of nonstationary Poisson processes in which the observables are the instants of the occurrences rather than their numbers in given intervals of time.**

## I. Introduction

In this paper the following mathematical model is analyzed. During a given time interval $(-T, +T)$, a realization of a Poisson point process of time-varying expectation $\lambda(t)$ is observed. The realization consists in general of randomly distributed points $t_j$, $|t_j| \leq T$, $j = 1, 2, \cdots, M$, with $M$ itself a random variable. Two different, though related, cases are considered. The first is a decision problem. It is assumed that $\lambda(t)$ can assume one of two possible a priori known functional forms, $\lambda_0(t)$ and $\lambda_1(t)$ corresponding, repectively, to the different hypotheses $H_0$ and $H_1$. It is required to decide between the two hypotheses on the basis of the observed points, $t_j$. The second case is an estimation problem. It is assumed that the expectation $\lambda(t : \alpha)$ depends on an additional parameter $\alpha$, the functional form of $\lambda(t : \alpha)$ being known in both $t$ and $\alpha$. It is required to estimate the parameter $\alpha$, again, on the basis of the observed points.

Both problems are solved in principle for arbitrary expectation functions $\lambda$, under a maximum-likelihood criterion. Expressions for the probability of correct decision and for the variance of the time-delay estimate are derived. The possibility of gross errors in the delay estimate is described by the probability of "threshold," and an upper-bounding expression for it is derived.

The solution is based on a representation of Poisson processes of time-varying expectation in which the observables are the instants of the occurrences $t_j$, rather than the number of occurrences in any specified interval. The $M$-dimensional joint probability density function of the $t_j$, derived in the next section, enables the description of the likelihood function in terms of these observables.

In optical communication systems, in which incident radiation is intercepted by means of photon-sensitive devices, the emission of the photoelectrons corresponds to the point process in the model introduced above. It has been shown [1] that if the transmitted beam is generated by a single-mode laser, the beam fluctuations, and hence the photoelectron count, obey Poisson statistics. Furthermore, the expectation of the count varies as the signal that modulates the laser beam, when noise is absent, and as the signal plus the noise average when noise is also present. The noise is due mainly to detector dark current and background radiation, which are also thought to obey Poisson statistics. Thermal (Gaussian) noise is usually negligible, in particular when high-gain photomultiplier tubes are used as detectors.

It should, however, be realized that if the transmitted beam is due to several interacting laser modes or, in extreme cases, to incoherent sources, the probability distribution of the photoelectron count is an average over Poisson distributions [1] and is not necessarily Poisson itself. In such cases, the model introduced previously only approximates the physical situation. Another limitation of the model is that it assumes accurate observation of the instants of electron emissions. Actually, slight variations (of the order of $10^{-11}$ seconds) exist in the outputs of some devices, notably of high-gain photomultiplier tubes. An attempt is presently being made to account for such variations in a more elaborate model.

Previous treatments [2], [3], [4] of the photon communication problem were restricted to cases in which the transmitted signal energy is piecewise constant. Imposing such a restriction enables the use of a number of photoelectrons in the subintervals of constant $\lambda$ as the observables of the process. A serious drawback in such a treatment is that delay can be estimated only up to the length of the subintervals. The representation of the Poisson processes in terms of the instants of arrival introduced in this paper enables the treatment of arbitrary signals. Some of the results of this paper, pertaining to the decision problem, can, however, also be obtained by proper interpretation of the previous results in the limit of vanishing lengths of the constant-$\lambda$ subintervals. This point is further discussed in Section III.

## II. A Representation of Poisson Processes

### *Probability Density Functions*

Given a Poisson process with time-varying expectation $\lambda(t) \geq 0$, the probability $P[k, (a, b)]$ that the number of occurrences in the time interval $(a, b)$ equals the integer $k$ is [5]

$$P[k, (a, b)] = \left\{\exp\left[-\int_a^b \lambda(t)\,dt\right]\right\}\cdot\left[\int_a^b \lambda(t)\,dt\right]^k/k!\,. \tag{1}$$

Manuscript received February 9, 1968; revised August 9, 1968.
The author is with the Scientific Department, Israel Ministry of Defense, Haifa, Israel.

A complete description of the process over an interval $(-T, +T)$, using (1), is obtained only by considering all possible partitions, $-T = a_0 < a_1 \cdots < a_K = T$ and observing the number of occurrences in each of intervals $(a_i, a_{i+1})$, $i = 0, 1, \cdots, K-1$. To cover all possibilities, $K$ would have to become infinitely large. An alternative representation, which seems to be natural for this process, uses the instants $t_j$ of the occurrences as the observables. One obvious advantage is that there are only a finite number of such instants.

One recalls that for the derivation of (1), the following axioms are postulated.

1) The probability of one occurrence in an infinitesimal interval $\Delta t$, $P[1, \Delta t]$, is given by

$$P[1, \Delta t] = \lambda(t)\,\Delta t, \qquad \Delta t \to 0. \tag{2}$$

2) The probability of more than one occurrence in $\Delta t$ is zero for $\Delta t \to 0$.
3) The number of occurrences in any interval is independent of those in all other disjoint intervals.

In particular, for $k = 0$, (1) reduces to

$$P[0, (a, b)] = \exp\left[-\int_a^b \lambda(t)\,dt\right]. \tag{3}$$

Consider now a possible realization of the process, as in Fig. 1. Denote by $\{t_M\}$ the set of $M$ numbers $-T \le t_1 < t_2 < \cdots < T_M \le T$. The $M$-dimensional joint probability density function $p\{t_M\}$ of such a realization can be calculated by first allowing infinitesimal intervals of width $\pm\,\Delta t_j/2$ about $t_j$, $j = 1, 2, \cdots, M$. The probability that one and only one point would fall within each one of these intervals and none outside them is $p\{t_M\}\,\Delta t_1\,\Delta t_2 \cdots \Delta t_M$ and is given by (2) and condition (3). Thus,

$$\begin{aligned} p\{t_M\}\,\Delta t_1\,\Delta t_2 \cdots \Delta t_M &= P[0, (-T, t_1 - \tfrac{1}{2}\Delta t_1)] \\ &\quad \cdot \lambda(t_1)\,\Delta t_1 \cdot P[0, (t_1 + \tfrac{1}{2}\Delta t_1, t_2 - \tfrac{1}{2}\Delta t_2)] \cdots \\ &\quad \cdot \lambda(t_M)\,\Delta t_M\, P[0, (t_M + \tfrac{1}{2}\Delta t_M, T)]. \end{aligned}$$

Using (3) in the limit of $\Delta t_j \to 0$, for all $j$, one obtains, for $M \ge 1$,

$$p\{t_M\} = e^{-Q} \prod_{j=1}^{M} \lambda(t_j), \qquad -T \le t_1 < t_2 \cdots < t_M \le T, \tag{4}$$

where $Q$ is given by

$$Q = \int_{-T}^{T} \lambda(t)\,dt. \tag{5}$$

If $M = 0$, $\{t_M\}$ is empty, i.e., no occurrence is observed, and by (3),

$$P[0, (-T, T)] = e^{-Q} \tag{6}$$

Thus, for $M = 0$, if $p\{t_M\}$ is interpreted as the probability of no occurrence and $\prod_{j=1}^{M} \lambda(t_j)$ is interpreted as 1, then (4) holds for all $M$ and provides a complete statistical description of the Poisson process in the interval $(-T, +T)$.

It should be pointed out that $p\{t_M\}$ is *not* a conditional density function since $M$ itself is a random variable.[1] The sample space of events is illustrated in Fig. 2, where $\Omega_M$ denotes the set of all possible sets $\{t_M\}$, $\Omega_0$ the event of no occurrence in $(-T, +T)$ and $\Omega$ the sure event, i.e., the event that any number of points occured at any instants in the interval $(-T, T)$. In particular, if the process is stationary and $\lambda(t) = \bar{k}$ is the constant mean, then all sample sequences of $M$ occurrences within the interval $(-T, +T)$, are equally likely, with a joint probability *density* given by

$$p\{t_M\} = (\bar{k})^M \exp(-2\bar{k}T). \tag{7}$$

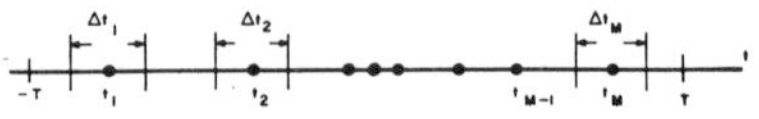

Fig. 1. A sample realization of a point process.

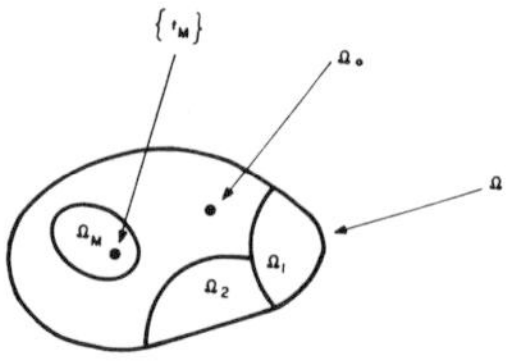


Fig. 2. The sample space of events.

*Expectation of Product Functions*

Of interest in what follows are expectations of product functions $f_\pi(\{t_M\})$, which are defined here by means of a function $f(t)$, as follows.

$$\begin{aligned} f_\pi(\{t_M\}) &= \prod_{j=1}^{M} f(t_j), \qquad j = 1, 2, \cdots, M, \quad M \ge 1 \\ &= 1, \qquad M = 0. \end{aligned} \tag{8}$$

Symbolically,

$$\begin{aligned} E[f_\pi] &= \int_\Omega p\{t_M\} \prod_{j=1}^{M} f(t_j) \\ &= \sum_{M=0}^{\infty} \int_{\Omega_M} p\{t_M\} \prod_{j=1}^{M} f(t_j) \triangleq \sum_{0}^{\infty} E_M(f_\pi). \end{aligned}$$

Using (4), the $M$th summand becomes

$$E_M[f_\pi] = \int_{-T}^{T} \int_{t_1}^{T} \cdots \int_{t_{M-1}}^{T} dt_1\,dt_2 \cdots dt_M \cdot p\{t_M\} \prod_{j=1}^{M} f(t_j) \tag{9}$$

$$= e^{-Q} \int_{-T}^{T} \int_{t_1}^{T} \cdots \int_{t_{M-1}}^{T} dt_1\,dt_2 \cdots dt_M \prod_{j=1}^{M} g(t_j), \tag{10}$$

where $g(t)$ is defined by

$$g(t) = f(t)\lambda(t).$$

[1] The conditional density function appears in (14).

The $M$-fold integral is over a region that is $(1/M!)$ of the hypercube $-T < t_j < T$, all $j$. By permuting the indices another integral of equal value over a similar, albeit different, region is obtained. By adding the $M!$ similarly obtained integrals one obtains

$$e^{-Q} \int_{-T}^{T} \int_{-T}^{T} \cdots \int_{-T}^{T} dt_1\, dt_2 \cdots dt_M \prod_{j=1}^{M} g(t_j) = e^{-Q} G^M(T)$$

where

$$G(T) = \int_{-T}^{T} g(t)\, dt. \tag{11}$$

Thus,[2]

$$E_M[f_\pi] = \frac{e^{-Q} G^M(T)}{M!}. \tag{12}$$

Finally,

$$E[f_\pi] = e^{-Q} \sum_{0}^{\infty} \frac{G^M(T)}{M!} = e^{-Q+G(T)} \tag{13}$$

In particular, if $f(t) = 1$, then $E_M[1] =$ probability of $\Omega_M$, i.e., the probability of exactly $M$ occurrences in the interval $(-T, +T)$. Indeed, from (11), $G(T) = Q$ and (12) reduces to (1), providing an alternative derivation of the latter. Also the expectation in (13) becomes the probability of the sure event and equals 1.

### *Conditional Probabilities*

The event $[\{t_M\}, M]$, i.e., that a given sequence $\{t_M\}$ occurs simultaneously with a total of $M$ occurrences in the interval $(-T, T)$, is evidently included in the event $\Omega_M$. Therefore the joint density function $p_J[\{t_M\}, M]$ equals

$$p_J[\{t_M\}, M] = p\{t_M\},$$

Also, evidently, the conditional probability of $\Omega_M$ given $\{t_M\}$ is

$$\Pr[M \mid \{t_M\}] = 1.$$

On the other hand, the conditional density function $p_c$, is the ratio of (4) and (12), with $G(T) = Q$:

$$p_c[\{t_M\} \mid M] = Q^{-M} M! \prod_{j=1}^{M} \lambda(t_j). \tag{14}$$

In the particular case that $\lambda(t) = \bar{k}$

$$p_c[\{t_M\} \mid M] = (2\bar{k}T)^{-M} M!\, \bar{k}^M = (2T)^{-M} M! \tag{15}$$

is uniform overall $\Omega_M$.

## III. The Decision Problem[3]

### *Decision Functions*

Let $\{t_M\}$ be, as before, the representation of the observed sample, assumed to be a realization of either of two Poisson processes. Under hypothesis $H_k$ the mean is $\lambda_k(t)$, its integral is $Q_k$, and the probability law is $p_k\{t_M\}$, $k = 0, 1$.

[2] This simplified proof has been suggested by the Editor. A different proof is given in [11].

[3] For a discussion of the philosophy of decision methods see [6].

Basing the decision between the two hypotheses on comparison of the likelihood ratio $L = p_1\{t_M\}/p_0\{t_M\}$ with a threshold $\gamma_L$, one has from (4),

$$L = e^{-(Q_1 - Q_0)} \prod_{j=1}^{M} \frac{\lambda_1(t_j)}{\lambda_0(t_j)} \gtrless \gamma_L. \tag{16}$$

It is assumed that the ratio $\lambda_1(t)/\lambda_0(t)$ is a finite number for all $t$.

It is assumed temporarily that during the interval of interest neither process has zero mean. The singular cases of zero-valued means are considered in a later section. The logarithm being a monotone function, the above is equivalent to

$$G \triangleq \log L + (Q_1 - Q_0)$$
$$= \sum_{j=1}^{M} \log \frac{\lambda_1(t_j)}{\lambda_0(t_j)} \gtrless \gamma_G \triangleq \log \gamma_L + (Q_1 - Q_0). \tag{17}$$

In particular, if costs and a priori probabilities are equal, $\gamma_L = 1$, and $\gamma_G = (Q_1 - Q_0)$. The implementation of the decision function $G$ is as follows: The time function

$$v(t) = \log \frac{\lambda_1(t)}{\lambda_0(t)}, \tag{18}$$

which is defined because by definition $\lambda_k(t)$ are nonnegative and by assumption nonzero, is generated locally and fed into a sampler that is operated at the instants $t_j$, as in Fig. 3(a). In a noncoherent optical communication channel, $t_j$ is the time when an electron is emitted at a photocathode. If the electrical pulse caused by such an emission is sufficiently narrow, i.e., if the band of the output circuit of the photomultiplier tube (PMT) is much wider than that of $v(t)$, then each electron causes an output signal that approximates a Dirac impulse. Then the above is equivalent to a correlation between the "received signal,"

$$r(t) = \sum_{j=1}^{M} \delta(t - t_j)$$

and $v(t)$, and it can be implemented either as a correlation receiver or as a time-invariant filter with impulse response $h(t) = v(T - t)$, Fig. 3(b). The particular case of communicating binary data over such a link can correspond to

$H_0$ : noise alone $\rightarrow \lambda_0(t) = \bar{n}$,
where $\bar{n}$ is the average of noise (background) photons,

$H_1$ : signal plus noise $\rightarrow \lambda_1(t) = \bar{n} + s(t)$,
where $s(t)$ is the shape of the envelope of the transmitted light pulse.

Then

$$v(t) = \log\left(\frac{n + s(t)}{\bar{n}}\right) = \log\left(1 + \frac{s(t)}{\bar{n}}\right). \tag{19}$$

For small SNR

$$v(t) \simeq \frac{s(t)}{\bar{n}}, \tag{20}$$

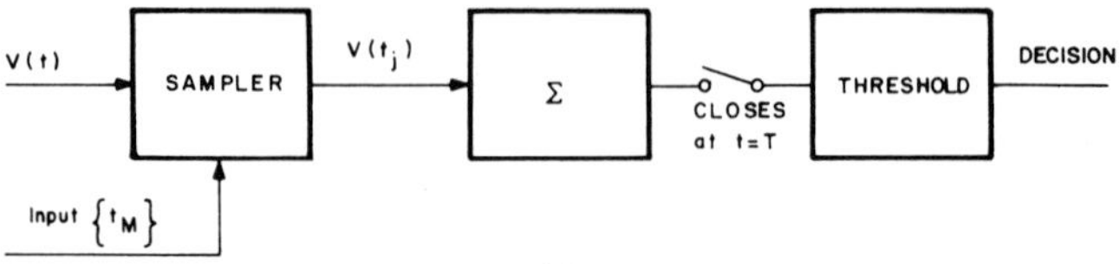

(a)

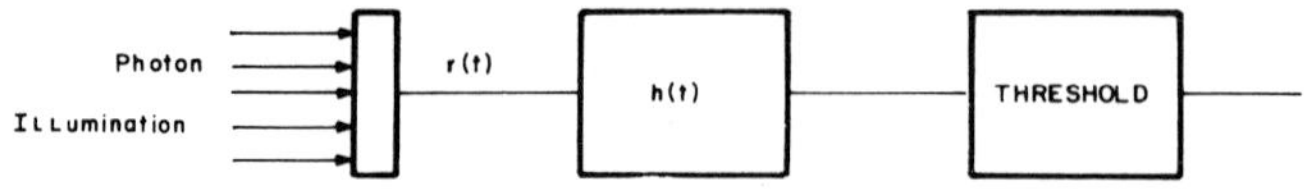

(b)

Fig. 3. Maximum-likelihood receiver: (a) correlation type, (b) matched-filter type.

which indicates a matched-filter receiver. For large SNR, however, logarithmic weighting is required. If $\lambda_1(t)$ and $\lambda_0(t)$ are both piecewise constant in $(-T, T)$, then there can be found subintervals $(t_k, t_{k+1})$ $k = 1, 2, \cdots, K$ such that both $\lambda_i(t)$ are constant within them, say $\lambda_{ik}$. Then the decision function $G$ of (17) reduces to

$$\sum_{j=1}^{M} \log \frac{\lambda_1(t_j)}{\lambda_0(t_j)} = \sum_{k=1}^{K} n_k \log \frac{\lambda_{1k}}{\lambda_{0k}} \tag{21}$$

where $n_k$ is the number of occurrences in the $k$th such interval, indicating that the set of $n_k$ is a sufficient statistic and observation of the set $\{t_M\}$ is not required. Equation (21) has been previously derived [2], by considering at the outset the piecewise constant case. On the basis of this result a processing scheme was suggested that first counts the number of occurrences $n_k$ in each subinterval and then performs the digital convolutions of (21). The generally valid schemes of Fig. 3, which require no counting, evidently cover such situations as well.

On the other hand the result (17), of this paper could be obtained from (2) by the following argument. Assume that $K \to \infty$, in such a way that the width of each subinterval $(t_k, t_{k+1}) \to 0$. Then, by axiom 2) of Section II, $n_k$ is either 0 or 1, and those $t_k$ that correspond to $n_k = 1$ denote the instants of occurrences, hence the set $\{t_M\}$. Then the test statistic (21) becomes

$$\sum_{k:n_k=1} \log \frac{\lambda_1(t_k)}{\lambda_0(t_k)} = \sum_{j=1}^{M} \log \frac{\lambda_1(t_j)}{\lambda_0(t_j)}, \qquad j = 1, 2, \cdots, M, \tag{22}$$

where the set $\{t_M\} = \{t_1, t_2, \cdots, t_i, \cdots, t_M\}$ denotes the infinitesimal intervals at which $n_k = 1$, as before. An analogous derivation has been used by Helstrom [8] for a spatial optical signal.

### *Decision Probabilities*

These can be calculated by deriving a Gram–Charlier series [7] for the distribution of the test statistic $G$. The cummulants $\chi_i$ of the distribution of $G$, which appear in this series, are given by

$$\chi_i = \int_{-T}^{T} \lambda_k(t) \log (\lambda_1(t)/\lambda_0(t))^i \, dt, \tag{23}$$

where the index $k = 0, 1$ denotes the two hypotheses. This result is obtained from the characteristic function $H_G(ix)$ of $G$,

$$H_G(ix) = E[\exp (ixG)]$$
$$= E\left\{\prod_{j=1}^{M} \exp \{ix \log [\lambda_1(t_j)/\lambda_0(t_j)]\}\right\}, \tag{24}$$

which, upon using (13), reduces to

$$H_G(ix) = \exp \left\{-Q_k + \int_{-T}^{T} \lambda_k(t)[\lambda_1(t)/\lambda_0(t)]^{ix} \, dt\right\}. \tag{25}$$

The influence of the third-order term in the Gram–Charlier series, in a typical case where $\lambda_1(t) = e^2\lambda_0(t)$, is seen from the corresponding correction term in the probability of correct decision, $P_D = 1 - 0.274 - 0.010 + \cdots$, [11].

### *Singular Cases*

If either $\lambda_1(t)$, or $\lambda_0(t)$, is zero over any finite subinterval, the test statistic can be modified so as to be itself zero over each such subinterval:

$$G_{\text{mod}}(t) = 0, \qquad t \text{ such that } \lambda_0(t) \text{ or } \lambda_1(t) = 0$$
$$= G(t), \quad \text{otherwise.}$$

If no occurence is recorded during these subintervals, $G_{\text{mod}}$ serves perfectly. If, however, an occurrence is recorded during the subinterval in which either $\lambda_k$ vanishes, evidently the alternative hypothesis holds with probability 1. The probability of such an event can be easily calculated.

## IV. Signal Parameter Estimation

Let the time-varying mean value of the process depend on a parameter $\alpha$ as follows.

$$\lambda(t : \alpha) = s(t, \alpha) + \lambda_n, \tag{26}$$

where the signal part $s(t, \alpha)$ is a known function of both $t$ and $\alpha$ and $\lambda_n$ is a constant, representing the average noise power. Let $\{t_M\}$ be the set of the observables, as before, and $Q(\alpha) = \int_{-T}^{T} \lambda(t : \alpha) \, dt$. Then the likelihood function is

$$p\{t_M\} = e^{-Q(\alpha)} \prod_{j=1}^{M} [s(t_j, \alpha) + \lambda_n]. \tag{27}$$

The maximum-likelihood estimate $\hat{\alpha}$ is that value of $\alpha$ that maximizes the above expression or, equivalently, that yields

$$\max_{\alpha} \left[ \sum_{i=1}^{M} \log (s(t_i, \alpha) + \lambda_n) - Q(\alpha) \right]. \tag{28}$$

A search procedure is in general required for the estimate $\hat{\alpha}$.

Assuming that $s(t, \alpha)$ is piecewise differentiable and denoting the derivative with respect to $\alpha$ by an upper dot, one obtains the following for $\hat{\alpha}$:

$$\sum_{i=1}^{M} \frac{\dot{s}(t_i, \alpha)}{\lambda_n + s(t_i, \alpha)} = \dot{Q}(\alpha). \tag{29}$$

A simple example is that of transmission of the parameter by amplitude modulation: $s(t, \alpha) = \alpha\lambda_0(t)$, with $\int_{-T}^{T} \lambda_0(t)\, dt = 1$. Then

$$\sum_{i=1}^{M} \frac{\lambda_0(t_i)}{\hat{\alpha}\lambda_0(t_i) + \lambda_n} = 1, \tag{30}$$

which is an algebraic equation of power $M$. An approximate solution is obtained by assuming high SNR,

$$\hat{\alpha} \simeq M - \frac{1}{M} \sum_{1}^{M} \frac{\lambda_n}{\lambda_0(t_i)}. \tag{31}$$

The above is exact if $\lambda_0(t)$ is constant within $(-T, T)$. Then also $\hat{\alpha} = M - \lambda_n/\lambda_0$, so that the number $M$ alone is a sufficient statistic for estimation of the parameter.

### *Pulse Position Modulation—Estimation of Delay*

This case is of considerable interest in a noncoherent communication link as well as in distance measurements. The parameter $\alpha$ is delay time $\tau$, and the signal can be written $s(t - \tau)$. Assuming that the signal duration $(\tau - D, \tau + D)$ is very short compared with the interval of a priori incertitude, and neglecting end effects (i.e., values of $\tau$ near $T$), $\dot{Q}(\tau) = 0$. Then the logarithm of the likelihood function (27), here denoted by $F(\tau)$, becomes

$$F(\tau) = \sum_{i} \log [s(t_i - \tau) + \lambda_n] \tag{32}$$

The search for $\hat{\tau}$ that yields a maximum of $F(\tau)$ can be mechanized by constructing the time function

$$v(t) = \log (s(t) + \lambda_n), \tag{33}$$

or the time function

$$q(t) = \dot{s}(t)/(\lambda_n + s(t)) \tag{34}$$

and passing impulses through a filter matched to either $v(t)$ or $q(t)$ at the instants $t_i$ of the occurrences (as in Fig. 3). The instants at which the outputs pass, respectively, through a maximum or a zero yield, in principle, the estimate $\hat{\tau}$. Several maxima or zero crossings, respectively, of the outputs of the filters may, however, be due to the noise process, yielding ambiguities in location of the estimate. One has to pick, therefore, the maximum, or the zero crossing, that appears in the neighborhood of the "strongest" reception, i.e., where the occurrences are densest. An erroneous decision as to this neighborhood causes an error which is very large compared with the error involved in locating the maximum, or the zero crossing, in its correct neighborhood. The probability $P_t$ of such an erroneous decision has been called the "threshold" probability [9], [10]. It is shown in the Appendix that $P_t$ for the assumed Poisson regime, is bounded above by the following expression

$$P_t \leq \frac{T}{2D} \left( \frac{2Q_n}{Q_D + Q_n} \right)^{1/2} \cdot \exp \{ -(Q_D + Q_n) + 2(2Q_n(Q_D + Q_n))^{1/2} \} \tag{35}$$

where

$$Q_n = 2D\lambda_n \quad \text{and} \quad Q_D = \int_{-D}^{D} s(t)\, dt$$

are, respectively, the expectations of the number of occurrences due to noise and to signal within the interval $(-D, +D)$ of signal duration. The bound increases linearly with the number of signal "bins" $T/D$ and decreases nearly exponentially with $Q_D$, with considerable similarity to the parallel case of known signal in Gaussian noise [9], [10]. As a numerical example, if $Q_D = 20$, $Q_n = 1$ and $T = 1000\, D$, then $P_t < 0.02$. For a tighter bound the double sum in (59) in the Appendix must be evaluated.

Assuming, now, that the maximum that has been selected *is* in the correct neighborhood, the variance of the estimator $\hat{\tau}$ can be approximated in terms of the first two derivatives of $F(\tau)$, calculated at the true value of the delay, $\tau_0$. This method of calculation has been used in similar problems [6, ch. VIII], [8], [9]. Thus, if $F(\tau)$ is twice differentiable about $\tau_0$, then $\dot{F}(\tau)$ can be expressed as

$$\dot{F}(\tau) = \dot{F}(\tau_0) + (\tau - \tau_0)\ddot{F}(\tau_0) + \cdots. \tag{36}$$

By the definition of $\hat{\tau}$,

$$0 = \dot{F}(\hat{\tau}) = \dot{F}(\tau_0) + (\hat{\tau} - \tau_0)\ddot{F}(\tau_0) + \cdots,$$

from which it follows that, provided $F''(\tau_0)$ does not vanish,[4]

$$\epsilon_\tau \triangleq \hat{\tau} - \tau_0 \doteq -\frac{\dot{F}(\tau_0)}{\ddot{F}(\tau_0)}.$$

It will be shown below that the mean of the numerator is zero; then letting $\dot{F}(\tau_0) = f_n$ and $\ddot{F}(\tau_0) = f_d + m_d$, where $m_d$ is the mean of $\ddot{F}(\tau_0)$, and assuming that $f_d \ll m_d$ with high probability, one can write

$$\epsilon_\tau = -\frac{f_n}{m_d + f_d} \doteq -\frac{f_n}{m_d}\left(1 - \frac{f_d}{m_d}\right), \tag{38}$$

whence it follows that

$$\overline{\epsilon_\tau^2} \doteq \frac{\overline{f_n^2}}{m_d^2} - 2\frac{\overline{f_n^2 f_d}}{m_d^3} + \frac{\overline{f_n^2 f_d^2}}{m_d^4}.$$

[4] Owing to the nature of $F(\tau)$, (32), this requirement excludes strictly flat-topped signals from the analysis. This is discussed in more detail in [11].

By the above assumption, $m_d^2 \gg \overline{f_d^2}$, so that the last two terms are negligible and

$$\overline{\epsilon_\tau^2} \doteq \frac{\overline{f_n^2}}{m_d^2}. \tag{40}$$

The characteristic functions of $\dot{F}(\tau_0)$ and $\ddot{F}(\tau_0)$ are, respectively,

$$E\left[\exp\left\{ix \sum_{i=1}^{M} \frac{\dot{s}(t_i - \tau_0)}{s(t_i - \tau_0) + \lambda_n}\right\}\right];$$

$$E\left[\exp\left\{ix \sum_{i=1}^{M} \frac{d}{d\tau} \frac{s(t_i - \tau_0)}{s(t_i - \tau_0) + \lambda_n}\right\}\right],$$

and can be evaluated using (13). Differentiating twice the results of the evaluations, the following expressions are obtained for the moments:

$$m_n = \int_{-T}^{T} \dot{s}(t)\, dt,$$

$$\overline{f_n^2} = m_d = -\int_{-T}^{T} (s(t) + \lambda_n) \frac{d}{dt}\left[\frac{\dot{s}(t)}{s(t) + \lambda_n}\right] dt,$$

$$\overline{f_d^2} = \int_{-T}^{T} (s(t) + \lambda_n)\left(\frac{d}{dt}\left[\frac{\dot{s}(t)}{s(t) + \lambda_n}\right]\right)^2 dt. \tag{41}$$

(Having set $\tau_0 = 0$ does not involve any loss in generality if end effects are neglected.) Evidently $m_n = 0$ and $\overline{f_d^2}/m_d^2$ goes to zero, as $s(t)$ increases, justifying the approximations. Finally from (40) and (41), one obtains

$$\overline{\epsilon_\tau^2} \doteq \frac{1}{m_d} = \left[\int_{-T}^{T} \frac{[\dot{s}(t)]^2}{s(t) + \lambda_n}\, dt\right]^{-1}, \tag{42}$$

where it has been assumed that pulse-type signals are used for which $s(\pm T) = \dot{s}(\pm T) = 0$.

According to the basic requirement that $\lambda(t) > 0$, one can set $s(t) = Qa^2(t)$, where $Q > 0$ denotes the total energy in the signal, if the normalizing constraint $\int_{-T}^{T} a^2(t)\, dt = 1$ is added. Then,

$$\overline{\epsilon_\tau^2} \doteq \left[4Q \int_{-T}^{T} (\dot{a}(t))^2 \frac{Qa^2(t)}{\lambda_n + Qa^2(t)}\, dt\right]^{-1} \tag{43}$$

For sufficiently large $Q$, the fractional term in the integral is close to 1 whenever $a(t)$ is nonzero. Then the integral is recognized as the square of the effective bandwidth of $a(t)$, usually denoted by $W_a$. Thus,

$$\overline{\epsilon_\tau^2} \doteq \tfrac{1}{4} Q^{-1} W_a^{-2} \tag{44}$$

which resembles somewhat the familiar result in the estimation problem involving a known signal in Gaussian noise, except that here $Q$ is the total energy in the signal, and not the SNR, indicating that the error has a finite nonzero value even in the case of vanishing noise. This behavior is due, of course. to the random nature of the signal process. In optical communication terminology such a situation is referred to as being *photon-limited.*

The problem of signal design is, nevertheless, the same as in the classical case; the square of any *real* large bandwidth signal $a(t)$ that would be used to amplitude-modulate an RF carrier can be used to modulate the energy of the laser beam. Phase-modulating (complex) $a(t)$ are of course excluded by the requirement that $s(t)$ be positive, reflecting the lack of sensitivity of photon detectors to the phase of the radiation.

Whenever peak-power constraints exist, the tendency to increase the effective bandwidth by using amplitude modulation alone leads by necessity to a signal made up of a sequence of nonoverlaping pulses. A sequence of $K$ identical pulses has the same effective bandwidth, but $K$ times the energy, of each elementary pulse. From (44), the improvement in $\overline{\epsilon^2}$ is, then, linear in $K$. Ostensibly, the same improvement results from averaging $K$ independent measurements, such as could be obtained by checking the $K$ maxima of the output of a filter "matched" (as prescribed by (34)) to one of the elementary pulses. The loss in using such a suboptimal processing scheme is apparent, first in the increase in the threshold probability, (35), which is nearly exponential in the total energy involved in any single measurement, and second in the increase in the error due to neglected terms in (43).

As a last point of interest, if a bell-shaped signal is used, e.g., $s(t) = Q(2\pi D^2)^{-1/2} \exp(-1/2\, t^2/D^2)$, then, for large $Q$, (29) yields $\hat{\tau} \doteq (1/M) \sum_1^M t_i$, i.e., the estimate of the delay is at the center of gravity of the observed times of emission. In this particular case, it can be shown by direct calculation [11], that (44) holds down to low values of signal energy.

## V. Conclusion

By using the instant-of-occurrence representation of Poisson processes, expressions for optimal decision and estimation procedures and their performance have been obtained. Unlike the cases of known signals in Gaussian noise, in which the performance of the system depends only on certain functionals of the transmitted wave form, e.g., total energy, equivalent bandwidth, etc., in the Poisson cases signal shape also influences the detectability. Even in the ideal noiseless situation the random nature of the received signal restricts the variance of the delay estimate to a finite value that depends on the expected number of occurrences, i.e., on signal energy. Such a result was to be expected considering that what has been modeled is a photon in which the quantum nature of the radiation sets a bound on the accuracy of delay measurement. The results on the probability of threshold have a strong similarity to the classical case.

## Appendix

### The Noise Threshold

The noise threshold, as defined in Section IV, is reached whenever another interval of length $2D$, disjoint from the interval in which the true delay is located, is chosen in order to estimate the delay within its limits. This happens whenever there is an interval of length $2D$ in $(-T, +T)$ such that it includes more points than does the correct interval. The probability $P_t$ ($t$ stands for threshold) of such an event is overbounded by

$$P_t \leq \sum_{k=0}^{\infty} P_1(k)P_2(k)$$

where $P_1(k) \equiv$ Pr [$k$ points in the proper interval] and $P_2(k) \equiv$ Pr [there is an interval of length $2D$ in the domain $(-T, +T)$ in which the number of points due to noise alone is larger than $k$]. This expression is an upper bound since the event of which $P_2(k)$ is the probability includes also the possibility that the number is larger than $k$ within the proper interval of width $2D$. This bound is, however, very tight since if there is a threshold problem at all, $T \gg D$. By (1),

$$P_1(k) = \exp(-Q_p)\, Q_p^k/k!, \quad Q_p \triangleq Q_D + Q_n,\ Q_n = 2D\lambda_n.$$

To calculate $P_2(k)$, assume first that in the interval $(-T, T)$ there are exactly $M$ points due to the noise of uniform mean $\lambda_n$. The probability of such an event is

$$P[M, (-T, T)] = \exp(-Q_N)\, Q_N^M/M!; \quad Q_N \triangleq Q_n T/D$$

The probability that exactly 2 points out of these $M$ be within $2D$ of each other somewhere in $(-T, T)$ is trivially overbounded by $(2D/T)$, if $M = 2$, and by $(2D/T)\binom{M}{2}$ if $M \geq 2$ and the probability that $m$ points out of $M$ be so close is by induction overbounded by $(2D/T)^{m-1}\binom{M}{m}$. Lifting the condition of a total of $M$ points yields

$$\Pr[m \text{ points within } (-D, D) \text{ somewhere in } (-T, T)]$$

$$\leq \sum_{M=m}^{\infty} e^{-Q_N} \frac{Q_N^M}{M!}\left(\frac{2D}{T}\right)^{m-1} \frac{M!}{(M-m)!\, m!}$$

$$= e^{-Q_N}\left(\frac{2D}{T}\right)^{m-1} \frac{Q_N^m}{m!} \sum_{M=m}^{\infty} \frac{Q_N^{M-m}}{(M-m)!} = \left(\frac{2D}{T}\right)^{m-1} \frac{Q_N^m}{m!}$$

$$= \frac{T}{2D}\frac{2^m Q_n^m}{m!}.$$

$P_2(k)$ is overbounded by summing this result over all $m$ larger than $k$,

$$P_2(k) < \frac{T}{2D} \sum_{k+1}^{\infty} \frac{(2Q_n)^m}{m!} \tag{58}$$

and therefore

$$P_t \leq \frac{T}{2D} [\exp(-Q_p)] \sum_{k=0}^{\infty} \frac{Q_p^k}{k!} \sum_{k+1}^{\infty} \frac{(2Q_n)^m}{m!}. \tag{59}$$

Using a Chernov-type upper bound,

$$P_t \leq \frac{T}{2D} e^{-Q_p} \sum_{k=0}^{\infty} \frac{Q_p^k}{k!} \sum_{0}^{\infty} \frac{(2Q_n)^m}{m!} c^{m-(k+1)}, \qquad c \geq 1$$

$$= \frac{T}{2D} e^{-Q_p} \frac{1}{c} e^{2cQ_n + Q_p/c}.$$

Minimizing the exponent over all possible values of $c \geq 1$, one has $c = (Q_p/2Q_n)^{1/2}$ from where (35) follows. This value of $c$ is larger than 1 whenever $Q_D > Q_n$.

## Acknowledgment

The author is pleased to acknowledge interesting discussions on photon receivers with I. Ziskind.

## References

[1] L. Mandel and E. Wolf, "Coherence properties of optical fields," *Rev. Mod. Phys.*, vol. 37, pp. 231–287, April 1965. L. Mandel, "Phenomenological theory of laser beam fluctuations and beam mixing," *Phys. Re.*, vol. 138, pp. B753–B762, May 1965.
[2] B. Reiffen and H. Sherman, "An optimum demodulator for Poisson processes: Photon source detectors," *Proc. IEEE*, vol. 51, pp. 1316–1320, October 1963.
[3] K. Abend, "Optimum photon detection," *IEEE Trans. Information Theory (Correspondence)*, vol. IT-12, pp. 64–65, January 1966.
[4] T. F. Curran and M. Ross, "Optimum detection thresholds in optical communications," *Proc. IEEE (Correspondence)*, vol. 53, pp. 1770–1771, November 1965.
[5] A. Papoulis, *Probability, Random Variables, and Stochastic Processes.* New York: McGraw-Hill, 1965, p. 74.
[6] C. W. Helstrom, *Statistical Theory of Signal Detection.* London: Pergamon, 1960, ch. 3.
[7] *Ibid.*, p. 177.
[8] C. W. Helstrom, "The detection and resolution of optical signals," *IEEE Trans. Information Theory*, vol. IT-10, pp. 275–287, October 1964.
[9] P. M. Woodward, *Probability and Information Theory with Applications to Radar.* London: Pergamon, 1957, chs. 5 and 6.
[10] J. M. Wozencraft and I. M. Jacobs, *Principles of Communications Engineering.* New York: Wiley, 1965, ch. 8.
[11] I. Bar-David, "Communication under Poissonian regime," Sci. Dept., Ministry of Defence, Israel, Rept. 40/07-526, January 1968.

# Editor's Comments on Papers 2, 3, and 4

2 **Rubin:** *Regular Point Processes and Their Detection*
3 **Snyder:** *Filtering and Detection for Doubly Stochastic Poisson Processes*
4 **Snyder:** *Smoothing for Doubly Stochastic Poisson Processes*

In these papers the subject is the detection, filtering, and smoothing of point processes. They represent the first attempts to depart from the restrictive assumption of Poisson statistics. In Paper 2 the regular point processes are defined, and a general likelihood-ratio formula is developed that is in some agreement in form with likelihood ratios for Gaussian processes. In Paper 3 the filtering and detection of compound Poisson processes are considered. This class of processes belongs to the class of regular processes and is an example of conditional independent increment processes [1], with conditional Poisson densities. The Poisson rate is itself an ordinary stochastic process. Paper 4 deals finally with the smoothing of such processes. Note that for filtering and smoothing the Markov assumption is needed on the modulating-intensity process. Subsequent work by the authors of these papers has extended many of the results and has generalized the class of point processes to that of jump processes, where the event occurrences are accompanied by Markov transitions of an associated ordinary process [2].

## References


1. P. A. Frost, Estimation and detection for a simple class of conditionally independent-increment processes, *Proc. IEEE Decision Contr. Conf.*, Dec. 1971.
2. D. L. Snyder, Information processing for observed jump processes, *Inform. Contr.*, **22,** 69–78 (1973).

# 2



Reprinted from *IEEE Trans. Inform. Theory,* **IT-18**(5), 547–557 (1972)

# Regular Point Processes and Their Detection

IZHAK RUBIN, MEMBER, IEEE

***Abstract*—A class of point processes that possess intensity functions are studied. The processes of this class, which seem to include most point processes of practical interest, are called regular point processes (RPP's). Expressions for the evolution of these processes and especially for their joint occurrence statistics are derived.**

**Compound RPP's, which are RPP's whose intensity functions are themselves stochastic processes, are shown to be RPP's whose intensity functions are given as the causal minimum mean-squared-error (MMSE) estimates of the given intensity functions.**

**The superposition of two independent RPP's is shown to yield an RPP whose intensity is given as a causal least squares estimate of the appropriate combination of the two given intensity functions.**

**A general likelihood-ratio formula for the detection of compound RPP's is obtained. Singular detection cases are characterized. Detection procedures that use only the total number of counts are discussed. As an example, the optimal detection scheme for signals of the random-telegraph type with unknown transition intensities is derived.**

## I. Introduction

THE PROBLEMS of detection, estimation, and filtering of stochastic point processes are of considerable interest in the engineering and medical sciences. Yet an analysis of these problems has been carried out for only special types of point processes, such as renewal processes [9], [11], and doubly stochastic Poisson processes [6].

In practice, it is very desirable that the point process used as a statistical model in our system be "constructively" characterized by a certain measurable function, in terms of which its evolution and various processings could be expressed. Such a function is the intensity function of the Poisson process.

In this paper we define a family of point processes, to be called regular point processes (RPP's), which possess intensity functions. However, these functions are now defined to be dependent on the past occurrences of the process and are hence themselves stochastic processes, to be called intensity processes. This dependence is required since in general the point process will not be memoryless, as the Poisson process is. For RPP's, which include almost any practical point process, we derive in this paper the important properties required for any detection, filtering, and estimation analysis. The evolution laws are studied, an expression for the joint occurrence density in the observation period is obtained, and a general likelihood-ratio formula is derived.

The idea of using a conditional intensity function that depends on all the past evolution of the process to characterize a stochastic point process was used by McFadden [15] and recently by Cox and Lewis [12]. The latter use second-order cross-intensity functions to express correlational properties of bivariate point processes. See also [14] regarding renewal intensity functions and [3] for the definition of Markov jump processes in terms of intensity functions. However, to the author's knowledge, no general studies associated with information processing and evolutional characteristics for RPP's have been reported.

We start in Section II by defining RPP's. Differential equations for the conditional probabilities of the process, corresponding to the Kolmogorov equations for Markov counting processes, are written. The intensity process is defined and an expression for the joint occurrence density is derived.

In Section III we obtain the corresponding properties for compound RPP's. These are defined to be RPP's whose intensity functions are themselves stochastic processes. This will often be the case in practice, owing to noise and uncertainties concerning the statistics of the observed point process. We show that a compound-RPP is itself an RPP whose intensity function is given as the causal minimum mean-squared-error (MMSE) estimate of the given intensity function.

In many systems the observed point process is very often the result of superposition of two RPP's. In order to filter the desired information, we have to know the statistical characteristics of this superposed process. We prove in Section IV that the latter is also an RPP, whose intensity is given as a causal MMSE estimate of the appropriate combination of the two intensity functions.

A general likelihood-ratio formula for the binary detection problem, when the received signal under the two hypotheses is a compound RPP, is derived in Section V. Singular detection cases are characterized. Perfect (zero-error-probability) detection is shown to always occur only with probability strictly less than one. Optimal detection procedures that use an observation of only the total counts are obtained. Finally, we note the constructional nature of the RPP being characterized by the intensity process and illustrate the direct applicability of our results to renewal processes and doubly stochastic Poisson processes. The latter serve as a model in optical communication and various biological systems [6]. As an example, the optimal detection scheme for signals of the random-telegraph type with unknown transition intensities is derived.

## II. Regular Point Processes

### *Definitions*

We consider a (separable) honest[1] counting process $\{N(t), 0 \leq t \leq T\}$ whose state space is the nonnegative

Manuscript received April 8, 1971; revised April 26, 1972.

The author is with the Department of System Science, School of Engineering and Applied Science, University of California, Los Angeles, Calif. 90024.

[1] The process is honest in the sense that (with probability one) only a finite number of occurrences are allowed in any finite time interval; i.e., $P\{N(t) = \infty\} = 0 \ \forall t \in [0,T]$. For dishonest outcomes $(\{N(t) = \infty\})$ let $\lambda_{N(t)}(t,\mathscr{B}_t) = 0$.

integers and that is defined on a probability space $(\Omega_N, \beta_N, P_N)$. $N(t)$ denotes the number of point occurrences in $[0,t)$, $N(0) = 0$. We denote by $\mathscr{B}_t$ the Borel field generated by $\{N(\tau), 0 \leq \tau \leq t\}$. We assume the process to be an RPP, which is defined as follows.

*Definition 1:* A counting process is called an RPP if the following limits hold for each $t \in [0,T]$ and for each realization,

$$\lim_{\Delta t \downarrow 0} \frac{1}{\Delta t} [1 - P\{N(t + \Delta t) = N(t) \mid \mathscr{B}_t\}]$$

$$= \lim_{\Delta t \downarrow 0} \frac{1}{\Delta t} [P\{N(t + \Delta t) = N(t) + 1 \mid \mathscr{B}_t\}]$$

$$\triangleq \lambda_{N(t)}(t,\mathscr{B}_t), \tag{1}$$

where, for each realization $\omega$, the intensity function $\lambda_{N(t)}(t,\omega)$ is a nonnegative piecewise continuous function over $[0,T]$. At its discontinuity points, the intensity function is taken to be left continuous. In addition, we require

$$E\{\lambda_{N(t)}(t,\mathscr{B}_t)\} < \infty \tag{2}$$

$$(|\Delta t|)^{-1} P\{N(t + \Delta t) = N(t) + 1 \mid \mathscr{B}_t\} \leq K(t,\mathscr{B}_t), \tag{3}$$

where $E\{|K(t,\mathscr{B}_t)|\} < \infty \ \forall t$, and similarly for

$$(|\Delta t|)^{-1}[1 - P\{N(t + \Delta t) = N(t) \mid \mathscr{B}_t\}].$$

Thus, for an RPP the probabilities of an event occurrence in $[t, t + \Delta t)$ satisfy

$$1 - P\{N(t + \Delta t) = N(t) \mid \mathscr{B}_t\}$$

$$= P\{N(t + \Delta t) = N(t) + 1 \mid \mathscr{B}_t\} + o(\Delta t)$$

$$= \lambda_{N(t)}(t,\mathscr{B}_t)\,\Delta t + o(\Delta t), \tag{4}$$

where

$$\lim_{\Delta t \downarrow 0} \frac{o(\Delta t)}{\Delta t} = 0, \qquad \forall \omega.$$

When conditioned on only the present state, (1) reduces to the definition

$$\lambda_{N(t)}(t) \triangleq \lim_{\Delta t \downarrow 0} \frac{1}{\Delta t} [1 - P\{N(t + \Delta t) = N(t) \mid N(t)\}]$$

$$= \lim_{\Delta t \downarrow 0} \frac{1}{\Delta t} [P\{N(t + \Delta t) = N(t) + 1 \mid N(t)\}], \tag{5}$$

which corresponds to the intensities $\lambda_n(t)$ defined for Markov counting processes (or equivalently pure-birth processes; see [1, ch. 7], [2, ch. 2], [3, ch. 7]).

More generally, intensity functions specified in terms of some period in the past may be written. Thus $\lambda_{N(t)}(t,\mathscr{B}_s)$, $s \leq t$, is defined by the limits in (1), when the probabilities there are now conditioned on the Borel field generated by $\{N(t);\ N(\tau), 0 \leq \tau \leq s\}$. One can then readily derive the following important relation between the intensities.

*Lemma 1:*

$$\lambda_{N(t)}(t,\mathscr{B}_s) = E[\lambda_{N(t)}(t,\mathscr{B}_t) \mid N(t),\mathscr{B}_s]. \tag{6}$$

*Proof:*

$$\lambda_{N(t)}(t,\mathscr{B}_s)$$

$$= \lim_{\Delta t \downarrow 0} \frac{1}{\Delta t} P\{N(t + \Delta t) = N(t) + 1 \mid N(t),\mathscr{B}_s\}$$

$$= \lim_{\Delta t \downarrow 0} \frac{1}{\Delta t} E^{\{N(t),\mathscr{B}_s\}} P\{N(t + \Delta t) = N(t) + 1 \mid \mathscr{B}_t\}$$

$$= E^{\{N(t),\mathscr{B}_s\}} \lim_{\Delta t \downarrow 0} \frac{1}{\Delta t} P\{N(t + \Delta t) = N(t) + 1 \mid \mathscr{B}_t\}$$

$$= E^{\{N(t),\mathscr{B}_s\}} \lambda_{N(t)}(t,\mathscr{B}_t),$$

where $E^{\{\mathscr{B}\}} X \triangleq E\{X \mid \mathscr{B}\}$. The interchange of limit and expectation above follows by the dominated convergence theorem for conditional probabilities (Doob [4, p. 23]) and (3). Q.E.D.

Subsequently, $\lambda_{N(t)}(t,\mathscr{B}_s) \underset{s \uparrow t}{\rightarrow} \lambda_{N(t)}(t,\mathscr{B}_t)$ (with probability one) follows (using Doob [4, th. 4.3, p. 355] and (2)). In particular, we will repeatedly use the following intensity,[2] $t \geq s \geq 0$

$$\lambda_{N(s)}(t,\mathscr{B}_s)$$

$$\triangleq \lim_{\Delta t \downarrow 0} \frac{1}{\Delta t} [1 - P\{N(t + \Delta t) = N(t) \mid N(t) = N(s),\mathscr{B}_s\}]. \tag{7}$$

Some characteristics of RPP's, which will be used in our present analysis, are derived next.

*The Evolution of the Process*

The conditional state occupancy probabilities of an RPP satisfy the following difference-differential equations.

*Lemma 2:* For an RPP, $\forall t > s \geq 0$, $n = 0,1,2,\cdots$, we have

$$\frac{\partial}{\partial t} P\{N(t) = n \mid \mathscr{B}_s\} = -\lambda_n(t,\mathscr{B}_s) P\{N(t) = n \mid \mathscr{B}_s\} + \lambda_{n-1}(t,\mathscr{B}_s) P\{N(t) = n - 1 \mid \mathscr{B}_s\}. \tag{8}$$

*Proof:* Write

$$\frac{\partial}{\partial t} P\{N(t) = n \mid \mathscr{B}_s\}$$

$$= \lim_{\Delta t \downarrow 0} \frac{1}{\Delta t} [P\{N(t + \Delta t) = n \mid \mathscr{B}_s\} - P\{N(t) = n \mid \mathscr{B}_s\}]$$

$$= \lim_{\Delta t \downarrow 0} \frac{1}{\Delta t} [P\{N(t + \Delta t) = n \mid N(t) = n,\mathscr{B}_s\} - 1]$$

$$P\{N(t) = n \mid \mathscr{B}_s\} + P\{N(t + \Delta t) = n \mid N(t) = n - 1,\mathscr{B}_s\} P\{N(t) = n - 1 \mid \mathscr{B}_s\} + o(\Delta t)\}$$

and use the intensity definition (7) to obtain (8). Q.E.D.

[2] If $A \in \beta_N$, the conditional probability $P[A \mid N(t) = n,\mathscr{B}_s]$ is defined by

$$P[A,N(t) = n \mid \mathscr{B}_s] = P[A \mid N(t) = n,\mathscr{B}_s] P[N(t) = n \mid \mathscr{B}_s],$$

if $P[N(t) = n \mid \mathscr{B}_s] \neq 0$, and is 0 otherwise.

We consequently obtain the following.

*Corollary 1:* $\forall t \geq s \geq 0$,

$$P\{N(t) = H(s) \mid \mathscr{B}_s\} = \exp\left[-\int_s^t \lambda_{N(s)}(u,\mathscr{B}_s)\, du\right]. \quad (9)$$

*Proof:* Since $P\{N(t) = N(s) - 1 \mid \mathscr{B}_s\} = 0$, we obtain from (8) that

$$\frac{\partial}{\partial t} P\{N(t) = N(s) \mid \mathscr{B}_s\} = -\lambda_{N(s)}(t,\mathscr{B}_s) P\{N(t) = N(s) \mid \mathscr{B}_s\} \quad (10)$$

from which (9) follows. Q.E.D.

For the counting probability $p_n(t) \equiv P\{N(t) = n\}$ of an RPP, we obtain Lemma 3.

*Lemma 3:* For an RPP

$$\frac{\partial}{\partial t} p_n(t) = -\lambda_n(t)p_n(t) + \lambda_{n-1}(t)p_{n-1}(t), \qquad n \geq 1$$

$$\frac{\partial}{\partial t} p_0(t) = -\lambda_0(t)p_0(t), \quad (11)$$

where $\lambda_n(t)$ is defined by (5).

*Proof:* (11) follows from (5), in the same way (8) has been derived. Note that, by Lemma 1, we have

$$\lambda_{N(t)}(t) = E\{\lambda_{N(t)}(t,\mathscr{B}_s) \mid N(t)\}.$$

Lemma 3 indicates that calculation of the counting law at each time requires information concerned only with the total number of the preceding counts. Moreover, (11) is identical to the forward Kolmogorov equation for a Markov counting process (see [1, sec. 7-3]), whose intensity is given by $\lambda_n(t)$. Consequently, the state occupancy probabilities of an RPP are the same as those of an equivalent Markov counting process. One can subsequently deduce the following sufficient condition for the honesty of the RPP.

*Lemma 4:* If

$$\sum_{k=0}^{\infty} [\sup_{0 \leq \tau \leq t} \lambda_k(\tau)]^{-1} = \infty \quad (12)$$

then

$$\sum_{n=0}^{\infty} p_n(t) = 1.$$

*Proof:* Follows essentially Feller ([16, p. 452]) and will therefore be omitted.

Since we are interested in the evolution of the process over $[0,T]$, and as $\sup_{0 \leq \tau \leq t} \lambda_n(\tau)$ is a nondecreasing function of $t$, it is sufficient to require

$$\sum_{n=0}^{\infty} [\sup_{0 \leq \tau \leq T} \lambda_n(\tau)]^{-1} = \infty. \quad (13)$$

Note, for example, that if $\lambda_n(t) = (n + a)^\alpha \lambda(t)$, (12) implies $-\infty < \alpha \leq 1$. A quadratic term in $n$ will cause too great a rate of increase of the occurrence rate of the process, and thus cause it to be dishonest.

Finally, we observe the character of the sample functions of the regular counting process. By Corollary 1, (9), or directly from the definition, one concludes that the counting process is stochastically continuous. Its sample functions have only jump discontinuities, at which points both the left and right limits exist. The realizations are actually nondecreasing step functions with unit jumps. We choose the sample functions to be left continuous.

*The Joint Occurrence Density*

Instead of using only the counting process $\{N(t), t \in [0,T]\}$ to describe occurrence properties of the given point process, we will find it advantageous to also use the discrete-parameter random process $\{W_n, n = 1,2,3,\cdots\}$, $W_0 = 0$, where $W_n$ is the instant of the $n$th occurrence. Consequently,

$$W_{N(t)}(\omega) = \inf_\tau \{\tau \geq 0: N(\tau,\omega) = N(t,\omega)\}, \quad (14)$$

denotes the instant of occurrence preceding $t$. The basic relation between the counting process and the corresponding sequence of occurrence times (often called waiting times) is

$$N(t) \leq n, \qquad \text{iff } W_{n+1} \geq t \quad (15)$$

for any $t > 0$ and $n = 1,2,\cdots$.

For purposes of detection, filtering, and estimation, it is necessary to know the joint occurrence distribution for our point process,

$$F(t_1,t_2,\cdots,t_n) = P\{W_1 < t_1, W_2 < t_2,\cdots, W_n < t_n\} \triangleq 1 - \mathscr{F}(t_1,t_2,\cdots,t_n),$$

and its density $f(t_1,t_2,\cdots,t_n)$. The latter is given by the following lemma.

*Lemma 5:* The joint occurrence density of an RPP is given by

$$f(t_1,t_2,\cdots,t_n) = \prod_{i=1}^{n} \lambda_{i-1}(t_i,t_{i-1},\cdots,t_1) \cdot \exp\left\{-\sum_{i=1}^{n} \int_{t_{i-1}}^{t_i} \lambda_{i-1}(u,t_{i-1},\cdots,t_1)\, du\right\}, \quad (16)$$

where

$$n \geq 1,\ t_n > t_{n-1} > \cdots > t_1 > t_0 = 0,$$

$$\lambda_{i-1}(u,t_{i-1},\cdots,t_1)\mid_{i=1} \triangleq \lambda_0(u)$$

and

$$\lambda_n(t,t_n,\cdots,t_1) = \lim_{\Delta t \downarrow 0} \frac{1}{\Delta t} [P\{N(t + \Delta t) = n + 1 \mid N(t) = n, W_n = t_n,\cdots,W_1 = t_1\}]. \quad (17)$$

*Proof:* Since $\{W_n = t_n,\cdots, W_1 = t_1\} \in \mathscr{B}_{t_n^+}$, using $s = t_n^+$ in (9), we obtain for

$n \geq 1, t > t_n > t_{n-1} > \cdots > t_1 > 0,$

$$\begin{aligned}\mathscr{F}_{W_{n+1}}(t \mid t_n,\cdots,t_1) &\triangleq P\{W_{n+1} \geq t \mid W_n = t_n,\cdots,W_1 = t_1\}\\ &= P\{N(t) = n \mid W_n = t_n,\cdots,W_1 = t_1\}\\ &= \exp\left[-\int_{t_n}^{t} \lambda_n(u,t_n,\cdots,t_1)\,du\right].\end{aligned}$$

The intensity $\lambda_n(u,t_n,\cdots,t_1)$ is a realization of $\lambda_{N(t_n+)}(t,\mathscr{B}_{t_n+})$ defined by (7) and is subsequently expressed as in (17). The corresponding conditional density is then

$$\begin{aligned}f_{W_{n+1}}(t \mid t_n,\cdots,t_1) &= \lambda_n(t,t_n,\cdots,t_1)\\ &\cdot \exp\left[-\int_{t_n}^{t} \lambda_n(u,t_n,\cdots,t_1)\,du\right]. \quad (18)\end{aligned}$$

The latter is used to calculate the joint occurrence density by

$$f(t_1,t_2,\cdots,t_n) = f_{W_1}(t_1)f_{W_2}(t_2 \mid t_1)\cdots f_{W_n}(t_n \mid t_{n-1},\cdots,t_1).$$

The first occurrence density is given by

$$f_{W_1}(t_1) = \lambda_0(t_1)\exp\left[-\int_0^{t_1} \lambda_0(u)\,du\right]. \quad (19)$$

Equation (19) follows from the second equation in (11), which yields

$$\begin{aligned}\mathscr{F}_{W_1}(t) = P\{W_1 \geq t\} &= P\{N(t) = 0\}\\ &= \exp\left[-\int_0^{t} \lambda_0(u)\,du\right].\end{aligned}$$

Equation (16) then follows. Q.E.D.

Since we consider a fixed observation interval $[0,T]$, it is important to express the joint occurrence density over this interval. The latter is the joint density of the occurrence times, $(W_1,W_2,\cdots,W_{N(T)})$ and the number $N(T)$ of occurrences in $[0,T]$. Denote this density by $f(t_1,t_2,\cdots,t_{N_T},N_T)$. We then have the following theorem.

*Theorem 1:* The joint occurrence density of an RPP over $[0,T]$ is given by

$$\begin{aligned}f(t_1,t_2,\cdots,t_{N_T},N_T) &= \prod_{i=1}^{N_T} \lambda_{i-1}(t_i,t_{i-1},\cdots,t_1)\\ &\exp\left\{-\left[\sum_{i=1}^{N_T}\int_{t_{i-1}}^{t_i} \lambda_{i-1}(u,t_{i-1},\cdots,t_1)\,du\right]\right.\\ &\left.-\int_{t_{N_T}}^{T} \lambda_{N_T}(u,t_{N_T},\cdots,t_1)\,du\right\}, \quad (20)\end{aligned}$$

where $\lambda_{i-1}(u,t_{i-1},\cdots,t_1)|_{i=1} \triangleq \lambda_0(u)$ and $N_T \geq 1, 0 = t_0 < t_1 < t_2 \cdots < t_{N_T} \leq T$. When $N_T = 0$, $f(\cdot) = \exp[-\int_0^T \lambda_0(u)\,du]$.

*Proof:* Using (9) with $s = t_{N_T}$, one obtains

$$\begin{aligned}&f(t_1,t_2,\cdots,t_{N_T},N_T)\\ &= f(t_1,t_2,\cdots,t_{N_T})P\{N(T) = N_T \mid W_{N_T} = t_{N_T},\cdots,W_1 = t_1\}\\ &= f(t_1,t_2,\cdots,t_{N_T})\exp\left[-\int_{t_{N_T}}^{T} \lambda_{N_T}(u,t_{N_T},\cdots,t_1)\,du\right].\end{aligned}$$

Equation (20) then follows when (16) is substituted in the preceding. When $N_T = 0, f(\cdot) = P\{N(t) = 0\} = \exp[-\int_0^t \lambda_0(u)\,du]$ by (11). Q.E.D.

Theorem 1 is our main result in this section. Equation (20) indicates how one should incorporate all past occurrences of the process in order to calculate the occurrence density over the whole observation period. This density is written in a more compact form as follows.

Denote the sample-function space of $\{N(t), 0 \leq t \leq T\}$ by $(\Omega_1,\beta_1,P_1)$, where each outcome $\omega_1 \in \Omega_1$ is a realization of the point process over $[0,T]$. We construct now over this space a stochastic process $\lambda(t,\omega_1)$ to be called the *intensity process*, so that $\lambda(t,\omega_1) \equiv \lambda_{N(t)}(t,\mathscr{B}_t)$; i.e., the intensity process $\lambda(t,\omega_1)$ is given for each outcome $\omega_1 = \{t_1,t_2,\cdots,t_{N_T},N_T\}$ by

$$\lambda(t,\omega_1) = \begin{cases}\lambda_n(t,t_n,\cdots,t_1), & t_n < t \leq t_{n+1}, n = 1,2,\cdots,N_T\\ \lambda_0(t), & 0 \leq t \leq t_1.\end{cases} \quad (21)$$

For fixed $t \in [0,T]$, $\lambda(t,\omega_1)$ is $\mathscr{B}_t$-measurable and is given by

$$\lambda(t,\omega_1) = \lambda_{N(t)}(t,\mathscr{B}_t). \quad (22)$$

The sample functions of $\lambda(t,\omega_1)$ are thus piecewise left continuous (see Fig. 1). As the counting process is honest, $N(T) < \infty$ (with probability one), and both $\lambda(t,\omega_1)$ and $N(t,\omega_1)$ are of bounded variation. Consequently, the following stochastic integrals are well defined.[3]

*Definition 2:* For almost all $N(T)$, define

$$\int_0^T \lambda(t,\omega_1)\,dt \triangleq \begin{cases}\displaystyle\sum_{i=1}^{N(T)}\int_{W_{i-1}}^{W_i} \lambda_{i-1}(u,W_{i-1},\cdots,W_1)\,du\\ \displaystyle\quad+\int_{W_{N(T)}}^{T} \lambda_{N(T)}(u,W_{N(T)},\cdots,W_1)\,du, & N(T) > 0\\ \displaystyle\int_0^T \lambda_0(u)\,du, & N(T) = 0.\end{cases} \quad (23)$$

$$\int_0^T \lambda(t,\omega_1)\,dN(t,\omega_1) \triangleq \begin{cases}\displaystyle\sum_{i=1}^{N(T)} \lambda_{i-1}(W_i,W_{i-1},\cdots,W_1), & N(T) > 0\\ 0, & N(T) = 0.\end{cases} \quad (24)$$

We denote by $f_T(\omega_1)$ the joint occurrence density in $[0,T]$ for the realization $\omega_1 \in \Omega_1$. Using (23) and (24) in (20) we conclude the following.

*Theorem 2:* The joint occurrence density $f_T(\omega_1)$ of an RPP satisfies

[3] Clearly, for almost any realization $\omega_1$, $\int_0^T \lambda(t,\omega_1)\,dt$ is regarded as a Lebesgue integral and (23) thus follows. Equation (24) defines the stochastic integral $\int_0^T \lambda(t,\omega_1)\,dN(t,\omega_1)$ by sampling $\lambda(t,\omega_1)$ at the occurrence points. One may show that, since $\lambda(t,\omega_1)$ is left continuous, the integral in (24) may be written using an Itô sampling procedure (in an a.s. sense).

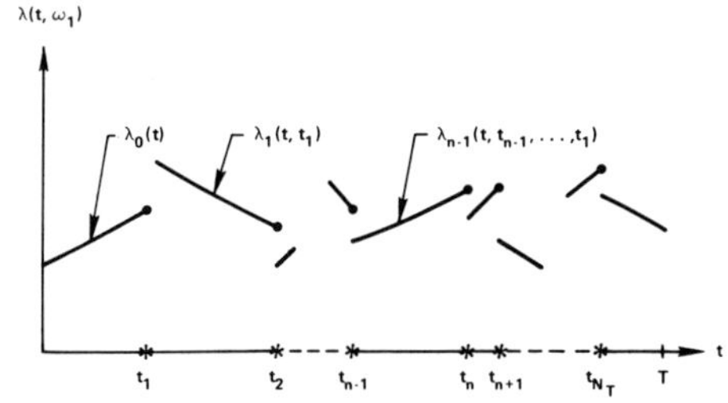

Fig. 1. The intensity process.

$$\ln f_T(\omega_1) = \int_0^T \ln \lambda(t,\omega_1)\, dN(t,\omega_1) - \int_0^T \lambda(t,\omega_1)\, dt \qquad (25)$$

whenever $\lambda_{i-1}(W_i,\cdots,W_1) > 0 \ \forall i \geq 1$, and vanishes otherwise.

This is a most important result. Detection, filtering, and estimation schemes for RPP's follow directly from (25) (see Section V).

## III. Compound Point Processes

*Definitions*

The statistical characteristics of an observed point process are many times determined by the evolution of a stochastic process $\{S(t), 0 \leq t \leq T\}$ defined over a sample-function space $(\Omega_s,\beta_s,P_s)$. The latter process can represent the information-bearing process, as is the case in optical and biomedical communications, or an underlying parameter process, as is the case when uncertainties concerning the statistics of the point process arise. This "message process" $\{S(t)\}$ will thus causally modulate the intensity function of the observed point process. We therefore assume the observed point process to be an RPP whose intensity function is given, for each realization $S_t$ of $\{S(t)\}$ over $[0,t]$, by $\lambda_{N(t)}(t,\mathscr{B}_t,S_t)\ \forall t \in [0,T]$. The observed RPP is thus defined for each realization $\omega_s \in \Omega_s$ over the space $(\Omega,\beta,P(\cdot \mid \omega_s))$. $P(B \mid \omega_s)$ is a probability defined over the product space $\Omega_s \times \beta$, such that $\forall \omega_s \in \Omega_s$, $P(\cdot \mid \omega_s)$ is a probability on $(\Omega,\beta)$; and $\forall B \in \beta$, $P(B \mid \cdot)$ is measurable on $(\Omega_s,\beta_s)$.

A major role is played in the applications mentioned above by the compound RPP, which is defined in the following way as the "unconditional" point process. The compound RPP is defined on the probability space $(\Omega,\beta,P_c)$, where the compound probability measure $P_c$ is given by

$$P_c(B) = E\{P(B \mid \omega_s)\} = \int_{\Omega_s} P_s(d\omega_s)P(B \mid \omega_s), \qquad B \in \beta. \qquad (26)$$

We will now show that the compound RPP is itself an RPP and derive a very useful expression for its intensity function.[4]

[4] We henceforth delete the subscripts of $P$. It will be clear from the text which probability measure is used in any specific case.

*The Evolution of the Compound Process*

Since conditioned on $S(t)$, the compound process is assumed to be regular, we have by Definition 1

$$\lambda_{N(t)}(t,\mathscr{B}_t,S_t) = \lim_{\Delta t \downarrow 0} \frac{1}{\Delta t}[1 - P\{N(t + \Delta t) = N(t) \mid \mathscr{B}_t,S_{t+\Delta t}\}]$$

$$= \lim_{\Delta t \downarrow 0} \frac{1}{\Delta t} P\{N(t + \Delta t) = N(t) + 1 \mid \mathscr{B}_t,S_{t+\Delta t}\}. \qquad (27)$$

Furthermore, $\lambda_{N(t)}(t,\mathscr{B}_t,S_t)$ is a nonnegative piecewise-continuous function over $[0,T]$, for any realization $\{\omega,S_t\}$ and, when conditioned on $S_{t+\Delta t}$, (3) holds. Also, by (2)

$$E\{\lambda_{N(t)}(t,\mathscr{B}_t,S_t)\} < \infty. \qquad (28)$$

In addition, we require $E\{\lambda_{N(t)}(t,\mathscr{B}_t,S_t) \mid \mathscr{B}_t\}$ to have piecewise-continuous realizations over $[0,T]$. The above conditions define the class of admissible processes $\{S(t)\}$. We can consequently derive the following important property.

*Theorem 3:* Assuming $\{S(t)\}$ to be an admissible stochastic process, a compound RPP is an RPP whose intensity function $\hat{\lambda}_{N(t)}(t,\mathscr{B}_t)$ is given by

$$\hat{\lambda}_{N(t)}(t,\mathscr{B}_t) = E\{\lambda_{N(t)}(t,\mathscr{B}_t,S_t) \mid \mathscr{B}_t\}. \qquad (29)$$

*Proof:*

$$\hat{\lambda}_{N(t)}(t,\mathscr{B}_t) \triangleq \lim_{\Delta t \downarrow 0} \frac{1}{\Delta t} P\{N(t + \Delta t) = N(t) + 1 \mid \mathscr{B}_t\}$$

$$= \lim_{\Delta t \downarrow 0} \frac{1}{\Delta t} E^{\{\mathscr{B}_t\}}\{P[N(t + \Delta t) = N(t) + 1 \mid \mathscr{B}_t,S_{t+\Delta t}]\}$$

$$= E^{\{\mathscr{B}_t\}}\left\{\lim_{\Delta t \downarrow 0} \frac{1}{\Delta t} P[N(t + \Delta t) = N(t) + 1 \mid \mathscr{B}_t,S_{t+\Delta t}]\right\}$$

$$= E^{\{\mathscr{B}_t\}}[\lambda_{N(t)}(t,\mathscr{B}_t,S_t)],$$

which is the compound intensity given by (29). We have used above (27) and the dominated convergence theorem to justify the interchange of limit and expectation using (3), which assumes now the form

$$\frac{1}{|\Delta t|} P[N(t + \Delta t) = N(t) + 1 \mid \mathscr{B}_t,S_{t+\Delta t}] \leq K(t,\mathscr{B}_t,S_t), \qquad E\{|K(\cdot)|\} < \infty.$$

Finally, $E\{\hat{\lambda}_{N(t)}(t,\mathscr{B}_t)\} = E\{\lambda_{N(t)}(t,\mathscr{B}_t,S_t)\} < \infty$ by (28), so that the compound process is an RPP. Q.E.D.

Since the compound process is an RPP, all its characteristics follow those derived in the previous section, when the intensity (29) is incorporated. In particular, the conditional and unconditional state occupancy probabilities are expressed as follows.

*Corollary 2:* The conditional state-occupancy probabilities of a compound RPP satisfy relation (8), where $\lambda_n(t,\mathscr{B}_s)$ is replaced by $\hat{\lambda}_n(t,\mathscr{B}_s)$. The latter satisfies

$$\hat{\lambda}_{N(t)}(t,\mathscr{B}_s) = E\{\lambda_{N(t)}(t,\mathscr{B}_t,S_t) \mid N(t),\mathscr{B}_s\}. \quad (30)$$

*Proof:* We have just to show (30), which follows directly from Lemma 1, as

$$\begin{aligned}\hat{\lambda}_{N(t)}(t,\mathscr{B}_s) &= E[\hat{\lambda}_{N(t)}(t,\mathscr{B}_t) \mid N(t),\mathscr{B}_s] \\ &= E\{E[\lambda_{N(t)}(t,\mathscr{B}_t,S_t) \mid \mathscr{B}_t] \mid N(t),\mathscr{B}_s\} \\ &= E\{\lambda_{N(t)}(t,\mathscr{B}_t,S_t) \mid N(t),\mathscr{B}_s\}\end{aligned}$$

since $\{N(t),\mathscr{B}_s\} \subset \mathscr{B}_t$, where $\{N(t),\mathscr{B}_s\}$ denotes the Borel field generated by $\{N(t);\ N(\tau),\ 0 \le \tau \le s\}$. Q.E.D.

*Corollary 3:* For a compound RPP we have

$$\frac{\partial}{\partial t} p_n(t) = -\hat{\lambda}_n(t)p_n(t) + \hat{\lambda}_{n-1}(t)p_{n-1}(t), \qquad n \ge 1$$

$$\frac{\partial}{\partial t} p_0(t) = -\hat{\lambda}_0(t)p_0(t), \quad (31)$$

where

$$\hat{\lambda}_n(t) = E\{\lambda_{N(t)}(t,\mathscr{B}_t,S_t) \mid N(t) = n\}. \quad (32)$$

*Proof:* Follows directly from Lemmas 3 and 1, using same considerations as in Corollary 2. Q.E.D.

Corollary 3 yields a very useful relation for the state-occupancy probabilities. In particular, (31) indicates that the latter probabilities of the compound RPP are the same as those of a Markov counting process whose intensity function is equal to $\hat{\lambda}_n(t)$. Incorporating $\hat{\lambda}_n(t)$ in (12), one subsequently obtains a sufficient condition for the honesty of the compound process.

In the same way, the joint occurrence density of the compound process follows from (20) and (25). Because of the importance of this density for deriving detection and estimation results, the result is summarized in the following.

*Theorem 4:* The joint occurrence density over $[0,T]$ for a compound RPP is given by

$$\ln f_T(\omega_1) = \int_0^T \ln \hat{\lambda}(t,\omega_1)\, dN(t,\omega_1) - \int_0^T \hat{\lambda}(t,\omega_1)\, dt \quad (33)$$

whenever $\hat{\lambda}_{i-1}(W_i,\cdots,W_1) > 0\ \forall i \ge 1$, and vanishes otherwise. For any outcome $\omega_1 = \{t_1,t_2,\cdots,t_{N_T}\}$ we define

$$\hat{\lambda}(t,\omega_1) = \begin{cases}\hat{\lambda}_n(t,t_n,\cdots,t_1), & t_n < t \le t_{n+1},\ n = 1,2,\cdots,N_T \\ \hat{\lambda}_0(t), & 0 \le t \le t_1.\end{cases} \quad (34)$$

For fixed $t \in [0,T]$ we have

$$\hat{\lambda}(t,\omega_1) \equiv \hat{\lambda}_{N(t)}(t,\mathscr{B}_t) \quad (35)$$

and for $n \ge 1$

$$\hat{\lambda}_n(t,t_n,\cdots,t_1) = E\{\lambda_{N(t)}(t,\mathscr{B}_t,S_t) \mid N(t) = n,\ W_n = t_n,\cdots,\ W_1 = t_1\}. \quad (36)$$

The compound occurrence density is equivalently expressed by (20), if the intensity (36) is incorporated.

It is particularly important to notice that the compound intensity functions are the appropriate causal MMSE estimates of the given conditional intensities. The observations utilized to derive these estimates consist of all past occurrences if $\hat{\lambda}_{N(t)}(t,\mathscr{B}_t)$ of (29) is required, while only the total past counts have to be observed if $\hat{\lambda}_{N(t)}(t)$ is to be calculated [see (32)].

## IV. Superposition of RPP's

In many systems, the observed point process is the result of superposition of two point processes. This is many times due to the "signal" point process being perturbed by a background point process, caused by noise or neighboring transmitters. In order to derive estimation and detection schemes, we have to know the statistical characteristics of the incoming superposed point process, especially its joint occurrence density. In this section, we show that when the original processes are RPP's the resulting superposed process is also an RPP, and obtain an expression for the superposed process intensity function. The evolution characteristics of the superposed process will then follow those obtained in Section II.

We assume the "signal" and "noise" processes to be statistically independent RPP's, with intensities $\lambda_n^{(2)}(t,t_n,\cdots,t_1)$ and $\lambda_n^{(1)}(t,t_n,\cdots,t_1)$, respectively. Superposition of the noise process, $\{N^{(1)}(t),\ 0 \le t \le T\}$, and the signal process, $\{N^{(2)}(t),\ 0 \le t \le T\}$, thus results in a superposed process $\{N(t),\ 0 \le t \le T\}$, so that $N(t) = N^{(1)}(t) + N^{(2)}(t)\ \forall t \in [0,T]$. Denote by $\mathscr{B}_t$, $\mathscr{B}_t^{(1)}$, and $\mathscr{B}_t^{(2)}$ the corresponding Borel fields of the above processes, generated by the corresponding counts over $[0,t]$. We then obtain the following.

*Theorem 5:* The superposed process that results from the superposition of two statistically independent RPP's is an RPP whose intensity function $\lambda_{N(t)}^{(c)}(t,\mathscr{B}_t)$ is given by

$$\lambda_{N(t)}^{(c)}(t,\mathscr{B}_t) = E^{\{\mathscr{B}_t\}}[\lambda^{(1)}_{N^{(1)}(t)}(t,\mathscr{B}_t^{(1)}) + \lambda^{(2)}_{N^{(2)}(t)}(t,\mathscr{B}_t^{(2)})]. \quad (37)$$

*Proof:* Denote by $I_A$ the indicator function of the set $A$, and by $\{\mathscr{B}_t^{(1)},\mathscr{B}_t^{(2)}\}$ the Borel field generated by $\{N^{(1)}(\tau), N^{(2)}(\tau),\ 0 \le \tau \le t\}$. Clearly $\mathscr{B}_t \subset \{\mathscr{B}_t^{(1)},\mathscr{B}_t^{(2)}\}$. We then have

$$\begin{aligned}P\{N(t+\Delta t) &= N(t) \mid \mathscr{B}_t\} \\ &= E^{\{\mathscr{B}_t\}}(I_{\{N(t+\Delta t)=N(t)\}}) \\ &= E^{\{\mathscr{B}_t\}}[E^{\{\mathscr{B}_t^{(1)},\mathscr{B}_t^{(2)}\}}(I_{\{N(t+\Delta t)=N(t)\}})] \\ &= E^{\{\mathscr{B}_t\}}[E^{\{\mathscr{B}_t^{(1)},\mathscr{B}_t^{(2)}\}} \\ &\quad \cdot (I_{\{N^{(1)}(t+\Delta t)=N^{(1)}(t)\}}I_{\{N^{(2)}(t+\Delta t)=N^{(2)}(t)\}})] \\ &= E^{\{\mathscr{B}_t\}}[E^{\{\mathscr{B}_t^{(1)}\}}(I_{\{N^{(1)}(t+\Delta t)=N^{(1)}(t)\}}) \\ &\quad \cdot E^{\{\mathscr{B}_t^{(2)}\}}(I_{\{N^{(2)}(t+\Delta t)=N^{(2)}(t)\}})] \\ &= E^{\{\mathscr{B}_t\}}[P\{N^{(1)}(t+\Delta t) = N^{(1)}(t) \mid \mathscr{B}_t^{(1)}\} \\ &\quad \cdot P\{N^{(2)}(t+\Delta t) = N^{(2)}(t) \mid \mathscr{B}_t^{(2)}\}],\end{aligned} \quad (38)$$

where the third equality follows from the counting nature of the processes and the fourth equality follows from the independence of the incoming processes. Hence, using (38) and the intensity definition, we obtain

$$
\begin{aligned}
&\lambda_{N(t)}{}^{(c)}(t,\mathscr{B}_t)\\
&\triangleq \lim_{\Delta t \downarrow 0} \frac{1}{\Delta t}\,[1 - P\{N(t+\Delta t) = N(t) \mid \mathscr{B}_t\}]\\
&= \lim_{\Delta t \downarrow 0} \frac{1}{\Delta t}\,\{1 - E^{\{\mathscr{B}_t\}}[P\{N^{(1)}(t+\Delta t) = N^{(1)}(t) \mid \mathscr{B}_t{}^{(1)}\}\\
&\quad \cdot P\{N^{(2)}(t+\Delta t) = N^{(2)}(t) \mid \mathscr{B}_t{}^{(2)}\}]\}\\
&= \lim_{\Delta t \downarrow 0} \frac{1}{\Delta t}\,E^{\{\mathscr{B}_t\}}\{[1 - P\{N^{(1)}(t+\Delta t) = N^{(1)}(t) \mid \mathscr{B}_t{}^{(1)}\}]\\
&\quad + [1 - P\{N^{(2)}(t+\Delta t) = N^{(2)}(t) \mid \mathscr{B}_t{}^{(2)}\}]\\
&\quad - [1 - P\{N^{(1)}(t+\Delta t) = N^{(1)}(t) \mid \mathscr{B}_t{}^{(1)}\}]\\
&\quad \cdot [1 - P\{N^{(2)}(t+\Delta t) = N^{(2)}(t) \mid \mathscr{B}_t{}^{(2)}\}]\}\\
&= E^{\{\mathscr{B}_t\}} \lim_{\Delta t \downarrow 0} \Big\{\lambda^{(1)}_{N^{(1)}(t)}(t,\mathscr{B}_t{}^{(1)}) + \lambda^{(2)}_{N^{(2)}(t)}(t,\mathscr{B}_t{}^{(2)})\\
&\quad - \lambda^{(1)}_{N^{(1)}(t)}(t,\mathscr{B}_t{}^{(1)})\lambda^{(2)}_{N^{(2)}(t)}(t,\mathscr{B}_t{}^{(2)})\,\Delta t + \frac{o(\Delta t)}{\Delta t}\Big\},
\end{aligned}
$$

which yields (37). The interchange of limit and expectation above follows from relation (3), which holds for both RPP's and the dominated convergence theorem. The regularity conditions of the superposed intensity (37) follow directly from those of the intensities of the incoming RPP. One also readily shows that relation (37) is obtained if

$$\lim_{\Delta t \downarrow 0} \frac{1}{\Delta t}\, P\{N(t+\Delta t) = N(t) + 1 \mid \mathscr{B}_t\}$$

is used above to calculate $\lambda_{N(t)}{}^{(c)}(t,\mathscr{B}_t)$. Q.E.D.

Notice that, given occurrences $(W_{N(t)},\cdots,W_1)$ and $(W^{(1)}_{N^{(1)}(t)},\cdots,W_1{}^{(1)})$, one has to consider in (37) as occurrences of $N^{(2)}(t)$ only those of $(W_{N(t)},\cdots,W_1) \cap (\overline{W^{(1)}_{N^{(1)}(t)},\cdots,W_1})$ (where $\bar{A}$ denotes the complement of the set $A$). Thus, one can express (37) as an expectation with respect to $\{W_n{}^{(1)}\}$ occurrences. Symbolically then,

$$
\begin{aligned}
&\lambda_{N(t)}{}^{(c)}(t,W_{N(t)},\cdots,W_1)\\
&= E^{\{N(t),W_{N(t)},\cdots,W_1\}}\{\lambda^{(1)}_{N^{(1)}(t)}(t,W^{(1)}_{N^{(1)}(t)},\cdots,W_1{}^{(1)})\\
&\quad + \lambda^{(2)}_{N(t)-N^{(1)}(t)}[t,(W_{N(t)},\cdots,W_1) \cap (\overline{W^{(1)}_{N^{(1)}(t)},\cdots,W_1{}^{(1)}})]\}.
\end{aligned}
\tag{39}
$$

Theorem 5 indicates that the class of RPP's is closed under superposition, which is an extremely useful property. It is also very important to observe that the superposed intensity is expressed as an expectation of the two given intensities, conditioned on the observed past occurrences. Thus an interpretation of it as a causal MMSE estimate of the appropriate sum of the two given intensities is possible.

We observe that the superposition of two compound RPP's will yield a superposed RPP with intensity given by (37) when the causal MMSE estimates of (29), $\hat{\lambda}_{N^{(i)}(t)}{}^{(i)}(t,\mathscr{B}_t{}^{(i)})$, $i = 1,2$, are incorporated.

Extension of Theorem 5 to the case of superposition of a finite number of RPP's is readily obtained.

## V. Detection of Point Processes

Under a wide range of performance criteria, optimal detection procedures for a binary communication system consist of a likelihood-ratio processor whose output is compared with a threshold. It is known ([7], [5, ch. 6]) that when the known signals are imbedded in white Gaussian noise, the optimal processor performs two types of operation on the incoming process, namely correlation and energy operations. Moreover, when the information-bearing signal is a stochastic process, the same detection procedure is used, except that the causal MMSE estimate of the signal is used now in the likelihood-ratio processor.

In this section, we derive the optimal likelihood-ratio processor for differentiating a compound RPP from a second compound RPP. The resulting detection procedure is then seen to be of the same nature as that mentioned above.

### *General Likelihood-Ratio Formula*

We observe the sample function of the counting process $\{N(t), 0 \le t \le T\}$, whose sample-function space is $(\Omega_1, \beta_1)$. A two-hypothesis problem is then considered. Under hypothesis $H_1$, we observe a noise compound RPP whose intensity function is $\hat{\lambda}^{(1)}(t,\omega)$; while under $H_2$, a second signal-plus-noise compound RPP is observed, with the intensity function $\hat{\lambda}^{(2)}(t,\omega)$. A decision has to be made at the end of the observation period $[0,T]$ as to the existence of the signal.

Denote the joint occurrence densities in $[0,T]$ under $H_1$ and $H_2$ by $f_T{}^{(1)}(\omega)$ and $f_T{}^{(2)}(\omega)$, respectively. The problem is thus of deciding between two regular counting measures $P^{(1)}$ and $P^{(2)}$ on the basis of observing a sample function $\{N(t,\omega), 0 \le t \le T\}$, where

$$P^{(i)}(A) = \int_A f_T{}^{(i)}\,(d\omega), \qquad \forall A \in \beta_1,\ i = 1,2. \tag{40}$$

If $P^{(2)}$ is absolutely continuous[5] with respect to $P^{(1)}$, $P^{(2)} \ll P^{(1)}$, one can compute the likelihood ratio $\Lambda_T(\omega)$ as the Radon-Nikodym derivative

$$\Lambda_T(\omega) = \frac{dP^{(2)}}{dP^{(1)}}\,(\omega) = \frac{f_T{}^{(2)}(\omega)}{f_T{}^{(1)}(\omega)}. \tag{41}$$

In general, however, one has to use the Lebesgue decomposition theorem (see, for example, [5, p. 210]), and obtain

$$P^{(2)}(A) = \int_A \Lambda_T(\omega)P^{(1)}\,(d\omega) + \mu(A) \tag{42}$$

for every $A \in \beta_1$, where $\mu$ is a finite measure singular[5] with respect to $P^{(1)}$. We first characterize the decomposition (42) in our case, and then deduce the optimal detection procedures.

By Theorem 4, $f_T(\omega)$ is given by (33). For a realization

[5] $P^{(2)}$ is defined to be *absolute continuous* with respect to $P^{(1)}(P^{(2)} \ll P^{(1)})$ if $\forall A \in \beta_1$ such that $P^{(1)}(A) = 0$, we have $P^{(2)}(A) = 0$. If $P^{(2)} \ll P^{(1)}$ and $P^{(1)} \ll P^{(2)}$, then $P^{(1)}$ and $P^{(2)}$ are said to be *equivalent* $(P^{(1)} \equiv P^{(2)})$. $P^{(1)}$ and $P^{(2)}$ are *singular* $(P^{(1)} \perp P^{(2)})$ if $\exists A \in \beta_1$ such that $P^{(1)}(A) = 0$ and $P^{(2)}(\Omega_1 - A) = 0$.

$\omega \equiv \{t_1,t_2,\cdots,t_{N_T}\}$, $f_T(\omega) = 0$ and if only if $\hat{\lambda}_{n-1}(t_n, t_{n-1},\cdots,t_1) = 0$ for some $1 \leq n \leq N_T$. The set of realizations for which the latter equality holds is denoted by $J_n(\omega)$. Thus, we define

$$L_n^{(i)}(\omega) = \{t : W_{n-1} < t \leq T, \hat{\lambda}_{n-1}^{(i)}(t,W_{n-1},\cdots,W_1) = 0\}$$

$$J_n^{(i)}(\omega) = \{\omega : W_n(\omega) \in L_n^{(i)}(\omega)\}$$

$$J^{(i)}(\omega) = \bigcup_n J_n^{(i)}(\omega), \qquad i = 1,2. \tag{43}$$

Clearly, by (43) and (40)

$$A \subset J^{(i)} \Rightarrow P^{(i)}(A) = 0. \tag{44}$$

Also, since $P_{W_n}{}^{(i)} \ll m$, where $m$ is Lebesgue measure over $R^1$, we have that $J_n^{(i)}(\omega) = \phi$ a.s. $(P^{(i)})$ if $m(L_n^{(i)}(\omega)) = 0$ $\forall \omega \in \Omega_1$. This is the case when $\hat{\lambda}_{n-1}(t,t_{n-1},\cdots,t_1)$ vanishes only at a countable number of points in $(t_{n-1},T]$. Decomposition (42) can now be completely characterized by the following theorem.

*Theorem 6:* For the regular counting measures (40), decomposition (42) holds with $\Lambda_T(\omega)$ given by

$$\ln \Lambda_T(\omega) = \int_0^T \ln \frac{\hat{\lambda}^{(2)}(t,\omega)}{\hat{\lambda}^{(1)}(t,\omega)} dN(t,\omega) - \int_0^T [\hat{\lambda}^{(2)}(t,\omega) - \hat{\lambda}^{(1)}(t,\omega)]\, dt, \tag{45}$$

where

$$\hat{\lambda}^{(i)}(t,\omega) = E\{\lambda_{N(t)}(t,\mathscr{B}_t,S_t^{(i)}) \mid \mathscr{B}_t,H_i\} \tag{46}$$

and $\mu(A)$ given by

$$\mu(A) = P^{(2)}(A)I_{\{J^{(1)}\}}(A) = P^{(2)}(A)I_{\{J^{(1)}\cap\overline{J^{(2)}}\}}(A) \tag{47}$$

$\forall A \in \beta_1$. The indicator function $I_{\{J\}}(A)$ is equal to 1 if $A \subset J$ and vanishes otherwise and $\bar{J}$ is the complement to the set $J$.

*Proof:* For any set $A \in \overline{J^{(1)}}$, we have that $P^{(1)}(A) > 0$. Then, $P^{(2)} \ll P^{(1)}$ and we must have $\mu(A) = 0$ in (42). This is the case when $\mu(A)$ is given by (47). Subsequently, $\Lambda_T(\omega)$ is expressed as the Radon–Nikodym derivative (41). Equation (45) then follows directly from (33).

For any set $A \in J^{(1)}$, one must have in (40) $P^{(2)}(A) = \mu(A)$. The latter follows from (47). Also, $\mu$ is singular with respect to $P^{(1)}$. This follows as for $A_1 \equiv \{J^{(1)}\}$, $P^{(1)}(A_1) = 0$ and $\mu(\Omega_1 - A_1) = \mu(\bar{J}_1) = 0$, so that $A_1$ is a separating set. Q.E.D.

Similarly, one obtains for the decomposition of $P^{(1)}$ the following.

*Lemma 6:* For each $A \in \beta_1$

$$P^{(1)}(A) = \int_A \Lambda_T^{-1}(\omega)P^{(2)}(d\omega) + \nu(A), \tag{48}$$

where

$$\nu(A) = P^{(1)}(A)I_{\{J^{(2)}\cap\overline{J^{(1)}}\}}(A) \tag{49}$$

and $\Lambda_T(\omega)$ is given by (45).

From Theorem 6 and Lemma 6, we readily obtain the form of the optimal likelihood detection procedure, summarized as follows.

*Theorem 7:* The optimal detection procedure is given by

$$\Lambda_T(\omega) \begin{cases} > K \text{ decide in favor of } P^{(2)}, & \omega \in \overline{\{J^{(1)} \cup J^{(2)}\}} \\ \leq K \text{ decide in favor of } P^{(1)}, & \omega \in \overline{\{J^{(1)} \cup J^{(2)}\}} \end{cases} \tag{50a}$$

$$\text{decide in favor of } P^{(2)}, \qquad \omega \in \{J^{(1)} \cup \overline{J^{(2)}}\} \tag{50b}$$

$$\text{decide in favor of } P^{(1)}, \qquad \omega \in \{J^{(2)} \cup \overline{J^{(1)}}\} \tag{50c}$$

where $K$ is a constant and $\Lambda_T(\omega)$ is given by (45).

We also observe that[5]

$$P^{(1)} \equiv P^{(2)}, \qquad \text{iff } J^{(1)} = J^{(2)}. \tag{51}$$

Under these conditions, the test is composed of part (50a) $\forall \omega \in \Omega_1$. Also

$$P_2 \ll P_1 \qquad \text{iff } J^{(1)} \subset J^{(2)}, \tag{52}$$

and the test will then be

$$\begin{array}{ll} \text{decide in favor of } P^{(1)}, & \omega \in \{J^{(2)} \cap \overline{J^{(1)}}\} \\ \Lambda_T(\omega) \gtrless K, & \text{otherwise.} \end{array} \tag{53}$$

*Singular Detection*

Theorem 7 indicates that under some outcomes the test is singular. Thus, if $\pi_1$ and $\pi_2 = 1 - \pi_1$ are the prior occurrence probabilities of $H_1$ and $H_2$, respectively, singular detection will occur with probability

$$p = \pi_2 P^{(2)}\{J^{(1)} \cap \overline{J^{(2)}}\} + \pi_1 P^{(1)}\{J^{(2)} \cap \overline{J^{(1)}}\}. \tag{54}$$

For singular detection to occur $(\forall \pi_i)$ with probability one, one must have $p = 1$, and subsequently require (since $P^{(2)}\{J^{(1)} \cap \overline{J^{(2)}}\} = P^{(2)}\{J^{(1)}\})$

$$P^{(2)}\{J^{(1)}\} = P^{(1)}\{J^{(2)}\} = 1. \tag{55}$$

The following shows this to be (a.s.) impossible.

*Lemma 7:* A completely singular test (50) over $[0,T]$, $T < \infty$, cannot occur with probability one.

*Proof:* We must show that (55) cannot hold; i.e.,

$$P^{(2)}\{J^{(1)}\} < 1 \qquad P^{(1)}\{J^{(2)}\} < 1.$$

Clearly,

$$J^{(i)}(\omega) \subset \{W_1(\omega) < T\}, \qquad i = 1,2.$$

But, by (19), for any RPP

$$P\{W_1(\omega) < T\} = 1 - P\{W_1(\omega) \geq T\} = 1 - \exp\left[-\int_0^T \hat{\lambda}_0(u)\, du\right] < 1$$

since $T < \infty$ and $\hat{\lambda}_0(u)$ is bounded. Q.E.D.

As a corollary, we observe that a completely singular case (i.e., correct decision probabilities equal to one a.s.)

can occur only if

$$\lim_{T\to\infty} \int_0^T \hat{\lambda}_0^{(i)}(u)\,du = \infty, \tag{56}$$

for those $i = 1,2$, for which $J_1^{(i)}(\omega) \neq \phi$. Thus, one has to observe the input a very long time, as well as impose a nonintegrability restriction over the intensity function, to ensure perfect detection with probability one. We illustrate a perfect detection situation by an example.

Assume $J^{(2)} = \phi$, $L_n^{(1)}(\omega) = \phi$ for $n \neq k$ and $L_k^{(1)}(\omega) = (W_{k-1}(\omega),T]$ for some $k \geq 1$, so that $J^{(1)}(\omega) = \{W_k(\omega) \in (W_{k-1}(\omega), T]\}$. Equivalently, we have that $P^{(1)}\{N(T) \geq k\} = 0$. For singularity one requires (55), $P^{(2)}\{J^{(1)}\} = P^{(2)}\{N(T) \geq k\} = 1$, or $P^{(2)}\{W_k(\omega) \leq T\} = 1$. Letting $T \to \infty$, we deduce from relation (18) that $W_k < \infty$ with probability one if for each $0 < t_1 < \cdots < t_{m-1} < \infty$ and each $m$, $1 \leq m \leq k$, we have

$$\lim_{T\to\infty} \int_{t_{m-1}}^T \lambda_{m-1}^{(2)}(u,t_{m-1},\cdots,t_1)\,du = \infty. \tag{57}$$

Equation (57) is thus a sufficient condition for complete singularity, provided the observation period is infinitely long.

In most practical cases, one expects $J^{(1)} = J^{(2)}$ $(= \phi$, usually). Consequently, $P^{(1)} \equiv P^{(2)}$ by (51) and the test consists of comparing the likelihood ratio (45) with a threshold. The first term in the latter test involves a correlation operation between the ratio of the causal MMSE estimates of the two intensity processes and the observed counting process. The second term represents the difference between the total "energy" of the two intensity estimates. When the incoming processes are noncompound RPP's, the intensity functions alone are involved in (45), while intensities (37) are to be incorporated if we observe superposed RPP's.

*Optimal Counting Detection Procedures*

In practice, one often utilizes only a counter at the input of the receiver. A decision between the two counting processes is then based only on the total number of occurrences $N(T)$. The latter is a random variable defined on $(\Omega_N,\beta_T)$, where $\beta_T$ is the Borel field generated by $N(T)$. To derive the likelihood-ratio test, one has to calculate the Radon–Nikodym derivative $dP_T^{(2)}/dP_T^{(1)}$, where

$$P_T^{(i)}(A) = \int_A P^{(i)}\{N(T, d\omega)\}, \qquad i = 1,2, \tag{58}$$

$\forall A \in \beta_T$. $P_T^{(i)}$ is the counting measure at $T$ of an RPP whose intensity (4) is $\lambda_n^{(i)}(t)$, $n \geq 0$. If $P_T^{(2)} \ll P_T^{(1)}$ the likelihood ratio is

$$\Lambda_n(T) = \frac{P_T^{(2)}\{N(T) = n\}}{P_T^{(1)}\{N(T) = n\}}. \tag{59}$$

To evaluate $\Lambda_n(T)$ expressions for the counting probabilities $p_n^{(i)}(t) = P^{(i)}\{N(t) = n\}$ of the incoming processes are required. Although the latter are generally difficult to calculate explicitly, difference–differential equations for them are given by (11). A recursive detection procedure can then be synthesized.

The singularity of the counting test is studied in the same way as above. For that purpose, the following property is essential.

*Lemma 8:* For an RPP, $\forall t > 0$ and $m \geq 1$

$$P\{N(t) = m\} = 0, \qquad \text{iff } \lambda_i(t) = 0 \text{ for some } 0 \leq i \leq m-1. \tag{60}$$

*Proof:* By (11), if $\lambda_{m-1}(t) = 0$, then $(\partial/\partial t)p_m(t) = -\lambda_m(t)p_m(t)$, which in turn implies $p_m(t) = 0$ since $p_m(0) = 0$. If $p_m(t) = 0$, we have by (11) that $\lambda_{m-1}(t)p_{m-1}(t) = 0$. Consequently, if $\lambda_{m-1}(t)$ does not vanish, one must have $p_{m-1}(t) = 0$. Subsequently, $\lambda_i(t) = 0$ for some $0 \leq i \leq m-1$ as $\lambda_0(t)p_0(t) = 0 \Rightarrow \lambda_0(t) = 0$ by (11), since $p_0(0) = 1$. Q.E.D.

As a corollary to Lemma 8, we obtain for any RPP that

$$P\{N(t) = n\} = 0 \Rightarrow P\{N(t) \geq n\} = 0, \qquad \forall n \geq 1, \forall t \in [0,T]. \tag{61}$$

Using properties (60) and (61) the singularity conditions are expressed as follows. Let

$$k^{(i)} = \min_{n\geq 1} \{n: \lambda_{n-1}^{(i)}(T) = 0\}, \qquad i = 1,2, \tag{62}$$

if it is defined, and $k^{(i)} = \infty$ otherwise. Define then the set

$$J^{(i)}(\omega) = \{\omega : N(T,\omega) \geq k^{(i)}\}, \qquad i = 1,2, \tag{63}$$

so that $J^{(i)}(\omega) = \phi$ (a.s.) if $k^{(i)} = \infty$, since the process is honest. From (60) and (61), $P^{(i)}\{J^{(i)}\} = 0$, $i = 1,2$. Lebesgue decomposition of $P_T^{(2)}$ and $P_T^{(1)}$ then follows directly as in Lemma 6. Corresponding to Theorem 7, one then deduces here the following detection procedures.

*Theorem 8:* For an RPP, if $k^{(1)} = k^{(2)}$, then $P_T^{(1)} \equiv P_T^{(2)}$ and the optimal detection procedure is the likelihood-ratio test (59). If $k^{(1)} > k^{(2)}$, we have $P_T^{(2)} \ll P_T^{(1)}$ and we will decide in favor of $H_1$ if $k^{(2)} < N(T,\omega) \leq k^{(1)}$ and use (59) otherwise. A similar result holds for $k^{(2)} > k^{(1)}$.

As an example, consider the following important case. Assume the $H_2$ process to be any RPP with a positive intensity function $\lambda_n^{(2)}(t)$. The noise $(H_1)$ process is taken to be an homogeneous Poisson process, with intensity $\lambda^{(1)} > 0$. Using (11) in (59), we obtain the following difference–differential relation for the likelihood ratio, $n \geq 1$,

$$\frac{\partial}{\partial t}\Lambda_n(t) = \Lambda_n(t)\left[\lambda^{(1)} - \frac{n}{t} - \lambda_n^{(2)}(t)\right] + \Lambda_{n-1}(t)\lambda_{n-1}^{(2)}(t)\frac{n}{\lambda^{(1)}t}. \tag{64}$$

When the $H_2$ process is the superposition of the noise (Poisson) process and an RPP $\{N^{(s)}(t)\}$ which is modulated by a stochastic process $S(t)$ and has intensity $\lambda_n^{(s)}(t,S_t)$, the likelihood ratio follows relation (64) with $\lambda_n^{(2)}(t)$ replace by [see (32), (37)]

$$\hat{\lambda}_n^{(2)}(t) = \lambda^{(1)} + E\{\lambda_{N^{(s)}(t)}^{(s)}(t,S_t) \mid N(t) = n, H_2\}. \quad (65)$$

## VI. Applications

An RPP is a most useful statistical model in practical applications due to its physically simple "constructive" nature. The process, as well as its joint occurrence density, are directly characterized by the intensity process. Since the latter expresses the occurrence density of the events at any instant of time, based upon the complete past evolution of the point process, one can directly incorporate into the model all possible dependencies and nonstationary effects which characterize the system.

Two important models of point processes that belong to the class of RPP's are doubly stochastic Poisson processes and renewal processes. The various results of the present paper can be easily applied to these processes. A doubly stochastic Poisson process [11] is a compound Poisson process, and thus an RPP for which $\lambda_{N(t)}(t,\mathscr{B}_t,S_t) = \lambda(t,S_t)$. It serves as a statistical model in medical and optical communication systems [6]. In the latter case $\lambda(t,S_t) = \alpha|S(t)|^2$, where $S(t)$ is the complex envelope of the received electric field and $\alpha$ is related to the quantum efficiency of the photodetector and the energy per photon at the carrier frequency. Using this $\lambda(t,S_t)$ as the intensity function, our results can be directly applied. In particular, the evolution of the likelihood function follows from (45). The latter expression, for the doubly stochastic Poisson processes, has been obtained in [6] and [10], and for inhomogeneous Poisson processes in [8].

A renewal process ([1], [13], [14]) is defined as a point process whose intervals between occurrences are independent and identically distributed. Denote the interval distribution and density function (the latter is assumed to exist) by $F_X(x)$ and $f_X(x)$, respectively. The sequence $\{W_n\}$ is now a Markov sequence with the transition density

$$f_{W_{n+1}|W_n}(t_{n+1},t_n) = f_X(t_{n+1} - t_n). \quad (66)$$

Using (17) and (66), the intensity function of the process is then given by

$$\lambda_{N(t)}(t, W_{N(t)}, \cdots, W_1) = \frac{f_X(t - W_{N(t)})}{\mathscr{F}_X(t - W_{N(t)})} \triangleq h_X(t - W_{N(t)}), \quad (67)$$

where $\mathscr{F}_X(x) = 1 - F_X(x)$ and $h_X(x) = f_X(x)/\mathscr{F}_X(x)$ is the hazard function corresponding to $X$ [11]. Now the intensity process $\lambda(t,\omega_1)$ is given for a specific outcome $\omega_1 = \{t_1, t_2, \cdots, t_{N_T}\}$ by $h_X(t - t_n)$ for $t_n < t \le t_{n+1}$, $n = 0,1,2, \cdots, N_T$. Various characteristics of the process, as well as filtering and detection procedures, then follow directly. In particular, when the hazard function depends on some random parameter, MMSE estimates are utilized.

As an illustrating example, we consider now the optimal detection procedure for the following signals of the random-telegraph type. Assume that, under hypothesis $H_i$, the observed process is a two-state homogeneous Markov jump process $\{Y^{(i)}(t), t \in [0,T]\}$, $i = 1,2$. Let the two states be denoted as $+1$ and $-1$. Thus, the observed signal is a process with randomly occurring jumps oscillating between states $+1$ and $-1$. Assume $Y^{(i)}(0^+) = 1$. Let $W_k^{(i)}$ denote the instant of occurrence of the $k$th jump (whether from 1 to $-1$ or vice versa), under $H_i$. Then, the evolution of the random-telegraph signal is clearly completely specified by the stochastic point process $\{W_k^{(i)}, k \ge 1\}$, $W_0^{(i)} \triangleq 0$, since no information is gained by incorporating the state observations. Denote the counting processes associated with the latter point process by $\{N^{(i)}(t), t \in [0,T]\}$, $i = 1,2$.

The homogeneous two-state Markov processes $\{Y^{(i)}(t)\}$ are specified by their generator matrix $Q^{(i)} = (q_{k,j}^{(i)})$, where $q_{k,j}^{(i)}$ is the passage intensity from state $k$ to state $j$; $k,j = 0,1$, under $H_i$ (see, for example, [1, p. 293]). Let these intensities be given by the following positive quantities, $i = 1,2: q_{-1,1}^{(i)} = \theta_{-1}^{(i)}, q_{+1,-1}^{(i)} = \theta_1^{(i)}$, $q_{1,1}^{(i)} = -\theta_1^{(i)}$, $q_{-1,1}^{(i)} = -\theta_{-1}^{(i)}$. One thus readily observes that $\{N^{(i)}(t)\}$ are RPP's with the intensity functions

$$\lambda_{N(t)}^{(i)}(t,\mathscr{B}_t) = \begin{cases} \theta_1^{(i)}, & N(t) = 2k,\ k \ge 0 \\ \theta_{-1}^{(i)}, & N(t) = 2k+1,\ k \ge 0. \end{cases} \quad (68)$$

Note that $\theta_1^{(i)}$ is the intensity of jumps from state 1 into state $-1$ under $H_i$.

Observing a sample function over $[0,T]$, we wish to decide between $\{Y^{(1)}(t)\}$ and $\{Y^{(2)}(t)\}$. Under a Bayes optimization criterion, the optimal detection procedure is given by the likelihood-ratio processor. Since only $\{N^{(i)}(t)\}$ are relevant, the optimal detection scheme is obtained by incorporating (68) into (20) or (25).

We thus have

$$\begin{aligned} \ln \Lambda_T(\omega) = {} & [(N(T) + 1)/2]_+ \ln (\theta_1^{(2)}/\theta_1^{(1)}) \\ & + [(N(T) + 1)/2]_- \ln (\theta_{-1}^{(1)}/\theta_{-1}^{(1)}) \\ & + (\theta_1^{(1)} - \theta_1^{(2)})\tau_T + (\theta_{-1}^{(1)} - \theta_{-1}^{(2)})\sigma_T, \end{aligned} \quad (69)$$

where $\tau_t(\sigma_t)$ denotes the total time the observed process has spent in state 1 ($-1$) during $[0,t]$, $\tau_t + \sigma_t = t$, $[x]_-$ denotes the largest integer that is not larger than $x$, and $[x]_+$ denotes the smallest integer that is not smaller than $x$. Note that for this problem the pair $(N(T),\tau_T)$ constitutes a sufficient statistic. Thus, one has to measure only the total number of occurrences and the total time the observed process spends in state 1 during $[0,T]$.

In practice, the observer will not often know the intensities $\theta_1^{(i)}$, $\theta_{-1}^{(i)}$. However, a statistical model for these parameters is usually available. Consequently, consider now $\theta_1^{(i)}$ and $\theta_{-1}^{(i)}$ to be positive random variables with the (continuously differentiable) moment-generating functions $\phi_{1,i}(t) = E\{\exp[-\theta_1^{(i)}t]\}$ and $\phi_{-1,i}(t) = E\{\exp[-\theta_{-1}^{(i)}t]\}$, respectively. The optimal detection procedure for an observation of a sample function of the incoming random-telegraph signal over $[0,T]$ is sought. Note that now under $H_i$ the observed counting process possesses the intensity function $\lambda_{N(t)}^{(i)}(t,\mathscr{B}_t,\theta_1^{(i)},\theta_{-1}^{(i)})$ given by (68) for any realization of $\{\theta_1^{(i)},\theta_{-1}^{(i)}\}$. Since the latter realization is unobserved we can consider it as a "nuisance" parameter. Under a Bayes criterion, it is well known that the resulting optimal detection procedure is given by the generalized likelihood ratio $\hat{f}_T^{(2)}(\omega)/\hat{f}_T^{(1)}(\omega)$, where $\hat{f}_T^{(i)}(\omega)$ is the compound (over realizations of $\theta_1^{(i)}$ and $\theta_{-1}^{(i)}$) joint occurrence density and is thus given by (29) where $S_t \equiv \{\theta_1,\theta_{-1}\}$. One then readily obtains that under $H_i$ the compound RPP possesses the intensity

$$\hat{\lambda}_{N(t)}^{(i)}(t,\mathscr{B}_t) = \begin{cases} \mu_{N(t)}^{(i)}(\tau_t), & N(t) = 2k,\ k \geq 0 \\ \nu_{N(t)}^{(i)}(\sigma_t), & N(t) = 2k+1,\ k \geq 0, \end{cases} \quad (70)$$

where

$$\mu_j^{(i)}(\tau_t) = |\phi_{1,i}^{(j+1)}(\tau_t)/\phi_{1,i}^{(j)}(\tau_t)|$$

$$\nu_j^{(i)}(\sigma_t) = |\phi_{-1,i}^{(j+1)}(\sigma_t)/\phi_{-1,i}^{(j)}(\sigma_t)|$$

and

$$\phi^{(j)}(x) \triangleq \frac{d^j}{dx^j}\phi(x).$$

By (33), the optimal detection procedure is thus given as

$$\begin{aligned} \ln \Lambda_T(\omega) &= \sum_{k=0}^{[(N(T)-1)/2]_+} \ln [\mu_{2k}^{(2)}(\tau_{W_{2k+1}})/\mu_{2k}^{(1)}(\tau_{W_{2k+1}})] \\ &+ \sum_{k=0}^{[(N(T)-1)/2]_-} \ln [\nu_{2k+1}^{(2)}(\sigma_{W_{2k+1}})/\nu_{2k+1}^{(1)}(\sigma_{W_{2k+1}})] \\ &- \sum_{k=0}^{[(N(T)-1)/2]_+} \int_{W_{2k}}^{W_{2k+1}} [\mu_{2k}^{(2)}(\tau_t) - \mu_{2k}^{(1)}(\tau_t)]\, dt \\ &- \sum_{k=0}^{[(N(T)-1)/2]_-} \int_{W_{2k+1}}^{W_{2k+2}} [\nu_{2k+1}^{(2)}(\sigma_t) - \nu_{2k+1}^{(1)}(\sigma_t)]\, dt, \end{aligned} \quad (71)$$

where we have set $W_{N(T)+1} = T$. We note that in the present problem, no simple sufficient statistic exists and one needs to observe the complete evolution of the incoming process; i.e., use measurements of $\{W_1,W_2,\cdots,W_{N(T)},N(T)\}$. To obtain the optimal detector when only the total number of counts $N(T)$ is observed, one has to generate the likelihood ratio (59). For that purpose, one computes $p_n^{(i)}(t)$ by solving the difference–differential equations (31), where for $k \geq 0$, one uses $\hat{\lambda}_{2k}(t) = E\{\theta_1 \mid N(t) = 2k\}$ and $\hat{\lambda}_{2k+1}(t) = E\{\theta_{-1} \mid N(t) = 2k+1\}$.

## VII. Conclusions

A class of regular point processes that possess intensity functions has been introduced. The occurrence characteristics of an RPP are expressed in terms of its intensity process. The same relations are shown to hold for a compound RPP, if the causal MMSE estimate of the intensity function is incorporated.

The superposition of two independent RPP's is shown to yield an RPP whose intensity is given as a causal MMSE estimate of the appropriate combination of the two intensity functions.

A general likelihood-ratio formula for the detection of compound RPP is derived. The known likelihood-ratio expressions, for doubly stochastic Poisson processes, are thus extended to include a larger class of point processes. Cases of singular detection are characterized. It is shown that perfect detection cannot occur with probability one. Optimal detection procedures which utilize observations only of the total counts are discussed.

We have presented here a "constructive" approach to the modeling and processing of point processes. This is most important in practice, since it indicates how one can incorporate into the model, or the processor, all possible dependencies and nonstationary effects that characterize the system. In particular, it provides us with insight as to the processing procedure one has to adopt when only partial information concerning the point process is available.

## References


[1] E. Parzen, *Stochastic Processes*. San Francisco: Holden-Day, 1962.
[2] A. T. Bharucha-Reid, *Elements of the Theory of Markov Processes and Their Applications*. New York: McGraw-Hill, 1960.
[3] I. I. Gikhman and A. V. Skorokhod, *Introduction to the Theory of Random Processes*. Philadelphia, Pa.: Saunders, 1969.
[4] J. L. Doob, *Stochastic Processes*. New York: Wiley, 1953.
[5] E. Wong, *Stochastic Processes in Information and Dynamical Systems*. New York: McGraw-Hill, 1971.
[6] D. L. Snyder, "Filtering and detection for doubly stochastic Poisson processes," *IEEE Trans. Inform. Theory*, vol. IT-18, pp. 91–102, Jan. 1972.
[7] T. Kailath, "A general likelihood ratio formula for random signals in Gaussian noise," *IEEE Trans. Inform. Theory*, vol. IT-15, pp. 350–361, May 1969.
[8] I. Bar-David, "Communication under the Poisson regime," *IEEE Trans. Inform. Theory*, vol. 15, pp. 31–37, Jan. 1969.
[9] I. Rubin, "Detection of point processes and applications to photon and radar detection," Inform. Sci. Syst. Lab., Dep. Elec. Eng., Princeton Univ., Princeton, N.J., Tech. Rep. 32, Sept. 1970.
[10] J. R. Clark, "Estimation for Poisson processes," Res. Lab. Electron., Massachusetts Inst. Technol., Cambridge, Quart. Progr. Rep. 100, pp. 146–149, Jan. 1971.
[11] D. R. Cox and P. A. W. Lewis, *The Statistical Analysis of Series of Events*. London: Methuen, 1966.
[12] ——, "Multivariate point processes," in *Proc. 6th Berkeley Symp.*, to be published.
[13] D. R. Cox, *Renewal Theory*. London: Methuen, 1962.
[14] W. L. Smith, "Renewal theory and its ramifications," *J. Roy. Statist. Soc. B*, vol. 20, pp. 284–320, 1958.
[15] J. A. McFadden, "The entropy of a point process," *SIAM J. Appl. Math.*, vol. 13, pp. 988–994, 1965.
[16] W. Feller, *An Introduction to Probability Theory and Its Applications*, vol. 1, 3rd ed. New York: Wiley, 1968.

3



Reprinted from *IEEE Trans. Inform. Theory,* **IT-18**(1), 91–102 (1972)

# Filtering and Detection for Doubly Stochastic Poisson Processes

DONALD L. SNYDER, MEMBER, IEEE

*Abstract*—**Equations are derived that describe the time evolution of the posterior statistics of a general Markov process that modulates the intensity function of an observed inhomogeneous Poisson counting process. The basic equation is a stochastic differential equation for the conditional characteristic function of the Markov process.**

**A separation theorem is established for the detection of a Poisson process having a stochastic intensity function. Specifically, it is shown that the causal minimum-mean-square-error estimate of the stochastic intensity is incorporated in the optimum Reiffen–Sherman detector in the same way as if it were known.**

**Specialized results are obtained when a set of random variables modulate the intensity. These include equations for maximum *a posteriori* probability estimates of the variables and some accuracy equations based on the Cramér–Rao inequality.**

**Procedures for approximating exact estimates of the Markov process are given. A comparison by simulation of exact and approximate estimates indicates that the approximations suggested can work well even under low count rate conditions.**

## I. Introduction

THE GENERAL mathematical model we formulate in Section II is motivated by the following procedure used in medical diagnosis and research. A quantity of a radioactive labeled substance (such as oxygen, carbon dioxide, water, and hemoglobin) is introduced into an organ (such as the lung and brain) and the radioactive emissions are then monitored externally with a particle counting device [1]–[4]. The observed-particle emission rate is generally time dependent because it decreases with time as the labeled substance is removed from the organ by natural processes such as blood circulation.

At least to a first approximation, it appears reasonable to model the counter registrations as an inhomogeneous Poisson counting process with an intensity $\lambda_t(x)$ counts per second, where $x$ represents a set of parameters describing the state of the organ. A commonly assumed form for $\lambda_t(x)$ is simply a sum of a few decaying exponentials in which the coefficients and decay constants are the elements of $x$, but other forms have also been suggested [4], [5]. The diagnostic problem is that of estimating the parameters $x$ from the observed counter registrations and then using these estimates with any additional clinical information that may be available to judge whether the organ is normal or abnormal. A frequently used procedure for estimating the parameters is to least-squares curve fit an assumed form for $\lambda_t(x)$ to a histogram of the counting rate. Moreover, it is often desired to estimate some function, say $\boldsymbol{h}_t(x)$, of the parameters. Some examples are: $\boldsymbol{h}_t(x) = x$, as before; $\boldsymbol{h}_t(x) = \lambda_t(x)$, the intensity; and $\boldsymbol{h}_t(x) = \lambda_0(x)/\int_0^\infty \lambda_\sigma(x)\, d\sigma$, a function used as a measure of blood flow [6]. In what follows, we shall offer an alternative to this procedure of curve fitting to count histograms for forming these estimates.

In the general mathematical model formulated below, we allow the parameters to vary stochastically with time as a vector Markov process; the case of constant parameters described above is then a special, but important, subclass of the model. While the applicability of the more general model to medical problems is presently unclear, there exist such applications, one being to optical communications in which photon counters are used as detectors. The intensity of the photon counting process varies stochastically due to two sources, one of which is message modulation of the incident optical field and the other is fading of the optical field introduced by turbulence and scattering in the optical link [7], [8].

Manuscript received March 27, 1970; revised December 28, 1970. This work was supported by the Division of Research Resources, National Institutes of Health, under Research Grant RR 00396.

The author is with the Department of Electrical Engineering and the Biomedical Computer Laboratory, Washington University, St. Louis, Mo. 63110.

## II. Model Formulation and Problem Statement

### *A. Model Formulation*

Let $\{N_t, t \geq t_0\}$ be a doubly stochastic Poisson counting process with a stochastic intensity function $\{\lambda_t, t \geq t_0\}$. These processes were first introduced by Cox [9] and later described by Cox and Lewis [10, ch. 7]. By a doubly stochastic Poisson process, we mean that $N_{t_0} = 0$ a.s., $\{N_t, t \geq t_0\}$ is an integer-valued process with independent increments given the intensity $\{\lambda_t, t \geq t_0\}$, and a.s. for $t > s \geq t_0$

$$\Pr[N_t - N_s = n \mid \lambda_\sigma, s < \sigma \leq t] = (n!)^{-1}\left(\int_s^t \lambda_\sigma\, d\sigma\right)^n \exp\left(-\int_s^t \lambda_\sigma\, d\sigma\right). \quad (1)$$

We assume that the following limits, which describe the incremental properties of $N_t$, exist a.s.:

i) $\lim_{\Delta t \to 0} (\Delta t)^{-1} \cdot \{1 - \Pr(\Delta N_t = 0 \mid \lambda_\sigma, t < \sigma \leq t + \Delta t)\} = \lambda_t$

ii) $\lim_{\Delta t \to 0} (\Delta t)^{-1} \Pr(\Delta N_t = 1 \mid \lambda_\sigma, t < \sigma \leq t + \Delta t) = \lambda_t$

iii) $\lim_{\Delta t \to 0} \Pr(\Delta N_t = m \mid \lambda_\sigma, t < \sigma \leq t + \Delta t) = 0, \quad m > 1,$

where $\Delta N_t = N_{t+\Delta t} - N_t$. Thus, for $\Delta t$ sufficiently small,

*Note:* The material in this paper appears in expanded form in Chapter 6 of D. L. Snyder, *Stochastic Point Processes,* Wiley-Interscience, A Division of John Wiley & Sons, Inc. (in preparation).

$$\Pr[\Delta N_t = i \mid \lambda_\sigma, t < \sigma \le t + \Delta t] = (1 - \lambda_t \Delta t)\,\delta_{0i} + \lambda_t \Delta t\, \delta_{1i} + o(\Delta t), \quad (2)$$

where

$$\lim_{\Delta t \to 0} (\Delta t)^{-1} o(\Delta t) = 0$$

and where $\delta_{ij}$ is the Kronecker delta function.

Certain statistics of a doubly stochastic Poisson process are given by Cox and Lewis [10, ch. 7] and Bartlett [11, p. 325]. A useful relation can be given for the characteristic functional of the process $\{N_t, t \ge t_0\}$ in terms of the characteristic functional of the process $\{m_t, t \ge t_0\}$, where $m_t = \int_{t_0}^t \lambda_\sigma \, d\sigma = E[N_t \mid \lambda_\sigma, t_0 < \sigma \le t]$. Let $\phi_y(v) = E[\exp(j\int_{t_0}^t v_\sigma \, dy_\sigma)]$ denote the characteristic functional for a process $\{y_t, t \ge t_0\}$. Then $\phi_N(v) = \phi_m[j\{1 - \exp(jv)\}]$. This relation is useful for investigating the probability density function, $r$th correlations $E[\prod_{j=1}^r N_{t_j}]$, and other statistics of $\{N_t, t \ge t_0\}$ when $\phi_m$ is known. Examples are given by Cox and Lewis [10, p. 183] and Bartlett [11, p. 325]. Karp and Clark [12] and Clark and Hoversten [13] have investigated the first-order statistics of $\{N_t, t \ge t_0\}$ for the special, but important case in optical communications when $\lambda_t = |a_t|^2$, where $\{a_t, t \ge t_0\}$ is a Gaussian process. Additional references on this case are given by Karp and Clark.

We shall assume in what follows that $\lambda_t = \lambda_t(\boldsymbol{x}_t)$ for $t \ge t_0$ is a positive function of an $n$-vector Markov process $\{\boldsymbol{x}_t, t \ge t_0\}$. For the following discussion of these processes, we refer to the work of Frost [14, p. 37]. Let $c_t(\boldsymbol{v})$ be the characteristic function for $\boldsymbol{x}_t$ at time $t$,

$$c_t(\boldsymbol{v}) = E\{\exp[j\langle \boldsymbol{v}, \boldsymbol{x}_t\rangle]\}, \quad (3)$$

where $\langle \cdot, \cdot \rangle$ denotes vector inner (dot) product. Assume that

a) $(\Delta t)^{-1} |E\{(\exp[j\langle \boldsymbol{v}, \Delta\boldsymbol{x}_t\rangle] - 1) \mid \boldsymbol{x}_t\}| \le g(\boldsymbol{v}; t, \boldsymbol{x}_t)$ a.s.

where $\Delta \boldsymbol{x}_t = \boldsymbol{x}_{t+\Delta t} - \boldsymbol{x}_t$ and $E[|g|] < \infty$; and

b) $p \lim_{\Delta t \to 0} (\Delta t)^{-1} E\{(\exp[j\langle \boldsymbol{v}, \Delta \boldsymbol{x}_t\rangle] - 1) \mid \boldsymbol{x}_t\} \triangleq \psi_t(\boldsymbol{v} \mid \boldsymbol{x}_t)$

exists.

The function $\psi_t(\boldsymbol{v} \mid \boldsymbol{x}_t)$ in b) is the characteristic form of the differential generator for $\boldsymbol{x}_t$. From these assumptions, it can be shown that the time evolution of the unconditional characteristic function for $\boldsymbol{x}_t$ is described by

$$(\partial/\partial t) c_t(\boldsymbol{v}) = E\{\exp[j\langle \boldsymbol{v}, \boldsymbol{x}_t\rangle] \psi_t(\boldsymbol{v} \mid \boldsymbol{x}_t)\}$$
$$c_{t_0}(\boldsymbol{v}) = E\{\exp[j\langle \boldsymbol{v}, \boldsymbol{x}_{t_0}\rangle]\}. \quad (4)$$

The proof is straightforward; because we need a similar proof later, we include it here. Still following Frost (also see Bartlett [11, p. 87]), we have the proof.

$$\begin{aligned} c_{t+\Delta t}(\boldsymbol{v}) &= E\{\exp[j\langle \boldsymbol{v}, \boldsymbol{x}_{t+\Delta t}\rangle]\} \\ &= E\{\exp[j\langle \boldsymbol{v}, \boldsymbol{x}_t\rangle] \exp[j\langle \boldsymbol{v}, \Delta \boldsymbol{x}_t\rangle]\} \\ &= E\{\exp[j\langle \boldsymbol{v}, \boldsymbol{x}_t\rangle] E\{\exp[j\langle \boldsymbol{v}, \Delta \boldsymbol{x}_t\rangle] \mid \boldsymbol{x}_t\}\}, \end{aligned}$$

where the last equality follows from the definition of conditional expectation. Thus,

$$\begin{aligned} (\Delta t)^{-1} \Delta c_t(\boldsymbol{v}) &= (\Delta t)^{-1}[c_{t+\Delta t}(\boldsymbol{v}) - c_t(\boldsymbol{v})] \\ &= E\{\exp[j\langle \boldsymbol{v}, \boldsymbol{x}_t\rangle] (\Delta t)^{-1} \\ &\quad \cdot E\{(\exp[j\langle \boldsymbol{v}, \Delta \boldsymbol{x}_t\rangle] - 1) \mid \boldsymbol{x}_t\}\}. \end{aligned}$$

Taking the limit as $\Delta t \to 0$ results in the desired expression. The interchange of limit and expectation is justified by assumption a) and Lebesgue's bounded convergence theorem [15, p. 110].

It is of interest to consider the case when $\{\boldsymbol{x}_t, t \ge t_0\}$ has a well-defined representation as the solution to a stochastic differential equation of the form

$$d\boldsymbol{x}_t = \boldsymbol{f}_t(\boldsymbol{x}_t)\, dt + \boldsymbol{G}_t(\boldsymbol{x}_t)\, d\boldsymbol{\chi}_t$$
$$\boldsymbol{x}_{t_0} = \boldsymbol{x}_0. \quad (5)$$

where $\{\boldsymbol{\chi}_t, t \ge t_0\}$ is a martingale with independent infinitely divisible increments. Three examples of the type of modulation process $\{\boldsymbol{x}_t, t \ge t_0\}$ included are as follows.

1) Let $\boldsymbol{f}_t(\boldsymbol{x}_t) = \boldsymbol{0}$ and $\boldsymbol{G}_t(\boldsymbol{x}_t) = \boldsymbol{0}$. Then $\boldsymbol{x}_t = \boldsymbol{x}_0$ is simply a collection of *random variables* for all $t \ge t_0$. It is easily seen that $\psi_t(\boldsymbol{v} \mid \boldsymbol{x}_t) = 0$ in this case. Substitution of this expression into (4) and then inverse Fourier transforming shows the obvious fact that $p_t(\boldsymbol{x}_t) = p(\boldsymbol{x}_0)$, the probability density for $\boldsymbol{x}_0$, for all $t \ge t_0$.

2) Let $\boldsymbol{\chi}_t$ be a standardized vector Wiener process. Then for appropriate restrictions on $\boldsymbol{f}_t$ and $\boldsymbol{G}_t$, $\boldsymbol{x}_t$ is a Markov diffusion process. If $\boldsymbol{f}_t$ is linear in $\boldsymbol{x}_t$ and $\boldsymbol{G}_t$ does not depend on $\boldsymbol{x}_t$, then $\boldsymbol{x}_t$ is a Gauss–Markov diffusion process. The characteristic form for the differential generator of $\boldsymbol{x}_t$ in this case is given by

$$\psi_t(\boldsymbol{v} \mid \boldsymbol{x}_t) = j\langle \boldsymbol{v}, \boldsymbol{f}_t(\boldsymbol{x}_t)\rangle - \tfrac{1}{2}\langle \boldsymbol{v}, \boldsymbol{G}_t(\boldsymbol{x}_t)\boldsymbol{G}_t'(\boldsymbol{x}_t)\boldsymbol{v}\rangle. \quad (6)$$

Substitution of this expression into (4) and then inverse Fourier transforming results in the forward Kolmogorov Fokker–Planck equation for the probability density $p_t(\boldsymbol{x}_t)$ of $\boldsymbol{x}_t$.

3) Let $\boldsymbol{\chi}_t = \tilde{\boldsymbol{\chi}}_t - E(\tilde{\boldsymbol{\chi}}_t)$, where $\tilde{\boldsymbol{\chi}}_t$ is an $m$-vector of independent Poisson counting processes with intensities $\mu_1, \mu_2, \cdots, \mu_m$ and assume $\boldsymbol{G}_t$ is not a function of $\boldsymbol{x}_t$. Then for appropriate restrictions on $\boldsymbol{f}_t$, $\boldsymbol{x}_t$ is a "Poisson driven" Markov process [16]. The characteristic form for the differential generator of $\boldsymbol{x}_t$ in this case is given by

$$\psi_t(\boldsymbol{v} \mid \boldsymbol{x}_t) = j\langle \boldsymbol{v}, \boldsymbol{f}_t(\boldsymbol{x}_t)\rangle + \sum_{i=1}^m \mu_i(\exp[j\langle \boldsymbol{v}, \boldsymbol{G}_t \boldsymbol{e}_i\rangle] - 1),$$

where $\boldsymbol{e}_i$ is an $m$-vector with a 1 in row $i$ and 0's elsewhere. Substitution of this expression into (4) and then inverse Fourier transforming results in the following equation for the probability density $p_t(\boldsymbol{x}_t)$ of $\boldsymbol{x}_t$:

$$(\partial/\partial t) p_t(\boldsymbol{x}_t) = -\langle \partial/\partial \boldsymbol{x}_t, \boldsymbol{f}_t(\boldsymbol{x}_t) p_t(\boldsymbol{x}_t)\rangle \sum_{i=1}^m \mu_i[p_t(\boldsymbol{x}_t - \boldsymbol{G}_t \boldsymbol{e}_i) - p_t(\boldsymbol{x}_t)],$$

where $\partial/\partial \boldsymbol{x}_t$ denotes the gradient operator.

*B. Problem Statement*

We consider the problem of causally estimating $\boldsymbol{h}_t = \boldsymbol{h}_t(\boldsymbol{x}_t)$, a given vector-valued function of $t$ and $\boldsymbol{x}_t$, from observations of the counting process on the interval $(t_0,t]$. Let $N_{t_0,t} = \{N_\sigma, t_0 < \sigma \leq t\}$ be the record of the observed counting process. Then the solution to this estimation problem depends on knowing the posterior density $p_t(\boldsymbol{x}_t \mid N_{t_0,t})$ of $\boldsymbol{x}_t$. For instance, the minimum-mean-square error (MMSE) and maximum *a posteriori* probability (MAP) estimates of $\boldsymbol{h}_t$ can be determined when this density is known. We therefore concentrate on the basic problem of describing the time evolution of $p_t(\boldsymbol{x}_t \mid N_{t_0,t})$ as additional observations are accumulated.

## III. The Evolution of the Posterior Statistics

Let $c_{t|t_0}(\boldsymbol{v} \mid N_{t_0,t})$ be the characteristic function for $\boldsymbol{x}_t$ given $N_{t_0,t}$,

$$c_{t|t_0}(\boldsymbol{v} \mid N_{t_0,t}) = E\{\exp[j\langle \boldsymbol{v},\boldsymbol{x}_t\rangle] \mid N_{t_0,t}\}. \tag{7}$$

Assume that

a) $(\Delta t)^{-1}|E\{(\exp[j\langle \boldsymbol{v},\Delta\boldsymbol{x}_t\rangle] - 1) \mid N_{t_0,t},\boldsymbol{x}_t\}| \leq g(\boldsymbol{v};t,N_{t_0,t},\boldsymbol{x}_t)$,

where $E[|g|] < \infty$; and

b) $p \lim_{\Delta t\to 0} (\Delta t)^{-1}E\{(\exp[j\langle \boldsymbol{v},\Delta\boldsymbol{x}_t\rangle] - 1) \mid N_{t_0,t},\boldsymbol{x}_t\} = \psi_t(\boldsymbol{v} \mid N_{t_0,t},\boldsymbol{x}_t)$

exists.

It then follows that the time evolution of the conditional characteristic function for $\boldsymbol{x}_t$ is described by the stochastic differential equation:

$$\begin{aligned} dc_{t|t_0}(\boldsymbol{v} \mid N_{t_0,t}) &= E\{\exp[j\langle \boldsymbol{v},\boldsymbol{x}_t\rangle]\psi_t(\boldsymbol{v}|N_{t_0,t},\boldsymbol{x}_t)|N_{t_0,t}\}\, dt \\ &\quad + E\{\exp[j\langle \boldsymbol{v},\boldsymbol{x}_t\rangle](\lambda_t(\boldsymbol{x}_t) - \hat{\lambda}_t) \mid N_{t_0,t}\} \\ &\quad \cdot \hat{\lambda}_t^{-1}(dN_t - \hat{\lambda}_t\, dt) \\ c_{t_0|t_0}(\boldsymbol{v} \mid N_{t_0,t_0}) &= E\{\exp[j\langle \boldsymbol{v},\boldsymbol{x}_{t_0}\rangle]\}, \end{aligned} \tag{8}$$

where $\hat{\lambda}_t \triangleq E[\lambda_t(\boldsymbol{x}_t) \mid N_{t_0,t}]$ is the causal MMSE estimate of the intensity $\lambda_t(\boldsymbol{x}_t)$ given $N_{t_0,t}$.

Before proving (8), let us interpret it briefly in terms of previous results. Suppose $\{\boldsymbol{x}_t, t \geq t_0\}$ is a solution to the stochastic differential equation in (5) and that $\{\boldsymbol{\chi}_t, t \geq t_0\}$ is a standard vector Wiener process that is independent of the past of the counting process $N_t$. It then follows that

$$\psi_t(\boldsymbol{v} \mid N_{t_0,t},\boldsymbol{x}_t) = j\langle \boldsymbol{v},\boldsymbol{f}_t(\boldsymbol{x}_t)\rangle - \tfrac{1}{2}\langle \boldsymbol{v},\boldsymbol{G}_t(\boldsymbol{x}_t)\boldsymbol{G}_t'(\boldsymbol{x}_t)\boldsymbol{v}\rangle.$$

Using this expression in (8) and inverse Fourier transforming then results in the following stochastic differential equation for the posterior probability density of $\boldsymbol{x}_t$:

$$\begin{aligned} dp_t(\boldsymbol{x}_t \mid N_{t_0,t}) &= L[p_t(\boldsymbol{x}_t \mid N_{t_0,t})]\, dt \\ &\quad + p_t(\boldsymbol{x}_t \mid N_{t_0,t})\{\lambda_t(\boldsymbol{x}_t) - \hat{\lambda}_t\} \\ &\quad \cdot \hat{\lambda}_t^{-1}\{dN_t - \hat{\lambda}_t\, dt\} \\ p_{t_0}(\boldsymbol{x}_{t_0} \mid N_{t_0,t_0}) &= p(\boldsymbol{x}_0), \end{aligned} \tag{9}$$

where $L[\cdot]$ is the forward Kolmogorov differential operator for the diffusion process $\boldsymbol{x}_t$. It is by now well known that if rather than the counting process $N_t$, the observations of $\lambda_t(\boldsymbol{x}_t)$ were of the additive form $dy_t = \lambda_t(\boldsymbol{x}_t)\, dt + dw_t$, where $w_t$ is an independent Wiener process with parameter $W$, then the last term on the right in (9) is $p_t(\boldsymbol{x}_t \mid y_{t_0,t}) \cdot \{\lambda_t(\boldsymbol{x}_t) - \hat{\lambda}_t\}W^{-1}\{dy_t - \hat{\lambda}_t\, dt\}$. The similarity between the two expressions is striking in view of the nonadditive way in which $\lambda_t(\boldsymbol{x}_t)$ enters the statistics of $N_t$.

*Proof of (8):* Let $B_{t_0}{}^s$ be the minimal $\sigma$-field induced by $N_{t_0,s} = \{N_\alpha, t_0 < \alpha \leq s\}$. The conditional characteristic function of $\boldsymbol{x}_s$ given $B_{t_0}{}^t$ is then

$$c_{s|t_0}(\boldsymbol{v} \mid B_{t_0}{}^s) = E[\exp(j\langle \boldsymbol{v},\boldsymbol{x}_s\rangle) \mid B_{t_0}{}^s].$$

Partition the interval $(t_0, t + \Delta t]$ into $(t_0,t]$ and $(t, t + \Delta t]$, and let $B_{t_0}{}^t \otimes B(\Delta N_t)$ denote the minimal $\sigma$-field induced by $N_{t_0,t}$ and the increment $\Delta N_t = N_{t+\Delta t} - N_t$.

Now examine the characteristic function for $\boldsymbol{x}_{t+\Delta t}$ given $B_{t_0}^{t+\Delta t}$, which is given by

$$\begin{aligned} c_{t+\Delta t|t_0}(\boldsymbol{v} \mid B_{t_0}^{t+\Delta t}) &= E[\exp(j\langle \boldsymbol{v},\boldsymbol{x}_t\rangle)\exp(j\langle \boldsymbol{v}, \Delta\boldsymbol{x}_t\rangle) \mid B_{t_0}^{t+\Delta t}] \\ &= \int_{R^{2n}} \exp(j\langle \boldsymbol{v},\boldsymbol{X}\rangle)\exp(j\langle \boldsymbol{v},\boldsymbol{Y}\rangle)\, d^{2n}P(\boldsymbol{X},\boldsymbol{Y} \mid B_{t_0}^{t+\Delta t}), \end{aligned}$$

where $\Delta\boldsymbol{x}_t = \boldsymbol{x}_{t+\Delta t} - \boldsymbol{x}_t$ and $P(\boldsymbol{X},\boldsymbol{Y} \mid B_{t_0}^{t+\Delta t})$ is the joint conditional probability distribution function of $\boldsymbol{x}_t$ and $\Delta\boldsymbol{x}_t$ given $B_{t_0}^{t+\Delta t}$.

To evaluate $c_{t+\Delta t|t_0}$, let us define

$$\begin{aligned} c^{\Delta}_{t+\Delta t|t_0}[\boldsymbol{v} \mid B_{t_0}{}^t \otimes B(\Delta N_t)] &= \int_{R^{2n}} \exp(j\langle \boldsymbol{v},\boldsymbol{X}\rangle) \\ &\quad \cdot \exp(j\langle \boldsymbol{v},\boldsymbol{Y}\rangle)\, d^{2n}P[\boldsymbol{X},\boldsymbol{Y} \mid B_{t_0}{}^t \otimes B(\Delta N_t)]. \end{aligned}$$

Then

$$c^{\Delta}_{t+\Delta t|t_0} \xrightarrow{\text{a.s.}} c_{t+\Delta t|t_0} \text{ as } t \to t + \Delta t$$

because $B_{t_0}{}^t \otimes B(\Delta N_t) \uparrow B_{t_0}^{t+\Delta t}$ and, consequently,

$$P(\boldsymbol{X},\boldsymbol{Y} \mid B_{t_0}{}^t \otimes B(\Delta N_t)) \xrightarrow{\text{a.s.}} P(\boldsymbol{X},\boldsymbol{Y} \mid B_{t_0}^{t+\Delta t}) \quad \text{as } t \to t + \Delta t$$

by the martingale convergence theorem (Feller [17, p. 236]). We evaluate $c^{\Delta}_{t+\Delta t|t_0}$ for fixed $\Delta N_t$; namely, for $\Delta N_t = 0$, $\Delta N_t = 1$, and $\Delta N_t = m$ where $m > 1$. For $\Delta N_t = 0$, we have

$$\begin{aligned} c^{\Delta}_{t+\Delta t|t_0}(\boldsymbol{v} \mid B_{t_0}{}^t \otimes B(0)) &= \int_{R^{2n}} \exp(j\langle \boldsymbol{v},\boldsymbol{X}\rangle) \\ &\quad \cdot \exp(j\langle \boldsymbol{v},\boldsymbol{Y}\rangle)\, d^{2n}P(\boldsymbol{X},\boldsymbol{Y} \mid B_{t_0}{}^t \otimes B(0)). \end{aligned}$$

The finite difference

$$\begin{aligned} &\delta^{2n}P(\boldsymbol{X},\boldsymbol{Y} \mid B_{t_0}{}^t \otimes B(0)) \\ &= \Pr[\boldsymbol{x}_t \in (\boldsymbol{X} - \delta\boldsymbol{X},\boldsymbol{X}], \Delta\boldsymbol{x}_t \in (\boldsymbol{Y} - \Delta\boldsymbol{Y},\boldsymbol{Y}] \mid B_{t_0}{}^t \otimes B(0)] \end{aligned}$$

can be evaluated as

$$\delta^{2n}P(X,Y \mid B_{t_0}{}^t \otimes B(0)) =$$

$$\Pr[\Delta N_t = 0 \mid x_t \in (X - \delta X, X], \Delta x_t \in (Y - \delta Y, Y], B_{t_0}{}^t] \times \delta^{2n}P(X,Y \mid B_{t_0}{}^t)/\Pr[\Delta N_t = 0 \mid B_{t_0}{}^t],$$

where as $\delta X \to 0$ and $\delta Y \to 0$

$$\Pr[\Delta N_t = 0 \mid x_t \in (X - \delta X, X], \Delta x_t \in (Y - \delta Y, Y], B_{t_0}{}^t] = 1 - \lambda_t(X)\,\Delta t + o(\Delta t)$$

and where

$$\Pr[\Delta N_t = 0 \mid B_{t_0}{}^t] = E\{\Pr[\Delta N_t = 0 \mid x_t, B_{t_0}{}^t] \mid B_{t_0}{}^t\} = 1 - \hat{\lambda}_t\,\Delta t + o(\Delta t),$$

where $\hat{\lambda}_t = E[\lambda_t(x_t) \mid B_{t_0}{}^t]$. Putting these results together, we obtain

$$\begin{aligned} c^{\Delta}_{t+\Delta t|t_0}[v \mid B_{t_0}{}^t \otimes B(0)] &= E\{\exp(j\langle v,x_t\rangle)\exp(j\langle v,\Delta x_t\rangle)[1 - \lambda_t(x_t)\,\Delta t] \mid B_{t_0}{}^t\} \\ &\quad \cdot (1 - \hat{\lambda}_t\,\Delta t)^{-1} + o(\Delta t) \\ &= E\{\exp(j\langle v,x_t\rangle)\exp(j\langle v,\Delta x_t\rangle) \\ &\quad \cdot [1 - \lambda_t(x_t)\Delta t + \hat{\lambda}_t\,\Delta t] \mid B_{t_0}{}^t\} + o(\Delta t). \end{aligned}$$

Similarly, by using the same procedure, we obtain

$$c^{\Delta}_{t+\Delta t|t_0}[v \mid B_{t_0}{}^t \otimes B(1)] = E[\exp(j\langle v,x_t\rangle)\exp(j\langle v,\Delta x_t\rangle)\lambda_t(x_t) \mid B_{t_0}{}^t]\hat{\lambda}_t^{-1} + o(\Delta t)$$

and

$$c^{\Delta}_{t+\Delta t|t_0}[v \mid B_{t_0}{}^t \otimes B(m)] = o(\Delta t), \qquad m > 1.$$

It follows that for $\Delta N_t$ variable, we have

$$\begin{aligned} c^{\Delta}_{t+\Delta t|t_0}[v \mid B_{t_0}{}^t \otimes B(\Delta N_t)] &= E[\exp(j\langle v,x_t\rangle)\exp(j\langle v,\Delta x_t\rangle) \\ &\quad \cdot [1 - \lambda_t(x_t)\,\Delta t + \hat{\lambda}_t\,\Delta t] \mid B_{t_0}{}^t]\delta_{0,\Delta N_t} \\ &\quad + E[\exp(j\langle v,x_t\rangle)\exp(j\langle v,\Delta x_t\rangle)\lambda_t(x_t) \mid B_{t_0}{}^t] \\ &\quad \cdot \hat{\lambda}_t^{-1}\,\delta_{1,\Delta N_t} + o(\Delta t). \end{aligned}$$

Because

$$\delta_{0,\Delta N_t} \xrightarrow{\text{a.s.}} 1 - \Delta N_t \quad \text{and} \quad \delta_{1,\Delta N_t} \xrightarrow{\text{a.s.}} \Delta N_t \quad \text{as } t \to t + \Delta t,$$

we can write

$$\begin{aligned} c^{\Delta}_{t+\Delta t|t_0}[v \mid B_{t_0}{}^t \otimes B(\Delta N_t)] &= E[\exp(j\langle v,x_t\rangle)\exp(j\langle v,\Delta x_t\rangle) \mid B_{t_0}{}^t] \\ &\quad + E[\exp(j\langle v,x_t\rangle)\exp(j\langle v,\Delta x_t\rangle)[\lambda_t(x_t) - \hat{\lambda}_t] \mid B_{t_0}{}^t] \\ &\quad \cdot \hat{\lambda}_t^{-1}(\Delta N_t - \hat{\lambda}_t\,\Delta t) + o(\Delta t). \end{aligned}$$

By subtracting the characteristic function for $x_t$ given $B_{t_0}{}^t$, we establish the desired theorem as follows:

$$\begin{aligned} dc_{t|t_0}(v \mid B_{t_0}{}^t) &= \lim_{\Delta t \to 0}[c_{t+\Delta t|t_0}(v \mid B_{t_0}^{t+\Delta t}) - c_{t|t_0}(v \mid B_{t_0}{}^t)] \\ &= \lim_{\Delta t \to 0}[c^{\Delta}_{t+\Delta t|t_0}(v \mid B_{t_0}{}^t \otimes B(\Delta N_t)) - c_{t|t_0}(v \mid B_{t_0}{}^t)] \\ &= E[\exp(j\langle v,x_t\rangle)\psi_t(v \mid B_{t_0}{}^t, x_t) \mid B_{t_0}{}^t]\,dt \\ &\quad + E\{\exp(j\langle v,x_t\rangle)[\lambda_t(x_t) - \hat{\lambda}_t] \mid B_{t_0}{}^t\}\hat{\lambda}_t^{-1}(dN_t - \hat{\lambda}_t\,dt), \end{aligned}$$

where the interchange of limit and expectation for the first term in the last equality is justified by assumption a) and the bounded convergence theorem.

Equation (8) is our basic result. The procedure for implementing an estimate of some specified function $h_t(x_t)$ of $x_t$ is clearly very complicated in general. First it is necessary to solve (8) for $c_{t|t_0}(v \mid N_{t_0,t})$; then this characteristic function must be inverse Fourier transformed to determine $p_t(x_t \mid N_{t_0,t})$, and finally the estimate must be determined from this probability density. These steps are generally analytically intractable, so that numerical techniques will be required as discussed in Sections V and VI.

## IV. Application to Detection

The detection model we consider in this section is motivated by an optical communication or radar system in which the optimum detector is placed at the output of an ideal photon-electron converter. The model is a generalization of the one first considered by Reiffen and Sherman [18], and we assume a familiarity with their formulation and results.

The generalization we include is to allow the intensity $\lambda_t$ to be stochastic rather than deterministic as assumed by Reiffen and Sherman. The motivation is to account in the model for stochastic effects introduced in the optical channel between the photon source and the photon converter. These arise, for instance, from atmospheric turbulence, target scintillation, and the use of an incoherent modulation.

Our results are similar in spirit to those obtained by Duncan [19] and Kailath [20] for the optimum detection of stochastic signals in additive white Gaussian noise. They obtained the interesting and fundamental result that the causal MMSE estimate of the stochastic signal should be incorporated in the optimum detector in exactly the same way as if the signal were known. The result we obtain is that the causal MMSE estimate of the intensity function of the Poisson process should be incorporated in the optimal detector in exactly the same way as if the function itself were known. This is surprising in view of the nonadditive way the intensity function affects the statistics of the Poisson process. The fact that the estimate is causal is important because it means that the detector can be updated continuously in time as the Poisson process is observed.

In this section, we shall use (8) to derive an equation for the log-likelihood ratio, which defines the optimum detector.

*A. Model Formulation and Problem Statement for Detection*

Let $\{N_t, t \geq t_0\}$ be a doubly stochastic Poisson process with either a known positive constant intensity $\lambda_0$ or a time-varying stochastic intensity $\lambda_0 + \lambda_t$. $\lambda_0$ represents the rate of arrival of photons from background radiation and $\{\lambda_t, t \geq t_0\}$ represents the stochastic rate of arrival of photons from the source. Thus we can write the intensity of $N_t$ as $\lambda_0 + \alpha\lambda_t$, where $\alpha$ is a discrete random variable that is 1 or 0. Let the prior probabilities of $\alpha$ be $P_1 = \Pr[\alpha = 1]$ and $P_0 = 1 - P_1 = \Pr[\alpha = 0]$. We assume as before that $\lambda_t = \lambda_t(\boldsymbol{x}_t)$ is a positive function of a general vector Markov process $\{\boldsymbol{x}_t, t \geq t_0\}$.

The problem we wish to consider is that of defining the optimum detector for deciding whether the random variable $\alpha$ is 0 or 1 given a record $N_{t_0,t} = \{N_\sigma, t_0 < \sigma \leq t\}$ of the Poisson counting process having an intensity $\lambda_0 + \alpha\lambda_t(\boldsymbol{x}_t)$.

*B. The Optimum Detector*

Let $l_t$ be the log-likelihood ratio defined by $l_t = \ln[p/(1-p)]$, where for notational convenience we define

$$p \triangleq \Pr(\alpha = 1 \mid N_{t_0,t})$$

as the posterior probability that $\alpha = 1$. It is well known that the optimum detector first computes $l_t$ from the observations and then compares the computed value to a preset decision level that depends on the criterion of performance, costs, etc. The result we wish to establish is that $l_t$ is given for $t \geq t_0$ by

$$l_t = l_{t_0} - \int_{t_0}^{t} \hat{\lambda}_\sigma \, d\sigma + \int_{t_0}^{t} \ln[\lambda_0^{-1}(\lambda_0 + \hat{\lambda}_\sigma)] \, dN_\sigma, \quad (10)$$

where $l_{t_0}$ depends on the prior probabilities of $\alpha$ according to $l_{t_0} = \ln(P_1/P_0)$. In this equation, $\hat{\lambda}_t$ is a causal functional of the observed data defined by $E[\lambda_t \mid N_{t_0,t}, \alpha = 1]$. Thus, if $\alpha = 1$, the functional $\hat{\lambda}_t$ is the MMSE estimate of $\lambda_t$ given the record $N_{t_0,t}$. However, if $\alpha = 0$, $\hat{\lambda}_t$ does not have an interpretation as an estimate.

The interpretation of (10) in terms of previous results is interesting. If (10) is compared to the log-likelihood ratio obtained by Reiffen and Sherman [18, eq. (14)], it is seen that $\hat{\lambda}_t$ simply replaces their known intensity function. This interpretation has practical implications because it suggests a structure for suboptimal detectors when $\hat{\lambda}_t$ is unknown or too complicated for practical realization. Namely, there is still a strong motivation to incorporate a suboptimal estimate directly in the Reiffen–Sherman detector.

The log-likelihood ratio for other detection problems that may be of interest can be obtained from (10) using the chain rule for likelihood ratios, as discussed by Kailath [20]. For instance, the optimum detector for the following two problems can be obtained easily this way:

i) $\lambda_t^{(0)}(\boldsymbol{x}_t) + \lambda_0$ versus $\lambda_t^{(1)}(\boldsymbol{x}_t) + \lambda_0$

and

ii) $s_t + \lambda_t(\boldsymbol{x}_t) + \lambda_0$ versus $\lambda_t(\boldsymbol{x}_t) + \lambda_0$,

where $s_t$ is a known intensity function. The first problem is that of deciding which of two stochastic intensities is present in $\{N_t, t \geq t_0\}$. The second problem is that of detecting a known signal in a stochastic background radiation.

We use the result in (8) for the derivation of (10). The intensity of $\{N_t, t \geq t_0\}$ is $\lambda_0 + \alpha\lambda_t(\boldsymbol{x}_t)$, where $\alpha$ is a discrete random variable, 0 or 1, and $\boldsymbol{x}_t$ is a vector-valued Markov process. As the collection $(\alpha, \boldsymbol{x}_t)$ is also a vector-valued Markov process, the general results in (8) can be used to describe the time evolution of the statistics of $(\alpha, \boldsymbol{x}_t)$ given $N_{t_0,t}$. Let the conditional characteristic function for $(\alpha, \boldsymbol{x}_t)$ be defined by

$$c_t(u,\boldsymbol{v} \mid N_{t_0,t}) = E\{\exp(ju\alpha) \exp[j\langle \boldsymbol{v},\boldsymbol{x}_t\rangle] \mid N_{t_0,t}\}.$$

Then from (8) $c_t$ satisfies the stochastic differential equation

$$\begin{aligned} dc_t(u,\boldsymbol{v} \mid N_{t_0,t}) &= E\{\exp(ju\alpha) \exp[j\langle \boldsymbol{v},\boldsymbol{x}_t\rangle]\psi(u,\boldsymbol{v} \mid N_{t_0,t},\alpha,\boldsymbol{x}_t) \mid N_{t_0,t}\} \, dt \\ &\quad + E\{\exp(ju\alpha) \exp[j\langle \boldsymbol{v},\boldsymbol{x}_t\rangle](\lambda_0 + \lambda_t(\boldsymbol{x}_t) \\ &\quad - e_t) \mid N_{t_0,t}\} e_t^{-1}(dN_t - e_t \, dt), \end{aligned} \quad (11)$$

where $e_t$ is the estimate defined by

$$e_t = E[\lambda_0 + \alpha\lambda_t(\boldsymbol{x}_t) \mid N_{t_0,t}]$$

and where $\psi_t$ is defined by

$$\begin{aligned} \psi_t(u,\boldsymbol{v} \mid N_{t_0,t},\alpha,\boldsymbol{x}_t) &= p \lim_{\Delta t \to 0} (\Delta t)^{-1} \\ &\quad \cdot E\{(\exp(ju\,\Delta\alpha) \exp[j\langle \boldsymbol{v},\Delta\boldsymbol{x}_t\rangle] - 1) \mid N_{t_0,t},\alpha,\boldsymbol{x}_t\}. \end{aligned}$$

Let $\hat{\lambda}_t = E[\lambda_t \mid N_{t_0,t}, \alpha = 1]$. Then, since $\alpha$ is 1 or 0, it follows that $e_t = \lambda_0 + p\hat{\lambda}_t$. Noting that $\Delta\alpha = 0$ and setting $\boldsymbol{v} = \boldsymbol{0}$ in (11), we obtain

$$\begin{aligned} dc_t(u,\boldsymbol{0} \mid N_{t_0,t}) &= E\{\exp(ju\alpha)(\alpha\lambda_t - p\hat{\lambda}_t) \mid N_{t_0,t}\}(\lambda_0 + p\hat{\lambda}_t)^{-1} \\ &\quad \cdot (dN_t - (\lambda_0 + p\hat{\lambda}_t) \, dt) \\ &= \exp(ju)\{p(1-p)\hat{\lambda}_t(\lambda_0 + p\hat{\lambda}_t)^{-1}(dN_t - (\lambda_0 + p\hat{\lambda}_t) \, dt)\} \\ &\quad - \{(1-p)p\hat{\lambda}_t(\lambda_0 + p\hat{\lambda}_t)^{-1}(dN_t - (\lambda_0 + p\hat{\lambda}_t) \, dt)\}. \end{aligned}$$

Upon inverse Fourier transforming, it follows that $p$ satisfies the following stochastic differential equation:

$$dp = -p(1-p)\hat{\lambda}_t \, dt + p(1-p)\hat{\lambda}_t(\lambda_0 + p\hat{\lambda}_t)^{-1} \, dN_t. \quad (12)$$

The log-likelihood ratio is defined by $l_t = \ln[p/(1-p)]$. Consequently, to establish (10), we need a stochastic differential rule relating the differential of $p$ to the differential of a function $l_t = l_t(p)$ of $p$. Such a rule is given formally by the following lemma.

*Lemma:* Let $\zeta_t$ satisfy $d\zeta_t = \alpha_t \, dt + \beta_t \, dN_t$, where $N_t$ is the jump process defined above. Let $\phi = \phi(\zeta)$ be a continuously differentiable scalar function of $\zeta$ with derivative $\phi_\zeta = d\phi/d\zeta$. Then

$$d\phi(\zeta_t) = \phi_\zeta(\zeta_t)\alpha_t \, dt + [\phi(\zeta_t + \beta_t) - \phi(\zeta_t)] \, dN_t. \tag{13}$$

*Proof:* This is a special case of the generalized Ito differential rule established by Kunita and Watanabe [21, theorem 5.1]. The following argument motivates the result. For $\Delta t$ sufficiently small, $\Delta\zeta_t = \alpha_t \, \Delta t$ or $\Delta\zeta_t = \alpha_t \, \Delta t + \beta_t$ because $\Delta N_t$ is 0 or 1. Thus, $\Delta\phi(\zeta_t) = \phi(\zeta_{t+\Delta t}) - \phi(\zeta_t)$ can be written as

$$\Delta\phi(\zeta_t) = [\phi(\zeta_t + \alpha_t \, \Delta t) - \phi(\zeta_t)](1 - \Delta N_t) + [\phi(\zeta_t + \alpha_t \, \Delta t + \beta_t) - \phi(\zeta_t)] \, \Delta N_t + o(\Delta t).$$

Observe that $\phi(\zeta_t + \alpha_t \, \Delta t) - \phi(\zeta_t) \to \phi_\zeta(\zeta_t)\alpha_t \, \Delta t + o(\Delta t)$ and

$$\phi(\zeta_t + \alpha_t \, \Delta t + \beta_t) - \phi(\zeta_t) \to \phi(\zeta_t + \beta_t) - \phi(\zeta_t) + 0(\Delta t) \qquad \text{as } \Delta t \to 0.$$

Consequently, for $\Delta t$ sufficiently small

$$\Delta\phi(\zeta_t) = \phi_\zeta(\zeta_t)\alpha_t \, \Delta t(1 - \Delta N_t) + [\phi(\zeta_t + \beta_t) - \phi(\zeta_t)] \, \Delta N_t + o(\Delta t).$$

Taking the limit as $\Delta t \to 0$ results in (13).

Now make the following identifications in the lemma: $\zeta_t = p$, $\alpha_t = -p(1 - p)\hat{\lambda}_t$, $\beta_t = p(1 - p)\hat{\lambda}_t(\lambda_0 + p\hat{\lambda}_t)^{-1}$, and $\phi_t = l_t = \ln [p/(1 - p)]$. It is easy to verify that (13) then becomes

$$dl_t = -\hat{\lambda}_t \, dt + \ln [\lambda_0^{-1}(\lambda_0 + \hat{\lambda}_t)] \, dN_t.$$

With the obvious initial condition $l_{t_0} = \ln [P_1/(1 - P_1)]$, this stochastic differential equation implies (10), which was to be established.

## V. Constant Parameters

An important special case of the model obtains when $\boldsymbol{x}_t = \boldsymbol{x}$ for $t \geq t_0$, where $\boldsymbol{x}$ is a vector of random variables. We wish to indicate briefly some results that apply for this situation. Let $p_0(\boldsymbol{x})$ be the prior probability density for $\boldsymbol{x}$ and $p_t(\boldsymbol{x} \mid N_{t_0,t})$ the posterior density given $\{N_\sigma, t_0 < \sigma \leq t\}$. Then (9) becomes

$$dp_t(\boldsymbol{x} \mid N_{t_0,t}) = p_t(\boldsymbol{x} \mid N_{t_0,t})\{\lambda_t(\boldsymbol{x}) - \hat{\lambda}_t\}\hat{\lambda}_t^{-1}\{dN_t - \hat{\lambda}_t \, dt\}$$
$$p_{t_0}(\boldsymbol{x} \mid N_{t_0,t_0}) = p_0(\boldsymbol{x}), \tag{14}$$

where $\hat{\lambda}_t = E[\lambda_t(\boldsymbol{x}) \mid N_{t_0,t}]$ in the causal MMSE estimate of $\lambda_t(\boldsymbol{x})$ given $\{N_\sigma, t_0 < \sigma \leq t\}$. This equation is a nonlinear integral-differential equation for the posterior density because $\hat{\lambda}_t$ requires an integration with respect to $p_t(\boldsymbol{x} \mid N_{t_0,t})$. In the following paragraphs, we discuss some applications of this equation.

### A. Numerical Solutions

Equation (14) is analytically intractible for most intensity functions $\lambda_t(\boldsymbol{x})$ so that numerical solutions are required. However, the equation is well suited for this because of its recursive form. We have been exploring the technique of replacing (14) by a finite difference equation, which is then used as a numerical algorithm for updating the posterior density as data arrives. Desired estimates are obtained by numerical integration with respect to the generated density. Some preliminary simulation results are given in Figs. 1 and 2. Note that no approximations are being made here beyond those required for digital computations.

The results in Fig. 1 were obtained by assuming that $\lambda_t(x) = x$, where $x$ had a uniform prior probability density between 1.0 and 2.0. The value of $x$ used in the simulation was selected at random with a random number generator. The numerically generated time evolution for $p_t(x \mid N_{t_0,t})$ is shown as well as for the MMSE estimate of $\lambda_t(x) = x$. The results shown are typical of those obtained with other randomly selected values for $x$.

The results in Fig. 2 were obtained by assuming that $\lambda_t(x) = 100 \exp(-xt)$ for $t > 0$, where $x$ had a uniform prior probability density between 0.5 and 1.0. As before, the value of $x$ used in the simulation was selected at random with a random number generator. The numerically generated time evolution for $p_t(x \mid N_{t_0,t})$ is shown as well as for $\hat{\lambda}_t$ and $\hat{x}_t$. The results shown are typical of those obtained with other randomly selected values for $x$.

A simulation for the parameterized intensity $\lambda_t(\boldsymbol{x}) = x_1 \exp(-x_2 t)$ for $t > 0$ has also been performed and the results are similar.

### B. Estimation of a Constant Intensity

For the homogeneous process with $\lambda_t(x) = x$, a scalar random variable, the solution to (14) is

$$p_t(x \mid N_{t_0,t}) = x^{N_t} \exp(-xt)p_0(x) \cdot \left[\int_0^\infty \xi^{N_t} \exp(-\xi t)p_0(\xi) \, d\xi\right]^{-1}.$$

This can be verified using the differential rule in (13) and may also be derived directly because $N_t$ is a sufficient statistic for the homogeneous process. Our simulation results in Fig. 2 are in good agreement with this analytic expression.

### C. MAP Estimates [22]

MAP estimate of $\boldsymbol{x}$ is the value of $\boldsymbol{x}$ that maximizes $l_t(\boldsymbol{x}) = \ln p_t(\boldsymbol{x} \mid N_{t_0,t})$. Using (14) and (13) it follows that

$$l_t(\boldsymbol{x}) = \ln p_0(\boldsymbol{x}) - \int_{t_0}^t (\lambda_\sigma(\boldsymbol{x}) - \hat{\lambda}_\sigma) \, d\sigma + \int_{t_0}^t \ln (\lambda_\sigma(\boldsymbol{x})/\hat{\lambda}_\sigma) \, dN_\sigma.$$

Let $\partial/\partial\boldsymbol{x}$ denote the gradient operator. Then the MAP estimate of $\boldsymbol{x}$ satisfies

$$\boldsymbol{0} = \frac{\partial}{\partial \boldsymbol{x}}\left\{\ln p_0(\boldsymbol{x}) - \int_{t_0}^t \lambda_\sigma(\boldsymbol{x}) \, d\sigma + \int_{t_0}^t \ln \lambda_\sigma(\boldsymbol{x}) \, dN_\sigma\right\}.$$

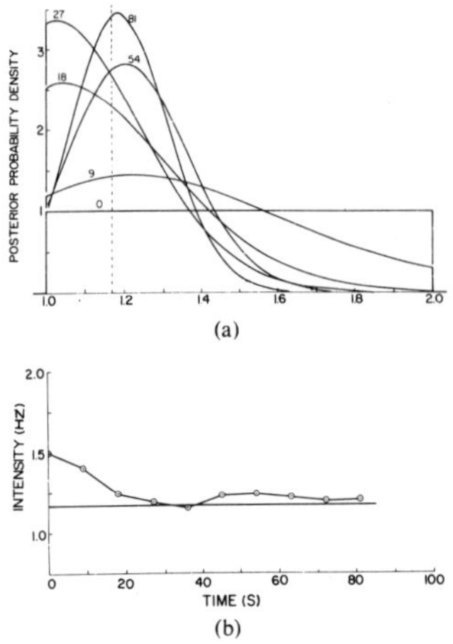


Fig. 1. (a) Time evolution for the posterior probability density function of $x$ when $\lambda_t(x) = x$. The true value of $x$ generated at random, uniformly between 1.0 and 2.0, is indicated by the dashed line at $x = 1.170$. The density is shown for $t = 0, 9, 18, 27, 54$, and 81 s. All densities are zero outside the interval [1,2]. (b) Time evolution for the MMSE estimate of $\lambda_t(x) = x$. The solid curve is the true value of $\lambda_t(x) = 1.170$, and the data points are the MMSE estimates of this value taken at 9.0 s intervals.

*D. Parameter Estimation Accuracy* [22]

Let $\Sigma_t = E[(x - \hat{x}_t)(x - \hat{x}_t)^T]$ be the error covariance matrix associated with an estimate $\hat{x}_t$ of $x$ given the record $N_{t_0,t}$. Then, under appropriate regularity conditions, $\Sigma_t \geq J_t^{-1}$ where $J_t$ is the information matrix given by $E[\partial l_t(x)/\partial x)(\partial l_t(x)/\partial x)^T]$. It can be shown using the above expression for $l_t(x)$ that the $(i,j)$ element of $J_t$ is given by

$$J_{ij} = -E\left[\frac{\partial^2 \ln p_0(x)}{\partial x_i\, \partial x_j}\right] + E\left[\int_{t_0}^{t} \frac{\partial^2 \lambda_\sigma(x)}{\partial x_i\, \partial x_j}\, d\sigma\right] - E\left[\int_{t_0}^{t} \lambda_\sigma(x) \frac{\partial^2 \ln \lambda_\sigma(x)}{\partial x_i\, \partial x_j}\, d\sigma\right],$$

where $E(\cdot)$ indicates integration with respect to $p_0(x)$.

## VI. Approximate Filtering

Let the modulation process $x_t$ satisfy the stochastic equation

$$dx_t = f_t(x_t)\, dt + G_t\, d\chi_t, \; x_{t_0} = x_0, \tag{15}$$

where $\{\chi_t, t \geq t_0\}$ is a standardized vector Wiener process. Then $p_t(x_t \mid N_{t_0,t})$ satisfies (9). We have described how (9) can be used to define a numerical algorithm for determining $p_t(x_t \mid N_{t_0,t})$, $\hat{\lambda}_t$, and $\hat{x}_t = E[x_t \mid N_{t_0,t}]$ computationally. However, at each stage of the numerical solution, the integration to determine $\hat{\lambda}_t$ must be performed. Consequently, the computation time can become excessive if the dimension of $x_t$ is more than one or two. Moreover, the array for storing the updated versions of $p_t(x_t \mid N_{t_0,t})$ can become so large that a small computer cannot be used. For these reasons, we are led to consider approximate techniques for generating estimates of $x_t$. The approximations we suggest here closely parallel those in Snyder [23, ch. 4]. The quasi-optimum estimates that result are *ad hoc* so their usefulness must be examined in individual applications.

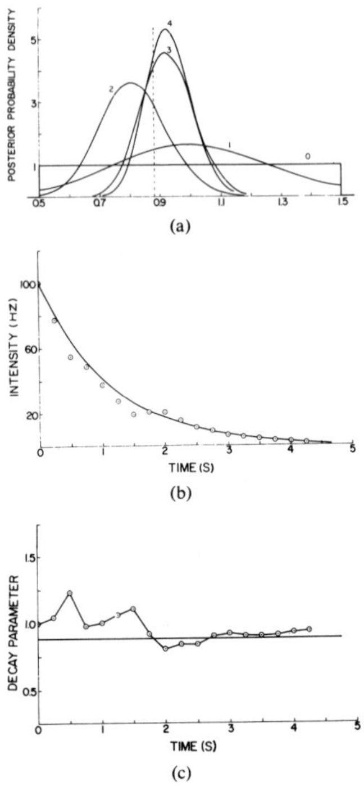


Fig. 2. (a) Time evolution for the posterior probability density of $x$ when $\lambda_t(x) = 100 \exp(-xt)$. The true value of $x$ generated at random, uniformly between 0.5 and 1.5, equals 0.8822. The posterior density is shown for $t = 0, 1, 2, 3$, and 4 s. All densities are zero outside the interval [0.5,1.5]. (b) Time evolution for the MMSE estimate for $\lambda_t(x) = 100 \exp[-xt]$. The solid curve is the true value of $\lambda_t(x) = 100 \exp[-0.8822t]$, and the data points are the MMSE estimates of this curve taken at 0.25 s intervals. (c) Time evolution for the MMSE estimate of $x$. The solid curve is the true parameter value of 0.8822 and the data points are the MMSE estimates of this value at 0.25 s intervals.

*A. Derivation for Quasi-Optimum Estimation*

Let

$$\hat{x}_t = E[x_t \mid N_{t_0,t}] = \int_{R^n} \xi p_t(\xi \mid N_{t_0,t}) \prod^{n} d\xi_i \tag{16}$$

be the causal MMSE estimate of $x_t$ given the record $N_{t_0,t}$. An equation for $\hat{x}_t$ can be derived by multiplying (9) by $x_t$ and then integrating according to (16). The result is

$$d\hat{x}_t = E[f_t(x_t) \mid N_{t_0,t}]\, dt + E[(x_t - \hat{x}_t)\lambda_t(x_t) \mid N_{t_0,t}]\hat{\lambda}_t^{-1}[dN_t - \hat{\lambda}_t\, dt]$$
$$\hat{x}_{t_0} = E(x_0) \tag{17}$$

We next assume that $f_t(x_t)$ and $\lambda_t(x_t)$ have Taylor series about the estimate $\hat{x}_t$ as

$$f_t(x_t) = f_t(\hat{x}_t) + [\partial f_t(\hat{x}_t)/\partial \hat{x}_t]^T(x_t - \hat{x}_t) + \tfrac{1}{2}\sum_{i,j}(x_i - \hat{x}_i)(x_j - \hat{x}_j)\, \partial^2 f_t(\hat{x}_t)/\partial \hat{x}_i\, \partial \hat{x}_j + \cdots \quad (18)$$

and

$$\lambda_t(x_t) = \lambda_t(\hat{x}_t) + [\partial \lambda_t(\hat{x}_t)/\partial \hat{x}_t]^T(x_t - \hat{x}_t) + \tfrac{1}{2}\sum_{i,j}(x_i - \hat{x}_i)(x_j - \hat{x}_j)\, \partial^2 \lambda_t(\hat{x}_t)/\partial \hat{x}_i\, \partial \hat{x}_j + \cdots, \quad (19)$$

where $\partial v/\partial x$ denotes the Jacobian matrix associated with the vector $v = v(x)$; the ($i$-row, $j$-column) element of $\partial v/\partial x$ is $\partial v_j/\partial x_i$.

Upon substituting these expansions into (17), we obtain

$$d\hat{x}_t = f_t(\hat{x}_t)\, dt + \tfrac{1}{2}\sum_{i,j}\sigma_{ij}\, \partial^2 f_t(\hat{x}_t)/\partial \hat{x}_i\, \partial \hat{x}_j\, dt + \Sigma_t[\partial \lambda_t(\hat{x}_t)/\partial \hat{x}_t]\hat{\lambda}_t^{-1}[dN_t - \hat{\lambda}_t\, dt] + o(x - \hat{x}_t) \quad (20)$$

in which

$$\Sigma_t = (\sigma_{ij}) = E[(x_t - \hat{x}_t)(x_t - \hat{x}_t)^T \mid N_{t_0,t}]$$

is the conditional error covariance matrix in estimating $x_t$ and $o(x_t - \hat{x}_t)$ denotes terms of order three or more in the error.

Note that no approximations have been introduced up to this point; $\hat{x}_t$ is the exact causal MMSE estimate of $x_t$ given $N_{t_0,t}$. We now introduce the following approximations.

i) Disregard all the higher than second-order error terms contained in $o(x_t - \hat{x}_t)$.

ii) Replace $\hat{\lambda}_t$ by $\lambda_t(\hat{x}_t)$; it is seen from (19) that this substitution implies disregarding second-order error terms.

These approximations are *ad hoc* and must be verified for specific functions $f_t$ and $\lambda_t$, but they appear reasonable if it is assumed that the error $x_t - \hat{x}_t$ is sufficiently small.

Thus, we are led to define the quasi-optimum estimate $x_t^*$ by

$$dx_t^* = f_t(x_t^*)\, dt + \tfrac{1}{2}\sum_{i,j}\sigma_{i,j}^*\, \partial^2 f_t(x_t^*)/\partial x_i^*\, \partial x_j^*\, dt + \Sigma_t^*[\partial \lambda_t(x_t^*)/\partial x_t^*]\lambda_t^{-1}(x_t^*)[dN_t - \lambda_t(x_t^*)\, dt]$$

$$x_{t_0}^* = E[x_0], \quad (21)$$

where $\Sigma_t^* = (\sigma_{ij}^*)$ is an approximation to the error covariance matrix $\Sigma_t$ as described below. The advantages of (21) compared to the exact equations are i) no integrations are required; and ii), a storage array for $p_t(x_t \mid N_{t_0,t})$ is not required—the number of data points to be stored for the updating of $x_t^*$ and $\Sigma_t^*$ is $n(n + 3)/2$. It is convenient for later use to rewrite (21) in the form

$$dx_t^* = f_t(x_t^*)\, dt + \tfrac{1}{2}\sum_{i,j}\sigma_{ij}^*\, \partial^2 f_t(x_t^*)/\partial x_i^*\, \partial x_j^*\, dt - \Sigma_t^*[\partial \lambda_t(x_t^*)/\partial x_t^*]\, dt + \Sigma_t^*[\partial \ln \lambda_t(x_t^*)/\partial x_t^*]\, dN_t$$

$$x_{t_0}^* = E[x_0]. \quad (22)$$

We next derive an equation for the conditional error covariance matrix

$$\Sigma_t = (\sigma_{ij}) = E[\varepsilon_t \varepsilon_t^T \mid N_{t_0,t}]$$

where $\varepsilon_t = x_t - \hat{x}_t$ is the error at time $t$. Note first that

$$\varepsilon_t \varepsilon_t^T = \varepsilon_{t+dt}\varepsilon_{t+dt}^T + \varepsilon_{t+dt}\, d\hat{x}_t^T + dx_t \varepsilon_{t+dt}^T + d\hat{x}_t\, d\hat{x}_t^T. \quad (23)$$

Multiply (9) for $p_t(x_t \mid N_{t_0,t})$ by $\varepsilon_t \varepsilon_t^T$ and integrate using (23) to obtain

$$d\Sigma_t + d\hat{x}_t\, d\hat{x}_t^T = E[f_t(x_t)\varepsilon_t^T + \varepsilon_t f_t^T(x_t) + G_t G_t^T]\, dt + E\{\varepsilon_t \varepsilon_t^T[\lambda_t(x_t) - \hat{\lambda}_t] \mid N_{t_0,t}\}\hat{\lambda}_t^{-1} \cdot [dN_t - \hat{\lambda}_t\, dt]$$

$$\Sigma_{t_0} = \operatorname{cov}(x_0). \quad (24)$$

For each of the expressions on the right in (24), we retain only the leading terms that result when the series (18) and (19) are substituted for $f_t(x_t)$ and $\lambda_t(x_t)$ and the following approximations are made.

i) $\hat{\lambda}_t$ is replaced by $\lambda_t(\hat{x}_t)$, as before.

ii) $\hat{x}_t$ is replaced by $x_t^*$.

iii) Fourth-order moments of the error are factored in products of second-order moments in the way Gaussian moments factor.

These approximations lead us to define $\Sigma_t^*$ by

$$d\Sigma_t^* + dx_t^*\, dx_t^{*T} = [\partial f_t(x_t^*)/\partial x_t^*]^T \Sigma_t^*\, dt + \Sigma_t^*[\partial f_t(x_t^*)/\partial x_t^*]\, dt + G_t G_t^T\, dt + \Sigma_t^*[\partial^2 \lambda_t(x_t^*)/\partial x_t^{*2}]\Sigma_t^* \lambda_t^{-1}(x_t^*) \cdot [dN_t - \lambda_t(x_t^*)\, dt], \quad (25)$$

where we use the notation $\partial^2 v/\partial x^2 = \partial\, [\partial v/\partial x]/\partial x$ for a vector $v = v(x)$. From (22) it is seen that to terms of order $dt$,

$$dx_t^*\, dx_t^{*T} = \Sigma_t^*[\partial \ln \lambda_t(x_t^*)/\partial x_t^*][\partial \ln \lambda_t(x_t^*)/\partial x_t^*]^T \Sigma_t^*\, dN_t.$$

Using this in (25) along with the observation that

$$\partial^2 \ln \lambda_t(x_t^*)/\partial x_t^{*2} = -[\partial \ln \lambda_t(x_t^*)/\partial x_t^*][\partial \ln \lambda_t(x_t^*)/\partial x_t^*]^T + [\partial^2 \lambda_t(x_t^*)/\partial x_t^{*2}]\lambda_t^{-1}(x_t^*),$$

we obtain the final equation defining $\Sigma_t^*$ as

$$d\Sigma_t^* = [\partial f_t(x_t^*)/\partial x_t^*]^T \Sigma_t^*\, dt + \Sigma_t^*[\partial f_t(x_t^*)/\partial x_t^*]\, dt + G_t G_t^T\, dt - \Sigma_t^*[\partial^2 \lambda_t(x_t^*)/\partial x_t^{*2}]\Sigma_t^*\, dt + \Sigma_t^*[\partial^2 \ln \lambda_t(x_t^*)/\partial x_t^{*2}]\Sigma_t^*\, dN_t$$

$$\Sigma_{t_0}^* = \operatorname{cov}(x_0). \quad (26)$$

We take (22) and (26) as our definitions for the quasi-optimum estimate of the state $x_t$ given the data record $N_{t_0,t}$. As mentioned previously, the utility of this definition depends on the form of $f_t(x_t)$ and $\lambda_t(x_t)$ and must be investigated in individual cases. The definition appears reasonable when the estimation error is small.

In the following two sections, we first specialize the approximation equations (22) and (26) for three intensity functions. Then we present some preliminary simulation results for these same functions. The results indicate the potential usefulness of the approximations introduced.

*B. Applications*

1) Let $\lambda_t(x) = A \exp(-xt)$, $t \geq 0$, where $A$ is a known positive constant and $x$ is a positive random variable with known mean $\bar{x}_0$ and variance $\sigma_0^2$. In this case (22) and (26) become

$$dx_t^* = At\Sigma_t^* \exp(-x_t^* t)\, dt - t\Sigma_t^*\, dN_t, \qquad x_0^* = \bar{x}_0 \tag{27}$$

$$d\Sigma_t^* = -At^2\Sigma_t^* \exp(-x_t^* t)\, dt, \qquad \Sigma_0^* = \sigma_0^2. \tag{28}$$

2) Let $\lambda_t(x_1,x_2) = x_1 \exp(-x_2 t)$, $t \geq 0$, where $x_1$ and $x_2$ are uncorrelated positive random variables with known means $\bar{x}_1$ and $\bar{x}_2$ and variances $\sigma_1^2$ and $\sigma_2^2$. In this case, (22) and (26) become

$$\begin{aligned} dx_t^* &= -\Sigma_t^*[1 - tx_1^*]^T \exp(-x_2^* t)\, dt \\ &\quad + \Sigma_t^*[x_1^{*-1} - t]^T\, dN_t, \qquad x_0^* = [\bar{x}_1 \bar{x}_2]^T \end{aligned} \tag{29}$$

$$\begin{aligned} d\Sigma_t^* &= -\Sigma_t^* \begin{bmatrix} 0 & -t \\ -t & t^2 x_1^* \end{bmatrix} \Sigma_t^* \exp(-x_2^* t)\, dt \\ &\quad - \Sigma_t^* \begin{bmatrix} x_1^{*-2} & 0 \\ 0 & 0 \end{bmatrix} \Sigma_t^*\, dN_t, \qquad \Sigma_0^* = \begin{bmatrix} \sigma_0^2 & 0 \\ 0 & \sigma_1^2 \end{bmatrix}. \end{aligned} \tag{30}$$

3) Let $\lambda_t(\boldsymbol{x}_t) = A[1 + m \cos(\omega_0 t + \theta_t)]$, $t \geq t_0$, be a phase-modulated intensity function, where $A$ ($A > 0$) and $m$ ($0 < m < 1$) and known constants and where $\theta_t$ is a Gaussian diffusion defined by $\theta_t = \boldsymbol{h}_t^T \boldsymbol{x}_t$, where $\boldsymbol{x}_t$ is defined by (15) when $\boldsymbol{f}_t(\boldsymbol{x}_t) = \boldsymbol{F}_t \boldsymbol{x}_t$ and $\boldsymbol{x}_0$ is normal, $p_0(\boldsymbol{x}_0) = N(\boldsymbol{0}, \boldsymbol{\Lambda}_0)$. This is a generalization of an intensity mentioned by Helstrom [25] in connection with optical communications. The simplest nonstationary example results when $\boldsymbol{F}_t = 0$, $\boldsymbol{G}_t =$ constant, and $\boldsymbol{h}_t = 1$, in which case $\theta_t$ is a Wiener process; our results may then be viewed as establishing a coherent phase reference when an unstable oscillator modulates the intensity [23]. A frequency-modulated intensity including preemphasis, would be treated in the same manner as this example and is, in fact, contained in it as a special case [23, ch. 5].

For this intensity, (21) becomes

$$\begin{aligned} d\boldsymbol{x}_t^* &= \boldsymbol{F}_t \boldsymbol{x}_t^*\, dt - m \sin(\omega_0 t + \theta_t^*) \\ &\quad \cdot [1 + m \cos(\omega_0 t + \theta_t^*)]^{-1} \boldsymbol{\Sigma}_t^* \boldsymbol{h}_t \\ &\quad \cdot \{dN_t - A[1 + m \cos(\omega_0 t + \theta_t^*)]\, dt\} \\ \boldsymbol{x}_{t_0}^* &= \boldsymbol{0}, \end{aligned} \tag{31}$$

where $\theta_t^* = \boldsymbol{h}_t^T \boldsymbol{x}_t^*$.

The following equation for $\boldsymbol{\Sigma}_t^*$ can be obtained by specializing (26) for the phase-modulated intensity

$$\begin{aligned} d\boldsymbol{\Sigma}_t^* &= \boldsymbol{F}_t^T \boldsymbol{\Sigma}_t^*\, dt + \boldsymbol{\Sigma}_t^* \boldsymbol{F}_t\, dt + \boldsymbol{G}_t \boldsymbol{G}_t^T\, dt \\ &\quad + Am \cos(\omega_0 t + \theta_t^*) \boldsymbol{\Sigma}_t^* \boldsymbol{h}_t \boldsymbol{h}_t^T \boldsymbol{\Sigma}_t^*\, dt \\ &\quad - m[m + \cos(\omega_0 t + \theta_t^*)] \\ &\quad \cdot [1 + m \cos(\omega_0 t + \theta_t^*)]^{-2} \boldsymbol{\Sigma}_t^* \boldsymbol{h}_t \boldsymbol{h}_t^T \boldsymbol{\Sigma}_t^*\, dN_t \\ \boldsymbol{\Sigma}_{t_0}^* &= \boldsymbol{\Lambda}_0. \end{aligned} \tag{32}$$

Equations (31) and (32) define the approximate estimate $\theta_t^*$ of the phase. However, if $\omega_0$ is sufficiently large, additional approximations that appear reasonable can be made. These result in estimation equations having the distinct advantage that the approximate covariance equation is uncoupled from both the approximate state estimate and the data process $N_t$; the equation is a Riccati equation of the type occurring commonly in Kalman–Bucy filtering. Furthermore, the estimation equations suggest the use of a form of tanlock loop [24] operating on the impulse process $\dot{N}_t$ to estimate $\theta_t$.

We assume in what follows that the elements of $\boldsymbol{F}_t$, $\boldsymbol{G}_t$, $\boldsymbol{h}_t$, $\boldsymbol{x}_t$, $\boldsymbol{x}_t^*$, and $\boldsymbol{\Sigma}_t^*$ are slowly varying compared to $\sin(\omega_0 t + \theta_t^*)$ and $\cos(\omega_0 t + \theta_t^*)$. Then for $\omega_0$ sufficiently large, it appears reasonable to neglect the subtractive term $A[1 + m \cos(\omega_0 t + \theta_t^*)]$ in (31) because of the implied time integration of the product of the slowly varying function $Am\boldsymbol{\Sigma}_t^* \boldsymbol{h}_t$ and $\sin(\omega_0 t + \theta_t^*)$.

Define the zero-mean jump process $\{\tilde{N}_t, t \geq t_0\}$ by

$$\tilde{N}_t = N_t - \int_{t_0}^{t} A[1 + m \cos(\omega_0 \sigma + \theta_\sigma)]\, d\sigma.$$

Then (32) can be written as

$$\begin{aligned} d\boldsymbol{\Sigma}_t^* &= \boldsymbol{F}_t^T \boldsymbol{\Sigma}_t^*\, dt + \boldsymbol{\Sigma}_t^* \boldsymbol{F}_t\, dt + \boldsymbol{G}_t \boldsymbol{G}_t^T\, dt \\ &\quad - Am^2[1 - \cos^2(\omega_0 t + \theta_t^*)] \\ &\quad \cdot [1 + m \cos(\omega_0 t + \theta_t^*)]^{-1} \boldsymbol{\Sigma}_t^* \boldsymbol{h}_t \boldsymbol{h}_t^T \boldsymbol{\Sigma}_t^*\, dt \\ &\quad - m[m + \cos(\omega_0 t + \theta_t^*)] \\ &\quad \cdot [1 + m \cos(\omega_0 t + \theta_t^*)]^{-2} \boldsymbol{\Sigma}_t^* \boldsymbol{h}_t \boldsymbol{h}_t^T \boldsymbol{\Sigma}_t^* \\ &\quad \cdot \{d\tilde{N}_t + A[\cos(\omega_0 t + \theta_t) - \cos(\omega_0 t + \theta_t^*)]\, dt\}. \end{aligned} \tag{33}$$

We first examine the fourth term on the right side in (33). The function

$$f(\phi) = (1 - \cos^2 \phi)(1 + m \cos \phi)^{-1}$$

is an even periodic function of $\phi$. Consequently, $f$ has a Fourier cosine series of the form

$$f(\phi) = a_0 + a_1 \cos \phi + a_2 \cos 2\phi + \cdots,$$

where it can be verified that $a_0$ is given by

$$a_0 = [1 - (1 - m^2)^{1/2}] m^{-2}.$$

If we let $\phi = \omega_0 t + \theta_t^*$ and substitute this series into the fourth term, then it appears reasonable to neglect all the harmonic components involving $\cos(n\omega_0 t + n\theta_t^*)$, $n \geq 1$, and retain only $a_0$ because of the implied time integration.

We shall arbitrarily drop the last term on the right side in (33). The motivation for doing so is as follows. $\tilde{N}_t$ is on the average zero and $d\tilde{N}_t$ is a future increment of an independent increment process. A Taylor series about $\theta_t^*$ shows that the difference $\cos(\omega_0 t + \theta_t) - \cos(\omega_0 t + \theta_t^*)$ is of the order of $\theta_t - \theta_t^*$. Consequently, the contribution of this difference in the last term is, on the average, of the order of the fifth moment of the error, which we have neglected.

The result of these approximations is the following pair of equations for the approximate estimate of the phase $\theta_t^*$:

$$dx_t^* = F_t x_t^* \, dt - m \sin(\omega_0 t + \theta_t^*) \cdot [1 + m\cos(\omega_0 t + \theta_t^*)]^{-1} \Sigma_t^* h_t \, dN_t$$

$$x_{t_0}^* = 0 \tag{34}$$

and

$$d\Sigma_t^* = F_t^T \Sigma_t^* \, dt + \Sigma_t^* F_t \, dt + G_t G_t^T \, dt - A[1 - (1 - m^2)^{1/2}] \Sigma_t^* h_t h_t^T \Sigma_t^* \, dt$$

$$\Sigma_{t_0}^* = \Lambda_0, \tag{35}$$

where $\theta_t^* = h_t^T x_t^*$. Equation (34) suggests the use of a form of tanlock loop to estimate $\theta_t$, and (35) is a Riccati equation.

### C. Simulation Results

1) The simulation results presented in Figs. 3 and 4 were obtained for the intensity $\lambda_t(x) = A \exp(-xt)$ described in Section VI-B1). The value $A = 100$ was used and the prior pdf for $x$ was taken to be uniform on the interval (0.5,1.5); thus, $\bar{x}_0 = 1.0$ and $\sigma_0^2 = \frac{1}{12}$. The exact and approximate estimates for $x$ and for $\lambda_t(x)$ are shown in Figs. 3 and 4, respectively, for three parameter values. The exact estimate was generated using the procedure described in Section V and is indicated by a circle. The approximate estimate is indicated by a star.

2) The simulation results presented in Figs. 5 and 6 were obtained for the intensity $\lambda_t(x_1,x_2) = x_1 \exp(-x_2 t)$ described in Section VI-B2). Both $x_1$ and $x_2$ were assumed to have a uniform prior pdf on the intervals (90,110) and (0.5,1.5), respectively; thus $\bar{x}_{10} = 100$, $\bar{x}_{20} = 1.0$, $\sigma_{10}^2 = \frac{100}{3}$, and $\sigma_{20}^2 = \frac{1}{12}$. The exact and approximate estimates for $x_1$, $x_2$, and $\lambda_t(x_1,x_2)$ are shown in Figs. 5 and 6. The exact estimates were generated using the procedure described in Section V and is indicated by a circle. The approximate estimate is indicated by a star.

3) The simulation results presented in Fig. 7 were obtained for the intensity $\lambda_t(\theta) = A[1 + m\cos(\omega_0 t + \theta)]$ described in Section VI-C3) for the special case of a constant phase parameter $\theta$, $-\pi \leq \theta \leq \pi$. This occurs when $F_t = 0$, $G_t = 0$, and $p_0(\theta)$ is uniform on the interval $(-\pi,\pi)$. For the simulation, it was assumed that $A = 500$, $m = 0.75$, and $\omega_0 = 2\pi(100)$. The count rate was such that about five counts per cycle of the modulation occurred.

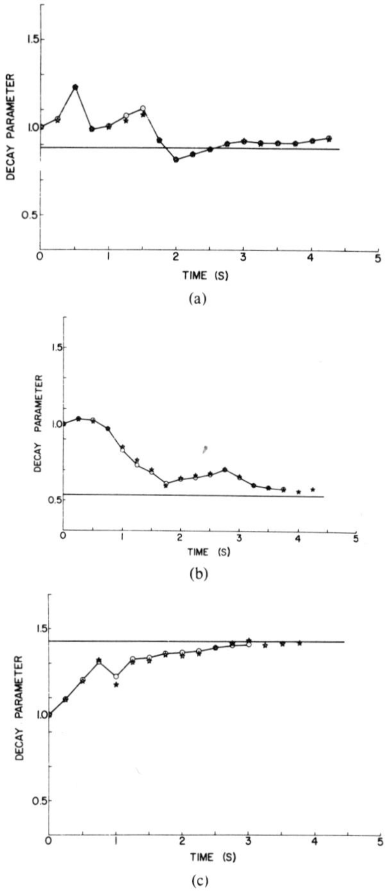


Fig. 3. Simulation record for the exact (circle) and approximate (star) estimates for the decay parameter $x$ of the intensity $\lambda_t(x) = 100 \exp(-xt)$, where $x$ is uniformly distributed on [0.5,1.5]. The values for $x$ are 0.8822, 0.538, and 1.429 in (a), (b), and (c), respectively. At $t = 4.25$ s, the total number of counts is 100 and 144 in (a) and (b), respectively. At $t = 3.00$ s, the total number of counts is 59 in (c).

The simulation time 0.7 s corresponds to 70 cycles of the modulation.

The results presented in Fig. 8 were obtained for the phase-modulated intensity $\lambda_t(\theta_t) = A[1 + m\cos(\omega_0 t + \theta_t)]$, where $\theta_t$ was a Wiener process with parameter $1/\tau_c$. The parameter $\tau_c$ may be interpreted as the coherence time of an unstable oscillator; it is the time at which 1 rad rms of phase drift is accumulated. This occurs when $F_t = 0$, $G_t = \tau_c^{-1/2}$, and $p_0(\theta) = \delta(\theta)$ in Section VI-B3). For the simulation, it was assumed that $A = 500$, $m = 0.75$, $\omega_0 = 2\pi(100)$, and $\tau_c = 0.1$.

The estimate of the constant phase and Wiener process were generated using (34) and (35) and is indicated by a star.

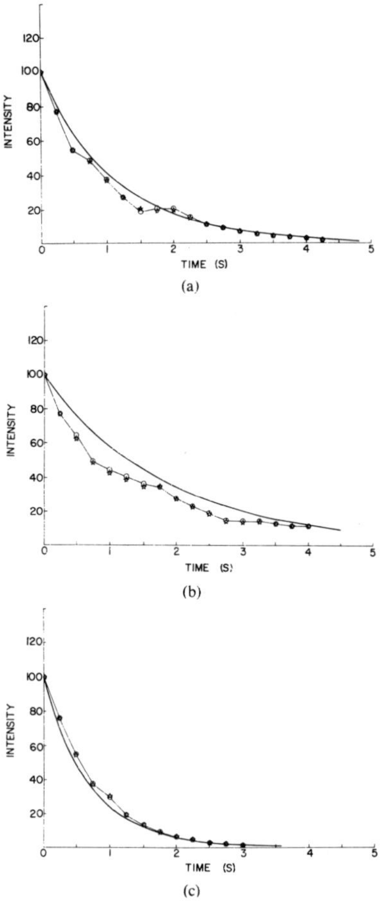


Fig. 4. Simulation record for the exact (circle) and approximate (star) estimates for the intensity $\lambda_t(x) = 100 \exp(-xt)$. Parameter values are identical to those of Fig. 3.

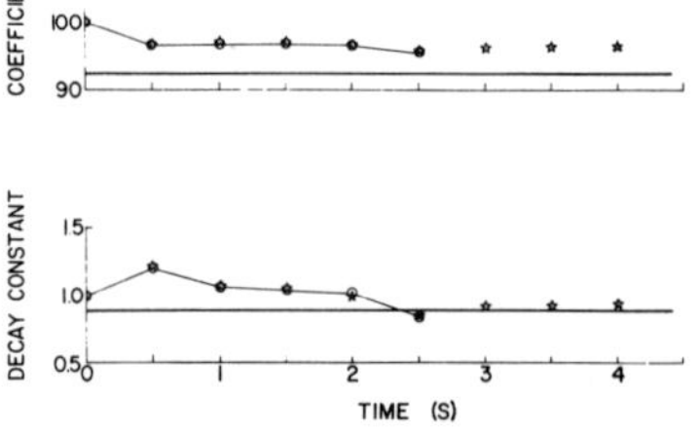


Fig. 5. Simulation record for the exact (circle) and approximate (star) estimates of the coefficient and decay parameters of the intensity $\lambda_t(x_1,x_2) = x_1 \exp(-x_2 t)$, where $x_1$ is uniformly distributed on [90,100] and $x_2$ is uniformly distributed on [0.5,1.5]. The values for $x_1$ and $x_2$ are 92.19 and 0.8822, respectively. At $t = 4.00$ s, the total number of counts is 94.

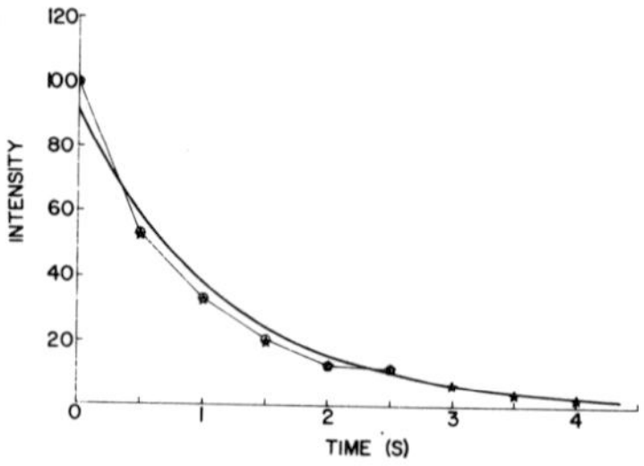


Fig. 6. Simulation record for the exact (circle) and approximate (star) estimate for the intensity $\lambda_t(x_1,x_2) = x_1 \exp(-x_2 t)$. Parameter values are identical to those of Fig. 5.

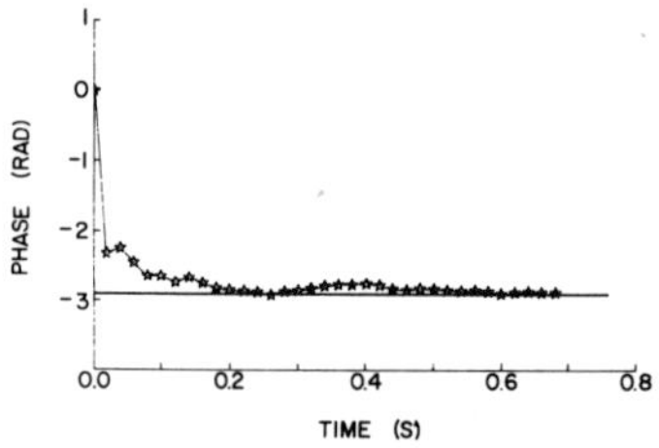


Fig. 7. Simulation record for the approximate (star) estimate of $\theta$ for the intensity $\lambda_t(\theta) = A(1 + m \cos(\omega_0 t + \theta))$, where $A = 500$, $m = 0.75$, $\omega_0 = 100(2\pi)$, and $\theta$ is uniformly distributed on $(-\pi,\pi)$. The value of $\theta$ is $-2.905$ rad. The total number of counts at $t = 0.6$ s is 267.

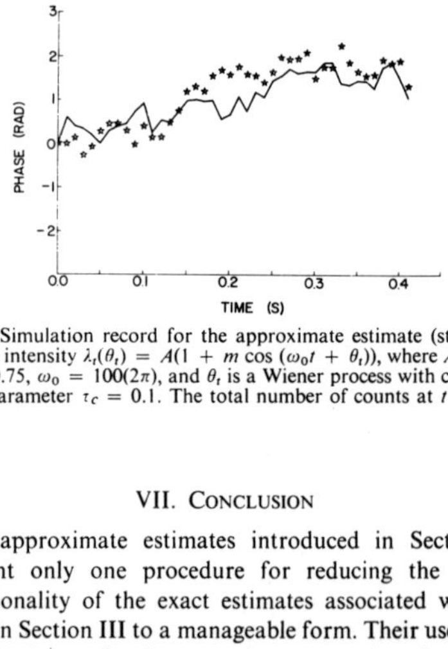


Fig. 8. Simulation record for the approximate estimate (star) of $\theta_t$ for the intensity $\lambda_t(\theta_t) = A(1 + m \cos(\omega_0 t + \theta_t))$, where $A = 500$, $m = 0.75$, $\omega_0 = 100(2\pi)$, and $\theta_t$ is a Wiener process with coherence time parameter $\tau_c = 0.1$. The total number of counts at $t = 0.4$ is 211.

## VII. Conclusion

The approximate estimates introduced in Section VI represent only one procedure for reducing the infinite dimensionality of the exact estimates associated with the results in Section III to a manageable form. Their usefulness for particular applications must be compared to alternatives that may be suggested by the particular functions involved. For the intensity functions chosen for simulation, the exact and approximate estimates introduced here appear to agree remarkably well considering the low count rates involved.

## Acknowledgment

The author would like to thank Prof. E. Hoversten and J. Clark of the Massachusetts Institute of Technology, Cambridge, for carefully reading the manuscript and making valuable suggestions. He would also like to thank the anonymous reviewers for their helpful comments.

## References

[1] J. B. West and C. T. Dollery, "Distribution of blood flow and ventilation perfusion ratio in the lung, measured with radioactive $CO_2$," *J. Appl. Physiol.*, vol. 15, 1960, pp. 405–410.
[2] J. B. West, C. T. Dollery, and P. Hugh-Jones, "The use of radioactive carbon-dioxide to measure regional blood flow in the lungs of patients with pulmonary disease," *J. Clin. Invest.*, vol. 40, Jan. 1961, pp. 1–12.
[3] M. M. Ter-Pogossian, J. O. Eichling, D. O. Davis, and M. J. Welch, "The measure in vivo of regional cerebral oxygen utilization by means of oxyhemoglobin labeled with radioactive oxygen-15," *J. Clin. Invest.*, vol. 49, 1970, pp. 381–391.
[4] C. W. Sheppard, *Basic Principles of the Tracer Method.* New York: Wiley, 1962.
[5] J. A. Jacquez, "Tracer kinetics," in *Principles of Nuclear Medicine*, H. N. Wagner, Jr., Ed. Philadelphia: Saunders, 1968, pp. 44–74.
[6] P. Meier and K. L. Zierler, "On the theory of the indicator-dilution method for measurement of blood flow and volume," *J. Appl. Physiol.*, vol. 12, June 1954, pp. 731–744.
[7] *Optical Space Communication*, Proc. M.I.T.–NASA workshop, Williams College, Williamstown, Mass., NASA-SP-217, Aug. 4–17, 1968.
[8] E. V. Hoversten, R. O. Harger, and S. J. Halme, "Communication theory for the turbulent atmosphere," *Proc. IEEE*, vol. 58, Oct. 1970, pp. 1626–1650.
[9] D. R. Cox, "Some statistical methods connected with series of events," *J. Res. Statist. Soc. B.*, vol. 17, 1955, pp. 129–164.
[10] D. R. Cox and P. A. W. Lewis, *The Statistical Analysis of Series of Events.* London: Methuen, 1966.
[11] M. S. Bartlett, *Stochastic Processes.* Cambridge: Cambridge Univ. Press, 1966.
[12] S. Karp and J. R. Clark, "Photon counting: A problem in classical noise theory," *IEEE Trans. Inform. Theory*, vol. IT-16, Nov. 1970, pp. 672–680.
[13] J. R. Clark and E. Hoversten, "Poisson process as a statistical model for photodetectors excited by Gaussian light," Res. Lab. Electron., M.I.T., Cambridge, Quart. Prog. Rep. 98, July 1970, pp. 95–101.
[14] P. A. Frost, "Nonlinear estimation in continuous time systems," Syst. Theory Lab., Stanford Univ., Stanford, Calif., Tech. Rep. 6304-4, May 1968.
[15] P. R. Halmos, *Measure Theory.* New York: Van Nostrand, 1950.
[16] H. J. Kushner, *Stochastic Stability and Control.* New York: Academic Press, 1967, p. 18.
[17] W. Feller, *An Introduction to Probability Theory and Its Applications*, vol. 2. New York: Wiley, 1966.
[18] B. Reiffen and H. Sherman, "An optimum demodulator for Poisson processes: Photon source detectors," *Proc. IEEE*, vol. 51, Oct. 1963, pp. 1316–1320.
[19] T. E. Duncan, "Evaluation of likelihood functions," *Inform. Contr.*, vol. 13, July 1968, pp. 62–74.
[20] T. Kailath, "A general likelihood-ratio formula for random signals in Gaussian noise," *IEEE Trans. Inform. Theory*, vol. IT-15, May 1969, pp. 350–361.
[21] H. Kunita and S. Watanabe, "On square-integrable martingales," *Nagoya Math. J.*, vol. 30, Aug. 1967, pp. 209–245.
[22] H. L. Van Trees, *Detection, Estimation and Modulation Theory, Part I.* New York: Wiley, 1968.
[23] D. L. Snyder, *The State-Variable Approach to Continuous Estimation, With Applications to Analog Communication Theory.* Cambridge, Mass.: M.I.T. Press, 1969.
[24] L. M. Robinson, "Tanlock: A phase-lock loop of extended tracking capability," in *Proc. Nat. Winter Conf. Military Electronics*, 1962.
[25] C. W. Helstrom, "Estimation of the modulation frequency of a light beam," in *Optical Space Communication*, Proc. M.I.T.–NASA workshop, Williams College, Williamstown, Mass., NASA SP-217, Aug. 1968, pp. 121–123.

# 4



Reprinted from *IEEE Trans. Inform. Theory,* **IT-18**(5), 558–562 (1972)

# Smoothing for Doubly Stochastic Poisson Processes

DONALD L. SNYDER, MEMBER, IEEE

***Abstract*—Some general equations are derived for the smoothing density of a Markov process that modulates the intensity of an observed doubly stochastic Poisson process. The equations are in terms of filtering densities that are specified by recursive equations.**

## I. INTRODUCTION

IN [1] we have discussed the problem of causally estimating, or filtering, a vector Markov process that modulates the intensity function of an observed Poisson counting process. We now examine estimates with the causality restriction removed. The theory parallels that for noncausally estimating, or smoothing, a vector Markov process from nonlinear additive-white-Gaussian-noise observations.

## II. RECURSIVE SMOOTHING

The problem setup and notation follow [1]. Let $\{N_\tau, t_0 < \tau \leq t_1\}$ be a doubly stochastic Poisson process with an intensity $\{\lambda_\tau, t_0 < \tau \leq t_1\}$ that is modulated by an $n$-vector Markov process $\{\boldsymbol{x}_\tau, t_0 < \tau \leq t_1\}$. Here, we shall assume that $\boldsymbol{x}$ is a diffusion with a well-defined probability density $p_t(X)$ for each $t \in (t_0,t_1]$.

Our aim in what follows is to develop the equations of smoothing in terms of the equations of filtering developed in [1]. Various expressions for smoothing estimates in terms of filtering estimates have been established for the additive Gaussian observation model. Lipster and Shiryaev [2] were evidently the first to do this. Frost and Kailath [3] use the innovation representation for the additive Gaussian model to develop similar results. Our approach for the doubly stochastic Poisson process observation model most closely parallels that of Lo [4] for the Gaussian model.

The following theorem is motivated by the fact that $\boldsymbol{x}_t$ for $t \in (t_0,t_1]$ splits the past and future of the observation $\{N_\tau, t_0 < \tau \leq t_1\}$ in the sense that $\{N_\tau, t_0 < \tau \leq t\}$ and $\{N_\tau, t \leq \tau \leq t_1\}$ are independent given $\boldsymbol{x}_t$. This obtains because $\boldsymbol{x}_t$ splits its own past and future in the sense that $\{\boldsymbol{x}_\tau, t_0 < \tau \leq t\}$ and $\{\boldsymbol{x}_\tau, t \leq \tau \leq t_1\}$ are independent given $\boldsymbol{x}_t$ by the basic properties of Markov processes and because $\{N_\tau, t_0 < \tau \leq t_1\}$ has independent increments given $\{\boldsymbol{x}_t, t_0 < \tau \leq t_1\}$. The theorem generalizes a similar theorem due to Lo [4, theorem 3.1], who established it from a Bucy-type representation theorem for smoothing with nonlinear observations in additive white Gaussian noise.

*Theorem 1:* Let $\{y_\tau, t_0 < \tau \leq t_1\}$ be a conditionally independent increment process given the $n$-vector Markov process $\{\boldsymbol{x}_\tau, t_0 < \tau \leq t_1\}$. Let $Y_{t_0,t_1} = \{Y_\tau, t_0 < \tau \leq t_1\}$ denote an observed record of $y$ on $(t_0,t_1]$. Let $t \in (t_0,t_1]$ and split $Y_{t_0,t_1}$ into two subrecords as $Y_{t_0,t} = \{Y_\tau, t_0 < \tau \leq t\}$ and $Y_{t,t_1} = \{Y_\tau, t \leq \tau \leq t_1\}$. Suppose $\boldsymbol{x}_t$ admits conditional densities. Then the conditional density of smoothing has the following decomposition:

$$p_t(X \mid Y_{t_0,t_1}) = k_t p_t(X \mid Y_{t_0,t}) p_t(X \mid Y_{t,t_1}) p_t^{-1}(X),$$

where $k_t$ is the normalization factor defined by

$$k_t^{-1} = \int_{R^n} p_t(\xi \mid Y_{t_0,t}) p_t(\xi \mid Y_{t,t_1}) p_t^{-1}(\xi) \prod_{i=1}^{n} d\xi_i.$$

Thus, the conditional density of smoothing can be decomposed into a conditional density of filtering $p_t(X \mid Y_{t_0,t})$, a conditional density of parameter estimation $p_t(X \mid Y_{t,t_1})$, and an unconditional density $p_t(X)$.

*Proof:* Partition $(t_0,t_1]$ as

$$t_0 \triangleq \tau_0 \leq \tau_1 \leq \tau_2 \leq \cdots \leq \tau_k$$

$$= t \leq \tau_{k+1} \leq \tau_{k+2} \leq \cdots \leq \tau_{k+m} \triangleq t_1,$$

where $k$ and $m$ are arbitrary positive integers. Define the increment random variables $b_i = y_{\tau_{i+1}} - y_{\tau_i}$ and the observed increment variables $B_i = Y_{\tau_{i+1}} - Y_{\tau_i}$ for $i = 0,1,\cdots, k + m - 1$. Then the observed record $Y_{t_0,t_1}$ is equivalent to the following event $E$ in the underlying probability space

$$E = \{\omega: B_i - \Delta B_i < b_i(\omega) \leq B_i; i = 1,2,\cdots, k + m - 1\}$$

as the partition of $(t_0,t_1]$ is refined indefinitely and as $\Delta B_i \to 0$ for each $i$. Similarly $Y_{t_0,t}$ and $Y_{t,t_1}$ are equivalent to the events

$$E_0 = \{\omega: B_i - \Delta B_i < b_i(\omega) \leq B_i; i = 1,2,\cdots, k - 1\}$$

and

$$E_1 = \{\omega: B_i - \Delta B_i < b_i(\omega) \leq B_i;$$
$$i = k, k + 1,\cdots, k + m - 1\}$$

as the partition is refined indefinitely and as $\Delta B_i \to 0$ for each $i$. Because $E = E_0 \cap E_1$, we can write $p_t(X \mid E) =$

Manuscript received October 1, 1971; revised March 20, 1972. This work was supported by the National Institutes of Health, Grant RR00396 from the Division of Research Resources and the National Science Foundation, Grant GK-32239.

The author is with the Biomedical Computer Laboratory, Washington University, St. Louis, Mo. 63130.

$p_t(X \mid E_0 \cap E_1)$. Then using Bayes' rule we have

$$p_t(X \mid E) = k_t' \Pr(E_0 \cap E_1 \mid x_t = X) p_t(X)$$

in which $k_t'$ is the normalization factor. From the smoothing property of conditional expectation and the conditional independence of the increments of $y$, we obtain the following factoring of the probability on the right side:

$$\begin{aligned}\Pr(E_0 \cap E_1 \mid x_t = X) &= E[\Pr(E_0 \cap E_1 \mid x_t = X; x_\tau, t_0 < \tau \leq t_1) \mid x_t = X] \\ &= E[\Pr(E_0 \mid x_t = X; x_\tau, t_0 < \tau \leq t) \\ &\quad \times \Pr(E_1 \mid x_t = X; x_\tau, t \leq \tau \leq t_1) \mid x_t = X] \\ &= E[\Pr(E_0 \mid x_t = X; x_\tau, t_0 < \tau \leq t) \mid x_t = X] \\ &\quad \times E[\Pr(E_1 \mid x_t = X; x_\tau, t \leq \tau \leq t_1) \mid x_t = X] \\ &= \Pr[E_0 \mid x_t = X] \Pr[E_1 \mid x_t = X],\end{aligned}$$

where the Markov property of $x$ has been used to factor the expectation. Thus, using Bayes' rule we obtain

$$\begin{aligned}p_t(X \mid E) &= k_t' \Pr[E_0 \mid x_t = X] \Pr[E_1 \mid x_t = X] p_t(X) \\ &= k_t p_t(X \mid E_0) p_t(X \mid E_1) p_t^{-1}(X),\end{aligned}$$

where $k_t$ is the normalization factor defined by

$$k_t^{-1} = \int_{R^n} p_t(\xi \mid E_0) p_t(\xi \mid E_1) p_t^{-1}(\xi) \prod_{i=1}^{n} d\xi_i.$$

Refining the partition of $(t_0, t_1]$ and letting $\Delta B_i \to 0$ for each $i$ establishes Theorem 1.

*Remark 1:* The decomposition of the theorem holds for additive observations $\{dy_\tau = h_\tau(x_\tau)\, d\tau + d\eta_\tau, t_0 < \tau \leq t_1\}$ where $\{\eta_\tau, t_0 < \tau \leq t_1\}$ is a Wiener process because $\{y_\tau, t_0 < \tau \leq t_1\}$ has independent increments given $\{x_\tau, t_0 < \tau \leq t_1\}$.

*Remark 2:* The decomposition of the theorem holds for doubly stochastic Poisson observations $\{dy_\tau = dN_\tau, t_0 < \tau \leq t_1\}$ because $\{y_\tau, t_0 < \tau \leq t_1\}$ has independent increments given $\{x_\tau, t_0 < \tau \leq t_1\}$.

The following theorem provides an expression for the conditional density of smoothing in terms of conditional densities of filtering for the Poisson observation model.

*Theorem 2:* Let $\{x_\tau, t_0 < \tau \leq t_1\}$ be a Markov process that modulates the intensity function $\{\lambda_\tau(x_\tau), t_0 < \tau \leq t_1\}$ of an observed doubly stochastic Poisson process $\{N_\tau, t_0 < \tau \leq t_1\}$. Let $N_{t_0,t_1}$ denote an observed record of $N$ and let $t \in (t_0, t_1]$ split $N_{t_0,t_1}$ into subrecords $N_{t_0,t}$ and $N_{t,t_1}$. Then the conditional density of smoothing can be expressed in terms of conditional densities of filtering as

$$p_t(X \mid N_{t_0,t_1}) = p_t(X \mid N_{t_0,t}) \phi_{t,t_1}(X) \hat{\phi}_{t,t_1}^{-1},$$

where

a)

$$\phi_{t,t_1}(X) = \exp\left(-\int_t^{t_1} a_\sigma(X)\, d\sigma + \int_t^{t_1} \ln[1 + a_\sigma(X) \hat{\lambda}_{\sigma|(t,\sigma)}^{-1}]\, dN_\sigma\right)$$

b)

$$a_\sigma(X) = \int_{R^n} [\hat{\lambda}_\sigma(\xi) - \hat{\lambda}_{\sigma|(t,\sigma)}] p_\sigma(\xi \mid x_t = X, N_{t,\sigma}) \prod_{i=1}^{n} d\xi_i$$

c)

$$\begin{aligned}\hat{\lambda}_{\sigma|(t,\sigma)} &= E[\lambda_\sigma(x_\sigma) \mid N_{t,\sigma}] \\ &= \int_{R^n} \lambda_\sigma(X) p_\sigma(X \mid N_{t,\sigma}) \prod_{i=1}^{n} dX_i\end{aligned}$$

and

d)

$$\begin{aligned}\hat{\phi}_{t,t_1} &= E[\phi_{t,t_1}(x_t) \mid N_{t_0,t}] \\ &= \int_{R^n} \phi_{t,t_1}(X) p_t(X \mid N_{t_0,t}) \prod_{i=1}^{n} dX_i.\end{aligned}$$

*Proof:* Let $\phi_{t,t_1}(X) = p_t(X \mid N_{t,t_1}) p_t^{-1}(X)$. Then from Corollary A of the Appendix, $\phi_{t,t_1}(X)$ has the form in a). From the definition of $k_t$, we have that $k_t = \hat{\phi}_{t,t_1}^{-1}$. Using these results in Theorem 1 then establishes Theorem 2.

*Remark:* The conditional densities of filtering $p_t(X \mid N_{t_0,t})$, $p_t(X \mid N_{t,t_1})$, and $p_{t_1}(\xi \mid x_t = X, N_{t,t_1})$ required in Theorem 2 satisfy recursive equations given in [1] with the initial conditions $p_{t_0}(X)$, $p_t(X)$, and $\delta(\xi - X)$, respectively.

The following differential rule for doubly stochastic Poisson processes will be used repeatedly in what follows.

*Differential Rule:* Let $\zeta_t$ satisfy

$$d\zeta_t = \alpha_t(\zeta_t)\, dt + \beta_t(\zeta_t)\, dN_t.$$

Let $\phi(\zeta_t)$ be a scalar function of $\zeta_t$ and denote the gradient of $\phi(\zeta_t)$ by $\partial\phi/\partial\zeta_t$. Then $\phi(\zeta_t)$ satisfies

$$d\phi(\zeta_t) = \langle \partial\phi/\partial\zeta_t, \alpha_t \rangle\, dt + [\phi(\zeta_t + \beta_t) - \phi(\zeta_t)]\, dN_t,$$

where $\langle v_1, v_2 \rangle$ denotes the inner or dot product of $v_1$ and $v_2$.

*Proof:* A rigorous proof is given in [5, theorem 2]. For a heuristic derivation see [1, Section IV-B].

Three smoothing problems of interest in practice are fixed-point smoothing, in which $t$ is a fixed point in $(t_0, t_1]$ and $t_1$ increases; fixed-interval sweep smoothing, in which $t$ increases in $(t_0, t_1]$ and $t_1$ is fixed; and fixed-lag smoothing, in which $t$ increases in $(t_0, t_1]$ and $t_1$ increases according to $t_1 = t + T$, where $T \geq 0$ is the lag time. Our purpose in what follows is to obtain recursive equations for the smoothing density for each of these three problems for Poisson observations.

*A. Fixed-Point Smoothing*

The following theorem provides a recursive equation for the evolution with $t_1$ of the conditional density of smoothing $p_t(X \mid N_{t_0,t_1})$ in terms of filtering densities.

*Theorem 3:* Under the conditions of Theorem 2 with $t$ fixed in $(t_0,t_1]$, the conditional density of smoothing evolves with increasing $t_1$, for $t_1 \geq t$, as

$$d_{t_1} p_t(X \mid N_{t_0,t_1}) = p_t(X \mid N_{t_0,t_1})[a_{t_1}(X) - \hat{a}_{t_1|(t_0,t_1)}] \cdot \hat{\lambda}_{t_1|(t_0,t_1)}^{-1}[dN_{t_1} - \hat{\lambda}_{t_1|(t_0,t_1)}\, dt_1],$$

where

$$a_{t_1}(X) - \hat{a}_{t_1|(t_0,t_1)} = \int_{R^n} [\lambda_{t_1}(\xi) - \hat{\lambda}_{t_1|(t_0,t_1)}] p_{t_1}(\xi \mid x_t = X, N_{t,t_1}) \prod_{i=1}^{n} d\xi_i$$

and

$$\hat{a}_{t_1|(t_0,t_1)} = E[a_{t_1}(x_t) \mid N_{t_0,t_1}].$$

*Proof:* From Theorem 2,

$$d_{t_1} p_t(X \mid N_{t_0,t_1}) = p_t(X \mid N_{t_0,t})\, d_{t_1}[\phi_{t,t_1}(X)\hat{\phi}_{t,t_1}^{-1}].$$

To evaluate the differential on the right side, we determine $d_{t_1}\phi_{t,t_1}(X)$ and $d_{t_1}\hat{\phi}_{t,t_1}$ and use the differential rule on $\phi_{t,t_1}(X)\hat{\phi}_{t,t_1}^{-1}$. From Theorem A of the Appendix, we have

$$d_{t_1}\phi_{t,t_1}(X) = \phi_{t,t_1}(X)a_{t_1}(X)\hat{\lambda}_{t_1|(t,t_1)}^{-1}[dN_{t_1} - \hat{\lambda}_{t|(t,t_1)}\, dt_1].$$

Multiplication of this expression by $p_t(X \mid N_{t_0,t})$, integration, and use of

$$E[\phi_{t,t_1}(x_t)a_{t_1}(x_t) \mid N_{t_0,t}] = \hat{\phi}_{t,t_1}\hat{a}_{t_1|(t_0,t_1)}$$

yield

$$d\hat{\phi}_{t,t_1} = \hat{\phi}_{t,t_1}\hat{a}_{t_1|(t_0,t_1)}\hat{\lambda}_{t_1|(t,t_1)}^{-1}[dN_{t_1} - \hat{\lambda}_{t_1|(t,t_1)}\, dt_1].$$

Straightforward application of the differential rule then shows

$$d_{t_1}[\phi_{t,t_1}(X)\hat{\phi}_{t,t_1}^{-1}] = \phi_{t,t_1}(X)\hat{\phi}_{t,t_1}^{-1}[a_{t_1}(X) - \hat{a}_{t_1|(t_0,t_1)}] \times [\hat{\lambda}_{t_1|(t,t_1)} + \hat{a}_{t_1|(t_0,t_1)}]^{-1} \times \{dN_{t_1} - [\hat{\lambda}_{t_1|(t,t_1)} + \hat{a}_{t_1|(t_0,t_1)}]\, dt_1\}.$$

Because $p_{t_1}(\xi \mid x_t = X, N_{t,t_1}) = p_{t_1}(\xi \mid x_t = X, N_{t_0,t_1})$, it follows that $\hat{a}_{t_1|(t_0,t_1)} = \hat{\lambda}_{t_1|(t_0,t_1)} - \hat{\lambda}_{t_1|(t,t_1)}$. Use of this, the definition for $a_t(X)$, and multiplication by $p_t(X \mid N_{t_0,t})$ then establishes Theorem 3.

*Remark:* The boundary condition for Theorem 3, $p_t(X \mid N_{t_0,t})$, corresponding to $t_1 = t$ satisfies a recursive equation given in [1].

*Lemma:* Under the conditions of Theorem 2, the conditional density of smoothing can be expressed in terms of conditional densities of filtering as

$$p_t(X \mid N_{t_0,t_1}) = p_t(X \mid N_{t_0,t}) \exp[\psi_{t,t_1}(X)],$$

where

$$\psi_{t,t_1}(X) = -\int_t^{t_1} [a_\sigma(X) - \hat{a}_{\sigma|(t_0,\sigma)}]\, d\sigma + \int_t^{t_1} \ln\{[a_\sigma(X) - \hat{a}_{\sigma|(t_0,\sigma)} + \hat{\lambda}_{\sigma|(t_0,\sigma)}]\hat{\lambda}_{\sigma|(t_0,\sigma)}^{-1}\}\, dN_\sigma.$$

*Proof:* Follows easily from Theorem 3, the differential rule on $\ln p_t(X \mid N_{t_0,t_1})$, and integration.

*Remark:* The second integral in $\psi_{t,t_1}(X)$ can be written as

$$\int_t^{t_1} \ln\left\{\left[\int_{R^n} \lambda_\sigma(\xi)p_\sigma(\xi \mid x_t = X, N_{t,\sigma}) \prod_{i=1}^{n} d\xi_i\right] \cdot \hat{\lambda}_\sigma^{-1} \mid (t_{0,\sigma})\right\} dN_\sigma.$$

*B. Fixed-Interval Sweep Smoothing*

The following theorem provides a recursive equation for the evolution with $t$ of the conditional density of smoothing $p_t(X \mid N_{t_0,t_1})$ in terms of filtering densities.

*Theorem 4:* Under the conditions of Theorem 2 with $(t_0,t_1]$ fixed, the conditional density of smoothing evolves with increasing $t$, for $t \in (t_0,t_1]$, as

$$d_t p_t(X \mid N_{t_0,t_1}) = L[p_t(X \mid N_{t_0,t}] \exp[\psi_{t,t_1}(X)]\, dt,$$

where $L[\cdot]$ is the forward Kolmogorov differential operator associated with the diffusion process $\{x_\tau, t_0 < \tau \leq t_1\}$.

*Proof:* From [1], we have

$$d_t p_t(X \mid N_{t_0,t}) = L[p_t(X \mid N_{t_0,t})]\, dt + p_t(X \mid N_{t_0,t})[\lambda_t(X) - \hat{\lambda}_{t|(t_0,t)}]\hat{\lambda}_{t|(t_0,t)}^{-1}[dN_t - \hat{\lambda}_{t|(t_0,t)}\, dt].$$

From the definition of $\psi_{t,t_1}(X)$ in the lemma following Theorem 3, the differential rule, and the identity $a_t(X) - \hat{a}_{t|(t_0,t)} = \lambda_t(X) - \hat{\lambda}_{t|(t_0,t)}$, we have

$$d_t \exp[\psi_{t,t_1}(X)] = (\exp[\psi_{t,t_1}(X)])[\lambda_t(X) - \hat{\lambda}_{t|(t_0,t)}]\, dt - \exp[\psi_{t,t_1}(X)][\lambda_t(X) - \hat{\lambda}_{t|(t_0,t)}]\lambda_t^{-1}(X)\, dN_t.$$

Use of the differential rule to evaluate $d_t\{p_t(X \mid N_{t_0,t}) \cdot \exp[\psi_{t,t_1}(X)]\}$ and straightforward manipulation then establish Theorem 4.

*Remark:* The initial condition $p_{t_0}(X \mid N_{t_0,t_1})$ is given in Corollary A of the Appendix on setting $t = t_0$.

*C. Fixed-Lag Smoothing*

The following theorem provides a recursive equation for the evolution with $t$ of the conditional density of smoothing $p_t(X \mid N_{t_0,t+T})$ in terms of filtering densities.

*Theorem 5:* Under the conditions of Theorem 2 with

$t_1 = t + T$, where $T \geq 0$, the conditional density of fixed-lag smoothing evolves with increasing $t$ as

$$d_t p_t(X \mid N_{t_0,t+T}) = L[p_t(X \mid N_{t_0,t})] \exp[\psi_{t,t+T}(X)]\, dt + p_t(X \mid N_{t_0,t+T})[a_{t+T}(X) - \hat{a}_{t+T|(t_0,t+T)}] \cdot \hat{\lambda}^{-1}_{t+T|(t_0,t+T)} [dN_{t+T} - \hat{\lambda}_{t+T|(t_0,t+T)}\, dt].$$

*Proof:* Theorem 5 follows from Theorems 3 and 5 by noting that

$$d_t p_t(X \mid N_{t_0,t+T}) = d_t p_t(X \mid N_{t_0,t_1}) + d_{t_1} p_t(X \mid N_{t_0,t_1}),$$

where $t_1 = t + T$.

*Remark:* An expression for the initial condition for Theorem 5 $p_{t_0}(X \mid N_{t_0,t_0+T})$ is given in Corollary A of the Appendix when $t = t_0$ and $t_1 = t_0 + T$.

## III. Conclusion

We have given several general expressions for the evolution of the conditional density of smoothing in terms of filtering densities for a doubly stochastic Poisson process observation model. These expressions can be viewed as updating algorithms useful in the numerical evaluation of the conditional density of smoothing. Also, they can form the point of departure in determining expressions for approximate or suboptimum smoothed estimates of an underlying Markov process that modulates the intensity function of the Poisson process. We have found no counterpart in the doubly stochastic Poisson-process observation model to the linear Gauss–Markov specialization that can arise with the additive white Gaussian-noise observation model. Thus, we have found no special case of the Poisson model in which neat closed-form expressions, not involving approximations, can be given for smoothed estimates of an underlying Markov process.


## Acknowledgment

The author would like to thank the anonymous reviewers for their careful reading of the manuscript. The detailed comments were very much appreciated. He would also like to thank Prof. T. Kailath for bringing the papers by Lipster and Shiryaev [2] and by Gihman and Dorogovcev [5] to his attention.


## Appendix

### Evolution of the Conditional Density of Parameter Estimation

The purpose of this appendix is to establish the following theorem describing the evolution with $t_1$ of the conditional density of parameter estimation $p_t(X \mid N_{t,t_1})$ for Poisson observations. Throughout, we assume these densities exist.

*Theorem A:* The conditional density of parameter estimation satisfies the following differential equation

$$d_{t_1} p_t(X \mid N_{t,t_1}) = p_t(X \mid N_{t,t_1}) a_{t_1}(X) \hat{\lambda}^{-1}_{t_1|(t,t_1)} [dN_{t_1} - \hat{\lambda}_{t_1|(t,t_1)}\, dt_1],$$

where $\hat{\lambda}_{t_1|(t,t_1)}$ denotes the estimate

$$\hat{\lambda}_{t_1|(t,t_1)} = E[\lambda_{t_1}(x_{t_1}) \mid N_{t,t_1}]$$

and where $a_{t_1}(X)$ satisfies

$$a_{t_1}(X) = \int_{R^n} [\lambda_{t_1}(\xi) - \hat{\lambda}_{t_1|(t,t_1)}] p_{t_1}(\xi \mid x_t = X, N_{t,t_1}) \prod_{i=1}^{n} d\xi_i.$$

*Proof:* Let $c_t(v \mid N_{t,t_1})$ be the conditional characteristic function of $x_t$ given the counting record $N_{t,t_1}$ as defined by

$$c_t(v \mid N_{t,t_1}) = E(\exp[j\langle v,x_t \rangle] \mid N_{t,t_1}).$$

To an incremental increase $t_1 \to t_1 + \Delta t_1$, there corresponds an increment in the counting record $\Delta N_{t_1} = N_{t_1+\Delta t_1} - N_{t_1}$ and an incremental change in the conditional characteristic function

$$\Delta_{t_1} c_t(v \mid N_{t,t_1}) = c_t(v \mid N_{t,t_1}, \Delta N_{t_1}) - c_t(v \mid N_{t,t_1}),$$

where

$$c_t(v \mid N_{t,t_1}, \Delta N_{t_1}) = \int_{R^n} \exp[j\langle v,X \rangle]\, d^n P_t(X \mid N_{t,t_1}, \Delta N_{t_1}),$$

where $P_t(X \mid N_{t,t_1}, \Delta N_{t_1})$ is the conditional distribution function of $x_t$. We evaluate this distribution function for fixed $\Delta N_{t_1}$; namely for $\Delta N_{t_1} = 0$, $\Delta N_{t_1} = 1$, and $\Delta N_{t_1} = m$ where $m > 1$. The finite difference

$$\delta^n P_t(X \mid N_{t,t_1}, \Delta N_{t_1} = 0) = \Pr(x_t \in (X - \delta X, X] \mid N_{t,t_1}, \Delta N_{t_1} = 0)$$

can be evaluated as

$$\delta^n P_t(X \mid N_{t,t_1}, \Delta N_{t_1} = 0) = \Pr(\Delta N_{t_1} = 0 \mid x_t \in (X - \delta X, X], N_{t,t_1}) \times \delta^n P_t(X \mid N_{t,t_1}) / \Pr(\Delta N_{t_1} = 0 \mid N_{t,t_1}),$$

where as $\delta X \to 0$

$$\Pr(\Delta N_{t_1} = 0 \mid x_t \in (X - \delta X, X], N_{t,t_1}) \to \int_{R^n} \Pr(\Delta N_{t_1} = 0 \mid x_{t_1} = \xi, x_t = X, N_{t,t_1}) \cdot p_{t_1}(\xi \mid x_t = X, N_{t,t_1}) \prod_{i=1}^{n} d\xi_i$$
$$= 1 - \int_{R^n} \lambda_{t_1}(\xi) p_{t_1}(\xi \mid x_t = X, N_{t,t_1}) \cdot \prod_{i=1}^{n} d\xi_i\, \Delta t_1 + o(\Delta t_1)$$

and where

$$\Pr(\Delta N_{t_1} = 0 \mid N_{t,t_1}) = E[\Pr(\Delta N_{t_1} = 0 \mid x_{t_1}, N_{t,t_1}) \mid N_{t,t_1}] = 1 - \hat{\lambda}_{t_1|(t,t_1)} \Delta t_1 + o(\Delta t_1).$$

Putting these results together, we have

$$c_t(v \mid N_{t,t_1}, \Delta N_{t_1} = 0) = E(\exp[j\langle v,x_t \rangle]\{1 - a_{t_1}(x_t)\, \Delta t_1\} \mid N_{t,t_1}) + o(\Delta t_1),$$

where

$$a_{t_1}(x_t) = \int_{R^n} [\lambda_{t_1}(\xi) - \hat{\lambda}_{t_1|(t,t_1)}] p_{t_1}(\xi \mid x_t, N_{t,t_1}) \prod_{i=1}^{n} d\xi_i.$$

Similarly, by the same procedure, we obtain

$$c_t(v \mid N_{t,t_1}, \Delta N_{t_1} = 1)$$

$$= E\left(\exp [j\langle v,x_t\rangle] \int_{R^n} \lambda_{t_1}(\xi) p_{t_1}(\xi \mid x_t, N_{t,t_1}) \prod_{i=1}^{n} d\xi_i \mid N_{t,t_1}\right)$$

$$\times \hat{\lambda}_{t_1|(t,t_1)}^{-1} + o(\Delta t_1)$$

$$= E(\exp [j\langle v,x_t\rangle]\{a_{t_1}(x_t) + \hat{\lambda}_{t_1|(t,t_1)}\} \mid N_{t,t_1})\hat{\lambda}_{t_1|(t,t_1)}^{-1}$$

$$+ o(\Delta t_1)$$

and

$$c_t(v \mid N_{t,t_1}, \Delta N_{t_1} = m) = 0(\Delta t_1), \qquad m > 1.$$

Thus, for $\Delta N_{t_1}$ variable we have

$$c_t(v \mid N_{t,t_1}, \Delta N_{t_1}) = E(\exp [j\langle v,x_t\rangle]$$

$$\{1 - a_{t_1}(x_t)\Delta t_1\} \mid N_{t,t_1})\delta_{0,\Delta N_{t_1}} + E(\exp [j\langle v,x_t\rangle]\{a_{t_1}(x_t)$$

$$+ \hat{\lambda}_{t_1|(t,t_1)}\} \mid N_{t,t_1})\hat{\lambda}_{t_1|(t,t_1)}^{-1}\delta_{1,\Delta N_{t_1}} + o(\Delta t_1).$$

Because $\delta_{0,\Delta N_{t_1}} \overset{\text{a.s.}}{\to} 1 - \Delta N_{t_1}$ and $\delta_{1,\Delta N_{t_1}} \overset{\text{a.s.}}{\to} \Delta N_{t_1}$ as $\Delta t_1 \to 0$, we can write

$$\Delta_{t_1} c(v \mid N_{t,t_1})$$

$$= E(\exp [j\langle v,x_t\rangle] a_{t_1}(x_t) \mid N_{t,t_1})\hat{\lambda}_{t_1|(t,t_1)}^{-1}(\Delta N_{t_1} - \hat{\lambda}_{t_1 t_1|(t,t_1)}\Delta t_1).$$

The limit as $\Delta t_1 \to 0$ and inverse Fourier transformation establishes Theorem A.

*Corollary A:* The conditional density of parameter estimation is given by

$$p_t(X \mid N_{t,t_1}) = p_t(X) \exp\left(-\int_t^{t_1} a_\sigma(X)\, d\sigma + \int_t^{t_1} \ln [a_\sigma(X)\hat{\lambda}_{\sigma|(t,\sigma)}^{-1}]\, dN_\sigma\right).$$

*Proof:* The differential rule and Theorem A imply

$$d_{t_1} \ln p_t(X \mid N_{t,t_1})$$

$$= -a_{t_1}(X)\, dt_1 + \ln [1 + a_{t_1}(X)\hat{\lambda}_{t_1|(t,t_1)}^{-1}]\, dN_{t_1}.$$

Integration establishes Corollary A.

## References


[1] D. L. Snyder, "Filtering and detection for doubly stochastic Poisson processes," *IEEE Trans. Inform. Theory*, vol. IT-18, pp. 91–102, Jan. 1972.

[2] R. Lipster and A. N. Shiryaev, "Non-linear interpolation of components of Markov diffusion processes," *Theory Prob. Appl.* (USSR), vol. 13, no. 4, 1968.

[3] P. Frost and T. Kailath, "An innovations approach to least squares estimation—Part III: Nonlinear estimation in white Gaussian noise," *IEEE Trans. Automat. Contr.*, vol. AC-16, pp. 217–224, June 1971.

[4] J. T. Lo, "On optimal nonlinear estimation—Part I: Continuous observation," in *Proc. 8th Allerton Conf. Circuit and System Theory*, Oct. 1970; also presented at Control Systems Science Seminar, Washington Univ., St. Louis, Mo., Jan. 1971.

[5] I. Gihman and A. Dorogovcev, "On stability of solutions of stochastic differential equations," *Ukran. Mat. Z.*, vol. 17, no. 6, pp. 3–21, 1965.

# Editor's Comments on Paper 5

5 **Rubin:** *Information Rates for Poisson Sequences*

As a first attempt to study exhaustively the information-carrying capabilities of Poisson and jump-point processes, this paper considers the rate-distortion function of Poisson sequences. Insight into the information-theoretic aspects of such a process is obtained by the derivation of bounds to the rate-distortion function and of coding schemes that achieve these bounds. Subsequent work by the author [1] has generalized these results.

## Reference

1. I. Rubin, Information rates and data compression schemes for Poisson processes, *IEEE Trans. Inform. Theory,* pp. 200–210 (Mar. 1974).

# 5



Reprinted from *IEEE Trans. Inform. Theory,* **IT-19**(3), 283–294 (1973)

# Information Rates for Poisson Sequences

IZHAK RUBIN

***Abstract*—The rate-distortion function of a Poisson sequence, under a single-letter magnitude-error distortion measure is derived and studied. Simple approximations to the rate-distortion curve for low and high distortions are obtained. A useful lower bound to this curve is derived and an upper bound is generated by a simple instrumentable coding scheme. The rate-distortion relationship for the latter is seen to be nearly ideal over a large distortion region.**

## I. Introduction

MANY stochastic systems that arise in the engineering, biological, and other sciences follow the statistics of a Poisson variable or process. A few examples are queueing systems, transportation systems, streams of telephone calls, radioactive radiations, output of photomultiplier tubes in a laser communication system, level-crossing processes, population processes, and many biological processes (see, for example, [3] and the references there). Moreover, in general whenever the system's evolution is described by a random sequence of point events (a point process), which is caused by a superposition of many low-intensity point processes, it is known that (under suitable regularity conditions) this process is governed asymptotically by Poisson statistics (see [6, ch. 5]). This asymptotic result, like that which leads to Gaussian statistics, explains the frequent occurrence of Poisson statistics in physical phenomena. We also know that the stream of level crossings by a stationary Gaussian process tends asymptotically (as the level increases) to a Poisson process (under suitable regularity conditions on the covariance function; see [7, ch. 12]).

Assume now that we wish to transmit with fidelity $D$, at each unit of time, the state of a Poisson process with intensity $\lambda$ to a remote user over a communication channel of capacity $C$. Our source is a sequence of independently identically distributed (i.i.d.) random variables that follow a Poisson distribution. Notice that the same source results if we consider transmitting the total counts that occur in each unit of time in a Poisson process with intensity $\lambda$ (since a Poisson process has independent increments). Associated with this source is a rate distortion function $R(D)$ which represents the channel capacity per source letter that is necessary and sufficient for transmitting the source to its destination with fidelity $D$ [1], [2]. The $R(D)$ function thus serves to identify the rate-distortion variation of an ideal data compression scheme. Although the rate-distortion function of a Gaussian sequence (under a per-letter squared-error distortion measure) is well known, this function for its discrete counterpart, the Poisson sequence, under a useful distortion measure which is proportional to the error, has not yet been derived and studied.

In this paper, we derive and study the rate-distortion function of a Poisson sequence, assuming a per-letter magnitude-error distortion measure. We obtain a useful lower bound to the rate-distortion curve, simple approximations to it for low and high distortions, and an upper bound that is generated by a simple instrumentable coding scheme. Preliminary properties are presented in Section II. The rate-distortion function is derived in Section III. In Section IV

Manuscript received September 26, 1972; revised December 14, 1972. This work was supported by the Office of Naval Research under Grant N00014-69-A-0200-4041.

The author is with the Department of System Science, School of Engineering and Applied Science, University of California, Los Angeles, Calif. 90024.

we obtain bounds and approximations to the $R(D)$ curve, and a useful coding scheme is presented. In Section V, several rate-distortion curves are presented and compared with the lower bounds and the coding schemes.

## II. Preliminaries

We consider a Poisson discrete memoryless source $\{x_i, i \geq 1\}$. Thus, the successive letters generated by the source are i.i.d. random variables, governed by a Poisson distribution with intensity $\lambda$, $0 < \lambda < \infty$. That is,

$$p_i = P\{x_j = i\} = \exp(-\lambda)\lambda^i/i!, \qquad i = 0,1,2,\cdots. \quad (1)$$

The output of this source is to be transmitted over a noisy channel and reconstructed at the receiver to within a prescribed accuracy. To calculate the latter, we have to specify a fidelity criterion. We choose a single-letter fidelity criterion [1], [2], with the single-letter distortion measure $\rho_{jk} \equiv \rho(j,k)$ given by

$$\rho_{jk} = |j - k|, \qquad j \in A_S, k \in A_R \quad (2)$$

where $A_S$ and $A_R$ represent the source alphabet and reproducing alphabet, respectively, and each of them is composed of the set of nonnegative integers. The distortion between a source letter and its reproducing letter thus equals the error's magnitude. The rate-distortion function of the source, with respect to the given distortion measure $\rho_{jk}$, is defined as follows. The set $Q_D$ of $D$-admissible conditional probabilities $q(k \mid j)$, $k \in A_R$, $j \in A_S$, is defined as

$$Q_D = \left\{q(k \mid j): d(Q) = \sum_j \sum_k p_j q(k \mid j)\rho_{jk} \leq D\right\} \quad (3)$$

where $d(Q)$ is the average distortion associated with the probabilities $Q = \{q(k \mid j)\}$. Also associated with $Q$ is the average mutual information

$$I(Q) = \sum_j \sum_k p_j q(k \mid j) \ln \frac{q(k \mid j)}{q_k} \quad (4)$$

where

$$q_k = \sum_j p_j q(k \mid j).$$

The rate-distortion function $R(D)$ is then defined, for each $D \in [0,\infty)$ as

$$R(D) = \inf_{Q \in Q_D} I(Q). \quad (5)$$

The source coding theorem[1] and its converse [1], [2] show that $R(D)$ actually represents the channel capacity per source letter that is necessary and sufficient for transmitting the source to its destination with average distortion $D$.

[1] The only assumption needed for the proof of the source coding theorem is that there exists a reproducing letter $k$ such that

$$\sum_i p_i \rho_{ik} < \infty.$$

In the present problem, for $k = 0$ we clearly have

$$\sum_i p_i \rho_{i0} = \sum_i i p_i = \lambda < \infty.$$

Solving the preceding variational problem for $R(D)$, one obtains the following useful property (see [2, theorem 2.5.2]). Assuming a set of reproducing probabilities $q = \{q_k, k \geq 0\}$ (i.e., a set of probabilities for the reproducing letters), let

$$B_q = \{k: q_k = 0\} \qquad V_q = \{k: q_k > 0\}.$$

Associate with $q$ a set of conditional probabilities, $Q(q) = \{q_{k|j}\}$, so that

$$q_{k|j} = \lambda_j q_k \exp(s\rho_{jk}) \quad (6)$$

where

$$\lambda_j^{-1} = \sum_k q_k \exp(s\rho_{jk}). \quad (7)$$

Then $Q(q)$ is said to be a tentative solution for that point on $R(D)$ where $(d/dD)R(D) = s$, if

$$c_k = \sum_j \lambda_j p_j \exp(s\rho_{jk}) = 1, \qquad k \in V_q. \quad (8a)$$

Thus $Q(q)$ is a tentative solution if its associated positive reproducing probabilities $\{q_k\}$ satisfy $c_k = 1$, a condition that results when solving the variational problem [2]. A necessary and sufficient condition for $Q(q)$ to yield a point on the $R(D)$ curve is that it be a tentative solution that satisfies

$$c_k = \sum_j \lambda_j p_j \exp(s\rho_{jk}) \leq 1, \qquad k \in B_q. \quad (8b)$$

The $R(D)$ curve is then given parametrically by

$$D = \sum_j \sum_k \lambda_j p_j q_k \exp(s\rho_{jk})\rho_{jk} \quad (9)$$

$$R = sD + \sum_j p_j \ln \lambda_j. \quad (10)$$

One can show that the parameter $s$ in (9) and (10) is the slope of $R(D)$, that $R(D)$ is a convex decreasing function, and that $R'(D) = (d/dD)R(D)$ is continuous in $(0,D_{\max})$ and $R'(D) \to -\infty$ as $D \to 0$. It can also be shown that $R(D)$, in the present case, is continuous[2] at $D = 0$. In addition, $R(D) > 0$, for $0 \leq D < D_{\max}$, and $R(D) = 0$, for $D \geq D_{\max}$, where

$$D_{\max} = \min_{k \in A_R} \sum_j p_j \rho_{jk}. \quad (11)$$

The Poisson distribution (1) has many interesting characteristics (see [3] and references there). The following properties will be helpful in the present analysis. For $\lambda$

[2] Berger [2, theorem 2.5.4] does not directly apply, as the size of source alphabet $M$, used there to upper bound an expression, is infinite in our case. However, using Poisson statistics we can proceed in the proof as there, upperbounding

$$\sum_{j \neq k} \exp(s\rho_{jk})$$

by $2\exp(s)/[1 - \exp(s)]$, instead of by $M \exp(s\rho_{\min})$, since

$$\sum_{j \neq k} \exp(s|j-k|) < 2\sum_{j=1}^{\infty} \exp(sj) = 2\exp(s)/[1 - \exp(s)].$$

integral,

$$\max_i p_i = p_\lambda = p_{\lambda-1}$$

further $p_{j+1} < p_j$, for $j \geq \lambda$, and $p_{j+1} > p_j$, for $j \leq \lambda - 2$. For $\lambda$ a nonintegral number, $p_i$ possesses a single maximum at $i = [\lambda]$, where $[\lambda]$ is the largest integer not larger than $\lambda$. The median of the Poisson distribution is defined as $n + a$, where

$$\sum_{i=0}^{n} p_i + a p_{n+1} = \tfrac{1}{2}, \qquad 0 \leq a < 1. \tag{12}$$

For integral $\lambda$, it is known (conjectured by Ramanujan and proved by Szego, see [4]) that $a = R_\lambda$ (known as Ramanujan's number) lies between $\frac{1}{3}$ and $\frac{1}{2}$ and tends rapidly to $\frac{1}{3}$ as $\lambda \to \infty$. For general $\lambda$, one can observe [5], [3] that the median of the Poisson distribution lies between $[\lambda] - 1$ and $[\lambda]$, or between $[\lambda]$ and $[\lambda] + 1$ according as $(\lambda - [\lambda])$ is $\lesssim$ or $\gtrsim$ $(1 - R_\lambda) \approx \frac{2}{3}$. (One can also show [4] that $R_\lambda = \frac{1}{3} + (4/135)\lambda^{-1} + (8/2835)\lambda^{-2} + 0(\lambda^{-3})$. The symbols $\lesssim$, $\gtrsim$, are henceforth used accordingly.)

## III. The Rate Distortion Function of a Poisson Sequence

*$R(0)$ and $D_{\max}$*

Since $\rho_{jk} = |j - k|$, we have $D_{\min} = 0$, where $D_{\min}$ denotes the minimum value that the average distortion can assume. Clearly, $R(0)$ is obtained by letting $q_{k|j} = \delta_{kj}$, where $\delta_{kj}$ is the Kronecker delta, so that $q_k = p_k$. Hence,

$$R(0) = H(\lambda) \triangleq -\sum_i p_i \ln p_i = \lambda(1 - \ln \lambda) + \sum_{i=0}^{\infty} p_i \ln (i!). \tag{13}$$

An upper bound on $R(0)$ is obtained as follows. Consider the problem of obtaining the discrete probability distribution $\{p_i, i \geq 0\}$, with given mean

$$\sum_0^{\infty} i p_i = \lambda$$

with maximum entropy measure

$$-\sum_i p_i \ln p_i.$$

Solving this variational problem one readily obtains as the solution the geometric distribution

$$p_j = \left(\frac{1}{1 + \lambda}\right)\left(\frac{\lambda}{1 + \lambda}\right)^j, \qquad j \geq 0$$

whose entropy is given by

$$H_G(\lambda) = (1 + \lambda) \ln (1 + \lambda) - \lambda \ln \lambda. \tag{14}$$

Hence, $R(0) \equiv H(\lambda) \leq H_G(\lambda) < \infty$, $\forall \lambda$. (For example, $H(0.5) \cong 0.93$, $H_G(0.5) \cong 0.95$; $H(5) \cong 2.2$, $H_G(5) \cong 2.7$.)

$D_{\max}$ is obtained by solving (11), which in the present case assumes the form

$$D_{\max} = \min_k \sum_j p_j |j - k|.$$

Subsequently, we find that the reproducing letter $k^*$ that achieves $D_{\max}$ is the *integral-median* of the distribution. The latter is defined as the nonnegative integer $k^*$ for which

$$\sum_{i=0}^{k^*-1} p_i < \tfrac{1}{2} \quad \text{and} \quad \sum_{i=0}^{k^*} p_i \geq \tfrac{1}{2}. \tag{15}$$

The distortion associated with $k^*$ is given by

$$\begin{aligned} D_{\max}^{(k^*)} &= \sum_{i=0}^{\infty} p_i |i - k^*| \\ &= \lambda - [k^* - 2k^* p_0 - 2(k^* - 1)p_1 - \cdots - 2p_{k^*-1}]. \end{aligned} \tag{16}$$

We observe that

$$2k^* p_0 + 2(k^* - 1)p_1 + \cdots + 2p_{k^*-1} \leq 2k^* \sum_0^{k^*-1} p_i \leq k^*$$

so that we have

$$D_{\max}^{(k^*)} \leq \lambda. \tag{17}$$

Equality holds in (17) if and only if $k^* = 0$.

Now applying the properties of the Poisson median, as defined by (12) and discussed thereafter, we readily deduce the following characteristics of the integral-median of a Poisson distribution.

*Lemma 1:* The reproducing letter $k^*$ that achieves $D_{\max}$ for a Poisson distribution with intensity $\lambda$ is given by

$$k^* = \begin{cases} [\lambda], & \text{if } \lambda - [\lambda] \lesssim 1 - R_\lambda \\ [\lambda] + 1, & \text{if } \lambda - [\lambda] \gtrapprox 1 - R_\lambda \end{cases} \tag{18}$$

where $R_\lambda$ is Ramanjuan's number, which tends rapidly to $\frac{1}{3}$ as $\lambda$ increases.

*Proof:* If $\lambda - [\lambda] \lessapprox 1 - R_\lambda$, we know that the median lies between $[\lambda] - 1$ and $[\lambda]$ and we have (approximately) [5]

$$\sum_0^{[\lambda]-1} p_i + (\lambda - [\lambda] + R_\lambda) p_{[\lambda]} = \tfrac{1}{2}$$

so that, by definition (15), $k^* = [\lambda]$. A similar argument holds when $\lambda - [\lambda] \gtrapprox 1 - R_\lambda$. Q.E.D.

In particular, note that $k^* = 0$, for $0 < \lambda < \ln 2 \sim 0.69$, so that $k^* = [\lambda] = 0$, for $\lambda - [\lambda] < \ln 2 \sim \frac{2}{3}$. Equation (18) thus indicates that the zero-rate source code which yields the minimal average distortion is composed of the single letter $k^*$ which equals $[\lambda]$ or $[\lambda] + 1$ according as $\lambda - [\lambda] \lesssim$ or $\gtrsim 1 - R_\lambda$.

*A Tentative Solution*

To solve for the rate-distortion curve, we assume a tentative solution, which has to satisfy (8a). We then verify that this solution also satisfies (8b), so that it is the optimal one. In addition, because of the complicated form in which the tentative solution $Q(q)$ is represented, we have to check that we actually have $q_k > 0$, for $k \in V_q$.

If we had started our calculations at low-distortion values, we could have applied the following reasoning. Since at $D = 0$, $q_k = p_k > 0$, $\forall k$, one might expect to have $V_q = A_R$ at very low distortion values. However, solving (8a) and then applying (8b), one fails to obtain any point on the $R(D)$ curve. Thus due to the infinite size of the alphabets, we find that $V_q \neq A_R$, $\forall D > 0$. Starting then at high distortions, we recall that at $D_{\max}$ we have $q_{k^*} = 1$. At lower distortion values we expect to have $V_q = \{k^*, k^* + 1\}$ or $V_q = \{k^* - 1, k^*\}$, and then as the distortion decreases to have $V_q = V_q^{(n,m)} \triangleq \{k^* - n, \cdots, k^* - 1, k^*, k^* + 1, \cdots, k^* + m\}$, with $n$ and $m$ appropriately increasing as $D$ decreases. We will show here that the latter pattern is the one that yields the rate-distortion curve of the Poisson sequence.

Assume thus that $V_q = V_q^{(n,m)}$ (to be called, henceforth, the state $(n,m)$). Then

$$q_i \begin{cases} > 0, & \text{for } k^* - n \le i \le k^* + m \\ = 0, & \text{for } i < k^* - n \text{ and } i > k^* + m \end{cases} \quad (19)$$

where $0 \le n \le k^*$, $m \ge 0$. Equations (8a) now assume the form

$$c_k = \sum_j \lambda_j p_j \alpha^{|j-k|} = 1, \qquad k^* - n \le k \le k^* + m \quad (20)$$

where

$$\lambda_j^{-1} = \sum_{k=k^*-n}^{k^*+m} q_k \alpha^{|j-k|} \quad (21)$$

and $\alpha \triangleq e^s$. Solving (20) and (21), we obtain

$$\sum_j q_j \alpha^{j-(k^*-n)} = (1 + \alpha) \sum_0^{k^*-n} p_j$$

$$\sum_j q_j \alpha^{|l-j|} = \frac{1+\alpha}{1-\alpha} p_l, \qquad \text{for } k^* - n + 1 \le l \le k^* + m - 1$$

$$\sum_j q_j \alpha^{k^*+m-j} = (1 + \alpha) \sum_{k^*+m}^{\infty} p_j. \quad (22)$$

Solving (22), we find, after some algebra, that the probabilities of the reproducing letters in state $(n,m)$ are given by[3]

$$(1-\alpha)^2 q_{k^*-n} = (1-\alpha)P(k^*-n) - \alpha p_{k^*-n+1}$$

$$(1-\alpha)^2 q_{k^*-n+1} = -\alpha(1-\alpha)P(k^*-n) + (1+\alpha^2)p_{k^*-n+1} - \alpha p_{k^*-n+2}$$

$$(1-\alpha)^2 q_i = -\alpha p_{i-1} + (1+\alpha^2)p_i - \alpha p_{i+1}, \qquad \text{for } k^* - n + 2 \le i \le k^* + m - 2$$

$$(1-\alpha)^2 q_{k^*+m-1} = -\alpha p_{k^*+m-2} + (1+\alpha^2)p_{k^*+m-1} - \alpha(1-\alpha)Q(k^*+m)$$

$$(1-\alpha)^2 q_{k^*+m} = -\alpha p_{k^*+m-1} + (1-\alpha)Q(k^*+m) \quad (23)$$

for $n + m > 2$, and where

$$P(i) \triangleq \sum_{j=0}^{i} p_j \qquad Q(i) \triangleq \sum_{j=i}^{\infty} p_j. \quad (24)$$

[3] Notice the similarity in the expressions for the optimal $\{q_k\}$ to the case where $|A_s| = |A_k| < \infty$ and $p_i \ge (p_{i-1} + p_{i+1})/2$ solved in [8]. However, the optimal set of reproducing letters is seen to be much different.

For states (0,1) and (1,0), we clearly have $V_q = \{k^* - n, k^* + m\}$ and $q_{k^*-n}, q_{k^*+m}$, are given as in (23). For states $(n,m) \in \{(1,1),(0,2),(2,0)\}$, i.e., $n + m = 2$, we have

$$(1-\alpha)^2 q_{k^*-n} = (1-\alpha)P(k^*-n) - \alpha p_{k^*-n+1}$$

$$(1-\alpha)^2 q_{k^*-n+1} = -\alpha(1-\alpha)P(k^*-n) + (1+\alpha^2) \cdot p_{k^*-n+1} - \alpha(1-\alpha)Q(k^*-n+2)$$

$$(1-\alpha)^2 q_{k^*-n+2} = -\alpha p_{k^*-n+1} + (1-\alpha)Q(k^*-n+2). \quad (25)$$

To obtain the distortion region in which state $(n,m)$ is optimal (i.e., yields $R(D)$), (8b) is to be satisfied. For that purpose, we make the following definitions:

$$\alpha_c^{(i)} \triangleq Q(i+1)/Q(i) \qquad \alpha_l^{(j)} \triangleq P(j-1)/P(j) \quad (26)$$

where $i \ge 0$, $j \ge 1$, $\alpha_l^{(0)} \triangleq 0$. The following property will be useful in our analysis.

*Proposition 1:* For a Poisson distribution,

$$\alpha_c^{(i+1)} < \alpha_c^{(i)} \qquad \alpha_l^{(j+1)} > \alpha_l^{(j)}, \qquad i \ge 0, j \ge 1. \quad (27)$$

*Proof:* $\alpha_c^{(i+1)} < \alpha_c^{(i)}$ if $Q(i+2)/Q(i+1) < Q(i+1)/Q(i)$ or, equivalently, if $[1 + p_{i+1}/Q(i+2)]^{-1} < [1 + p_i/Q(i+1)]$ or if $(p_i/p_{i+1})Q(i+2) < Q(i+1)$. But since $p_i$ is Poisson, we have

$$(p_i/p_{i+1})Q(i+2) = \frac{i+1}{\lambda} e^{-\lambda} \sum_{j=i+2}^{\infty} \frac{\lambda^j}{j!} = e^{-\lambda} \sum_{j=i+2}^{\infty} \frac{\lambda^{j-1}}{(j-1)!} \frac{i+1}{j} < Q(i+1)$$

since $i + 1 < j$, for $j \ge i + 2$. Similarly, $\alpha_l^{(j+1)} > \alpha_l^{(j)}$ if $(p_j/p_{j+1})P(j+1) > P(j)$. But

$$(p_j/p_{j+1})P(j+1) = \frac{j+1}{\lambda} e^{-\lambda} \sum_{i=0}^{j+1} \frac{\lambda^i}{i!} = e^{-\lambda} \sum_0^{j+1} \frac{(j+1/i)\lambda^{i-1}}{(i-1)!} > P(j).$$

Q.E.D

To check (8b) we have to derive expressions for $c_k$, $k \ge k^* + m + 1$ and $k \le k^* - n - 1$. The following relationships are thus important.

*Proposition 2:* For state $(n,m)$,

$$c_{i+1} = \alpha c_i + (1-\alpha)[\alpha^{i+1-(k^*+m)}]^{-1}[Q(i+1)/Q(k^*+m)], \qquad i \ge k^* + m \quad (28a)$$

$$c_{i-1} = \alpha c_i + (1-\alpha)[\alpha^{k^*-n+1-i}]^{-1}[P(i-1)/P(k^*-n)], \qquad i \le k^* - n. \quad (28b)$$

*Proof:* By its definition (8), $c_i$ is given as

$$c_i = \sum_{j=0}^{\infty} \lambda_j p_j \alpha^{|i-j|} = \sum_0^{i-1} \lambda_j p_j \alpha^{(i-j)} + \lambda_i p_i + \sum_{i+1}^{\infty} \lambda_j p_j \alpha^{j-i}.$$

Subsequently, we obtain the following relationships:

$$c_{i+1} = \alpha c_i + \frac{(1-\alpha^2)}{\alpha} \sum_{j=i+1}^{\infty} \lambda_j p_j \alpha^{(j-i)}$$

and

$$c_{i-1} = \alpha c_i + \frac{(1-\alpha^2)}{\alpha} \sum_{j=0}^{i-1} \lambda_j p_j \alpha^{(i-j)}.$$

For $i \geq k^* + m$, we obtain by (7), (8), and (22)

$$\sum_{i+1}^{\infty} \lambda_j p_j \alpha^{(j-i)} = Q(i+1)[\alpha^{i-(k^*+m)} \sum_j q_j \alpha^{k^*+m-j}]^{-1}$$
$$= Q(i+1)[(1+\alpha)\alpha^{i-(k^*+m)} Q(k^*+m)]^{-1}$$

which, when substituted in the preceding expression for $c_{i+1}$, yields (28a). Similarly, for $i \leq k^* - n$, using (7), (8), and (22), we obtain

$$\sum_{0}^{i-1} \lambda_j p_j \alpha^{(i-j)} = \alpha^i P(i-1) \left[\sum_j q_j \alpha^j\right]^{-1}$$
$$= \alpha^i P(i-1)[\alpha^{(k^*-n)}(1+\alpha)P(k^*-n)]^{-1}$$

which yields (28b). Q.E.D.

Propositions 1 and 2 are now used to deduce a lower bound to the distortion interval in which state $(n,m)$ can be the optimal one. This bound is expressed in terms of the parameter $\alpha = e^s$, which increases from $\alpha = 0$ at $D_{\min} = 0$ to $\alpha_{\max} \leq 1$ at $D_{\max}$.

*Lemma 2:* For state $(n,m)$, if

$$\alpha \geq \max [\alpha_l^{(k^*-n)}, \alpha_c^{(k^*+m)}] \tag{29}$$

then $c_k \leq 1, \forall k \in A_R$.

*Proof:* Clearly $c_k = 1$, for $k^* - n \leq k \leq k^* + m$. For $i \geq k^* + m$,

$$\frac{Q(i+1)}{Q(k^*+m)} = \prod_{j=k^*+m}^{i} \frac{Q(j+1)}{Q(j)} = \prod_{j=k^*+m}^{i} \alpha_c^{(j)}.$$

By (27), $\alpha_c^{(j+1)} < \alpha_c^{(j)}$, so that we have

$$\frac{Q(i+1)}{Q(k^*+m)} < [\alpha_c^{(k^*+m)}]^{i+1-(k^*+m)}.$$

Using (29), $\alpha \geq \alpha_c^{(k^*+m)}$, and (28a) one obtains $c_{i+1} \leq \alpha c_i + (1-\alpha)$. The proof is thus completed by induction on $i \geq k + m$. For $i = k^* + m$, $c_{k^*+m} = 1 \Rightarrow c_{k^*+m+1} \leq \alpha + 1 - \alpha = 1$. Then assuming $c_i \leq 1$, we conclude $c_{i+1} \leq \alpha + 1 - \alpha = 1$. Hence $c_k \leq 1, \forall k \geq k^* + m$. Similarly, for $i \leq k^* - n$, using (27) we have

$$\frac{P(i-1)}{P(k^*-n)} = \prod_{j=i}^{k^*-n} \frac{P(j)}{P(j-1)}$$
$$= \prod_{j=i}^{k^*-n} \alpha_l^{(j-1)} < [\alpha_l^{(k^*-n)}]^{k^*-n+1-i}.$$

Subsequently, using (28a), (29), and $\alpha \geq \alpha_l^{(k^*-n)}$, we obtain

$$c_{i-1} \leq \alpha c_i + 1 - \alpha.$$

By induction, as before, we conclude that $c_k \leq 1$ also, for $k \leq k^* - n$. Q.E.D.

The parametric representation of $R(D)$ in the $(n,m)$ state is obtained in the next lemma.

*Lemma 3:* For state $(n,m)$, the parametric representation of the rate-distortion curve is given by[4]

$$D_\alpha^{(n,m)} = D_0^{(n,m)} + \alpha/(1+\alpha) + [\alpha/(1-\alpha)] \sum_{k^*-n+1}^{k^*+m-1} p_i \tag{30}$$

$$R_\alpha^{(n,m)} = H^{(n,m)} - H_2\left(\frac{1}{1+\alpha}\right) - (1-\alpha)^{-1} H_2(\alpha) \sum_{k^*-n+1}^{k^*+m-1} p_i \tag{31a}$$

$$= H^{(n,m)} + (D_\alpha^{(n,m)} - D_0^{(n,m)}) \ln \alpha - \ln(1+\alpha)$$
$$+ [\ln(1-\alpha)] \sum_{k^*-n+1}^{k^*+m-1} p_i \tag{31b}$$

where

$$H_2(p) \triangleq -p \ln p - (1-p) \ln(1-p)$$

$$H^{(n,m)} = H\left(\sum_{0}^{k^*-n} p_i, p_{k^*-n+1}, p_{k^*-n+2}, \cdots, p_{k^*+m-1}, \sum_{k^*+m}^{\infty} p_i\right)$$
$$\triangleq -P(k^*-n) \ln P(k^*-n)$$
$$- p_{k^*-n+1} \ln p_{k^*-n+1} - \cdots - p_{k^*+m-1} \ln p_{k^*+m-1}$$
$$- Q(k^*+m) \ln Q(k^*+m) \tag{33}$$

$$D_0^{(n,m)} \triangleq \sum_{i=k^*+m}^{\infty} p_i[i - (k^*+m)]$$
$$+ \sum_{0}^{k^*-n} p_i[(k^*-n) - i]. \tag{34}$$

*Proof:* By definition (7),

$$\lambda_j^{-1} = \sum_{k=k^*-n}^{k^*+m} q_k \alpha^{|j-k|}.$$

Using expression (22) we obtain

$$\lambda_i^{-1} = \begin{cases} \alpha^{k^*-n-i}(1+\alpha)P(k^*-n), & i \leq k^*-n \\ [(1+\alpha)/(1-\alpha)]p_i, & k^*-n+1 \leq i \leq k^*+m-1 \\ \alpha^{i-(k^*+m)}(1+\alpha)Q(k^*+m), & i \geq k^*+m. \end{cases} \tag{35}$$

$D_\alpha$ is given by (9), but can equivalently be written in the form (see, for example, [2, eq. (2.5.24)])

$$D_\alpha = -\sum_j p_j \lambda_j^{-1} \frac{d\lambda_j}{ds}. \tag{36}$$

Using (35) and (36) one obtains, after some straightforward algebra, expression (30). Equation (31a) for $R_\alpha$ is obtained by incorporating (35) into (10) and observing that $-H_2[1/(1+\alpha)] = [\alpha/(1+\alpha)] \ln \alpha - \ln(1+\alpha)$. Q.E.D.

[4] We define

$$\sum_{k^*-n+1}^{+m-1} p_i \triangleq 0$$

when $k^* - n + 1 > k^* + m - 1$.

Notice that the $R^{(n,m)}(D)$ curve corresponding to state $(n,m)$ and given by (30) and (31) has not yet been shown to constitute a part of the $R(D)$ curve. This will be the case if we can show that the reproducing probabilities $\{q_i, k^* - n \leq i \leq k^* + m\}$ given by (23) are strictly positive in a distortion interval lowerbounded according to (29). To find this distortion interval, we observe that due to the continuity of the $R(D)$ curve and its derivative $s = R'(D)$ (and $\alpha = e^s$, as well), at the intersection of two distortion intervals generated by two different states, the $R(D)$ curves of these two states must have the same slope (and hence, same $\alpha$ values). We subsequently derive the following characterization of these intersection points.

*Lemma 4:* The slopes at the tangency points of curves $R^{(n,m)}(D)$ and $R^{(n,m+1)}(D)$ and curves $R^{(n,m)}(D)$ and $R^{(n-1,m)}(D)$, are given by $\ln \alpha_c^{(k^*+m)}$ and $\ln \alpha_l^{(k^*-n+1)}$, respectively.

*Proof:* Using (30), we have $D_\alpha^{(n,m)} - D_\alpha^{(n,m+1)} = Q(k^* + m) - (1 - \alpha)^{-1}p_{k^*+m}$. Hence, $D_\alpha^{(n,m)} = D_\alpha^{(n,m+1)}$ at $\alpha = \alpha_c^{(k^*+m)}$. By (31),

$$R_\alpha^{(n,m+1)} - R_\alpha^{(n,m)} = H^{(n,m+1)} - H^{(n,m)} - (1 - \alpha)^{-1}H_2(\alpha)p_{k^*+m}.$$

Consequently, using the following identity (readily proved),

$$H(p_1,p_2,\cdots,p_{n+1},Q(n + 2)) = H(p_1,p_2,\cdots,p_n,Q(n + 1)) + Q(n + 1)H_2(p_{n+1}Q(n + 1)^{-1})$$

we conclude that $R_\alpha^{(n,m+1)} = R_\alpha^{(n,m)}$ at $\alpha = \alpha_c^{(k^*+m)}$. We similarly show that at $\alpha = \alpha_l^{(k^*-n+1)}$, $D_\alpha^{(n,m)} = D_\alpha^{(n-1,m)}$, and $R_\alpha^{(n,m)} = R_\alpha^{(n-1,m)}$, observing now the identity $H(P(n),p_{n+1},\cdots) = H(P(n + 1),p_{n+2},\cdots) + P(n + 1)H_2(p_{n+1}P(n + 1)^{-1})$. Lemma 7 will show that the preceding intersection points are actually tangency points. Q.E.D.

*The Optimal Solution*

Lemma 4 indicates that we can expect an optimal state $(n,m)$ to change into state $(n, m + 1)$ at $\alpha = \alpha_c^{(k^*+m)}$, if $\max(\alpha_l^{(k^*-n)},\alpha_c^{(k^*+m)}) = \alpha_c^{(k^*+m)}$, and into state $(n + 1, m)$ at $\alpha = \alpha_l^{(k^*-n)}$ if the above maximum is $\alpha_l^{(k^*-n)}$. The distortion interval in which a state $(n,m)$ is optimal is thus expected to be given by

$$\max(\alpha_l^{(k^*-n)},\alpha_c^{(k^*+m)}) \leq \alpha < \min(\alpha_l^{(k^*-n+1)},\alpha_c^{(k^*+m-1)}). \quad (37)$$

Clearly, if the minimum on the right-hand side (RHS) is not larger than the maximum at the left-hand side (LHS) of the preceding inequality, state $(n,m)$ is not expected to be an optimum state. By Lemma 2, we already know that for state $(n,m)$ in region (37), we have $c_k \leq 1, \forall k$. To show that state $(n,m)$ is optimal in interval (37), it is left to show that the probabilities $\{q_i, k^* - n \leq i \leq k^* + m\}$ of the reproducing letters associated with state $(n,m)$ in region (37) are positive. This is established by the next two lemmas. In Lemma 5 we prove the positivity of $\{q_{k^*-j}, q_{k^*+i}, 1 < j \leq k^*, i > 1\}$, for which the following proposition is required.

*Proposition 3:* For Poisson statistics,

$$\frac{p_n - p_{n+1}}{p_{n-1} - p_n} > \frac{p_n}{p_{n-1}} > \alpha_c^{(n-1)} > \alpha_c^{(n+1)}, \qquad n > k^* \quad (38a)$$

$$\frac{p_n - p_{n-1}}{p_{n+1} - p_n} > \frac{p_n}{p_{n+1}} > \alpha_l^{(n+1)} > \alpha_l^{(n-1)}, \qquad n < k^* - 1. \quad (38b)$$

*Proof:* We have noted in Section II that $\{p_i\}$ possesses a single maximum value at $i = [\lambda]$, except that for $\lambda$ integral $p_\lambda = p_{\lambda-1}$. We have also shown that $k^*$ equals either $[\lambda]$ or $[\lambda] + 1$. Hence, the maximum is attained by $p_{k^*}$ or $p_{k^*-1}$. Subsequently $p_n >$ or $< p_{n+1}$ according as $n > k^*$ or $n < k^* - 1$. The expressions on the LHS of (38) are thus positive. We can then write for $n > k^*$,

$$\frac{p_n - p_{n+1}}{p_{n-1} - p_n} = \frac{p_n}{p_{n-1}} \frac{1 - p_{n+1}/p_n}{1 - p_n/p_{n-1}} = \frac{p_n}{p_{n-1}} \frac{1 - \lambda/(n + 1)}{1 - \lambda/n} > \frac{p_n}{p_{n-1}}.$$

We have already shown in Proposition 1 that $\alpha_c^{(n)} < \alpha_c^{(n-1)}$. Hence, $1 - \alpha_c^{(n)} > 1 - \alpha_c^{(n-1)}$, which implies that $p_n/Q(n) > p_{n-1}/Q(n - 1)$, or equivalently $p_n/p_{n-1} > Q(n)/Q(n - 1) = \alpha_c^{(n-1)}$, which proves (38a). Equation (38b) follows similarly. Q.E.D.

*Lemma 5:* For $n > 1, m > 1$ when the states' distribution over the distortion interval is chosen according to (37), we have for each optimal state $(n,m)$

$$q_i > 0, \qquad k^* - n \leq i \leq k^* + m.$$

*Proof:* 1) Consider first $q_{k^*-i}$, $1 < i \leq k^*$. The reproducing letter $(k^* - i)$ is introduced into the optimal set at $\alpha = \alpha_l^{(k-i+1)}$. It is the smallest reproducing letter in $\alpha_l^{(k^*-i)} \leq \alpha < \alpha_l^{(k^*-i+1)}$. In $\alpha_l^{(k^*-i-1)} \leq \alpha < \alpha_l^{(k^*-i)}$, the letter $(k^* - i)$ is the second smallest reproducing letter. Observing expressions (23) for the optimal reproducing probabilities, we have to consider the following three distortion regions.

1-a) $\alpha_l^{(k^*-i)} \leq \alpha < \alpha_l^{(k^*-i+1)}$: by (23),

$$(1 - \alpha)^2 q_{k^*-i} = (1 - \alpha)P(k^* - i) - \alpha p_{k^*-i+1}$$

so that $q_{k^*-i} > 0$, if and only if $\alpha < \alpha_l^{(k^*-i+1)}$, as is the case.

1-b) $\alpha_l^{(k^*-i-1)} \leq \alpha < \alpha_l^{(k^*-i)}$: by (23),

$$\begin{aligned}(1 - \alpha)^2 q_{k^*-i} &= -\alpha(1 - \alpha)P(k^* - i - 1) + (1 + \alpha^2)p_{k^*-i} - \alpha p_{k^*-i+1} \\ &= [p_{k^*-i} - \alpha p_{k^*-i+1}] - \alpha[P(k^* - i - 1) - \alpha P(k^* - i)] \\ &\triangleq y_1(\alpha) - \alpha y_2(\alpha)\end{aligned}$$

where $y_1(\alpha) \triangleq p_{k^*-i} - \alpha p_{k^*-i+1}$, $y_2(\alpha) \triangleq P(k^* - i - 1) - \alpha P(k^* - i)$. We show that in the present distortion region, $y_1(\alpha) > y_2(\alpha)$, and subsequently $y_1(\alpha) > \alpha y_2(\alpha)$ so that $q_{k^*-i} > 0$. For that purpose, notice that $y_1(\alpha_l^{(k^*-i)}) = [1 - \alpha_l^{(k^*-i)}]^2 q_{k^*-i}(\alpha_l^{(k^*-i)}) > 0$, while $y_2(\alpha_l^{(k^*-i)}) = 0$. Let $\alpha_1$ be defined as the intersection point of lines $y_1(\alpha)$ and $y_2(\alpha)$;

i.e., $y_1(\alpha_I) = y_2(\alpha_I)$. Then, $y_1(\alpha) > y_2(\alpha)$ in the present region, if and only if $\alpha_I < \alpha_l^{(k^*-i-1)}$. But we have, using Proposition 3, (38b), with $n = k^* - i$,

$$\alpha_I = \frac{P(k^* - i - 1) - p_{k^*-i}}{P(k^* - i) - p_{k^*-i+1}}$$

$$= \alpha_l^{(k^*-i-1)} \frac{1 - (p_{k^*-i} - p_{k^*-i-1})[P(k^* - i - 2)]^{-1}}{1 - (p_{k^*-i+1} - p_{k^*-i})[P(k^* - i - 1)]^{-1}}$$

$$< \alpha_l^{(k^*-i-1)}.$$

Hence, $q_{k^*-i} > 0$ in the present region.

1-c) $0 \le \alpha < \alpha_l^{(k^*-i-1)}$: by (23) we have

$$(1 - \alpha)^2 q_{k^*-i} = (p_{k^*-i} - \alpha p_{k^*-i+1}) - \alpha(p_{k^*-i-1} - \alpha p_{k^*-i})$$

$$\triangleq y_3(\alpha) - \alpha y_4(\alpha)$$

where $y_3(\alpha) \triangleq p_{k^*-i} - \alpha p_{k^*-i+1}$, $y_4(\alpha) \triangleq p_{k^*-i-1} - \alpha p_{k^*-i}$. We show that $y_3(\alpha) > y_4(\alpha)$, for $\alpha < \alpha_l^{(k^*-i-1)}$, so that $q_{k^*-i} > 0$ in the region. We first notice that $y_3(0) = p_{k^*-i} > y_4(0) - p_{k^*-i-1}$, since we have already observed that $p_{k^*-i} > p_{k^*-i-1}$, for $i \ge 1$. Let $\alpha_{II}$ be the intersection point of lines $y_3(\alpha)$ and $y_4(\alpha)$; i.e., $y_3(\alpha_{II}) = y_4(\alpha_{II})$. Then, $y_3(\alpha) > y_4(\alpha)$, for $\alpha < \alpha_l^{(k^*-i-1)}$, if and only if $\alpha_{II} > \alpha_l^{(k^*-i-1)}$. But using Proposition 3, (38b), with $n = k^* - i$, we have

$$\alpha_{II} = (p_{k^*-i} - p_{k^*-i-1})(p_{k^*-i+1} - p_{k^*-i})^{-1} > \alpha_l^{(k^*-i-1)}$$

so that $q_{k^*-i} > 0$ in this last region as well.

2) We now consider $q_{k^*+i}$, $i > 1$. We show that $q_{k^*+i} > 0$, following the same procedure as in part 1). Thus indicating the main points, we have the following.

2-a) $\alpha_c^{(k+i)} \le \alpha < \alpha_c^{(k^*+i-1)}$: by (23),

$$(1 - \alpha)^2 q_{k^*+i} = -\alpha p_{k^*+i-1} + (1 - \alpha)Q(k^* + i)$$

so that $q_{k^*+i} > 0$, if and only if $\alpha < \alpha_c^{(k^*+i-1)}$.

2-b) $\alpha_c^{(k^*+i+1)} \le \alpha < \alpha_c^{(k^*+i)}$: by (23),

$$(1 - \alpha)^2 q_{k^*+i} = [p_{k^*+i} - \alpha p_{k^*+i-1}] - \alpha[Q(k^* + i + 1) - \alpha Q(k^* + i)]$$

$$\triangleq z_1(\alpha) - \alpha z_2(\alpha).$$

We show $z_1(\alpha) > z_2(\alpha)$. We have $z_1(\alpha_c^{(k^*+i)}) > 0$ and $z_2(\alpha_c^{(k^*+i)}) = 0$. Define $\alpha_{III}$ as $z_1(\alpha_{III}) = z_2(\alpha_{III})$. Then, using (38a) with $n = k^* + i$, we obtain

$$\alpha_{III} = \frac{Q(k^* + i + 1) - p_{k^*+i}}{Q(k^* + i) - p_{k^*+i-1}}$$

$$= \alpha_c^{(k^*+i+1)} \frac{1 - (p_{k^*+i} - p_{k^*+i+1})[Q(k^* + i + 2)]^{-1}}{1 - (p_{k^*+i-1} - p_{k^*+i})[Q(k^* + i + 1)]^{-1}}$$

$$< \alpha_c^{(k^*+i+1)}$$

so that $z_1(\alpha) > z_2(\alpha)$ in this region, and $q_{k^*+i} > 0$.

2-c) $0 \le \alpha < \alpha_c^{(k^*+i+1)}$: by (23),

$$(1 - \alpha)^2 q_{k^*+i} = (p_{k^*+i} - \alpha p_{k^*+i-1}) - \alpha(p_{k^*+i+1} - \alpha p_{k^*+i})$$

$$\triangleq z_3(\alpha) - \alpha z_4(\alpha).$$

We have that $z_3(0) = p_{k^*+i} > z_4(0) = p_{k^*+i+1}$, $i \ge 1$. Thus $z_3(\alpha) > z_4(\alpha)$, if and only if $\alpha_{IV} > \alpha_c^{(k^*+i+1)}$, where $z_3(\alpha_{IV}) = z_4(\alpha_{IV})$. But, by Proposition 3, (38a), $\alpha_{IV} = (p_{k^*+i} - p_{k^*+i+1})(p_{k^*+i+1} - p_{k^*+i})^{-1} > \alpha_c^{(k^*+i+1)}$, so that $q_{k^*+i} > 0$ in this region as well. Q.E.D.

A criterion for choosing the first state (following state (0,0) which is chosen at $\alpha = \alpha_{max}$) which is either (0,1) or (1,0), and a proof of the positivity of $q_k, q_{k+1}, q_{k-1}$, in their optimal regions, are established by the next lemma. For that purpose, we will make use of the following propositions.

*Proposition 4:* For $k^* \ge 1$,

$$\max(\alpha_l^{(k^*-1)}, \alpha_c^{(k^*)}) < \alpha_{max}^{(1,0)}(k^*) \Leftrightarrow P(k^* - 1) > (1 - p_{k^*})/2 \quad (39a)$$

$$\max(\alpha_l^{(k^*)}, \alpha_c^{(k^*+1)}) < \alpha_{max}^{(0,1)}(k^*) \Leftrightarrow P(k^* - 1) < (1 - p_{k^*})/2 \quad (39b)$$

where

$$\alpha_{max}^{(1,0)}(k^*) = P(k^* - 1)/Q(k^*)$$

$$\alpha_{max}^{(0,1)}(k^*) = Q(k^* + 1)/P(k^*). \quad (40)$$

*Proof:* Note that

$$P(k^* - 1) \gtrless (1 - p_{k^*})/2 \Leftrightarrow P(k^* - 1) \gtrless Q(k^* + 1) \Leftrightarrow P(k^*) \gtrless Q(k^*). \quad (41)$$

By definition,

$$\alpha_c^{(k^*)} < \alpha_{max}^{(1,0)}(k^*) \Leftrightarrow Q(k^* + 1)/Q(k^*) < P(k^* - 1)/Q(k^*) \Leftrightarrow Q(k^* + 1) < P(k^* - 1)$$

as required in (39a). Also,

$$\alpha_l^{(k^*-1)} < \alpha_{max}^{(1,0)}(k^*), \quad \text{if } \alpha_l^{(k^*)} < \alpha_{max}^{(1,0)}(k^*)$$

$$\Leftrightarrow P(k^* - 1)/P(k^*) < P(k^* - 1)/Q(k^*)$$

$$\Leftrightarrow Q(k^*) < P(k^*)$$

since $\alpha_l^{(k^*-1)} < \alpha_l^{(k^*)}$. Hence, we have proved (39a). Equation (39b) follows similarly:

$$\alpha_c^{(k^*+1)} < \alpha_{max}^{(0,1)}(k^*), \quad \text{if } \alpha_c^{(k^*)} < \alpha_{max}^{(0,1)}(k^*) \Leftrightarrow Q(k^*) > P(k^*)$$

$$\alpha_l^{(k^*)} < \alpha_{max}^{(0,1)}(k^*) \Leftrightarrow P(k^* - 1) < Q(k^* + 1).$$

Q.E.D.

*Proposition 5:* For $k^* \ge 1$,

$$\alpha_l^{(i)} > \alpha_c^{(i)}, \quad \text{for } i \ge k^* + 1 \quad (42a)$$

$$\alpha_l^{(i)} < \alpha_c^{(i)}, \quad \text{for } i \le k^* - 1 \quad (42b)$$

$$\alpha_l^{(k^*)} \begin{cases} > \alpha_c^{(k^*)}, & \text{if } P(k^* - 1) > (1 - p_{k^*})/2 \\ < \alpha_c^{(k^*)}, & \text{if } P(k^* - 1) < (1 - p_{k^*})/2. \end{cases} \quad (42c)$$

*Proof:* We have

$$\alpha_l^{(i)} \gtrless \alpha_c^{(i)} \Leftrightarrow P(i - 1)/P(i) \gtrless Q(i + 1)/Q(i)$$

$$\Leftrightarrow p_i/P(i) \gtrless p_i/Q(i) \Leftrightarrow P(i) \gtrless Q(i)$$

$$\Leftrightarrow P(i - 1) \gtrless (1 - p_i)/2 \Leftrightarrow P(i) \gtrless (1 + p_i)/2.$$

For $i \ge k^* + 1$, $P(i - 1) \ge P(k^*) \ge \frac{1}{2} > (1 - p_i)/2$, so that (42a) holds. For $i \le k^* - 1$, $P(i) \le P(k^* - 1) < \frac{1}{2} < (1 + p_i)/2$, so that (42b) holds. Finally, when $i = k^*$, $\alpha_l^{(k^*)} \gtrless \alpha_c^{(k^*)} \Leftrightarrow P(k^* - 1) \gtrless (1 - p_{k^*})/2$, so that (42c) holds. Q.E.D.

The following result can now be established.

*Lemma 6:* We choose the initial optimal state to be (0,1) over $\max(\alpha_l^{(k^*-1)}, \alpha_c^{(k^*)}) \leq \alpha < \alpha_{\max}^{(0,1)}(k^*)$, if $k^* = 0$ and for $k^* \geq 1$, if $P(k^* - 1) < (1 - p_{k^*})/2$, and let it be (1,0) over $\max(\alpha_l^{(k^*)}, \alpha_c^{(k^*+1)}) \leq \alpha < \alpha_{\max}^{(1,0)}(k^*)$, otherwise. The rest of the optimal states are then chosen according to (37). Then, for each optimal state $(n,m)$

$$q_k > 0, \qquad k^* - n \leq k \leq k^* + m, 0 \leq n \leq k^*, m \geq 0.$$

*Proof:* Utilizing Lemma 5, it is left to show that $q_{k^*} > 0$, $q_{k^*-1} > 0$, $q_{k^*+1} > 0$ in the appropriate regions when the indicated choice of states is adopted. We consider first the initial states. By (23), if the initial optimal state is (1,0), we have

$$(1 - \alpha)q_{k^*-1} = P(k^* - 1) - \alpha Q(k^*)$$
$$(1 - \alpha)q_{k^*} = Q(k^*) - \alpha P(k^* - 1).$$

At $\alpha_{\max}$ we have $q_{k^*} = 1$ and $q_{k^*-1} = 0$, so that $\alpha_{\max} = \alpha_{\max}^{(1,0)}(k^*)$ as given by (40). We observe that $q_{k^*} > 0$ and $q_{k^*-1} > 0$, for $\alpha < \alpha_{\max}^{(1,0)}(k^*)$. By Lemma 2, this state will be optimal in the distortion interval $\max(\alpha_l^{(k^*)}, \alpha_c^{(k^*+1)}) \leq \alpha < \alpha_{\max}^{(1,0)}(k^*)$ if this region is not empty. The latter is the case, by Proposition 4, if and only if $P(k^* - 1) > (1 - p_{k^*})/2$. Similarly, if (0,1) is the initial optimal state, from (23) we obtain the $\alpha_{\max} = \alpha_{\max}^{(0,1)}(k^*)$ as given by (40), and $q_{k^*} > 0$, $q_{k^*+1} > 0$, for $\alpha < \alpha_{\max}$. By Proposition 4 and Lemma 2, state (0,1) is optimal in $\max(\alpha_l^{(k^*-1)}, \alpha_c^{(k^*)}) \leq \alpha < \alpha_{\max}^{(0,1)}(k^*)$, if and only if $P(k^* - 1) < (1 - p_{k^*})/2$, $k^* \geq 1$. For $k^* = 0$, one readily observes (0,1) to be optimal in $1 - p_0 = \alpha_c^{(k^*)} \leq \alpha < \alpha_{\max}^{(0,1)}(k^*) = (1 - p_0)/p_0$. We have thus proved the statement concerning the optimal initial state.

We now show that, under the stated optimal policy for choosing the states, $q_{k^*-1} > 0$, $k^* \geq 1$, in the appropriate region. Consider first the case where $P(k^* - 1) < (1 - p_{k^*})/2$. For $\alpha_l^{(k^*-1)} \leq \alpha < \alpha_l^{(k^*)}$, we have by (23),

$$(1 - \alpha)^2 q_{k^*-1} = (1 - \alpha)P(k^* - 1) - \alpha p_{k^*}$$

so that $q_{k^*-1} > 0$. For $\alpha_l^{(k^*-2)} \leq \alpha < \alpha_l^{(k^*-1)}$, we have by (23)

$$\begin{aligned}(1 - \alpha)^2 q_{k^*-1} &= -\alpha(1 - \alpha)P(k^* - 2) + (1 + \alpha^2)p_{k^*-1} - \alpha p_{k^*} \\ &> -\alpha p_{k^*-2} + (1 + \alpha^2)p_{k^*-1} - \alpha p_{k^*},\end{aligned}$$

since $\alpha > \alpha_l^{(k^*-2)} \Rightarrow (1 - \alpha) < p_{k^*-2}/P(k^* - 2)$. One then readily observes that a sufficient condition for $q_{k^*-1} > 0$ is that $p_{k^*-1} > (p_{k^*} + p_{k^*-2})/2$, or, equivalently, $(p_{k^*} + p_{k^*-2})/p_{k^*-1} < 2$. However, $k^* = [\lambda]$ or $k^* = [\lambda] + 1$. For $k^* = [\lambda]$, we have

$$\begin{aligned}(p_{k^*} + p_{k^*-2})/p_{k^*-1} &= ([\lambda] - 1)/\lambda + \lambda/[\lambda] \\ &= 2 - \{[\lambda] - (\lambda - [\lambda])^2\}/\lambda[\lambda] < 2,\end{aligned}$$

as $[\lambda] > \lambda - [\lambda] \geq (\lambda - [\lambda])^2$, since $[\lambda] \geq 1$ and $(\lambda - [\lambda]) < 1$. For $k^* = [\lambda] + 1$,

$$\begin{aligned}(p_{k^*} + p_{k^*-2})/p_{k^*-1} &= [\lambda]/\lambda + \lambda/([\lambda] + 1) \\ &= 2 - \{2\lambda - [\lambda] - (\lambda - [\lambda])^2\}/\{\lambda([\lambda] + 1)\} < 2,\end{aligned}$$

as $2\lambda > [\lambda] + (\lambda - [\lambda]) \geq [\lambda] + (\lambda - [\lambda])^2$, since $0 \leq (\lambda - [\lambda]) < 1$. Hence, $q_{k^*-1} > 0$, for $\alpha_l^{(k^*-2)} \leq \alpha < \alpha_l^{(k^*+1)}$. For $0 \leq \alpha < \alpha_l^{(k^*+2)}$, we have

$$(1 - \alpha)^2 q_{k^*-1} = -\alpha p_{k^*-2} + (1 + \alpha^2)p_{k^*-1} - \alpha p_{k^*}$$

so that following the preceding argument we conclude that $q_{k^*-1} > 0$.

Consider now $q_{k^*-1}$ when $P(k^* - 1) > (1 - p_{k^*})/2$. In that case, we have already seen that $q_{k^*-1} > 0$, for $\max(\alpha_c^{(k^*)}, \alpha_l^{(k^*-1)}) \leq \alpha < \alpha_{\max}^{(1,0)}(k^*)$. If now $\max(\alpha_c^{(k^*)}, \alpha_l^{(k^*-1)}) = \alpha_c^{(k^*)}$, the next state is (1,1). By (25) we obtain that $q_{k^*-1} > 0$ in region $\alpha_l^{(k^*-1)} \leq \alpha < \alpha_c^{(k^*)}$, if $\alpha < \alpha_l^{(k^*)}$. But by Proposition 5, (42c) indicates that $\alpha_c^{(k^*)} < \alpha_l^{(k^*)}$ in the present case, so that $\alpha < \alpha_c^{(k^*)} \Rightarrow \alpha < \alpha_l^{(k^*)}$. For the case where $\max(\alpha_c^{(k^*)}, \alpha_l^{(k^*-1)}) = \alpha_l^{(k^*-1)}$, and generally for $\alpha < \alpha_l^{(k^*-1)}$, the proof that $q_{k^*-1} > 0$ proceeds identically to that written previously for case $P(k^* - 1) < (1 - p_{k^*})/2$.

We show now that $q_{k^*+1} > 0$, in the appropriate region. First consider the case where $P(k^* - 1) > (1 - p_{k^*})/2$. We have then seen that optimal initial state is (1,0). The proof that $q_{k^*+1} > 0$, for $\alpha < \alpha_c^{(k^*)}$ is seen to be identical to that of Lemma 5, in which we have shown that $q_{k^*+i} > 0$, for $\max(\alpha_l^{(k^*)}, \alpha_c^{(k^*+1)}) \leq \alpha < \alpha_{\max}^{(0,1)}(k^*)$. If now $\max(\alpha_l^{(k^*)}, \alpha_c^{(k^*+1)}) = \alpha_c^{(k^*+1)}$, next state is (0,2), and by (25)

$$\begin{aligned}(1 - \alpha)^2 q_{k^*+1} &= -\alpha(1 - \alpha)P(k^*) + (1 + \alpha^2)p_{k^*+1} - \alpha(1 - \alpha)Q(k^* + 2) \\ &< -\alpha p_{k^*} + (1 + \alpha^2)p_{k^*+1} - \alpha(1 - \alpha)Q(k^* + 2)\end{aligned}$$

since $\alpha > \alpha_l^{(k^*)} \Rightarrow 1 - \alpha < p_{k^*}/P(k^*)$. However, for $\alpha < \alpha_c^{(k^*+1)}$, the latter expression is shown to be positive, following the proof of Lemma 5. Hence, $q_{k^*+1} > 0$, for $\alpha < \alpha_c^{(k^*+1)}$, under present conditions. If, on the other hand, $\max(\alpha_l^{(k^*)}, \alpha_c^{(k^*+1)}) = \alpha_l^{(k^*)}$, the next optimal state is (1,1). By (25), we see that then $q_{k^*+1} > 0$, for $\max(\alpha_l^{(k^*-1)}, \alpha_c^{(k^*+1)}) \leq \alpha < \alpha_l^{(k^*)}$, if and only if $\alpha < \alpha_c^{(k^*)}$. But by Proposition 5 we have $\alpha_l^{(k^*)} < \alpha_c^{(k^*)}$ here, so that $\alpha < \alpha_l^{(k^*)} \Rightarrow \alpha < \alpha_c^{(k^*)}$. The proof that $q_{k^*+1} > 0$, for $\alpha < \alpha_c^{(k^*+1)}$ then follows as before.

Finally, we show that $q_{k^*} > 0$ for the stated optimal policy, $\alpha \leq \alpha_{\max}$. Consider first the case where $P(k^* - 1) < (1 - p_{k^*})/2$. The initial state is (0,1) and we have seen that $q_{k^*} > 0$, for $\max(\alpha_l^{(k^*)}, \alpha_c^{(k^*+1)}) \leq \alpha < \alpha_{\max}^{(1,0)}(k^*)$. If now $\max(\alpha_l^{(k^*)}, \alpha_c^{(k^*+1)}) = \alpha_c^{(k^*+1)}$, we observe from (23) that for $\max(\alpha_l^{(k^*)}, \alpha_c^{(k^*+2)}) \leq \alpha < \alpha_c^{(k^*+1)}$, $q_{k^*} > 0$, if and only if $\alpha < \alpha_l^{(k^*+1)}$. But by Proposition 5 we have that $\alpha_c^{(k^*+1)} < \alpha_l^{(k^*+1)}$, so that $\alpha < \alpha_c^{(k^*+1)} \Rightarrow \alpha < \alpha_l^{(k^*+1)}$ as required. If $\max(\alpha_l^{(k^*)}, \alpha_c^{(k^*+1)}) = \alpha_l^{(k^*)}$, then for $\max(\alpha_l^{(k^*-1)}, \alpha_c^{(k^*+1)}) \leq \alpha < \alpha_l^{(k^*)}$ state (1,1) follows and we have by (25)

$$\begin{aligned}(1 - \alpha)^2 q_{k^*} &= -\alpha(1 - \alpha)P(k^* - 1) + (1 + \alpha^2)p_{k^*} \\ &\quad - \alpha(1 - \alpha)Q(k^* + 1) \\ &> -\alpha p_{k^*-1} + (1 + \alpha^2)p_{k^*} - \alpha(1 - \alpha)Q(k^* + 1) \\ &> -\alpha p_{k^*-1} + (1 + \alpha^2)p_{k^*} - \alpha p_{k^*+1}.\end{aligned}$$

The latter expression is now shown to be positive for the case where $k^* = [\lambda]$, by proving that then $p_{k^*} > (p_{k^*-1} +$

$p_{k^*+1})/2$. We have for $k^* = [\lambda]$

$$(p_{k^*-1} + p_{k^*+1})/p_{k^*}$$
$$= [\lambda]/\lambda + \lambda/([\lambda] + 1)$$
$$= 2 - \{2\lambda - [\lambda] - (\lambda - [\lambda])^2\}/\{\lambda(1 + [\lambda])\} < 2$$

as $2\lambda > [\lambda] + (\lambda - [\lambda]) > [\lambda] + (\lambda - [\lambda])^2$. Hence one concludes that $q_{k^*} > 0, \forall\alpha < \alpha_l^{(k^*)}$, when $k^* = [\lambda]$. When $k^* = [\lambda] + 1$, we have that $p_{k^*-1} > p_{k^*}$ (since $p_{[\lambda]}$ or $p_{[\lambda]-1}$ are the only maximal values) and can therefore apply Proposition 3, (38a) with $n = k^*$, and use the same proof procedure as in Lemma 5 to deduce that $q_{k^*} > 0, \forall\alpha < \alpha_l^{(k^*)}$. The proof that $q_{k^*} > 0$ when $P(k^* - 1) < (1 - p_{k^*})/2$ is analogous to that above, and will therefore be omitted. Q.E.D.

Utilizing the specific properties of the median of a Poisson distribution, as indicated in Section II, the following characteristic of the initial optimal state can be deduced from Lemma 6.

*Corollary 1:* For any Poisson distribution whose intensity $\lambda \geq 1$ is integral, the optimal initial state is (1,0). For general $\lambda$, the optimal initial state is (0,1) when (approximately)

$$\tfrac{1}{2} - R_\lambda \sim \tfrac{1}{6} < \lambda - [\lambda] < 1 - R_\lambda \sim \tfrac{2}{3} \tag{43}$$

and is (1,0) otherwise.

*Proof:* For $\lambda \geq 1$ integral, $k^* = \lambda$ and we have seen that

$$P(k^* - 1) + R_\lambda p_{k^*} = \tfrac{1}{2}$$

where $\frac{1}{3} < R_\lambda < \frac{1}{2}$. Hence, $P(k^* - 1) = \frac{1}{2} - R_\lambda p_\lambda > (1 - p_{k^*})/2$ and by Lemma 6 the optimal initial state is (1,0).

For general $\lambda$, $k^* = [\lambda]$ if $\lambda - [\lambda] \lesssim 1 - R_\lambda$ by Lemma 1, and we then (approximately) have (see [5, p. 290])

$$P(k^* - 1) + (\lambda - [\lambda] + R_\lambda)p_{k^*} = \tfrac{1}{2}$$

so that

$$P(k^* - 1) = \tfrac{1}{2} - (\lambda - [\lambda] + R_\lambda)p_{k^*} \begin{cases} > (1 - p_{k^*})/2, & \text{if } \lambda - [\lambda] < \frac{1}{2} - R_\lambda \\ < (1 - p_{k^*})/2, & \text{if } \lambda - [\lambda] > \frac{1}{2} - R_\lambda. \end{cases}$$

If $\lambda - [\lambda] > 1 - R_\lambda$, $k^* = [\lambda] + 1$ and then $P(k^* - 1) = \frac{1}{2} - (\lambda - [\lambda] + R_\lambda - 1)p_{k^*} > (1 - p_{k^*})/2$, as $(\lambda - [\lambda] + R_\lambda - 1) < R_\lambda < \frac{1}{2}$. Finally recall that $R_\lambda \to \frac{1}{3}$ rapidly as $\lambda$ increases. Q.E.D.

Note that Corollary 1 indicates that (approximately) the optimal initial state is (0,1) for $n + \frac{1}{6} < \lambda < n + \frac{2}{3}$, and is (1,0) otherwise, where $n$ is any nonnegative integer.

We have obtained the optimal state distribution and thus derived the rate-distortion curve for a Poisson sequence. For a fixed given $\lambda$, the optimal state distribution is easily obtained graphically by plotting an $m$-axis line on which the values $\{\alpha_c^{(k^*+i)}, i \geq 1$ when $P(k^* - 1) < (1 - p_{k^*})/2$ and $i \geq 0$, otherwise$\}$ are indicated, and an $n$-axis line on which the values $\{\alpha_l^{(k^*-i)}, 0 \leq i \leq k^*$ when $P(k^* - 1) < (1 - p_{k^*})/2$ and $1 \leq i \leq k^*$, otherwise$\}$ are indicated (Fig. 1). The optimal state distribution is obtained from the intersection of the intervals of the previous two lines. We summarize our main result by the following theorem.

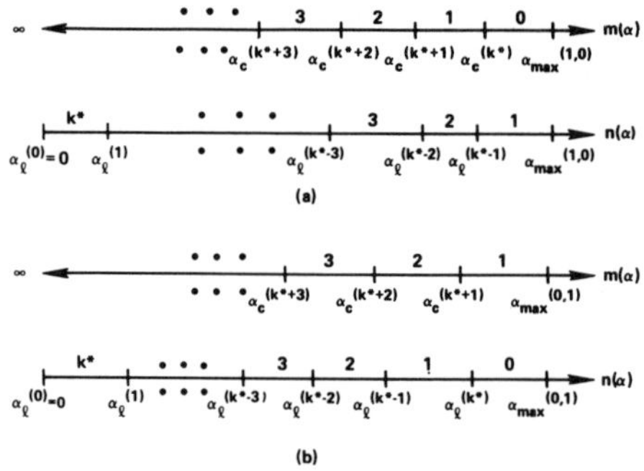


Fig. 1. Flow diagram of optimal states. (a) Case where $P(k^* - 1) \geq (1 - p_{k^*})/2$, holds for integral $\lambda \geq 1$. (b) Case where $P(k^* - 1) < (1 - p_{k^*})/2$, holds for $0 < \lambda \leq \ln 2$ and approximately for $n + 1/6 < \lambda < n + 2/3$, $n = 1,2,3,\cdots$.

*Theorem 1:* The rate-distortion function of a Poisson sequence is given parametrically in terms of the optimal state $(n,m)$, $k^* \geq n \geq 0$, $m \geq 0$, by the $D_\alpha^{(n,m)}$ and $R_\alpha^{(n,m)}$ of (30) and (31). The optimal state distribution is determined by (37), and is initially (1,0), if $P(k^* - 1) > (1 - p_{k^*})/2$, $k^* \geq 1$, and (0,1) otherwise.

We note that the number of optimal states is countably infinite. Thus as $(n,m) \to (k^*,\infty)$ the length of the distortion interval associated with each state tends to zero. In particular, the state $(k^*,\infty)$ is therefore associated with a distortion interval of length zero. Hence, we use the whole set of reproducing letters only at the point $D = 0$.

## IV. Bounds and Approximations to the Rate-Distortion Function

### *Behavior at Low and High Distortions*

At low distortion values we have $\alpha \ll 1$ and $D - D_0^{(n,m)} < 1$. Using there the approximations $\alpha(1 + \alpha)^{-1} \sim \alpha$, $\alpha(1 - \alpha)^{-1} \sim \alpha$, (30) yields

$$D_\alpha^{(n,m)} \cong D_0^{(n,m)} + \alpha[1 + P(k^* + m - 1) - P(k^* - n + 1)]. \tag{44}$$

Using (44) in (31) we obtain the following approximation to the rate-distortion function at low distortions, for the state $(n,m)$:

$$R^{(n,m)}(D) \cong R_1^{(n,m)}(D) \triangleq H^{(n,m)} + [D - D_0^{(n,m)}] \cdot \ln \frac{D - D_0^{(n,m)}}{1 + P(k^* + m - 1) - P(k^* - n + 1)}. \tag{45}$$

Equation (45) can be further simplified by noting that at low distortions $m \gg 1$, $n \approx k^*$, so that

$$P(k^* + m - 1) - P(k^* - n + 1) = \sum_{k^*-n+1}^{k^*+m-1} p_i \cong Q(1) = 1 - p_0$$

and $D_0^{(n,m)} \approx 0$, $H^{(n,m)} \approx H$. Hence, we have $D \approx \alpha(2 - p_0)$ and the following low-distortion approximation results:

$$R(D) \approx R_2(D) \triangleq H + D[\ln \{D(2 - p_0)^{-1}\} - 1]. \quad (46)$$

In particular, when $\lambda > 1$ we have $p_0 \approx 0$ and consequently obtain for $D \ll 1$ the simple expression

$$R(D) \approx \tilde{R}_2(D) \triangleq H + D[\ln (D/2) - 1]. \quad (47)$$

At high distortion values, we can consider the rate-distortion function associated with the initial optimal state. By Lemma 6, (30), and (31), we obtain for $P(k^* - 1) > (1 - p_{k^*})/2$ and high distortions

$$\begin{aligned} R(D) &= R^{(0,1)}(D) \\ &= H_2(P(k^* - 1)) - H_2(D - D_{\max} + P(k^* - 1)) \end{aligned} \quad (48)$$

while for $P(k^* - 1) < (1 - p_{k^*})/2$ and high distortions we have

$$\begin{aligned} R(D) &= R^{(0,1)}(D) \\ &= H_2(Q(k^* + 1)) - H_2(D - D_{\max} + Q(k^* + 1)) \end{aligned} \quad (49)$$

where $D_{\max}$ is given by (16). The distortion interval in which the LHS equality in (48), (49) holds is indicated by Lemma 6. For somewhat lower distortion values, (48) and (49) can serve as approximations.

*Lower Bounds*

We wish now to consider the relation between the $R^{(n,m)}(D)$ curve and the neighboring curves $R^{(n-1,m)}(D)$ and $R^{(n,m+1)}(D)$. First, we observe (using (30) and (31) and $\alpha = 0$) that at state $(n,m)$

$$D_{\min}^{(n,m)} = D_0^{(n,m)} \qquad R^{(n,m)}(D_{\min}^{(n,m)}) = H^{(n,m)}. \quad (50)$$

Notice that $H^{(n,m)} \uparrow H$ as $n \to k^*$, $m \to \infty$. We also have

$$\begin{aligned} D_\alpha^{(n,m)} - D_\alpha^{(n-1,m)} &= (1 - \alpha)^{-1} p_{k^*-n+1} - P(k^* - n + 1) \\ R_\alpha^{(n-1,m)} - R_\alpha^{(n,m)} &= H^{(n-1,m)} - H^{(n,m)} \\ &\quad + (1 - \alpha)^{-1} H_2(\alpha) p_{k^*-n+1}. \end{aligned} \quad (51)$$

Thus from (51) we conclude that for $\alpha = \alpha_l^{(k^*-n+1)}$ we have

$$R^{(n,m)}(D) = R^{(n-1,m)}(D)$$

and

$$\frac{d}{dD} R^{(n,m)}(D) = \frac{d}{dD} R^{(n-1,m)}(D)$$

while for $\alpha > \alpha_l^{(k^*-n+1)}$ we have

$$\frac{d}{dD} R^{(n-1,m)} < \frac{d}{dD} R^{(n,m)}$$

and for $\alpha < \alpha_l^{(k^*-n+1)}$ one obtains that

$$\frac{d}{dD} R^{(n-1,m)}(D) > \frac{d}{dD} R^{(n,m)}(D)$$

in the appropriate definition interval of $R^{(n-1,m)}(D)$. Hence, curves $R^{(n,m)}(D)$ and $R^{(n-1,m)}(D)$ are tangent at $\alpha = \alpha_l^{(k^*-n+1)}$, while for $\alpha \neq \alpha_l^{(k^*-n+1)}$ we have $R^{(n-1,m)}(D) > R^{(n,m)}(D)$. A similar analysis follows for the relation between $R^{(n,m)}(D)$ and $R^{(n,m+1)}(D)$. We have thus obtained the following property.

*Lemma 7:* We have, for all $m$ and $n$ in the definition regions of the following function,

$$\begin{aligned} R^{(n-1,m)}(D) &> R^{(n,m)}(D), & \alpha &\neq \alpha_l^{(k^*-n+1)} \\ R^{(n-1,m)}(D) &= R^{(n,m)}(D), & \alpha &= \alpha_l^{(k^*-n+1)} \end{aligned} \quad (52)$$

$$\begin{aligned} R^{(n,m)}(D) &> R^{(n,m+1)}(D), & \alpha &\neq \alpha_c^{(k^*+m)} \\ R^{(n,m)}(D) &= R^{(n,m+1)}(D), & \alpha &= \alpha_c^{(k^*+m)}. \end{aligned} \quad (53)$$

Hence, for any optimal state $(n,m)$,

$$R(D) \geq R^{(n,m)}(D), \qquad \text{for } \alpha \geq \max (\alpha_c^{(k^*+m)}, \alpha_l^{(k^*-n)}). \quad (54)$$

*Proof:* We have to show (54). State $(n,m)$ is optimal in interval (37), so that $R(D) = R^{(n,m)}(D)$ in this distortion region. In the next higher distortion region either state $(n, m - 1)$ or state $(n - 1, m)$ is optimal. In the first case, using (53), $R(D) = R^{(n,m-1)}(D) \geq R^{(n,m)}(D)$, while in the second case, using (52), $R(D) = R^{(n-1,m)}(D) \geq R^{(n,m)}(D)$, in the appropriate distortion region. Continuing recursively, one readily obtains (54). Q.E.D.

Equation (54) yields a useful set of lower bounds to $R(D)$, which can be used in the appropriate distortion range of interest. In particular, a useful simple lower bound follows from (54) when we let $n = k^*$ and $m \to \infty$. We then obtain

$$R(D) \geq R_L(D) \triangleq R^{(k^*,\infty)}(D), \qquad \forall 0 \leq D \leq D_{\max}. \quad (55)$$

Using (30) and (31), the parametric representation of $R_L(D)$ is obtained as

$$\begin{aligned} R_L(D,\alpha) &= H + D \ln \alpha + \ln \{(1 - \alpha)(1 + \alpha)^{-1}\} \\ &\quad - p_0 \ln (1 - \alpha) \\ D_L(\alpha) &= 2\alpha(1 - \alpha^2)^{-1} - p_0\alpha(1 - \alpha)^{-1}. \end{aligned} \quad (56)$$

For $\lambda > 1$, $p_0 \approx 0$ and $R_L(D)$ is then approximately given by

$$\begin{aligned} R_L(D) &\cong H + D \ln \{[(1 + D^2)^{1/2} - 1]D^{-1}\} \\ &\quad + \ln \frac{D + 1 - (1 + D^2)^{1/2}}{D - 1 - (1 + D^2)^{1/2}}. \end{aligned} \quad (57)$$

Notice that for low distortions, $\alpha \ll 1$, and $\lambda > 1$, we have by (56) that $D_L(\alpha) \approx 2\alpha$ and $R_L(D) \approx H + D(\ln (D(2) - 1)$, so that $R_L(D) \equiv \tilde{R}_2(D)$ as given by (47), and for low distortions $R(D)$ and $R_L(D)$ are very close. We will observe in the next sections, when plotting some rate-distortion curves, that $R_L(D)$ is actually a close lower bound over most of the distortion range.

It is interesting to compare $R_L(D)$ to a Shannon-type lower bound obtained by using (see [2, p. 37]) the relationship

$$R(D) = \sup_{s \leq 0,\, \lambda_i \in \Lambda_s} \left[ sD + \sum_i p_i \ln \lambda_i \right]$$

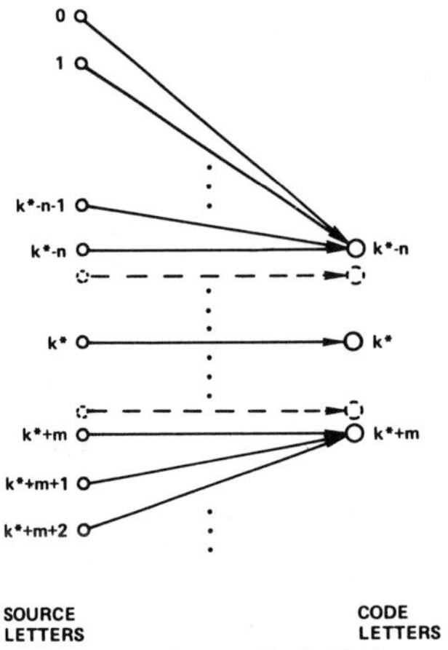


Fig. 2. Diagram of code $B^{(n,m)}$.

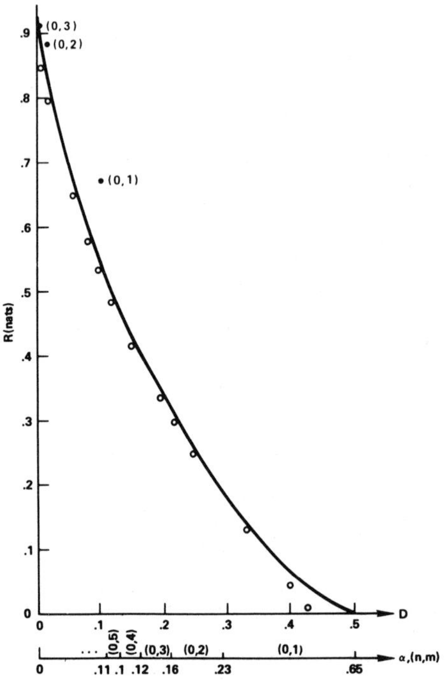


Fig. 3. $R(D)$ curve for $\lambda = 0.5$.○—$R_L(D)$.●$(n,m)$—code $B^{(n,m)}$.

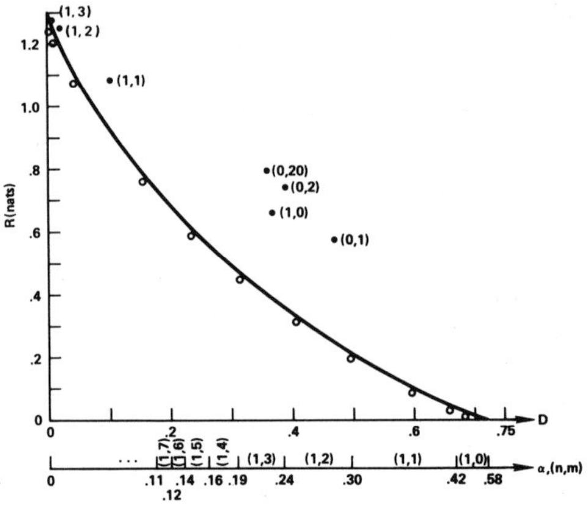


Fig. 4. $R(D)$ curve for $\lambda = 1$.○—$R_L(D)$.●$(n,m)$—code $B^{(n,m)}$.

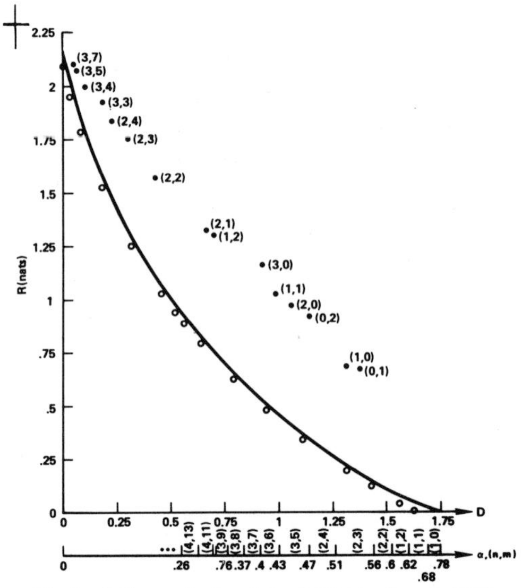


Fig. 5. $R(D)$ curve for $\lambda = 5$.○—$R_L(D)$.●$(n,m)$—code $B^{(n,m)}$.

where

$$\Lambda_s = \left\{\lambda_j : c_k = \sum p_j \lambda_j \exp(s|j-k|) \le 1, \ \forall k\right\}.$$

As in deriving the Shannon lower bound (see [2, p. 92]), let $\lambda_j = K/p_j$. Then

$$c_k = K \sum_{j=0}^{\infty} \alpha^{|j-k|} \le K\left(2 \sum_{i=0}^{\infty} \alpha^i - 1\right)$$
$$= K(1+\alpha)(1-\alpha)^{-1}.$$

We thus choose $K = (1-\alpha)(1+\alpha)^{-1}$, so that $c_k \le 1, \forall k$. Using the set $\{\lambda_j = K/p_j\}$, the preceding relationship yields the lower bound

$$R_{SL}(D,\alpha) = D \ln \alpha + \sum_j p_j \ln (K/p_j)$$
$$= H + D \ln \alpha + \ln (1 - \alpha)(1 + \alpha)^{-1}. \quad (58a)$$

Now we choose $\alpha$ to maximize $R_{SL}(D,\alpha)$. We have $(d/ds)R_{SL}(D,\alpha) = D - 2\alpha(1 - \alpha^2)^{-1}$; $(d^2/ds^2)R_L(D,\alpha) < 0$. Hence, by choosing

$$D_{SL}(\alpha) = 2\alpha(1 - \alpha^2)^{-1} \quad (58b)$$

we obtain the tightest lower bound for this choice of $\{\lambda_j\}$. The resulting Shannon-type lower bound $R_{SL}(D)$ is given parametrically by (58), and is seen to be identical to the $R_L(D)$ given by (56), when $\lambda \gg 1$. We recall now that for Gaussian sources $R_{SL}(D) < R(D)$, $\forall D > 0$ (see [2, p. 97]). In our case, as well, as shown by Lemma 7, $R_L(D) < R(D)$, $\forall D > 0$. Note that the Poisson distribution converges to a Gaussian distribution as $\lambda \to \infty$ (and then also $R_L(D) \to R_{SL}(D)$).

*An Upper Bound—A Coding Scheme*

The derivation of the rate distortion function for Poisson sequences, and the resulting specific form of the set of reproducing letters, suggest using the following simple coding scheme $B^{(n,m)}$, $0 \leq n \leq k^*$, $m \geq 0$ (Fig. 2). For a state $(n,m)$, the code letters are $\{k: k^* - n \leq k \leq k^* + m\} \triangleq A^{(n,m)}$. A source letter $j$, $k^* - n \leq j \leq k^* + m$, is encoded as a code letter $k = j$, while $k = k^* - n$ serves as the code letter of any source letter $j$ in the range $0 \leq j \leq k^* - n$, and $k = k^* + m$ encodes any source letter $j$ in the range $j \geq k^* + m$. The average distortion associated with $B^{(n,m)}$ is clearly

$$D^{(n,m)} = \sum_{i=0}^{k^*-n} p_i(k^* - n - i) + \sum_{i=k^*+m}^{\infty} p_i(i - k^* - m)$$
$$\equiv D_0^{(n,m)}.$$

The rate of the source code $B^{(n,m)}$, as a block code, is $\ln (n + m + 1)$. However, using Huffman encoding procedures (and thus variable-length codewords) we can reduce the effective rate to the entropy associated with the code letters. However, the probabilities of the code letters are $\{P(k^* - n), p_{k^*-n+1}, \cdots, p_{k^*+m-1}, Q(k^* + m)\}$, so that the entropy measure is $H^{(n,m)}$. Consequently, the coding scheme $B^{(n,m)}$ attains the point $(D_0^{(n,m)}, H^{(n,m)})$ on the $(D,R)$ plane. The curve $\{(D_0^{(n,m)}, H^{(n,m)}), 0 \leq n \leq k^*, m \geq 0\}$ is thus an upper bound to $R(D)$, and also indicates the $R_B(D)$ characteristic associated with the simple instrumentable code $B^{(n,m)}$.

An upper bound to $(R_B^{(n,m)}(D) - R(D))$ is readily obtained by using Lemma 7, (30), and (31). In particular, we have $R_B^{(k^*,m)}(D) - R(D) \leq H^{(n,m)} - R^{(k^*,m)}(\alpha_c^{(k^*+m)})$, which indicates that $R_B(D) - R(D) \to 0$ rapidly as $D \to 0$. The calculations presented in the next section verify the excellent performance of code $B^{(n,m)}$.

## V. Discussion and Conclusions

The rate-distortion function of a Poisson sequence, derived in Section III, is plotted in Figs. 3, 4, and 5 for intensities $\lambda = 0.5$, $\lambda = 1$, and $\lambda = 5$, respectively. On these figures we have also plotted the lower bound $R_L(D)$ curves and the $(R,D)$ points associated with the entropy-coded $B^{(n,m)}$ codes. We observe that the $R_L(D)$ curve is an excellent (lower-bound) approximation for the $R(D)$ curve, over most of the distortion region. We also observe the excellent performance of the $B^{(n,m)}$ codes. For example, for $\lambda = 0.5$ (in which case the source emits mainly zeros, ones with lower probability, etc.), we have $k^* = 0$ and the simple codes $B^{(0,1)}$, $B^{(0,2)}$, and $B^{(0,3)}$ yield average distortions of 0.1, 0.016, and 0.002, and require an incremental information rate (above the rate obtained from the $R(D)$ curve) of only 0.1, 0.03, and $\sim 10^{-3}$ nat, respectively. For $\lambda = 1$, $k^* = 1$, code $B^{(1,1)}$ yields an average distortion of 0.1 and requires an incremental information rate of 0.15 nat, while code $B^{(1,3)}$ yields an average distortion of 0.004 and requires an information rate essentially equal to that of the corresponding $R(D)$ (and approximately equal to $H$). For $\lambda = 5$, $k^* = 5$, codes $B^{(1,1)}$, $B^{(2,2)}$, and $B^{(3,7)}$ achieve average distortions of 0.93, 0.43, and 0.05, with incremental information rates of 0.58, 0.45, and 0.12 nat, respectively.

Finally, we observe that for large values of $\lambda$, one can use the normal distribution to approximate the Poisson distribution [4]. Also, under large $\lambda$, when a large average distortion is allowed, one can modify code $B^{(n,m)}$ to incorporate larger differences between $k^*$ and the neighboring code letters.

Rate-distortion curves for Poisson sequences under distortion criteria different from the minimum mean-absolute error criterion used here are yet to be studied.

## References

[1] R. G. Gallager, *Information Theory and Reliable Communication.* New York: Wiley, 1968.
[2] T. Berger, *Rate Distortion Theory.* Englewood Cliffs, N.J.: Prentice-Hall, 1971.
[3] F. A. Haight, *Handbook of the Poisson Distribution.* New York: Wiley, 1967.
[4] T. T. Cheng, "The normal approximation to the Poisson distribution and a proof of a conjecture of Ramanujan," *Bull. Amer. Math. Soc.*, ser. 2, vol. 55, pp. 396–401, 1949.
[5] G. J. Lidstone, "Notes on the Poisson frequency distribution," *Inst. Actuaries J.*, vol. 71, pp. 284–291, 1941.
[6] A. Y. Khintchine, *Mathematical Methods in the Theory of Queueing.* New York: Hafner, 1969.
[7] H. Cramér and M. R. Leadbetter, *Stationary and Related Stochastic Processes.* New York: Wiley, 1967.
[8] A. M. Gerrish, "Estimation of information rates," Ph.D. dissertation, Dep. Elec. Eng., Yale Univ., New Haven, Conn., 1963.

# II

# Statistical Analysis and Applications of Shot Noise

# Editor's Comments on Papers 6 and 7

**6 Beutler and Leneman:** *The Spectral Analysis of Impulse Processes*

**7 Beutler and Leneman:** *On the Statistics of Random Pulse Processes*

The shot-noise process has been a useful model in the analysis of sampling and information processing systems. The authors of the next two papers continue their previous work on stationary point processes [1, 2], which represented the earliest applications of the theory to engineering problems. They consider here general classes of impulse processes (shot noise) and compute their spectral density functions and their characteristic functions. In Paper 6 they use the results in sampling techniques with read-in, read-out jitter, loss of samples, and scaling errors. In Paper 7 they apply the results in pulse-duration modulation and in telephone traffic. These papers represent a shift from the previous ones in this volume in that they are concerned with different applications, thereby needing different theoretical and structural models that come closer to the statistical, rather than the probabilistic theory of point processes.

## References


1. F. J. Beutler and O. A. Z. Leneman, Random sampling of random processes: stationary point processes, *Inform. Contr.,* **9,** 325–346 (1966).
2. F. J. Beutler and O. A. Z. Leneman, The theory of stationary point processes, *Acta Math.,* **116,** 159–197 (1966).

# 6



Reprinted from *Inform. and Control,* **12**(3), 236–258 (1968)

# The Spectral Analysis of Impulse Processes*

FREDERICK J. BEUTLER

*Computer, Information and Control Engineering Program, The University of Michigan, Ann Arbor, Michigan 48104*

AND

OSCAR A. Z. LENEMAN

*Lincoln Laboratory, Massachusetts Institute of Technology, Lexington, Massachusetts 02173*

An expression for the spectral density of the impulse process $s(t) = \sum_{-\infty}^{\infty} \alpha_n \delta(t - t_n)$ is derived under the assumption that $\{\alpha_n\}$ is a stationary process, and that $\{t_n\}$ is a stationary point process independent of $\{\alpha_n\}$. The spectral density appears as an infinite series in terms of the correlation of $\{\alpha_n\}$ and the interval statistics of $\{t_n\}$. The same result was obtained by Leneman by a different argument under considerably more restrictive conditions of validity.

Various models of impulse processes are discussed relative to random sampling of random processes. Random and systematic loss of samples, separate read-in and read-out jitters, and correlated random scaling errors can all be represented by appropriate assumptions on $\{\alpha_n\}$ and $\{t_n\}$.

Finally, closed form expressions are calculated for the spectral density of $s(t)$ and the sampled process under combinations of the sampling errors mentioned in the preceding paragraph.

## I. INTRODUCTION

The impulse process

$$s(t) = \sum_{-\infty}^{\infty} \alpha_n \delta(t - t_n) \tag{1.1}$$

* This study was supported by the National Aeronautics and Space Administration under Research Grant NsG-2-59, and by Lincoln Laboratory, a center for research operated by the Massachusetts Institute of Technology with support from the U. S. Advanced Research Projects Agency.

is often encountered in the analysis of communication and control systems. Although (1.1) is an obvious model for noise appearing as sharp pulses (Stratonovich, 1963; Mazzetti, 1962 and 1964; Khurgin, 1957; Lee, 1960), $s(t)$ plays an even more important role as an intermediary or modulating process. For instance, $s(t)$ may be multiplied by another random process $x(t)$ to represent impulse sampling; the $t_n$ are (possibly randomly irregular) sampling times, and the $\alpha_n$ can be chosen to introduce random multiplicative errors, plus-minus sampling, etc. In other applications, such as to shot noise, $s(t)$ is passed through a linear time-invariant filter. Further examples dealing with modulation processes (Lee, 1960 and Nelsen, 1964) and pulse-modulated control systems (see Gupta and Jury, 1962 for a bibliography) are scattered throughout the literature.

Whenever an impulse process (1.1) appears in a system, successful analysis or synthesis demands that at least some of the statistics of $s(t)$ be known. Although the studies cited above attempt to obtain such statistics, they do so only under severely restrictive assumptions on $\{t_n\}$, and their *ad hoc* approach fails to suggest systematic techniques applicable to large classes of impulse processes. Typically, it is supposed that sampling is periodic except for small jitter perturbations (Balakrishnan, 1962 and Brown, 1963), or that intervals between noise pulses are independent, perhaps even with an interval distribution related to the exponential (Banta, 1964; Mazzetti, 1962). Even so, the resulting calculations are usually tedious and difficult.

A recent paper by Leneman (1966a) suggests a new and more powerful approach to the statistical analysis of pulse processes. It is based on general properties of stationary point processes (Beutler and Leneman, 1966a, 1966b) (hereafter abbreviated s.p.p.), a class of $\{t_n\}$ that seems to embrace all those point processes of interest to communication theorists. Using these properties, Leneman (1966a) was able to both simplify and generalize earlier results on pulse processes.

Subsequent to the appearance of Leneman's paper (Leneman, 1966a), the authors have made further progress in the analysis of impulse processes. The general expression for second-order statistics is now derived by a different method that permits relaxed assumption, and is also of greater intuitive appeal. Furthermore, the authors have gained experience with the application of the principal formula, and are now able to apply it to a larger variety of impulse processes of more general type.

In Part II, first- and second-order statistics of impulse processes

(1.1) are derived. For this purpose $\{t_n\}$ may be any s.p.p. with finite second moment. A remarkably simple formula is then obtained for the correlation of $s(t)$; this formula corresponds to equation (69) of Leneman (1966a) but the intervals between successive $t_n$ need be neither identically distributed nor mutually independent[1] as in Leneman (1966a).

Part III introduces models of impulse processes, and discusses their physical interpretation and applicability. Combinations of randomly-skipped and variously jittered sampling sequences are considered, correlated amplitude errors being taken into account. Special cases include plus-minus sampling, systematic skipping (as in time multiplexing), combined read-in and read-out jitters, etc. Computation of spectra (or correlations) for each of these models is carried out in Part IV.

## II. FIRST- AND SECOND-ORDER STATISTICS

Of the statistics of a random process, the first and second moments are perhaps the most useful. Correlations and spectra, in particular, are required for the analysis of bandwidth occupancy, signal detectability, and message reconstruction (Leneman, 1966b; Leneman and Lewis, 1966). Indeed, first- and second-order moments provide necessary and sufficient information for those problems involving linear systems and/or Gaussian random processes. It is therefore natural that efforts to obtain statistical knowledge of impulse processes be centered on means and second moments.

Consider then the impulse process

$$s(t) = \sum_{-\infty}^{\infty} \alpha_n \delta(t - t_n), \tag{2.1}$$

consisting of an infinite train of delta functions occurring at random times $t_n$ with random intensities $\alpha_n$. It is assumed throughout that $\{\alpha_n\}$ is a stationary discrete parameter random process, with $\{t_n\}$ an s.p.p. (cf. Beutler and Leneman, 1966a, 1966b) independent of $\{\alpha_n\}$. In order that the second moment of $s(t)$ be finite, the finiteness of the

[1] S.p.p. for which the $t_n$ are dependent and/or differently distributed from one another include many models of physical interest. Typical examples of such s.p.p. are jitter processes, processes with dependent skips (burst erasures), and non-uniformly spaced periodic sampling times. See Beutler and Leneman (1966a, 1966b) for precise definitions, discussion of properties, and examples.

expectations $E[(\alpha_n)^2]$ and $E[\{N(t, x)\}^2]$ are supposed.[2] Further hypotheses are not required for the validity of the formulas for the second moments of $s(t)$. Although these formulas hold generally, they appear as infinite sums, and summation to closed form becomes convenient only when additional conditions are imposed.

In order to avoid expectations of delta function products, and to utilize the knowledge of moments of $N(t, x)$, it is convenient to define moments of the impulse process indirectly. To this end, let $N(t)$ be a stationary increment stochastic process which is continuous from the right with

$$N(0) = 0, \tag{2.2}$$

and such that for $u \leqq v$

$$N(v) - N(u) = \sum_{n=-\infty}^{\infty} \alpha_n I_{(u,v]}(t_n). \tag{2.3}$$

In (2.3), $I_{(u,v]}(t_n)$ is an indicator function that is one or zero according as $t_n \in (u, v]$ or not. This means that

$$N(t) = \sum_{n=k}^{k+m-1} \alpha_n \tag{2.4}$$

if $t_k \leqq t$ is the first point to the right of the origin, and there are $m$ points in the interval $(0, t]$. Since $\{\alpha_n\}$ is stationary, the moments of $N(t)$ depend only on $m$, and not on $k$.

The desired impulse process (2.1) is now obtained from $N(t)$ by differentiation, i.e.,

$$s(t) = \frac{dN(t)}{dt}. \tag{2.5}$$

Thus, the discontinuities of $N(t)$ become impulses of $s(t)$ with the intensity of each delta function determined by the corresponding $\alpha_n$. This relationship, with typical $N(t)$ and $s(t)$ processes, is depicted by Fig. 2.1.

The computation of the expectation of a linear functional of a random process is often facilitated by interchanging the functional operation

[2] Here $N(t, x)$ refers to the number of points of $\{t_n\}$ occurring in the interval $(t, t + x]$. This notation, as well as that used elsewhere in the paper in referring to s.p.p., is consistent with that of Beutler and Leneman (1966a, 1966b). The reader is advised to familiarize himself with these two references, as properties of s.p.p. are basic to the present work.

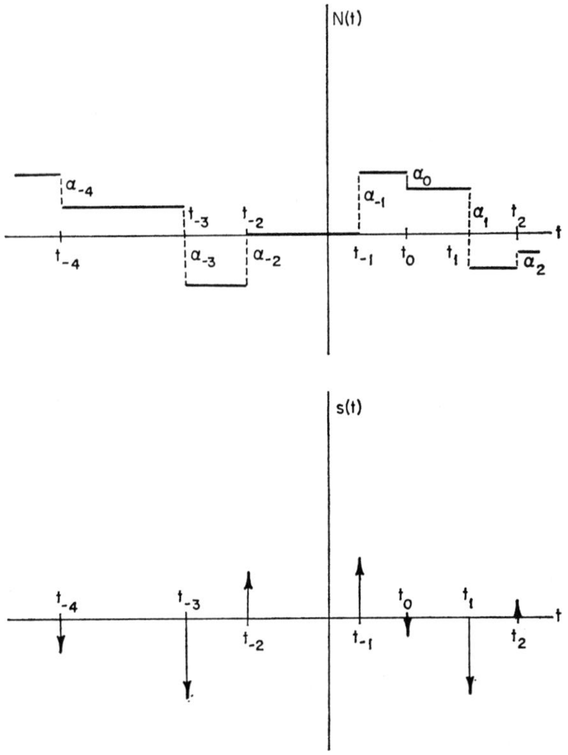


Fig. 2.1. Stationary Increment Process, and Corresponding Impulse Process.

with the expectation. Without inquiring into its validity here, we employ this interchange to determine moments of $s(t)$. Since $s(t)$ is the derivative of $N(t)$, its joint $k$th order moment becomes

$$E[s(t_1)s(t_2) \cdots s(t_k)] = \frac{\partial^k E[N(t_1)N(t_2) \cdots N(t_k)]}{\partial t_1 \, \partial t_2 \cdots \partial t_k}. \tag{2.6}$$

In applying (2.6), it may be supposed without loss of generality that all the $t_j$ are nonnegative and ordered according to magnitude. The ordering is irrelevant if it can be assumed that the order of differentiation is immaterial, and the time origin is unimportant because $N(t)$ is a stationary increment process.

Use of (2.6) makes it easy to show that the mean of $s(t)$ is

$$E[s(t)] = \alpha\beta \tag{2.7}$$

where $\alpha$ is defined by

$$E[\alpha_n] = \alpha \tag{2.8}$$

and $\beta$ is the average number of points per unit time interval. To verify (2.7), first apply the expectation to $N(t)$ as given by (2.3). Taking the expectation first with respect to $\{\alpha_n\}$ produces $\alpha$, and $E[\sum I_{(0,t]}(t_n)] = E[N(0, t)] = \beta t$ by (5.4) of Beutler and Leneman (1966a). Thus,

$$E[N(t)] = \alpha\beta t \tag{2.9}$$

for $t \geqq 0$. Differentiating both sides on $t$ and applying (2.6) to the left side then yields (2.7).

Calculation of the correlation of $s(t)$ is again based on (2.6); hence, $E[N(u)N(v)]$ must be obtained first. The expression for the latter is simplified by the expansion

$$\begin{aligned} &E[N(u)N(v)] \\ &\quad = \tfrac{1}{2}E[N^2(u)] + \tfrac{1}{2}E[N^2(v)] - \tfrac{1}{2}E[\{N(v) - N(u)\}^2] \end{aligned} \tag{2.10}$$

from which it follows that only $E[N^2(t)]$ need be determined. Indeed, $N(t)$ is a stationary increment process with $N(0) = 0$, so that the last term of (2.10) can be replaced by $E[N^2(v - u)]$ whenever $0 \leqq u \leqq v$. With this substitution (2.10) becomes

$$E[N(u)N(v)] = \tfrac{1}{2}\{E[N^2(u)] + E[N^2(v)] - E[N^2(v - u)]\}. \tag{2.11}$$

In view of the representation (2.4) for $N(t)$, each of the expectation terms on the right of (2.11) above is

$$E[N^2(t)] = \sum_{n=1}^{\infty} E\left[\left\{\sum_{k=1}^{n} \alpha_k\right\}^2\right] p(n, t), \tag{2.12}$$

in which $p(n, t)$ represents the probability that there are precisely $n$ points in an interval of length $t$. Now $p(n, t) = G_n(t) - G_{n+1}(t)$, where $G_n$ is the distribution of the waiting time from the origin up to the $n$th point occurring thereafter (compare (2.12) of Beutler and Leneman, 1966b). This means that (2.12) can be rewritten as

$$E[N^2(t)] = \sum_{n=1}^{\infty} E\left[\left\{\sum_{k=1}^{n} \alpha_k\right\}^2\right]\{G_n(t) - G_{n+1}(t)\}. \tag{2.13}$$

But

$$E\left\{\left[\sum_{k=1}^{n} \alpha_k\right\}^2\right] \leqq n^2 E[\alpha_j^2],$$

and $n^2G_{n+1} \leqq n^2G_n \to 0$, as shown in the proof of Theorem 3.2.2 in Beutler and Leneman (1966b); hence, a change in the index of summation on the $G_{n+1}$ term in (2.13) is legitimate, and the same argument as in Theorem 3.2.2 of Beutler and Leneman (1966b) produces

$$E[N^2(t)] = E[\alpha_1^2]G_1(t) + \sum_{n=1}^{\infty} E\left[\alpha_{n+1}\left(\alpha_{n+1} + 2\sum_{k=1}^{n} \alpha_k\right)\right] G_{n+1}(t). \quad (2.14)$$

It is seen that the mean square value of $N(t)$ appears in terms of the correlation function for $\{\alpha_n\}$, which is hereafter denoted by

$$\rho(k) = E[\alpha_{j+k}\alpha_j] \quad (\text{any } j). \quad (2.15)$$

With this notation, (2.14) is written

$$E[N^2(t)] = \rho(0)G_1(t) + \sum_{n=1}^{\infty} \left[\rho(0) + 2\sum_{k=1}^{n} \rho(k)\right] G_{n+1}(t). \quad (2.16)$$

It is possible to express (2.16) in even more compact form, using the interval distribution functions[3] $F_n$ in place of the forward occurrence (waiting) time distribution $G_n$. From $g_n = s_n - s_{n-1}$ (lower case symbols represent derivatives of the corresponding upper case letters) and (6.1) of Beutler and Leneman (1966a), one deduces that

$$g_n(t) = \beta[F_{n-1}(t) - F_n(t)], \quad (2.17)$$

with $F_0(t) = 1$ for $t > 0$. Thus, substituting (2.17) into (2.16) yields

$$\begin{aligned} E\,[N^2(t)] = \beta \int_0^t \Big\{ & \rho(0)[1 - F_1(u)] \\ & + \sum_{n=1}^{\infty} \left[\rho(0) + 2\sum_{k=1}^{n} \rho(k)\right] [F_n(u) - F_{n+1}(u)]\Big\}\, du \end{aligned} \quad (2.18)$$

in which the interchange of integration and summation is valid because the integrand summands are dominated by an integrable series of non-negative terms (compare proof of Theorem 3.3.3 in Beutler and Leneman, 1966b). Further, $nF_n \to 0$ as $n \to \infty$, so that a change in the index of summation on the right-most term in (2.18) leads to the simplified form

$$E\,[N^2(t)] = \beta\rho(0)t + 2\beta \int_0^t \sum_{n=1}^{\infty} \rho(n)F_n(u)\, du. \quad (2.19)$$

[3] As noted in Section 3.4 of Beutler and Leneman (1966b), $F_n$ is actually the conditional probability distribution function for the $n$th point after a given starting reference (say $t$), given that there is a point at $t$. In other words, $F_n$ may be viewed as the distribution function for $n$ successive intervals.

It is convenient to call

$$K(x) = \sum_{n=1}^{\infty} \rho(n) F_n(x); \tag{2.20}$$

then substitution of (2.19) into (2.11) yields for the correlation of $N(t)$

$$E\,[N(u)N(v)] = \beta\rho(0)u + \beta\left\{\int_0^u K(x)\,dx + \int_0^v K(x)\,dx - \int_0^{v-u} K(x)\,dx\right\}, \tag{2.21}$$

whenever $0 \leqq u \leqq v$. Considerations of symmetry lead to the same expression for $v < u$, except that these two symbols are interchanged in (2.21). The cases $u \leqq v$ and $v < u$ can therefore be combined in a single relation that holds for both:

$$E\,[N(u)N(v)] = \beta\left\{\rho(0)\min(u, v) + \int_0^u K(x)\,dx + \int_0^v K(x)\,dx - \int_0^{|v-u|} K(x)\,dx\right\}. \tag{2.22}$$

It remains to differentiate (2.22) in accordance with (2.6) to obtain the correlation function for the impulse process $s(t)$ from the correlation of $N(t)$. For the derivative on $u$, one has

$$\frac{\partial\{E[N(u)N(v)]\}}{\partial u} = \beta\{\rho(0)U(v-u) + K(u) + K(|v-u|)\operatorname{sgn}(v-u)\}, \tag{2.23}$$

where $U$ is the unit step function. Upon differentiating (2.23) with respect to $v$, one finally obtains for the correlation $R_s(u, v)$

$$E[s(u)s(v)] = \beta\rho(0)\delta(v-u) + \beta\sum_{n=1}^{\infty} \rho(n) f_n(|v-u|). \tag{2.24}$$

Here $f_n$ is the derivative of $F_n$; $f_n$ may well contain delta functions corresponding to discontinuities of $F_n$. Because of the intuitive meaning imputed to $F_n$, $f_n$ can be regarded as the probability density function associated with $n$ consecutive intervals of the s.p.p. $\{t_n\}$.

Unless the sum in (2.24) can be evaluated, further explicit results cannot be readily obtained. Frequently, however, summation in closed form becomes possible when (2.24) is subjected to a Fourier transformation. This suggests that it may be easier to calculate directly the spectral density $\Phi_s(\omega)$ of $s(t)$, than to evaluate (2.24) to find its correlation. For this purpose, let

$$f_n^*(s) = \int_0^\infty f_n(t)e^{-st}\,dt \qquad (2.25)$$

which is related to the characteristic function for $n$ successive interval lengths, since $f_n(t) = 0$ for negative argument. The definition (2.25) can be extended to negative indices by taking

$$f_{-n}^*(i\omega) = f_n^*(-i\omega) \qquad (2.26)$$

and adopting the convention $f_0(i\omega) = 1$. Taking the Fourier transform of the correlation $R_s(\tau)$ (with $\tau = v - u$) furnished by (2.24) yields

$$\Phi_s(\omega) = \beta \sum_{n=-\infty}^{\infty} \rho(n) f_n^*(i\omega). \qquad (2.27)$$

The doubly-infinite sum results because

$$\int_{-\infty}^{\infty} \rho(n)f_n(|\tau|)\,e^{-i\omega\tau}\,d\tau = \int_0^\infty \rho(n)f_n(\tau)e^{-i\omega\tau}\,d\tau$$
$$+ \int_0^\infty \rho(n)f_n(\tau)e^{+i\omega\tau}\,d\tau = \rho(n)f_n^*(i\omega) + \rho(n)f_n^*(-i\omega), \qquad (2.28)$$

and $\rho(n) = \rho(-n)$. Equation (2.27) and its equivalent

$$\Phi_s(\omega) = \beta\{\rho(0) + \sum_{n=1}^{\infty} \rho(n)[f_n^*(i\omega) + f_n^*(-i\omega)]\} \qquad (2.29)$$

are relations central to this paper. They represent remarkably simple expressions for the spectrum of $s(t)$, and may be explicitly evaluated for a wide variety of pulse trains.

Even for special cases of (2.1), the second-order properties are often not well known. Yet, a simple application of (2.24) may yield useful second-order properties. For example,

$$E\left[\sum_{-\infty}^{\infty} \delta(t - t_n)\delta(t + \tau - t_n)\right] = \beta\delta(\tau) \qquad (2.30)$$

follows immediately from (2.24) with $\rho(n) = \delta_{0n}$. Similarly, $\rho(0) = 2$, $\rho(\pm k) = 1$, and other $\rho(n) = 0$ leads to a result from which (2.30) is subtracted to give

$$E\left[\sum_{n=-\infty}^{\infty}\delta(t+\tau-t_n)\delta(t-t_{n-k}) + \sum_{n=-\infty}^{\infty}\delta(t+\tau-t_n)\delta(t-t_{n+k})\right] = \beta f_k(|\tau|). \tag{2.31}$$

It is emphasized that (2.24), (2.27), and (2.29) require neither statistical independence nor identically-distributed interval lengths, as was required for the derivation in Leneman (1966a). In the latter (but not here), it was also supposed that the interval lengths are bounded away from zero [Leneman, 1966a, Eq. (27)]. Thus, the validity of many of the examples of spectral computation in the above paper was limited; the present paper permits results of greater generality.

## III. MODELS OF IMPULSE PROCESSES

Although the spectrum for the $s(t)$ of (2.1) may be discussed without reference to specific physical applications, it appears desirable to emphasize those $\{\alpha_n\}$ and $\{t_n\}$ statistics that correspond to technologically interesting $s(t)$. A large class of $s(t)$ is associated with impulse sampling of another (ordinary wide-sense stationary) random process $x(t)$; most of the examples of the next section are motivated by this application.

The desirability of a spectrum (or correlation) in closed form restricts the $\{t_n\}$ that can be usefully considered. In particular, the infinite series in (2.24) or (2.27) ought to be summable to a closed form expression. One such $\{t_n\}$ is that of a Poisson s.p.p., in which the probability of $n$ points in an interval of length $x$ is $(\beta x)^n e^{-\beta x}/n!$. This type of sampling might be encountered as pseudo-randomly timed PAM, or as an approximation to outputs from a random access memory. For the Poisson s.p.p.,

$$f_n^*(i\omega) = \left(\frac{\beta}{i\omega+\beta}\right)^n. \tag{3.1}$$

It may be that certain of the samples are lost or expunged. If these deletions are random and mutually independent, the new point process is called a skip Poisson process. Then $f_n^*$ has the same form (3.1) as before, except that the parameter $\beta$ is replaced by $(1-q)\beta$ where $q$ is the probability that a given sample is skipped (compare Parzen (1962) and Beutler and Leneman (1966a)); thus, the skip Poisson process does not require separate analysis. Another variation of the Poisson point process is obtained through systematic skipping. For instance, if $k$ separate signals are sampled in turn (e.g., time multiplexed), the $f_n^*$ for each signal becomes

$$f_n^*(i\omega) = \left(\frac{\beta}{i\omega + \beta}\right)^{kn}, \tag{3.2}$$

in which $\beta$ is the average number of points per unit time for all $k$ signals combined.

The second major class of sampling schemes considered here represents uniformly-spaced sampling modified by the introduction of interference or errors. Random mutually-independent erasures (skips), each occurring with probability $q$, may be applied to uniform sampling of period $T$ to yield

$$f_n^*(i\omega) = \left[\frac{(1-q)e^{-i\omega T}}{1 - qe^{-i\omega T}}\right]^n. \tag{3.3}$$

The sample times $t_n$ may also be jittered, that is, displaced from their nominal position (which may be called $t_n'$) by a small[4] amount $u_n$, so that the actual sampling time is

$$t_n = t_n' + u_n. \tag{3.4}$$

Now let the jitters $u_n$ applied to the $t_n'$ [of a skip process as in (3.4)] be identically distributed and pairwise independent. If each $u_n$ has characteristic function $\gamma$, the $f_n^*$ for the jittered skip process is

$$f_n^*(i\omega) = |\gamma(i\omega)|^2\left[\frac{(1-q)e^{-i\omega T}}{1 - qe^{-i\omega T}}\right]^n, \tag{3.5}$$

as shown in equation (7.20) of Beutler and Leneman (1966a). Since (3.5) generalizes (3.3), which in turn generalizes uniformly spaced sampling, only the jittered skip process of (3.5) need be considered as an example in Section IV.

There are at least two ways of relating the impulse train

$$s(t) = \sum_{-\infty}^{\infty} \alpha_n \delta(t - t_n) \tag{3.6}$$

to the sampling of a (wide-sense stationary) random process $x(t)$. At first glance, it would seem that the computation of the spectral density

[4] A "small" displacement is any that does not alter the original ordering of the $t_n$. It suffices, for instance, if the $u_n$ are restricted in their range to $[-T/2, T/2)$ or $[0, T)$.

of the sample impulses is most easily achieved by taking $\alpha_n = x(t_n)$, so that $s(t)$ itself becomes the sampled sequence. But the $\rho(n)$ defined by (2.15) is then the correlation $R_x(t_{k+n} - t_k)$ of $x(t)$, which in general depends on $t_{k+n} - t_k$ rather than just on $n$. An awkward condition on $x(t)$ would then be required to assure that $R_x(t_{k+n} - t_k)$ is a function only of $n$ for almost all realizations of $\{t_n\}$. For this reason it is generally preferable to proceed otherwise, regarding $s(t)$ as a linear modulation of $x(t)$. The sampled sequence now becomes $y(t) = s(t)x(t)$. If [as is usually true] $x(t)$ and $s(t)$ are independent random processes [or even only orthogonal], the correlation of $y(t)$ is obtained from $R_y(\tau) = R_s(\tau)R_x(\tau)$. In the frequency domain, the equivalent expression in terms of spectra becomes a convolution, viz.

$$\Phi_y(\omega) = \frac{1}{2\pi}\int_{-\infty}^{\infty} \Phi_x(\omega - u)\Phi_s(u)\, du = \Phi_x * \Phi_s. \tag{3.7}$$

Thus, the evaluation of $\Phi_y$ remains contingent on the computation of $\Phi_s$, which is the purpose of this paper.

It follows from (2.24) or (2.27) that $\{\alpha_n\}$ influences the second-order properties of $s(t)$ only through $\rho(n)$. For most sampling modulations $s(t)$, it suffices to consider $\{\alpha_n\}$ with rational spectral density (in $e^{i\omega}$); hence, one assumes that $\rho(n)$ is of the form

$$\rho(n) = \sum_{k=1}^{m}\sum_{j=0}^{r_k} a_{jk}\,|\,n\,|^j\,\rho_k^{|n|}. \tag{3.8}$$

in which $-1 \leqq \rho_k \leqq +1$. However, the correlation and spectrum of $s(t)$ is linear in $\rho(n)$, so that it is enough to calculate $R_s$ or $\Phi_s$ for a general term on the right of (3.8). For the sake of simplicity, we shall be content with the somewhat more specialized result corresponding to distinct roots in the spectrum of $\{\alpha_n\}$. Then one need only take $\rho(n)$ to be of the form

$$\rho(n) = \rho^{|n|}, \qquad -1 \leqq \rho \leqq +1. \tag{3.9}$$

The $\rho(n)$ of (3.9) and its variants cover many cases of interest. For sampling without amplitude error, $\alpha_n \equiv 1$, so that $\rho(n) = 1$ for all $n$. Plus-minus sampling corresponds to $\rho(n) = (-1)^n$, whence $\rho = -1$. It is also possible to introduce amplitude error in the sampling procedure, taking

$$\alpha_n = 1 + w_n, \tag{3.10}$$

$w_n$ being a scaling error in the magnitude of the sample taken at $t_n$. If $w_n$ has zero mean and variance $\sigma^2$, and the $w_n$ are exponentially correlated, one has

$$\rho(n) = 1 + \sigma^2 \rho^{|n|}. \tag{3.11}$$

It is easy to specialize (3.11) to uncorrelated amplitude errors by taking $\rho = 0$, with $\rho^0 = 1$.

It will be observed that the correlation between the pulse amplitudes $\alpha_n$ appearing in (3.6) depends not on the time intervals between pulses, but only on the count of pulses. For instance, $\{t_n\}$ might be a skip process, in which case the correlation between successive pulse intensities would fail to depend on the number of skips intervening. The latter situation suggests that a more appropriate model (for some applications) would render such correlation a function of the time between samples. To this end, consider

$$s(t) = \sum_{-\infty}^{\infty} \alpha_n' y_n \delta(t - t_n), \tag{3.12}$$

in which each $y_n$ is zero or unity according as the corresponding $t_n$ is to be skipped or not. If skipping is again to occur with probability $q$, and the erasures are mutually independent, $E[y_{m+n} y_m] = (1 - q)^2 + q(1 - q)\delta_{0n}$, where $\delta_{0n}$ is the Kronecker delta. Further, it may be assumed that the $\alpha_n'$ are correlated in accordance with (3.9). Then, if one writes $\alpha_n = \alpha_n' y_n$ to reduce (3.12) to (3.6), one obtains for the correlation $\rho(n)$ of $\{\alpha_n\}$

$$\rho(n) = (1 - q)^2 \rho^{|n|} + q(1 - q)\delta_{0n}. \tag{3.13}$$

The model just described is called the time correlated skip model, whereas the earlier one is designated as the number interval correlated skip model.

Spectra of jittered sampling have been investigated by others (Balakrishnan, 1962; Brown, 1963), but the work presented here generalizes these studies by also permitting skips as well as correlated amplitude errors. Moreover, Brown's distinction between locked jitter and separate read-in and read-out jitters (Brown, 1963) can also be carried through here. As in Brown's paper, read-in jitter denotes the displacement of the samples in time by a jitter perturbation, whereas read-out jitter refers to a sample at $t_n'$, [i.e., $x(t_n')$] being read out at a different time $t_n$. The appropriate expression for separate read-in and read-out jittered sampling with skips and time interval correlated amplitude errors is

$$y(t) = \sum_{-\infty}^{\infty} \alpha_n' y_n x(t_n') \delta(t - t_n), \tag{3.14}$$

in which $\{t_n'\}$ is the original sampling process with jitters $u_n$, i.e.,

$$t_n' = t_{00} + nT + u_n . \tag{3.15}$$

Here $t_{00}$ is uniformly distributed on the interval $[0, T)$, and the $u_n$ (jitter process) are pairwise independent, independent of $t_{00}$, and distributed in some manner over $0 \leqq u_n < T$. $\{t_n\}$ is also a jitter process; the $t_n$ are specified by

$$t_n = t_{00} + nT + v_n . \tag{3.16}$$

It is assumed that $\{v_n\}$ is independent of $t_{00}$ and $\{u_n\}$, and that the $v_n$ are pairwise-independent, identically-distributed random variables, each taking on values in the interval $[0, T)$. The other notations and assumptions of (3.14) are identically those introduced earlier in the section. For locked jitter (with time correlated amplitude errors under skipping), (3.16) is replaced by $t_n = t_n'$; this corresponds precisely to the previously discussed (3.12).

Although there are many other impulse processes whose spectra can (and have) been calculated by the methods suggested in this paper, computations for the above processes will suffice to illustrate the power and nature of the methods proposed herein.

## IV. MOMENTS OF IMPULSE PROCESSES: EXAMPLES

This section is devoted to the computation of spectra and/or correlations of $s(t)$ [or $y(t)$, as applicable]. Although the section's title might imply that other moments (the mean of $s(t)$ and cross-correlation $R_{xy}$) are also to be found, these latter will receive little further attention. Indeed, the mean of the impulse process $s(t)$ is obtained almost by inspection from (2.7), while for the cross-correlation one has

$$R_{xy}(\tau) = E[x(t + \tau)y(t)] = E[x(t + \tau)x(t)s(t)] = \alpha\beta R_x(\tau)$$

by virtue of the assumed independence of $x(t)$ and $s(t)$. Thus, the significant task is the computation of the correlation and/or spectrum of $s(t)$ [or $y(t)$], and it is with this that the remainder of the paper is concerned.

For the first example, consider *Poisson sampling with exponentially* *correlated amplitudes*. Here $\rho(n)$ is given by (3.9), and $f_n^*$ by (3.1); these are substituted into (2.29), which may also be written as

$$\Phi_s(\omega) = \beta\left\{\rho(0) + 2\Re\left[\sum_{n=1}^{\infty} \rho(n) f_n^*(i\omega)\right]\right\}. \tag{4.1}$$

In (4.1), $\Re$ denotes "real part of," the formula being valid because $f_n^*(i\omega)$ and $f_n^*(-i\omega)$ are complex conjugates. The principal task in the evaluation of (4.1) is the summation of the series

$$\sum_{n=1}^{\infty} \rho(n) f_n^*(i\omega).$$

In the case of the Poisson s.p.p., the latter is a power series, and the relation

$$\sum_{n=1}^{\infty} z^n = z(1 - z)^{-1}$$

is applicable. Upon performing the indicated operations on the series, and taking the real part of the result, one obtains for the spectral density

$$\Phi_s(\omega) = \beta \frac{\omega^2 + \beta^2(1 - \rho^2)}{\omega^2 + \beta^2(1 - \rho)^2}. \tag{4.2}$$

It is easy to find the spectral density for *plus-minus Poisson sampling* from (4.2); one simply sets $\rho = -1$ in (4.2). Then

$$\Phi_s(\omega) = \frac{\beta\omega^2}{\omega^2 + 4\beta^2}. \tag{4.3}$$

Similarly, one could set $\rho = +1$ to model *ordinary Poisson sampling*. However, the behavior of $\Phi_s(\omega)$ near $\omega = 0$ is then incompletely specified. The possible anomaly can be avoided by using (2.24) to determine the correlation $R_s$. Since $\rho(n) = 1$, and

$$f_n(\tau) = \beta(\beta\tau)^{n-1}e^{-\beta\tau}/(n - 1)!, \qquad \tau \geqq 0, \tag{4.4}$$

$$R_s(\tau) = \beta[\delta(\tau) + \beta], \tag{4.5}$$

whence (taking the Fourier transform of $R_s$)

$$\Phi_s(\omega) = \beta[1 + 2\pi\beta\delta(\omega)]. \tag{4.6}$$

The *alternated Poisson sampling* process consists of Poisson skip sampling with every other point deleted. This means that $f_n^*$ is specified by (3.2) with $k = 2$. One may again substitute in (4.1) with $\rho(n) = 1$, thereby obtaining a power series which is well behaved except at $\omega = 0$. To find the value of $\Phi_s(0)$, it suffices to note that $s(t)$ has mean $\beta/2$, so that $\Phi_s$ has a delta function of intensity $\beta^2\pi/2$ at the origin. The complete expression for $\Phi_s$ is then

$$\Phi_s(\omega) = \beta\left[\frac{\omega^2 + 2\beta^2}{\omega^2 + 4\beta^2} + \frac{\pi\beta\delta(\omega)}{2}\right]. \tag{4.7}$$

This formula was found via a different approach by Mazzetti, 1962, and (along with the others related to Poisson sampling) also appears in Leneman, 1966a.

The remainder of the results presented here are motivated by consideration of errors arising in (supposedly) uniformly-spaced sampling. The spectral density of a *skip jittered sampling sequence with exponentially number interval correlated amplitudes* is calculated first. This means that $s(t)$ is given by (3.6), with the $\rho(n)$ of (3.9) and $f_n^*$ of (3.5). Evaluation of

$$\sum_{n=1}^{\infty} \rho(n) f_n^*(i\omega)$$

once more amounts to the summation of a power series, the sum being

$$\sum_{n=1}^{\infty} \rho(n) f_n^*(i\omega) = \frac{\rho(1-q)e^{-i\omega T}}{1 - \mu e^{-i\omega T}}, \tag{4.8}$$

where the parameter $\mu$ is given by

$$\mu = (1-q)\rho + q = \rho + (1-\rho)q. \tag{4.9}$$

Now (4.8) is substituted into (4.1), in which $\beta = (1-q)/T$ and $\rho(0) = 1$. Some manipulation leads to an expression for $\Phi_s$ in terms of the Poisson kernel (Hoffman, 1962)

$$P(\mu, \omega) = \frac{1 - \mu^2}{1 - 2\mu \cos \omega T + \mu^2}, \tag{4.10}$$

that is,

$$\Phi_s(\omega) = \frac{1-q}{T}\left\{1 - \frac{(1-q)\rho\,|\gamma(i\omega)|^2}{\mu} + \frac{(1-q)\rho\,|\gamma(i\omega)|^2}{\mu} P(\mu, \omega)\right\}. \tag{4.11}$$

The general result (4.11) may be specialized in various directions. If, for instance, there is no jitter, $\gamma$ is taken as unity, while no skipping makes $q = 0$. Other interesting cases are those of the *ordinary skip jittered sampling sequence* and the *plus-minus skip jittered sampling sequence*.[5] For the former, $\rho(n) = 1$ (since all $\alpha_n = 1$), so that $\rho = 1$, and hence $\mu = 1$. The latter is characterized by $\rho(n) = (-1)^n$, whence $\rho = -1$ and $\mu = 2q - 1$. An attempt to apply (4.11) directly to ordinary skip jittered sampling then fails because both numerator and denominator of (4.10) are zero. However, $P(\mu, \omega)$ is an approximate identity (Hoffman, 1962) so that it is proper to use the interpretation (Hoffman, 1962; Lighthill, 1958)

$$\lim_{\mu \to +1} P(\mu, \omega) = \frac{2\pi}{T} \sum_{-\infty}^{\infty} \delta\left(\omega - \frac{2\pi n}{T}\right). \tag{4.12}$$

The spectral density for ordinary skip jittered sampling then becomes

$$\begin{aligned} \Phi_s(\omega) = \frac{1-q}{T}\Bigg\{1 - (1-q)\,|\gamma(i\omega)|^2 \\ + \frac{2\pi(1-q)}{T} \sum_{n=-\infty}^{\infty} \left|\gamma\left(\frac{2\pi n i}{T}\right)\right|^2 \delta\left(\omega - \frac{2\pi n}{T}\right)\Bigg\}. \end{aligned} \tag{4.13}$$

Interestingly enough, the format of the spectrum for plus-minus skip jittered sampling depends on the skip probability. For high skip probabilities, i.e., $q > \frac{1}{2}$, $\mu > 0$, (4.11) remains applicable; as before, $P(\mu, \omega)$ attains its maxima at $\omega = 2\pi n/T$. When $q = \frac{1}{2}$, $\mu = 0$, so that direct evaluation of (4.11) is impracticable. However, one may return to (4.8), noting that twice its real part is now merely $-\cos \omega T$. According to (4.1), the spectrum is then

$$\Phi_s(\omega) = \frac{1}{2T}\{1 - |\gamma(i\omega)|^2 \cos \omega T\}. \tag{4.14}$$

With passage to smaller skip probabilities, $0 < q < \frac{1}{2}$, $\mu$ becomes negative. Since

$$P(\mu, \omega) = P\left(-\mu, \omega + \frac{\pi}{T}\right), \tag{4.15}$$

[5] It is characteristic of this model that successive samples alternate in sign, regardless of the multiple of $T$ that (due to skipping) separates adjacent sample times $t_n$.

the periodic minima of $P(\mu, \omega)$ occur at $\omega = 2\pi n/T$. Since $\mu$ is negative, $P(\mu, \omega)/\mu$ has its maxima at these $\omega$; hence, there are definite maxima at the same $\omega$ for all $0 < q < 1$ except $q = \frac{1}{2}$. Only $q = 0$ (no skipping) remains to be considered. This $q$ corresponds to $\mu = -1$, so that it is necessary to use

$$\lim_{\mu \to -1} P(\mu, \omega) = \frac{2\pi}{T} \sum_{-\infty}^{\infty} \delta\left(\omega - \frac{(2n+1)\pi}{T}\right) \tag{4.16}$$

in applying (4.11) to plus-minus jittered sampling (without skips). The spectral density for this type of sampling is now

$$\Phi_s(\omega) = \frac{1}{T}\left\{[1 - |\gamma(i\omega)|^2] + \frac{2\pi}{T} \sum_{-\infty}^{\infty} \left|\gamma\left(\frac{[2n+1]\pi i}{T}\right)\right|^2 \delta\left(\omega - \frac{(2n+1)\pi}{T}\right)\right\}. \tag{4.17}$$

The calculations made earlier suffice for finding the spectral density of *skip jittered sampling with exponentially number interval correlated scaling errors*. In fact, the desired result is a weighted linear combination of (4.11) and (4.13), because of (3.11) and the linearity of $\Phi_s$ with $\rho$. For such sampling, therefore, the sampling sequence spectral density is given by

$$\Phi_s(\omega) = \frac{1-q}{T}\left\{\sigma^2\left[1 - \frac{(1-q)\rho\,|\gamma(i\omega)|^2}{\mu}\right] + [1 - (1-q)\,|\gamma(i\omega)|^2] + (1-q)\,|\gamma(i\omega)|^2 \cdot\left[\frac{2\pi}{T}\sum_{-\infty}^{\infty}\delta\left(\omega - \frac{2\pi n}{T}\right) + \frac{\rho\sigma^2}{\mu} P(\mu, \omega)\right]\right\}. \tag{4.18}$$

Each of the above skip jitter sampling models has a counterpart in which the impulse strengths are time correlated rather than number correlated. The impulse train is described by (3.12), with the $\rho(n)$ furnished by (3.13). Upon substituting (3.13) and $|\gamma(i\omega)|^2 e^{-i\omega nT}$ into (4.1), one need only sum the resulting power series. The spectral density for a *skip jittered sampling sequence with exponentially time correlated amplitudes* is therefore

$$\Phi_s(\omega) = \frac{1-q}{T}\{1 - (1-q)\,|\gamma(i\omega)|^2 + (1-q)\,|\gamma(i\omega)|^2 P(\rho, \omega)\}. \tag{4.19}$$

Term-by-term comparison of (4.19) with (4.11) (the corresponding spectral density for number interval correlated amplitudes) shows the two to be identical iff $\rho = 1$ (all pulses unit intensity) or $q = 0$ (no skipping), just as would be expected. In fact, both models of ordinary skip jittered sampling sequences represent the same impulse process. However, the *plus-minus skip jittered sampling sequence* derived from (3.12) differs from that considered earlier. Now (compare footnote 5) successive samples have the same sign if they are separated by an odd number of skipped $t_n$, and opposite signs if the number of skipped $t_n$ is odd. In contrast to the dependence of the format of the spectral density on skip probability $q$ as in the earlier model, the plus-minus skip jittered sampling of (3.12) always has line spectrum components at $\omega = (2n + 1)\pi/T$ (all integer $n$). More precisely, its spectral density is

$$\Phi_s(\omega) = \frac{1-q}{T}\Bigg\{1 - (1-q)\,|\,\gamma(i\omega)\,|^2 + \frac{2\pi(1-q)}{T}\sum_{-\infty}^{\infty}\left|\gamma\left(\frac{[2n+1]\pi i}{T}\right)\right|^2 \delta\left(\omega - \frac{(2n+1)\pi}{T}\right)\Bigg\}. \tag{4.20}$$

A linear combination of (4.13) and (4.19) yields the spectral density of *skip jittered sampling with exponentially time correlated scaling errors*. This is the model represented by (3.14), with read-in and read-out times furnished by (3.15) and (3.16), respectively. Now (3.14) may be reduced to (3.6) by redefining $\alpha_n = \alpha_n' y_n x(t_n')$, and taking $\{t_n\}$ to be a jitter process without skips, the characteristic function of the jitters $v_n$ being designated $\mu$. Then the spectral density of the sampled signal is

$$\Phi_y(\omega) = \rho(0) + |\,\gamma(i\omega)\,|^2\left(\sum_{-\infty}^{\infty}\rho(n)e^{-i\omega nT} - \rho(0)\right). \tag{4.22}$$

In order to complete the calculation of $\Phi_y$, it is necessary to evaluate $\rho(n)$, and to find the indicated sum in (4.22). Because of the assumed independence of the pertinent random processes, and in view of their wide-sense stationarity,

$$\rho(n) = \rho'(n)E[R_x(t_{m+n}' - t_m')]E[y_{m+n}y_m]. \tag{4.23}$$

In (4.23), $\rho'(n)$ refers to $E[\alpha_{m+n}'\alpha_m']$,

$$E[y_{m+n}y_m] = \begin{cases}(1-q) & n = 0\\ (1-q)^2 & n \neq 0\end{cases} \tag{4.24}$$

as in the discussion following (3.12), and $E[R_x(t'_{m+n} - t_m')]$ is meant to be the expectation on $\{u_n\}$. The latter can be conveniently expressed in terms of the spectral density $\Phi_x$ of $x(t)$. If $\lambda'(n)$ is used to denote $E[R_x(t'_{m+n} - t_m')]$, an interchange of expectation and integration yields

$$\lambda'(n) = \frac{1}{2\pi}\int_{-\infty}^{\infty} \Phi_x(\omega) E[e^{i\omega(t'_{m+n} - t_m')}]\, d\omega. \tag{4.25}$$

Now $t'_{m+n} - t_m' = nT + (u_{m+n} - u_m)$, so that for $n \neq 0$

$$\lambda'(n) = \frac{1}{2\pi}\int_{-\infty}^{\infty} \Phi_x(\omega) \mid \mu(i\omega) \mid^2 e^{i\omega nT}\, d\omega, \tag{4.26}$$

$\mu$ being the characteristic function of each read-in jitter variable $u_n$ (the $u_n$ are assumed pairwise independent). The role of $\lambda'$ is clarified by dividing up the real line [interval of integration in (4.26)] into intervals of length $2\pi$, so that (4.26) becomes

$$\lambda'(n) = \frac{1}{2\pi}\int_{-\pi}^{\pi} \left[\sum_{-\infty}^{\infty} \Phi_x(\omega - 2\pi k) \mid \mu(i\omega - 2\pi ik) \mid^2\right] e^{i\omega n}\, d\omega; \tag{4.27}$$

this exhibits $\lambda'(n)$, $n \neq 0$, as the $n$th Fourier coefficient of the bracketed expression in (4.27). In general, one should choose the intervals into which the integral (4.26) is divided to be of length $2\pi/T$ rather than just $2\pi$; however, for convenience (only) we are assuming here and henceforth that $T = 1$. Since $\lambda'(n)$ represents the Fourier coefficients of

$$\sum_{-\infty}^{\infty} \Phi_x(\omega - 2\pi k) \mid \mu(i\omega - 2\pi ik) \mid^2$$

only for $n \neq 0$, one defines

$$\lambda(n) = \begin{cases} \lambda'(n) & n \neq 0 \\ \dfrac{1}{2\pi}\displaystyle\int_{-\infty}^{\infty} \Phi_x(\omega) \mid \mu(i\omega) \mid^2 d\omega & n = 0, \end{cases} \tag{4.28}$$

which gives the Fourier coefficients over $(-\pi, \pi)$ of this sum for all $n$. In other words

$$\sum_{-\infty}^{\infty} \lambda(n) e^{-i\omega n} = \sum_{-\infty}^{\infty} \Phi_x(\omega - 2\pi k) \mid \mu(i\omega - 2\pi ik) \mid^2. \tag{4.29}$$

With the further simplifying assumption (made without loss of generality) that $E[x^2(t)] = 1$, $\lambda'(0) = 1$, and the coefficients $\rho(n)$ in (4.22) become

$$\rho(0) = (1 - q)(1 + \sigma^2) \tag{4.30}$$

and since $\lambda'$ is even,

$$\rho(n) = (1 - q)^2(1 + \sigma^2\rho^{|n|})\lambda'(|n|), \qquad n \neq 0. \tag{4.31}$$

Substitution of this $\rho(n)$ into (4.22) yields

$$\begin{aligned}\Phi_y(\omega) = (1 - q)\Big\{&(1 + \sigma^2)[1 - (1 - q) \mid \gamma(i\omega) \mid^2 \lambda(0)] \\ &+ (1 - q) \mid \gamma(i\omega) \mid^2 \Big[\sum_{-\infty}^{\infty} \lambda(n)e^{-i\omega n} \\ &+ \sigma^2 \sum_{-\infty}^{\infty} \lambda(n)\rho^{|n|}e^{-i\omega n}\Big]\Big\}.\end{aligned} \tag{4.32}$$

The first sum in (4.32) is evaluated from (4.29). The second sum is the Fourier expansion at $z = \rho e^{-i\omega}$ of the analytic function specified on the unit circle by the right side of (4.29). It is well known (Hoffman, 1962) that this function is furnished by a convolution with the Poisson kernel[6], viz.

$$\begin{aligned}\sum_{-\infty}^{\infty} \lambda(n)\rho^{|n|}e^{-i\omega n} &= \frac{1}{2\pi}\int_{-\pi}^{\pi} \sum_{k=-\infty}^{\infty} \Phi_x(u - 2\pi k) \mid \mu(iu - 2\pi ik) \mid^2 \\ &\qquad \cdot P(\rho, \omega - u)\, du \\ &= \Big[\sum_{-\infty}^{\infty} \Phi_x(\omega - 2\pi k) \mid \mu(i\omega - 2\pi ik) \mid^2\Big] * P(\rho, \omega).\end{aligned} \tag{4.33}$$

Using (4.29) and (4.33) in (4.32) leads to the final form

$$\begin{aligned}\Phi_y(\omega) = (1 - q)\Big\{&(1 + \sigma^2)\Big[1 - (1 - q) \mid \gamma(i\omega) \mid^2 \\ &+ \frac{1}{2\pi}\int_{-\infty}^{\infty} \Phi_x(\omega) \mid \mu(i\omega) \mid^2 d\omega\Big] \\ &+ (1 - q) \mid \gamma(i\omega) \mid^2\Big[\sum_{-\infty}^{\infty} \Phi_x(\omega - 2\pi k) \mid \mu(i\omega - 2\pi ik) \mid^2 \\ &+ \sigma^2\Big(\sum_{-\infty}^{\infty} \Phi_x(\omega - 2\pi k) \mid \mu(i\omega - 2\pi ik) \mid^2\Big) * P(\rho, \omega)\Big]\Big\}.\end{aligned} \tag{4.34}$$

[6] The right-hand sum in (4.29) converges almost everywhere, and is integrable over $[-\pi, \pi]$; hence the asserted representation as a convolution with the Poisson kernel is valid for $0 < \rho < 1$. For $-1 < \rho < 0$, the result is still valid, but with $\rho$ replaced by $|\rho|$, and $\omega$ by $\omega + \pi$.

It is interesting to compare the above result with the spectral density for locked (in place of independent) jitters. If the jitters are locked, $s(t)$ is furnished by (3.12), since

$$y(t) = x(t)s(t) = \sum_{-\infty}^{\infty} \alpha_n' x(t_n) y_n \delta(t - t_n).$$

For an $s(t)$ of this form, the spectral density is already available from (4.21). Specializing the latter with $T = 1$, and carrying out the convolution of spectra implied by $y(t) = x(t)s(t)$, yields for a *sampled signal with locked read-in and read-out jitters, skips, and time-correlated scaling errors*

$$\Phi_y(\omega) = (1 - q)\Big\{(1 + \sigma^2)[1 - (1 - q)(|\gamma|^2 \,\bar{*}\, \Phi_x)] + (1 - q)\Big[\sum_{-\infty}^{\infty} \Phi_x(\omega - 2\pi k)\,|\gamma(\omega - 2\pi k)|^2 + \sigma^2(|\gamma|^2 P(\rho, \cdot) \,\bar{*}\, \Phi_x)\Big]\Big\}. \tag{4.35}$$

The symbol $\bar{*}$ has been introduced to denote convolution over the entire real axis, rather than over the interval $[-\pi, \pi]$. Since (except in the trivial case of no jitter) "small" jitter variables preclude that $\gamma$ be periodic with period $2\pi$, (4.35) cannot be modified to a convolution form similar to that of (4.34).

*Note added in proof:* The authors thank one of the referees for directing their attention to the work of Kryukov, 1967. His results unify some earlier calculations of spectra of impulse processes by deriving a formula like our (2.24); however, he treats only impulses of the same fixed intensity and sampling points specified by a renewal process.

RECEIVED: June 21, 1967.

REFERENCES

BALAKRISHNAN, A. (1962), On the problem of time jitter in sampling. *IRE Trans. Inform. Theory* **IT-8**, 226–236.

BANTA, E. D. (1964), A note on the correlation function of non-independent, overlapping pulse trains. *IEEE Trans. Inform. Theory* **IT-10**, 160–161.

BEUTLER, F. J. AND LENEMAN, O. A. Z. (1966a), Random sampling of random processes: stationary point processes. *Inform. Control* **9**, 325–346.

BEUTLER, F. J. AND LENEMAN, O. A. Z. (1966b), The theory of stationary point processes. *Acta Math.* **116**, 159–197.

BROWN, W. M. (1963), Sampling with random jitter. *J. Soc. Ind. Appl. Math.* **11**, 460–473.

GUPTA, S. C., AND JURY, E. I. (1962), Statistical study of pulse-width modulated control systems. *J. Franklin Inst.* **273**, 292–321.

HOFFMAN, K. (1962), "Banach Spaces of Analytic Functions." Prentice-Hall, Englewood Cliffs, N.J., 1962.

KHURGIN, Y. I. (1957), A class of random impulse processes. *Radiotekhn. Elektron.* **2**, 371–379.

KRYUKOV, V. I. (1967), Calculation of the correlation function and the spectral power density of random sampling. *Radio Engr. and Elec. Phys.* **12**, 169–176.

KUZNETSOV, P. I., AND STRATONOVICH, R. L. (1956), On the mathematical theory of correlated random points. *Izv. Akad. Nauk SSR, Ser. Mat.* **20**, 167–178. Edited transl. by J. A. McFadden.

LEE, Y. W. (1960), "Statistical Theory of Communication." Wiley, New York.

LENEMAN, O. A. Z. (1966a), Random sampling of random processes: impulse processes. *Inform. Control* **9**, 347–363.

LENEMAN, O. A. Z. (1966b), Random sampling of random processes: optimum linear interpolation. *J. Franklin Inst.* **281**, 302–314.

LENEMAN, O. A. Z., AND LEWIS, J. B. (1966), Random sampling of random processes: mean-square comparison of various interpolators. *IEEE Trans. Autom. Control* **AC-11**, 396–403.

LIGHTHILL, M. J. (1958), "Introduction to Fourier Analysis and Generalized Functions." Cambridge Univ. Press, London.

MAZZETTI, P. (1962), Study of nonindependent random pulse trains, with application to the Barkhausen noise. *Nuovo Cimento* **25**, 1323–1342.

MAZZETTI, P. (1964), Correlation function and power spectrum of a train of nonindependent overlapping pulses having random shape and amplitude. *Nuovo Cimento* **31**, 88–97.

NELSEN, D. E. (1964), Calculation of power density spectra for a class of randomly jittered waveforms. *Quart. Progr. Rept.* **74**, 168–179. (Research Laboratory of Electronics, Massachusetts Institute of Technology, Cambridge, Mass.)

PARZEN, E. (1962), "Stochastic Processes." Holden-Day, San Francisco.

STRATONOVICH, R. L. (1963), "Topics in the Theory of Random Noise." Vol. 1, trans. by R. A. Silverman. Gordon and Breach, New York.

# 7



Reprinted from *Inform. and Control,* **18**(4), 326–341 (1971)

## On the Statistics of Random Pulse Processes*

FREDERICK J. BEUTLER

*Computer, Information and Control Engineering Program,*
*University of Michigan, Ann Arbor, Michigan 48104*

AND

OSCAR A. Z. LENEMAN

Statistics are obtained for pulse trains in which the pulse shapes as well as the time base are random. The general expression derived for the mean and spectral density of the pulse train require neither independence of intervals between time base points nor independence of the pulses. The spectral density appears as an infinite series that can be summed to closed form in many applications (e.g., pulse duration modulation with skipped and jittered samples). If the time base is a Poisson point process and the pulse shapes are independent, stronger results become available; we are then able to calculate joint characteristic functions for the pulse process, thus providing a more complete statistical description. Examples are given, illustrating use of the above results for pulse duration modulation (with arbitrary pulse shapes) and telephone traffic.

### INTRODUCTION

In various applications involving pulse trains, both the pulse shape and the time base are random in nature. As one example, consider pulse duration modulation (PDM) of a random signal with irregular sampling times caused by jitter and the random loss of pulses. A second example concerns disturbances in a receiver due to an electrical storm; the times and effects of lightning bolts are each random. There are also phenomena not ordinarily

* Research sponsored by the Air Force Office of Scientific Research, AFSC, USAF, under Grant No. AFOSR-70-1920, and by Lincoln Laboratory, a center for research operated by the Massachusetts Institute for Technology with support from the U.S. Air Force. The United States Government is authorized to reproduce and distribute reprints for Governmental purposes notwithstanding any copyright notation hereon.

regarded as having random pulse shapes and time base, but which may be interpreted as such a pulse train. An example of this type is the number of telephone lines in use when the length of calls as well as their origination times are random.

In this paper, we show how some of the statistics of pulse trains with random pulse shapes and random time base may be calculated. Two techniques are discussed. The first of these results in general expressions for the means and spectra of such pulse trains; these expressions are valid also for correlated pulses and time bases with intervals between pulses that may be neither independent nor identically distributed. The other technique yields even more information, namely the first and second order probability densities for the pulse process, but under the more restrictive condition that the time base is a Poisson point process.[1]

The second order statistics of the impulse train

$$s(t) = \sum_{-\infty}^{\infty} \alpha_n \delta(t - t_n) \tag{1.1}$$

were considered by the authors in an earlier paper (1968). The time base $\{t_n\}$ was assumed to be a stationary point process [Beutler and Leneman (1966a) and (1966b)], while $\{\alpha_n\}$ was taken to be a wide stationary discrete parameter process with specified covariance. From the second order properties of $s(t)$ it is easy to deduce similar results for $\sum_{-\infty}^{\infty} \alpha_n h(t - t_n)$, thus treating pulses of fixed shape with random amplitude and time base; the pulse train $\sum_{-\infty}^{\infty} \alpha_n h(t - t_n)$ merely represents the $s(t)$ of (1.1) after its passage through a linear time-invariant filter with response function $h(\cdot)$. However, this model is incapable of generalization to pulse trains in which the shapes of the respective pulses may vary also. For that case we must analyze the statistics of

$$y(t) = \sum_{-\infty}^{\infty} h_n(t - t_n), \tag{1.2}$$

in which $\{t_n\}$ is again the random time base (a stationary point process) and $h_n(\cdot)$ is the $n$-th pulse. A typical pulse train of this type is shown in Fig. 1. It is seen that $\sum_{-\infty}^{\infty} \alpha_n h(t - t_n)$ becomes a special case of $y(t)$ when we take $h_n(t) = \alpha_n h(t)$ in (1.2)

In the next section, we shall find universal formulas for the mean and spectral density of the $y(t)$ of (1.2) under the following hypotheses. It is

[1] For this restricted case, the spectrum (only) is calculated in Mazzetti (1964).

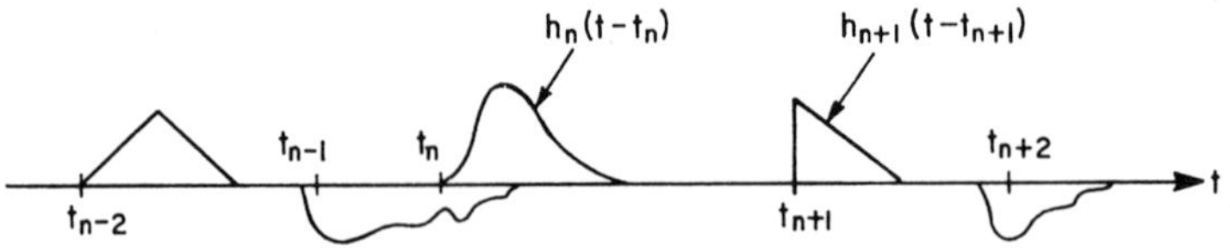


FIG. 1. A realization of a train of randomly shaped pulses.

supposed that $\{t_n\}$ is an ergodic stationary point process, and that the random functions $\{h_n(t)\}$ are independent of $\{t_n\}$ with means

$$E[h_n(t)] = m(t) \tag{1.3}$$

that do not depend on $n$. The transform covariance for $\{h_n(t)\}$ is

$$\Gamma_n{}^*(\omega) = E[H_{m+n}(\omega)\, \overline{H_m(\omega)}], \tag{1.4}$$

where the overline denotes complex conjugacy and $H_k(\omega)$ is the Fourier transform of $h_k(t)$. The point of (1.4) is that the indicated expectation satisfies the weak stationarity condition that it does not depend on $m$, but only on $n$.

The class of stationary point processes for which the spectral density expression is obtained embraces most $\{t_n\}$ considered to be realistic time bases. Poisson point processes are included, as well as uniformly timed sampling that has been subjected to random jitter and/or random deletion (skipping) of pulses. Other possible variations on the stationary point processes include systematic skipping of some originally existent points, and points at intervals of varying lengths following a planned or random sequence. Stationary point processes are analyzed in Beutler and Leneman, (1966a) and (1966b), and the statistics of point processes required for this paper are calculated therein.

## First and Second Order Statistics

The mean and spectral density for the $y(t)$ of (1.2) can be derived in terms of simple closed form expressions. The spectral density appears as an infinite series in terms of $\Gamma_n{}^*$ and $f_n{}^*$, where the latter is the generating function of the distance separating $n$ successive points, i.e., of $t_{k+n} - t_k$. As will be seen from the examples that follow the derivation, the infinite series representing the spectral density of the pulse train can be summed to an analytical expression for many models of interest in applications. The arguments used will be heuristic, but the validity of the final results can be established either by alternative methods (in the time domain) or by justifying the various types in the calculation.

The mean $y(t)$ is computed by taking expectations of (1.2) successively on $\{h_n(t)\}$ and $\{t_n\}$. Because of the independence of these two random processes

$$E[y(t)] = E\left[\sum_{-\infty}^{\infty} h_n(t - t_n)\right] = E\left[\sum_{-\infty}^{\infty} m(t - t_n)\right]. \tag{2.1}$$

Now if we let $s(t) = \sum \delta(t - t_n)$ it is possible to write

$$m(t - t_n) = \int_{-\infty}^{\infty} m(t - \tau)\, s(\tau)\, d\tau \tag{2.2}$$

and hence

$$E[y(t)] = E\left[\int_{-\infty}^{\infty} m(t - \tau)\, s(\tau)\, d\tau\right]. \tag{2.3}$$

From an interchange of expectation and integration in (2.3) one then obtains

$$E[y(t)] = \beta \int_{-\infty}^{\infty} m(u)\, du. \tag{2.4}$$

In the formula (2.4) $E[s(t)] = \beta$ represents the average number of pulses per unit time. The expectation of $s(t)$ has been derived in Beutler and Leneman (1968), and values of the mean number of points per unit time $\beta$ are available for a wide variety of stationary point processes in Beutler and Leneman (1966b).

The spectral density $S_y$ can be adduced by first computing the correlation $E[y(t + \tau)\, y(t)]$ and then taking the Fourier transform of the expectation. This method has been used for the $s(t)$ of (1.1) in Beutler and Leneman (1968), but becomes inconvenient when an attempt is made to generalize the same technique to $y(t)$. The same result may be attained more simply by utilizing the direct method [Davenport and Root (1958), p. 108], which means that we use the formula

$$S_y(\omega) = \lim_{T\to\infty} E\left(\frac{1}{T}\left|\int_0^T y(t)\, e^{-i\omega t}\, dt\right|^2\right). \tag{2.5}$$

The indicated limit is best taken by letting $T = \beta^{-1}N$, with $N$ then tending toward infinity through the integers to attain the desired limit. Such $T$ is convenient because it allows us to suppose that for large $N$ approximately $N$ pulses fall into the interval $(0, \beta^{-1}N]$. This is indeed true if $\{t_n\}$ is an ergodic stationary point process as defined in Section 3.6 of Beutler and Leneman (1966a); i.e., if the average number of points in $(0, T]$ tends toward $\beta$ for almost every realization as $T \to \infty$.[2] We also assume that the interval $(0, \beta^{-1}N]$ is sufficiently large so that the contributions of pulses intruding from outside the interval and tails of pulses lost by restricting the interval are negligible compared with $N$. Then over $(0, \beta^{-1}N]$ $y(t)$ is approximated $\sum_k^{k+N-1} h_n(t - t_n)$, where $t_k$ is the first point past the origin. Insofar as the statistics of the sum are concerned, $k$ is irrelevant because of the stationarity of $\{t_n\}$ and the assumption (1.4) which permits us to translate the indices of $H_n$. Accordingly, we take $k = 1$ and obtain asymptotically

$$\int_0^{\beta^{-1}N} y(t)\, e^{-i\omega t}\, dt = \sum_1^N H_n(\omega)\, e^{-i\omega t_n}. \tag{2.6}$$

This expression is substituted into (2.5). On multiplying it by its conjugate and taking its expectation we find that

$$E\left|\int_0^{\beta^{-1}N} y(t)\, e^{-i\omega t}\, dt\right|^2 = \sum_{m,n=1}^N \Gamma^*_{n-m}(\omega)\, E\{\exp[-i\omega(t_n - t_m)]\}. \tag{2.7}$$

The right hand expectation represents (for $n \geqslant m$) the characteristic function for $n - m$ successive intervals between points. If the probability density function for the length of $k$ successive intervals[3] is called $f_k$, we may define $f_k^*$ as the corresponding characteristic function and write $f_k^*$ as

$$f_k^*(i\omega) = \int_0^\infty e^{-i\omega x} f_k(x)\, dx = E\{\exp[-i\omega(t_{j+k} - t_j)]\}. \tag{2.8}$$

For many stationary point processes of interest in applications, the $f_k^*$ have been calculated in Beutler and Leneman (1966b). The negative indices on the right side of (2.8) produce expectations of the complex conjugate for each term, so that it is consistent to define $f^*_{-n}(i\omega) = \overline{f_n^*(i\omega)}$ and $\Gamma^*_{-n}(\omega) = \overline{\Gamma_n^*(\omega)}$. With this convention the left side of (2.7) becomes

$$E\left|\int_0^{\beta^{-1}N} y(t)\, e^{-i\omega t}\, dt\right|^2 = \sum_{m,n=1}^N \Gamma^*_{n-m}(\omega) f^*_{n-m}(i\omega). \tag{2.9}$$

[2] Neither this assumption nor the one following are needed to effect the final result, but they greatly facilitate its derivation. The alternative approach through a time domain argument also yields the same final expression for the spectral density, and this provides an additional check on its validity.

[3] There exists stationary point processes for which different sets of lengths of $n$ successive intervals do not all have the same distribution functions, but these do not appear to be of physical interest. See Beutler and Leneman (1966a), Section 4.2.

The calculation of the spectral density $S_y$ is completed by dividing the double sum in (2.9) by $\beta^{-1}N$ and taking the limit on $N$, in conformance with the expression (2.5) for $S_y$. Thus

$$S_y(\omega) = \beta \lim_{N\to\infty} \left[ \frac{1}{N} \sum_{m,n=1}^{N} \Gamma_{n-m}^{*}(\omega) f_{n-m}^{*}(i\omega) \right]. \tag{2.10}$$

The double sum is replaced by a single sum and the denominator moved inside the summation, viz.,

$$S_y(\omega) = \beta \lim_{N\to\infty} \left[ \sum_{-N}^{+N} \left[1 - \frac{|k|}{N}\right] \Gamma_k{}^*(\omega) f_k{}^*(i\omega) \right]. \tag{2.11}$$

The desired spectral density is therefore

$$S_y(\omega) = \beta \sum_{-\infty}^{\infty} \Gamma_k{}^*(\omega) f_k{}^*(i\omega), \tag{2.12}$$

which can also be written

$$S_y(\omega) = \beta \left\{ \Gamma_0{}^*(\omega) + 2 \operatorname{Re} \left[ \sum_{1}^{\infty} \Gamma_k{}^*(\omega) f_k{}^*(i\omega) \right] \right\}. \tag{2.13}$$

The first formula (2.12) for $S_y$ is certainly more elegant than the second, but the latter has proved more useful in the actual computation of spectral densities.

The expression (2.12) for the spectral density $S_y$ generalizes the $S_s$ for (1.1) as obtained in Eq. (2.27) of Beutler and Leneman (1968). To see this, we observe that $y(t) = \sum h_n(t - t_n)$ specializes to $s(t) = \sum \alpha_n \delta(t - t_n)$ if we let $h_n(t) = \alpha_n \delta(t)$. Then $H_k(\omega) = \alpha_k$ and so $\Gamma_n{}^*(\omega) = E[\alpha_{m+n}\alpha_m] = \rho(n)$ [in the notation of Beutler and Leneman (1968)]; this yields Eq. (2.27) of Beutler and Leneman (1968) directly.

As a first example, consider pulse duration modulation (PDM) with rectangular unit height pulses whose pulse width $a_n$ is given by a signal $x(t)$ sampled at time $t_n$, i.e., $a_n = x(t_n)$. Then $y(t) = \sum h_n(t - t_n)$ with

$$h_n(t) = \begin{cases} 1 & 0 \leqslant t < a_n \\ 0 & \text{otherwise.} \end{cases} \tag{2.14}$$

To find $\Gamma_k{}^*$ we first take the Fourier transform of $h_n$, viz.,

$$H_n(\omega) = \int_0^{a_n} e^{-i\omega t}\, dt = \frac{1 - e^{-i\omega a_n}}{i\omega}. \tag{2.15}$$

We assume that the samples $a_n$ are pairwise independent identically distributed random variables so that we have

$$\Gamma_k^*(\omega) = | E[H_n(\omega)]|^2, \qquad k \neq 0, \tag{2.16}$$

and also

$$\Gamma_0^*(\omega) = E[| H_n(\omega)|^2]. \tag{2.17}$$

Accordingly,

$$\Gamma_k^*(\omega) = \frac{1}{\omega^2}[| 1 - \phi(\omega)|^2] \tag{2.18}$$

for nonzero $k$, and

$$\Gamma_0^*(\omega) = \frac{2}{\omega^2}\{1 - \text{Re}[\phi(\omega)]\}. \tag{2.19}$$

In the preceding two equations, $\phi$ denotes the characteristic function of any $a_n$,

$$\phi(\omega) = \int_0^\infty e^{i\omega a} dG(a). \tag{2.20}$$

It only remains to substitute the $\Gamma_k^*$ into the appropriate spectral density relation (2.12) or (2.13). Since $f_0^*(i\omega) = 1$, the first of these formulas yields for the spectral density of PDM with rectangular pulses:

$$S_y(\omega) = \frac{\beta}{\omega^2}\left\{1 - |\phi(\omega)|^2 + | 1 - \phi(\omega)|^2 \left[\sum_{-\infty}^{\infty} f_k^*(\omega)\right]\right\}. \tag{2.21}$$

The alternative form of $S_y$ which features a one-sided infinite series in the $f_k^*$ is

$$S_y(\omega) = \frac{2\beta}{\omega^2}\left\{1 - \text{Re}[\phi(\omega)] + | 1 - \phi(\omega)|^2 \,\text{Re}\left[\sum_{1}^{\infty} f_k^*(\omega)\right]\right\}. \tag{2.22}$$

Although $S_y$ appears to have a singularity at $\omega = 0$ due to the $1/\omega^2$ term, such is not the case because of the behavior of $\phi$ near the origin when $a_n$ has finite variance. However, $\sum f_k^*(0)$ diverges, reflecting the existence of a delta function at the origin. The intensity of this delta function is the square of the mean of $y(t)$, and this mean is seen to be

$$E[y(t)] = \beta \int_{-\infty}^{\infty} m(t)\, dt = \beta \left\{E\left[\int_{-\infty}^{\infty} h_n(t)\, dt\right]\right\} = \beta\{E(a_n)\} \tag{2.23}$$

by (1.3) followed by an interchange of integration and expectation. We have also used $E[h_n(t)] = m(t)$ (by definition), and the fact that the integral of $h_n(t)$ is merely $a_n$.

We continue this example with a generalization to pulses of arbitrary shape. Now

$$h_n(t) = h\left(\frac{t}{a_n}\right), \qquad a_n > 0, \tag{2.24}$$

where $h(\cdot)$ has a Fourier transform, is differentiable (we admit delta function derivatives), and $h(-\infty) = h(\infty) = 0$. Then

$$H_n(\omega) = \int_{-\infty}^{\infty} h\left(\frac{t}{a_n}\right) e^{-i\omega t}\, dt = a_n \int_{-\infty}^{\infty} h(u)\, e^{-ia_n\omega u}\, du, \tag{2.25}$$

which we may integrate by parts to obtain

$$H_n(\omega) = \frac{1}{i\omega} \int_{-\infty}^{\infty} h'(u)\, e^{-ia_n\omega u}\, du. \tag{2.26}$$

The independence of the $a_n$ permits us to find $\Gamma_k^*$ easily from (2.16) and (2.17); for nonzero $k$,

$$\Gamma_k^*(\omega) = \frac{1}{\omega^2} \left| \int_{-\infty}^{\infty} h'(u)\, \phi(u\omega)\, du \right|^2; \tag{2.27}$$

and for $k = 0$,

$$\Gamma_0^*(\omega) = \frac{1}{\omega^2} \iint_{-\infty}^{\infty} h'(u)\, h'(v)\, \phi(\omega[v - u])\, du dv. \tag{2.28}$$

As before, $\phi$ is the characteristic function of any $a_n$, and the prime denotes differentiation of a function with respect to its argument. In some instances it may be more convenient to once more integrate by parts; this rephrases (2.27) in terms of $h$ and $\phi'$, and (2.28) as a function of $h$ and $\phi''$.

The above expressions for $\Gamma_k^*$ are somewhat simplified by the change of variable $u - v = s$, $v = t$. If we then put

$$\Lambda(t, \omega) = \frac{1}{\omega} \int_{-\infty}^{\infty} h'(s + t)\, \phi(\omega s)\, ds, \tag{2.29}$$

we shall have

$$\Gamma_0^*(\omega) = \frac{1}{\omega} \int_{-\infty}^{\infty} h'(t)\, \Lambda(t, \omega)\, dt \tag{2.30}$$

and

$$\Gamma_k^*(\omega) = |\Lambda(0, \omega)|^2, \qquad k \neq 0. \tag{2.31}$$

The reader can easily verify that these two formulas agree with the $\Gamma_k^*$ previously obtained for the rectangular pulse, for which $h'(u) = \delta(u) - \delta(u - 1)$. Moreover, substitution into the formulas (2.12) or (2.13) for the spectral density is routine and will not be carried out here. As in the case of rectangular pulses, the spectral density is obtained in closed form whenever $\sum f_n^*(i\omega)$ can be summed.

The second example is concerned with the theory of telephone traffic, and more particularly with the number of lines in use at any specified time $t$.[4] We assume that the lengths of calls are independent random variables with identical probability distributions $G(\cdot)$. The $n$-th call is initiated at time $t_n$ ($n = 0, \pm 1, \pm 2, \ldots$), and $\{t_n\}$ constitutes a Poisson point process (over the entire real line) for which $\beta$ is the average number of calls initiated in any unit period. Finally, it is supposed that there are a sufficient number of lines to assure that every potential caller can in fact initiate a call whenever desired.

In the example, we determine the mean and autocorrelation of the number of lines in use. This number is modelled by $y(t) = \sum h_n(t - t_n)$, where $h_n(t)$ is taken to be the rectangular function defined by (2.14), with $a_n$ the duration of the $n$-th call. Hence the general results we have already derived are applicable to this problem. For instance, the mean number of lines in use is

$$E[y(t)] = \beta[E(a_n)] = \beta \int_0^\infty x \, dG(x). \tag{2.32}$$

The autocorrelation function is in theory also available, since we may substitute for the $f_k^*$ in the spectral density formula (2.12), and then take the inverse Fourier transformation for the autocorrelation function. However, we shall find it more instructive to start with the general autocorrelation expression, and to evaluate it directly.

We assert that the autocorrelation $E[y(t + \tau)\, y(t)]$ is

$$R_y(\tau) = \beta \left\{ \int_{-\infty}^{\infty} \Gamma_0(\tau + u, u)\, du + \sum_{k=1}^{\infty} \iint_{-\infty}^{\infty} \Gamma_k(\tau + v, u) f_k(|\, u - v\,|)\, du\, dv \right\}, \tag{2.33}$$

in which

$$\Gamma_k(u, v) = E[h_{m+k}(u)\, \overline{h_m(v)}], \tag{2.34}$$

[4] The same model has been used to represent the number of units being serviced by a system with an infinite number of servers, and the number of fibers in a cord consisting of fibers of random lengths. Consequently, the results of this example have been obtained earlier by alternate methods; see Rao (1966) and Haji and Newell (1970).

and $f_k$ represents the density function for $k$ successive intervals between points. Verification of the correctness of (2.33) is accomplished by taking the Fourier transform on $\tau$; the result should be the spectral density $S_y$ as given by (2.12). The double integral in (2.33) may be written

$$\iint \Gamma_k(v, u) f_k(| u - v + \tau |) \, du \, dv,$$

so that its transform on $\tau$ gives rise to the integral

$$\int_{-\infty}^{\infty} f_k(| u - v + \tau |) \, e^{-i\omega\tau} \, d\tau$$
$$= e^{i\omega(u-v)} \left[ \int_0^{\infty} f_k(x) \, e^{-i\omega x} \, dx + \int_0^{\infty} f_k(x) \, e^{+i\omega x} \, dx \right]. \qquad (2.35)$$

It will be recalled that $f_k$ is the probability density function for $k$ successive intervals, and that $f_k{}^*$ is the corresponding characteristic function according to (2.8). Hence the right side of (2.35) gives rise to $f_k{}^*$ as well as $\overline{f_k{}^*} = f_{-k}^*$. To complete the verification of (2.33) we obbserve that $\Gamma_k$ and $\Gamma_k{}^*$ [as defined by (2.34) and (1.4), respectively] are connected by the transform relation

$$\Gamma_k{}^*(\omega) = \iint_{-\infty}^{\infty} \Gamma_k(u, v) \, e^{-i\omega(u-v)} \, du \, dv. \qquad (2.36)$$

We require that $\Gamma_k(u, v) = \Gamma_k(v, u)$; since, in any case, $\Gamma_k(u, v) = \overline{\Gamma_{-k}(v, u)}$, we have $\Gamma_k{}^*(\omega) = \Gamma_{-k}^*(\omega)$. It follows from the latter and (2.35) that the $k$ index term in (2.33) transforms into the $-k$ and $+k$ terms of (2.12). The single integral term in (2.33) becomes the zero index term of (2.12).

With the aid of (2.33) we now evaluate the correlation $R_y$ for the number of telephone lines in use at any given two times. Because of the symmetry of $R_y(\tau)$, it suffices to consider $\tau \geqslant 0$. Then for the $h_n(\cdot)$ defined by (2.14),

$$\Gamma_0(u + \tau, u) = E[h_m(u + \tau) \, h_m(u)] = E[h_m(u + \tau)], \qquad (2.37)$$

if $u \geqslant 0$, and $\Gamma_0(u + \tau, u) = 0$ otherwise. This means that $\Gamma_0$ is specified for $u \geqslant 0$ by the distribution function $G$ of the length of any call since

$$\begin{aligned} E[h_m(u + \tau)] = P[(u + \tau) \leqslant a_m] &= 1 - P[a_m < (u + \tau)] \\ &= 1 - G(u + \tau). \end{aligned} \qquad (2.38)$$

These considerations, together with the change of variable $u + \tau = x$, permit us to write the first integral in (2.33) as

$$\int_{-\infty}^{\infty} \Gamma_0(\tau + u, u) \, du = \int_{\tau}^{\infty} [1 - G(x)] \, dx, \qquad \tau \geqslant 0. \qquad (2.39)$$

In the second integral of the autocorrelation (2.33), we have by the assumed independence of the $\{h_n(t)\}$

$$\Gamma_k(x, y) = E[h_n(x)]\, E[h_n(y)], \qquad k \neq 0. \tag{2.40}$$

Thus $\Gamma_k$ fails to depend on its index, and the summation may be applied only to the $f_k$. But for a Poisson point process $\{t_n\}$ it follows that whenever $u \neq v$

$$\sum_{k=1}^{\infty} f_k(| u - v |) = \beta, \tag{2.41}$$

as shown in Beutler and Leneman (1966a), Eq. (4.1.2). Accordingly, the summation of the double integrals in (2.33) becomes

$$\beta \iint_{-\infty}^{\infty} \Gamma_k(\tau + v, u)\, du\, dv = \beta \left( \int_{-\infty}^{\infty} E[h_n(u)]\, du \right)^2 = \beta \{E(a_n)\}^2, \tag{2.42}$$

in which the right side is attained by interchanging expectation and integration, and noting that the integral of $h_n(t)$ is $a_n$. The values of the integrals (2.39) and (2.42) are substituted into (2.33), the expression for $R_y$. When use is made of the symmetry of the autocorrelation, the final result is seen to be

$$R_y(\tau) = \beta \int_{|\tau|}^{\infty} [1 - G(x)]\, dx + \{\beta[E(a_n)]\}^2. \tag{2.43}$$

In the above example, the special role played by the Poisson point process and the assumed independence of telephone call durations made it possible to evaluate $R_y$ explicitly. In the absence of these specialized conditions it is generally easier to calculate the spectral density $S_y$, in large part because the $f_k{}^*$ usually constitute terms of a power series.

## Statistics for Poisson Point Processes

When the underlying time base of a pulse process is a Poisson point process, the numbers of pulses in disjoint intervals are mutually independent, and the number of pulses originating in a given interval depends only on the length of the interval. These special properties [which almost serve to specify the Poisson point process (see Beutler and Leneman (1966a), Section 4)] can be exploited to obtain more complete statistics than the first and second order moments found in the preceding section. Indeed, when $\{t_n\}$ is a Poisson point process and the $h_n(t)$ are mutually independent random functions, we can determine the characteristic function for the pulse process $y(t) = \Sigma h_n(t - t_n)$; once this characteristic function is known, any statistic of $y(t)$ is (at least in theory) available. Joint statistics depend on multivariate characteristic functions, and these are complicated indeed. Nevertheless, we will indicate how these are obtained, and give an explicit formula for the joint characteristic function of $y(t_1)$, $y(t_2)$. The utility of these results will then be demonstrated by applying them to the number of telephone lines in use, thereby generalizing the last example in the preceding section.

We consider again the $y(t)$ of the form

$$y(t) = \sum_{-\infty}^{\infty} h_n(t - t_n), \tag{3.1}$$

with the specializing assumptions that $\{t_n\}$ is a Poisson stationary point process and that the $h_n(t)$ are mutually independent. For this $y(t)$ we seek its characteristic function $E\{\exp[i\lambda y(t)]\}$. The indicated expectation is taken in two stages. First, the expectation with respect to $\{h_n(t)\}$ is denoted by

$$E_1[e^{i\lambda y(t)}] = E_1\left\{\exp\left[i\lambda \sum_{-\infty}^{\infty} h_n(t - t_n)\right]\right\}. \tag{3.2}$$

Because of the hypothesized independence of the $h_n$, this expectation can be written

$$E_1[e^{i\lambda y(t)}] = \prod_{-\infty}^{\infty} \Psi(t - t_n, \lambda), \tag{3.3}$$

in which $\Psi$ is defined

$$\Psi(u, \lambda) = E_1\{\exp[i\lambda h_n(u)]\}; \tag{3.4}$$

since the $h_n$ are identically distributed, $\Psi$ does not depend on the index $n$. We define further

$$g(u, \lambda) = \frac{1}{i\lambda} \log \Psi(u, \lambda) \tag{3.5}$$

so that the expectation (3.3) becomes

$$E_1[e^{i\lambda y(t)}] = \exp\left[i\lambda \sum_{-\infty}^{\infty} g(t - t_n, \lambda)\right]. \tag{3.6}$$

Since $E[e^{i\lambda y(t)}] = E_2 E_1[e^{i\lambda y(t)}]$, where $E_2$ is the expectation with respect to $\{t_n\}$, completing the calculation of the characteristic function requires that we apply $E_2$ to the expectation (3.6) immediately above. To facilitate this operation, we observe that the exponential

$$\sum_{-\infty}^{\infty} g(t - t_n, \lambda) = \int_{-\infty}^{\infty} g(t - u, \lambda)\, dN(u), \tag{3.7}$$

where $N(t)$ is the stationary increment process with $N(0) = 0$ and a unit jump at each $t_n$ [compare Beutler and Leneman (1968)]. Since $N(t)$ may be assumed continuous from the right, the integral in (3.7) is of the Riemann–Stieltjes type and may be regarded as the limit (as the intervals between variates tend toward zero) of the sums $\sum_k g(u_k, \lambda)[N(u_{k+1}) - N(u_k)]$, where $\{u_n\}$ is an increasing (nonrandom) sequence on the real line. Now since $\{t_n\}$ is a Poisson point process $\{N(u_{k+1}) - N(u_k)\}$ constitutes a mutually independent set of random variables and so

$$E_2\left(\exp\left\{\sum_k i\lambda g(t - u_k, \lambda)[N(u_{k+1}) - N(u_k)]\right\}\right)$$
$$= \prod_k E_2\{\exp\left(i\lambda g(t - u_k, \lambda)[N(u_{k+1}) - N(u_k)]\right)\}. \tag{3.8}$$

Moreover, $N(t)$ is a stationary increment process, which means that $N(v) - N(u)$ and $N(v - u)$ have the same statistics. Hence

$$E[e^{i\lambda y(t)}] = \lim \prod_k E_2\{\exp[i\lambda g(t - u_k, \lambda)\, N(u_{k+1} - u_k)]\}. \tag{3.9}$$

The right side expectation is easily evaluated because $N(t)$ is known to be a simple Poisson process whose characteristic function [see Parzen (1962), pp. 13 and 30] is

$$E[e^{i\gamma N(t)}] = \exp\{\beta t(e^{i\gamma} - 1)\}. \tag{3.10}$$

Thus, with the role of $\gamma$ being played by $\lambda g(t - u_k, \lambda)$ and that of $t$ by $(u_{k+1} - u_k)$ the right side expectation in (3.9) becomes

$$\prod_k \exp\left((\beta(u_{k+1} - u_k)\{\exp[i\lambda g(t - u_k, \lambda)] - 1\}\right)$$
$$= \exp\left(\beta\left[\sum \{\exp[i\lambda g(t - u_k, \lambda)] - 1\}(u_{k+1} - u_k)\right]\right)$$
$$\to \exp\left\{\beta \int_{-\infty}^{\infty} [\Psi(t - u, \lambda) - 1]\, du\right\}$$
$$= \exp\left\{\beta \int_{-\infty}^{\infty} [\Psi(u, \lambda) - 1]\, du\right\}. \tag{3.11}$$

The right side of (3.11) above is the limit of the indicated Riemann sums, and use has been made of the relation between $g(u, \lambda)$ and $\Psi(u, \lambda)$ [see (3.5)] in arriving at the final form. The characteristic function of $y(t)$, according to (3.9) and (3.11), is therefore[5]

$$E[e^{i\lambda y(t)}] = \exp\left\{\beta \int_{-\infty}^{\infty} [\Psi(u, \lambda) - 1]\, du\right\}. \tag{3.12}$$

An extension of the preceding arguments is used to derive higher-order characteristic functions such as

$$E[e^{i\lambda_1 y(t) + i\lambda_2 y(t+\tau)}] = \exp\left\{\beta \int_{-\infty}^{\infty} [\Psi(u, u+\tau, \lambda_1, \lambda_2) - 1]\, du\right\}, \tag{3.13}$$

in which

$$\Psi(x, y, \lambda_1, \lambda_2) = E_1\{\exp[i\lambda_1 h_n(x) + i\lambda_2 h_n(y)]\} \tag{3.14}$$

by definition. From the joint characteristic function the autocorrelation can be obtained, and similar methods are applicable to higher joint moments. In view of the apparent difficulty of dealing with $y(t) = \sum h_n(t - t_n)$ [a very general form of pulse train], the characteristic function forms (3.12) and (3.13) are remarkably simple.

As an example, we continue the telephone line usage problem of the preceding section, with the same assumptions as before. For this process, we obtained the mean and autocorrelation function (2.32) and (2.43), respectively. The techniques of the present section enable us to go further. In particular, we shall derive first- and second-order characteristic functions, and hence in principle *all* first and second-order statistics.

Although the second-order characteristic function (3.13) clearly includes the first order one (3.12) by taking $\lambda_2 = 0$, we shall find it instructive to compute the two separately. To find $E[e^{i\lambda y(t)}]$, we first obtain $\Psi$ as defined by (3.4). Since $h_n(t)$ is specified by (2.14) this random function can take on only the values zero or unity. Now if $h_n(t) = 0$, $\exp[i\lambda h_n(t)] = 1$, and this is the case for $t < 0$ and $t \geqslant a_n$ ; thus for $t \geqslant 0$, there is the probability $G(t)$ that

[5] This result is not entirely new. For a Poisson renewal process $\{t_n\}$ specified on the positive half-axis and with $y(0) = 0$, the equivalent result for arbitrary $t \geqslant 0$ is found in Parzen (1962); if $t \to \infty$, this result agrees with our (3.12).

$h_n(t) = 0$ and $[1 - G(t)]$ that $h_n(t) = 1$. Here $G$ is again the probability distribution function of any $a_n$. These considerations imply that

$$\Psi(u, \lambda) = \begin{cases} 1 & u < 0 \\ e^{i\lambda}[1 - G(u)] + G(u) & u \geqslant 0, \end{cases} \tag{3.15}$$

$$E[e^{i\lambda y(t)}] = \exp\left\{\beta(e^{i\lambda} - 1) \int_0^\infty [1 - G(u)]\, du\right\}, \tag{3.16}$$

by substituting in (3.12) for $\Psi$. The form of the characteristic function (3.16) shows that $y(t)$ is Poisson distributed with parameter $\beta \int_0^\infty [1 - G(u)]\, du$. Essentially the same result is obtained when $\{t_n\}$ is a Poisson renewal process over the positive half-axis and $y(0) = 0$ [see Parzen (1962), Example 5E on pp. 147–148], except that the characteristic function asymptotically approaches ours as $t \to \infty$.

Since $E[h_n(u)] = 1 - G(u)$ from (2.38), the characteristic function (3.16) also takes on either of the alternative forms

$$E[e^{i\lambda y(t)}] = \exp\{\beta(e^{i\lambda} - 1)\, E(a_n)\} = \exp\{(e^{i\lambda} - 1)\, E[y(t)]\} \tag{3.17}$$

through an application of the identity (2.23). Therefore, the probability distribution of $y(t)$ depends on $\{t_n\}$ only through the mean number of calls per unit time, and on $a_n$ only through its mean $E(a_n)$.

The bivariate characteristic function $E[e^{i\lambda_1 y(t) + i\lambda_2 y(t+\tau)}]$ is calculated as follows: for arbitrary $\tau$,

$$E[e^{i\lambda_1 y(t) + i\lambda_2 y(t+\tau)}] = E[e^{i\lambda_2 y(t) + i\lambda_1 y(t-\tau)}] \tag{3.18}$$

from considerations of stationarity and symmetry, so it suffices to get this characteristic function for $\tau \geqslant 0$. This means that the $\Psi(x, y, \lambda_1, \lambda_2)$ of (3.14) is needed only for $x \leqslant y$, since the latter argument is always greater than the former in (3.13), where $\Psi$ is used in the expression for $E[e^{i\lambda_1 y(t) + i\lambda_2 y(t+\tau)}]$. There are three cases. If $y < 0$, then $\Psi(x, y, \lambda_1, \lambda_2) = 1$. If $x < 0 \leqslant y$, then $\Psi(x, y, \lambda_1, \lambda_2)$ coincides with $\Psi(y, \lambda_2)$ as specified by (3.15). Finally, for $x \geqslant 0$, we have both $h_n(x)$ and $h_n(y)$ unity with probability $P[y < a_n] = 1 - G(y)$, $h_n(x)$ unity and $h_n(y)$ zero with $P[x < a_n \leqslant y] = G(y) - G(x)$, and both $h_n(x)$ and $h_n(y)$ zero with probability $P[a_n \leqslant x] = G(x)$. Hence for $-\tau \leqslant u < 0$,

$$\Psi(u, u + \tau, \lambda_1, \lambda_2) = e^{i\lambda_2}[1 - G(u + \tau)] + G(u + \tau), \tag{3.19}$$

and for $u \geqslant 0$

$$\Psi(u, u + \tau, \lambda_1, \lambda_2) = e^{i\lambda_1 + i\lambda_2}[1 - G(u + \tau)] + e^{i\lambda_1}[G(u + \tau) - G(u)] + G(u). \tag{3.20}$$

The final step consists of substituting $\Psi$ from (3.19) and (3.20) into the expression (3.13) for the bivariate characteristic function, viz.,

$$E[e^{i\lambda_1 y(t)+i\lambda_2 y(t+\tau)}] = \exp\left(\beta \int_0^\infty \{e^{i\lambda_1+i\lambda_2}[1 - G(u+\tau)] + e^{i\lambda_1}[G(u+\tau) - G(u)] + [G(u) - 1]\}\, du + \beta(e^{i\lambda_2} - 1)\int_0^\tau [1 - G(u)]\, du\right). \tag{3.21}$$

Various specializations of this characteristic function (e.g., $\lambda_2 = 0$ or $\tau = 0$) are left to the reader, as is the computation of the autocorrelation or other moments dependent jointly only on $y(t_1)$ and $y(t_2)$.

RECEIVED: August 19, 1970

## REFERENCES

BEUTLER, F. J. AND LENEMAN, O. A. (1966a), The theory of stationary point processes, *Acta Math.* **116**, 159–197.

BEUTLER, F. J. AND LENEMAN, O. A. (1966b), Random sampling of random processes: stationary point processes, *Information and Control* **9**, 325–346.

BEUTLER, F. J. AND LENEMAN, O. A. (1968), The spectral analysis of impulse processes, *Information and Control* **12**, 236–258.

DAVENPORT, W. B. AND ROOT, W. L. (1958), "An Introduction to the Theory of Random Signals and Noise," McGraw-Hill, New York.

HAJI, R. AND NEWELL, G. F. (1970), Variance of the number of customers in an infinite channel server, to appear.

LENEMAN, O. A. (1967), Correlation function and power spectrum of randomly shaped pulse trains, *IEEE Trans. Aerospace and Elec. Sys. AES-3*, 774–778.

MAZZETTI, P. (1964), Correlation function and power spectrum of a train of non-independent overlapping pulses having random shape and amplitude, *Nuovo Cimento* **31**, 88–97.

PARZEN, E. (1962), "Stochastic Processes," Holden-Day, San Francisco.

RAO, J. S. (1966), An application of stationary point processes to queueing theory and textile research, *J. Appl. Probability* **3**, 231–246.

# Editor's Comments on Paper 8

8 **Bar-David and Nemirovsky:** *Level Crossings of Nondifferentiable Shot Processes*

The consideration of a point process as being generated by level crossings of an ordinary process is appealing in both mathematical and physical terms. It ties the point process to an associated ordinary process for which a stronger, fully developed theory exists that facilitates analysis. The advantages of such a description can be understood from the detailed study of the level-crossing mechanism in Paper 9.

In Paper 8 a particular class of shot processes is considered which is only piecewise continuous and which models the output of a photon-multiplier tube. The main result is the statistical description of this class of processes.

# 8



Reprinted from *IEEE Trans. Inform. Theory,* **IT-18**(1), 27–34 (1972)

# Level Crossings of Nondifferentiable Shot Processes

ISRAEL BAR-DAVID, MEMBER, IEEE, AND AMIKAM NEMIROVSKY

***Abstract*—An expression for the expectation of level crossings of a class of nondifferentiable shot processes that involve impulse responses having discontinuities is derived. Its first term is essentially the Rician formula [1, pp. 51–53] except that the random variables ($y_0, \dot{y}_0$) in the integrand are conditioned on nonoccurrence of discontinuities and can be interpreted as yielding the contribution of "smooth" crossings; the second term then describes the direct contribution of the jumps.**

**The moments of ($y_0, \dot{y}_0$) reflect the influence, at the points of continuity of the process $y(t)$, of the jumps at its points of discontinuity. Whereas in differentiable processes ($y, \dot{y}$) are orthogonal, here ($y_0, \dot{y}_0$) are correlated; furthermore, although $y_0$ converges in distribution to $y$ and $E[\dot{y}_0]$ is finite and nonzero in general, evidently $\dot{y}$ has no finite moments.**

**In the Gaussian limit of large densities of counts of the underlying Poisson process, an explicit formula is obtained in terms of known parameters. The Rician term is slightly altered by the correlation between $y_0$ and $\dot{y}_0$. On the other hand, the additional term has a component that increases as the square root of the average number of counts. In various practical cases either the bounded Rician or the diverging term can be dominant. An example of particular interest is examined in detail.**

Manuscript received November 5, 1970; revised May 18, 1971.
I. Bar-David is with the Department of Electrical Engineering, City College of New York, New York, N.Y., on a leave of absence from the Scientific Department, Ministry of Defense, Tel-Aviv, Israel.
A. Nemirovsky is with the Scientific Department, Ministry of Defense, Tel-Aviv, Israel.

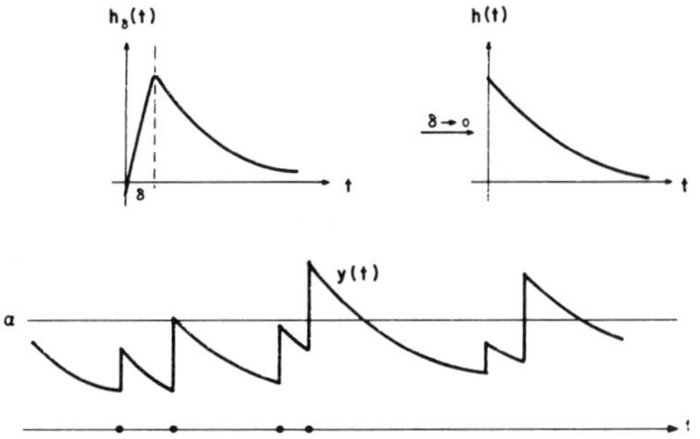


Fig. 1. Example of a piecewise continuous shot process.

## I. Introduction

THE MOTIVATION for this work is best illustrated by the simple practical example of the output of a photon-multiplier tube (PMT) excited by a flux of photons (Fig. 1). Assuming a Poisson distribution to the instants of emissions at the cathode $\{t_k\}$ and a single-photon response stylized by $h_\delta(\tau)$, the resulting current can be described by the shot process

$$y_\delta(t) = \sum_k x_k h_\delta(t - t_k),$$

where $x_k$ are statistically independent random variables (allowing for the variations in the tube gain). Of interest in many applications is the "alarm rate" identified with the expectation of the number of upward crossings of some level $\alpha$ by the process, per unit time, here denoted by $C_\alpha^{\ \delta}$. According to the general formula derived by Rice [1, pp. 51–53],

$$C_\alpha^{\ \delta} = \int_0^\infty x P_{y_\delta,\dot{y}_\delta}(\alpha,x)\, dx, \tag{1}$$

where $P_{y_\delta,\dot{y}_\delta}(y,\dot{y})$ is the joint probability density of $y_\delta(t)$ and its derivative $\dot{y}_\delta(t)$.

With the advent of the very fast PMTs the value of $\delta$ (cf. Fig. 1) became practically negligible as compared to the duration of $h_\delta(t)$. Furthermore, it is intuitively clear that for fixed expectation of emissions $\lambda$ and small $\delta$, $\delta \ll 1/\lambda$, $C_\alpha^{\ \delta}$ must be practically independent of the exact value of $\delta$ one picks while stylizing $h_\delta(t)$ to fit some practical situation. One is tempted, therefore, to settle on a mathematical model with $\delta = 0$ and speak about the corresponding process $y(t)$, as in Fig. 1, rather than go into the details of calculating $p_{y_\delta,\dot{y}_\delta}(y_1,\dot{y}_2)$ for any particular continuous $h_\delta(t)$ in order to use the classical formula (1). This last alternative could be more than just tedious, since as $\delta \to 0$, $p_{y_\delta,\dot{y}_\delta}(y_1,y_2)$ obtains significant values for arbitrarily large $\dot{y}_\delta$ so that the amount of computation involved in the integration in (1) is unbounded as $\delta \to 0$. Arbitrary truncation in the calculations could yield unpredictable errors.

On the other hand, the difficulty with an attempt to set $\delta = 0$ is that then $\dot{y}$ does not exist unconditionally[1] and (1) is meaningless. This reflects the fact that Rice's derivation [1, pp. 51–53] is based on the assumption that the process under consideration can be approximated in any infinitesimal interval $\Delta t$, by a straight line of (an expected) finite slope, which is related to the differentiability of the process. The purpose of this paper is to extend Rice's formula to cover nondifferentiable shot processes by modifying the derivation so as to account for the possible advent of discontinuities in the intervals of observation.

In Section II a general formula (13) for the expectation $C_\alpha$ of level crossings, valid for arbitrary piecewise continuous $h(t)$ (having a finite number of discontinuities), is derived. Section IV considers the limiting case of "large" $\lambda$ in which the Gaussian approximation to the statistics of the process is justifiable. The resulting expression for $C_\alpha$ shows a linear dependence on $\sqrt{\lambda}$; whereas (1), with a normal law for $p_{y,\dot{y}}(y,\dot{y})$, yields an expression (Rice's formula [1, pp. 54–55]) that does not contain $\lambda$ and is infinite for $\delta = 0$.

[1] This point is discussed in more detail in the context of (14).

The expressions for the joint statistics of the (generally) nondifferentiable process and its derivative, at their points of continuity, are discussed in Section III. Section V is devoted to the inspection of the main result by applying it to a simple version of the above introduced example. The proofs of the various propositions are collected in the appendixes.

## II. The Expectation of the Level Crossings

The model under consideration is the shot process

$$y(t) = \sum_k x_k h(t - t_k), \qquad -\infty < t < \infty, \tag{2}$$

where $\{t_k\}$ is a Poisson point process of constant parameter $\lambda$, and $\{x_k\}$ are statistically independent identically distributed random variables having finite first and second moments and also statistically independent of $\{t_k\}$. It follows that $y(t)$ is stationary. It is assumed that $h(t)$ is a known, bounded, integrable and square-integrable, piecewise continuous and piecewise differentiable function.

The instants of the assumedly finite number of discontinuities in $h(\tau)$ and in its derivative $\dot{h}(\tau)$ are ordered according to their occurrences and denoted by $\tau_j$, $j = 1,2,\cdots,N$.

The values of $h(\tau)$ to the left and to the right of $\tau_j$ are denoted, respectively, by $h_j^- = h(\tau_j - 0)$ and $h_j^+ = h(\tau_j + 0)$ and the jump $h_j^+ - h_j^-$ is denoted by $a_j$.

The real line $R = [-\infty, \infty]$, less the set $\{\tau_j\}_1^N$, is denoted by $R_0$. It is assumed that $\dot{h}(\tau)$ is square integrable over $R_0$, i.e.,

$$\int_{R_0} [\dot{h}(\tau)]^2\, d\tau < \infty.$$

Consider the infinitesimal time interval $[T_0, T_0 + \Delta t]$ and a given level $\alpha$. The following events within the interval are identified.

- $C$ At least one upward $\alpha$-crossing occurred.
- $C_1$ Exactly one upward $\alpha$-crossing occurred.
- $D_0$ No discontinuity occurred.
- $D_1$ Exactly one discontinuity occurred.

By the second axiom of the Poisson process (Appendix I) the probability of more than one discontinuity within any infinitesimal interval is of the order of $(\Delta t)^2$. It can also be shown [2] that in a stationary process the expected number of upward (or downward) $\alpha$-crossings within any interval of time is proportional to the length of the interval. It follows that, while passing to the limit of $\Delta t \to 0$, the occurrence of multiple discontinuities in $y(t)$ within $[T_0, T_0 + \Delta t]$ can be discarded.

Furthermore, since $h(t)$ is by assumption piecewise differentiable, it follows that, within the interval $[T_0, T_0 + \Delta t]$, if $D_0$ is the case, $y(t)$ is linear, whereas if $D_1$ is the case, then $y(t)$ is piecewise linear.

If $(CD)$ denotes the intersection of $C$ and $D$, then (discarding multiple discontinuities)

$$C = (CD_0) \cup (CD_1).$$

The event $(CD_1)$ is the union of the following three

events, the first of which is disjoint with the other two.

$(CD_1)^0$ Upward crossing and discontinuity are simultaneous.
$(CD_1)^+$ An upward crossing follows the discontinuity.
$(CD_1)^-$ An upward crossing precedes the discontinuity.

The only types of upward $\alpha$-crossings possible under the above assumptions are illustrated in Fig. 2.

It is shown in Appendix II that if the probability density[2] of the random variable $y_0$, to be defined later (see (7)), is bounded, then the probabilities of $(CD_1)^+$ and $(CD_1)^-$ are of the order of $(\Delta t)^2$ or less. Furthermore, the event that more than one upward $\alpha$-crossing occur within the interval is $[(CD_1)^+,(CD_1)^-]$ (see Fig. 2) and hence the probability of this event is also of the order of $(\Delta t)^2$ or less, as $\Delta t \to 0$. Thus, assuming that the above mentioned condition on $y_0$ holds, it follows that, as $\Delta t \to 0$,

$$\Pr(C) \to \Pr(C_1) \tag{3}$$

and

$$\Pr(C_1) = \Pr(CD_1)^0 + \Pr(CD_0) + 0((\Delta t)^2) \tag{4}$$

where $0((\Delta t)^2)$ is of the order of $(\Delta t)^2$.

It follows from (3) and (4) that the expectation of upward $\alpha$-crossing $C_\alpha$, as defined before [1, pp. 51–53], is given by

$$C_\alpha = \lim_{\Delta t \to 0} \frac{1}{\Delta t} \Pr(C_1) = \lim_{\Delta t \to 0} \frac{1}{\Delta t} [\Pr(CD_0) + \Pr(CD_1)^0]. \tag{5}$$

The first term inside the brackets in (5) is the contribution of the "smooth" crossings (i.e., conditioned on non-occurrence of discontinuities within the interval) and can be written as

$$\begin{aligned}\Pr(CD_0) &= \Pr(C \mid D_0)\Pr(D_0)\\ &= \Pr(C \mid D_0)[1 - \lambda\,\Delta t]^N \to \Pr(C \mid D_0),\\ &\qquad \text{as } \Delta t \to 0,\end{aligned} \tag{6}$$

where the "first" axiom of the Poisson process has been used (see Appendix I). Under the condition $D_0$ the following random variables can be defined:

$$y_0 \triangleq y(T_0 + \tfrac{1}{2}\Delta t) \qquad \dot{y}_0 \triangleq \dot{y}(T_0 + \tfrac{1}{2}\Delta t). \tag{7}$$

Their joint probability density function $p_{y_0,\dot{y}_0}(y_0,\dot{y}_0;\Delta t)$ may depend on $\Delta t$ but not on $T_0$. It is assumed that its limit, as $\Delta t \to 0$, exists and is denoted by $p_{y_0,\dot{y}_0}(y_0,\dot{y}_0)$. Then the Rician formula [1, pp. 51–53] can be applied to calculate the conditional probability:

$$\Pr(C \mid D_0) = \Delta t \int_0^\infty z\, p_{y_0,\dot{y}_0}(\alpha,z)\, dz. \tag{8}$$

The second term inside the brackets in (5) is the probability of the event $(CD_1)^0$ that the upward $\alpha$-crossing occurred simultaneously with the discontinuity. It is

[2] This density can be calculated from (27).

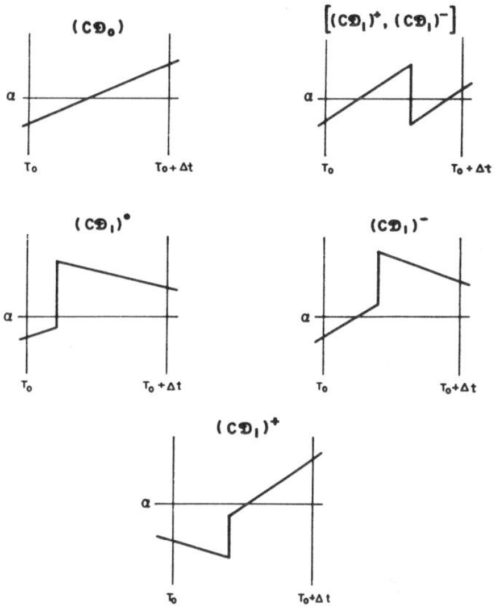

Fig. 2. The set of possible upwards crossings.

convenient to distinguish between the $N$ various possibilities.

Let it be said that a $j$-type discontinuity in $y(t)$ occurred within $[T_0, T_0 + \Delta t]$ if within $[T_0 - \tau_j, T_0 - \tau_j + \Delta t]$ a count of the $\{t_k\}$ counting process is recorded, i.e., if the discontinuity is identified as being caused by the discontinuity that $h(t)$, or $\dot{h}(t)$, exhibits at $t = \tau_j$. Denote this event by $D_1{}^j$. The simultaneous occurrence of an upward $\alpha$-crossing and a $j$-type discontinuity is then $((CD_1)^0, D_1{}^j)$ and

$$(CD_1)^0 = \bigcup_{j=1}^{N} ((CD_1)^0, D_1{}^j). \tag{9}$$

Since the events $((CD_1)^0 \mid D_1{}^j)$, $j = 1,2,\cdots,N$, are disjoint, we have

$$\begin{aligned}\Pr(CD_1)^0 &= \sum_{j=1}^{N} \Pr((CD_1)^0 \mid D_1{}^j)\Pr(D_1{}^j)\\ &= \lambda\,\Delta t \sum_{j=1}^{N} \Pr((CD_1)^0 \mid D_1{}^j),\end{aligned} \tag{10}$$

where the first axiom of Appendix I has been applied again.

Under the condition $D_1{}^j$, denote by $t'$ the instant of the discontinuity. Then $t_l = t' - \tau_j$ is an element of the $\{t_k\}$ process, and associated with it there is a random amplitude $x_l$. Denote by $p_\theta(y)$ the conditional probability density function of the random variable $\theta_j$, defined by

$$\theta_j \triangleq y(t' - 0) - x_l h_j{}^- = y(t' + 0) - x_l h_j{}^+. \tag{11}$$

It equals the value of the process with the contribution of the particular count, giving rise to the discontinuity, removed. It follows that $x_l$ and $\theta_j$ are statistically independent. Given these definitions, the probability of an upward $\alpha$-crossing simultaneous with a $j$-type discontinuity within

$[T_0, T_0 + t]$ is given by inspection:

$$\Pr\left((CD_1)^0 \mid D_1{}^j\right) = \Delta t \int_{-\infty}^{\infty} U(xa_j)p_x(x)\,dx \cdot \int_{\alpha - xh_j^+}^{\alpha - xh_j^-} p_\theta(y)\,dy. \tag{12}$$

Here $p_x(x)$ denotes the density of $x_k$ for all $k$, $a_j = h_j^+ - h_j^-$, and $U(x) = 1;\ x \geq 0$, and $U(x) = 0;\ x < 0$.

It is shown in Appendix II that as $\Delta t \to 0$, $\theta_j$ converges in distribution to $y(t)$, i.e.,

$$\lim_{\Delta \to 0} p_\theta(y) \to p_y(y),$$

where the latter denotes the probability density function of $y(t)$. Substituting (6), (8), (10), and (12) in (5) obtains the final result

$$C_\alpha = \int_0^\infty z p_{y_0,\dot{y}_0}(\alpha,z)\,dz + \lambda \sum_{j=1}^{N} \int_{-\infty}^{\infty} U(xa_j)p_x(x)\,dx \cdot \int_{\alpha - xh_j^+}^{\alpha - xh_j^-} p_y(y)\,dy. \tag{13}$$

Of the various quantities appearing in (13), $\lambda$, $p_x(x)$, $\alpha$, $h_j^+$, $h_j^-$, and $a_j$, $j = 1,2,\cdots,N$, are data of the problem; $p_y(y)$ and $p_{y_0,\dot{y}_0}(\alpha,z)$, on the other hand, can be calculated from the latter and from $h(t)$, as indicated in the next section.

It should be noted that in (1) $C_\alpha{}^\delta$ stands for the crossings of a physical process, $\delta$ symbolizing the finite duration of sharp edges. In (13) on the other hand, $C_\alpha$ without the superscript, stands for the crossings of the limiting mathematical model in which all such durations are nullified for convenience. The objection that (1) is accurate in all physical situations while (13) is only an approximation in such cases can be rightfully raised. However, as argued in the Introduction, the computation of $p_{y\dot{y}}(\cdot,\cdot)$ for very small $\delta$ can be prohibitively large (because of $\dot{y}$) and truncating the computations to practical limits might lead to unpredictable errors. From this point of view, (13) lumps together the "easy" part of the computation in the first term, which depends only on the smooth part of $h(t)$ and solves the difficulties that would be caused by the sharp edges by idealizing them into discontinuities and collecting their contributions into the second term. Formidable as it looks, the second term is actually simpler than the first since it includes only the one-dimensional density function of the process.

In any practical problem only engineering judgement can be relied upon to decide whether to accept the consequences of modeling the process by discontinuities and use (13) or rather those of truncating the calculation required for $p_{y\dot{y}}(\cdot,\cdot)$ in (1). The example of Section V provides an illustration, in the form of the right-hand side of (18), of how simple the use of (13) can be in a practical case.

## III. Statistics of the Process and of Its Derivative at Their Points of Continuity

The purpose of this section is to derive the joint characteristic function of the process and its derivative at their points of continuity, i.e., that of $y_0$, $\dot{y}_0$. In particular, it is shown that the existence of discontinuities in the process causes a nonzero mean in $\dot{y}_0$ as well as a nonzero correlation between $y_0$ and $\dot{y}_0$; whereas in any differentiable process both these quantities vanish.

The joint characteristic function of $(y_0,\dot{y}_0)$ is derived in Appendix I. The expression, as $\Delta t \to 0$, is

$$G_{y_0,\dot{y}_0}(i\omega_1,i\omega_2) = \exp\left\{\lambda \int_{-\infty}^{\infty} p_x(x)\,dx \int_{R_0} d\tau[\exp\{i\omega_1 xh(\tau) + i\omega_2 x\dot{h}(\tau)\} - 1]\right\}. \tag{14a}$$

It should be noted that, as before, $R_0$ is the real line less the points of discontinuity $\{\tau_j\}_1{}^N$. For any particular case of interest $p_{y_0,\dot{y}_0}(y_1,y_2)$ can be calculated by transforming (14a).

It follows from (14a) that the characteristic function of $y_0$ involves only $h(\tau)$ and not $\dot{h}(\tau)$ so that, considering the assumed properties of $h(\tau)$, the integration over $R_0$ is equivalent to that over the entire real line $R$. Since the expression for the characteristic function of $y(t)$, obtained in a similar way, is

$$G_y(i\omega_1) = \exp\left\{\lambda \int_{-\infty}^{\infty} p_x(x)\,dx \cdot \int_R d\tau[\exp(i\omega_1 xh(\tau)) - 1]\right\}, \tag{14b}$$

it follows that, as $\Delta t \to 0$, $y_0$ converges to $y(t)$ in distribution.

On the other hand, the random variable $\dot{y}_0$ has no unconditional counterpart, since $y(t)$ is not differentiable, if $a_j \neq 0$, for some $j$. The proper interpretation of $p_{y_0,\dot{y}_0}(y_1,y_2)$ is the following. Even though $y(t)$ is not differentiable, the measure of the sample functions that do not have jumps nor discontinuities in their derivative in an interval of width $\Delta t \ll 1/\lambda$ is $(1 - \lambda \cdot \Delta t)^N$, which is close to 1. One can therefore speak about the "derivative of $y(t)$ at its points of continuity" $\dot{y}_0$ and about the joint probability density function of $y(t)$ and its derivative at their common points of continuity $p_{y_0,\dot{y}_0}(y_1 y_2)$.

The first- and second-order moments of $y_0$ and $\dot{y}_0$ are obtained from (14a) by repeated differentiations. It is convenient to tabulate the results, for $\Delta t \to 0$.

| | Moment | Notation | Definition |
|---|---|---|---|
| Means | $E\{y\} = E\{y_0\} = \lambda m$ | $m \triangleq E\{x\} \cdot H_1$ | $H_1 \triangleq \int_R h(\tau)\,d\tau$ |
| | $E\{\dot{y}_0\} = \lambda \dot{m}$ | $\dot{m} \triangleq -E\{x\} \cdot H_0$ | $H_0 \triangleq \sum_{j=1}^N (h_j^+ - h_j^-)$ |
| Variances | $\sigma_{y_0}{}^2 = \lambda\sigma^2$ | $\sigma^2 \triangleq E\{x^2\} \cdot H_2$ | $H_2 \triangleq \int_R h^2(\tau)\,d\tau$ |
| | $\sigma_{\dot{y}_0}{}^2 = \lambda(\dot{\sigma})^2$ | $(\dot{\sigma})^2 \triangleq E\{x^2\} \cdot H_3$ | $H_3 \triangleq \int_{R_0} [\dot{h}(\tau)]^2\,d\tau$ |
| Covariance | $\rho_{y_0,\dot{y}_0} = \rho = -\frac{1}{2}H_4(H_2H_3)^{-1/2}$ | | $H_4 \triangleq \sum_{j=1}^N [(h_j^+)^2 - (h_j^-)^2]$. (15) |

Here, $E\{x\}$ and $E\{x^2\}$ are the first and second moments of $x_k$ for all $k$. $H_1$ and $H_2$ are known, respectively, as the area and the norm of $h(t)$. The additional functionals of $h(t)$: $H_0$, $H_3$, and $H_4$, naturally defined on the piecewise-linear impulse response, may be denominated, respectively, the equivalent jump, the norm of the "smooth" part (or the "smooth norm") of the derivative, and the equivalent jump in the square—of $h(\tau)$. Evidently, if all jumps vanish ($a_j = 0$ for all $j$), then $H_0 = H_4 = 0$, $(y_0,\dot{y}_0) = (y,\dot{y})$, the mean of the derivative $E\{\dot{y}\}$ and the covariance $\rho$ vanish (as they should in a differentiable process) and $H_3$ reduces to the unqualified norm of the derivative $\dot{y}(t)$. Otherwise, $\dot{y}_0$, $\sigma_{\dot{y}_0}$, and $\rho_{y_0,\dot{y}_0}$ reflect the influence, at the points of continuity of $y(t)$, of the jumps at its points of discontinuity.

## IV. The Gaussian Limit

The purpose of this section is to show that, in the limit of large $\lambda$, (13) for $C_\alpha$ can be integrated into a closed form expression that depends on readily calculable parameters of the impulse response $h(t)$ and of the statistics of the generating Poisson process. The meaning of "large $\lambda$" is discussed by applying the results to three simple cases.

A power series decomposition of the inner exponential in (14a) indicates that, as $\lambda \to \infty$, $(y_0,\dot{y}_0)$ become jointly Gaussian and are determined by the moments in (15). This result, together with the observation that $y_0 \to y$ in distribution as $\Delta t \to 0$, enables the integration of both terms in (13) to yield:

$$C_\alpha = \{[(1-\rho^2)^{1/2} \exp(-Q^2/2) + (2\pi)^{1/2} \rho q \beta] W_s + (\lambda W_d)^{1/2}\} \exp(-\beta^2/2), \quad (16)$$

where $\beta \triangleq (\alpha - E\{y\})\sigma_y^{-1}$ is the normalized level and $\sigma_y = (\lambda)^{1/2}\sigma = \sigma_{y_0}$ is the standard deviation of $y(t)$. Here $W_s$ is defined by

$$W_s = (2\pi)^{-1} \cdot (H_3/H_2)^{1/2}$$

and is termed the *effective "smooth" bandwidth* of $h(\tau)$, considering that $H_3$ is the norm of its "smooth" part. The *effective bandwidth associated with the discontinuities of the process* (at the normalized level $\beta$) is denoted by $W_d$ and defined by:

$$W_d \triangleq (2\pi T_h)^{-1} \cdot [r^+ s^+ + r^- s^- - qrs]^2,$$

where $T_h$ is an effective "duration" of $h(t)$, defined to be its norm divided by the square of its modulus $h_m$,

$$T_h = H_2/h_m^2 \qquad h_m \triangleq \max_t |h(t)|.$$

Furthermore, $r^+$, $r^-$, $r$ are numerical jumps defined by

$$r^+ \triangleq H_0^+/h_m, \qquad r^- \triangleq H_0^-/h_m, \qquad r \triangleq r^+ + r^-,$$

where

$$H_0^+ = \sum_{j=1}^{N} a_j U(a_j), \qquad H_0^- = H_0 - H_0^+.$$

Also $s^+$, $s^-$, and $s$ are defined by

$$s^+ \triangleq E\{x^+\} \cdot (E\{x^2\})^{-1/2},$$
$$s^- \triangleq E\{x^-\} \cdot (E\{x^2\})^{-1/2},$$
$$s \triangleq s^+ + s^-,$$

where

$$E\{x^+\} \triangleq \int_0^\infty x p_x(x)\, dx, \qquad E\{x^-\} \triangleq E\{x\} - E\{x^+\}.$$

Finally, $Q$ and $q$ are given by

$$Q \triangleq (\dot{m}/\dot{\sigma})[\lambda(1-\rho^2)^{-1}]^{1/2} + \rho\beta(1-\rho^2)^{-1/2},$$
$$q \triangleq 1 - \operatorname{erf}(-Q).$$

It can easily be proved that $W_d$ is nonnegative and vanishes if and only if $r^+ = r^- = 0$, i.e., $h(t)$ is "smooth." Then the coefficient of $W_s$ in (16) becomes 1, $W_d$ vanishes and (16) reduces to the, by now, classical result of Rice [1],

$$C_\alpha = W_s \exp(-\beta^2/2)$$
$$= (2\pi)^{-1}[-R''(0)/R(0)]^{1/2} \exp(-\beta^2/2),$$

where $R(\tau)$ is the autocorrelation function of the process, and where Parseval's theorem has been invoked.

Jumps in $h(t)$ have two effects: i) they modify the above Rician term that describes smooth crossings, by the factor within the square brackets in (16) and ii) they add a term that corresponds to the abrupt crossings and diverges as the square root of $\lambda$.

### *Discussion of the Approximations*

Equation (16), which assumes Gaussian statistics, can be considered reliable if within the duration of $h(t)$ a large number of counts add up on the average, i.e., if $\lambda T_h \gg 1$, say 50. Fig. 3 illustrates the behavior of $C_\alpha$ for three cases that share a common duration and smooth bandwidth but differ widely in $W_d$.

*Case A:*

$$h(\tau) = \begin{cases} \tau \cdot \exp(-\tau), & \tau \geq 0 \\ 0, & \tau < 0. \end{cases}$$

*Case B:*

$$h(\tau) = \begin{cases} \tau \cdot \exp(-\tau), & \tau \geq 10^{-7} \\ 0, & \tau < 10^{-7}. \end{cases}$$

*Case C:*

$$h(\tau) = \begin{cases} \exp(-\tau), & \tau \geq 0 \\ 0, & \tau < 0. \end{cases}$$

For the simplicity of the illustration the coefficient of $W_s$ in (16) has been taken as 1.

Case A is trivial. Case B, on the other hand, shows that even a small jump can offset the Rician formula by orders of magnitude for sufficiently large $\lambda$. In extreme cases like Case C, where $W_d$ is large, the diverging term dominates even for relatively small $\lambda$.

There are two additional observations to be made. For $\lambda$ well below $T_d^{-1}$ the responses to the occurrences are distinct, so that if $\beta$ is not larger than the value correspond-

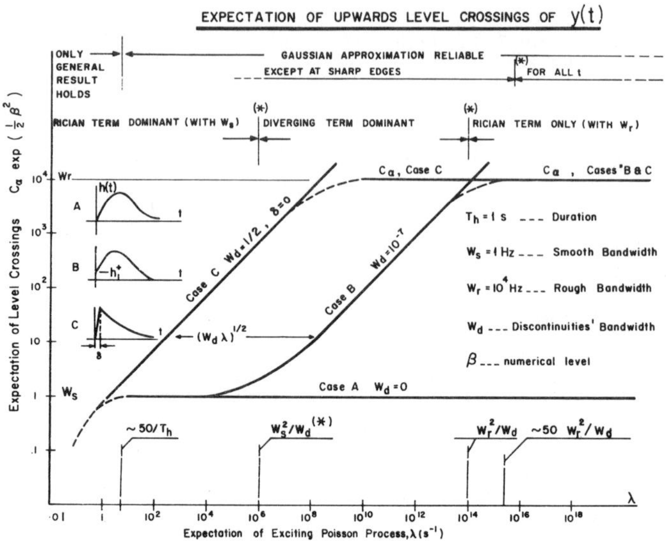


Fig. 3. Expectation of upwards crossings. (*) refers to Case B.

ing to

$$\alpha = \max_t |h(t)|,$$

then evidently $C_\alpha$ increases linearly in $\lambda$ if $x_k = 1$ for all $k$. The last observation is of a physical nature. There must be a finite nonzero value, say $\delta$, to the duration of the rise time of the edges in $h(t)$ (at the points $\tau_j$), which have been modeled by discontinuities (see Fig. 1). As long as $\lambda$ is small compared to $\delta^{-1}$, the edges are salient in $y(t)$ and modeling them by discontinuities is plausible and useful. However, as $\lambda$ increases so that even $\lambda\delta \gg 1$, the model breaks down since if the intervals of time $\Delta t$ are small enough for the Poisson assumptions to hold, they are small compared to $\delta$ too, so that transitions within $\Delta t$ are smooth. Furthermore, if $\lambda\delta \gg 1$, there is piling up also of the leading edges so that the Gaussian approximation is valid everywhere. In such a case it is expedient to consider the effective bandwidth of the "rough" $h(t)$, i.e., inclusive its sharp edges. Denote it by $W_r$, which is of the order of $\delta^{-1}$. Then

$$C_\alpha = W_r \exp(-\beta^2/2)$$

by rightfully using the Rician formula again. Clearly $C_\alpha$ cannot increase beyond this value in physical situation. This sets the upper-bounding line in Fig. 3.

## V. Inspection of the Basic Result—An Example

Consider the example of Fig. 1, with $x_k = 1$, with probability 1, $h(t) = \exp(-\gamma t)$; $t > 0$, and $h(t) = 0$; $t < 0$ and $\gamma > 0$. In this case $\dot{y}_0 = -\gamma y_0$ and hence

$$p_{y_0,\dot{y}_0}(y_1,y_2) = p_{y_0}(y_1)\,\delta(\gamma y_1 + y_2), \tag{17}$$

where $\delta(y)$ is the Dirac function. Upward crossings through a level $\alpha > 0$ are only of the abrupt type while downward crossings only of the smooth type. Indeed, upon substituting (17) in (13), one notices that the first term vanishes while the second yields

$$C_\alpha = \lambda \int_{\alpha-1}^{\alpha} p_y(y)\,dy. \tag{18}$$

On the other hand, one can easily transcribe (13) to yield the expectation of downward crossings per unit time. As expected the second term vanishes upon substitution of (17) and the first yields

$$-\int_{-\infty}^{0} y p_{y_0,\dot{y}_0}(\alpha, y)\,dy = \gamma\alpha p_y(\alpha). \tag{19}$$

Since in a stationary process the expectation of up- and downward crossings are equal [3], then if the basic result (13) is correct, (18) and (19) should be equal:

$$\lambda \int_{\alpha-1}^{\alpha} p_y(y)\,dy = \gamma\alpha p_y(\alpha), \tag{20}$$

or in other words, $p_y(y)$, as given by the transform of the characteristic function $G_y(i\omega)$ (14) with $p_x(x)$ and $h(\tau)$ as above, should solve this integral equation.

Transforming both sides of (20), one obtains $\lambda G_y(i\omega)\cdot[\exp(i\omega) - 1] = \omega\gamma(d/d\omega)[G_y(i\omega)]$; $G_y(0) = 1$, which is satisfied by (14b), with $p_x(x)$ and $h(\tau)$ as above, i.e., by

$$G_y(i\omega) = \exp\left\{\lambda \int_0^\infty [\exp(i\omega e^{-\gamma u}) - 1]\,du\right\}.$$

In this example the one-dimensional density $p_y$ is sufficient for the calculation of $C_\alpha$.

## VI. Conclusion

It has been shown that the expectation $C_\alpha$ of the $\alpha$-level crossings of a nondifferentiable shot process, generated by a piecewise continuous impulse response is composed of two terms. Their functional form indicates that the one that accounts for "smooth" crossings is essentially the Rician term, while the second, which is due solely to the jumps in the process, increases asymptotically as the square root of the expectation $\lambda$ of the counts of the underlying Poisson process. The main result (13) is valid for arbitrary $\lambda$; on the other hand, using the Gaussian approximation for large $\lambda$ the more concise formula (16) has been explicitly integrated.

A particular example (Fig. 3) illustrates the fact that a small jump (of relative magnitude $10^{-7}$) in an otherwise smooth impulse response, can cause a tenfold increase in $C_\alpha$, for $\lambda$ of the order of $10^8$.

A particular feature of these processes is that, although not differentiable, they possess a derivative almost everywhere. However, the jumps at the discontinuities introduce correlation between the values of the process and its derivative where the latter exists (14a), (15).

## Appendix I

Poisson point processes are governed by the following three axioms.

i) The probability of one event within the infinitesimal interval $[T, T + \Delta t]$ is $\lambda(T)\,\Delta t$, where $\lambda(t)$ is the time-varying parameter of the process.

ii) The probability for more than one event within $[T, T + \Delta t]$ approaches zero as $(\Delta t)^2$ when $\Delta t \to 0$.

iii) The numbers of events in disjoint intervals are statistically independent.

On the basis of these axioms it has been shown [3] that a complete statistical description of a Poisson point process with parameter $\lambda(t)$, in an interval $-\varepsilon \le t \le \varepsilon$ over which

$$\infty > \int_{-\varepsilon}^{\varepsilon} \lambda(t)\, dt \triangleq Q,$$

is given by the $M$-dimensional density function

$$p_{t_1,t_2,\cdots,t_M,M}(y_1,y_2,\cdots,y_M,m) = \begin{cases} \exp(-Q)\cdot \prod_{k=1}^{m} \lambda(y_k), & m = 1,2,\cdots \\ \exp(-Q), & m = 0, \end{cases} \tag{21}$$

where $t_1 < t_2 < \cdots < t_M$ are random variables denoting the instants of occurrence of the $M$ events, $M$ itself being a random variable.

It follows from (21) that the conditional probability density of $t_1,t_2,\cdots,t_M$ and $M$, given that no event occurs within any of the following intervals: $[T_0 - \tau_j, T_0 - \tau_j + \Delta t]$, $j = 1,2,\cdots,N$, for which

$$\varepsilon > \max_{j=1,2,\cdots,N} |T_0 - \tau_j \pm \Delta t|,$$

is given by

$$p_{t_1,t_2,\cdots,t_M,M|D_0}(y_1,y_2,\cdots,y_M,m) = \exp\left\{-Q + \sum_{j=1}^{N} \int_{T_0-\tau_j}^{T_0-\tau_j+\Delta t} \lambda(y)\, dy\right\} \prod_{k=1}^{m} \lambda_0(y_k)$$

$$= \exp(-Q_0)\cdot \prod_{k=1}^{m} \lambda_0(y_k), \tag{22}$$

where

$$Q_0 \triangleq Q - \sum_{j=1}^{N} \int_{T_0-\tau_j}^{T_0-\tau_j+\Delta t} \lambda(y)\, dy$$

and

$$\lambda_0(y) \triangleq \lambda(y)\left\{1 - \sum_{j=1}^{N} [U(y - T_0 + \tau_j) - U(y - T_0 + \tau_j - \Delta t)]\right\}. \tag{23}$$

Therefore, a possible realization of the conditional random variables $y_0$, $\dot{y}_0$ defined earlier, is by defining a pair of random variables $\zeta_0$, $\dot{\zeta}_0$:

$$\zeta_0 \triangleq \sum_{k=1}^{M} x_k h(T_0 + \tfrac{1}{2}\Delta t - t_k)$$

$$\zeta_0 \triangleq \sum_{k=1}^{M} x_k h(T_0 + \tfrac{1}{2}\Delta t - t_k), \tag{24}$$

where in (24) $\{t_k\}$ are governed by the probability density (22) with

$$\lambda(y) = [U(y + \varepsilon) - U(y - \varepsilon)]\cdot \lambda. \tag{25}$$

The random variables $\{x_k\}$ are equally distributed and statistically independent and also independent of the point process. Thus it is now possible to calculate the joint characteristic function of $\zeta_0$, $\dot{\zeta}_0$ for arbitrary $\varepsilon$, along lines similar to those in [3] from which the joint characteristic function of $y_0$, $\dot{y}_0$ is obtained by passing to the limit of $\varepsilon \to \infty$. The expression obtained is, of course, independent of $T_0$ but depends on $\Delta t$:

$$G_{y_0,\dot{y}_0}(i\omega_1,i\omega_2;\Delta t) = \exp\left[\lambda \int_{-\infty}^{\infty} p_x(x)\, dx \int_{-\infty}^{\infty} du \left\{1 - \sum_{j=1}^{N} [U(u - \tau_j + \tfrac{1}{2}\Delta t) - U(u - \tau_j - \tfrac{1}{2}\Delta t)]\right\} \cdot \{\exp[i\omega_1 x h(u) + i\omega_2 x \dot{h}(u)] - 1\}\right]. \tag{26}$$

Here, as before, $p_x(x)$ denotes the probability density of each of the $x_k$. As $\Delta t \to 0$, the limit of the last expression is

$$\lim_{\Delta t \to 0} G_{y,\dot{y}_0}(i\omega_1,i\omega_2;\Delta t) \triangleq G_{y,\dot{y}_0}(i\omega_1,i\omega_2) = \exp\left[\lambda \int_{-\infty}^{\infty} p_x(x)\, dx \int_{R_0} du\{\exp[i\omega_1 x h(u) + i\omega_2 x \dot{h}(u)] - 1\}\right], \tag{27}$$

where, as mentioned before, $R_0$ is the real axis less the set of points $\{\tau_j\}_1^N$.

The moments of $y_0$, $\dot{y}_0$ (in the limit of $\Delta t \to 0$) can now be obtained by repeated differentiation of (27).

## Appendix II

In addition to the definition of the random variable $\theta_j$ (see (11)), one can define a random variable $\dot{\theta}_j$ describing the value of the derivative of the process (at the instant $t'$) after the contribution of the particular count, giving rise to the discontinuity at $t = t'$ has been removed. Such a definition is possible as multiple discontinuities in $y(t)$, within the infinitesimal interval $[T_0, T_0 + \Delta t]$, are disconsidered. Since the random vector $(\theta_j,\dot{\theta}_j)$ is constructed only from the contributions of counts outside the intervals $[T_0 - \tau_k, T_0 - \tau_k + \Delta t]$, $k = 1,2,\cdots,N$, it follows from the third axiom of Poisson point processes that, as $\Delta t \to 0$, $(\theta_j,\dot{\theta}_j)$ approaches $(y_0,\dot{y}_0)$ in distribution. Since it was shown (see the text following (14b)) that, as $\Delta t \to 0$,

$y_0$ converges to $y(t)$ in distribution, it follows that $\theta_j$ converges to $y(t)$ in distribution when $\Delta t \to 0$, i.e.,

$$\lim_{\Delta t \to 0} p_{\theta_j}(y) = p_y(y), \qquad \text{for all } j = 1,2,\cdots,N.$$

In Section II we denoted by $x_l$ the amplitude associated with the count responsible for the discontinuity at the instant $t'$. The random vector $(\xi_j,\dot{\xi}_j)$, defined by

$$\xi_j \triangleq \theta_j + x_l h(\tau_j + 0)$$
$$\dot{\xi}_j = \dot{\theta}_j + x_l \dot{h}(\tau_j + 0) \tag{28}$$

describes the value of $(y(t),\dot{y}(t))$ at the instant $t = t' + 0$, i.e., just after the $j$-type discontinuity at $t = t'$. It follows that $x_l$ is statistically independent of the random vector $(\theta_j,\dot{\theta}_j)$. The probability of an upward $\alpha$-crossing within $(t', T_0 + \Delta t)$ (that is, *after* the $j$-type discontinuity at $t'$) is proportional to $T_0 - t' + \Delta t$ (see [2]). Therefore this probability is upper-bounded by assuming $t' = T_0$. Hence, using Rice's formula [1, pp. 51–53] and a decomposition of the event $(CD_1)^+$ to disjoint events as follows:

$$(CD_1)^+ = \bigcup_{j=1}^{N} [(CD_1)^+, D_1{}^j],$$

we get, for infinitesimal $\Delta t$,

$$P((CD_1)^+) = \sum_{j=1}^{N} P((CD_1)^+ \mid D_1{}^j) \cdot P(D_1{}^j)$$
$$= \lambda \cdot \Delta t \sum_{j=1}^{N} P((CD_1)^+ \mid D_1{}^j)$$
$$\leq \lambda \cdot (\Delta t)^2 \sum_{j=1}^{N} \int_0^\infty y p_{\xi_j,\dot{\xi}_j}(\alpha, y)\, dy. \tag{29}$$

The probability densities $p_{\xi_j,\dot{\xi}_j}(y_1,y_2)$, $j = 1,2,\cdots,N$, denote the limits of the probability densities of the random vectors $(\xi_j,\dot{\xi}_j)$, $j = 1,2,\cdots,N$, respectively, as $\Delta t \to 0$.

Using the following one-to-one transformation

$$\theta_j = \xi_j - x_l h(\tau_j + 0)$$
$$\dot{\theta}_j = \dot{\xi}_j - x_l \dot{h}(\tau_j + 0)$$
$$x_l = x_l \tag{30}$$

and recalling that $x_l$ is statistically independent of the random vector $(\xi_j,\dot{\xi}_j)$ and that $(\theta_j,\dot{\theta}_j) \to (y_0,\dot{y}_0)$ in distribution as $\Delta t \to 0$, one can show that, in the limit of $\Delta t \to 0$,

$$p_{\xi_j,\dot{\xi}_j,x_l}(y_1,y_2,x) = p_{y_0,\dot{y}_0}(y_1 - xh(\tau_j + 0), y_2 - x\dot{h}(\tau_j + 0))p_x(x), \tag{31}$$

where $p_{\xi_j,\dot{\xi}_j,x_l}(y_1,y_2,x)$ denotes the limit of the joint probability density of $\xi_j$, $\dot{\xi}_j$, $x_l$ as $\Delta t \to 0$.

It now follows from (29) and (31) that

$$P((CD_1)^+) \leq \lambda \cdot (\Delta t)^2 \sum_{j=1}^{N} \int_{-\infty}^{\infty} p_x(z)\, dz \int_0^\infty y p_{y_0,\dot{y}_0}$$
$$\cdot (\alpha - zh(\tau_j + 0), y - z\dot{h}(\tau_j + 0))\, dy. \tag{32}$$

We now observe that for all $z$

$$0 \leq \int_0^\infty y p_{y_0,\dot{y}_0}(\alpha - zh(t_j + 0), y - z\dot{h}(\tau_j + 0))\, dy$$
$$= \int_{-z\dot{h}(\tau_j+0)}^{\infty} [y_1 + z\dot{h}(\tau_j + 0)] p_{y_0,\dot{y}_0}$$
$$\cdot (\alpha - zh(\tau_j + 0), y_1)\, dy_1$$
$$\leq \int_0^\infty y_1 p_{y_0,\dot{y}_0}(\alpha - zh(\tau_j + 0), y_1)\, dy_1$$
$$+ |z\dot{h}(\tau_j + 0)| p_{y_0}(\alpha - zh(\tau_j + 0)). \tag{33}$$

It follows from the Schwartz inequality that

$$\int_{-\infty}^{\infty} p_x(z)|z| p_{y_0}(\alpha - zh(\tau_j + 0))\, dz$$
$$\leq [E\{x^2\} \int_{-\infty}^{\infty} p_x(x)\{p_{y_0}(\alpha - zh(\tau + 0))\}^2\, dz]^{1/2}, \tag{34}$$

where $E\{x^2\} \triangleq \int_{-\infty}^{\infty} z^2 p_x(z)\, dz$ and $p_{y_0}(y)$ is the probability density of $y_0$. Now, $\int_0^\infty y_1 p_{y_0,\dot{y}_0}(\alpha - zh(\tau_j + 0), y_1)\, dy_1$ is simply the Rician term at the level $\alpha - zh(\tau_j + 0)$, i.e., it equals the expectation per unit time of the smooth crossings at the level $\alpha - zh(\tau_j + 0)$. Under the assumptions on $h(t)$ this term is maximized by some $z$ and hence bounded by some $K_1 > 0$. Therefore, combining (32)–(34), we have

$$P((CD_1)^+) \leq \lambda(\Delta t)^2 N K_1 + \lambda(\Delta t)^2 \cdot (E\{x^2\})^{1/2} \cdot \sum_{j=1}^{N} |\dot{h}(\tau_j + 0)|$$
$$\cdot \left[ \int_{-\infty}^{\infty} p_x(z)\{p_{y_0}(\alpha - zh(\tau_j + 0))\}^2\, dz \right]^{1/2}. \tag{35}$$

It was assumed that each of the $\{x_k\}$ has first and second moments. Therefore, a sufficient condition for $P((CD_1)^+)$ to approach zero as $(\Delta t)^2$ when $\Delta t \to 0$ is the finiteness of the integral in (35) for all $j = 1,2,\cdots N$. This condition is certainly fulfilled if $p_{y_0}(y)$ is bounded.

A similar argument holds for the event $(CD_1)^-$.

## References


[1] S. O. Rice, "Mathematical analysis of random noise," *Bell Syst. Tech. J.*, vol. 24, 1945, pp. 46–156.

[2] H. Cramér and H. R. Leadbetter, *Stationary and Related Stochastic Processes, Sample Functions and Their Applications.* New York: Wiley, 1967, pp. 190–198.

[3] I. Bar-David, "Communication under the Poisson regime," *IEEE Trans. Inform. Theory*, vol. IT-15, Jan. 1969, pp. 31–37; see also *Proc. IEEE*, vol. 56, Dec. 1968, pp. 2167–2168.

# III
# General Point Processes

# Editor's Comments on Paper 9

9 **Leadbetter:** *Point Processes Generated by Level Crossings*

This is the first paper of this volume drawn from the statistical literature. There is no specific underlying engineering problem but rather an effort to obtain various properties of the level crossings and curve crossings by stochastic processes and to thus characterize the point processes that can be generated in this way. The paper is mathematical in nature and provides a thorough review of related work in the literature.

# 9



Reprinted by permission from *Stochastic Point Processes,* P. A. W. Lewis, ed., Wiley, 1972, pp. 436–467

## POINT PROCESSES GENERATED BY LEVEL CROSSINGS

M. R. Leadbetter
*University of North Carolina at Chapel Hill*

SUMMARY

This paper consists primarily of a review of available literature (and especially more recent work) concerning the crossings of levels and curves by stochastic processes. Attention is particularly directed towards those properties for which it is most profitable to emphasize the point process nature of the crossings. The topics considered are summarized in the following list of contents:

Section 1 *Introduction*

Section 2 *The Point Process of Level Crossings. Counting Procedures for the Mean Number of Events*

Section 3 *Applications and Generalizations*

Section 4 *Moments of the Number of Crossings*

Section 5 *Distribution of the Time Between Crossings by a Stationary Process*

Section 6 *"Crossings" by Vector Processes and Fields*

Section 7 *Poisson Approximations for Level Crossings*

Section 8 *Local Extremes.*

## 1. INTRODUCTION

The problems concerning crossings of levels and curves by stochastic processes are very closely related to a number of areas of stochastic process theory. Such areas include local properties (continuity, etc.) of stochastic process sample functions, extreme value theory of stochastic processes, and the theory of point processes (cf. Cramér and Leadbetter, 1967). While other aspects must necessarily enter, it is the latter connection--the particular emphasis on purely point process properties--which we wish especially to develop in this paper. The selection of topics reflects this interest and has resulted in the exclusion of some problems which might have been treated.

Within this framework, the aim of the paper is to review the currently available literature on a spectrum of level- and curve-crossing problems, with particular reference to recent work. The historical references will be largely confined to this introductory section and the summary of the contents of the paper given below. A much fuller discussion of work up to 1967 may be found in Cramér and Leadbetter (1967).

The interest in crossing problems really dates back to the original papers of M. Kac (1943) and S. O. Rice (1945). In particular, Rice obtained the now familiar formula for the mean number E(C) of crossings of a level u by a stationary (zero mean) normal stochastic process $\xi(t)$ in an interval $0 \leq t \leq T$, viz.,

$$E(C) = \frac{T}{\pi}\left(\frac{\lambda_2}{\lambda_0}\right)^{1/2} \exp(-u^2/2\lambda_0) , \tag{1.1}$$

where, if $r(\tau)$ denotes the covariance function of $\xi(t)$, $\lambda_0 = r(0) = \text{var}\,\xi(t)$ and $\lambda_2 = -r''(0)$, the second derivative of r at the origin. ($\lambda_2$ is also the "second spectral moment", $\lambda_2 = \int \lambda^2\, dF(\lambda)$ if F denotes the spectral function for $\xi(t)$.)

The conditions under which (1.1) holds were successively weakened by various authors, including Ivanov (1960), Bulinskaya (1961), Ito (1964) and Ylvisaker (1965), the latter two authors giving minimal conditions. In particular, Ylvisaker used a counting procedure for the number of zeros which may be readily adapted to a general point process framework. This will be discussed in Section 2 following the definition of terms concerning crossings and a description of the previous counting procedures used (following Kac).

In Section 2 and throughout the paper, we shall mainly think in terms of upcrossings of levels, rather than all crossings, for reasons of "cleanliness" of exposition in the later sections. The modifications required to deal with downcrossings or all crossings will be evident. The notation N(a,b) will be used in two senses; first to denote the number of upcrossings of some fixed level (or curve) in the interval $a < t \leq b$, and also to denote the number of events of an arbitrary point process in that interval. It seems preferable to do this to avoid duplicating notation, since it will always be clear which use is intended, and the first use is, of course, a special case of the second. In later sections, we will need also to use the notation $N_u(a,b)$ where the level u considered will be changing.

Section 3 contains applications of the general results of Section 2. The standard results for crossings of levels and curves by normal (stationary and non-stationary) processes are given, and a general result for non-normal processes, including, in particular, application to the envelope of a stationary normal process. This section is concluded with some recent general results of Fieger concerning the generalization of the crossing framework to include possibly discontinuous curves and sample paths.

The higher (factorial) moments of the number N(0,T) of upcrossings are considered in Section 4. Again a general point process framework is used in which the kth factorial moment of N(0,T) is exhibited as the mean number of events of a process, the "kth derived process", formed from the original one, but in k-dimensional Euclidean space $R^k$. This follows essentially the treatment of the problem by Belayev (1969). The specific methods used for obtaining the moments are indicated from this basic viewpoint. Questions of *finiteness* of the moments are briefly mentioned.

One of the main uses of the factorial moments of the number of upcrossings of a level in a given time, is to describe the distribution of the time between successive upcrossings by a stationary normal process. Series expressions, of which one was given by Rice (1945) and many more, later, by Longuet-Higgins (1962a), may be given for such distributions. It turns out that the terms in the series are in fact (derivatives of) the factorial moments.

Again these are special cases of results which hold in a much wider framework--that of stationary point processes. This is described in Section 5, from which the specific application to the intervals between say, upcrossings may be obtained. The concept of a "mixture" of point processes is also mentioned in that section--leading in particular to the distribution of the length of, say, an upwards excursion of a level u (i.e., the time from an upcrossing to the next downcrossing).

In Section 6, we consider generalizations of crossing problems to include vector processes and fields. Specific results are described, and it is shown that these are typically special cases of a crossing of a fixed vector by a "vector field", or equivalently the solutions of n random equations in n unknowns.

The behavior of a sequence of stationary point processes on the line, with intensities tending to zero, tends to take on more and more a Poisson character in certain cases. The important application for our purposes here concerns the upcrossings of an increasingly high level by a normal stationary process. (In particular, this leads to the asymptotic distribution of the maximum of such a process.) These questions are discussed in Section 7.

The final topic of the paper--in Section 8--concerns the occurrence of local extremes of a stationary normal process. In particular, we indicate some interesting recent work of G. Lindgren (1970) on the behavior of such a process near a local maximum and the asymptotic properties of crest-trough times and heights.

## 2. THE POINT PROCESS OF LEVEL CROSSINGS. COUNTING PROCEDURES FOR THE MEAN NUMBER OF EVENTS

In this section, we shall review the basic theory for calculation of the mean number of crossings of a level by a stochastic process, including the original "counting procedure" due to Kac (1943), and the now more often used method due to Ylvisaker (1965). This latter procedure will be cast here within a point process framework. Specific applications will be given in the next section.

It will be assumed throughout this section that the process $\xi(t)$ considered has continuous sample functions (see e.g. Cramér and Leadbetter,

1967, for a variety of sufficient conditions for this to hold). The relaxation of the continuity condition will be considered in the next section.

Following Cramér and Leadbetter (1967, Section 10.2), we say that $\xi(t)$ has an *upcrossing* of the level u at $t_0$ if for some $\varepsilon > 0$, $\xi(t) \leq u$ for $t_0-\varepsilon < t < t_0$, and $\xi(t) \geq u$ for $t_0 < t < t_0+\varepsilon$. Downcrossings are defined by simply reversing the inequalities $\xi(t) \leq u$, $\xi(t) \geq u$, whereas $\xi(t)$ has a *crossing* of the level u at $t_0$ if in each neighborhood of $t_0$ there are points $t_1$, $t_2$ with $\{\xi(t_1)-u\}\{\xi(t_2)-u\} < 0$. (For a discussion of these definitions, we refer to Cramér and Leadbetter, 1967, Section 10.2.)

To obtain the mean number of, say upcrossings, of u in an interval I, it is necessary to approximate the number of upcrossings as the limit of a sequence of quantities whose means can be calculated from the process distributions. (This point will be developed further in relation to a general point process later in this section.) For example, Kac (1943) used a counting procedure of the form

$$W_n = \int_I \delta_n\{\xi(t)-u\}\, \xi_+'(t)\, dt$$

in which $\xi_+'(t)$ is the derivative $\xi'(t)$ of $\xi$ where this is non-negative, and zero otherwise, and $\delta_n(\cdot)$ is a sequence of functions "becoming more like a $\delta$-function" as n increases (e.g., $\delta_n(x) = n$ for $|x| \leq 1/2n$, $\delta_n(x) = 0$ otherwise). That $W_n$ approximates the number N(I) of upcrossings of u by $\xi(t)$ in I may be seen intuitively by regarding I as being composed of disjoint intervals in each of which $\xi'(t)$ has constant sign. The integrand vanishes on the intervals on which $\xi'(t) \leq 0$ and on each of the other intervals may be transformed to give a contribution $\int_\alpha^\beta \delta_n(v)\, dv$ where $\alpha < 0 < \beta$ if and only if that interval contains an upcrossing. For such intervals $\int_\alpha^\beta \delta_n(v)\, dv \to 1$ whereas for the others (with $\alpha < \beta < 0$ or $0 < \alpha < \beta$) $\int_\alpha^\beta \delta_n(v)\, dv \to 0$. Thus in the limit $W_n$ "counts" the number of upcrossings of u by $\xi(t)$ in I. The mean number of upcrossings is then obtained as $\lim_{n\to\infty} E(W_n)$.

Later authors (e.g., Bulinskaya, 1961; Ivanov, 1960; Leadbetter, 1965) followed Kac in using similar counting procedures. More recently, it has become customary to use a very simple and in some ways more natural procedure (due to Ylvisaker, 1965) which does not (at least explicitly) make any differentiability assumption necessary. It does, however, appear that the "Kac counting procedure" may provide a rather useful and natural method of dealing with certain crossing problems for vector processes (see Section 6).

Instead of describing the counting procedure used by Ylvisaker directly, we give a modified general version within a purely point process framework. This, we feel, provides an illuminating viewpoint and is certainly relevant to the aims of the present paper. Specifically, the following result holds. (We shall consider the interval (0,1] for simplicity--the required alterations for any other interval will be obvious.)

*Theorem 2.1.* Consider a point process without multiple events and let $N(s,t) = N(I)$ denote the number of events in the semiclosed interval $(s,t] = I$. Divide the interval (0,1] into n sub-intervals

$$I_{ni} = ((i-1)/n,\ i/n], \qquad i = 1,2,\ldots,n; \qquad n = 1,2,\ldots .$$

Then

$$E\{N(0,1)\} = \lim_{n\to\infty} \sum_{i=1}^{n} \text{prob}\{N(I_{ni}) \geq 1\} \quad . \tag{2.1}$$

The proof of (2.1) is obtained very simply by writing $\chi_{ni} = 1$ if $N(I_{ni}) \geq 1$, $\chi_{ni} = 0$ otherwise and $N_n = \Sigma_{i=1}^{n} \chi_{ni}$. Then it is clear that $N_n \to N(0,1)$ with probability one, and hence by Fatou's lemma, since $N_n \leq N(0,1)$, it follows that $E(N_n) \to E\{N(0,1)\} \leq \infty$, from which (2.1) follows.

It may be noticed that this argument can be regarded also as the heart of simple proofs of (a) the equivalence of the "principal" and "parametric" measures of a point process on the line ("Korolyuk's Theorem"--cf. Belayev, 1969) and (b) the expression of $E\{N(0,1)\}$ as the "Burkill integral" $\int_0^1 P\{N(\cdot) \geq 1\}$ (cf. Fieger, 1971).

Equation (2.1) expresses the mean number of events in the interval (0,1] in terms of distributions of numbers of events in (small) intervals. If the events are, say, upcrossings of a level by a process $\xi(t)$, we wish to express $E\{N(0,1)\}$ in terms of the finite-dimensional distributions of $\xi(t)$. It is intuitively clear that we should be able to replace $\text{prob}\{N(I_{ni}) \geq 1\}$ in (2.1) by $\text{prob}[\xi\{(i-1)/n\} < u < \xi(i/n)]$ in such a case. Specifically, we have the following result.

*Theorem 2.2.* Let $\xi(t)$ be a stochastic process whose sample functions are continuous with probability one, and such that for the given level u, $\text{prob}\{\xi(t) = u\} = 0$ for all t. Then if $N(s,t) = N(I)$ denote the number of upcrossings of u by $\xi(t)$ in $I = (s,t]$, it follows that

$$E\{N(0,1)\} = \lim_{n\to\infty} \sum_{i=1}^{n} \text{prob}\{\xi(\tfrac{i-1}{n}) < u < \xi(\tfrac{i}{n})\} . \tag{2.2}$$

This result may be proved from Theorem (2.1) by defining $\chi_{ni}$ as in the proof of that theorem and $\chi'_{ni} = 1$ if $\xi\{(i-1)/n\} < u < \xi(i/n)$, $\chi'_{ni} = 0$ otherwise. Clearly $N'_n = \Sigma_{i=1}^n \chi'_{ni} \leq \Sigma_{i=1}^n \chi_{ni}$ and hence $\limsup E(N'_n) \leq E\{N(0,1)\}$ by Theorem 2.1. But it is apparent that with probability one for n fixed, $N_n \leq N'_m$ when m is sufficiently large, since then an upcrossing of u in $((i-1)/n, i/n]$ implies $\xi\{(j-1)/m\} < u < \xi(j/m)$ for some subinterval $I_{mj}$ of $I_{ni}$. Thus, by Fatou's lemma $\liminf_m E(N'_m) \geq E(N_n)$ and hence

$$\liminf_m E(N'_m) \geq \liminf_n E(N_n) = E\{N(0,1)\}$$

by Theorem 2.1, showing that $E(N'_n) \to E\{N(0,1)\}$, which yields (2.2).

Thus the calculation of the mean number of upcrossings in an interval is better carried out by substituting the simpler event "$\xi\{(i-1)/n\} < u < \xi(i/n)$" for "$N\{(i-1)/n, i/n\} \geq 1$". This is rather obvious and indeed it is easy to proceed *directly* to Theorem 2.2 without using Theorem 2.1.

The mean number of *downcrossings* of the level u in (0,1) is, of course, obtained under the same conditions by reversing the inequalities in (2.2), whereas the mean number of crossings is obtained by adding the results for upcrossings and downcrossings.

These results may be applied at once to give the standard formulae for normal and other processes. Such applications are noted in the next section. To conclude this section, we mention that the above method for calculation the mean number of events from a simpler result such as (2.2) rather than (2.1) may be given considerable generality. Such very general considerations have been given by Fieger (1971) in a related, but differently organized framework. We shall use a somewhat less general and simplified version of what Fieger terms an "ausschöpfend" set function (Fieger, 1971, Section 3), designed to handle standard applications.

Specifically, let $(\Omega, F, P)$ denote the basic probability space on which a given point process is defined. For each $n = 1,2,\ldots$ , $i = 0,\pm 1,\pm 2,\ldots$ let $S_{ni} = S(I_{ni})$ be an $F$-measurable set determined by the interval $I_{ni} = ((i-1)/n, i/n]$. Then $S_{ni}$ will be called a *sufficient set function* for the point process if for each n, i

(a) $S_{ni} \subset \{\omega : N(I_{ni}) \geq 1\}$

and

(b) with probability one, if $N(I_{ni}) \geq 1$, there exists an integer $m_0 = m_0(\omega)$ such that for any $m \geq m_0$ an integer j may be found with $\omega \in S_{mj}$ and $I_{mj} \subset I_{ni}$.

Theorem 2.2 may then be generalized as follows.

*Theorem 2.3.* Let $S_{ni}$ be a sufficient set function for the point process considered in Theorem 2.1. Then

$$E\{N(0,1)\} = \lim_{n\to\infty} \sum_{i=1}^{n} P(S_{ni}) ,$$

(cf. Fieger, 1971).

## 3. APPLICATIONS AND GENERALIZATIONS

For a *stationary* process $\xi(t)$ satisfying the conditions of Theorem 2.2, we have at once, for the intensity $E\{N(0,1)\}$ of upcrossings of the level u;

$$E\{N(0,1)\} = \lim_{n\to\infty} \text{prob}\{\xi(0) < u < \xi(n^{-1})\}/n^{-1} \quad . \tag{3.1}$$

In the case of a stationary normal process (zero mean, unit variance, covariance function r(t)), this easily yields the familiar formula of Rice (1945) viz.,

$$E\{N(0,1)\} = (\lambda_2^{1/2}/2\pi)\ \exp(-u^2/2), \tag{3.2}$$

where $\lambda_2$ is the "second spectral moment" taking the value $-r''(0)$ if r is twice differentiable, and $+\infty$ otherwise. The mean number of downcrossings of u in $0 \le t \le 1$ has the same value and the mean number of crossings, twice the value given by (3.2).

For a non-stationary normal process $\xi(t)$ the mean number of upcrossings of the *zero* level in $0 \le t \le 1$ may be similarly obtained and has the expression

$$E\{N(0,1)\} = \int_0^1 \gamma\sigma^{-1}(1-\mu^2)^{1/2}\ \phi(m/\sigma)\,[\phi(\eta) + \eta\{\Phi(\eta) - 1/2\}]\ dt\ , \tag{3.3}$$

in which (if $\xi(t)$ has mean $m = m(t)$ and covariance function $r(t,s)$),

$$\sigma^2 = r(t,t); \qquad \gamma = \partial^2 r(t,s)/\partial t\partial s\big|_{s=t};$$

$$\mu = \partial r(t,s)/\partial s\big|_{s=t}/(\gamma\sigma);$$

$$\eta = (\frac{dm}{dt} - \gamma\mu m/\sigma)/\{\gamma(1-\mu^2)^{1/2}\}\ ,$$

it being assumed that dm/dt and $\partial^2 r(t,s)/\partial r\partial s$ are continuous functions and that $\sigma > 0$, $|\mu| < 1$ for each t. Here $\phi$ is the standard normal density (with d.f. $\Phi$). A discussion of this result, and details of proof, are contained in Cramér and Leadbetter (1967, Section 13.2). While it applies to upcrossings of *zero*, it can be modified to apply to any level u by simply writing $m(t)-u$ for $m(t)$ (since $\xi(t)-u$ is a normal process with mean $m(t)-u$ and covariance function $r(t,s)$ which crosses zero whenever $\xi(t)$ crosses u). Indeed, we may clearly consider upcrossings of a (continuously differentiable) *curve* $u(t)$ (defined to be upcrossings of zero by $\xi(t) - u(t)$) by simply writing $m(t) - u(t)$ in place of $m(t)$ in (3.3).

Another way of writing (3.3) is

$$E\{N(0,1)\} = \int_0^1 \int_0^\infty y p_t(0,y)\, dy\, dt \tag{3.4}$$

where $p_t(x,y)$ denotes the joint density for the normal process $\xi(t)$ and its q.m. derivative $\xi'(t)$. In fact, this result holds for a wide variety of stochastic processes $\xi(t)$--not necessarily stationary or normal. A variety of conditions are possible to ensure (3.3) for an arbirary process. Those in the following theorem--given in Leadbetter (1966a)--are sometimes useful.

*Theorem 3.1.* Let $\xi(t)$ be a stochastic process with continuous sample functions and joint density $f_{t,s}(x,y)$ for $\xi(t)$, $\xi(s)$, $t \neq s$. Write $g_{t,\tau}(x,y) = \tau f_{t,t+\tau}(x,x+\tau y)$ (i.e., the joint density for $\xi(t)$ and $\{\xi(t+\tau) - \xi(t)\}/\tau$). Assume that $\xi(t)$ and its q.m. derivative $\xi'(t)$ have a joint density $p_t(x,y)$. Then the following three conditions imply the truth of Equation (3.4):

(i) $g_{t,\tau}(x,y)$ is continuous in $(t,x)$ for each $y$, $\tau$;

(ii) $g_{t,\tau}(x,y) \to p_t(x,y)$ as $\tau \to 0$ uniformly in $(t,x)$ for each $y$;

(iii) $g_{t,\tau}(x,y) \leq h(y)$ for all $t$, $\tau$, $x$, where $\int_0^\infty y h(y)\, dy < \infty$.

Equation (3.3) for normal processes, may be obtained from Theorem 3.1. As another application we mention the upcrossings of a level u by the *envelope* $R(t)$ of a stationary normal (zero mean, unit variance) stochastic process $\xi(t)$, defined (Cramér and Leadbetter, 1967) to be

$$R(t) = \{\xi^2(t) + \hat{\xi}^2(t)\}^{1/2} ,$$

where, if $\xi(t)$ has the spectral representation

$$\xi(t) = \int_0^\infty \cos \lambda t \, du(\lambda) + \int_0^\infty \sin \lambda t \, dv(\lambda) ,$$

$\hat{\xi}(t)$ is its Hilbert transform, defined by

$$\hat{\xi}(t) = \int_0^\infty \sin \lambda t \, du(\lambda) - \int_0^\infty \cos \lambda t \, dv(\lambda) .$$

Application of Theorem 3.1 yields, after calculation,

$$E\{N(0,1)\} = (\Delta/2\pi)^{1/2} \, u \exp(-u^2/2) , \tag{3.5}$$

in which $\Delta$ is a constant determined by the first two spectral moments $\lambda_1$, $\lambda_2$ of $\xi$, $\Delta = \lambda_2 - \lambda_1^2$ ($\lambda_i = \int_0^\infty \lambda^i \, dF(\lambda)$ if F denotes the "real form" of the spectrum of $\xi$). The details of this calculation may be found in Leadbetter (1966a). We will describe another method for obtaining this result in Section 6.

Our final topic in this section concerns the possibility of relaxing the requirement of sample function continuity. As far as *stationary normal* processes are concerned, the question is of little importance since it is known (Belayev, 1971) that for a stationary normal process if the sample functions are not continuous with probability one, then they are unbounded (above and below) in every finite interval. Thus in this case, one should certainly regard the number of crossings of a level as being infinite with probability one. This combined with Equation (3.2) (with a value $\infty$ if $\lambda_2 = \infty$) describes the mean number of (up)crossings for a stationary normal process in all circumstances.

On the other hand, for other types of discontinuous processes, it may be of interest to obtain the mean number of crossings of a level. A result of this type could then be used also to calculate the mean number of crossings of a possibly discontinuous curve by a process with continuous or discontinuous sample paths.

Fieger (1971) has recently investigated this problem in considerable generality. He uses a slightly different definition of crossings and upcrossings from ours--especially relative to the endpoints of the interval considered, and obtains an equation like (2.2), expressed as a Burkill integral. For a normal process $\xi(t)$ (not necessarily stationary), Fieger is then able to give necessary and sufficient conditions for finiteness of the mean number of crossings of a level in a given interval. Temporarily using his notation, in which $m(a,b;g)$ denotes the number of crossings (computed according to his definition) of the curve $g(\cdot)$ in the interval with endpoints a, b, Fieger obtains the following result.

*Theorem 3.2 (Fieger).* If $\xi(t) - g(t)$ is separable, $\xi(t)$ being normal with zero mean, unit variance and covariance function $r(t,s)$, then $E\{m(a,b;g)\}$ exists if and only if

(a) $g(t)$ is of bounded variation on $[a,b]$

and

(b) $\int_a^b \{1 - r(\cdot,\cdot)\}^{1/2}$ exists as a Burkill integral.

The formula for the mean number of crossings also appears compactly in this framework. Specifically, Fieger (1971) defines a function $S(t)$ as the Burkill integral $\int_a^t \{1 - r(.,.)\}^{1/2}$ and gives a formula for the mean number $E\{m(a,b;\gamma)\}$ of crossings of a level $\gamma$ by the (same) normal process $\xi(t)$ in the interval with endpoints a, b. When $S(\cdot)$ is a continuous function this becomes

$$E\{m(a,b;\gamma)\} = (2^{1/2}/\pi) \exp(-\gamma^2/2) \int_a^b \{1 - r(\cdot,\cdot)\}^{1/2} . \qquad (3.6)$$

For a *stationary* normal process for which $1 - r(t,s) \sim \frac{1}{2} \lambda_2 (t-s)^2$ (i.e., with second spectral moment $\lambda_2$) the Burkill integral $\int_a^b \{1 - r(\cdot,\cdot)\}^{1/2}$ clearly becomes $(\lambda_2/2)^{1/2}$ (b-a), which gives

$$E\{m(a,b;\gamma)\} = (\lambda_2^{1/2}/\pi)\ (b-a) \exp(-\gamma^2/2)$$

(consistently with (3.2) in view of the difference between *crcssings* and *upcrossings*). If $\lambda_2 = \infty$ this again gives $E\{m(a,b;\gamma)\} = \infty$.

Equation (3.6) is a pleasant and very compact way of expressing the mean number of crossings of a level. Of course, in particular cases one would still need to make assumptions about the behavior of r(t,s) (such as those leading to (3.3)) in order to evaluate the Burkill integral $\int_a^b \{1 - r(\cdot,\cdot)\}^{1/2}$.

## 4. MOMENTS OF THE NUMBER OF CROSSINGS

Again, to be definite, we shall consider *upcrossings* of a level u by the stochastic process $\xi(t)$ and write N(s,t) for the number in (s,t]. One is interested in the moments of the random variables N(s,t) for at least two reasons. First, since the distributions of these random variables are usually unknown, the moments are helpful quantities to calculate, particularly if limiting results of some kind are of interest. Second--as discussed further in the next section--knowledge of the moments permits a calculation (even though it may be complicated) of the distribution of the time from an "arbitrary" upcrossing to the next or of the length of an "arbitrary excursion above the level u".

Both for neatness of expression and for usefulness of application, it is more convenient to calculate the *factorial* moments $M_k(T) = E[N(0,T)\{N(0,T) - 1\} \cdots \{N(0,T) - k + 1\}]$ of N(0,T) rather than the moments themselves. A history of the calculation of such moments is given in Cramér and Leadbetter (1967) for the case when $\xi(t)$ is a stationary normal process. These calculations are summarized by the following result from that reference.

*Theorem 4.1.* Let $\xi(t)$ be a stationary normal process whose spectrum possesses a continuous component, and finite second (spectral) moment $\lambda_2$. Then for any positive integer k

$$M_k(T) = \int_0^T \cdots \int dt_1 \ldots dt_k \int_0^\infty \cdots \int y_1 \ldots y_k \, p_{\underline{t}}(u,\underline{y}) \, dy_1 \ldots dy_k, \qquad (4.1)$$

in which $p_{\underline{t}}(u,\underline{y})$ denotes the joint density of the random variables $\xi(t_1) \ldots \xi(t_k)$ and the q.m. derivatives $\xi'(t_1) \ldots \xi'(t_k)$, evaluated at $(u, \ldots u, y_1 \ldots y_k)$. Equation (4.1) holds whether both sides are finite or infinite.

Equation (4.1) can be written in more specific forms for $k = 1$ (Equation 3.2), 2 and 3 (cf. Cramér and Leadbetter, 1967, and Longuet-Higgins, 1962b), whereas for larger values of k such results have not been obtained, to our knowledge.

For non-stationary and non-normal processes, conditions can be given under which Equation (4.1) still holds. For example sufficient conditions --analogous to those of Theorem 3.1--are given in Leadbetter (1967). Before quoting this result, we shall indicate briefly the "counting procedure" which we feel is simplest for the calculation of the moments. While not being simplified in any way, the calculation is again illuminated by focussing on the purely point-process properties of the upcrossings, this time in a way developed in some generality by Belayev (1969). For simplicity, we shall again consider $T = 1$.

Consider, then, an arbitrary point process without multiple events on the real line R. Given a fixed integer $k > 1$, define a new point process, the "kth derived process", on $R^k$ (k-dimensional Euclidean space) to consist of all points $(t_1 \ldots t_k) \in R^k$ such that $t_1 \ldots t_k$ are times of occurrence of (distinct) events of the original point process. (Note that even if the original point process is stationary, the new one will not be.) Write N for the number of events of the original point process in the unit interval and $N^{(k)}$ for the number in the new process which lie in the unit cube. Clearly

$$N^{(k)} = N(N-1) \cdots (N-k+1)$$

and thus the kth factorial moment of N is

$$M_k = E\{N^{(k)}\} . \tag{4.2}$$

That is, the kth factorial moment of the number of events in the unit interval is simply the mean number of events of the kth derived process in the unit cube of $R^k$.

Now the method for obtaining the mean number of events of a point process in the unit interval outlined in Section 2, involved splitting the interval (0,1] into subintervals of length 1/n, for n = 1,2,... . Similarly, here we may calculate $E\{N^{(k)}\}$ by splitting the unit cube $\{0 < t_i \le 1 : i = 1 \dots k\}$ into smaller and smaller cubes. (This method may be generalized and set in an abstract framework--cf. Belayev, 1969, or Leadbetter, 1972).

Specifically, for each n let $I_{n\underline{i}}$ denote the small cube consisting of points $(t_1 \dots t_k)$ with $(i_j - 1)/n < t_j \le i_j/n$ where $\underline{i} = (i_1 \dots i_k)$, $1 < i_j \le n$. Then it follows as for (2.1) that

$$E\{N^{(k)}\} = \lim_{n\to\infty} \sum_{\underline{i}} \text{prob}\{N^{(k)}(I_{n\underline{i}}) \ge 1\} , \tag{4.3}$$

where the sum is over all the small cubes (i.e., all vectors $\underline{i}$) and $N^{(k)}(I_{n\underline{i}})$ denotes the number of events of the kth derived process in $I_{n\underline{i}}$.

Looking now at the case where the original events are upcrossings of a level u by a stochastic process $\xi(t)$ (with continuous sample functions and such that $\text{prob}\{\xi(t) = u\} = 0$), we may slavishly proceed to the analogue of Equation (2.2). To avoid degeneracies of the joint distribution of $\xi(t)$ at points close together, it is more convenient to consider only those small cubes, the coordinates of whose points do not lie too close together. To be specific, let $\varepsilon > 0$ and for fixed n let $C_{n\varepsilon}$ index the cubes with the following property: $\underline{i} = (i_1 \dots i_k) \in C_{n\varepsilon}$ when, if $\underline{t} = (t_1 \dots t_k) \in I_{n\underline{i}}$, then $|t_r - t_s| > \varepsilon$ for all $r \ne s$.

For $\underline{i} = (i_1 \dots i_k)$, write $\chi_{n\underline{i}} = 1$ if $N^{(k)}(I_{n\underline{i}}) \ge 1$, ($\chi_{n\underline{i}} = 0$ otherwise) and $\chi'_{n\underline{i}} = 1$ if $\xi\{(i_j - 1)/n\} < u < \xi(i_j/n)$ all $j = 1 \dots k$ ($\chi'_{n\underline{i}} = 0$ otherwise). Instead of approximating $\Sigma\chi_{n\underline{i}}$ by $\Sigma\chi'_{n\underline{i}}$ we use just $\Sigma^*\chi_{n\underline{i}}$ where the * denotes that the summation is only taken over $\underline{i} \in C_{n\varepsilon}$. As before of course $\chi'_{n\underline{i}} = 1$ implies that $\chi_{n\underline{i}} = 1$ and hence $\Sigma^*\chi'_{n\underline{i}} \le \Sigma\chi_{n\underline{i}}$ (the latter sum being over all $\underline{i} = (i_1 \dots i_k)$, $i \le i_j \le n$), and it follows from (4.3) that

$$E\{N^{(k)}\} \ge \liminf_{\varepsilon \to 0} \liminf_{n \to \infty} \Sigma^* E(\chi'_{n\underline{i}}) . \tag{4.4}$$

But if $\varepsilon$ is sufficiently small and n is fixed, it is not difficult to see that

$$\Sigma \chi_{n\underline{i}} \le \Sigma^* \chi'_{m\underline{i}} \qquad \text{(summing over } C_{m\varepsilon})$$

when m is sufficiently large, which gives

$$\Sigma \chi_{ni} \le \liminf_{\varepsilon \to 0} \liminf_{m \to \infty} \Sigma^* \chi'_{mi}$$

and thus from (4.3) and two applications of Fatou's lemma, the reverse inequality to (4.4) holds. We thus have

$$E\{N^{(k)}\} = \liminf_{\varepsilon \to 0} \liminf_{n \to \infty} \sum_{\underline{i} \varepsilon C_{n\varepsilon}} \text{prob}\left\{\xi\left(\frac{i_j - 1}{n}\right) < u < \xi\left(\frac{i_j}{n}\right),\ j = 1 \ldots k\right\}. \tag{4.5}$$

This formula may be used to obtain Theorem 4.1, or to give the conditions referred to above for the validity of Equation (4.1) for an arbitrary process $\xi(t)$. In these conditions, it is assumed first of all that the 2k-dimensional distributions of $\xi(t)$ are defined by densities $f_{t_1 \ldots t_k\, s_1 \ldots s_k}(x_1 \ldots x_k,\ y_1 \ldots y_k)$ from which a function $g_{\underline{t}\tau}(\underline{x},\underline{y})$ is defined for $\underline{t} = (t_1 \ldots t_k)$, $\underline{x} = (x_1 \ldots x_k)$, $\underline{y} = (y_1 \ldots y_k)$ by

$$g_{\underline{t}\tau}(x,y) = \tau^k f_{t_1 \ldots t_k,\ t_1+\tau \ldots t_k+\tau}(x_1 \ldots x_k,\ y_1 \ldots y_k)$$

($g_{\underline{t},\tau}$ is the joint density for $\xi(t_1) \ldots \xi(t_k)$ and the increments $\{\xi(t_i+\tau) - \xi(t_i)\}/\tau$). Now $g_{\underline{t},\tau}$ is assumed to satisfy the following three conditions:

(i) $g_{\underline{t}\tau}(\underline{x},\underline{y})$ is continuous in $(\underline{t},\underline{x})$ for each $\underline{y}$, $\tau$;

(ii) For each $\varepsilon > 0$, $g(\underline{t},\tau)(x,y) \to p_{\underline{t}}(\underline{x},\underline{y})$ as $\tau \to 0$ uniformly in the region $D(\varepsilon) = \{\underline{t} = (t_1 \ldots t_k) : |t_i - t_j| \ge \varepsilon \text{ for all } i \ne j\}$ and each y;

(iii) For each $\varepsilon > 0$ there is a function $h_\varepsilon(\underline{y})$ such that for $\underline{t} \in D(\varepsilon)$, $g_{\underline{t},\tau}(\underline{x},\underline{y}) \le h_\varepsilon(\underline{y})$ and

$$\int_0^\infty \cdots \int y_1 \cdots y_k \, h_\varepsilon(\underline{y}) \, d\underline{y} < \infty .$$

Under these conditions (4.1) holds for the process $\xi(t)$.

Finally, we note that simple modifications of Equation (4.1) yield the factorial moments of the number of downcrossings and of the total number of crossings. In the former case $y_1 \cdots y_k$ are replaced by $|y_1| \cdots |y_k|$ and the y-integrals are each taken from $-\infty$ to 0. For the total number of crossings $|y_1| \cdots |y_k|$ again appear and the integrals are each taken over the entire range $(-\infty,\infty)$.

Our final comments of this section concern *finiteness* of these factorial moments. Under the conditions stated, Equation (4.1) gives the factorial moments for the number of upcrossings of a level u by a process $\xi(t)$, whether or not that moment is finite. Even for stationary normal processes, it is not known in general precisely when the $M_k(T)$ are finite. For $k = 1$, the situation is clear. For $k = 2$, a sufficient condition for finiteness given in Cramér and Leadbetter (1967) is that the covariance function $r(\tau)$ should satisfy

$$\int_0^\delta \tau^{-1}\{\lambda_2 + r''(\tau)\} \, d\tau < \infty$$

for some $\delta > 0$. We understand that it has been shown by D. Geman that this condition is, in fact, also necessary for finiteness of the second moment. Belayev (1966) has shown that a sufficient condition for finiteness (still in the normal case) of $M_k(T)$ is that $\xi(t)$ should possess k q.m. derivatives. (This condition is, as noted by Belayev, clearly not a necessary one.) Aside from that, the results are scattered. For example, Longuet-Higgins (1962b) does some calculations which seem to imply finiteness of moments under certain assumptions, and some criteria (for particular kinds of covariance behavior) are given by Piterbarg (1968).

## 5. DISTRIBUTION OF THE TIMES BETWEEN CROSSINGS BY A STATIONARY PROCESS

The statistical properties of the intervals between zero crossings or between crossings of some level by a stationary stochastic process, have important engineering applications--for example, with reference to the "limiting" of stochastic waveforms. Further, it is often of importance to consider intervals such as that between an upcrossing of a level and the next downcrossing--or vice versa. For example, the interval that the envelope of a radio signal spends below some level may represent fading and consequent communication loss.

The interest in this problem again dates back to the pioneering work of S. O. Rice (1945) who gives a series expression and a very simple approximation for the case of successive zero crossings by a stationary normal process. More generally, one may consider the distribution of times between an axis crossing and the nth subsequent axis crossing or between an upcrossing of zero and the nth subsequent downcrossing, and so on. Problems of this latter type have been discussed by Longuet-Higgins (1962b), with particular reference to the normal case. In particular, Longuet-Higgins calculates (by somewhat heuristic methods) a series for the probability density of the time between an "arbitrary" upcrossing of zero and the (r+1)st subsequent upcrossing. (Precise definitions of what is meant by an "arbitrary" upcrossing are not usually given in the relevant literature, but this will be commented on below.) The series just referred to may be written as

$$f(\tau) = \sum_{i=0}^{\infty} (-)^i \binom{r+1}{i} \int \cdots \int_{0<t_2<\cdots<t_{n-1}<\tau} W(0,t_2\ldots t_{n-1},\tau)/W(0)\, dt_2\ldots dt_{n-1} \tag{5.1}$$

where $W(t_1\ldots t_n)\, dt_1\ldots dt_n$ represents the "probability of an upcrossing of the axis in each of the intervals $(t_i,\ t_i+dt_i)$". (These W-functions were used originally by Ramakrishnan (cf. Bartlett, 1956) and termed "product densities".)

Again, in these situations it is useful to think in terms of a purely (now stationary) point process framework, and ask for the distribution of such quantities as the time from an "arbitrary event" to say the nth subsequent event. Precisely, this means the distribution of the time to the nth event after that at zero under the "Palm distribution". For a more pedestrian, but more intuitive viewpoint it is the conditional distribution of the time to the nth event after time zero, given an event "at" zero in the limiting sense:

$$F_n(t) = \lim_{\delta \downarrow 0} \text{prob}\{N(0,t) \geq n | N(-\delta,0) \geq 1\} \tag{5.2}$$

(using $N(s,t)$ for the number of events in $(s,t]$ again). Now $N(0,t) \geq n$, of course, if and only if the nth event after zero occurs before time t. We note that $F_n(t)$ as defined is a distribution function, but is *not* the same in general as distribution functions "defined with reference to a fixed time point" such as that for the interval from the first event prior to zero to the nth event after zero. The reason for the importance of $F_n(t)$ as opposed to these other possible distribution functions is its frequency interpretation under ergodic assumptions. (These points are discussed further in Leadbetter, 1966a.)

It turns out that bounds, and exact series expressions for $F_n(t)$ may be obtained in terms of the factorial moments

$$\beta_k(t) = E\{N(N-1) \ldots (N-k+1)\} \qquad (k = 1,2,\ldots)$$

of $N = N(0,t)$, under general conditions. When the point process consists of, say, upcrossings of a level by a stochastic process, the factorial moments may be obtained from the expressions of the previous section, leading to equations such as (5.1) of Longuet-Higgins (1962b).

The specific results obtainable for a stationary point process are as follows (from Cramér, et al., 1971).

*Theorem 5.1 (bounds for $F_n(t)$):* Suppose that for given positive integers n, k, $E\{N^{n+k+1}(0,t)\} < \infty$ for some (and hence all) $t > 0$. Then if k is even

$$F_n(t) \le \lambda^{-1} \sum_{j=n+1}^{n+k+1} (-)^{j-n-1} \binom{j-2}{n-1} \beta_j'/j! \,, \tag{5.3}$$

where $\beta_j'$ is written for the right hand derivative of $\beta_j(t)$ and $\lambda$ is the intensity, $E\{N(0,1)\}$, of the process. If k is odd, the inequality is reversed.

*Theorem 5.2 (series for $F_n(t)$):* If $E\{N^k(0,t)\} < \infty$ for all $k = 1,2,...$ then

$$F_n(t) = \lambda^{-1} \sum_{j=n+1}^{\infty} (-)^{j-n-1} \binom{j-2}{n-1} \beta_j'/j! \,, \tag{5.4}$$

provided the terms of the series tend to zero.

The proof of these results is quite straightforward and will not be given in detail here. It basically relies on easily obtained bounds for the distribution of any discrete random variable in terms of its factorial moments. Using this result, the $F_n$'s may be bounded by expressions involving "conditional factorial moments" $\alpha_k(t)$ which are like the $\beta_k(t)$ but defined conditional on the occurrence of an event at the origin, in the same way as the $F_n$ were defined by (5.2). The quantity $\alpha_k$ is then related to $\beta_{k+1}$ by means of "Palm's formulae" to give Theorem 5.1. Theorem 5.2 follows from Theorem 5.1.

It should be noted that Theorem 5.1 may be applied to give bounds for $F_n(t)$ whenever a sufficient (but finite) number of moments of $N(0,t)$ are finite. For "crossing problems", the difficulties of determining whether the moments are finite were mentioned in the last section. Bounds may, of course, be obtained in both directions by altering k. Theorem 5.2 gives an exact expression for $F_n(t)$, but requires knowledge and finiteness of all the moments. The series (5.4) incidentally converges, but not necessarily absolutely, under the stated assumptions.

Using these results--together with the expressions of the previous section for the factorial moments, we may obtain (at least in principle), the distributions of the time from one upcrossing of zero (or a level) by a stationary process to the nth subsequent upcrossing, or from a downcrossing to the nth later downcrossing, or indeed from an arbitrary crossing (unidentified as to direction) to the nth later one. The point is that we deal with a single point process--upcrossings, downcrossings, or all crossings. The problem of determining the distribution of the time from say an *upcrossing* to the nth later *downcrossing* is somewhat different. There we are really dealing with a point process composed of two point processes consisting of events of "type 1" (e.g., upcrossings) and "type 2" (e.g., downcrossings) which occur alternately. Previously, we considered the point process of each type of event separately, or else together without identifying the types. Now it is important to consider them to be "mixed" in this way but to retain their identities. (Or we may regard them as "marked" in the sense of Matthes, 1963.)

Similar results to those in Theorem 5.1, 5.2 are possible here. One may define, for example, the distribution function $F_n^{(1)}(t)$ for the time from an arbitrary event of type 1 to the nth subsequent event of type 2. The factorial moments $\nu_k(t)$ of a random variable M now enter, M being defined so that M-1 is the number of those type 1 events in (0,t) for which the following type 2 event is also in (0,t). We then obtain, analogously to (5.4),

$$F_n^{(1)}(t) = \lambda_1^{-1} \sum_{j=n+1}^{\infty} (-)^{j-n-1} \binom{j-2}{n-1} \nu_j'/j\,! \,,$$

where $\lambda_1$ is the mean number of type 1 events in (0,1), provided all moments $\nu_j$ are finite (cf. also Leadbetter, 1969a), and the terms tend to zero.

In view of the difficulty of calculating factorial moments of numbers of level crossings, or zeros, of a stochastic process (because of the multiple integrations involved), we feel that bounds of the type given in Theorem 5.1, for small values of n, k are likely to be the most useful of these results in practice. Series such as (5.4) are, of course, exact, and widely applicable in principle. When these series fail to converge, "Euler's q-transform" may be used to give other double series which may converge. The form of this result corresponding to (5.4) is

$$F_n(t) = \lambda^{-1} \sum_{k=n+1}^{\infty} (1+q)^{-k-1} \sum_{s=n+1}^{k} (-)^{s-k-1} \binom{k}{s} \binom{s-2}{n-1} q^{k-s} \beta_s'/s! \,.$$

While this result (which applies when q is large enough) is theoretically interesting, it is not likely to be very helpful in practice (cf. Leadbetter, 1969b).

6. "CROSSINGS" BY VECTOR PROCESSES AND FIELDS

One obvious generalization of the problem of obtaining the mean (or moments) of the number of zeros of a stochastic process, is to consider a *vector* process $\underline{\xi}(t) = (\xi_1(t)\ldots\xi_n(t))$. This is a curve in n-dimensional space and it is sensible to consider the (one-dimensional) point process consisting of the instants at which this curve intersects a surface, say $\phi(x_1\ldots x_n) = 0$.

There is no difficulty in principle in solving this problem since if we define a stochastic process

$$\zeta(t) = \phi\{\xi_1(t)\ldots\xi_n(t)\}$$

we are simply concerned with the zeros of $\zeta(t)$--and the results of Section 4 may be applied. That is, the vector case really reduces to the familiar scalar situation. Of course, the vector process $\xi(t)$ and the function $\phi$ must be suitably restricted in order to use these results.

Belayev (1968) treats this topic and gives the following version for the kth factorial moment $M_k$ of the number of intersections of the vector process with the subset $\Gamma$ of the surface for t in the time interval $\Delta$

$$M_k = \int\cdots\int_{t_i\varepsilon\Delta} \int\cdots\int_{x_i\varepsilon\Gamma} E\{\prod_{i=1}^{k} |\underline{n}(\underline{x}_i)'\ \dot{\underline{\xi}}_{t_i}| \,\big|\, \underline{\xi}_{t_i} = \underline{x}_i,\ i=1\ldots k\}$$
$$\times\ p_{t_1\ldots t_k}(\underline{x}_1\ldots\underline{x}_k)\ dS(\underline{x}_1)\ldots dS(\underline{x}_k)\ dt_1\ldots dt_k\ , \qquad (6.1)$$

in which $n(\underline{x})$ denotes the normal to the surface at $\underline{x}$, the dot denotes time differentiation, $p_{t_1\ldots t_k}$ is the joint density for $\underline{\xi}(t_1)\ldots\underline{\xi}(t_k)$ and $dS(\underline{x})$ is the element of surface area at $\underline{x}$.

The conditions for the validity of (6.1) are naturally fairly complicated and we refer to Belayev (1968) for the details. Belayev applies (a modified version of) this result in an interesting way to obtain the mean number of upcrossings of a level by the envelope of a stationary normal process--thus providing an alternative derivation to that in Section 3. Specifically, with the notation leading to Equation (3.5) it can be seen that the envelope R(t) crosses the level u when the vector process $\{\xi(t), \hat{\xi}(t)\}$ crosses the circle $x^2 + y^2 = u^2$. Application of the version of (6.1) applicable to "outward crossings", with k = 1, yields Equation (3.5) again. Of course, while the point of view is illuminating, no different mathematics is really involved since, as noted, the vector case can be reduced to a scalar one.

Crossing problems for (scalar) stochastic processes may also be regarded as the discussion of the solutions to a random equation $\xi(t) = 0$, $\xi(t) - u = 0$, etc. We typically ask, "How many solutions are there (for fixed "sample point" $\omega$) to the single equation ($\xi(t) = 0$) in one unknown (t) in some interval, and what are the mean and moments of this number?" As we saw, the case of a vector process really belongs within this framework.

A more general question is to consider the point process (in $R^n$) consisting of the solutions to n (random) equation in n unknowns. That is, we consider a vector stochastic process $\underline{\xi}(\underline{t}) = \{\xi_1(\underline{t})\ldots\xi_n(\underline{t})\}$ where the parameter $\underline{t} = (t_1\ldots t_n)$ is also a member of n-dimensional Euclidean space $R^n$. (We will call such a process a "vector field".) One may, of course, even more generally let $\underline{\xi}$ have n components and $\underline{t}$ m-components, and this may lead to interesting results (e.g., in terms of Hausdorff dimension and measure of the set of zeros) when n < m. We will not need this extra generality here, however.

It is not our intention to pursue any general theory for the zeros of vector-fields, but merely to point out that it is this framework which is really appropriate for a number of applications. Particularly (in addition to all the cases considered with n = 1), we would refer to work by Longuet-Higgins (1962a) and especially Belayev (1967b) concerning certain point processes associated with (ordinary) random fields.

Specifically Belayev (1967b) considers a real random field $\{\zeta_{\underline{s}}: \underline{s} = (s_1 \ldots s_n) \in R^n\}$. He deals with three point processes in $R^n$ formed from such a field, which he terms "bursts", "shines" (alias "flashes", "splashes" according to translational preferences) and saddle points. A "burst" occurs at the point $\underline{s}$ if $\zeta_{\underline{s}}$ has a local maximum of height greater than (some fixed) u at that point. A "shine" occurs at $\underline{s}$ if $\zeta_{\underline{s}} > u$ and the normal to the $\zeta$-surface $s_{n+1} = \zeta(s_1 \ldots s_n)$ has fixed direction--which means that a light ray along this direction should be reflected straight back by the element of surface there. A saddle point occurs at $\underline{s}$ if the normal to the surface there is parallel to the (n+1)-axis and the principal curvatures have opposite sign.

Thus, bursts, shines and saddle points are defined primarily by conditions on the direction of the normal to the surface--which immediately leads to n equations to be satisfied in each case. (Of course, in working out, say, the mean number of "bursts" $\underline{s}$ in a set, we must use the added condition that $\xi_{\underline{s}} > u$.)

The point processes of bursts, shines and saddle points are homogenous with respect to the group of parallel shifts if the field $\zeta_s$ is homogeneous. Belayev gives conditions--based on the covariance function for $\zeta_s$--for these point processes to have finite intensities. He further obtains explicit formulae (generalizing (4.1)) for the factorial moments of each of the number of bursts, shines and saddle points in a given set. We refer to Belayev (1967b) for the details.

## 7. POISSON APPROXIMATIONS FOR LEVEL CROSSINGS

If a stationary point process on the line is "thinned out" by making events rarer in some way, it is natural to ask whether the remaining events tend (in some sense) to behave approximately like a Poisson process. Clearly the "less dependency" there is in the process between distinct time points, the "more likely" such a result will be. Such questions were investigated first (to our knowledge) by Volkonski and Rozanov (1959, 1961) who used *strong mixing* assumptions to describe the "dependence decay".

One most useful situation in which this has been thoroughly investigated is that for the upcrossings of a high level u, by a stationary normal process. As the level increases, the upcrossings become rarer, thus raising the possibility of Poisson-like behavior. Let us now write $N_u(0,T)$ for the number of upcrossings of the level u in (0,T) by a stationary normal process $\xi(t)$ (with zero mean, unit variance and covariance function $r(\tau)$). As u increases, $N_u(0,T)$ will tend to become smaller. Hence we consider a normalized version of $N_u(0,T)$ formed by letting $T \to \infty$ as $u \to \infty$, in a suitably coordinated way. Specifically, writing $\mu = E\{N_u(0,1)\} = (\lambda_2^{1/2}/2\pi)\exp(-u^2/2)$, and fixing $\tau > 0$ we wish to have

$$\lim_{u\to\infty} \text{prob}\{N_u(0,T) = k\} = \exp(-\tau)\tau^k/k! \tag{7.1}$$

with corresponding independent Poisson limits for the joint distributions of $N(a_i b_i)$ in disjoint (normalized) intervals.

Volkonski and Rozanov (1959, 1961) obtained this result under strong mixing conditions on the normal process, as an application of their general result referred to above. For normal processes, however, conditions on the covariance function are much preferable to mixing conditions and the Poisson limit was obtained first under such assumptions by Cramér (1966). Specifically, Cramér's basic assumptions were that the process possessed a finite fourth spectral moment (i.e., $r(\tau)$ is four times differentiable at $\tau = 0$) and that $r(t) = O(t^{-\alpha})$ for some $\alpha > 0$, as $t \to \infty$.

These conditions were subsequently weakened by Belayev (1967a), Qualls (1968) and finally recently by Berman (1971). We quote Berman's result.

*Theorem 7.1 (Berman).* With the above notation, let the stationary normal process $\xi(t)$ have finite second spectral moment $\lambda_2 = -r''(0)$ and suppose that either (i) $r(t)\log t \to 0$ as $t \to \infty$, or (ii) $\int_0^\infty r^2(s)\,ds < \infty$. Then the upcrossings asymptotically approximate a Poisson process in the sense that (7.1), and the corresponding limits for the joint distributions, hold.

In fact Berman proves more than this. He shows that the upcrossings of a high level and downcrossings of a low level are independently distributed in Poisson fashion asymptotically as the levels tend to $\pm\infty$.

An important use for Theorem 7.1 concerns the evaluation of the asymptotic distribution for the maximum M(T) of the stationary normal process $\xi(t)$ in $0 \leq t \leq T$. This connection is easily seen since

$$\text{prob}\{N_u(0,T) = 0\} = \text{prob}\{\xi(0) > u,\ N_u(0,T) = 0\} + \text{prob}\{M(T) \leq u\}.$$

The first term on the right is dominated by $\text{prob}\{\xi(0) > u\}$ which tends to zero as $u \to \infty$. Hence $\text{prob}\{M(T) \leq u\}$ can be approximated by $\text{prob}\{N_u(0,T) = 0\}$ as $u, T \to \infty$ in a coordinated manner. This leads in fact to

$$\text{prob}[(2 \log T)^{1/2} \{M(T) - (2 \log T)^{1/2}\} - \log(\lambda_2^{1/2}/2\pi) \leq z] \to \exp(-e^{-z})$$

as $T \to \infty$ (cf. Cramér and Leadbetter, 1967, Section 12.3).

Other topics related to the Poisson nature of the upcrossings of a high level include the distribution of the total time spent above a high level in an interval, and of the length of a single excursion above a high level. This latter quantity is again the distribution of time from an "arbitrary" upcrossing to the next downcrossing, for which the series expression holds. However, if the level is very high, it may be shown that such an excursion--suitably scaled--has an asymptotic distribution with density $\frac{1}{2}\pi t \exp(-(\pi/4)t^2)$. A discussion of the history of results of this kind appears in Cramér and Leadbetter (1967, 12.4, 12.5). More recent work appears in Belayev and Nosko (1969) and closely related work in Berman (1972).

The basic assumption made in considering the Poisson nature of the upcrossings of a very high level was that the stationary normal process $\xi(t)$ had a finite second spectral moment $\lambda_2$. If $\lambda_2 = \infty$, then the mean number of upcrossings of any level u is infinite and indeed there may be positive probability that the number of upcrossings itself is infinite. This of course does not provide a point process with any of the usual properties of good behavior. However, some interesting properties may still be obtained under useful assumptions, in particular when the covariance function $r(\tau)$ satisfies

$$1 - r(\tau) \sim C|t|^{\alpha} \qquad \text{as } |t| \to 0, \tag{7.2}$$

where C is a finite non-zero constant and $0 < \alpha < 2$. The case $\alpha = 2$ is that previously considered ($\lambda_2 < \infty$). The case $\alpha = 1$ includes the Ornstein-Uhlenbeck process with $r(\tau) = \exp(-a|\tau|)$.

It has been shown by S. Orey (1970) that when $r(\tau)$ satisfies (7.2) (and certain other assumptions) then the set of crossings has Hausdorff dimension $1 - \alpha/2$. Thus even though infinitely many crossing events occur in finite intervals, their "density" may be described via their Hausdorff dimension.

There is, of course, no hope of obtaining a Poisson result for upcrossings of a high level. However, a device of Pickands (1969a) for "thinning" the upcrossings to get a well-behaved point process does allow a Poisson result to be derived, and this result is useful in discussing extreme value distributions for such processes.

To be precise, Pickands (1969a) discussed "$\varepsilon$-upcrossings" which are defined for $\varepsilon > 0$ to be those upcrossing points t for which $(t-\varepsilon, t)$ contains no other upcrossing. The number of $\varepsilon$-upcrossings of a level u in any finite interval is finite--indeed a bounded random variable since it cannot exceed (length of interval)/$\varepsilon$. Pickands (1969a) shows that if, in addition to (7.2), either $r(t) \log t \to 0$ as $t \to \infty$ or $\int_0^\infty r^2(t)\, dt < \infty$, then an asymptotic Poisson property holds for the $\varepsilon$-upcrossings. This result may again be used to obtain the asymptotic distribution of the maximum Pickands (1969b).

Finally, we note that other forms of limiting result are possible (for, say, the zeros of a stationary normal process with $\lambda_2 < \infty$). In the case considered the crossings were made rare and hence approximately

Poisson by letting the level $u \to \infty$. For a fixed level, it may be shown under certain conditions that the number of zeros (suitably normalized) has an asymptotic normal distribution (cf. Malevich, 1969) in long time intervals.

## 8. LOCAL EXTREMES

In this final section, we shall briefly consider some aspects of the occurrence of local extremes of a stationary normal process $\xi(t)$ (again with zero mean, unit variance and covariance function $r(\tau)$).

A local maximum or minimum may be defined in terms of "continuity properties" of the sample path (e.g., a local maximum may be said to occur at $t_0$ if $\xi(t) < \xi(t_0)$ for all t in some neighborhood of $t_0$). However, there is little point in so doing, since the conditions one wishes to assume will virtually always imply the existence of a continuous sample derivative. This being so, the local maxima (minima) of $\xi(t)$ are simply the down crossings (upcrossings) of zero by $\xi'(t)$. Since $\xi'(t)$ has covariance function $-r''(\tau)$, it follows that the mean number of local maxima and minima per unit time are finite if and only if $\lambda_4 = -r^{(4)}(0) < \infty$ and are each given by $(1/2\pi)(\lambda_4/\lambda_2)^{1/2}$. These and other properties of the local extremes are developed in Leadbetter (1966). (See also Fieger (1969) for a development via "continuity properties".)

A problem of some interest--which has recently been studied in considerable detail by G. Lindgren (1970)--concerns the behavior of a stationary normal process $\xi(t)$ in the neighborhood of a local maximum. In particular, what Lindgren calls the "wavelength" (time to the next minimum or "crest-trough time") and the "wave-height" (drop in height from the maximum to the minimum or "crest-trough height") have had some attention in the past (cf. Cartwright and Longuet-Higgins, 1956).

Lindgren (1970) shows that given a local maximum of height u at $t = 0$, $\xi(t)$ has the same finite dimensional distributions as a process $uA(t) + \Delta_1(t) - \Delta_2(t)$, where $A(t)$ is a certain deterministic function, $\Delta_1$ is a non-stationary zero mean normal process with a certain covariance function, and $\Delta_2$ is an independent deterministic process of the form $\zeta B(t)$, where $\zeta$ is a random variable and B a known function. (The condition "given an event at t = 0" must be appropriately interpreted, of course--cf. Lindgren (1970) for the details of this, the specific functional forms of A, B and the distribution of $\xi$.) This representation is, incidentally, motivated by one of Slepian in a different context.

Lindgren studies the behavior of $\xi(t)$ in the neighborhood of a very low maximum (Lindgren, 1970) and uses the results in Lindgren (1971a) to obtain the limiting distribution of the wavelength and wave-height as $u \to -\infty$. Similar questions are studied in Lindgren (1971b) for the (perhaps most interesting) case when $u \to +\infty$.

## ACKNOWLEDGMENTS

This research was supported by the Office of Naval Research under contract N00014-67-A-0321-0002.

## REFERENCES

Bartlett, M.S. (1956). *An Introduction to Stochastic Processes*. Cambridge University Press.

Belayev, Yu. K. (1961). Continuity and Holder's conditions for sample functions of stationary Gaussian processes. Proc. 4th Berkeley Symp. 2, 23-33.

Belayev, Yu. K. (1966). On the number of intersections of a level by a Gaussian stochastic process. Teor. Veroyatnost i Primenen 11, 120-8.

Belayev, Yu. K. (1967a). On the number of intersections of a level by a Gaussian stochastic process II. Teor. Veroyatnost i Primenen 12, 444-57.

Belayev, Yu. K. (1967b). Bursts and shines of random fields. Doklady Akad. Nauk SSSR 176, 495-7.

Belayev, Yu. K. (1968). On the number of exists across a boundary of a region by a vector stochastic process. Teor. Veroyatnost i Primenen 13, 333-7.

Belayev, Yu. K. (1969). Elements of the general theory of random streams. Appendix to Russian edition of *Stationary and Related Stochastic Processes* by H. Cramér and M. R. Leadbetter, MIR Moscow 1969 (English translation in University of North Carolina Mimeo Series No. 703).

Belayev, Yu. K. & Nosko, V.P. (1969). Characteristics of excursions above a high level for a Gaussian stochastic process and its envelope. Teor. Veroyatnost i Primenen 14, 302-14.

Berman, S. M. (1971). Asymptotic independence of the numbers of high and low level crossings of a stationary Gaussian process. Ann. Math. Statist. 42, 927-45.

Berman, S. M. (1972). Excursions above high levels for stationary Gaussian processes. Pacific J. Math. to appear.

Bulinskaya, E. V. (1961). On the mean number of crossings of a level by a stationary Gaussian process. Teor. Veroyatnost i Primenen 6, 474-7.

Cartwright, D. E. & Longuet-Higgins, M. S. (1956). The statistical distribution of the maxima of a random function. Proc. Roy. Soc. A 237, 212-32.

Cramér, H. (1966). On the intersections between the trajectories of a normal stationary process and a high level. Ark. Mat. 6, 337-49.

Cramér, H. and Leadbetter, M. R. (1967). *Stationary and Related Stochastic Processes*. New York: Wiley.

Cramér, H., Leadbetter, M. R. & Serfling, R. J. (1971). On distribution function-moment relationships in a stationary point process. Z. Wahrscheinlichkeitstheorie verw. Geb. 18, 1-8.

Fieger, W. (1969). The number of local maxima of a stationary normal process. Math. Scand. 25, 218-26.

Fieger, W. (1971). The number of $\gamma$-level crossing points of a stochastic process. Z. Wahrscheinlichkeitstheorie verw. Geb. 18, 227-60.

Ito, K. (1964). The expected number of zeros of continuous stationary Gaussian processes. J. Math. Kyoto Univ. 3-2, 207-16.

Ivanov, V. A. (1960). On the average number of crossings of a level by sample functions of a stochastic process. Teor. Veroyatnost i Primenen 5, 219-23.

Kac, M. (1943). On the average number of real roots of a random algebraic equation. Bull. Amer. Math. Soc. 49, 314-20.

Leadbetter, M. R. (1965). On crossing of arbitrary curves by certain Gaussian processes. Proc. Amer. Math. Soc. 16, 60-8.

Leadbetter, M. R. (1966a). On crossings of levels and curves by a wide class of stochastic processes. Ann. Math. Statist. 37, 260-7.

Leadbetter, M. R. (1966b). On streams of events and mixtures of streams. J. R. Statist. Soc. B 28, 218-27.

Leadbetter, M. R. (1966c). Local maxima of stationary processes. Proc. Camb. Phil. Soc. 62, 263-8.

Leadbetter, M. R. (1967). A note on the moments of the number of axis crossings by a stochastic process. Bull. Amer. Math. Soc. 73, 129-32.

Leadbetter, M. R. (1969a). On the distributions of the times between events in a stationary stream of events. J. R. Statist. Soc. B 31, 295-302.

Leadbetter, M. R. (1969b). On certain results for stationary point processes and their application. Bull. I.S.I. 43, 309-20.

Leadbetter, M. R. (1972). On basic results of point process theory. Proc. 6th Berkeley Symp., to appear.

Lindgren, G. (1970). Some properties of a normal process near a local maximum. Ann. Math. Statist. 41, 1870-83.

Lindgren, G. (1971a). Extreme values of stationary normal processes. Z. Wahrscheinlichkeitstheorie verw. Geb. 17, 39-47.

Lindgren, G. (1971b). Wavelength and amplitude for a stationary process after a high maximum-decreasing covariance function. University of North Carolina Institute of Statistics Mimeo Series No. 745.

Longuet-Higgins, M. S. (1962a). The statistical geometry of random surfaces. Hydrodynamic Instability. Proc. Symp. Appl. Math. 13, Amer. Math. Soc., 105-43.

Longuet-Higgins, M. S. (1962b). The distribution of intervals between zeros of a stationary random function. Phil. Trans. Roy. Soc. 254, 557-99.

Malevich, T. L. (1969). Asymptotic normality of the number of crossings of level zero by a Gaussian process. Teor. Veroyatnost i Primenen 14, 287-309.

Matthes, K. (1963). Stationäre Zufällige Punktfolgen I. Jber. Deutsh. Math.-Verein 66, 66-79.

Orey, S. (1970). Gaussian sample functions and the Hausdorff dimension of level crossings. Z. Wahrscheinlichkeitstheorie verw. Geb. 15, 249-56.

Pickands, J. (1969a). Upcrossing probabilities for stationary Gaussian processes. Trans. Amer. Math. Soc. 145, 51-73.

Pickands, J. (1969b). Asymptotic properties of the maximum in a stationary Gaussian process. Trans. Amer. Math. Soc. 145, 75-86.

Pitèrbarg, V. I. (1968). The existence of moments for the number of level crossings by a stationary Gaussian process. Doklady Akad. Nauk. SSSR 182, 46-8.

Qualls, C. (1968). On a limit distribution of high level crossings of a stationary Gaussian process. Ann. Math. Statist. 39, 2108-13.

Rice, S. O. (1945). Mathematical analysis of random noise. Bell Syst. Tech. J. 24, 46-156.

Volkonski, V. A. & Rozanov, Yu. A. (1959). Some limit theorems for random functions I. Teor. Veroyatnost i Primenen 4, 186-207.

Volkonski, V. A. & Rozanov, Yu. A. (1961). Some limit theorems for random functions II. Teor. Veroyatnost i Primenen 6, 202-15.

Ylvisaker, N. D. (1965). The expected number of zeros of a stationary Gaussian process. Ann. Math. Statist. 36, 1043-6.

# Editor's Comments on Paper 10

**10 Leadbetter:** *On Basic Results of Point Process Theory*

In this paper M. R. Leadbetter proves several theorems concerning the fundamental structural properties of point processes. The approach of the author and the resulting level of presentation achieve a combination of the abstract nature of the probabilitic intrinsic models for point processes and of the more analytical nature of statistical and operations-research approaches. It should be noted that much work along similar lines has been done by a number of authors in the Soviet Union. The reference lists of Papers 9 and 10 provide a basic set of samples of Soviet work on point processes.

# 10



# ON BASIC RESULTS OF POINT PROCESS THEORY

M. R. LEADBETTER
UNIVERSITY OF NORTH CAROLINA

## 1. Introduction

There are many existing approaches to the theory of point processes. Some of these—following the original work of Khinchin [9] are "analytical" and others (for example, [15], [8]) quite abstract in nature. Here we will take a position somewhat in the middle in describing the development of some of the basic theory of point processes in a relatively general setting, but by using largely the simple techniques of proof described for the real line in [11]. We shall survey a number of known results—giving simple derivations of certain existing theorems (or their adaptations in our setting) and obtain some results which we believe to be new. Our framework for describing a general point process will be essentially that of Belyayev [2], while that for Section 4 concerning Palm distributions is developed from the approach of Matthes [14].

First we give the necessary background and notation. There are various essentially equivalent ways of defining the basic structure of a point process. For example, for point processes on the line, one may consider the space of integer valued functions $x(t)$ with $x(0) = 0$, which increase by a finite number of jumps in any finite interval. The events of the process then correspond to jumps of $x(t)$. One advantage of such a specification is that multiple events fit naturally into the framework.

To define point processes on an arbitrary space $T$, it is often appropriate to consider the "sample points" $\omega$ to be subsets of $T$. This is the point of view taken in [18], where each $\omega$ is itself a countable subset of the real line, the set of points "where events occur." Sometimes, however, a point process arises from some existing probabilistic situation (such as the zeros of a continuous parameter stochastic process) and one may wish to preserve the existing framework in the discussion. A convenient structure for this is the following, used in [2]. Let $(\Omega, \mathscr{F}, P)$ be a probability space and $(T, \mathscr{T})$ a measurable space ($T$ is the space "in which the events will occur"). For each $\omega \in \Omega$, let $S_\omega$ be a subset of $T$. If for each $E \in \mathscr{T}$

$$N(E) = N_\omega(E) = \text{card}\,(E \cap S_\omega) \tag{1.1}$$

is a (possibly infinite valued) random variable, then $S_\omega$ is called a *random set* and the family $\{N(E): E \in \mathscr{T}\}$ a *point process*. The "events" of the process are, of course, the points of $S_\omega$.

The model may be generalized slightly to take account of *multiple events*—that is, the possible occurrence of more than one event at some $t \in T$. The definition of $N(E)$ as card $(E \cap S_\omega)$ shows that $N(E)$ is an integer valued measure (on the subsets of $T$) for each $\omega$. As a measure, $N_\omega(\cdot)$ has its mass confined to $S_\omega$ and $N_\omega(\{t\}) = 1$ for each $t \in S_\omega$.

To allow multiple events, we may simply redefine $N_\omega(E)$ to be an integer valued measure with all its mass confined to $S_\omega$, with $N_\omega(\{t\}) \geqq 1$ for each $t \in S_\omega$ and such that $N_\omega(E)$ is a random variable for each $E \in \mathscr{T}$. If $N_\omega(\{t\}) > 1$, we say a *multiple event* occurs at $t$. If there is zero probability that any $t \in S_\omega$ is multiple, we say the process is *without multiple events.*

If we say a process may have multiple events, we shall be referring to this framework and shall write $M(E)$ for the number of multiple events in $E$. In such a case, we shall write $N^*(E)$ for card $\{S_\omega \cap E\}$ and refer to $N^*(E)$ as the number of events in $E$ *without regard to their multiplicities.* (Of course, $N(E)$ is the total number of events in $E$.)

In the manner just described, a point process may be regarded as a special type of *random measure.* This concept has been developed in considerable generality for stationary cases (see, for example, [15]), but this generality will not be pursued here.

Another method of taking account of multiple events is to replace each $t \in S_\omega$ by a pair $(t, k_t)$, where $k_t$ is a "mark" associated with $t$ denoting the multiplicity. This again is capable of considerable generalization by considering rather arbitrary kinds of "marks" and the appropriate additional measure theoretic structure. These ideas have been developed by Matthes (see, for example, [14]) for stationary point processes on the real line and provide an elegant framework for obtaining results, for example, in relation to Palm distributions. In such cases, the marks are chosen to be highly dependent on the set $S_\omega$ (for example, translates of $S_\omega$). At the same time, most results of interest can be obtained by using essentially these techniques, but without explicit reference to marks. Hence, we here use the framework previously explained.

For stationary point processes on the real line, there are several important basic theorems. Included among these are (writing $N(s, t)$ for the number of events in $(s, t]$):

(i) the theorem of Khinchin regarding the existence of the *parameter* $\lambda = \lim_{t \downarrow 0} Pr\{N(0, t) \geqq 1\}/t$;

(ii) Korolyuk's theorem which, in its sharpest form, says that for a stationary point process without multiple events, $\lambda$ is equal to the *intensity* $\mu = \mathscr{E}N(0, 1)$ that is, the mean number of events per unit time; $\lambda$ and $\mu$ may be infinite; if multiple events may occur, we replace $\mu$ by $\mathscr{E}N^*(0,1)$;

(iii) for the regular (orderly, ordinary) case (that is, when $Pr\{N(0, t) > 1\} = o(t)$ as $t \downarrow 0$) multiple events have probability zero;

(iv) "Dobrushin's lemma"—a converse to (iii)—stating that if $\lambda < \infty$ and multiple events have probability zero, then the process is regular.

Various analogues of these results have been studied for nonstationary point processes on the real line in [20], [4], [5], largely by using properties of Burkhill integrals. A clarifying and general viewpoint has been more recently given by Belyayev [2]. Specifically in [2], generalizations of the two constants $\lambda$, $\mu$ are made in terms of *measures* $\lambda(\cdot)$, $\mu(\cdot)$ on the space $T$, instead of in terms of point functions. The *principal measure* $\mu(\cdot)$ is defined (as customarily) on $\mathscr{T}$ simply by $\mu(E) = \mathscr{E}N(E)$—countable additivity of $N$ guaranteeing countable additivity of $\mu(\cdot)$. On the other hand, the *parametric measure* $\lambda(\cdot)$ is defined in [2] by

$$(1.2) \qquad \lambda(E) = \sup\left\{\sum_1^\infty Pr\,\{N(E_i) > 0\} : E_i \in T,\ E_i \text{ disjoint},\ \bigcup_1^\infty E_i = E\right\}.$$

It is easily shown that $\lambda(\cdot)$ is a measure and it is clear that $\lambda(E) \leqq \mu(E)$ for all $E \in \mathscr{T}$. For a stationary point process on the real line, $\lambda(E) = \lambda m(E)$ and $\mu(E) = \mu m(E)$, where $m$ denotes Lebesgue measure.

Using these definitions, it is possible to extend the basic results quoted above to apply to point processes which may be nonstationary, on spaces $T$ more general than the line (including any Euclidean space). These generalizations are systematically described in Section 2. In Section 3, stationarity is discussed in general terms (with particular reference to Khinchin's theorem) when $T$ is a topological group. In both these sections, the general lines of development are those of [2], with adaptation of the results in presenting a somewhat different viewpoint, and with emphasis on simplicity of proofs obtained by direct analogy with those of [11].

Finally, in Section 4, we discuss some basic results relative to Palm distributions (and their expressions as limits of conditional probabilities), for stationary point processes on the real line. The approach is essentially that of [14] (without explicit reference to marks), again with emphasis on the simplicity of proofs obtained from the techniques of [11].

## 2. The basic general theorems

The notation already developed will be used throughout this section. We shall systematically obtain the generalizations of the basic theorems referred to in Section 1. This development follows the same general lines as [2] but with differences of detail and perspective.

All that is to be said in *general* relative to Khinchin's theorem concerning the existence of the intensity, is contained in Belyayev's definition of the parametric measure (1.2) given in Section 1. (For special cases, when $T$ has a group structure and the point process is stationary, it is possible to say more that is directly analogous to the real line case—mention of this will be made later.)

It is shown in [2] that the truth of the generalized version of Korolyuk's theorem, namely, $\lambda(E) = \mu(E)$ for all $E \in \mathscr{T}$ (for a point process without multiple events or $\lambda(E) = \mathscr{E}N^*(E)$ if multiple events may occur), depends on the structure of $T$ rather than on any stationarity assumption. The proof given directly generalizes that of [11] for stationary processes on the real line. This is most clearly seen for a nonstationary process on the real line ($\mathscr{T}$ then being the Borel sets). For then if $E$ is an interval $(a, b]$, we may divide $E$ into $n$ equal subintervals $E_{ni}$, $i = 1, \cdots, n$, and write $\chi_{ni} = 1$ if $N(E_{ni}) \geqq 1$, $\chi_{ni} = 0$ otherwise. Assuming there are no multiple events, it is easily seen that $N_n = \Sigma_{i=1}^n \chi_{ni} \to N(E)$ with probability one, as $n \to \infty$, and hence by Fatou's lemma,

$$\mu(E) \leqq \liminf \mathscr{E} N_n = \liminf \sum_{i=1}^{n} Pr\{\chi_{ni} = 1\} \leqq \lambda(E). \tag{2.1}$$

But $\lambda(E) \leqq \mu(E)$, and hence, $\lambda(E) = \mu(E)$ for all $E$ of the form $(a, b]$. Thus, $\lambda(E) = \mu(E)$ for all Borel sets $E$, provided $\mu$ is $\sigma$-finite.

For the above proof to be useful when $T$ is a more general space, we require $T$ to have sets playing the role of intervals. A suitable definition of such a class of sets is given by Belyayev [2] and called a "fundamental system of dissecting sets" for $T$. Here we shall use a somewhat different definition to achieve the desired results. Specifically, we here say that a class $\mathscr{C} = \{E_{nk}: n, k = 1, 2 \cdots\}$ of sets $E_{nk} \in \mathscr{T}$ is a *dissecting system* for $T$ if

(i) $\mathscr{C}$ is a "determining class" (see [3]) for $\sigma$-finite measures on $\mathscr{T}$; that is, two $\sigma$-finite measures equal on $\mathscr{C}$ are equal on $\mathscr{T}$ (for example, $\mathscr{C}$ may be a semiring generating $\mathscr{T}$);

(ii) for any given set $E \in \mathscr{C}$, there is corresponding to each $n = 1, 2, 3, \cdots$ a set $I_n$ of integers such that

(a) $E_{nk}$ are disjoint subsets of $E$ for $k \in I_n$ with $E - \bigcup_{k \in I_n} E_{nk} \subset F_n \in \mathscr{T}$, where $F_n \downarrow \varnothing$, the empty set, as $n \to \infty$ and

(b) given any two points $t_1 \neq t_2$ of $E$, for all sufficiently large values of $n$ (that is, for all $n \geqq$ some $n_0(t_1, t_2)$), there are sets $E_{nk_1}, E_{nk_2}$, $k_1, k_2 \in I_n (k_1 \neq k_2$, such that $t_1 \in E_{nk_1}$, $t_2 \in E_{nk_2}$.

For example, for the real line, we may take $E_{nk}$ to be any interval $(a, b]$ with rational endpoints and of length $1/n$. We note also that the requirement in (ii) (a) that $\lim F_n = \varnothing$ may be replaced by $Pr\{N(\lim F_n) = 0\} = 1$, but this, of course, depends on the process as well as the structure of $T$.

The proof of Korolyuk's theorem given for the real line now generalizes at once to apply to a point process on a space $T$ possessing a dissecting system. This is easily seen from the following lemma.

LEMMA 2.1. *Consider a point process on a space $T$ possessing a dissecting system $C = \{E_{nk}\}$. With the above notation for $E \in C$, $k \in I_n$, write $\chi_{nk} = 1$ if $N(E_{nk}) > 0$, $\chi_{nk} = 0$ otherwise. Let*

$$N_n = \sum_{k \in I_n} \chi_{nk}. \tag{2.2}$$

*Then*

$$N_n \to N^*(E) \leqq \infty \text{ with probability one,} \tag{2.3}$$

*as $n \to \infty$.*

*Further, if* $\chi_{nk}^* = 1$ *when* $N(E_{nk}) > 1$ *and* $\chi_{nk}^* = 0$ *otherwise, and if* $N(E) < \infty$ *with probability one, then*

$$\sum_{k \in I_n} \chi_{nk}^* \to M(E) \text{ with probability one,} \tag{2.4}$$

*as* $n \to \infty$.

PROOF. It is clear that $N_n \leqq N(E)$. On the other hand, if $\infty \geqq N(E) \geqq m$, there are points $t_1, \cdots, t_m$, where events occur. For large $n$, these are eventually contained in different sets $E_{nk}$ and hence $N_n \geqq m$. Equation (2.3) follows by combining these results.

The second part follows by noting that since (with probability one) only a finite number of distinct events occur, they are eventually contained in different $E_{nk}$ sets when $n$ is large, and thus for such $n$, $N_n^* = M(E)$.

By using the first part of this lemma, Korolyuk's theorem follows as for the real line by a simple application of Fatou's lemma. Stated specifically we have (see [2]):

THEOREM 2.1 (Generalized Korolyuk's theorem). *For a point process, with* $\sigma$*-finite principal measure, on a space* $T$ *possessing a dissecting system, we have* $\lambda(E) = \mathscr{E}N^*(E)$ *for all* $E \in \mathscr{T}$. *In particular if there are no multiple events, then the principal and parametric measures coincide on* $\mathscr{T}$.

If $\lambda(\cdot)$ or $\mu(\cdot)$ is absolutely continuous with respect to some $\sigma$-finite measure $\nu$ on $T$, then under the above conditions the densities $d\lambda/d\nu$, $d\mu/d\nu$ coincide a.e. This reduces again to the usual statement of Korolyuk's theorem for stationary point processes on the line.

A point process on $T$ is called regular (orderly, ordinary—of [20], [5] and especially [2]) with respect to a dissecting system $\mathscr{C} = \{E_{nk}\}$ if

$$\lim_{n \to \infty} \sup_k \frac{Pr\,\{N(E_{nk}) > 1\}}{Pr\,\{N(E_{nk}) > 0\}} = 0. \tag{2.5}$$

(For simplicity, we shall always assume $Pr\,\{N(E_{nk}) > 0\} \neq 0$ for any $n$, $k$.) This definition applies to a point process which may conceivably have multiple events. However, the next result shows that in fact regularity precludes the occurrence of multiple events under simple conditions on $T$.

THEOREM 2.2. *Consider a point process (allowing multiple events) on a space* $T$ *possessing a dissecting system* $\mathscr{C}$. *Suppose the process is regular and that there exist* $E_n \in \mathscr{C}$, $E_n \uparrow T$ *such that* $\lambda(E_n) < \infty$. *Then, with probability one, the process has no multiple events.*

PROOF. Let $E \in \mathscr{C}$ be such that $\lambda(E) < \infty$. Write again $M(E)$ for the number of *multiple* events in $E$. Then by Lemma 2.1, $M(E) = \lim_{n\to\infty} \Sigma_{k \in I_n} \chi_{nk}^*$ (with the usual notation), where $\chi_{nk}^*$ is one or zero according as $N(E_{nk}) > 1$ or not. Hence,

$$\begin{aligned} \mathscr{E}M(E) &\leqq \liminf_n \Big[\sum_{k \in I_n} Pr\,\{N(E_{nk}) > 1\}\Big] \\ &\leqq \liminf_n \left[\sup_k \frac{Pr\,\{N(E_{nk}) > 1\}}{Pr\,\{N(E_{nk}) > 0\}} \sum_{j \in I_n} Pr\,\{N(E_{nj}) > 0\}\right], \end{aligned} \tag{2.6}$$

which is zero since by regularity the first term in the braces tends to zero, and the sum does not exceed $\lambda(E) < \infty$. Since $\mathscr{E}M(E)$ is a measure on $\mathscr{T}$, $\mathscr{E}M(T) = \lim_{n\to\infty} \mathscr{E}M(E_n) = 0$, and hence, $M(T) = 0$ with probability one.

A converse result of Theorem 2.2 is "Dobrushin's lemma." A general form of this given in [2] assumes a "homogeneous" point process—for which $T$ possesses a fundamental system $\mathscr{C}$ of dissecting sets such that $p_{nk}(0) = Pr\{N(E_{nk}) > 0\}$, $p_{nk}(1) = Pr\{N(E_{nk}) > 1\}$ are each dependent on $n$ but not on $k$ for $E_{nk} \in \mathscr{C}$. This assumption does not imply stationarity of the point process (indeed there may be no "translations" defined on $T$), but it may well be that the only interesting homogeneous processes are stationary ones. We give a less restricted result below. It may still be of greatest interest in the stationary case, but it does allow considerable variation in the quantities $p_{nk}(0)$, $p_{nk}(1)$ for fixed $n$.

Specifically to obtain Dobrushin's lemma, we shall assume the existence of a dissecting system $\mathscr{C} = \{E_{nk}\}$ for which there is a sequence $\{\theta_n\}$ of nonnegative real numbers, and a function $\phi(\theta) \to 0$ as $\theta \to 0$, such that for each $n$

$$\theta_n \leqq \frac{Pr\{N(E_{nk}) > 1\}}{Pr\{N(E_{nk}) > 0\}} \leqq \phi(\theta_n) \tag{2.7}$$

for all $k$.

THEOREM 2.3 (Generalized version of Dobrushin's lemma). *Consider a point process without multiple events, on a space $T$ possessing a dissecting system $\mathscr{C}$ satisfying* (2.7). *Suppose $\lambda(E) < \infty$ for some $E \in \mathscr{C}$. Then the point process is regular.*

PROOF. Using the notation of Lemma 2.1, we have

$$\sum_{k\in I_n} \chi_{nk} \to N(E), \qquad \sum_{k\in I_n} \chi^*_{nk} \to 0 \tag{2.8}$$

with probability one, as $n \to \infty$. Since both sums are dominated by $N(E)$ and $\mathscr{E}N(E) = \mu(E) = \lambda(E) < \infty$, it follows by dominated convergence that

$$\sum_{k\in I_n} Pr\{N(E_{nk}) > 0\} = \mathscr{E}\{\sum_{k\in I_n} \chi_{nk}\} \to \mu(E) = \lambda(E), \tag{2.9}$$

and similarly that

$$\sum_{k\in I_n} Pr\{N(E_{nk}) > 1\} \to 0. \tag{2.10}$$

Hence by (2.7),

$$\theta_n \sum_{k\in I_n} Pr\{N(E_{nk}) > 0\} \leqq \sum_{k\in I_n} Pr\{N(E_{nk}) > 1\} \to 0, \tag{2.11}$$

and thus by (2.9), $\theta_n \to 0$ $(\lambda(E) \geqq Pr\{N(E) > 0\} > 0$ since $E \in \mathscr{C})$.

Finally, from (2.7) again,

$$\sup_k \left[\frac{Pr\{N(E_{nk}) > 1\}}{Pr\{N(E_{nk}) > 0\}}\right] \leqq \phi(\theta_n) \to 0 \tag{2.12}$$

as $n \to \infty$.

## 3. Stationarity generalities

A very great deal of literature exists relative to stationary point processes on the real line (see Section 4). One expects to be able to say less about stationary point processes on the plane or in $R^n$ (see, for example, [6]). However, there is quite a good deal that may be said even when $T$ is just assumed to be a (locally compact) topological group. In this section, we comment briefly on a few aspects of such results.

If $T$ is a locally compact (Hausdorff) group, the natural $\sigma$-field $\mathscr{T}$ is the class of Borel sets—generated by the open sets of $T$. It is usually convenient to assume (and we here do) that $T$ is also $\sigma$-compact, and then $\mathscr{T}$ is also generated by the compact sets of $T$. (It is, in fact, sometimes assumed that $T$ is second countable; for example, [15]. While this additional assumption may be necessary for some purposes it does, however, imply that the group is also metrizable.)

For a point process on such a group $T$, stationarity may be defined in terms of the invariance of the joint distributions of $N(tE_1), \cdots, N(tE_n)$ for $t \in T$, where $n$ is any fixed positive integer and the $E_i$ are any fixed sets of $\mathscr{T}$ $(tE = \{ts : s \in E\}$, $ts$ denoting the group operation). If $T$ is not abelian this gives a concept of "left stationarity," "right stationarity" being correspondingly defined.

Under (say, left) stationarity, the principal and parametric measures $\mu(\cdot)$, $\lambda(\cdot)$ are (left) invariant Borel measures which are regular provided their values on compact sets are finite ([7], Theorem 64I)—which we will assume. Thus, $\lambda(\cdot)$ and $\mu(\cdot)$ are just constant multiples of the Haar measure $m(\cdot)$ on $T$, $\lambda(E) = \lambda m(E)$, $\mu(E) = \mu m(E)$, say, for all $E \in \mathscr{T}$, where $\lambda$ and $\mu$ are constants, the *parameter* and the *intensity* of the stationary point process, respectively. Questions concerning the parameter and intensity in such a setting have been discussed to some extent in [1]. The general line of argument above is that of [2].

If in addition $T$ possesses a dissecting system $\mathscr{C} = \{E_{nk}\}$ of, say, bounded sets (that is, having compact closures) and if a stationary point process on $T$ is without multiple events, then Theorem 2.1 shows that $\lambda = \mu < \infty$. This is Korolyuk's theorem in the stationary case. Further, in such a case it is not unreasonable to suppose that $P\{N(E_{nk}) > 0\}$ and $m(E_{nk})$ are independent of $k$ (which will hold if, for example, for fixed $n$ the $E_{nk}$ are translates of each other). Then using the notation of Theorem 2.3 we have, from the proof of that theorem,

$$r_n Pr\,\{N(E_{n0}) > 0\} \to \lambda(E) = \lambda m(E) \tag{3.1}$$

for $E \in \mathscr{C}$, where $r_n$ is the (necessarily finite) number of integers in the set $I_n$ and $E_{n0}$ is any given $E_{nk}$ for $k \in I_n$.

But since by definition of $\mathscr{C}$.

$$E - \bigcup_{k \in I_n} E_{nk} \subset F_n \downarrow \varnothing, \tag{3.2}$$

it follows that

$$r_n m(E_{n0}) = \sum_{k \in I_n} m(E_{nk}) \to m(E), \tag{3.3}$$

and hence, that

$$\frac{Pr\{N(E_{n0}) > 0\}}{m(E_{n0})} \to \lambda \tag{3.4}$$

as $n \to \infty$. It is this latter property that the parameter satisfies in Khinchin's existence theorem. We summarize this as a theorem. For convenience of statement, we will *here* call a dissecting system $\mathscr{C}$ *homogeneous* if the distribution of $N(E_{nk})$ and $m(E_{nk})$ do not depend on $k$ for each fixed $n$.

THEOREM 3.1. *Consider a stationary point process without multiple events on locally compact group $T$. Suppose $T$ is also $\sigma$-compact. Then there exist constants $\lambda$, $\mu$ such that $\lambda(E) = \lambda m(E)$, $\mu(E) = \mu m(E)$ for all $E \in \mathscr{T}$, where $m(\cdot)$ is the Haar measure of $T$, $0 \leqq \lambda \leqq \mu < \infty$.*

*Suppose, in addition, that $T$ has a homogeneous dissecting system $\mathscr{C} = \{E_{nk}\}$ of bounded sets $E_{nk}$. Then the point process is regular, $\lambda = \mu$ and*

$$\lim_{n\to\infty} \frac{Pr\{N(E_{n0}) > 0\}}{m(E_{n0})} = \lambda, \tag{3.5}$$

*where $E_{n0}$ is any $E_{nk}$.*

COROLLARY 3.1. *The stated results hold if the condition that $\mathscr{C}$ be a homogeneous dissecting system is replaced by the requirement that for each fixed $n$, the sets $E_{nk}$ are all translates of each other.*

The above remarks have been concerned with a stationary process without multiple events. When multiple events are allowed, the appropriate generalizations of the real line results occur. For example, if $E$ is a set of $\mathscr{T}$ with $\mu(E) < \infty$ (for example, $E$ compact), and if $N_s(E)$ denotes the number of those events in $E$ which have "multiplicity" $s = 1, 2, \cdots$, then $p_s = \mathscr{E}N_s(E)/\lambda(E)$ is a probability distribution on the integers $1, 2, \cdots$. we may interpret $\{p_s\}$ as the "probability that an event has multiplicity $s$." If in addition $T$ has a homogeneous dissecting system $\mathscr{C} = \{E_{nk}\}$ and we choose $E \in \mathscr{C}$ with $\mu(E) < \infty$ writing $\chi^s_{nk} = 1$ if $N(E_{nk}) = s$ and $\chi^s_{nk} = 0$ otherwise, then, similarly to Lemma 2.1,

$$\sum_{k\in I_n} \chi^s_{nk} \to N_s(E) \tag{3.6}$$

as $n \to \infty$, with probability one. The familiar argument of taking expectations and using dominated convergence shows that $r_n Pr\{N(E_{n0}) = s\} \to \mathscr{E}N_s(E)$, where $E_{n0}$ is any $E_{nk}$ and $r_n$ is the number of points in $I_n$. Similarly, $r_n Pr\{N(E_{n0}) \geqq 1\} \to \lambda(E)$. Thus,

$$p_s = \lim_{n\to\infty} Pr\{N(E_{n0}) = s \mid N(E_{n0}) \geqq 1\}, \tag{3.7}$$

giving intuitive justification to the description of $p_s$ as the probability that an event has multiplicity $s$ (under these assumptions $p_s$ does not depend on $E$). Further questions of this type are considered in [16] when $T = R^n$. We note that the above calculation may also be considered as a special case of that in the next section concerning Palm distributions.

## 4. Concerning Palm distributions

For a stationary point process, the Palm distribution $P_0$ gives a precise meaning to the intuitive notion of conditional probability "given an event of the process occurred at some point (for example, $t = 0$)." When $T$ is the real line, we may write (for certain sets $F \in \mathscr{F}$)

$$P_0(F) = \lim_{\delta \downarrow 0} Pr\{F \mid N((-\delta, 0)) \geqq 1\}. \tag{4.1}$$

That is, $P_0(F)$ is then the limit of the conditional probability of $F$ given an event occurred in an interval near $t = 0$ as that interval shrinks. For example, if $F$ denotes the occurrence of at least one event in the interval $(0, t]$ (that is, $\{N(0, t) \geqq 1\}$), then $P_0(F) = F_1(t)$, the distribution function for the time to the first event after time zero given an event occurred "at" time zero.

This kind of procedure for particular sets $F$ was used by Khinchin [9] and is useful in providing an "analytical" approach to such conditional probabilities (see, for example, [12]). More sophisticated and general measure theoretic treatments involving the definition and properties of $P_0$ have been given by a variety of authors (for example, [14], [15], [17], [18], [19]). In this section, we shall use a "middle of the road" approach to the definition of $P_0$ (based essentially on [14]) which is capable of considerable generality. Our main purpose will be to give simple proofs for formulae such as (4.1) and its generalizations to include "conditional expectations" of functions. Such results have application, for example, to the evaluation of the distributions of the times between events in terms of conditional moments [13].

We give the construction of the Palm distribution $P_0$ for stationary point process on the real line in the manner of [14], though, from a somewhat different viewpoint. The construction generalizes to apply to point processes on groups (see also [15]), but we consider just the real line case for simplicity relative to the later results.

Consider, then, a stationary point process (without multiple events for simplicity) with finite parameter $\lambda$ on the real line. Again for simplicity, we take the sample points $\omega$ to be themselves the subsets $S_\omega$ of $T = R^1$, that is, $\omega$ is a countable set of real numbers (without finite limit points, since $\lambda < \infty$). Denote by $\mathscr{T}$ the Borel sets of $T = R^1$ and by $\mathscr{F}$ the smallest $\sigma$-field on $\Omega$ making $N(B) = N_\omega(B)$ measurable for each $B \in \mathscr{T}$. Finally, we shall again write $N(s, t)$ for $N\{(s, t]\}$, the number of events (card $\{\omega \cap (s, t]\}$) in the semiclosed interval $(s, t]$.

For any real $t$, and $\omega \in \Omega$, let $\omega_t \in \Omega$ denote the set of points of $\omega$ translated to the left by $t$; that is, if $\omega = \{t_i\}$, $\omega_t = \{t_i - t\}$. If $F$ is any set of $\mathscr{F}$ and $\omega \in \Omega$, $\omega = \{t_i\}$, say, we define $\omega^* \in \Omega$ to consist of precisely those points $t_i \in \omega$ for which $\omega_{t_i} \in F$. In other words, to form $\omega^*$, we "thin" $\omega$ by retaining only the points $t_i$ such that $\omega_{t_i}$ (that is, $\omega$ translated to $t_i$ as origin) is in $F$. The $\omega^*$ define a stationary point process formed from some of the events in the original point process. For example, if $F = \{\omega : N(0, t) \geqq 1\}$, the new process contains precisely those events $t_i$ of the old process which are followed by a further event within a further time $t$ (that is, no later than $t_i + t$). Write $N_F$ for the number of events of the thinned process in the interval (0, 1), that is, card $\{\omega^* \cap (0, 1)\}$. Then the thinned process has intensity $\lambda_F = \mathscr{E} N_F$.

Now this procedure may be carried out for any $F \in \mathscr{F}$, and for fixed $\omega$, $N_F$ is countably additive as a function on $\mathscr{F}$. It follows at once that $\lambda_F$ is a measure on $\mathscr{F}$, and hence, that

$$P_0(F) = \frac{\lambda_F}{\lambda} \tag{4.2}$$

is a probability measure on $\mathscr{F}$, $\lambda = \lambda_\Omega = \mathscr{E} N(0, 1)$. This $P_0$ is the desired *Palm distribution*.

To give $P_0$ an intuitive interpretation, one wishes to prove relations such as (4.1). Equation (4.1) is not universally true, however, as can be seen by considering a "periodic" stationary point process in which the events occur at a regular spacing $h$, where the distance to the first one after $t = 0$ is a uniform random variable on $(0, h)$. For this process take $F$ to be the occurrence of at least one event in the open interval $(h - \eta, h)$. Clearly, $Pr\{F \mid N(-\delta, 0) \geqq 1\} = 1$ when $\delta < \eta$. But $N_F = 0$, and hence $P_0(F) = 0$.

We give now a class of sets for which (4.1) does hold. Specifically, we shall call a set $F \in \mathscr{F}$ *right continuous* if its characteristic function $\chi_F(\omega)$ is such that $\chi_F(\omega_t)$ is continuous to the right in $t$; that is $\chi_F(\omega_s) \to \chi_F(\omega_t)$ as $s \downarrow t$. Equivalently, this means that for any $t$, if $\omega_t \in F$ then $\omega_s \in F$ when $s$ is sufficiently close to $t$ on the right, and conversely.

THEOREM 4.1. *Suppose $F \in \mathscr{F}$ is a right continuous set. Then*

$$Pr\{F \mid N(-\delta, 0) \geqq 1\} \to P_0(F) \tag{4.3}$$

*as $\delta \downarrow 0$.*

PROOF. Let $\delta_m$ be any sequence of nonnegative numbers converging to zero as $m \to \infty$. Write $r_m$ for the integer part $[\delta_m^{-1}]$ of $\delta_m^{-1}$. Divide the interval (0, 1) into $r_m$ intervals of length $\delta_m$ (with perhaps an interval of length less than $\delta_m$ left over). Write $\chi_{mi} = 1$ if $N((i-1)\delta_m, i\delta_m) \geqq 1$, $\chi_{mi} = 0$ otherwise, $i = 0, 1 \cdots r_m$. Let

$$N_m = \sum_{i=1}^{r_m} \chi_{mi} \chi_F(\omega_{i\delta_m}). \tag{4.4}$$

Then $N_m$ denotes the number of intervals $((i-1)\delta_m, i\delta_m]$ containing an event and such that the translate $\omega_{i\delta_m}$ is in $F$. But by the right continuity assumption, if an event occurs at $t_0$, then $\omega_{t_0} \in F$ if and only if $\omega_{i\delta_m} \in F$ for that interval $((i-1)\delta_m, i\delta_m]$ containing $t_0$ when $m$ is sufficiently large. Further, with probability one, when $m$ is sufficiently large the events all lie in different intervals and there is no event in the last short interval. Hence, with probability one,

$N_m \to N_F$ as $m \to \infty$. Since $N_m \leqq N(0, 1)$ and $\mathscr{E}N(0, 1) < \infty$, it follows by dominated convergence that $\mathscr{E}N_m \to \lambda_F$ as $m \to \infty$. That is,

$$\sum_{i=1}^{r_m} Pr\{\chi_{mi} = 1, \omega_{i\delta_m} \in F\} \to \lambda_F \tag{4.5}$$

or by stationarity, $r_m Pr\{\chi_{m0} = 1, \omega \in F\} \to \lambda_F$. But

$$Pr\{\chi_{m0} = 1, \omega \in F\} = Pr\{F \mid N(-\delta_m, 0) \geqq 1\} \, Pr\{N(-\delta_m, 0) \geqq 1\}. \tag{4.6}$$

Hence, since $r_m \sim \delta_m^{-1}$ and $Pr\{N(-\delta_m, 0) \geqq 1\} \sim \lambda\delta_m$, we have

$$Pr\{F \mid N(-\delta_m, 0) \geqq 1\} \to \frac{\lambda_F}{\lambda} = P_0(F), \tag{4.7}$$

as required.

As an example, consider the set $F = \{\omega : N(0, t) \geqq r\}$, $r = 1, 2, \cdots$. This is easily seen to be right continuous, and hence the theorem applies. In this case,

$$P_0(F) = \lim_{\delta \downarrow 0} Pr\{N(0, t) \geqq r \mid N(-\delta, 0) \geqq 1\} \tag{4.8}$$

is interpreted as the distribution function for the time to the $r$th event after time zero, given an event occurred "at" time zero. (Note that at least $r$ events occur in $(0, t)$ if and only if the time to the $r$th event after time zero does not exceed $t$.)

Similarly, if we take $0 < t_1 \leqq t_2 \cdots \leqq t_k$, $0 \leqq r_1 \leqq r_2 \cdots \leqq r_k$, and

$$F = \{\omega : N(0, t_1) \geqq r_1, N(0, t_2) \geqq r_2, \cdots, N(0, t_k) \geqq r_k\}, \tag{4.9}$$

then $F$ is right continuous, leading to what could naturally be termed the joint distribution function for the time to the $r_1$st, $r_2$nd, $\cdots$, $r_k$th events after the origin given an event occurred at the origin.

The convergence in Theorem 4.1 does not occur for all $F \in \mathscr{F}$ in general. However, we may regard the probability space $\Omega$ as consisting of real integer valued functions increasing by unit jumps where events occur, and consider it as a subspace of $D$, the space of functions with discontinuities of the first kind (see [3]) where $D$ has the "Skorohod topology." Then Theorem 4.1 may be shown to imply weak convergence of $P_\delta = P(\cdot \mid N(-\delta, 0) > 0)$ to $P_0$.

A slightly different definition given by Matthes ([14]) does give convergence similar to Theorem 4.1 for all $F \in \mathscr{F}$. Specifically, let $s = s(\omega)$ denote the time of the first event prior to the origin. Then instead of $P_\delta(F) = P\{\omega : \omega \in F \mid N(-\delta, 0) > 0\}$, we may consider $P_\delta^*(F) = P\{\omega : \omega_s \in F \mid N(-\delta, 0) > 0\}$. That is, the "origin is moved" slightly to the point $s$ of $(-\delta, 0)$, where an event occurs. Then the following theorem (which is virtually identical to that of [10], Section 1(f)) holds.

THEOREM 4.2. *For each $F \in \mathscr{F}$,*

$$P_\delta^*(F) \to P_0(F) \tag{4.10}$$

*as $\delta \downarrow 0$ (hence the total variation of $P_\delta^* - P_0$ tends to zero $\delta \downarrow 0$).*

PROOF. This can be proved as in [10], Section 1. However, a very easy proof follows by a simplification of the method of Theorem 4.1. In fact, using the notation of that proof, we consider $N_m^*$ (instead of $N_m$), where

$$N_m^* = \sum_{i=1}^{r_m} \chi_{mi} \chi_F(\omega_{s_{mi}}) \tag{4.11}$$

with $s_{mi}$ denoting the position of the last event prior to (or at) $i\delta_m$. (A contribution to the sum only occurs if this event is in $((i - 1)\delta_m, i\delta_m]$.) Then, with probability one, $N_m^*$ converges to the number of events $t_i \in (0, 1)$ for which $\omega_{t_i} \in F$. It follows as before by dominated convergence and stationarity that $r_m Pr\{\chi_{m0} = 1, \omega_s \in F\} \to \lambda_F$, from which the desired result follows (for any sequence $\delta_m \downarrow 0$) using the fact that $Pr\{N(-\delta_m, 0) \geqq 1\} \sim \lambda/r_m$.

The fact that the limit in (4.10) holds for all $F \in \mathscr{F}$ is, of course, more satisfying than that in (4.1) which requires "continuity sets." However, the definition of $P_\delta^*$ is more complicated than that of $P_\delta$ and the limit in (4.1) may be more useful in practice. The difference between $P_\delta$ and $P_\delta^*$ is, of course, slight (but we feel it worthy of exploration).

Theorems 4.1 and 4.2 concerned conditional expectations of the function $\chi_F$, given an event near the origin. One may ask whether similar results hold for other functions. To answer this in relation to Theorem 4.1, we will call a measurable function $\phi(\omega)$ *continuous to the right* if $\phi(\omega_t)$ is continuous to the right in $t$.

Before stating the generalization of Theorem 4.1, we give a lemma (the result of which is contained in [14]) which is useful in a number of contexts.

LEMMA 4.1. *If $\phi$ is a measurable function on $\Omega$ and $\phi$ is either nonnegative, or integrable with respect to $P_0$, then*

$$\lambda \int \phi dP_0 = \mathscr{E}\{\Sigma\, \phi(\omega_{t_j}): t_j \in \omega \cap (0, 1)\}. \tag{4.12}$$

The statement of this lemma, when $\phi = \chi_F$, $F \in \mathscr{F}$, is just the definition of $P_0(F)$. Its truth for nonnegative measurable or $P_0$ integrable $\phi$ follows at once by the standard approximation technique.

The following result generalizes Theorem 4.2.

THEOREM 4.3. *Let $\phi$ be measurable (on $\Omega$), continuous to the right and such that $|\phi(\omega_t)| < \psi(\omega)$ for all $t \in (0, 1)$, where $\mathscr{E}\{\psi N(0, 1)\} < \infty$. Then*

$$\mathscr{E}\{\phi \,|\, N(-\delta, 0) \geqq 1\} \to \int \phi dP_0 \tag{4.13}$$

*as $\delta \downarrow 0$.*

PROOF. The pattern of the proof of Theorem 4.1 applies, with $\phi$ written for $\chi_F$ Specifically,

$$S_m = \sum_{i=1}^{r_m} \chi_{mi} \phi(\omega_{i\delta_m}) \to \sum \{\phi(\omega_{t_j}): t_j \in \omega \cap (0, 1)\} \tag{4.14}$$

with probability one. But $|S_n| \leqq \psi(\omega) \cdot N(0, 1)$ which has finite expectation, and thus, by dominated convergence and Lemma 4.1,

$$\int \phi \, dP_0 = \lambda^{-1} \lim_{m\to\infty} \mathscr{E} S_m \tag{4.15}$$

$$= \lambda^{-1} \lim_{m\to\infty} r_m \mathscr{E}\{\chi_{m0}\phi(\omega)\}$$

$$= \lim_{m\to\infty} \mathscr{E}\{\phi \mid \chi_{m0} = 1\}$$

since $Pr(\chi_{m0} = 1) \sim \lambda\delta_m \lambda r_m^{-1}$. This is the desired result (writing $N(-\delta_m, 0) \geqq 1$ for $\chi_{m0} = 1$).

COROLLARY 4.1. *If $\phi$ is a bounded, right continuous function, the result holds. For if $|\phi| \leqq K$ we may take $\psi(\omega) = K$ and $\mathscr{E}\{\psi N(0, 1)\} = K\lambda < \infty$.*

This corollary is similar to a theorem of Ryll-Nardzewski [18] (there two sided continuity of $\phi(\omega_t)$ is required and the condition $N(-\delta, 0) \geqq 1$ replaced by $N(-\delta, \delta) \geqq 1$).

COROLLARY 4.2. *Suppose $\mathscr{E}N^{k+1}(0, \tau) < \infty$ for some positive integer $k$, $\tau > 0$. Then*

$$\lim_{\delta\downarrow 0} \mathscr{E}\{N^k(0, \tau) \mid N(-\delta, 0) \geqq 1\} = \mathscr{E}_{P_0} N^k(0, \tau), \tag{4.16}$$

*where $\mathscr{E}_{P_0}$ denotes expectation with respect to the Palm distribution. That is, the $k$th moment of $N(0, \tau)$ with respect to the Palm distribution is simply the $k$th conditional moment (defined as a limit) given an event "at" the origin.*

The proof is immediate on noting that $\phi(\omega) = N_\omega^k(0, \tau)$ is continuous to the right, and for all $t \in [0, 1]$,

$$\phi(\omega_t) = N_\omega(t, t + \tau) \leqq N(0, 1 + \tau) = \psi(\omega), \tag{4.17}$$

where $\mathscr{E}\{\psi(\omega)N(0, 1)\} \leqq \mathscr{E}N^{k+1}(0, 1 + \tau)$. This latter quantity is finite since it is easily seen by Minkowski's inequality and stationarity that $\mathscr{E}N^{k+1}(0, s) < \infty$ for all $s > 0$.

Finally, we note the corresponding generalization of Theorem 4.2. For this, the condition required above that $\phi$ be continuous to the right can be omitted, but the origin must "be moved" to measure from the time $s$ of the first event prior to zero. We state this formally.

THEOREM 4.4. *Let $\phi$ be measurable and such that $|\phi(\omega_t)| < \psi(\omega)$ for all $t \in (0, 1)$, where $\mathscr{E}\{\psi N(0, 1)\} < \infty$. Then*

$$\mathscr{E}\{\phi(\omega_s) \mid N(-\delta, 0) \geqq 1\} \to \int \phi \, dP_0 \tag{4.18}$$

*as $\delta \downarrow 0$, where $s = s(\omega)$ denotes the position of the first event prior to $t = 0$.*

## REFERENCES

[1] R. A. AGNEW, "Transformations of uniform and stationary point processes," Ph.D. thesis, Northwestern University, 1968.

[2] YU. K. BELYAYEV, "Elements of the general theory of random streams," Appendix to Russian edition of *Stationary and Related Stochastic Processes* by H. Cramér and M. R. Leadbetter, MIR, Moscow, 1969. (English translation under preparation for University of North Carolina Statistics Mimeograph Series, No. 703, 1970.)

[3] P. Billingsley, *Convergence of Probability Measures*, New York, Wiley, 1968.
[4] W. Fieger, "Eine für beliebige Call-Prozesse geltende Verallgemeinerung der Palmschen Formeln," *Math. Scand.*, Vol. 16 (1965), pp. 121–147.
[5] ———, "Zwei Verallgemeinerungen der Palmschen Formeln," *Transactions of the Third Prague Conference on Information Theory*, Prague,—Czechoslovak Academy of Sciences, 1964, pp. 107–122.
[6] J. R. Goldman, "Infinitely divisible point processes in $R^n$," *J. Math. Anal. Appl.*, Vol. 17 (1967), pp. 133–146.
[7] P. R. Halmos, *Measure Theory*, Princeton, Van Nostrand, 1950.
[8] T. E. Harris, "Random measures and motions of point processes," *Z. Wahrscheinlichkeitstheorie und verw. Gebiete*, Vol. 18 (1971), pp. 85–115.
[9] Y. A. Khinchin, *Mathematical Methods in the Theory of Queueing*, London, Griffin, 1960.
[10] D. König and K. Matthes, "Verallgemeinerungen der Erlangschen Formeln, I," *Math. Nachr.*, Vol 26 (1963), pp. 45–56.
[11] M. R. Leadbetter, "On three basic results in the theory of stationary point processes," *Proc. Amer. Math. Soc.*, Vol. 19 (1968), pp. 115–117.
[12] ———, "On streams of events and mixtures of streams," *J. Roy. Statist. Soc. Ser. B*, Vol. 28 (1966), pp. 218–227.
[13] ———, "On certain results for stationary point processes and their application," *Bull. Inst. Internat. Statist.*, Vol. 43 (1969) pp. 309–319.
[14] K. Matthes, "Stationäre zufällige Punktfolgen I," *Jber. Deutsch. Math.-Verein.*, Vol. 66 (1963), pp. 66–79.
[15] J. Mecke, "Stationäre zufällige Masse auf lokalkompakten Abelschen Gruppen," *Z. Wahrscheinlichkeitstheorie und verw. Gebiete*, Vol. 9 (1967), pp. 36–58.
[16] R. K. Milne, "Simple proofs of some theorems on point processes," *Ann. Math. Statist.*, Vol. 42 (1971), pp. 368–372.
[17] J. Neveu, "Sur la structure des processus ponctuels stationnaires," *C. R. Acad. Sci. Paris, Ser. A*, Vol. 267 (1968), pp. 561–564.
[18] C. Ryll-Nardzewski, "Remarks on processes of calls," *Proceedings of the Fourth Berkeley Symposium on Mathematical Statistics and Probability*, Berkeley and Los Angeles, University of California Press, 1961, Vol. 2, pp. 455–466.
[19] I. M. Slivnyak, "Stationary streams of homogeneous random events," *Vestnik Harkov. Gos. Univ.*, Vol. 32 (1966), pp. 73–116. (In Russian.)
[20] F. Zitek, "On the theory of ordinary streams," *Czechoslovak Math. J.*, Vol. 8 (1958), pp. 448–458. (In Russian.)

# Editor's Comments on Papers 11 and 12

11 **Cox and Lewis:** *Multivariate Point Processes*

12 **Solomon and Wang:** *Nonhomogeneous Poisson Fields of Random Lines with Applications to Traffic Flow*

The next two papers are included to show the development of two generalizations of point-process models. The first one (Paper 11) develops the theory of multivariate processes, which represent occurrences of events of more than one type. A basic assumption in the theory of point processes precludes the simultaneous occurrence of more than one event. It is possible, however, to have two correlated point processes such that one event of the first and one event of the second occur simultaneously; an example is the input–output streams of customers in a service station.

The second one (Paper 12) generalizes the point process to a random field much as an ordinary random process can be generalized to a random field. One motivation for such a generalization is the use of the random-field model in the study of traffic flow. The events of such a field are lines occurring on the plane under Poisson-like statistics, similar to the way that points occur on the line in a simple point process.

# 11



# MULTIVARIATE POINT PROCESSES

D. R. COX
Imperial College, University of London
and
P. A. W. LEWIS*
Imperial College, University of London
and
IBM Research Center

## 1. Introduction

We consider in this paper events of two or more types occurring in a one dimensional continuum, usually time. The classification of the events may be by a qualitative variable attached to each event, or by their arising in a common time scale but in different physical locations. Such multivariate point processes, or multitype series of events, are to be distinguished from events of one type occurring in an $n$ dimensional continuum and considered, for example, by Bartlett [2]. It is of course possible to have multivariate point processes in, say, two dimensions, for example, the locations of accidents labelled by day of occurrence, but we do not consider this extension here.

Multivariate series of events arise in many contexts; the following are a few examples.

Example 1.1. Queues are a well-known situation in which bivariate point processes arise as the input and output, although interest in the joint properties of the input and output processes is fairly recent (for example, Daley [16] and Brown [7]). The two processes occur simultaneously in time. Many of the variants on simple queueing situations which have been considered give rise to more than two point processes.

Example 1.2. An important and rich source of multivariate point processes is neurophysiology (Perkel, Gerstein, and Moore [41]). Information is carried along nerve bundles by spikes which occur randomly in time. (The spikes are extremely narrow and, at least in many situations, their shape and height do not appear to vary or carry information.) The neuronal spike trains of different types may be observations at different locations with no definite knowledge of physical connection, or may be the inputs and outputs to nerve connections (neurons).

Example 1.3. When the events are crossings of a given level by a real valued stochastic process in continuous time, the up crossings and down crossings of the

*Support under a National Institutes of Health Special Fellowship (2–FO3–GM 38922–02) is gratefully acknowledged. Present address: Naval Postgraduate School, Monterey, California.

level constitute a very special bivariate point process in which the two types of events alternate (Leadbetter [27]). However, up crossings of two different levels produce a general type of bivariate point process which is of interest, for example, in reliability investigations.

EXAMPLE 1.4. In reliability studies over time, of continuously operating machines such as computers, the failures are more often than not labelled according to the part of the system in which they occurred, or according to some other qualitative characterization of the failure, for example, mechanical or electrical. One might also be interested in studying interactions between preventive maintenance points and failures occurring during normal operation. Again a comparison between failure patterns in separately located computers (Lewis [29]) might be of interest in determining whether some unknown common variable, such as temperature and/or humidity, influences reliability.

EXAMPLE 1.5. Cox [11] has considered the problem of analyzing events of two types in textile production. The two types of event may be breakdowns in the loom and faults in the cloth, or different types of breakdown of the loom. The continuum is length of thread rather than time.

EXAMPLE 1.6. In the analysis of electrocardiograms the trace is continuous, but both regular heart beats and various types of ectopic heart beats occur. It is therefore of interest to analyze electrocardiograms as bivariate event processes, even though defining the precise time of occurrence of the event (heartbeat) may present some problems.

EXAMPLE 1.7. Traffic studies are a rich source of multivariate point processes. Just two possibilities are that the events may be the passage of cars by a point on a road when the type of event is differentiated by direction of travel, or we may consider passage of cars past two different positions.

EXAMPLE 1.8. Finally, physical phenomena such as volcanoes or earthquakes (Vere-Jones [45], [46], [47]) may have distinguishing features of many kinds—generally highly compacted attributes of the process, for example, the general location of the origin of the earthquake.

Multivariate point processes can be regarded as very special cases of univariate point processes in which a real valued quantity is associated with each point event, that is, special cases of what Bartlett [3] has called, rather generally, line processes. In particular, if the real valued quantity takes only two possible values, we have in effect a bivariate process of events of two types.

Three broad types of problems arise for multivariate point processes. The first are general theoretical and structural problems of which the most outstanding is the problem of characterizing the dependence and interaction between a number of processes. This is the only general theoretical question we will consider in any detail; it is intimately connected with the statistical analysis of bivariate point processes.

The second type of problem is the calculation of the properties of special stochastic models suggested, for example, by physical considerations. This in general is a formidable task even for quite simple models.

Thirdly, there are problems of statistical analysis. These include:

(a) comparing rates in independent processes (Cox and Lewis [14], Chapter 9) from finite samples;

(b) assessing possible dependence between two processes from finite samples;

(c) determining, again from finite samples, the probabilistic structure of a mechanism which transforms one process into a second quite clearly dependent process.

The range of the problems will become clear in the main body of the paper. The topics considered are briefly as follows.

In Section 2, we give some notation and define various types of interevent sequences and counting processes which occur in bivariate point processes. Concepts such as independence of the marginal processes and stationarity and regularity of the complete, bivariate process are defined. The ideas of this section are illustrated by considering two independent renewal processes and also the semi-Markov process (Markov renewal process).

In Section 3, we study dependence and correlation in bivariate point processes, defining complete intensity functions and second order cross intensity functions and cross spectra, giving their relationship to covariance time surfaces. Doubly stochastic bivariate point processes are defined and their cross intensity function is given. Other simple models of bivariate point processes are defined through the complete intensity and cross intensity functions. In this way, various degrees of interaction between events in the bivariate process can be specified. A class of bivariate Markov interval processes is defined.

In Section 4, a simple delay model with marginal Poisson processes is considered in some detail. Other special physical models are considered briefly in Section 5.

General comments on bivariate Poisson processes are given at the end of Section 5; a bivariate Poisson process is defined simply as a bivariate point process whose marginal processes are Poisson processes.

Statistical procedures are considered in Section 6, including the estimation of second order cross intensity functions and cross spectra, as well as covariance time surfaces. Tests for dependence in general and particular situations are considered, and statistical procedures for some special processes are given.

Throughout, emphasis is placed on concepts rather than on mathematical details and a number of open questions are indicated. For the most part we deal with bivariate processes, that is, with events of two types; the generalization of more than two types of events is on the whole straightforward.

## 2. General definitions and ideas

2.1. *Regularity.* Throughout Section 2, we deal with bivariate processes, that is, processes of events of two types called type $a$ and type $b$. The process of, say, type $a$ events alone is called a *marginal process.*

In a univariate point process such as a marginal process in a bivariate point process, regularity is defined by requiring that in any interval of length $\Delta t$

$$Pr\{(\text{number events in } \Delta t) > 1\} = o(\Delta t). \tag{2.1}$$

Regularity is intuitively the nonoccurrence of multiple events.

For bivariate processes, we say the process is *marginally regular* if its marginal processes, considered as univariate point processes, are both regular. The bivariate process is said to be *regular* if the process of superposed marginal events is regular, that is, if the process of events regardless of type is regular. This type of regularity, of course, implies *marginal regularity*.

A simple, rather degenerate, bivariate process is obtained by taking three Poisson processes, say I, II, and III, and superposing processes I and II to obtain the events of type $a$ and superposing II and III to obtain the events of type $b$ (Marshall and Olkin [33]). Clearly, the bivariate process is marginally regular but not regular. However, if the events of type $b$ are made up of process III events superposed with process II events delayed by a fixed amount, the resulting bivariate process is regular. A commonly used alternative to the word *regular* is *orderly*.

2.2. *Independence and stationarity.* Independence of the marginal processes in a bivariate process is intuitively defined as independence of the number of events (counts) in any two sets of intervals in the marginal processes. The more difficult problem of specifying dependence (and correlation) in the bivariate process is central to this paper and will be taken up in the next section.

In the sequel, we will be primarily concerned with *transient* or *stationary* bivariate point processes, as opposed to *nonhomogeneous* processes. The latter type of process is defined roughly as one with either an evolutionary or cyclic trend, whereas a *transient* process is roughly one whose probabilistic structure eventually becomes stationary (time invariant). There are a number of types of stationarity which need to be defined more carefully.

DEFINITION 2.1 (Simple stationarity). *Let* $N^{(a)}(t_1^{(1)}, t_1^{(1)} + \tau_1^{(1)})$ *be the number of events of type a in the interval* $(t_1^{(1)}, t_1^{(1)} + \tau_1^{(1)}]$ *and* $N^{(b)}(t_2^{(1)}, t_2^{(1)} + \tau_2^{(1)})$ *be the number of events of type b in the interval* $(t_2^{(1)}, t_2^{(1)} + \tau_2^{(1)}]$. *The bivariate point process is said to have* simple stationarity *if*

$$\begin{aligned} Pr\{N^{(a)}(t_1^{(1)}, t_1^{(1)} + \tau_1^{(1)}) = n^{(a)}; N^{(b)}(t_2^{(1)}, t_2^{(1)} + \tau_2^{(1)}) = n^{(b)}\} \\ = Pr\{N^{(a)}(t_1^{(1)} + y, t_1^{(1)} + \tau_1^{(1)} + y) = n^{(a)}; \\ N^{(b)}(t_2^{(1)} + y, t_2^{(1)} + \tau_2^{(1)} + y) = n^{(b)}\}, \end{aligned} \tag{2.2}$$

*for all* $t_1, t_2, \tau_1^{(1)}, \tau_2^{(1)}, y > 0$.

In other words, the joint distribution of the number of type $a$ events in a fixed interval and the number of type $b$ events in another fixed interval is invariant under translation.

Simple stationarity of the bivariate process implies an analogous property for the individual marginal processes and for the superposed process.

In the sequel, we assume that for the marginal processes considered individually the probabilities of more than one type $a$ event in $\tau_1$ and more than one type $b$ event in $\tau_2$ are, respectively, $\rho_a \tau_1 + o(\tau_1)$ as $\tau_1 \to 0$ and $\rho_b \tau_2 + o(\tau_2)$ as $\tau_2 \to 0$, where $\rho_a$ and $\rho_b$ are finite.

Simple stationarity and these finiteness conditions imply that the univariate forward recurrence time relationships in the marginal processes and the pooled processes hold (Lawrance [25]).

If in addition the process is regular, Korolyuk's theorem implies that $\rho_a$, $\rho_b$, and $\rho_a + \rho_b$ are, respectively, the rates of events of types $a$, events of types $b$, and events regardless of type.

DEFINITION 2.2 (Second order stationarity). *By extension, we say that the bivariate point process has* second order stationarity (*weak stationarity*) *if the joint distribution of the number of type a events in two fixed intervals and the number of type b events in another two fixed intervals is invariant under translation.*

This type of stationarity is necessary in the sequel for the definition of a time invariant cross intensity function. Clearly, it implies second order stationarity for the marginal processes considered individually and for the superposed marginal processes.

DEFINITION 2.3 (Complete stationarity). *By extension,* complete stationarity *for a bivariate point process is invariant under translation for the joint distribution of counts in arbitrary numbers of intervals in each process.*

2.3. *Asynchronous counts and intervals.* In specifying stationarity, we did not mention the time origin or the method of starting the process. There are three main possibilities.

(i) The process is started at time $t = 0$ with initial conditions which produce stationarity, referred to as *stationary initial conditions.*

(ii) The process is transient and is considered beyond $t = 0$ as its start moves off to the left. The process then becomes stationary as the start moves to minus infinity. There is generally a specification of the state of the process at $t = 0$ known as the *stationary equilibrium conditions.*

Note that in both (i) and (ii) stationarity is defined by invariance under shifts to the right.

(iii) In a stationary point process, a time is specified without knowledge of the events and is taken to be the origin, $t = 0$. The time $t = 0$ is said to be an *arbitrary time* in the (stationary) process, selected by an *asynchronous sampling* of the process.

Now there is associated with the stationary bivariate point process a counting process $\mathbf{N}(t_1, t_2) = \{N^{(a)}(t_1), N^{(b)}(t_2)\}$, where

$$\begin{aligned} &N^{(a)}(t_1) \text{ is the number of type } a \text{ events in } (0, t_1], \\ &N^{(b)}(t_2) \text{ is the number of type } b \text{ events in } (0, t_2], \end{aligned} \tag{2.3}$$

and a bivariate sequence of intervals $\{X^{(a)}(i), X^{(b)}(j)\}$, where, assuming regularity of the process, $X^{(a)}(1)$ is the forward recurrence time in the process of type $a$ events (that is, the time from $t = 0$ to the first type $a$ event), $X^{(a)}(2)$ is the time between the first and second type $a$ events, and so forth; and the $\{X^{(b)}(j)\}$ sequence is defined similarly.

Note that for asynchronous sampling of a stationary process the indices $i$ and $j$ can take negative values; in particular, $\{X^{(a)}(-1), X^{(b)}(-1)\}$ are the bivariate backward recurrence times.

There is a fundamental relationship connecting the bivariate counting processes with the bivariate interval processes; this is a direct generalization of the relationship for the univariate case:

$$N^{(a)}(t_1) < n^{(a)}, \qquad N^{(b)}(t_2) < n^{(b)}, \tag{2.4}$$

if and only if

$$\begin{aligned} S^{(a)}(n^{(a)}) &= X^{(a)}(1) + \cdots + X^{(a)}(n^{(a)}) > t_1, \\ S^{(b)}(n^{(b)}) &= X^{(b)}(1) + \cdots + X^{(b)}(n^{(b)}) > t_2. \end{aligned} \tag{2.5}$$

Probability relationships are written down directly from these identities connecting the bivariate distribution of counts with the bivariate distribution of the sums of intervals $S^{(a)}(n^{(a)})$ and $S^{(b)}(n^{(b)})$.

Equations (2.4) and (2.5) can be used, for example, to prove the asymptotic bivariate normality of $\{N^{(a)}(t_1), N^{(b)}(t_2)\}$ for a broad class of bivariate point processes.

2.4. *Semisynchronous sampling.* In a univariate point process, *synchronous* sampling of the stationary process refers to the placement of the time origin at an arbitrary event and the examination of the counts and intervals following this arbitrary event (Cox and Lewis [14], Chapter 4, and McFadden [35]). In more precise terms (Leadbetter [27], [28], and Lawrance [24]), the notion of an arbitrary event in a stationary point process is the event $\{N(0, \tau) \geqq 1\}$ as $\tau$ tends to zero, and the distribution function $F(t)$ of the interval between the arbitrary event and the following event is defined to be

$$1 - F(t) = \lim_{\tau \to 0+} Pr\{N(\tau, \tau + t) = 0 | N(0, \tau) \geqq 1\}. \tag{2.6}$$

In bivariate point processes, the situation is more complex. Synchronous sampling of the marginal process of type $a$ events produces *semisynchronous sampling* of the process of $b$ events from an arbitrary $a$ event, and *vice versa*.

The bivariate counting processes and intervals following these two types of sampling are denoted as follows:

(a) for semisynchronous sampling of $b$ by $a$,

$N_a^{(a)}(t_1)$ is the number of type $a$ events following an origin at a type $a$ event;

$N_a^{(b)}(t_1)$ is the number of type $b$ events following an origin at a type $a$ event;

$\{X_a^{(a)}(i)\}$ is, for $i = 1$, the time from the origin at a type $a$ event to the next event of type $a$, and for $i = 2, 3, \cdots$, the intervals between subsequent type $a$ events;

$\{X_a^{(b)}(j)\}$ is, for $j = 1$, the time from the origin at a type $a$ event to the first subsequent type $b$ event, and for $j = 2, 3, \cdots$, the intervals between subsequent type $b$ events;

(b) for semisynchronous sampling of $a$ by $b$, the subscript becomes $b$ instead of $a$, in the above expressions, indicating the nature of the origin.

Note that in general (Slivnyak [44]) the sequences $\{X_a^{(a)}(i)\}$ and $\{X_b^{(b)}(j)\}$, being the synchronous interval processes in the marginal point processes, are stationary, whereas $\{X_a^{(b)}(i)\}$ and $\{X_b^{(a)}(j)\}$, the semisynchronous intervals, are in general not stationary. Also for independent processes, the semisynchronous sequences are identical with the asynchronous sequences $\{X^{(a)}(i)\}$ and $\{X^{(b)}(j)\}$.

2.5. *Pooling and superposition of processes.* In discussing regularity, we referred to the superposition of the two marginal processes in the bivariate process. This is the univariate process of events of both types considered without specification of the event type and is referred to simply as the *superposed process.* Study of the superposed process of rate $\rho_a + \rho_b$ is an intimate part of the analysis of the bivariate process. Asynchronous sampling of the superimposed process gives counts and intervals denoted by $N^{(\cdot)}(t_1)$ and $\{X^{(\cdot)}(i)\}$, whereas synchronous sampling, that is, the process considered conditionally (in the Khinchin sense) on the existence of an event of an unspecified type at the origin, gives $N_{\cdot}^{(\cdot)}(t_1)$ and $\{X_{\cdot}^{(\cdot)}(i)\}$.

Semisynchronous sampling of the superposed process by events of type $a$ or type $b$ is also possible and the notation should be clear.

We call the superposed process with specification of the event type the *pooled* process. The original bivariate process can then be respecified in terms of the process

$$\{X_{\cdot}^{(\cdot)}(i), \qquad T_{\cdot}(i)\}, \tag{2.7}$$

where $T_{\cdot}(i)$ is a binary valued process indicating the type of the $i$th event after the origin in the superposed process with synchronous sampling. Clearly, the marginal processes of event types, that is, $\{T(i)\}$, $\{T_{\cdot}(i)\}$, $\{T_a(i)\}$ and $\{T_b(i)\}$ are themselves of interest. Note that they are in general not stationary processes for all types of sampling and are related to the processes defined in Sections 2.3 and 2.4. Thus, for example,

$$\{X_a^{(\cdot)}(1) \leqq x; T_a(1) = a\} \Leftrightarrow \{X_a^{(a)} < X_a^{(b)}; X_a^{(a)} \leqq x\}, \tag{2.8}$$

with much more complicated statements relating events of higher index $i$. The binary sequence of event types has no counterpart in univariate point process.

Thus, there are many possible representations of a bivariate point process. Which is the most fruitful is likely to depend on the particular application.

As a very simple practical example of these representations, consider a generalization of the alternating renewal process. We have a sequence of positive random variables $W(1)$, $Z(1)$, $W(2)$, $Z(2)$, $\cdots$, representing operating and repair intervals in a machine. It is natural to assume that $W(i)$ and $Z(i)$ are mutually correlated but independent of other pairs of operating and repair times. Type $a$ events, occurring at the end of the $W(i)$ variables, are machine failures. Type $b$ events occur at the end of $Z(i)$ variables and represent times at which the machine goes back into service.

Specification of the process is straightforward and simple in terms of the pooled process variables $\{X_{\cdot}^{(\cdot)}(i), T_{\cdot}(i)\}$, $\{X_a^{(\cdot)}(i), T_a(i)\}$, and so forth. However, marginally the type $b$ events are a renewal process, whereas the type $a$ events are a nonrenewal, non-Markovian point process and the dependency structure expressed through the intervals in the marginals is complex.

2.6. *Successive semisynchronous sampling.* Finally, we mention the possibility of successive semisynchronous samples of the marginal process of type $b$ events by $a$ events. The origin is at an $a$ event, as in ordinary semisynchronous sampling and connected with this $a$ event is the time forward (or backward) to the next $b$ event. Subsequent $a$ events are associated with the times forward (or backward) to the next $b$ event. It is not clear how generally useful this procedure is in studying bivariate point processes. It has been used, however, by Brown [7] in studying identifiability problems in $M/G/\infty$ queues; see also Section 6.4.

2.7. *Palm-Khinchin formulae.* In the theory of univariate point processes, there are relations connecting the distributions of sums of synchronous intervals and sums of asynchronous intervals. Similar relationships connect the synchronous and asynchronous counting processes. These relationships are sometimes called the Palm-Khinchin formulae and are given, for example, by Cox and Lewis ([14], Chapter 4).

The best known of these relations connects the distributions of the synchronous and asynchronous forward recurrence times in a stationary point process with finite rate $\rho$ (Lawrance [25]). In the context of the marginal process of type $a$ events,

$$\rho_a\{1 - F_{X_a^{(a)}}(t)\} = D_t^+ F_{X^{(a)}}(t), \tag{2.9}$$

where $D_t^+$ denotes a right derivative. For moments when the relevant moments exist we have

$$E\{(X^{(a)})^r\} = \frac{\rho_a E\{(X_a^{(a)})^{r+1}\}}{r+1}. \tag{2.10}$$

Palm-Khinchin type formulae for bivariate point processes have been developed by Wisniewski [50], [51]. They are far more complex than those for univariate processes, both in terms of the number of relationships involved and in the analytical problems encountered. Thus, on the first point there are not only interval relationships, but also relationships between the probabilistic structures of the binary sequences $\{T(i)\}$ and $\{T_{\cdot}(i)\}$ and between the probabilistic structures of the binary sequence $\{T(i)\}$ and the binary sequences $\{T_a(i)\}$ and $\{T_b(i)\}$.

On the second point, the analytical problems are illustrated by the following argument. It is easily shown that an arbitrarily selected point in the (univariate) superposed process is of type $a$ with probability $\rho_a/(\rho_a + \rho_b)$. Thus, any probabilistic statement about the variables $\{X_\cdot^{(\cdot)}(i), T_\cdot(i)\}$, say $g(X_\cdot^{(\cdot)}(1), T_\cdot(1), \cdots)$, is expressible in terms of the same probabilistic statement for $\{X_a^{(\cdot)}(i), T_a(i)\}$ and $\{X_b^{(\cdot)}(i), T_b(i)\}$,

$$g(X_\cdot^{(\cdot)}(1), T_\cdot(1), \cdots) = \frac{\rho_a}{\rho_a + \rho_b} g(X_a^{(\cdot)}(1), \cdots) + \frac{\rho_b}{\rho_a + \rho_b} g(X_b^{(\cdot)}(1), \cdots). \tag{2.11}$$

Now if a relationship between $g(X^{(\cdot)}(1), T(1), \cdots)$, and $g(X_\cdot^{(\cdot)}(1), T_\cdot(1), \cdots)$ exists, we can relate the asynchronous sequence to the two semisynchronous sequences through (2.11). But the usual univariate Palm-Khinchin formulae relate univariate distributions of *sums* of asynchronous intervals to univariate distributions of sums of synchronous intervals. Clearly, formulae relating *joint* properties of asynchronous intervals and types to joint properties of synchronous intervals $X_\cdot(i)$ and types $T_\cdot(i)$ are needed if one is, for example, to relate, through (2.11) and generalizations of (2.8), bivariate distributions of asynchronous forward recurrence times $\{X^{(a)}(1), X^{(b)}(1)\}$ to the bivariate distributions of the semisynchronous forward recurrence times $\{X_a^{(a)}(1), X_a^{(b)}(1)\}$ and $\{X_b^{(a)}(1), X_b^{(b)}(1)\}$,

Lawrance [26] has noted this need for extended Palm-Khinchin formulae and conjectured results in the univariate case.

Of Wisniewski's results [50], [51], we cite here only two moment formulae. These relate the moments of the joint asynchronous forward recurrence times $\{X^{(a)}(1), X^{(b)}(1)\}$ with the moments of both of the semisynchronous forward recurrence times, $\{X_a^{(a)}(1), X_a^{(b)}(1)\}$ and $\{X_b^{(a)}(1), X_b^{(b)}(1)\}$. The feature that probabilistic properties of both semisynchronous sequences are needed to determine probabilistic properties of the asynchronous sequence is characteristic of all these relationships, and follows from (2.11).

We have for the bivariate analogues to (2.10), for $r = 1$,

$$\begin{aligned} &\tfrac{1}{2}\rho_a E[\{X_a^{(a)}(1)\}^2] + \tfrac{1}{2}\rho_b E[\{X_b^{(b)}(1)\}^2] \\ &\quad = E\{X^{(a)}\} + E\{X^{(b)}\} \\ &\quad = \rho_a E\{X_a^{(a)}(1)\, X_a^{(b)}(1)\} + \rho_b E\{X_b^{(a)}(1)\, X_b^{(b)}(1)\} \end{aligned} \tag{2.12}$$

and

$$\begin{aligned} &12E\{X^{(a)}(1)\, X^{(b)}(1)\} \\ &\quad = \rho_a E[3X_a^{(a)}(1)\,\{X_a^{(b)}(1)\}^2 + 3\{X_a^{(a)}(1)\}^2\, X_a^{(b)}(1) - \{X_a^{(a)}(1)\}^3] \\ &\qquad + \rho_b E[3X_b^{(b)}(1)\,\{X_b^{(a)}(1)\}^2 + 3\{X_b^{(b)}(1)\}^2\, X_b^{(a)}(1) - \{X_b^{(b)}(1)\}^3]. \end{aligned} \tag{2.13}$$

The interesting feature of (2.12) is that the correlation between semisynchronous forward recurrence times is a function only of the properties of the marginal processes and not of the dependency structure of the bivariate point process. Moreover, (2.13) shows that if we use correlation between the asynchronous forward recurrence times as a measure of dependence in the bivariate point process, this dependence only affects the third order joint moments of the semisynchronous forward recurrence times.

2.8. *Examples.* To illustrate the definitions and concepts introduced above, we consider two very simple bivariate point processes. The analytical details developed here will be used in Section 6 in considering the statistical analysis of bivariate point processes.

EXAMPLE 2.1. *Independent renewal processes.* Consider two *delayed* renewal processes $\{X^{(a)}(1); X_a^{(a)}(i), i = 2, 3, \cdots\}$ and $\{X^{(b)}(1); X_b^{(b)}(j), j = 2, 3, \cdots\}$, where using a shortened notation,

$$G^{(a)}(x) = Pr\{X^{(a)}(1) \leqq x\} = \frac{\int_0^x \{1 - F^{(a)}(u)\}\, du}{E_a(X)}, \tag{2.14}$$

$$Pr\{X_a^{(a)}(i) \leqq x\} = F^{(a)}(x), \qquad E_a(X) = \int_0^\infty x\, dF^{(a)}(x), \tag{2.15}$$

with similar definitions for the process of type $b$ events. The distribution of the variable $X^{(a)}(1)$ in (2.14) and the analogous distribution for $X^{(b)}(1)$ are the stationary initial conditions for the marginal renewal processes, and clearly the independence of the processes implies that these distributions (jointly) give stationarity to the bivariate process. Because of independence there is no difference between semisynchronous and asynchronous sampling; the process is defined completely in terms of the properties of the asynchronous and synchronous intervals.

Properties of intervals in the superposed process, and properties of successive intervals and event types in the pooled process, that is, $\{X^{(\cdot)}(i), T(i)\}$ are very difficult to obtain explicitly. The sequences $X^{(\cdot)}(i)$ and $T(i)$ are neither stationary nor independent, but contain transient effects. We have for example

$$\begin{aligned} Pr\{X^{(\cdot)}(1) > x; T(1) = a\} &= Pr\{X^{(b)}(1) > X^{(a)}(1) > x\} \\ &= \int_x^\infty \{1 - G^{(b)}(y)\}\, dG^{(a)}(y) \end{aligned} \tag{2.16}$$

and, marginally,

$$Pr\{T(1) = a\} = \int_0^\infty \{1 - G^{(b)}(y)\}\, dG^{(a)}(y). \tag{2.17}$$

The only simple case is where the two renewal processes are Poisson processes with parameters $\rho_a$ and $\rho_b$. Then, of course, $\{X^{(\cdot)}(i)\}$ is a Poisson process of rate $\rho_a + \rho_b$ and $T(i)$ is an independent binomial sequence

$$Pr\{T(1) = a\} = Pr\{T(1) = a | X^{(\cdot)} > x\} = \frac{\rho_a}{\rho_a + \rho_b}. \tag{2.18}$$

EXAMPLE 2.2. *Semi-Markov processes (Markov renewal processes).* The two state semi-Markov process is the simplest bivariate process with dependent structure and plays, in bivariate process theory, a role similar to that played in univariate process theory by the renewal process. It is, in a sense, the closest one gets in bivariate processes to a regenerative process. The process is defined in terms of the sequences $\{X_a^{(\cdot)}(i), T_a(i)\}$, and $\{X_b^{(\cdot)}(i), T_b(i)\}$, the type processes $\{T_a(i)\}$ and $\{T_b(i)\}$ being Markov chains with transition matrix

$$\mathbf{P} = \begin{pmatrix} p_{aa} & p_{ab} \\ p_{ba} & p_{bb} \end{pmatrix} = \begin{pmatrix} \alpha_1 & 1 - \alpha_1 \\ 1 - \alpha_2 & \alpha_2 \end{pmatrix}, \tag{2.19}$$

while the distributions of the random variables $X_a^{(\cdot)}(i)$, $X^{(\cdot)}(i)$, and $X_b^{(\cdot)}(i)$ depend only on the type of events at $i$ and $(i - 1)$. Thus, illustrating the regenerative nature of the process, we define $F_{aa}(x)$ to be, for $i \geqq 2$,

$$\begin{aligned} F_{aa}(x) &= Pr\{X_a^{(\cdot)}(i) \leqq x \,|\, T_a(i) = a, T_a(i - 1) = a\} \\ &= Pr\{X_\cdot^{(\cdot)}(i) \leqq x \,|\, T_\cdot(i) = a, T_\cdot(i - 1) = a\} \\ &= Pr\{X^{(\cdot)}(i) \leqq x \,|\, T(i) = a, T(i - 1) = a\} \end{aligned} \tag{2.20}$$

with equivalent definitions for $F_{ab}(x)$, $F_{ba}(x)$, $F_{bb}(x)$. Thus, the effect of the initial sampling disappears when the type of the first subsequent events is known.

The joint distributions of the time from the origin to the first event and the type of the first event $(i = 1)$ are either quite arbitrary initial conditions, or initial conditions established by the kind of sampling involved at the origin and denoted by the subscript on the interval random variable. Thus for asynchronous sampling, we get stationary initial conditions which are specified by the joint distribution of $X^{(\cdot)}(i)$ and $T(1)$.

These stationary equilibrium conditions (Pyke and Schaufele [43]) are that $T(1) = a$ and $T(1) = b$ have probabilities $p_a$ and $p_b$, where

$$\{p_a, p_b\} = \{p_a, p_b\}\, \mathbf{P} = \left\{\frac{1 - \alpha_2}{2 - \alpha_1 - \alpha_2}, \frac{1 - \alpha_1}{2 - \alpha_1 - \alpha_2}\right\}, \tag{2.21}$$

the equilibrium probabilities of the Markov chain, and the time from the origin to an event of type $a$ has distribution function

$$\frac{p_{ba} \int_0^x R_{ba}(u)\, du}{E(X_b^{(b)}(1))} + \frac{p_{aa} \int_0^x R_{aa}(u)\, du}{E(X_a^{(a)}(1))}, \tag{2.22}$$

with a similar definition for the time to an event of type $b$.

Cinlar [9] has reviewed the properties of semi-Markov processes. Our view of these processes, being related to statistical problems arising in the analysis of bivariate point processes, will be somewhat different from the usual one. Thus, note that in the marginal processes the regenerative property of the semi-Markov process implies that the times between events of type $a$, $X_a^{(a)}(i)$, $i = 1, 2, \cdots$, are independent and identically distributed, as are the $X_b^{(b)}(j)$, $j = 1, 2, \cdots$. Therefore, the marginal processes are renewal processes and we say that the semi-Markov process is a *bivariate renewal process*. Since the types of successive renewals (events) form a Markov chain, the process is also called a Markov renewal process ([9], p. 130). However, the two marginal renewal processes together with the Markov chain of event types do not determine the process.

The dependency structure of this bivariate renewal process can also be examined through joint properties of forward recurrence times in the process. The joint forward recurrence times $\{X_a^{(a)}(1), X_a^{(b)}(1)\}$ for semisynchronous sampling of $b$ by $a$ are, in the terminology of semi-Markov process theory, the first passage times from state $a$ to state $a$ and from state $a$ to state $b$, with similar definitions for $\{X_b^{(a)}(1), X_b^{(b)}(1)\}$. Denoting the marginal distributions of these random variables by $F_a^{(a)}(x)$ and so forth, we have the equations

$$F_a^{(a)}(x) = p_{aa}F_{aa}(x) + p_{ab}F_{ab}(x) * F_b^{(a)}(x), \tag{2.23}$$

$$F_a^{(b)}(x) = p_{ab}F_{ab}(x) + p_{aa}F_{aa}(x) * F_a^{(b)}(x), \tag{2.24}$$

$$F_b^{(a)}(x) = p_{ba}F_{ba}(x) + p_{bb}F_{bb}(x) * F_b^{(a)}(x), \tag{2.25}$$

$$F_b^{(b)}(x) = p_{bb}F_{bb}(x) + p_{ba}F_{ba}(x) * F_a^{(b)}(x), \tag{2.26}$$

where $*$ denotes Stieltjes convolution and $F_{aa}(x)$ and so forth, are defined in (2.20).

These equations can be solved using Laplace–Stieltjes transforms. Thus, if $\mathscr{F}_a^{(a)}(s)$ is the Laplace–Stieltjes transform of $F_a^{(a)}(x)$, and so forth, we get

$$\mathscr{F}_a^{(a)}(s) = \alpha_1 \mathscr{F}_{aa}(s) + \frac{(1 - \alpha_1)(1 - \alpha_2)\mathscr{F}_{ab}(s)\mathscr{F}_{ba}(s)}{1 - \alpha_2 \mathscr{F}_{bb}(s)}, \tag{2.27}$$

$$\mathscr{F}_b^{(b)}(s) = \alpha_1 \mathscr{F}_{bb}(s) + \frac{(1 - \alpha_1)(1 - \alpha_2)\mathscr{F}_{ab}(s)\mathscr{F}_{ba}(s)}{1 - \alpha_1 \mathscr{F}_{aa}(s)}. \tag{2.28}$$

From these results, we can write down joint forward recurrence time distributions using the regenerative properties of the process. For example,

$$\begin{aligned} &R_{X_a^{(a)}(1), X_a^{(b)}}(x_1, x_2) \\ &\quad = Pr\{X_a^{(a)}(1) > x_1, X_a^{(b)} > x_2\} \\ &\quad = \begin{cases} \alpha_1 R_{aa}(x_1) + (1 - \alpha_1)\left\{R_{ab}(x_1) + \displaystyle\int_{x_2}^{x_1} [1 - F_b^{(a)}(x_1 - u)]\, dF_{ab}(u)\right\} & \text{if } x_1 \geqq x_2, \\ (1 - \alpha_1)R_{ab}(x_2) + \alpha_1 \left\{R_{aa}(x_2) + \displaystyle\int_{x_1}^{x_2} [1 - F_a^{(b)}(x_2 - u)]\, dF_{aa}(u)\right\} & \text{if } x_2 \geqq x_1. \end{cases} \end{aligned} \tag{2.29}$$

It is actually much simpler, because of the regenerative nature of the process, to express results in terms of the order statistics and order types associated with $R(x_1, x_2)$. These aspects of the process are worked out in greater detail by Wisniewski [50].

Note that the process derived previously as two independent Poisson processes is a very particular form of semi-Markov process. The question then arises whether there are any other semi-Markov processes with Poisson marginals and the answer is clearly yes. For example, when $\alpha_1 = \alpha_2 = 0$ we have the special case of an alternating renewal process and choosing $F_{ab}(x)$ and $F_{ba}(x)$ to be distributions of random variables proportional to chi square variables with one degree of freedom gives Poisson marginals. The example shows in fact that one can produce any desired marginal renewal processes in a semi-Markov process, as is also clear from (2.27) and (2.28).

From equations such as (2.14) and (2.15), it can be shown that no bivariate process of independent renewal marginals is a semi-Markov process unless the marginals are also Poisson processes. The dependency structure in a semi-Markov process is actually better characterized by the second order cross intensity function, which we introduce in the next section, rather than by joint moments of forward recurrence times. This cross intensity function together with the two distributions of intervals in the marginal renewal processes (or equivalently the intensity functions of the marginal renewal processes) completely specifies the semi-Markov process.

## 3. Dependence and correlation in bivariate point processes

3.1. *Specification.* We now consider in more detail the specification of the structure of bivariate point processes. It is common in the study of particular stochastic processes to find that physically the same process can be specified in several equivalent but superficially different ways. A simple and familiar example is the stationary univariate Poisson process which can be specified as:

(a) a process in which the numbers of events in disjoint sets have independent Poisson distributions with means proportional to the measures of the sets;

(b) a renewal process with exponentially distributed intervals;

(c) a process in which the probability of an event in $(t, t + \Delta t]$ has an especially simple form, as $\Delta t \to 0$.

We call these three specifications, respectively, the counting, the interval, and the intensity specifications. Univariate point processes can in general be specified in these three ways, if the initial conditions are properly chosen.

While the counting specification (a) for bivariate point processes is in principle fundamental, it is often too complicated to be very fruitful. If the joint characteristic functional of the process, defined by an obvious generalization of the univariate case, can be obtained in a useful form, this does give a concise representation of all the joint distributions of counts; even then, such a characteristic functional would usually give little insight into the physical mechanism generating the process.

Often, special processes are most conveniently handled through some kind of interval specification, especially when this corresponds rather closely to the physical origin of the process. In particular, the two state semi-Markov process is most simply specified in this way, as shown in Section 2.8. The two main types of interval specifications discussed in Section 2 were the specifications in terms of the intervals in the marginal processes, or the intervals and event types in the pooled process. The latter is the basic specification for the semi-Markov process. Other processes, such as various kinds of inhibited processes and the bivariate Poisson process of Section 4.1 are specified rather less directly in terms of relations between intervals and event types.

However, in some ways the most convenient general specification is through the intensity. Denote by $\mathscr{H}_t$ the history of the process at time $t$, that is, a complete specification of the occurrences in $(-\infty, t]$ measured backwards from an origin at $t$, then two time points $t'$, $t''$ have the same history if and only if the observed sequences $\{x^{(a)}(-1), x^{(a)}(-2), \cdots\}$, $\{x^{(b)}(-1), x^{(b)}(-2), \cdots\}$ are identical if measured from origins at $t'$ and at $t''$.

Then a marginally regular process is specified by

$$\lambda^{(a)}(t; \mathscr{H}_t) = \lim_{\Delta t \to 0+} \frac{Pr\{N^{(a)}(t, t + \Delta t) \geqq 1 | \mathscr{H}_t\}}{\Delta t}, \tag{3.1}$$

$$\lambda^{(b)}(t; \mathscr{H}_t) = \lim_{\Delta t \to 0+} \frac{Pr\{N^{(b)}(t, t + \Delta t) \geqq 1 | \mathscr{H}_t\}}{\Delta t}, \tag{3.2}$$

$$\lambda^{(ab)}(t; \mathscr{H}_t) = \lim_{\Delta t \to 0+} \frac{Pr\{N^{(a)}(t, t + \Delta t) N^{(b)}(t, t + \Delta t) \geqq 1 | \mathscr{H}_t\}}{\Delta t}. \tag{3.3}$$

We call these functions the *complete intensity functions* of the process. If the process is regular $\lambda^{(ab)}(t; \mathscr{H}_t) = 0$. Given the functions (3.1) through (3.3) and some initial conditions, we can construct a discretized realization of the process, although this is, of course, a clumsy method of simulation if the interval specification is at all simple.

One advantage of the complete intensity specification is that one can generate families of models of increasing complexity by allowing more and more complex dependency on $\mathscr{H}_t$. This may be useful, for instance, in testing consistency of data with a given type of model, for example, a semi-Markov process. Further, if the main features of $\mathscr{H}_t$ that determine the intensity functions can be found, an appropriate type of model may be indicated.

As an example of a complete intensity specification, consider the two state semi-Markov process. Here the only aspects of $\mathscr{H}_t$ that are relevant, if at least one event has occurred before $t$, are the backward recurrence time to the previous event and the type of that event $\{x^{(\cdot)}(-1), t(-1)\}$. Any initial conditions disappear once one event has occurred. For convenience, we write the partial history as $(u, a)$, if the preceding event is of type $a$ and $(u, b)$ if it is of type $b$. Then assuming that the process is regular, that is, that none of the interval distributions has an atom at zero, we have

$$\lambda^{(a)}\{t; (u, a)\} \equiv \lambda_a^{(a)}(u) = \frac{p_{aa} f_{aa}(u)}{p_{aa} R_{aa}(u) + p_{ab} R_{ab}(u)}, \tag{3.4}$$

$$\lambda^{(b)}\{t;\,(u,a)\} \equiv \lambda_a^{(b)}(u) = \frac{p_{ab} f_{ab}(u)}{p_{aa} R_{aa}(u) + p_{ab} R_{ab}(u)}, \tag{3.5}$$

with similar expressions defining $\lambda_b^{(a)}(u)$ and $\lambda_b^{(b)}(u)$ when the partial history is $(u, b)$. These complete intensities are analogues of the hazard function, or age specific failure rate, which can be used to specify a univariate renewal process.

The semi-Markov process is characterized by the dependence on $\mathscr{H}_t$ being only on $u$ and the type of the preceding event. We can generalize the semi-Markov process in many ways, for instance by allowing a dependence on both of the backward recurrence times $x^{(a)}(-1)$ and $x^{(b)}(-1)$; see Section 3.8.

3.2. *Properties of complete intensity functions.* We now consider briefly some properties of complete intensity functions. It is supposed for simplicity that the process is regular and that it is observed for a time long enough to allow initial conditions to be disregarded. For the semi-Markov process "long enough" is the occurrence of at least one event.

(i) If the process is completely stationary, as defined in Section 2.3, the intensity functions depend only on $\mathscr{H}_t$ and not on $t$.

(ii) Nonstationary generalizations of a given stationary process can be produced by inserting into the intensity a function either of $t$, for example, $e^{\gamma t}$, $\exp\{\gamma\cos(\omega_0 t + \phi)\}$, or of the numbers of events that have occurred since the start of the process.

(iii) The intensity specification of a stationary process is unique in the sense that if we have two different intensity specifications and can find a set of histories of nonzero probability such that, say, the first intensity specification gives greater intensity of events of type $a$ than the second, then the two processes are distinguishable from suitable data. Note that this is not the same question as whether two different specifications containing unknown parameters are distinguishable.

(iv) The events of different types are independent if and only if $\lambda^{(a)}$ and $\lambda^{(b)}$ involve $\mathscr{H}_t$ only through the histories of the separate processes of events of type $a$ and type $b$, denoted, respectively, by $\mathscr{H}_t^{(a)}$ and $\mathscr{H}_t^{(b)}$.

(v) We can call the process purely $a$ dependent if both $\lambda^{(a)}$ and $\lambda^{(b)}$ depend on $\mathscr{H}_t$ only through $\mathscr{H}_t^{(a)}$. In many ways the simplest example of such a process is obtained when both intensities depend only on the backward recurrence time in the process of events of type $a$, that is, on the time $u^{(a)}$ measured back to the previous event of type $a$. Denote the intensities by $\lambda^{(a)}(u^{(a)})$ and $\lambda^{(b)}(u^{(a)})$. Then the events of type $a$ form a renewal process; if in particular $\lambda^{(a)}(\cdot)$ is constant, the events of type $a$ form a Poisson process. If simple functional forms are assumed for the intensities, the likelihood of data can be obtained in a fairly simple form and hence an efficient statistical analysis derived.

(vi) A different kind of purely $a$ dependent process is derived from a shot noise process based on the $a$ events, that is, by considering a stochastic process $Z^{(a)}(t)$ defined by

$$Z^{(a)}(t) = \int_0^\infty g(u)\, dN^{(a)}(t-u). \tag{3.6}$$

We then take $\lambda^{(b)}(t)$ and possibly also $\lambda^{(a)}(t)$ to depend only on $Z^{(a)}(t)$. In particular if $g(u) = 1(u < \Delta)$ and $g(u) = 0(u \geqq \Delta)$, the intensities depend only on the number of events of type $a$ in $(t - \Delta, t)$. Hawkes [22] has considered some processes of this type.

(vii) The intensity functions look in one direction in time. This approach is therefore rather less suitable for processes in a spatial continuum, where there may be no reason for picking out one spatial direction rather than another.

(viii) Some simple processes, for example, the bivariate Poisson process of Section 4.1, have intensity specifications that appear quite difficult to obtain.

3.3. *Second order cross intensity functions.* In Section 3.2, we considered the complete intensity functions which specify probabilities of occurrence given the entire history $\mathscr{H}_t$. For some purposes, it is useful with stationary (second order) processes to be less ambitious and to consider probabilities of occurrence conditionally on much less information than the entire history $\mathscr{H}_t$. We then call the functions corresponding to (3.1) through (3.3) incomplete intensity functions. For example, using the notation of (3.4) and (3.5), both

$$\lim_{\Delta t \to 0+} Pr \frac{\{N^{(a)}(t, t + \Delta t) \geqq 1 | (u, a)\}}{\Delta t} \tag{3.7}$$

and the corresponding function when the last event is of type $b$ are defined for any regular stationary process, even though they specify the process completely only for semi-Markov processes.

A particularly important incomplete intensity function is obtained when one conditions on the information that an event of specified type occurs at the time origin. Again for simplicity, we consider stationary regular processes. Write

$$h_a^{(a)}(t) = \lim_{\Delta t \to 0+} Pr \frac{\{N^{(a)}(t, t + \Delta t) \geqq 1 | \text{type } a \text{ event at } 0\}}{\Delta t}, \tag{3.8}$$

$$h_a^{(b)}(t) = \lim_{\Delta t \to 0+} Pr \frac{\{N^{(b)}(t, t + \Delta t) \geqq 1 | \text{type } a \text{ event at } 0\}}{\Delta t}, \tag{3.9}$$

with similar definitions for $h_b^{(a)}(t)$, $h_b^{(b)}(t)$ if an event of type $b$ occurs at 0. We call the function (3.9) a second order cross intensity function. For nonregular processes, it may be helpful to introduce intensities conditionally on events of both types occurring at 0.

Note that the cross intensity functions $h_a^{(b)}(t)$ and $h_b^{(a)}(t)$ will contain Dirac delta functions as components if, for example, there is a nonzero probability that an event of type $b$ will occur exactly $\tau$ away from a type $a$ event. For the process to be regular, rather than merely marginally regular, the cross intensity functions must not contain delta functions at the origin.

Note too that $h_a^{(b)}(t)$ is well defined near $t = 0$ and will typically be continuous there.

If following an event of type $a$ at the origin, subsequent events of type $a$ are at times $S_a^{(a)}(1), S_a^{(a)}(2), \cdots$ and those of type $b$ at $S_a^{(b)}(1), S_a^{(b)}(2), \cdots$, we can write

$$h_a^{(a)}(t) = \sum_{r=1}^{\infty} f_{S_a^{(a)}(r)}(t), \tag{3.10}$$

$$h_a^{(b)}(t) = \sum_{r=1}^{\infty} f_{S_a^{(b)}(r)}(t), \tag{3.11}$$

where $f_U(\cdot)$ is the probability density function of the random variable $U$.

If the process of type $a$ events is a renewal process, (3.10) is a function familiar as the renewal density. For small $t$ the contribution from $r = 1$ is likely to be dominant in all these functions.

The intensities are defined for all $t$. However, $h_a^{(a)}(t)$ and $h_b^{(b)}(t)$ are even functions of $t$. Further, it follows from the definition of conditional probability that

$$h_b^{(a)}(t)\rho_b = h_a^{(b)}(-t)\rho_a, \tag{3.12}$$

where $\rho_a$ and $\rho_b$ are the rates of the two processes. For processes without long term effects, we have that as $t \to \infty$ or $t \to -\infty$

$$h_a^{(a)}(t) \to \rho_a, \qquad h_b^{(a)}(t) \to \rho_a, \qquad h_b^{(b)}(t) \to \rho_b. \tag{3.13}$$

Sometimes it may be required to calculate the intensity function of the superposed process, that is, the process in which the type of event is disregarded. Given an event at the time origin, it has probability $\rho_a/(\rho_a + \rho_b)$ of being a type $a$, and hence the intensity of the superposed process is

$$h_{\cdot}^{(\cdot)}(t) = \frac{\rho_a}{\rho_a + \rho_b} \{h_a^{(a)}(t) + h_a^{(b)}(t)\} + \frac{\rho_b}{\rho_a + \rho_b} \{h_b^{(a)}(t) + h_b^{(b)}(t)\}. \tag{3.14}$$

This is a general formula for the intensity function of the superposition of two, possibly dependent, processes.

3.4. *Covariance densities.* For some purposes, it is slightly more convenient to work with covariance densities rather than with the second order intensity functions; see, for example, Bartlett [4]. To define the *cross covariance density*, we consider the random variables $N^{(a)}(0, \Delta' t)$ and $N^{(b)}(t, t + \Delta'' t)$ and define

$$\begin{aligned} \gamma_a^{(b)}(t) &= \lim_{\Delta' t, \Delta'' t \to 0+} \frac{\operatorname{Cov}\{N^{(a)}(0, \Delta' t), N^{(b)}(t, t + \Delta'' t)\}}{\Delta' t \, \Delta'' t} \\ &= \rho_a h_a^{(b)}(t) - \rho_a \rho_b. \end{aligned} \tag{3.15}$$

It follows directly from (3.14) or from (3.12) and (3.15), that $\gamma_a^{(b)}(t) = \lambda_b^{(a)}(-t)$. Note that an *autocovariance density* such as $\gamma_a^{(a)}(t)$ can be written

$$\gamma_a^{(a)}(t) = \rho_a \delta(t) + \gamma_{a,\text{cont}}^{(a)}(t) = \rho_a \delta(t) + \rho_a\{h_b^{(a)}(t) - \rho_a\}, \tag{3.16}$$

where the second terms are continuous at $t = 0$ and $\delta(t)$ denotes the Dirac delta function.

We denote by $V^{(ab)}(t_1, t_2)$ the covariance between $N^{(a)}(t_1)$ and $N^{(b)}(t_2)$ in the stationary bivariate process. This is called the *covariance time surface*. Then

$$V^{(ab)}(t_1, t_2) = \text{Cov}\,\{N^{(a)}(t_1), N^{(b)}(t_2)\} = \text{Cov}\left\{\int_0^{t_1} dN^{(a)}(u), \int_0^{t_2} dN^{(b)}(v)\right\} = \int_0^{t_1}\int_0^{t_2} \gamma_b^{(a)}(u - v)\,du\,dv. \tag{3.17}$$

In the special case $t_1 = t_2 = t$, we write $V^{(ab)}(t, t) = V^{(ab)}(t)$. It follows from (3.17) that

$$V^{(ab)}(t) = \int_0^t (t - v)\{\gamma_b^{(a)}(v) + \gamma_a^{(b)}(v)\}\,dv. \tag{3.18}$$

Note that in (3.18) a delta function component at the origin can enter one but not both of the cross covariance densities. If, in (3.18), we take the special highly degenerate case when the type $b$ and type $a$ processes coincide point for point, we obtain the well-known variance time formula

$$V^{(aa)}(t) = \text{Var}\,\{N^{(a)}(t)\} = \rho_a t + 2\int_{0+}^t (t - v)\gamma_a^{(a)}(v)\,dv. \tag{3.19}$$

An interesting question concerns the conditions under which a set of functions $\{\gamma_a^{(a)}(t), \gamma_b^{(a)}(t), \gamma_a^{(b)}(t), \gamma_b^{(b)}(t)\}$ can be the covariance densities of a bivariate point process. Now for all $\alpha$ and $\beta$

$$\text{Var}\,\{\alpha N^{(a)}(t_1) + \beta N^{(b)}(t_2)\} = \alpha^2 V^{(aa)}(t_1) + 2\alpha\beta V^{(ab)}(t_1, t_2) + \beta^2 V^{(bb)}(t_2) \geqq 0. \tag{3.20}$$

Thus for all $t_1$ and $t_2$,

$$V^{(aa)}(t_1) \geqq 0, \qquad \{V^{(ab)}(t_1, t_2)\}^2 \leqq V^{(aa)}(t_1)V^{(bb)}(t_2), \qquad V^{(bb)}(t_2) \geqq 0. \tag{3.21}$$

The conditions (3.21) can be used to show that certain proposed functions cannot be covariance densities. It would be interesting to know whether corresponding to any functions satisfying (3.21) there always exists a corresponding stationary bivariate point process.

Nothing special is learned by letting $t_1$ and $t_2 \to 0$ in (3.21). If, however, we let $t_1 = t_2 \to \infty$, we have under weak conditions that

$$V^{(aa)}(t) \sim t\left\{\rho_a + 2\int_{0+}^{\infty} \gamma_a^{(a)}(v)\,dv\right\} = \rho_a t I^{(aa)}, \tag{3.22}$$

$$V^{(ab)}(t) \sim t\int_0^{\infty} \{\gamma_b^{(a)}(v) + \gamma_a^{(b)}(v)\}\,dv = (\rho_a\rho_b)^{1/2} t I^{(ab)}, \tag{3.23}$$

$$V^{(bb)}(t) \sim t\left\{\rho_b + 2\int_0^\infty \gamma_b^{(b)}(v)\,dv\right\} = \rho_b t I^{(bb)}, \tag{3.24}$$

where the right sides of these equations define three asymptotic measures of dispersion $I$. The conditions

$$I^{(aa)} \geqq 0, \qquad \{I^{(ab)}\}^2 \leqq I^{(aa)} I^{(bb)}, \qquad I^{(bb)} \geqq 0 \tag{3.25}$$

must, of course, be satisfied, in virtue of (3.21).

3.5. *Some special processes.* The second order intensity functions, or equivalently the covariance densities, are not the most natural means of representing the dependencies in a point process, if these dependencies take special account of the nearest events of either or both types. Thus for the semi-Markov process, the second order intensity functions satisfy integral equations; see, for example, Cox and Miller [15], pp. 352–356. The relation with the defining functions of the process is therefore indirect. Thus, while in principle the distributions defining the process could be estimated from data via the second order intensity functions, this would be a roundabout approach, and probably very inefficient.

We now discuss briefly two processes for which the second order intensity functions are more directly related to the underlying mechanism of the process.

Consider an arbitrary regular stationary process of events of type $a$. Let each event of type $a$ be displaced by a random amount to form a corresponding event of type $b$; the displacements of different points are independent and identically distributed random variables with probability density function $p(\cdot)$. Denote the probability density function of the difference between two such random variables by $q(\cdot)$. Then a direct probability calculation for the limiting, stationary, process shows that (Cox [12])

$$h_a^{(b)}(t) = p(t) + \int_{-\infty}^{\infty} h_a^{(b)}(v)p(t - v)\,dv, \tag{3.26}$$

$$h_b^{(b)}(t) = \int_{-\infty}^{\infty} h_a^{(a)}(v)q(t - v)\,dv. \tag{3.27}$$

In particular, if the type $a$ events form a Poisson process, $h_a^{(a)}(v) = \rho_a$, so that

$$h_a^{(b)}(t) = p(t) + \rho_a, \qquad h_b^{(b)}(t) = \rho_a. \tag{3.28}$$

The constancy of $h_b^{(b)}(t)$ is an immediate consequence of the easily proved fact that the type $b$ events on their own form a Poisson process. The results (3.28) lead to quite direct methods of estimating $p(\cdot)$ from data and to tests of the adequacy of the model. For positive displacements the type $a$ events could be the inputs to an $M/G/\infty$ queue, the type $b$ events being the outputs. Generalizations of this delay process are considered in Sections 4 and 5.

As a second example, consider a *bivariate doubly stochastic Poisson process.* That is, we have an unobservable real valued (nonnegative) stationary bivariate process $\{\mathbf{\Lambda}(t)\} = \{\Lambda_a(t), \Lambda_b(t)\}$. Conditionally on the realized value of this process, we observe two independent nonstationary Poisson processes with rates, respectively, $\Lambda_a(t)$ for the type $a$ events and $\Lambda_b(t)$ for the type $b$ events. Then, by first arguing conditionally on the realized value of $\{\mathbf{\Lambda}(t)\}$, we have a stationary bivariate point process with

$$\begin{aligned}\gamma_a^{(a)}(t) &= \rho_a\delta(t) + c_\Lambda^{(aa)}(t), \qquad \gamma_b^{(a)}(t) = c_\Lambda^{(ab)}(t),\\ \gamma_b^{(b)}(t) &= \rho_b\delta(t) + c_\Lambda^{(bb)}(t),\end{aligned} \tag{3.29}$$

where $E\{\mathbf{\Lambda}(t)\} = (\rho_a, \rho_b)$ and the $c_\Lambda$ are the auto and cross covariance functions of $\{\mathbf{\Lambda}(t)\}$.

Again there is a quite direct connection between the covariance densities and the underlying mechanism of the process. Two special cases are of interest. One is when $\Lambda_a(t) = \Lambda_b(t)\,\rho_a/\rho_b$, leading to some simplification of (3.29). Another special case is

$$\begin{aligned}\Lambda_a(t) &= \rho_a + R_a\cos(\omega_0 t + \theta + \Phi),\\ \Lambda_b(t) &= \rho_b + R_b\cos(\omega_0 t + \Phi).\end{aligned} \tag{3.30}$$

In this

$$\begin{aligned}E(R_a) = E(R_b) &= 0,\\ E(R_a^2) = \sigma_{aa}, \qquad E(R_{ab}) &= \sigma_{ab}, \qquad E(R_{bb}) = \sigma_{bb},\end{aligned} \tag{3.31}$$

and the random variable $\Phi$ is uniformly distributed over $(0, 2\pi)$ independently of $R_a$ and $R_b$. Further, $\rho_a$, $\rho_b$, $\omega_0$, and $\theta$ are constants and, to keep the $\Lambda$ nonnegative, $|R_a| \leqq \rho_a$, $|R_b| \leqq \rho_b$. This defines a stationary although nonergodic process $\{\mathbf{\Lambda}(t)\}$.

Specifications (3.30) and (3.31) yield

$$\begin{aligned}\gamma_a^{(a)}(t) &= \rho_a\delta(t) + \sigma_{aa}\cos(\omega_0 t), \qquad \gamma_b^{(a)}(t) = \sigma_{ab}\cos\{\omega_0(t + \theta)\},\\ \gamma_b^{(b)}(t) &= \rho_b\delta(t) + \sigma_{bb}\cos(\omega_0 t).\end{aligned} \tag{3.32}$$

Of course this process is extremely special. Note, however, that fairly general processes with a sinusoidal component in the intensity can be produced by starting from the complete intensity functions of a stationary process and either adding a sinusoidal component or multiplying by the exponential of a sinusoidal component; the latter has the advantage of ensuring automatically a nonnegative complete intensity function.

3.6. *Spectral analysis of the counting process.* For Gaussian stationary stochastic processes, study of spectral properties is useful for three rather different reasons:

(a) the spectral representation of the process itself may be helpful;

(b) the spectral representation of the covariance matrix may be helpful;

(c) the effect on the process of a stationary linear operator is neatly expressed.

For point processes a general representation analogous to (a) has been discussed by Brillinger [6]. Bartlett [1] has given some interesting second order theory and applications in the univariate case. For doubly stochastic Poisson processes, which are of course very special, we can often use a full spectral representation for the defining $\{\mathbf{\Lambda}(t)\}$ process; indeed the $\{\mathbf{\Lambda}(t)\}$ process may be nearly Gaussian.

If we are content with a spectral analysis of the covariance density, we can write, in particular for the complex valued *cross spectral density function*,

$$g_b^{(a)}(\omega) = \frac{1}{2\pi}\int_{-\infty}^{\infty} e^{-i\omega t}\gamma_b^{(a)}(t)\,dt = g_a^{(b)}(-\omega). \tag{3.33}$$

Because of the mathematical equivalence between the covariance density and the spectral density, the previous general and particular results for covariance densities can all be expressed in terms of the spectral properties. While these will not be given in full here, note first that the measures of dispersion in (3.22) through (3.24) are given by

$$\begin{gathered} \rho_a I^{(aa)} = 2\pi g_a^{(a)}(0), \qquad (\rho_a\rho_b)^{1/2} I^{(ab)} = 2\pi g_b^{(a)}(0), \\ \rho_b I^{(bb)} = 2\pi g_b^{(b)}(0). \end{gathered} \tag{3.34}$$

All the results (3.26) through (3.32) can be expressed simply in terms of the spectral properties. Thus, from (3.29), the spectral analysis of the bivariate doubly stochastic Poisson process leads directly to the spectral properties of the process $\{\mathbf{\Lambda}(t)\}$ on subtracting the "white" Poisson spectra. Thus, spectral analysis of a doubly stochastic Poisson process is likely to be useful whenever the process $\{\mathbf{\Lambda}(t)\}$ has an enlightening spectral form. In the special case (3.32) where $\{\mathbf{\Lambda}(t)\}$ is sinusoidal,

$$g_a^{(a)}(\omega) = \frac{\rho_a}{2\pi} + \frac{\sigma_{aa}}{2\pi}\delta(\omega - \omega_0), \tag{3.35}$$

$$g_b^{(a)}(\omega) = \frac{\sigma_{ab}}{2\pi} e^{i\omega\theta}\delta(\omega - \omega_0). \tag{3.36}$$

The complex valued cross spectral density can be split in the usual way into real and imaginary components, which indicate the relative phases of the fluctuations in the processes of events of type $a$ and type $b$. We can also define the coherency as $|g_b^{(a)}(\omega)|^2/\{g_a^{(a)}(\omega)g_b^{(b)}(\omega)\}$; for the doubly stochastic process driven by proportional intensities, $\Lambda_b(t) \propto \Lambda_a(t)$, and the coherency is one for all $\omega$, provided that the "white" Poisson component is removed from the denominator.

The natural analogue for point processes of the stationary linear operators on a real valued process is random translation, summarized in (3.26) and (3.27). It follows directly from these equations and from the relation between covariance densities and intensity functions that

$$g_a^{(b)}(\omega) = \rho_a p^{\dagger}(\omega) + g_a^{(a)}(\omega)p^{\dagger}(\omega), \tag{3.37}$$

(3.38) $$\left\{g_b^{(b)}(\omega) - \frac{\rho_b}{2\pi}\right\} = q^\dagger(\omega)\left\{g_a^{(a)}(\omega) - \frac{\rho_a}{2\pi}\right\},$$

where $p^\dagger(\omega)$, $q^\dagger(\omega)$ are the Fourier transforms of $p(t)$ and $q(t)$. A more general type of random translation for bivariate processes is discussed in Section 5.

3.7. *Variance and covariance time functions.* For univariate point processes the covariance density or spectral functions are mathematically equivalent to the variance time function $V^{(aa)}(t)$ of (3.19), which gives as a function of $t$ the variance of the number of events in an interval of length $t$. This function is useful for some kinds of statistical analysis; examination of its behavior for large $t$ is equivalent analytically to looking at the low frequency part of the spectrum.

For bivariate point processes, it might be thought that the variance time function $V^{(aa)}(t)$, $V^{(bb)}(t)$, and the covariance time function $V^{(ab)}(t)$ of (3.18) are equivalent to the other second order specifications. This is not the case, however, because it is clear from (3.18) that only the combinations $\gamma_b^{(a)}(\omega) + \gamma_a^{(b)}(\omega)$ can be found from $V^{(ab)}(t)$ and this is not enough to fix the cross covariance function of the process.

The cross covariance density can, however, be found from the covariance time surface, $V^{(ab)}(t_1, t_2)$ of (3.17).

The covariance time function and surface are useful for some rather special statistical purposes.

The variance time function of the superposed process is

(3.39) $$V^{(\cdot\cdot)}(t) = V^{(aa)}(t) + 2V^{(ab)}(t) + V^{(bb)}(t);$$

this is equivalent to the relation (3.14) for intensity functions.

3.8. *Bivariate interval specifications; bivariate Markov interval processes.* As has been mentioned several times in this section, the second order intensity functions and their equivalents are most likely to be useful when the dependencies in the underlying mechanism do not specifically involve nearest neighbors, or other features of the process that are most naturally expressed serially, that is, through event number either in the pooled process or in the marginal processes rather than through real time.

For processes in which an interval specification is more appropriate, there are many ways of introducing functions wholly or partially specifying the dependency structure of the process. For a stationary univariate process we can consider the sequence of intervals between successive events as a stochastic process, indexed by serial number, that is, as a real valued process in discrete time. The second order properties are described by an autocovariance sequence which, say for events of type $a$, is

(3.40) $$\gamma_x^{(aa)}(j) = \text{Cov}\,\{X_a^{(a)}(k), X_a^{(a)}(k+j)\}, \qquad j = 0, \pm 1, \cdots.$$

McFadden [35] has shown that the autocovariance sequence is related to the distribution of counts by the simple, although indirect, formula

$$\gamma_x^{(aa)}(j) = \frac{1}{\rho_a}\left[\int_0^\infty Pr\{N^{(a)}(t) = j\}\,dt - \frac{1}{\rho_a}\right]. \tag{3.41}$$

Stationarity of the $X_a^{(a)}(i)$ sequence is discussed in Slivnyak [44].

If the distribution of $N^{(a)}(t)$ is given by the probability generating function

$$\phi^{(a)}(z, t) = \sum_{j=0}^{\infty} z^j Pr\{N^{(a)}(t) = j\} \tag{3.42}$$

with Laplace transform $\phi^{(a)*}(z, s)$, it will be convenient to substitute in (3.41) the result

$$\int_0^\infty Pr\{N^{(a)}(t) = j\}\,dt = \left[\frac{1}{j!}\frac{\partial^j \phi^{(a)*}(z, s)}{\partial z^j}\right]_{z=0, s=0+}. \tag{3.43}$$

The sequence (3.40) and the analogous one for events of type $b$ summarize the second order marginal properties. To study the joint properties of various kinds of intervals between events, the following are some of the possibilities.

(i) The two sets of intervals $\{X_a^{(a)}(r), X_b^{(b)}(r)\}$ may be considered as a bivariate process in discrete time, that is, we may use serial number in each process as a common discrete time scale. Cross covariances and cross spectra can then be defined in the usual way. While this may occasionally be fruitful, it is not a useful general approach, because for almost all physical models events in the two processes with a common serial number will be far apart in real time. Another problem is that if the process is sampled semisynchronously, say on a type $a$ event, the sequence $X_a^{(b)}(r)$ is not a stationary sequence, although it will generally "converge" to the sequence $X_b^{(b)}(r)$. Again, sufficiently far out from the sampling point, events in the two processes with common serial number will be far apart in real time.

(ii) We may consider the intervals between successive events in the process taken regardless of type, that is, the superposed process. This gives a third covariance sequence, namely, $\gamma_x^{(\cdot\cdot)}(j)$. For particular processes this can be calculated from (3.41) applied to the pooled process, particularly if the joint distribution of the count $N^{(a)}(t)$ and $N^{(b)}(t)$ are available.

In fact, if the joint distribution of $\{N^{(a)}(t), N^{(b)}(t)\}$ is specified by the joint probability generating function $\phi^{(ab)}(z_a, z_b, t)$ with Laplace transform $\phi^{(ab)*}(z_a, z_b, s)$, we have from (3.41) and (3.43) that

$$\gamma_x^{(\cdot\cdot)}(j) = \frac{1}{\rho_a + \rho_b}\left\{\frac{1}{j!}\frac{\partial^j \phi^{(ab)*}(z, z, s)}{\partial z^j} - \frac{1}{\rho_a + \rho_b}\right\}, \tag{3.44}$$

the derivative being evaluated at $z = 0$, $s = 0+$.

A limitation of this approach is, however, that independence of the type $a$ and type $b$ events is not reflected in any simple general relation between the three covariance sequences; this is clear from (3.44). Consider also the process of two independent renewal processes of Section 2.3; the covariance sequence for the superposed sequence is complex and not directly informative.

(iii) The discussion of (i) and (ii) suggests that we consider some properties of the intervals in the pooled sequence, that is, the superposed process with the type of each event being distinguished. Possibilities and questions that arise include the following.

(a) The sequence of event types can be considered as a binary time series. In particular, it might be useful to construct a simple test of dependence of the two series based on the nonrandomness of the sequence of event types. Such a test would, however, at least in its simplest form, require the assumption that the marginal processes are Poisson processes.

(b) We can examine the distributions and in particular the means of the backward recurrence times from events of one type to those of the opposite type, that is, $X_b^{(a)}(-1)$ and $X_a^{(b)}(-1)$. If the two types of events are independently distributed, the two "mixed" recurrence times should have marginal distributions corresponding to the equilibrium recurrence time distributions in the marginal process of events of types $a$ and $b$.

(c) A more symmetrical possibility similar in spirit to (b) is to examine the joint distribution of the two backward recurrence times measured from an arbitrary time origin, that is, of $X^{(a)}(-1)$ and $X^{(b)}(-1)$; the marginal distributions are, of course, the usual ones from univariate theory. If the events of the two types are independent, the two recurrence times are independently distributed with the distribution of the equilibrium recurrence times. Note, however, the discussion following (2.13). It would be possible to adapt (b) and (c) to take account of forward as well as of backward recurrence times.

(d) Probably the most useful general procedure for examining dependence in a bivariate process through intervals is to consider intensities conditional on the two separate asynchronous backward recurrence times. This is not quite analogous to the use of second order intensities of Section 3.3. Denote the realized backward recurrence times from an arbitrary time origin in the stationary process by $u_a$, $u_b$, that is, $u_a = x^{(a)}(-1)$, $u_b = x^{(b)}(-1)$. We then define the *serial intensity functions* for a stationary regular process by

$$\lambda^{(a)}(u_a, u_b) = \lim_{\Delta t \to 0+} \frac{Pr\{N^{(a)}(\Delta t) \geqq 1 \mid U_a = u_a, U_b = u_b\}}{\Delta t}, \tag{3.45}$$

with an analogous definition for $\lambda^{(b)}(u_a, u_b)$. These are, in a sense, third order rather than second order functions, since they involve occurrences at three points.

Now these two serial intensities are defined for all regular stationary processes, but they are complete intensity functions in the sense of Section 3.1 only for a very special class of process that we shall call *bivariate Markov interval processes*. These processes include semi-Markov processes and independent renewal processes; note, however, that in general the marginal processes associated with a bivariate Markov interval process are not univariate renewal processes (as with semi-Markov processes) and this is why we have not called the processes bivariate renewal processes.

As an example of this type of process, consider the alternating process of Section 2.5 with disjoint pairwise dependence. Denote the marginal distribution of the $W(i)$ by $G(x)$, and the conditional distribution of the $Z(i)$, given $W(i) = w$, by $F(z|w)$. If $\bar{G}(x) = 1 - G(x)$, $\bar{F}(z|w) = 1 - F(z|w)$, and the probability densities $g(x)$ and $f(z|w)$ exist, then

$$(3.46) \qquad \gamma^{(a)}(u_a, u_b) = \frac{g(u_a)}{\bar{G}(u_a)}, \qquad \gamma^{(b)}(u_a, u_b) = \frac{f(u_a|u_b - u_a)}{\bar{F}(u_a|u_b - u_a)}.$$

These are essentially hazard (failure rate) functions.

Thorough study of bivariate Markov interval processes would be of interest. The main properties can be obtained in principle because of the fairly simple Markov structure of the process. In particular if $p(u, v)$ denotes the bivariate probability density function of the backward recurrence times from an arbitrary time, that is, of $(U_a, U_b)$ or $(X^{(a)}(-1), X^{(b)}(-1))$, then

$$(3.47) \qquad \frac{\partial p(u, v)}{\partial u} + \frac{\partial p(u, v)}{\partial v} = -\{\lambda^{(a)}(u, v) + \lambda^{(b)}(u, v)\}p(u, v),$$

and

$$(3.48) \qquad p(0, v) = \int_0^\infty p(u, v)\lambda^{(a)}(u, v)\, du, \qquad p(u, 0) = \int_0^\infty p(u, v)\lambda^{(b)}(u, v)\, dv.$$

From the normalized solution of these equations, some of the simpler properties of the process can be deduced.

More generally, (3.45) may be a useful semiqualitative summary of the local serial properties of a bivariate point process. It does not seem possible to deduce the properties of the marginal processes given just $\lambda^{(a)}(u_a, u_b)$ and $\lambda^{(b)}(u_a, u_b)$, except for very particular processes such as the Markov interval process. For the alternating process with pairwise disjoint dependence, we indicated this difficulty in Section 2.5.

## 4. A bivariate delayed Poisson process model with Poisson noise

In previous sections, we defined bivariate Poisson processes to be those processes whose marginal processes (processes of type $a$ events and type $b$ events) are Poisson processes. Bivariate Poisson processes with a dependency structure which is completely specified by the second order intensity function arise from semi-Markov (Markov renewal) processes. The complete intensity function is also particularly simple.

Other bivariate Poisson processes can be constructed and in the present section we examine in some detail one such process. Its physical specification is very simple, although the specification of its dependency structure via a complete intensity function is difficult. The details of the model also illustrate the definitions introduced in Section 2.

General considerations on bivariate Poisson processes will be given in the next section.

4.1. *Construction of the model.* Suppose we have an unobservable main or generating Poisson process of rate $\mu$. Events from the main process are delayed (independently) by random amounts $Y_a$ with common distribution $F_a(t)$ and superposed on a "noise" process which is Poisson with rate $\lambda_a$. The resulting process is the observed marginal process of type $a$ events. Similarly, the events in the main process are delayed (independently) by random amounts with common distribution $F_b(t)$ and superposed with another independent noise process which is Poisson with rate $\lambda_b$. The resulting process is then the marginal process of type $b$ events. It is not observed which type $a$ and which type $b$ events originate from common main events.

In what follows, we assume for simplicity that the two delays associated with each main point are independent and positive random variables. The process has a number of possible interpretations. One is as an immigration death process with immigration consisting of couples "arriving" and type $a$ events being deaths of men and type $b$ events being deaths of women. Other queueing or service situations should be evident. The Poisson noise processes are added for generality and because they lead to interesting complications in inference procedures. In particular applications, it might be known that one or both noise processes are absent.

Various special cases are of interest. Thus, if delays of both types are equal with probability one, we have the Marshall–Olkin process [34] mentioned in Section 2. Without the added noise and if delays on one side (say, the $a$ event side) are zero with probability one, we have the delay process of Section 3.5 or, equivalently, an $M/G/\infty$ queue, where type $a$ events are arrivals and type $b$ events are departures. The noise process on the $a$ event side would correspond to independent balking in the arrival process.

4.2. *Some simple properties of the model.* If we consider the transient process from its initiation, it is well known (for example, Cox and Lewis [14], p. 209) that the processes are nonhomogeneous Poisson processes with rates that are, respectively,

$$\rho_a(t_1) = \lambda_a + \mu F_a(t_1), \tag{4.1}$$

$$\rho_b(t_2) = \lambda_b + \mu F_b(t_2). \tag{4.2}$$

Furthermore, the superposed process is a generalized branching Poisson process whose properties are given by Lewis [30] and Vere-Jones [47]. Thus, at each point in the main or generating process there are, with probability $(\lambda_a + \lambda_b)/$

$(\lambda_a + \lambda_b + \mu)$, no subsidiary events, and, with probability $\mu/(\lambda_a + \lambda_b + \mu)$, two subsidiary events. In the second case, the two subsidiary events are independently displaced from the main or parent event by amounts having distributions $F_a(\cdot)$ and $F_b(\cdot)$.

It is also known (Doob [17]) that as $t \to \infty$, or the origin moves off to the right, the marginal processes become simple stationary Poisson processes of rates

$$\rho_a = \lambda_a + \mu, \qquad \rho_b = \lambda_b + \mu, \tag{4.3}$$

respectively, for any distributions $F_a(u)$ and $F_b(u)$. The superposed process is then a stationary generalized branching Poisson process of rate $\lambda_a + \lambda_b + 2\mu$. The bivariate process is unusual in this respect, since there are very few dependent point processes whose superposition has a simple structure. The properties of the process of event types $\{T(i)\}$ or $\{T.(i)\}$ are, however, by no means simple to obtain, as will be evident when we consider bivariate properties below. Note too that stationarity of the marginal and superposed process does not imply stationarity of the bivariate process. A counterexample will be given later when initial conditions are discussed.

Asymptotic results for the bivariate counting process $\{N^{(a)}(t_1), N^{(b)}(t_2)\}$ can be obtained by a simple generalization of the methods of Lewis [30]. If, for simplicity, $t_1 = t_2 = t$, the intuitive basis of the method is that when $t$ is very large, the proportion of events that are delayed from the generating process until after $t$ goes (in some sense) to zero and the process behaves as though all events are concentrated at their generating event, that is, like the Marshall–Olkin process. Thus,

$$E\{N^{(a)}(t)\} = \text{Var}\,\{N^{(a)}(t)\} = V^{(aa)}(t) \sim \rho_a t, \tag{4.4}$$

$$E\{N^{(b)}(t)\} = \text{Var}\,\{N^{(b)}(t)\} = V^{(bb)}(t) \sim \rho_b t, \tag{4.5}$$

$$\text{Var}\,\{N^{(\cdot)}(t)\} \sim (\rho_a + \rho_b + 2\mu)t, \tag{4.6}$$

and therefore

$$\text{Cov}\,\{N^{(a)}(t),\ N^{(b)}(t)\} = V^{(ab)}(t) \sim \mu t. \tag{4.7}$$

The asymptotic measures of dispersion $I^{(aa)}$, $I^{(ab)}$, and $I^{(bb)}$ defined in equations (3.22) to (3.24) are therefore 1, $\mu/(\rho_a\rho_b)^{1/2}$, and 1. Result (4.7) will be useful in a statistical analysis of the process. By similar methods (Lewis, [30]), one can establish the joint asymptotic normality of the bivariate counting process.

Another property of the process which is simple to derive is the second order cross intensity function (3.8) or the covariance density function (3.14). In fact because of the Poisson nature of the main process and the independence of the noise processes from the main process, there is a contribution to the covariance density only if the type $b$ event is a delayed event and the event at $\tau$ is the same event appearing in the type $a$ event process with its delay of $Y_a$. Thus using (3.10), we get the cross covariance function

$$\gamma_b^{(a)}(\tau) = \mu f_{Y_a - Y_b}(\tau) = \gamma_a^{(b)}(-\tau) \tag{4.8}$$

if $F_{Y_a}(\cdot)$ and $F_{Y_b}(\cdot)$ are absolutely continuous.

If $F_{Y_a}(\cdot)$ and $F_{Y_b}(\cdot)$ have jumps, there will be delta function components in the cross intensity. In particular, when $Y_a$ and $Y_b$ are zero with probability one, there is a delta function component at zero and the process is marginally regular but not regular.

Result (4.8) will be verified from the more detailed results we derive next for the asynchronously sampled, stationary bivariate process. For this we must first consider detailed results for the transient process.

4.3. *The transient counting process.* The number of events of type $a$ in an interval $(0, t_1]$ following the start of the process is denoted by $N_0^{(a)}(t_1)$ and the number of events of type $b$ in $(0, t_2]$ by $N_0^{(b)}(t_2)$.

Assume first that $t_2 \geqq t_1 > 0$.

Now if a main event occurs at time $v$ in the interval $(0, t_1]$, then it contributes either one or no events to the type $a$ event process in $(0, t_1]$ and one or no events to the type $b$ event process in $(0, t_2]$. This bivariate binomial random variable has generating function

$$\begin{aligned} 1 &+ (1 - z_1)(1 - z_2)F_a(t_1 - v)F_b(t_2 - v) \\ &+ (z_2 - 1)F_b(t_2 - v) + (z_1 - 1)F_a(t_1 - v). \end{aligned} \tag{4.9}$$

Since we will be using the conditional properties of Poisson processes in our derivation, we require the time $v$ to be uniformly distributed over $(0, t_1]$ and the resulting generating function for the contribution of each main point is obtained by integrating (4.9) with respect to $v$ from 0 to $t_1$ and dividing by $t_1$. After some manipulation, this gives

$$\begin{aligned} 1 &+ \frac{(1 - z_1 - z_2 + z_1 z_2)}{t_1} \int_0^{t_1} F_a(v)F_b(t_2 - t_1 + v)\,dv \\ &+ \frac{(z_2 - 1)}{t_1} \int_0^{t_1} F_b(t_2 - t_1 + v)\,dv + \frac{(z_1 - 1)}{t_1} \int_0^{t_1} F_a(v)\,dv \\ &= Q(z_1, z_2, t_2, t_1). \end{aligned} \tag{4.10}$$

Now assume that there are $k_1$ events from the main Poisson process of rate $\mu$ in $(0, t_1]$, and $k_2$ main events in $(t_1, t_2]$. Then using the conditional properties of the Poisson process and the independence of the number of main events in $(0, t_1]$ and $(t_1, t_2]$, we get for the conditional generating function of $N_0^{(a)}(t_1)$ and $N_0^{(b)}(t_2)$

$$\begin{aligned} &\exp\{\lambda_a t_1(z_1 - 1) + \lambda_b t_2(z_2 - 1)\}\{Q(z_1, z_2, t_2, t_1)\}^{k_1} \\ &\qquad \cdot \left\{1 + \frac{(z_2 - 1)}{(t_2 - t_1)} \int_0^{t_2 - t_1} F_b(u)\,du\right\}^{k_2}. \end{aligned} \tag{4.11}$$

Removing the conditioning on the independently Poisson distributed number of events $k_1$ and $k_2$, we have for the logarithm of the joint generating function of $N_0^{(a)}(t_1)$ and $N_0^{(b)}(t_2)$

$$(4.12)\quad \begin{aligned}\psi_0(z_1, z_2; t_1, t_2) &= \log \phi(z_1, z_2; t_1, t_2)\\ &= \rho_a t_1(z_1 - 1) + \rho_b t_2(z_2 - 1)\\ &\quad - \mu(z_2 - 1)\int_0^{t_2} R_b(u)\,du - \mu(z_1 - 1)\int_0^{t_1} R_a(u)\,du\\ &\quad + \mu(1 - z_1 - z_2 + z_1 z_2)\int_0^{t_1} F_a(u)F_b(t_2 - t_1 + u)\,du,\end{aligned}$$

where $\rho_b = \lambda_a + \mu$, $\rho_b = \lambda_b + \mu$, $R_b(u) = 1 - F_b(u)$, and we still have $t_2 \geqq t_1$.

A similar derivation gives the result for $t_1 \geqq t_2$ and we can write for the general case

$$(4.13)\quad \begin{aligned}\psi_0(z_1, z_2; t_1, t_2) &= \rho_a t_1(z_1 - 1) + \rho_b t_2(z_2 - 1)\\ &\quad - \mu(z_2 - 1)\int_0^{t_2} R_b(v)\,dv - \mu(z_1 - 1)\int_0^{t_1} R_a(v)\,dv\\ &\quad + \mu(1 - z_1)(1 - z_2)\int_0^{\min(t_1, t_2)} F_a(t_1 - v)F_b(t_2 - v)\,dv.\end{aligned}$$

The expected numbers of events (4.1) and (4.2) in the marginal processes also come out of (4.13), as do the properties of the transient, generalized branching Poisson process obtained by superposing events of type $a$ and type $b$. Moreover, when the random variables $Y_a$ and $Y_b$ have fixed values, $\psi_0(0, 0; t_1, t_2)$ gives the logarithm of the survivor function of the bivariate exponential distribution of Marshall and Olkin [33], [34].

Note that $\psi_0(z_1, z_2; t_1, t_2)$ is the generating function of a bivariate Poisson variate, that is, a bivariate distribution with Poisson marginals. It is, in fact, the bivariate form of the multivariate distribution which Dwass and Teicher [18] showed to be the only infinitely divisible Poisson distribution:

$$(4.14)\quad \phi(\mathbf{z}) = \exp\left\{\sum_{i=1}^{n} a_i(z_i - 1) + \sum_{i<j} a_{ij}(z_i - 1)(z_j - 1) + \cdots + a_{1,2,\cdots,n}\prod_{i=1}^{n}(z_i - 1)\right\}.$$

However, since the coefficients in (4.13) depend on $t_1$ and $t_2$, the joint distribution of events of type $a$ in two disjoint intervals and events of type $b$ in another two disjoint intervals will not have the form (4.14). This is clearly only true for the highly degenerate Marshall–Olkin process of Section 2.

4.4. *The stationary asynchronous counting process.* To derive the properties of the generating function of counts in the stationary limiting process, or equivalently the asynchronously sampled stationary process, we consider first the number of events of type $a$ in $(t, t_1]$ and of type $b$ in $(t, t_2]$. Because of the independent interval properties of the main and noise Poisson processes of rates $\lambda_a$, $\lambda_b$, and $\mu$, respectively, this is made up independently from noise and main events occurring in $(t, \max(t_1, t_2)]$, whose generating function is given by (4.13), and by main events occurring in $(0, t]$ and delayed into $(t, t_1]$ or $(t, t_2]$.

Consider, therefore, the generating function of the latter type of events. A main event at $v$ in $(0, t]$ generates either one or no type $a$ events in $(t, t_1]$ and either one or no events of type $b$ in $(t, t_2]$. The generating function of this bivariate binomial random variable is

$$1 + (z_1 - 1)p_a + (z_2 - 1)p_b + (z_1 - 1)(z_2 - 1)p_a p_b, \tag{4.15}$$

where

$$p_a = p_a(1; t_1; t; v) = R_a(t - v) - R_a(t + t_1 - v) \tag{4.16}$$

and

$$p_b = p_b(1; t_2; t; v) = R_b(t - v) - R_b(t + t_2 - v). \tag{4.17}$$

If the start time $v$ is assumed to be uniformly distributed over $(0, t]$, then the generating function becomes

$$1 + (z_1 - 1)\frac{\bar{p}_a}{t} + (z_2 - 1)\frac{\bar{p}_b}{t} + (z_1 - 1)(z_2 - 1)\frac{\overline{p_a p_b}}{t}, \tag{4.18}$$

where

$$\bar{p}_a = \int_0^t \{R_a(v) - R_a(v + t_1)\}\, dv, \tag{4.19}$$

$$\bar{p}_b = \int_0^t \{R_b(v) - R_b(v + t_2)\}\, dv, \tag{4.20}$$

$$\overline{p_a p_b} = \int_0^t \{R_a(v) - R_a(v + t_1)\}\{R_b(v) - R_b(v + t_2)\}\, dv. \tag{4.21}$$

It follows from (4.19) and (4.20) that if $t_1$ and $t_2$ are finite, we have, even if $E(Y_a)$ and $E(Y_b)$ are infinite,

$$\lim_{t\to\infty} \bar{p}_a = \int_0^{t_1} R_a(v)\, dv, \qquad \lim_{t\to\infty} \bar{p}_b = \int_0^{t_2} R_b(v)\, dv; \tag{4.22}$$

and since $\overline{p_a p_b} \leqq \bar{p}_b$ for all $t, t_1, t_2$, we have that

$$\lim_{t\to\infty} \overline{p_a p_b} = \int_0^{\infty} \{R_a(v) - R_a(v + t_1)\}\{R_b(v) - R_b(v + t_2)\}\, dv \tag{4.23}$$

exists for finite $t_1$ and $t_2$.

The results (4.19) through (4.23) are used, as in the derivation of (4.12), to obtain the cumulant generating function of the contribution of delayed events of type $a$ and type $b$ to $(t, t_1]$ and $(t, t_2]$ when $t \to \infty$. This is

$$
\begin{aligned}
(4.24)\quad & \psi^+(z_1, z_2; t_1, t_2) \\
&= \mu(z_1 - 1)\int_0^{t_1} R_a(v)\,dv + \mu(z_2 - 1)\int_0^{t_2} R_b(v)\,dv \\
&\quad + \mu(z_1 - 1)(z_2 - 1)\int_0^{\infty}\{R_a(v) - R_a(v + t_1)\}\{R_b(v) - R_b(v + t_2)\}\,dv.
\end{aligned}
$$

Combined with (4.13), we have for the stationary bivariate process the result

$$
\begin{aligned}
(4.25)\quad & \psi(z_1, z_2; t_1, t_2) \\
&= \rho_a t_1(z_1 - 1) + \rho_b t_2(z_2 - 1) + \mu(z_1 - 1)(z_2 - 1) \\
&\quad \cdot\left[\int_0^{\min(t_1,t_2)} F_a(t_1 - v)F_b(t_2 - v)\,dv\right. \\
&\quad \left. + \int_0^{\infty}\{R_a(v) - R_a(v + t_1)\}\{R_b(v) - R_b(v + t_2)\}\,dv\right].
\end{aligned}
$$

Note that this is the cumulant generating function of a bivariate Poisson distribution and that the covariance time function (3.17) is the term in (4.25) multiplying $(z_1 - 1)(z_2 - 1)$;

$$
\begin{aligned}
(4.26)\quad V^{(ab)}(t_1, t_2) &= \mu\int_0^{\min(t_1,t_2)} R_a(t - v_1)R_b(t_2 - v)\,dv \\
&\quad + \mu\int_0^{\infty}\{R_a(v) - R_a(v + t_1)\}\{R_b(v) - R_b(v + t_2)\}\,dv.
\end{aligned}
$$

Differentiation of this expression with respect to $t_1$ and $t_2$ gives, after some manipulation, the covariance density (4.8), as predicted by the general formula (3.17).

Thus, if the densities associated with $R_a(\cdot)$ and $R_b(\cdot)$ exist, we can express (4.25) as

$$
\begin{aligned}
(4.27)\quad & \psi(z_1, z_2; t_1, t_2) \\
&= \rho_a t_1(z_1 - 1) + \rho_b t_2(z_2 - 1) \\
&\quad + (z_1 - 1)(z_2 - 1)\mu\int_0^{t_1}\int_0^{t_2} f_{Y_a - Y_b}(u - v)\,du\,dv.
\end{aligned}
$$

There are a number of alternative forms for and derivations of this distribution.

The behavior of $V^{(ab)}(t_1, t_2)$, although it is clearly a monotone nondecreasing function of both $t_1$ and $t_2$, is complex and will not be studied further here. In (4.7), we saw that along the line $t_1 = t_2 = t$ it is asymptotically $\mu t$.

We have also not established the complete stationarity of the limiting bivariate process; this follows from the fact that the delay depends only on the distance from the Poisson generating event, and can be established rigorously using bivariate characteristic functionals.

The complete intensity functions for this process (3.1) cannot be written down and although the second order intensity function is simple it does not specify the dependency structure of the process completely, as it does for the bivariate semi-Markov process. Note too that the cross covariance function (4.8) is always positive, so that there is in effect no inhibition of type $a$ events by $b$ events. In fact from the construction of the process, it is clear that just the opposite effect takes place. We examine the dependency structure of the delay process in more detail here by looking at the joint asynchronous forward recurrence time distribution. This distribution is of some interest in itself.

4.5. *The joint asynchronous forward recurrence times.* In the asynchronous process of the previous section, the time to the $k$th event of type $a$, $S^{(a)}(k)$, has a gamma distribution with parameter $k$ and $S^{(b)}(h)$ has a gamma distribution with parameter $h$. Thus, the joint distribution of these random variables is a bivariate gamma distribution of mixed marginal parameters $k$ and $h$ which is obtained from the generating function (4.25) via the fundamental relationship (2.5). We consider only the joint forward recurrence times $S^{(a)}(1) = X^{(a)}(1)$ and $S^{(b)}(1) = X^{(b)}(1)$ which have a bivariate exponential distribution:

$$\begin{aligned}R_{ab}(t_1, t_2) &= Pr\{X^{(a)}(1) > t_1, X^{(b)}(1) > t_2\} \\ &= \exp\{\psi(0, 0; t_1, t_2)\} \\ &= \exp\{-\rho_a t_1 - \rho_b t_2 + V^{(ab)}(t_1, t_2)\}.\end{aligned} \tag{4.28}$$

Clearly, this bivariate exponential distribution reduces to the distribution discussed by Marshall and Olkin [33] in the degenerate case when there are no delays (or fixed delays [34]). For no delays

$$R_{ab}(t_1, t_2) = -\rho_a t_1 - \rho_b t_2 + \mu \min(t_1, t_2). \tag{4.29}$$

The bivariate exponential distribution (4.27) is not the same as the infinitely divisible exponential distribution discussed by Gaver [20], Moran and Vere-Jones [38], and others. Whenever the delay distributions $R_a(\cdot)$ and $R_b(\cdot)$ have jumps, $R_{ab}(t_1, t_2)$ will have singularities.

For the correlation coefficient, we have

$$\rho_a \rho_b \operatorname{Corr}\{X^{(a)}(1), X^{(b)}(1)\} = \int_0^\infty \int_0^\infty R_{ab}(t_1, t_2)\, dt_1\, dt_2 - \frac{1}{\rho_a \rho_b}. \tag{4.30}$$

It is not possible to integrate this expression explicitly except in special cases. However, since $V^{(ab)}(t_1, t_2) \geqq 0$, we clearly have that the correlation coefficient is greater than zero.

For the special case (4.29) the correlation (4.30) is $1/\{(1 + (\lambda_a + \lambda_b)/\mu)\}$.

We do not pursue further here the properties of the process obtainable from the joint distribution of counts (4.25) of the synchronous counting process $\{N^{(a)}(t_1), N^{(b)}(t_2)\}$. However, it is useful to summarize what useful properties can be derived for this or any other bivariate process such as those given in the next section, from this bivariate distribution.

(i) The marginal generating functions ($z_1 = 0$ or $z_2 = 0$) give the correlation structure of the marginal interval process through equation (3.43). This is trivial for the delay process.

(ii) The generating function with $z_1 = z_2$ gives the correlation structure of the intervals in the superposed process through (3.44). For the delay process this is the interval correlation structure of a clustering (branching) Poisson process.

(iii) The covariance time surface and cross intensity and marginal intensity functions can be obtained. Again for the delay process this is trivial.

(iv) The joint distribution of the asynchronous forward recurrence times $\{X^{(a)}(1), X^{(b)}(1)\}$ can be calculated. Other functions of interest are the smaller and larger of $X^{(a)}(1)$ and $X^{(b)}(1)$, and the conditional distributions and expectations, for example, $E\{X^{(a)}(1) | X^{(b)}(1) = x\}$. The latter is difficult to obtain for the delay process, the regression being highly nonlinear.

(v) In principle, one can obtain not only the distributions of the smaller and larger of $X^{(a)}(1)$ and $X^{(b)}(1)$, but also the order type (jointly or marginally) since

$$Pr\{T(1) = a\} = Pr\{X^{(a)}(1) < X^{(b)}(1)\}. \tag{4.31}$$

(vi) It is not possible to obtain the complete distributions of types, for example, $Pr\{T(1) = a; T(2) = a\}$ from the bivariate distribution of asynchronous counts, since these counts are related to the sums of intervals by (2.5). For this information, we need more complete probability relationships, that is, for the pooled process $\{X^{(\cdot)}(1), T(1); X^{(\cdot)}(2), \cdots\}$. Note too that $\{T(i)\}$ is not a stationary binary sequence.

It is possible to obtain distributions of semisynchronous counting processes for the delay processes although we do not do this here. One reason for doing this is to obtain information on the distribution of the stationary sequences $T.(i)$. Thus,

$$Pr\{T.(0) = a, T.(1) = b\} = \frac{\rho_a}{\rho_a + \rho_b} Pr\{X_a^{(b)}(1) < X_a^{(a)}(1)\}, \tag{4.32}$$

and so forth, from which the correlation coefficient of lag one is obtained. It is not possible to carry the argument to lags of greater than one solely with joint distributions of sums of semisynchronous intervals.

4.6. *Stationary initial conditions.* We discuss here briefly the problem of obtaining stationary initial conditions for the delay process, since this has some bearing on the problems considered in this paper.

Note that for the marginal processes in the delayed Poisson process the numbers of events generated before $t$ which are delayed beyond $t$ have, if $E(Y_a) < \infty$ and $E(Y_b) < \infty$, Poisson distributions with parameters $\mu E(Y_a)$ and $\mu E(Y_b)$, respectively, when $t \to \infty$. Denote these random variables by $Z^{(a)}$ and $Z^{(b)}$. If the transient process of Section 4.3 is started with an additional number

$Z_a$ of type $a$ events which occur independently at distances $\bar{Y}_a(1), \cdots, \bar{Y}_a(Z_a)$ from the origin, where

$$(4.33) \qquad Pr\{\bar{Y}_a(i) \leqq t\} = \int_0^t \frac{R_a(u)\,du}{\{E(Y_a)\}},$$

and with an additional number $Z_b$ of type $b$ events which occur independently at distances $\bar{Y}_b(1), \cdots, \bar{Y}_b(z_b)$ from the origin, where the common distribution of the $\bar{Y}_b(j)$ is directly analogous to that of the $\bar{Y}_a(i)$, then the marginal processes are stationary Poisson processes (Lewis [30]). However, the bivariate process is not stationary. This can be verified, for instance, by obtaining the covariance density from the resulting generating function and noting that it depends on $t_1$ and $t_2$ separately, and not just on their difference.

In obtaining stationary initial conditions, the joint distribution of $Z_a$ and $Z_b$ is needed. Without going into the details of the limiting process, the generating function for these random variables is clearly (4.24) when $t_1 \to \infty$ and $t_2 \to \infty$. Thus,

$$(4.34) \quad \psi_{Z_a, Z_b}(z_1, z_2) = (z_1 - 1)\mu E(Y_a) + (z_2 - 1)\mu E(Y_b) + (z_1 - 1)(z_2 - 1)\mu \cdot E\{\min(Y_a, Y_b)\},$$

where $E\{\min(Y_a, Y_b)\} = \int_0^\infty R_a(v)R_b(v)\,dv$. This is the generating function (4.14) of a bivariate Poisson distribution.

Further details of this model, including the complete stationary initial conditions, will be given in another paper.

## 5. Some other special processes

We discuss here briefly several important models for bivariate point processes. The specification of the models is through the structure of intervals and is based on direct physical considerations, unlike, say, the bivariate Markov process with its specification of degree of dependence through the complete intensity functions. At the end of the section we consider the general problem of specifying the form of bivariate Poisson processes.

5.1. *Single process subject to bivariate delays.* The bivariate delayed Poisson process of the previous section can be generalized in several ways. First, the delays $Y_a$ and $Y_b$ might be correlated since, for instance, in the example of a man and wife in a bivariate immigration death process, their residual lifetimes would be correlated. Again $Y_a$ and $Y_b$ may take both positive and negative values. The stationary analysis of the previous section goes through essentially unchanged although specifying initial conditions is difficult. The covariance function (4.8) is the same except that $f_{Y_a - Y_b}(t)$ is, of course, no longer a simple convolution.

Another extension is to consider main processes which are, say, regular stationary point processes with rate $\mu$ and intensity function $h_\mu(t)$. Then the cross intensity function for the bivariate process, $h_a^{(b)}(t)$, becomes

$$\frac{\lambda_a}{\lambda_a + \mu}\rho_b + \frac{\mu}{\lambda_a + \mu}\left\{\lambda_b + f_{Y_a - Y_b}(t) + \int_{-\infty}^{\infty} h_\mu(u) f_{Y_a - Y_b}(t - u)\, du\right\}, \tag{5.1}$$

with a similar expression for $h_b^{(a)}(t)$. These should be compared with (3.26). Except when the main process is a renewal process, explicit results beyond the intensity function are difficult to obtain. For the renewal case an integral equation can be written down, as also for branching renewal processes (Lewis, [32]); from the integral equation higher moments of the bivariate counting process can be derived.

5.2. *Bivariate point process subject to delays.* Instead of having a univariate point process in which each point (say the $i$th) is delayed by two different amounts $Y_a(i)$ and $Y_b(i)$ to form the bivariate process, one can have a main bivariate point process in which the $i$th type $a$ event is delayed by $Y_a(i)$ and the $j$th type $b$ event is delayed by $Y_b(j)$, thus forming a new bivariate point process. This does not reduce to the bivariate delay process of Section 5.1 although it is conceptually similar.

The simplest illustration is where there is error (jitter) in recording the positions of the points. Usually the errors are taken to be independently distributed, although $Y_a$ and $Y_b$ may have different distributions. Another situation is an immigration death process with two different types of immigrants.

If the main process has cross intensities $\bar{h}_a^{(b)}(t)$ and $\bar{h}_b^{(a)}(t)$, then the delayed bivariate process (with no added Poisson noise) has cross intensity

$$h_a^{(b)}(t) = \int_{-\infty}^{\infty} \bar{h}_a^{(b)}(t - v) f_{Y_a - Y_b}(v)\, dv. \tag{5.2}$$

It will not be possible from data to separate properties of the jitter process from those of the underlying main process, unless strong special assumptions are made.

An interesting situation occurs when the main process is a semi-Markov process with marginal processes which are Poisson processes as, for example, in Section 2. Then the delayed bivariate point process is, in equilibrium, a bivariate Poisson process.

5.3. *Clustering processes.* Univariate clustering processes (Neyman and Scott [39], Vere-Jones [47], and Lewis [30]) are important. Each main event generates one subsidiary sequence of events and the subsidiary sequences have a finite number of points with probability one. The subsidiary processes are independent of one another but can be of quite general structure. When the subsidiary processes are finite renewal processes, the clustering process is known as a Bartlett–Lewis process; when the events are generated by independent delays from the initiating main event, the process is known as a Neyman–Scott cluster process.

The bivariate delay process and delayed bivariate process described in the previous two subsections are special cases of bivariate cluster processes and clearly both types of main process are possible for these cluster processes. As an example of a bivariate main process generating two different types of subsidiary process, Lewis [29] considered computer failure patterns and discussed the possibility of two types of subsidiary sequences, one generated by permanent component failures and the other by intermittent component failures.

There are many possibilities that will not be discussed here. Some general points of interest are, however, the following.

(i) When the main process is a univariate Poisson process, producing a bivariate clustering Poisson process, bivariate superposition of such processes again produces a bivariate clustering Poisson process. The process is thus infinitely divisible.

(ii) Both the marginal processes and the superposed processes are (generalized) cluster processes. Thus, we can use known results for these processes and expressions such as (3.39) and (3.14) to find variance time curves and cross intensities for the bivariate process. When the main process is a semi-Markov process, the marginal processes are clustering (or branching) renewal processes (Lewis, [32]).

(iii) The analysis in Section 4 can be used for these processes when the main process is a univariate Poisson process. Bivariate characteristic functionals are probably also useful.

5.4. *Selective inhibition.* A simple, realistic and analytically interesting model arises in neurophysiological contexts. We have two series of events, the first called the inhibitory series of events and the second the excitatory series of events, occurring on a common time scale. Each event in the inhibitory series blocks only the next excitatory event (and blocks it only if no following inhibitory event occurs before the excitatory event). This is the simplest of many possibilities.

Although only the sequence of noninhibited excitatory events (the responses) is usually studied, Lawrance has pointed out that there are a number of bivariate processes generated by this mechanism, in particular the inhibitory events and the responses [24], [25]. These may constitute the input and output to a neuron, and are the only pair we consider here. In particular, we take the excitatory process to be a Poisson process with rate $\rho_a$ and the inhibiting process to be a renewal process with interevent probability distribution function $F_b(x)$. The response process has dependent intervals unless the inhibitory process also is a Poisson process.

When the excitatory process is a renewal process with interevent probability distribution function $F_a(x)$ and the inhibitory process is Poisson with rate $\rho_b$, the process of responses is a renewal process. This follows because the original renewal process is in effect being thinned at a rate depending only on the time since the last recorded response and such an operation preserves the renewal property. This bivariate renewal process is not a semi-Markov process, as can be seen by attempting to write down the complete intensity functions (3.4) and (3.5). The complete intensity functions become simple only for the trivariate process of inhibitory events, responses, and nonresponses.

Coleman and Gastwirth [10] have shown that it is possible to pick $F_a(x)$ so that the responses also form a Poisson process. The covariance density of this bivariate Poisson process can be obtained; it is always negative (personal communication, T. K. M. Wisniewski).

Other forms of selective inhibition can be postulated; some have been discussed by Coleman and Gastwirth [10]. Another possibility is the simultaneous inhibition, as above, of two excitatory processes by a single, unobservable inhibitory process. When the inhibitory process is Poisson and the excitatory processes are renewal processes, the two response processes are a bivariate renewal process.

There are, of course, many other neurophysiological models, generally more complicated than the selective inhibition models and many times involving the doubly stochastic mechanism discussed in Section 3.5. An interesting example is given by Walloe, Jansen, and Nygaard [48].

5.5. *General remarks on bivariate Poisson processes.* In this and previous sections, we have encountered several examples of bivariate Poisson processes, defined as bivariate point processes in which the marginal processes are Poisson processes.

(i) The degenerate Poisson process of Marshall and Olkin was discussed in Section 2.

(ii) The process in (i) is a special case of a broad family of bivariate Poisson processes generated by bivariate delays on univariate Poisson processes. Several other examples arise in considering delays on bivariate Poisson processes.

(iii) Semi-Markov processes have renewal marginals and a broad class of bivariate Poisson processes is obtained by choosing the marginal processes to be Poisson processes. Delays added to these particular semi-Markov processes again produce bivariate Poisson processes.

(iv) A rather special case arises when a Poisson process inhibits a renewal process.

Another example is mentioned because it illustrates the problem considered in Section 3.8 of specifying dependency structure in terms of the bivariate, discrete time sequence of marginal intervals. Thus, we can start the process and require that the intervals in the marginals with the same serial index be bivariate exponentials. Any bivariate exponential distribution may be used, such as (4.28) or those of Gaver [20], Plackett [42], Freund [19], and Griffiths [21]. The interval structure is stationary, as is the counting process of the marginals, which are Poisson processes. The bivariate counting process is, however, not stationary. It is not clear whether one gets the counting process to be stationary, as defined in Section 2, when moving away from the origin, but since the time lag between the dependent intervals increases indefinitely as $n \to \infty$ the process is degenerate and tends to almost independent Poisson processes a long time from the origin.

No general structure is known for bivariate Poisson processes. There follow some general comments and some open questions.

(i) The bivariate Poisson process as defined is infinitely divisible in that bivariate superposition produces bivariate Poisson processes. However, of the above models of bivariate Poisson processes, only the bivariate delayed Poisson process keeps the same dependency structure under bivariate superposition.

(ii) Does unlimited bivariate superposition produce two independent Poisson processes? The answer is, generally, yes (Cinlar [8]).

(iii) It can be shown that successive independent delays on bivariate Poisson processes (and most bivariate processes) produces in the limit a process of independent Poisson processes. This can be seen from (5.2) and (5.3), but needs bivariate characteristic functionals for a complete proof.

(iv) The numbers of events of the two types in an interval $(0, t]$ in a bivariate Poisson process have a bivariate Poisson distribution. Some general properties of such distributions are known (Dwass and Teicher [18]); the bivariate Poisson distribution (4.33) is the only infinitely divisible bivariate Poisson distribution. An open question of interest in investigating bivariate Poisson processes is whether, when $Z_1$, $Z_2$, and $Z_1 + Z_2$ have marginally Poisson distributions of means $\mu_1$, $\mu_2$, and $\mu_1 + \mu_2$, $Z_1$ and $Z_2$ are independent. If this is so, a bivariate Poisson process in which the superposed marginal process is a Poisson process must have the events of two types independent.

(v) The broad class of stationary bivariate Poisson processes arising from delay mechanisms have positive cross covariance densities, that is, no "inhibitory effect." For the semi-Markov process with Poisson marginals, it is an open question as to whether cross covariance densities which take on negative values exist. In particular, for the alternating renewal process with identical gamma distributions of index one for up and down times, the cross covariance is strictly positive. The only model which is known to produce a bivariate Poisson process with strictly negative covariance density is the Poisson inhibited renewal process described earlier in this section.

## 6. Statistical analysis

6.1. *General discussion.* We now consider in outline some of the statistical problems that arise in analyzing data from a bivariate point process. If a particular type of model is suggested by physical considerations, it will be required to estimate the parameters and test goodness of fit. In some applications, a fairly simple test of dependence between events of different types will be the primary requirement. In yet other cases, the estimation of such functions as the covariance densities will be required to give a general indication of the nature of the process, possibly leading to the suggestion of a more specific model. In all cases, the detection and elimination of nonstationarity may be required.

There is one important general distinction to be drawn, parallel to that between correlation and regression in the analysis of quantitative data. It may be that both types of event are to be treated symmetrically, and that in particular the stochastic character of both types needs analysis. This is broadly the attitude implicit in the previous sections. Alternatively one type of event, say $b$, may be causally dependent on previous $a$ events, or it may be required to predict events of type $b$ given information about the previous occurrences of events of both types. Then it will be sensible to examine the occurrence of the $b$'s conditionally on the observed sequence of $a$'s and not to consider the stochastic mechanism generating the $a$'s; this is analogous to the treatment of the independent variable in regression analysis as "fixed." Note in particular that the pattern of the $a$'s might be very nonstationary and yet if the mechanism generating the $b$'s is stable, simple "stationary" analyses may be available.

In the rest of this section, we sketch a few of the statistical ideas required in analyzing this sort of data.

6.2. *Likelihood analyses.* If a particular probability model is indicated as the basis of the analysis when the model is specified except for unknown parameters, in principle it will be a good thing to obtain the likelihood of the data from which exactly or asymptotically optimum procedures of analysis can be derived, for example, by the method of maximum likelihood; of course, this presupposes that the usual theorems of maximum likelihood theory can be extended to cover such applications. Unfortunately, even for univariate point processes, there are relatively few models for which the likelihood can be obtained in a useful form. Thus, one is often driven to rather *ad hoc* procedures.

Here we note a few very particular processes for which the likelihood can be calculated.

In a semi-Markov process, the likelihood can be obtained as a product of a factor associated with the two state Markov chain and factors associated with the four distributions of duration; if sampling is for a fixed time there will be one "censored" duration. Moore and Pyke [36] have examined this in detail with particular reference to the asymptotic distributions obtained when sampling is for a fixed time, so that the numbers of intervals of various types are random variables.

A rather similar analysis can be applied to the bivariate Markov process of intervals of Section 3.8, although a more complex notation is necessary. Let

$$L^{(a)}(x; v, w) = \exp\left\{-\int_0^x \lambda^{(a)}(z + v, z + w)\, dz\right\}, \tag{6.1}$$

$$L^{(b)}(x; v, w) = \exp\left\{-\int_0^x \lambda^{(b)}(z + v, z + w)\, dz\right\}. \tag{6.2}$$

We can summarize the observations as a sequence of intervals between successive events in the pooled process, where the intervals are of type $aa$, $ab$, $ba$, or $bb$. We characterize each interval by its length $x$ and by the backward recurrence time at the start of the interval measured to the event of opposite type. Denote this by $v$ if measured to a type $a$ event and by $w$ if measured to a type $b$ event.

Then the contribution to the likelihood of the length of the interval and the type of the event at the end of the interval is

$$\lambda^{(a)}(x, w + x)\, L^{(a)}(x; 0, w)\, L^{(b)}(x; 0, w) \quad \text{for an } aa \text{ interval,} \tag{6.3}$$

$$\lambda^{(b)}(x, w + x)\, L^{(a)}(x; 0, w)\, L^{(b)}(x; 0, w) \quad \text{for an } ab \text{ interval,} \tag{6.4}$$

$$\lambda^{(a)}(v + x, x)\, L^{(a)}(x; v, 0)\, L^{(b)}(x; v, 0) \quad \text{for a } ba \text{ interval,} \tag{6.5}$$

$$\lambda^{(b)}(v + x, x)\, L^{(a)}(x; v, 0)\, L^{(b)}(x; v, 0) \quad \text{for a } bb \text{ interval.} \tag{6.6}$$

Thus, once the intensities are specified parametrically the likelihood can be written down and, for example, maximized numerically.

Now the above discussion is for the "correlational" approach in which the two types of event are treated symmetrically. If, however, we treat the events of type $b$ as the dependent process and argue conditionally on the observed sequence of events of type $a$, the analysis is simplified, in effect by replacing $\lambda^{(a)}(\cdot, \cdot)$ and $L^{(a)}(\cdot, \cdot, \cdot)$ by unity.

A particular case of interest is when the intensities are linear functions of their arguments. This, of course, precludes having the semi-Markov process as a special case.

A further example of when a likelihood analysis is feasible is provided by the bivariate sinusoidal Poisson process of (3.30) with $R_a$, $R_b$, and $\Phi$ regarded as unknown parameters. An analysis in terms of exponential family likelihoods is obtained by taking (3.20) to refer to the log intensity; for the univariate analysis see Lewis [31].

In the bivariate case, we reparametrize and have

$$\lambda_a(t) = \frac{\rho_a \exp\{R_a \cos(\omega_0 t + \theta + \Phi)\}}{I_0(R_a)} \tag{6.7}$$

and

$$\lambda_b(t) = \frac{\rho_b \exp\{R_b \cos(\omega_0 t + \Phi)\}}{I_0(R_b)}, \tag{6.8}$$

where $I_0(R_b)$ is a zero order modified Bessel function of the first kind. It is convenient to assume that observation on both processes is for a common fixed period $t_0$, where $\omega_0 t_0$ is an integral multiple of $2\pi$, say $2\pi p$. Then $\int_0^{t_0} \lambda_a(u)\, du = \rho_a t_0$ and $\int_0^{t_0} \lambda_b(u)\, du = \rho_b t_0$.

If $n^{(a)}$ type $a$ events are observed in $(0, t_0]$ at times $t_1^{(a)}, \cdots, t_{n^{(a)}}^{(a)}$ and $n^{(b)}$ type $b$ events at times $t_1^{(b)}, \cdots, t_{n^{(b)}}^{(b)}$, then, using the likelihood for the nonhomogeneous bivariate Poisson process

$$\prod_{i=1}^{n^{(a)}} \lambda_a(t_i^{(a)}) \prod_{j=1}^{n^{(b)}} \lambda_b(t_j^{(b)}) \exp\{-\rho_a t_0 - \rho_b t_0\}, \tag{6.9}$$

we find that the set of sufficient statistics for $\{\rho_a, \rho_b, R_a \cos(\theta + \Phi), R_a \sin(\theta + \Phi), R_b \cos \Phi, R_b \sin \Phi\}$ are $\{n^{(a)}, n^{(b)}, \mathscr{A}_a(\omega_0), \mathscr{B}_a(\omega_0), \mathscr{A}_b(\omega_0), \mathscr{B}_b(\omega_0)\}$, where

$$(6.10) \qquad \mathscr{A}_a(\omega_0) = \sum_{i=1}^{n^{(a)}} \cos(\omega_0 t_i^{(a)}), \qquad \mathscr{B}_a(\omega_0) = \sum_{j=1}^{n^{(b)}} \sin(\omega_0 t_j^{(a)}),$$

with similar definitions for $\mathscr{A}_b(\omega_0)$ and $\mathscr{B}_b(\omega_0)$.

Typically, if $R_a = R_b = R$, maximum likelihood estimates of $R$ and tests of $R = 0$ are based on monotone functions of $\mathscr{A}_a(\omega_0)$, $\mathscr{B}_a(\omega_0)$, $\mathscr{A}_b(\omega_0)$, and $\mathscr{B}_b(\omega_0)$. The estimation and testing procedures are formally equivalent to tests for directionality on a circle from two independent samples when the direction vector has a von Mises distribution (Watson and Williams, [49]).

Other trend analyses can be carried out with a similar type of likelihood analysis if the model is a nonhomogeneous bivariate Poisson process.

For most other special models, including quite simple ones such as the delayed Poisson process of Section 4, it does not seem possible to obtain the likelihood in usable form; it would be helpful to have ways of obtaining useful pseudo-likelihoods for such processes.

For testing goodness of fit, it may sometimes be possible to imbed the model under test in some richer family; for instance, agreement with a parametric semi-Markov model could be tested by fitting some more general bivariate Markov interval process and comparing the maximum likelihoods achieved. More usually, however, it will be a case of finding relatively *ad hoc* test statistics to examine various aspects of the model.

In situations in which the model of independent renewal processes or the semi-Markov model may be relevant, the following procedures are likely to be useful. To test consistency with an independent renewal process model, we may:

(a) examine for possible nonstationarity,

(b) test the marginal processes for consistency with a univariate renewal model (Cox and Lewis [14], Chapter 6),

(c) test for dependence using the estimates of the cross intensity given in the next section, or test that the event types do not have the first order Markov property.

If dependence is present, it may be natural to see whether the data are consistent with a semi-Markov process. (Note, however, that the family of independent renewal models is not contained in the family of semi-Markov models.) To test for the adequacy of an assumed parametric semi-Markov model, we may, for example, proceed as follows:

(a) examine for possible nonstationarity,

(b) test the sequence of event types for the first order Markov property (Billingsley [5]),

(c) examine the distributional form of the four separate types of interval,

(d) examine the dependence of intervals on the preceding interval and the preceding event type.

6.3. *Estimation of intensities and associated functions.* If a likelihood based analysis is not feasible, we must use the more empirical approach of choosing aspects of the process thought to be particularly indicative of its structure and estimating these aspects from the data. In this way we may be able to obtain estimates of unknown parameters and tests of the adequacy of a proposed model.

In the following discussion, we assume that the process is stationary. With extensive data, it will be wise first to analyze the data in separate sections, pooling the results only if the sections are reasonably consistent.

The main aspects of the process likely to be useful as a basis for such procedures are the frequency distributions of intervals of various kinds, the second order functions of Section 3.3 through 3.7 and, the bivariate interval properties, in particular the serial intensity functions (3.42). As stressed in Section 3, it will often happen that one or other of the above aspects is directly related to the underlying mechanism of the process and hence is suitable for statistical analysis.

Estimation of the univariate second order functions does not need special discussion here. We therefore merely comment briefly on the estimation of the serial intensity functions and the cross properties; for the latter the procedures closely parallel the corresponding univariate estimation procedures.

6.3.1. *Cross intensity function.* To obtain a smoothed estimate of the cross intensity function $h_a^{(b)}(t)$, choose a grouping interval $\Delta$ and count the total number of times a type $b$ event occurs a distance between $t$ and $t + \Delta$ to the right of a type $a$ event; let the random variable corresponding to this number be $R_a^{(b)}(t, t + \Delta)$. In practice, we form a histogram from all possible intervals between events of type $a$ and events of type $b$. We now follow closely the argument of Cox and Lewis ([14], p. 122) writing, for observations over $(0, t_0)$,

$$(6.11)\quad R_a^{(b)}(t, t + \Delta) = \left\{\int_{u=0}^{t_0 - t - \Delta} \int_{x=t}^{t+\Delta} + \int_{u=t_0-t-\Delta}^{t_0 - t} \int_{x=t}^{t_0 - u}\right\} dN^{(a)}(u)\, dN^{(b)}(u + x).$$

Now for a stationary process

$$(6.12)\qquad E\{dN^{(a)}(u)\, dN^{(b)}(u + x)\} = \rho_a h_a^{(b)}(x)\, du\, dx,$$

and a direct calculation, plus the assumption that $h_a^{(b)}(x)$ varies little over $(t, t + \Delta)$, gives

$$(6.13)\qquad E\{R_a^{(b)}(t, t + \Delta)\} = (t_0 - t - \tfrac{1}{2}\Delta)\rho_a \int_t^{t+\Delta} h_a^{(b)}(x)\, dx,$$

thus leading to a nearly unbiased estimate of the integral of the cross intensity over $(t, t + \Delta)$.

If the type $b$ events are distributed in a Poisson process independently of the type $a$ events, we can find the exact moments of $R_a^{(b)}(t, t + \Delta)$, by arguing conditionally both on the number of type $b$ events and on the whole observed process of type $a$ events (see Section 6.4). To a first approximation, $R_a^{(b)}(t, t + \Delta)$

has (conditionally) a Poisson distribution of mean $n^{(a)}n^{(b)}\Delta/t_0$ provided that $\Delta$ is small and, in particular, that few type $a$ events occur within $\Delta$ of one another. This provides the basis for a test of the strong null hypothesis that the type $b$ events follow an independent Poisson process; it would be interesting to study the extent to which the test is distorted if the type $b$ events are distributed independently of the type $a$ events, although not in a Poisson process.

6.3.2. *Cross spectrum.* Estimation of the cross spectrum is based on the cross periodogram, defined as follows. For each marginal process, we define the finite Fourier–Stieltjes transforms of $N^{(a)}(t)$ and $N^{(b)}(t)$ (Cox and Lewis [14], p. 124) to be

$$H_{t_0}^{(a)}(\omega) = (2\pi t_0)^{-1/2} \sum_{\ell=1}^{n^{(a)}} \exp\{i\omega t_\ell^{(a)}\} = (2\pi t_0)^{-1/2}\{\mathscr{A}_{t_0}^{(a)}(\omega) + i\mathscr{B}_{t_0}^{(a)}(\omega)\}, \tag{6.14}$$

$$H_{t_0}^{(b)}(\omega) = (2\pi t_0)^{-1/2} \sum_{j=1}^{n^{(b)}} \exp\{i\omega t_j^{(b)}\} = (2\pi t_0)^{-1/2}\{\mathscr{A}_{t_0}^{(b)}(\omega) + i\mathscr{B}_{t_0}^{(b)}(\omega)\}. \tag{6.15}$$

The cross periodogram is then

$$\mathscr{I}_{t_0}^{(ab)}(\omega) = H_{t_0}^{(a)}(\omega)\,\bar{H}_{t_0}^{(b)}(\omega) \tag{6.16}$$

(Jenkins [23]). Thus, the estimates of the amplitude and phase of harmonic components of fixed frequencies in a nonhomogeneous bivariate Poisson model considered in the previous section are functions of the empirical spectral components. It can also be shown, as for the univariate case (Lewis [31]), that $\mathscr{I}_{t_0}^{(ab)}(\omega)$ is the Fourier transform of the unsmoothed estimator of the cross intensity function obtained from all possible intervals between events of type $a$ and events of type $b$.

The distribution theory of $\mathscr{I}_{t_0}^{(ab)}(\omega)$ for independent Poisson processes follows simply from the conditional properties of the Poisson processes. Thus, we find that $A_{t_0}^{(a)}(\omega)$ and $B_{t_0}^{(a)}(\omega)$ have the (conditional) joint generating function

$$[I_0\{(\xi_a^2 + \xi_b^2)^{1/2}\}]^{n^{(a)}} \tag{6.17}$$

if $\omega t_0 = 2\pi p$, from which it can be shown, for example, that $\mathscr{A}_{t_0}^{(a)}(\omega)$ and $\mathscr{B}_{t_0}^{(b)}(\omega)$ go rapidly to independent normal random variables with means 0 and standard deviations $\frac{1}{2}t_0\rho_a$ as $n^{(a)}$ becomes large. Consequently, the real and imaginary components of the cross periodogram have double exponential distributions centered at zero with a variance which does not decrease as $t_0$ increases.

At two frequencies $\omega_1$ and $\omega_2$ such that $\omega_1 t_0 = 2\pi p_1$ and $\omega_2 t_0 = 2\pi p_2$, the real components of $\mathscr{I}_{t_0}^{(ab)}(\omega_1)$ and $\mathscr{I}_{t_0}^{(ab)}(\omega_2)$ are asymptotically uncorrelated, as are the imaginary components. Consequently, smoothing of the periodogram is required to get consistent estimates of the in phase and out of phase components of the cross spectrum. The problems of bias, smoothing, and computation of the spectral estimates are similar to those for the univariate case discussed in detail by Lewis [31].

Note that the smoothed intensity function or the smoothed spectral estimates can be used to estimate the delay probability density function in the one sided Poisson delay model (see equations (3.26) and (3.27)) and the difference of the delays in the two sided (bivariate) Poisson delay model. In the first case, the estimation procedure is probably much more efficient, in some sense, than the procedure discussed by Brown [7] unless the mean delay is much shorter than the mean time between events in the main Poisson process.

6.3.3. *Covariance time function.* Another problem that arises with the bivariate Poisson delay process is to test for the presence of the Poisson noise and to estimate the rate $\mu$ of the unobservable main process. Since the covariance time curve $V^{(ab)}(t) \sim \mu t$, we can estimate $\mu$ by estimating $V^{(ab)}(t)$ and also test for Poisson noise by comparing the estimated measures of dispersion $I^{(aa)}$, $I^{(bb)}$, and $I^{(ab)}$, defined in (3.22), (3.23), and (3.24). Care will be needed over possible nonstationarity.

The simplest method for estimating $V^{(ab)}(t)$ is to estimate the variance time curves $V^{(aa)}(t)$, $V^{(bb)}(t)$, and $V^{(\cdot\cdot)}(t)$ with the procedures given by Cox and Lewis ([14], Chapter 5) and to use (3.39) to give an estimate of $V^{(ab)}(t)$.

There is no evident reason for estimating the covariance time surface $C(t_1 t_2)$ along any line except $t_1 = t_2$.

6.3.4. *Serial intensity function.* Estimation of the serial intensity functions raises new problems, somewhat analogous to the analysis of life tables. Consider the estimation of $\lambda^{(a)}(u_a, u_b)$ of (3.42). One approach is to pass to discrete time, dividing the time axis into small intervals of length $\Delta$. Each such interval is characterized by the values of $(u_a, u_b)$ measured from the center of the interval if no type $a$ event occurs within the interval, and by the values of $(u_a, u_b)$ at the type $a$ event in question if one such event occurs; we assume for simplicity of exposition that the occurrence of multiple type $a$ events can be ignored. Thus, each time interval contributes a binary response plus the values of two explanatory variables $(u_a, u_b)$; the procedure extends to the case of more than two explanatory variables, and to the situation in which multiple type $a$ events occur within the intervals $\Delta$.

We can now do one or both of the following:

(a) assume a simple functional form for the dependence on $(u_a, u_b)$ of the probability $\lambda^{(a)}(u_a, u_b)\Delta$ of a type $a$ event and fit by weighted least squares or maximum likelihood (Cox [13]);

(b) group into fairly coarse "cells" in the $(u_a, u_b)$ plane and find the proportion of "successes" in each cell.

It is likely that standard methods based on an assumption of independent binomial trials are approximately applicable to such data and, if so, specific assumptions about the form of the serial intensities can be tested. In particular, we can test the hypothesis that the process is, say, purely $a$ dependent, making the further assumption to begin with that the dependence is only on $u_a$.

By extensions of this method, that is, by bringing in dependencies on more aspects of the history at time $t$ than merely $u_a$ and $u_b$, it may be possible to build up empirically a fairly simple model for the process.

6.4. *Simple tests for dependence.* As noted previously, it may sometimes be required to construct simple tests of the null hypothesis that the type $a$ and type $b$ events are independent, as defined in Section 2.2. This may be done in various ways. Much the simplest situation arises when we consider the dependence of, say, the type $b$ events on the type $a$ events, argue conditionally on the observed type $a$ process, and consider the strong null hypothesis that the type $b$ events form an independent Poisson process. Then, conditionally on the total number of events of type $b$, the positions of the type $b$ events, $t_1^{(b)}, \cdots, t_{n(a)}^{(b)}$ are independently and uniformly distributed over the period of observation. Thus in principle, the exact distribution of any test statistic can be obtained free of nuisance parameters.

The two simplest of the many possible test statistics are probably:

(a) particular ordinates of the cross intensity function, usually that near the origin; equivalently we can use the statistic $R_a^{(b)}(0, \Delta)$ of Section 6.3, directly;

(b) the sample mean recurrence time backwards from a type $b$ event to the nearest preceding type $a$ event.

The null distribution of $R_a^{(b)}(0, \Delta)$ can be found as follows. Place an interval of length $\Delta$ to the right of each type $a$ event. (It is assumed for convenience that either there is a type $a$ event at the origin, or that the position of the last type $a$ event before the origin is available.) Let $\pi_0, \pi_1, \pi_2, \cdots, \pi_{n(a)}$ be the proportion of the observed interval $(0, t_0)$ covered jointly by $0, 1, 2, \cdots, n^{(a)}$ of these intervals $\Delta$. Then, if there are $n^{(b)}$ events of type $b$ in all, the null distribution of $R_a^{(b)}(0, \Delta)$ is that of the sum of $n^{(b)}$ independent random variables each taking the value $i$ with probability $\pi_i$, $i = 1, \cdots, n^{(a)}$.

Similarly, for the second test statistic, we can find the null distribution as follows. Regard the sequence of intervals between successive type $a$ events as a finite population $x = \{x_1, \cdots, x_N\}$, say. This includes the intervals from 0 to the first type $a$ event and from the last type $a$ event to $t_0$. If $t_0$ is preassigned, $N = n^{(a)} + 1$. Note that $\Sigma\, x_i = t_0$. Then the null distribution of the test statistic is that of the mean of $n_b$ independent and identically distributed random variables each with probability density function

$$\frac{1}{t_0} \sum_{i=1}^{N} U(x; x_i), \tag{6.18}$$

where

$$U(x; x_i) = \begin{cases} 1, & 0 \leqq x \leqq x_i, \\ 0, & \text{otherwise.} \end{cases} \tag{6.19}$$

Thus, in particular, the null mean and variance of the test statistic are

$$\frac{\sum x_i^2}{2t_0}, \qquad \frac{1}{n^{(b)}} \left\{ \frac{1}{3t_0} \sum x_i^3 - \frac{(\sum x_i^2)^2}{4t_0^2} \right\}. \tag{6.20}$$

A strong central limit effect may be expected.

The tests derived here may be compared with similar ones in which the null distribution is derived by computer simulation, permuting at random the observed sequences of intervals (Perkel [40]; Moore, Perkel, and Segundo [37]; Perkel, Gerstein, and Moore [41]). In both types of procedure, it is not clear how satisfactory the tests are in practice as general tests of independence, when the type $b$ process is not marginally Poisson. Note, however, that in order to obtain a null distribution for (a) and (b) above it is necessary to assume only that one of the marginal processes is a Poisson process.

If it is required to treat the two processes symmetrically, taking the null hypothesis that there are two mutually independent Poisson processes, there are many possibilities, including the use of the estimated cross spectral or cross intensity functions or of a two sample test based on the idea that, conditionally on $n^{(a)}$ and $n^{(b)}$, the times to events in the two processes are the order statistics from two independent populations of uniformly distributed random variables. Again, in the symmetrical case when both marginal processes are clearly not Poisson processes, tests of independence based on the cross spectrum are probably the best broad tests. For this purpose, investigation of the robustness of the distribution theory given in Section 6.3 would be worthwhile.

◇ ◇ ◇ ◇ ◇

We are indebted to Mr. T. K. M. Wisniewski, Dr. A. J. Lawrance, and Professor D. P. Gaver for helpful discussions during the growth of this paper.

## REFERENCES

[1] M. S. Bartlett, "The spectral analysis of point processes," *J. Roy. Statist. Soc. Ser. B*, Vol. 25 (1963), pp. 264–296.

[2] ———, "The spectral analysis of two-dimensional point processes," *Biometrika*, Vol. 51 (1964), pp. 299–311.

[3] ———, "Line processes and their spectral analysis," *Proceedings of the Fifth Berkeley Symposium on Mathematical Statistics and Probability*, Berkeley and Los Angeles, University of California Press, 1967, Vol. 3, pp. 135–154.

[4] ———, *An Introduction to Stochastic Processes*, Cambridge, Cambridge University Press, 1966 (2nd ed.).

[5] P. Billingsley, "Statistical methods in Markov chains," *Ann. Math. Statist.*, Vol. 32 (1961), pp. 12–40.

[6] D. R. Brillinger, "The spectral analysis of stationary interval functions," *Proccedings of the Sixth Berkeley Symposium on Mathematical Statistics and Probability*, Berkeley and Los Angeles, University of California Press, 1972, Vol. 1, pp. 483–513.

[7] M. Brown, "An $M/G/\infty$ estimation problem," *Ann. Math. Statist.*, Vol. 41 (1970), pp. 651–654.

[8] E. Cinlar, "On the superposition of $m$-dimensional point processes," *J. Appl. Prob.*, Vol. 5 (1968), pp. 169–176.

[9] ———, "Markov renewal theory," *Adv. Appl. Prob.*, Vol. 1 (1969), pp. 123–187.

[10] R. Coleman and J. L. Gastwirth, "Some models for interaction of renewal processes related to neuron firing," *J. Appl. Prob.*, Vol. 6 (1969), pp. 38–58.

[11] D. R. Cox, "Some statistical methods connected with series of events," *J. Roy. Statist. Soc. Ser. B*, Vol. 17 (1955), pp. 129–164.

[12] ———, "Some models for series of events," *Bull. Inst. Internat. Statist.*, Vol. 40 (1963), 737–746.

[13] ———, *Analysis of Binary Data*, London, Methuen; New York, Barnes and Noble, 1970.

[14] D. R. Cox and P. A. W. Lewis, *The Statistical Analysis of Series of Events*, London, Methuen; New York, Barnes and Noble, 1966.

[15] D. R. Cox and H. D. Miller, *The Theory of Stochastic Processes*, London, Methuen, 1966.

[16] D. J. Daley, "The correlation structure of the output process of some single server queueing systems," *Ann. Math. Statist.*, Vol. 39 (1968), pp. 1007–1019.

[17] J. L. Doob, *Stochastic Processes*, New York, Wiley, 1953.

[18] M. Dwass and H. Teicher, "On infinitely divisible random vectors," *Ann. Math. Statist.*, Vol. 28 (1957), pp. 461–470.

[19] J. E. Freund, "A bivariate extension of the exponential distribution," *J. Amer. Statist. Assoc.*, Vol. 56 (1961), pp. 971–977.

[20] D. P. Gaver, "Multivariate gamma distributions generated by mixture," *Sankhyā Ser. A*, Vol. 32 (1970), pp. 123–126.

[21] R. C. Griffiths, "The canonical correlation coefficients of bivariate gamma distributions," *Ann. Math. Statist.*, Vol. 40 (1969), pp. 1401–1408.

[22] A. G. Hawkes, "Spectra of some self-exciting and mutually exciting point processes," *Biometrika*, Vol. 58 (1971), pp. 83–90.

[23] G. M. Jenkins, "Contribution to a discussion of paper by M. S. Bartlett," *J. Roy. Statist. Soc. Ser. B*, Vol. 25 (1963), pp. 290–292.

[24] A. J. Lawrance, "Selective interaction of a Poisson and renewal process: First-order stationary point results," *J. Appl. Prob.*, Vol. 7 (1970), pp. 359–372.

[25] ———, "Selective interaction of a stationary point process and a renewal process," *J. Appl. Prob.*, Vol. 7 (1970), pp. 483–489.

[26] ———, "Selective interaction of a Poisson and renewal process: The dependency structure of the intervals between responses," *J. Appl. Prob.*, Vol. 8 (1971), pp. 170–184.

[27] M. R. Leadbetter, "On streams of events and mixtures of streams," *J. Roy. Statist. Soc. Ser. B*, Vol. 28 (1966), pp. 218–227.

[28] ———, "On the distribution of times between events in a stationary stream of events," *J. Roy. Statist. Soc. Ser. B*, Vol. 31 (1969), pp. 295–302.

[29] P. A. W. Lewis, "A branching Poisson process model for the analysis of computer failure patterns," *J. Roy. Statist. Soc. Ser. B*, Vol. 26 (1964), pp. 398–456.

[30] ———, "Asymptotic properties and equilibrium conditions for branching Poisson processes," *J. Appl. Prob.*, Vol. 6 (1969), pp. 355–371.

[31] ———, "Remarks on the theory, computation and application of the spectral analysis of series of events," *J. Sound Vib.*, Vol. 12 (1970), pp. 353–375.

[32] ———, "Asymptotic properties of branching renewal processes," *J. Appl. Prob.*, to appear.

[33] A. W. Marshall and I. Olkin, "A multivariate exponential distribution," *J. Amer. Statist. Assoc.*, Vol. 62 (1967), pp. 30–44.

[34] ———, "A generalized bivariate exponential distribution," *J. Appl. Prob.*, Vol. 4 (1967), pp. 291–302.

[35] J. A. McFadden, "On the lengths of intervals in a stationary point process," *J. Roy. Statist. Soc. Ser. B*, Vol. 24 (1962), pp. 364–382.

[36] E. H. Moore and R. Pyke, "Estimation of the transition distributions of a Markov renewal process," *Ann. Inst. Statist. Math.*, Vol. 20 (1968), pp. 411–424.

[37] G. P. Moore, D. H. Perkel, and J. P. Segundo, "Statistical analysis and functional interpretation of neuronal spike data," *Ann. Rev. Psychology*, Vol. 28 (1966), pp. 493–522

[38] P. A. P. Moran and D. Vere-Jones, "The infinite divisibility of multivariate gamma distributions," *Sankhyā Ser. A*, Vol. 31 (1969), pp. 191–194.

[39] J. Neyman and E. L. Scott, "Statistical approach to problems of cosmology," *J. Roy. Statist. Soc. Ser. B*, Vol. 20 (1958), pp. 1–29.

[40] D. H. Perkel, "Statistical techniques for detecting and classifying neuronal interactions," *Symposium on Information Processing in Sight Sensory Systems*, Pasadena, California Institute of Technology, 1965, pp. 216–238.

[41] D. H. Perkel, G. L. Gerstein, and G. P. Moore, "Neuronal spike trains and stochastic point processes II. Simultaneous spike trains," *Biophys. J.*, Vol. 7 (1967), pp. 419–440.

[42] R. L. Plackett, "A class of bivariate distributions," *J. Amer. Statist. Assoc.*, Vol. 60 (1965), pp. 516–522.

[43] R. Pyke and R. A. Schaufele, "The existence and uniqueness of stationary measures for Markov renewal processes," *Ann. Math. Statist.*, Vol. 37 (1966), pp. 1439–1462.

[44] I. M. Slivnyak, "Some properties of stationary flows of homogeneous random events," *Theor. Probability Appl.*, Vol. 7 (1962), pp. 336–341.

[45] D. Vere-Jones, S. Turnovsky, and G. A. Eiby, "A statistical survey of earthquakes in the main seismic region of New Zealand. Part I. Time trends in the pattern of recorded activity," *New Zealand J. Geol. Geophys.*, Vol. 7 (1964), pp. 722–744.

[46] D. Vere-Jones and R. D. Davies, "A statistical survey of earthquakes in the main seismic region of New Zealand, Part II. Time series analysis," *New Zealand J. Geol. Geophys.*, Vol. 9 (1966), pp. 251–284.

[47] D. Vere-Jones, "Stochastic models for earthquake occurrence," *J. Roy. Statist. Soc. Ser. B*, Vol. 32 (1970), pp. 1–62.

[48] L. Walloe, J. K. S. Jansen, and K. Nygaard, "A computer simulated model of a second order sensory neuron," *Kybernetik*, Vol. 6 (1969), pp. 130–140.

[49] G. S. Watson and E. J. Williams, "On the construction of significance tests on the circle and the sphere," *Biometrika*, Vol. 43 (1956), pp. 344–352.

[50] T. K. M. Wisniewski, "Forward recurrence time relations in bivariate point processes," *J. Appl. Prob.*, Vol. 9 (1972).

[51] ———, "Extended recurrence time relations in bivariate point processes," to appear.

# 12



# NONHOMOGENEOUS POISSON FIELDS OF RANDOM LINES WITH APPLICATIONS TO TRAFFIC FLOW

HERBERT SOLOMON[1]
STANFORD UNIVERSITY
and
PETER C. C. WANG[2]
NAVAL POSTGRADUATE SCHOOL, MONTEREY

## 1. Introduction

This study was prompted by investigations of models of traffic flow on a highway through analyses of the structure and properties of Poisson fields of random lines in a plane. It is possible to view the trajectory of a car produced by its time and space coordinates on the highway as a straight line in that plane if the car travels at a constant speed once it enters the highway and then never leaves the highway. These traffic considerations plus the property of time invariance for traffic flow distributions lead to one model for traffic flow on a divided highway developed by Rényi [10]. This idealized model is simpler to study than the more realistic situation that provided Rényi's motivation and which he also subjects to analysis, namely, cars do lose time because of an overtaking of one car by another even on a divided highway with two lanes for traffic moving in one direction.

In his paper, Rényi found it convenient to start from the stochastic process of entrance times of the cars at a fixed point on the highway. Other authors start from the spatial process of cars distributed in locations along the highway at some fixed time according to some random law. The traffic flow results of Weiss and Herman [13] who study the spatial process for the idealized model are analogous to Rényi's results which stem from the temporal process. To demonstrate the equivalence of the two results, care must be taken to employ the appropriate measure in deriving distributions related to traffic flow. Both Rényi, and Weiss and Herman, achieved asymptotic results for traffic flow distributions. We will reproduce both results in Section 4 as special cases of our development of traffic flow models through the structure of random lines in the plane. It should be mentioned here that Brown [3] reconsiders Rényi's idealized model and derives exact distributions rather than asymptotic distributions for spatial and speed distributions of cars.

[1]This research partially supported by Contract No. FH11-7698 U.S. Department of Transportation.
[2]This research partially supported by Contract No. NRO42-268 U.S. Office of Naval Research.

To this point we have not been specific about the random processes governing entrance times of cars on a highway, positions of cars on a highway, and speed distributions of cars on the highway. The Poisson process is the assumed machinery governing car entrance times or equivalently car positions and the speed distributions for each car are assumed to be identically and independently distributed (i.i.d.). Starting from the spatial process, Breiman [2] considered the idealized model and proved that the Poisson process is the only process obeying the time invariance property—namely if at a time $t_0$, the spatial process is Poisson with specific parameter, and the speeds of the cars are i.i.d. with respect to each other and the positions of the cars at time $t_0$, then the process will have the same properties at any other time $t$.

Obviously, other results for Poisson processes can be germane to traffic flow situations and similarly this can be so for results in queueing processes. There is a vast literature in both subjects. However, it is pertinent to this exposition to mention some results for the $M/G/\infty$ queue. The highway can be regarded as the infinite server for each car suffers no delay when it enters the highway in our model; in addition the input is Poisson and the service time distribution is the distribution of the distances traveled by each car before it overtakes or is overtaken by another car on the highway or equivalently the distribution of the time expended until an overtaking occurs. In a paper on Markov processes, Kingman [6] arrives at a general formulation that can be reduced to our idealized traffic flow model or equivalently the $M/G/\infty$ queue. This produces the result that the distribution of cars on the highway is Poisson with parameter

$$\omega \int_0^\infty \frac{1}{v} \, dG(v). \tag{1.1}$$

where $\omega$ is the parameter of the Poisson process for cars entering the highway and $G(v)$ is the cumulative distribution function for the speed of each car. This result is employed by Rényi in his paper where he cites other authors who have produced it. It also falls out of the development in this paper and appears in Theorem 4.2.

Along these lines there is a recent paper by Brown [4] in which he discusses an estimation procedure for $G$ in the $M/G/\infty$ queue for which data are kept only on the times cars enter or leave the highway without identification of cars (that is, no pairing of entering and departing times for any one car). This is a different model from the one to which we give central attention in this paper. In its representation in the time-space plane we would have one straight line going through an origin on the time axis or equivalently on the spatial axis to indicate an arbitrary car (or observer car) always traveling on the highway at some constant speed, $v_0$, but all the other cars would be indicated by line segments from whose lengths we could get distance traveled on highway (still assumed to be i.i.d.) and from whose orientation angle with the $t$ axis we could get the speed of the car. This produces the problem of the distribution of the number of intersections made by the line segments with the fixed line, an interesting but unsolved problem in geometrical probability.

However, this serves to return us to the central issue of intersections of random lines in the plane and its relationship to traffic flow models. We now turn to the formulation where the arbitrary car and all other cars are indicated by straight lines in the plane. The number of intersections of the arbitrary line (observer car) by the other lines determines the number of overtakings of slower cars made by the observer car plus the number of times it was overtaken by faster cars. We are interested in this distribution and also in the distributions of faster car overtakings of the observer car and the overtaking of slower cars by the observer car.

The structure of random lines in the plane and the properties resulting from a specific structure are therefore pertinent to analyses of traffic flow for our idealized model. The notion of a homogeneous Poisson field of random lines in the plane and its consequences have been developed by Miles in several papers [7], [8]. Additional development for nonhomogeneous Poisson fields of random lines is required for study of traffic flow models. In subsequent sections, we provide a formulation for a nonhomogeneous Poisson field of random lines and develop its structure and characteristics. This makes it possible to provide a different proof of Rênyi's theorem and the Weiss and Herman result on traffic flow and allows for further understanding of traffic flow models. It also provides a format for viewing their results as special cases of a more general model. In fact, this model provides a unified treatment for viewing any aspect of the idealized traffic flow model.

## 2. Development

First we formalize the notion of straight lines distributed "at random" throughout the plane. We will describe the plane in terms of $(t, x)$ coordinates for subsequently the $t$ axis will be employed to register time of arrival of cars at a fixed point on a highway and the $x$ axis will in similar fashion report on spatial positions of cars on a highway at a fixed point in time. Naturally the time invariance property will insure that the conditions will prevail at any point in time. Any line in the $(t, x)$ plane can be represented as

$$p = t \cos \alpha + x \sin \alpha, \qquad -\infty < p < \infty, 0 \leqq \alpha < \pi, \tag{2.1}$$

where $p$ is the signed length of the perpendicular to the line from an arbitrary origin 0, and $\alpha$ is the angle this perpendicular makes with the $t$ axis (Figure 1). Note that if the intersection of the perpendicular with the line is in the third or fourth quadrant, $p$ is taken to be negative. A set of lines $\{(p_i, \alpha_i): i = 0, \pm 1, \pm 2, \cdots\}$ constitutes a Poisson field under the following conditions.

(1) The distances $\cdots \leqq p_{-2} \leqq p_{-1} \leqq p_0 \leqq p_1 \leqq p_2 \leqq \cdots$ of the lines from an arbitrary origin 0, arranged according to magnitude represent the coordinates of the events of a Poisson process with constant parameter, say $\lambda$. Thus, the

number of $p_i$ in an interval of length $L$ has a Poisson distribution with mean $\lambda L$.

(2) The orientations $\alpha_i$ of each line with a fixed but arbitrary axis (say the $t$ axis) in the plane are independent and obey a uniform distribution in the interval $[0, \pi)$.

Thus, a reasonable representation of random lines in the plane is that of the Poisson field. This definition of randomness for lines in the plane also has the property that the randomness is unaffected by the choice of origin or line to serve as $t$ axis, since it can be demonstrated that except for a constant factor $\int dp d\alpha$ is the only invariant measure under the group of rotations and translations that transform the line $(p, \alpha)$ to the line $(p', \alpha')$. We will return to this structure and its characteristics, but now we employ it as a point of departure to initiate discussion of a nonhomogeneous Poisson field of random lines. To achieve this we will relax condition (2) above and ask only that the $\alpha_i$ be identically and independently distributed (i.i.d.).

For ease in the algebra of our traffic flow models, we will employ instead of $\alpha_i$ an angle formed by the intersection of the $t$ axis with a line in the plane and we label this $\theta$ (Figure 1); note that $v = \tan \theta$. Also we will only be concerned with

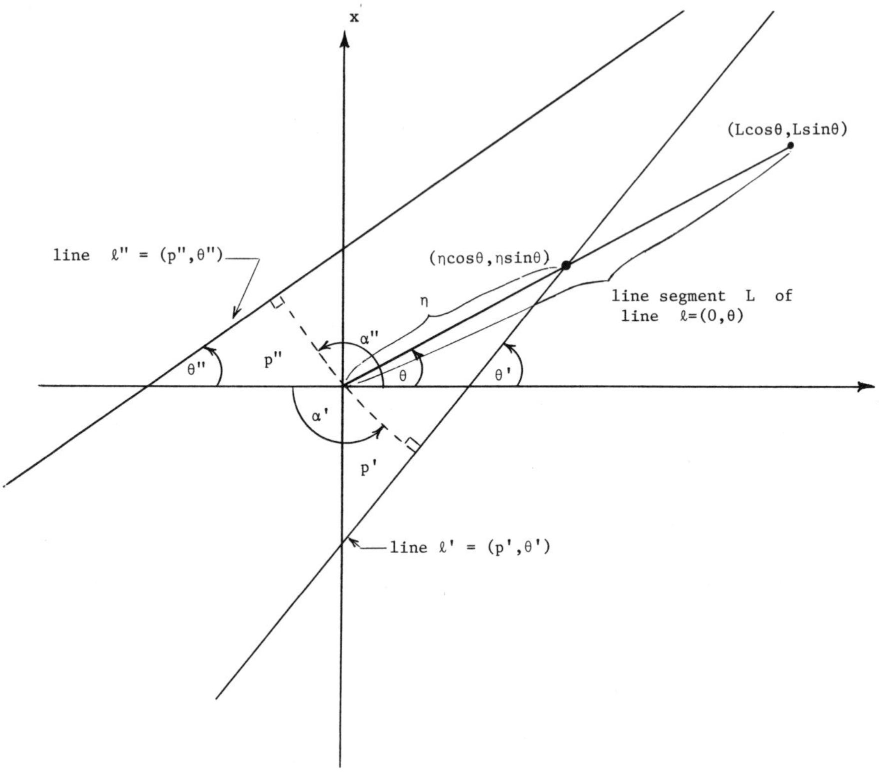


FIGURE 1

those lines where $p_i$ falls in the second or fourth quadrant since this will yield all positive car velocities. The inclusion of the $p_i$ in the first and third quadrant does not complicate the mathematical development, but they are not relevant. Thus, $\alpha = \frac{1}{2}\pi + \theta$ and the lines of interest will now be parametrized by $(p, \theta)$ where

$$p = -t \sin \theta + x \cos \theta, \qquad 0 \leqq \theta < \tfrac{1}{2}\pi. \tag{2.2}$$

Equation (2.2) takes care of the sign of $p$ for it insures that $p$ will be positive if it is in the second quadrant and negative in the fourth quadrant.

The set $\mathscr{L}$ of lines $\{(p_i, \alpha_i): i = 0, \pm 1, \pm 2, \cdots\}$ becomes a nonhomogeneous Poisson field if we require invariant measure only under translation, and we look into this situation because it will be helpful in our traffic flow models. Under this constraint, we now have the same conditions except that the orientation angles $\alpha_i$ of each line are i.i.d. random variables with common distribution function in the interval $[0, \pi)$. Thus, $\int dpd\alpha$ is no longer the appropriate measure. The diagram in Figure 1 delineates the situation where the origin can be arbitrarily chosen at any point on a specific and fixed $t$ axis because invariance is preserved now only under translation.

The orientations $\theta_i$ are independent and identically distributed with common distribution $F$ in the interval $[0, \frac{1}{2}\pi)$ and further the sequence of values $\langle\theta_i\rangle$ are independent of $\langle p_i\rangle$. This is equivalent to the statement that the velocities of cars, namely, $v_i = \tan \theta_i$ are independent and identically distributed with common distribution $G$ on $[0, \infty)$ and thus $\langle v_i = \tan \theta_i\rangle$ are independent of $\langle p_i\rangle$.

When $\theta_0 = 0, p_0 = 0$, the traffic flow is characterized by a distribution of time intercepts on the $t$ axis; when $\theta_0 = \frac{1}{2}\pi, p_0 = 0$, the traffic flow is characterized by a distribution of cars spaced along the $x$ axis. For any other value of $\theta$, the traffic flow is measured along a trajectory line. In the traffic literature, trajectories for low density traffic flow (no delays in overtaking) may be assumed to be linear in the time-space plane. Thus in any development, we must employ the appropriate measure to characterize distributions of traffic flow in such matters, for example, as distribution of number of overtakings. For our purposes where Poisson processes will be the underpinning for traffic flow in both spatial and temporal processes, the evaluation of the appropriate Poisson intensity parameter will be paramount as will be the relationships between these parameters for different measures.

The following exposition and the diagram in Figure 2 are included to make clear how the departure to nonhomogeneous Poisson fields occurs. Consider the $(p, \theta)$ plane. The homogeneous Poisson field occurs when points on the $p$ axis follow a Poisson process with parameter $\lambda$ independent of $p$ and $\theta$ is uniformly distributed from 0 to $\frac{1}{2}\pi$. Given a fixed interval on $p$ containing exactly $n$ points, each follows a uniform distribution whose range is the length of the interval. When the interval is of unit length the density is $dp$. Similarly the density for $\theta$ is $d\theta$ and the joint density is $dpd\theta$ leading to $\int dpd\theta$ as the measure. This is invariant under rotations and translations. If $\theta_i$ is i.i.d. but not uniformly

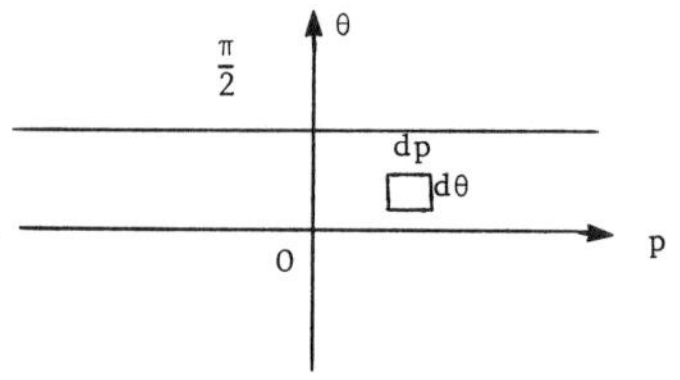


FIGURE 2

distributed, then the Poisson process for points of intersection along any trajectory line $(p, \theta)$ is maintained but the density for $\theta$ is no longer $d\theta$. Thus, any $dpd\theta$ rectangle as in Figure 2 will have the same measure only under translation on the $p$ axis.

Also if $\theta$ is uniformly distributed but the points on the $p$ axis follow a Poisson with parameter $\lambda(p)$, we obtain a nonhomogeneous Poisson field of random lines. If there are departures in the structure of both $\theta_i$ and $p_i$ as listed above, then we obviously have a nonhomogeneous Poisson field of random lines where a Poisson process for points of intersections along any trajectory line $(p, \theta)$ will be maintained but the counting will be measured by the values of $(p, \theta)$ or equivalently the values of $(t, x)$.

## 3. Basic results

The main results for nonhomogeneous Poisson fields of random lines $\mathscr{L}$ are discussed in this section. All sets under investigation are assumed to be measurable and events of probability zero are neglected. For instance, a possible realization of $\mathscr{L}$ is one in which there are no lines at all with probability zero and this is omitted. Many of the following results must be qualified by the phrase "with probability one"; however, this is often omitted for brevity. One basic feature of a special nonhomogeneous Poisson field of random lines, where $p$ is Poisson with parameter $\lambda$ and $\theta$ is i.i.d. is given in the following theorem.

THEOREM 3.1. *Points of intersections of such random lines $\mathscr{L}$ and any arbitrary and fixed line $(p_0, \theta_0)$ form a Poisson process with parameter $\lambda(\theta_0)$, where*

$$\lambda(\theta_0) = \lambda \cos \theta_0 \int_0^\infty |v - \tan \theta_0| (1 + v)^{-1/2} \, dG(v) \tag{3.1}$$

*and $\lambda$ is the parameter of the Poisson field of random lines and $v = \tan \theta$.*

NOTE. The counting is done on the arbitrary and fixed line $(p_0, \theta_0)$ and of course $\langle v = \tan \theta \rangle$ for all the lines in $\mathscr{L}$. In our traffic model, a point of intersection on the line $(p_0, \theta_0)$ when represented in the coordinates of the time-space plane $(t_0, x_0)$ may be viewed in the following traffic sense—$t_0$ is the actual time of car overtaking and $x_0$ is the actual spatial position where the car overtaking event occurs. This is developed more fully in Section 4.

PROOF. We note that the random mechanism in $\mathscr{L}$ is invariant under translation and is thus unaffected by the choice of origin; hence, we can have the arbitrary line go through the origin such that the segment of line $(0, \theta_0)$ with length $L$ emanates from the origin and $\theta_0$ is the fixed angle associated with this arbitrary line. Now denote $\eta$ as the length of this segment measured from the origin to the point of intersection with another line $\ell' = (p', \theta') \in \mathscr{L}$ (see Figure 1). We can classify lines in $\mathscr{L}$ that intersect with line segment $L$ into two groups, namely:

(1) for $\theta$ such that $0 < \theta < \theta_0$, $p > 0$ we have $\eta \sin(\theta_0 - \theta) = p$, if and only if

$$0 < \eta = p \csc(\theta_0 - \theta) < L. \tag{3.2}$$

(2) for $\theta$ such that $\theta_0 < \theta < \frac{1}{2}\pi$, $p < 0$ we have $\eta \sin(\theta - \theta_0) = -p$, if and only if

$$0 < \eta = -p \csc(\theta - \theta_0) < L. \tag{3.3}$$

Let $N_L$ denote the number of lines in $\mathscr{L}$ intersecting the segment of length $L$. Then we will show that

$$Pr\{N_L = n\} = \exp\{-L\lambda\mu\} \frac{(L\lambda\mu)^n}{n!}, \tag{3.4}$$

and upon evaluation, that

$$\mu = \cos\theta_0 \int_0^\infty |v - \tan\theta_0| (1 + v^2)^{-1/2} \, dG(v). \tag{3.5}$$

Recall that $\cos\theta_0$ and $\tan\theta_0$ are constants depending on the $\theta_0$ of the arbitrary line. Denote $N_p$ the number of random lines whose signed distance $p$, to the origin is between $-L\sin\theta_0$ and $L\cos\theta_0$. Then

$$Pr\{N_L = n\} = \sum_{m=0}^{\infty} Pr\{N_L = n \mid N_p = m\} Pr\{N_p = m\}. \tag{3.6}$$

Clearly, no line can intersect the segment $L$ unless its minimum distance to the origin is between $-L\sin\theta_0$ and $L\cos\theta_0$. Thus, $N_p$ must be more than $N_L$; that is,

$$Pr\{N_L = n \mid N_p = m\} = 0 \quad \text{for } n > m, \tag{3.7}$$

and therefore

$$Pr\{N_L = n\} = \sum_{m=n}^{\infty} Pr\{N_L = n \mid N_p = m\} Pr\{N_p = m\}. \tag{3.8}$$

Let $\mu = Pr\{N_L = 1 \mid N_p = 1\}$. Then since the random lines are independent, that is, sequences $\langle v_i \rangle$ and $\langle p_i \rangle$ are independent, we have

$$Pr\{N_L = n \mid N_p = m\} = \binom{m}{n} \mu^n (1 - \mu)^{m-n} \quad \text{for } m \geqq n. \tag{3.9}$$

By the definition of random lines $\mathscr{L}$, we have

$$(3.10)\qquad Pr\,\{N_p = m\} = \exp\{-\lambda L(\sin\theta_0 + \cos\theta_0)\}\frac{[\lambda L(\cos\theta_0 + \sin\theta_0)]^m}{m!}.$$

Thus,

$$(3.11)\quad Pr\,\{N_L = n\} = \sum_{m=n}^{\infty}\binom{m}{n}\mu^n(1-\mu)^{m-n}$$
$$\exp\{-\lambda L(\sin\theta_0 + \cos\theta_0)\}\frac{[\lambda L(\cos\theta_0 + \sin\theta_0)]^m}{m!}$$
$$= \exp\{-\lambda L\mu(\sin\theta_0 + \cos\theta_0)\}\frac{[\lambda L\mu(\sin\theta_0 + \cos\theta_0)]^n}{n!}.$$

Now we evaluate $\mu$, the probability that a line whose minimum signed distance to the origin is between $-L\sin\theta_0$ and $L\cos\theta_0$, will intersect the segment $L$. Write

$$\begin{aligned}(3.12)\qquad \mu &= Pr\,\{N_L = 1 \mid N_p = 1\}\\ &= Pr\,\{0 < \eta < L \mid -L\sin\theta_0 < p < L\cos\theta_0\}\\ &= Pr\,\{0 < \eta < L; 0 < \theta < \theta_0 \mid -L\sin\theta_0 < p < L\cos\theta_0\}\\ &\quad + Pr\,\{0 < \eta < L; \theta_0 < \theta < \tfrac{1}{2}\pi \mid -L\sin\theta_0 < p < L\cos\theta_0\}\\ &= \frac{1}{L(\sin\theta_0 + \cos\theta_0)}\Bigg[\int_{-L\sin\theta_0}^{0} Pr\,\{0 < \eta < L, 0 < \theta < \theta_0 \mid p\}\,dp\\ &\quad + \int_{0}^{L\cos\theta_0} Pr\,\{0 < \eta < L; \theta_0 < \theta < \tfrac{1}{2}\pi \mid p\}\,dp\Bigg].\end{aligned}$$

Therefore, we have

$$\begin{aligned}(3.13)\qquad L\mu(\cos\theta_0 + \sin\theta_0) &= \int_{-L\sin\theta_0}^{0} Pr\,\{0 < \eta < L; 0 < \theta < \theta_0 \mid p\}\,dp\\ &\quad + \int_{0}^{L\cos\theta_0} Pr\,\{0 < \eta < L; \theta_0 < \theta < \tfrac{1}{2}\pi \mid p\}\,dp\\ &= L\cos\theta_0\Bigg[\int_{0}^{\tan\theta_0}(\tan\theta_0 - v)(1 + v^2)^{-1/2}\,dG(v)\\ &\quad + \int_{\tan\theta_0}^{\infty}(v - \tan\theta_0)(1 + v^2)^{-1/2}\,dG(v)\Bigg].\end{aligned}$$

Hence, we may conclude that

$$(3.14)\qquad \mu = \frac{\cos\theta_0}{\cos\theta_0 + \sin\theta_0}\int_0^\infty |v - \tan\theta_0|(1 + v^2)^{-1/2}\,dG(v),$$

and this in turn gives the result that

$$(3.15)\qquad Pr\{N_L = n\} = \exp\left\{-\lambda L \cos\theta_0 \int_0^\infty |v - \tan\theta_0|(1+v^2)^{-1/2}\,dG(v)\right\}$$

$$\cdot\left[\lambda L \cos\theta_0 \int_0^\infty |v - \tan\theta_0|(1+v^2)^{-1/2}\,dG(v)\right]^n (n!)^{-1}.$$

That is, $N_L$, the number of intersections with segment $L$ from lines in $\mathscr{L}$, follows the Poisson distribution with parameter

$$(3.16)\qquad \lambda \cos\theta_0 \int_0^\infty |v - \tan\theta_0|(1+v^2)^{-1/2}\,dG(v).$$

Let us denote $N_L^+$ the number of lines in $\mathscr{L}$ intersecting the segment $L$ with $\theta_0 < \theta < \frac{1}{2}\pi$ and denote $N_L^-$ the number of lines in $\mathscr{L}$ intersecting the segment $L$ with $0 < \theta < \theta_0$. (Clearly, $N_L = N_L^+ + N_L^-$.) Theorem 3.1 permits us to state the following result immediately.

THEOREM 3.2. *Let* $\langle\tau_i^-\rangle$ *be points of intersections of random lines* $\mathscr{L}$ *with* $\theta_0 < \theta < \frac{1}{2}\pi$ *and any arbitrary line* $(p_0, \theta_0)$ *and let* $\langle\tau_i^+\rangle$ *be points of intersections of random lines* $\mathscr{L}$ *with* $0 < \theta < \theta_0$ *and line* $(p_0, \theta_0)$. *Then* $\langle\tau_i^+\rangle$ *and* $\langle\tau_i^-\rangle$ *form two independent Poisson processes, with parameters*

$$(3.17)\qquad \lambda^+(\theta_0) = \lambda \cos\theta_0 \int_0^{\tan\theta_0} (\tan\theta_0 - v)(1+v^2)^{-1/2}\,dG(v)$$

*and*

$$(3.18)\qquad \lambda^-(\theta_0) = \lambda \cos\theta_0 \int_{\tan\theta_0}^\infty (v - \tan\theta_0)(1+v^2)^{-1/2}\,dG(v).$$

In traffic terms, $\lambda^+(\theta_0)$ is the intensity of the Poisson process generated by the fixed car $K(p_0, \theta_0)$ overtaking slower cars and $\lambda^-(\theta_0)$ for faster cars overtaking $K(p_0, \theta_0)$. We remark here that if $\theta_0 = 0$, $p_0 = 0$, namely the $t$ axis, then $\lambda^+(0) = 0$ and $\lambda^-(0) = \lambda \int_0^\infty v(1+v^2)^{-1/2}\,dG(v)$, that is, if the random variable $N_p$ is distributed according to the Poisson distribution with parameter $\lambda$, then the points of intersection of random lines $\mathscr{L}$ with the $t$ axis form a point process distributed according to the Poisson distribution with parameter $\lambda \int_0^\infty v(1+v^2)^{-1/2}\,dG(v)$. Similarly, if $\theta_0 = \frac{1}{2}\pi$, $p_0 = 0$, namely the $x$ axis, then

$$(3.19)\qquad \lambda(\tfrac{1}{2}\pi) = \lambda \int_0^\infty (1+v^2)^{-1/2}\,dG(v),$$

and the counting is done along the spatial axis. The corresponding $\lambda^+(\frac{1}{2}\pi) = \lambda(\frac{1}{2}\pi)$ and $\lambda^-(\frac{1}{2}\pi) = 0$. Hence, we have established the following result.

THEOREM 3.3. (i) *Points of intersection of the field* $\mathscr{L}$ *and the* $t$ *axis (temporal counting) form a Poisson process with parameter* $\lambda_t$ *where*

$$(3.20)\qquad \lambda_t = \lambda \int_0^\infty v(1+v^2)^{-1/2}\,dG(v).$$

(ii) *Points of intersection of the field $\mathscr{L}$ and the x axis (spatial counting) form a Poisson process with parameter $\lambda_x$, where*

$$\lambda_x = \lambda \int_0^\infty (1 + v^2)^{-1/2}\, dG(v). \tag{3.21}$$

Let the sequence $\langle \tau_{1k} \rangle$ denote the instants when the arbitrary line $(p_0, \theta_0)$ segment of length $L$ intersects random lines of $\mathscr{L}$ whose orientations $\theta_i$ belong to a given set $\Theta_1$ and sequence $\langle \tau_{2k} \rangle$ denote the instants when the arbitrary line $(p_0, \theta_0)$ segment of length $L$ intersects random lines of $\mathscr{L}$ whose orientations $\theta_i$ belong to a given set $\Theta_2$. We now state a generalized version of the results in Theorem 3.4.

THEOREM 3.4. *If $\Theta_1 \cap \Theta_2 = \varnothing$, then the two sequences $\langle \tau_{1k} \rangle$ and $\langle \tau_{2k} \rangle$ form two independent Poisson processes with parameters $\lambda_1(\theta_0)$ and $\lambda_2(\theta_0)$, respectively, where*

$$\lambda_i(\theta_0) = \lambda \int_{\tan \Theta_i} |v - \tan \theta_0| (1 + v^2)^{-1/2}\, dG(v), \qquad i = 1, 2, \tag{3.22}$$

*and*

$$\tan \Theta_i = \{v \,|\, v = \tan \theta \text{ such that } \theta \in \Theta_i\}, \qquad i = 1, 2. \tag{3.23}$$

The details of the proof are omitted since it is essentially the proof used in Theorem 3.1.

In the next paragraphs, we establish some similar results employing $\langle \tau_i \rangle$ and $\langle \eta_i \rangle$, where the $\tau_i$ are the arrival times of cars on a highway measured from a fixed position, say $x = 0$, and $\eta_i$ are corresponding positions of these cars on the highway at a fixed time, say $t_i$. Let us denote $\langle \tau_i \rangle$ the sequence of points of intersections of a given random family of lines $\mathscr{A}$ with the $t$ axis. Let $\langle v_i = \tan \theta_i \rangle$ be the sequence of i.i.d. random variables. Those $\theta_i$ are the orientations of random lines in $\mathscr{A}$. Denote $\langle \eta_i \rangle$ the sequence of points of intersections of random lines in $\mathscr{A}$ with the $x$ axis. We employ $\mathscr{A}$ instead of $\mathscr{L}$ for now we do not wish to assume as in $\mathscr{L}$ that $\langle p_i \rangle$ and $\langle v_i \rangle$ are independent sequences. In the following theorems, we will employ $\langle \eta_i \rangle$ and $\langle v_i \rangle$, or $\langle \tau_i \rangle$ and $\langle v_i \rangle$ as independent sequences and these assumptions will be made specific in each statement of the theorem. The results can be stated as follows.

THEOREM 3.5. *If $\langle \tau_i \rangle$ forms a Poisson process with parameter $\lambda_\tau$ and sequences $\langle \tau_i \rangle$ and $\langle v_i \rangle$ are independent, then $\langle p_i \rangle$ forms a Poisson process with parameter $\lambda_\eta \int_0^\infty [(1 + v^2)^{1/2}/v]\, dG(v)$.*

Similarly, we have:

THEOREM 3.6. *If $\langle \eta_i \rangle$ forms a Poisson process with parameter $\lambda_\eta$ and sequence $\langle \eta_i \rangle$ and $\langle v_i \rangle$ are independent, then $\langle p_i \rangle$ forms a Poisson process with parameter $\lambda_\eta \int_0^\infty (1 + v^2)^{1/2}\, dG(v)$.*

We shall give a proof of Theorem 3.5. The proof of Theorem 3.6 is similar and hence is omitted.

PROOF OF THEOREM 3.5. Based on the proof similar to that used in Theorem 3.1, we denote $N_t(c)$ the number of lines in $\mathscr{A}$ intersecting the $t$ axis in an interval of length $c$ and denote $N_p$ for the number of lines in $\mathscr{A}$ whose $p_i$ is bounded by $0 < p_i < p$. Then it is clear we want to show that

$$(3.24)\quad Pr\,\{N_p = n\} = \exp\left\{-\lambda p \int_0^\infty \frac{(1+v^2)^{1/2}}{v}\,dG(v)\right\}\left[\lambda p \int_0^\infty \frac{(1+v^2)^{1/2}}{v}\,dG(v)\right]^n (n!)^{-1}.$$

Following the previous development, we arrive at

$$(3.25)\qquad Pr\,\{N_p = n\} = \lim_{c\to\infty} \exp\,\{-\lambda_1 C\mu_c\}\,\frac{(\lambda_1 C\mu_c)^n}{n!}$$

and

$$(3.26)\qquad \mu_c = Pr\,\{N_p = 1 \,|\, N_t(c) = 1\}.$$

It remains to show that

$$(3.27)\qquad \lim_{c\to\infty} c\mu_c = p\int_0^\infty \frac{(1+v^2)^{1/2}}{v}\,dG(v),$$

$$(3.28)\qquad \mu_c = Pr\,\{N_p = 1\,|\,N_t(c) = 1\} = \frac{1}{c}\int_0^c Pr\,\{N_p = 1\,|\,\tau\}\,d\tau,$$

$$(3.29)\qquad c\mu_c = \int_0^c Pr\,\{N_p = 1\,|\,\tau\}\,d\tau,$$

$$(3.30)\qquad \begin{aligned}\lim_{c\to\infty} c\mu_c &= \int_0^\infty Pr\,\{N_p = 1\,|\,\tau\}\,d\tau\\ &= \int_0^\infty Pr\left\{0 < \theta < \sin^{-1}\frac{p}{\tau}\,\middle|\,\tau\right\}d\tau\\ &= \int_0^\infty \int_0^{p/\mathrm{sintan}^{-1}v} d\tau\, dG(v)\\ &= p\int_0^\infty \frac{(1+v^2)^{1/2}}{v}\,dG(v).\end{aligned}$$

This completes the proof of Theorem 3.5.

## 4. Traffic flow applications

The purpose of this section is to discuss a number of results that can be related to low density traffic flow models on an infinite highway in the light of the developments in Section 3. These models were initiated and developed principally in papers by Rényi [10], Weiss and Herman [13], and Breiman [2], sometimes without specific reference to low density traffic flow. Of the theorems presented in this section, some are known but all the proofs are new and developed in a unified manner.

Rényi [10] has developed and analyzed a model of traffic flow on a divided highway that extends in one direction out to infinity without traffic lights or other barriers. It is assumed that the speed of each car is constant but its value is governed by a random variable and passing is always achieved without delays. Assuming that the temporal distribution of cars is described by a Poisson process, Rényi obtained some asymptotic results for the spatial distribution of cars along the highway. In what follows, we shall reproduce Rényi's theorems and include other results dealing with low density traffic flow. It will also be demonstrated for Rényi's model, that if the spatial distribution of cars is assumed to obey a Poisson process then the temporal distribution of cars (that is, arrival times at some fixed position) is again a Poisson process. This new result establishes a crucial structural property of Rényi's model for low density traffic. In detail, the assumptions of Rényi's model are:

(a) instants $\langle t_i \rangle_{i=1}^{\infty}$ at which cars enter the highway at a fixed position form a homogeneous Poisson process with parameter $\omega$;

(b) a car arriving at a certain point on the highway at instant $t_i$ chooses a velocity $V_i$ and then moves with this constant velocity; the random variables $\langle V_k \rangle$ are independently and identically distributed with distribution function $G(v) = Pr\{V \leqq v\}$ and sequences $\{V_k\}$ and $\langle t_k \rangle$ are independent;

(c) $\int_0^{\infty} (1/v)\, dG(v) < \infty$, that is, the mean value of $1/v$ is finite; without this condition a traffic jam would arise and make all traffic flow impossible;

(d) no delay in overtaking a car traveling at a slower speed when it is approached.

Suppose an arbitrary car $K(t_0, v_0)$ arrives at some fixed point of the highway at time $t_0$, where it assumes and maintains the fixed velocity $v_0$. Let $\langle t_k^+ \rangle$ denote the instants at which the car $K(t_0, v_0)$ overtakes slower cars and $\langle t_k^- \rangle$ denote instants at which car $K(t_0, v_0)$ is overtaken by faster cars. Rényi has obtained the following asymptotic result.

THEOREM 4.1. (Rényi). *The instants* $\{t_k^+\}$ *and* $\{t_k^-\}$ *form two independent homogeneous Poisson processes, with parameters:*

$$\omega^+(v_0) = \omega \int_0^{v_0} \frac{v_0 - v}{v}\, dG(v), \qquad \omega^-(v_0) = \omega \int_{v_0}^{\infty} \frac{v - v_0}{v}\, dG(v). \tag{4.1}$$

Rényi's proof of the above theorem is based on the following two properties of Poisson processes:

(A) if $\langle t_i \rangle$ are the instants of time when an event occurs in a homogeneous Poisson process with parameter $\omega$, and $\zeta_1, \zeta_2, \cdots$, is a sequence of independent positive random variables, each having the same distribution $G(\zeta)$ and each is independent of the process $\{t_k\}$, then the time instants $t_k \zeta_k$, $k = 1, 2, \cdots$, also form a homogeneous Poisson process with density

$$\omega^* = \omega \int_0^\infty \frac{1}{\zeta}\, dG(\zeta); \tag{4.2}$$

(B) if a subsequence $\{t_{v_k}\}$ of the instants $\{t_k\}$, in which an event occurs in a Poisson process with density $\omega$, is selected at random in such a way that for each $j$ the probability of the event $A_j$ that $j$ should belong to the subsequence $\{v_k\}$ is equal to $r$, $0 < r < 1$, and the events $A_j, j = 1, 2, \cdots$, are independent, and if $\{t_{u_k}\}$ are the instants that are not selected, (that is, $j$ belongs to the sequence $\{u_k\}$ if and only if it does not belong to the sequence $\{v_k\}$), then $\{t_{v_j}\}$ and $\{t_{u_k}\}$ are two independent Poisson processes with density $\omega r$ and $\omega(1 - r)$.

It is now known from a result of Wang [12] that property (B), in some sense, is a characteristic property for Poisson processes. We shall establish Theorem 4.1 without using property (A). Thus, it may be inferred that property (B) implies property (A).

PROOF OF THEOREM 4.1. The trajectory of any car in the time-space diagram in the preceding section for Rényi's low density traffic model is realized by a straight line. Let us denote the trajectories of all cars on the highway as a set $\mathscr{A}$. Then it is clear that $\mathscr{A}$ possesses the properties of a nonhomogeneous Poisson field of random lines. Denote $M_L^+$ the number of lines in $\mathscr{A}$ that intersect segment $L$ from below and $M_p$ the number of lines in $\mathscr{A}$ whose arrival times are in $(0, t_0)$. Then

$$\begin{aligned} Pr\,\{M_L^+ = n\} &= \sum_{m=n}^{\infty} \binom{m}{n} \mu^n (1 - \mu)^{m-n} \exp\{-\omega t_0\} \frac{(\omega t_0)^m}{m!} \\ &= \exp\{-\omega t_0 \mu\} \frac{(\omega t_0 \mu)^n}{n!}, \end{aligned} \tag{4.3}$$

where

$$\begin{aligned} \mu &= Pr\,\{M_L^+ = 1 \mid M_p = 1\} \\ &= Pr\left\{\theta \geqq \tan^{-1} \frac{x_0}{t_0 - p} \,\middle|\, 0 < p < t_0\right\} \\ &= \frac{1}{t_0} \int_0^{t_0} Pr\left\{V \geqq \frac{x_0}{t_0 - p}\right\} dp \\ &= \int_{v_0}^{\infty} \frac{v - v_0}{v}\, dG(v), \end{aligned} \tag{4.4}$$

and $v_0 = x_0/t_0$.

Similarly, we define $M_L^-$ as the number of lines in $\mathscr{A}$ intersecting $L$ from above and $M_p^c$ as the number of lines in $\mathscr{A}$ whose arrival times fall in the interval $-c$ and $0$, $c > 0$. We can compute

$$Pr\,\{M_L^- = n\} = \lim_{c \to \infty} \exp\{-\omega c \mu_c^*\} \frac{(\omega c \mu_c^*)^n}{n!} \tag{4.5}$$

where $\mu_c^* = Pr\{M_L^- = 1 \mid M_p^c = 1\}$ and

$$\begin{aligned}(4.6)\qquad \lim_{c\to\infty} c\mu_c^* &= \lim_{c\to\infty} cPr\{M_L^- = 1 \mid M_p^c = 1\}\\ &= \lim \int_{-c}^{0}\int_{0}^{x_0/(t_0-p)} dG(v)\,dp\\ &= \int_{-\infty}^{0}\int_{0}^{x_0/(t_0-p)} dG(v)\,dp\\ &= \int_{0}^{v_0} \frac{x_0 - vt_0}{v}\,dG(v)\\ &= t_0 \int_{0}^{v_0} \frac{v_0 - v}{v}\,dG(v).\end{aligned}$$

Random variables $M_L^-$ and $M_L^+$ are independent because the events involved come from disjoint intervals. This completes the proof of Theorem 4.1.

The counting interval employed in the above theorem is on the time axis. In what follows, a similar approach to the problem dealing with a spatial counting interval is employed and produces some interesting results.

Denote $M^-$ the number of lines in $\mathscr{A}$ intersecting $L$ from above and $M^+$ the number of lines from below. Denote $M_{x_0}$ the number of lines in $\mathscr{A}$ whose spatial positions at $t = 0$ are between 0 and $x_0$ and similarly $M_{x_0}^c$ for 0 and $-c$. Let $\lambda^*$ be the spatial density. Then we have

$$(4.7)\qquad Pr\{M^- = n\} = \exp\{-\lambda^* x_0 \mu\} \frac{(\lambda^* x_0 \mu)^n}{n!},$$

where

$$\begin{aligned}(4.8)\qquad \mu &= Pr\{M^- = 1 \mid M_{x_0} = 1\}\\ &= \frac{t_0}{x_0}\int_{0}^{v_0} (v_0 - v)\,dG(v),\end{aligned}$$

and

$$\begin{aligned}(4.9)\qquad Pr\{M^+ = n\} &= \lim_{c\to\infty} \sum_{m=n}^{\infty} Pr\{M^+ = n \mid M_{x_0}^c = m\}\, Pr\{M_{x_0}^c = m\}\\ &= \lim_{c\to\infty} \exp\{-\lambda^* c_1^c\} \frac{(\lambda^* c\mu_1^c)^n}{n!}\end{aligned}$$

where $\mu_1^c = Pr\{M^+ = 1 \mid M_{x_0}^c = 1\}$. It can be easily verified that

$$(4.10)\qquad \lim_{c\to\infty} c\mu_1^c = t_0 \int_{v_0}^{\infty} (v - v_0)\,dG(v)$$

and random variables $M^-$ and $M^+$ are independent. Now denote $M = M^+ + M^-$. We conclude that

$$(4.11)\qquad Pr\{M = n\} = \exp\left\{-\lambda^* t_0 \int_0^\infty |v_0 - v|\, dG(v)\right\} \cdot \left[\lambda^* t_0 \int_0^\infty |v_0 - v|\, dG(v)\right]^n (n!)^{-1}.$$

The above result appeared initially in the paper [13] by Weiss and Herman mentioned previously.

In the next paragraph, results are derived about the spatial distribution of vehicles if the temporal distribution (distribution of arrival times) is assumed to be Poisson.

Denote by $S^+$ the number of lines in $\mathscr{A}$ intersecting $(0, x_0)$ and $x_0 > 0$ at time zero and by $S_c^+$ the number of lines in $\mathscr{A}$ whose arrival times are in the interval $(-c, 0)$. We further denote by $S^-$ the number of lines in $\mathscr{A}$ intersecting $(-x_0, 0)$, $x_0 > 0$ at time zero and by $S_c^-$ the number of lines in $\mathscr{A}$ whose arrival times are in the interval $(0, c)$. Let us compute the quantities $Pr\{S^+ = n\}$, $Pr\{S^- = n\}$, and $Pr\{S = S^+ + S^- = n\}$. We have

$$(4.12)\qquad Pr\{S^+ = n\} = \lim_{c\to\infty} \exp\{-\omega c \mu_2\} \frac{(\omega c \mu_2)^n}{n!},$$

where $\omega$ is the temporal density and $\mu_2 = Pr\{S^+ = 1 | S_c^+ = 1\}$. It can be shown easily that

$$(4.13)\qquad \lim_{c\to\infty} c\mu_2 = x_0 \int_0^\infty \frac{1}{v}\, dG(v).$$

We conclude that

$$(4.14)\qquad Pr\{S^+ = n\} = \exp\left\{-\omega x_0 \int_0^\infty \frac{1}{v}\, dG(v)\right\} \left[\omega x_0 \int_0^\infty \frac{1}{v}\, dG(v)\right]^n (n!)^{-1}.$$

Similarly, we obtain $Pr\{S_n^- = n\} = Pr\{S^+ = n\}$ and

$$(4.15)\qquad Pr\{S = S^+ + S^- = n\} = \exp\left\{-2\omega x_0 \int_0^\infty \frac{1}{v}\, dG(v)\right\} \cdot \left[2\omega x_0 \int_0^\infty \frac{1}{v}\, dG(v)\right]^n (n!)^{-1}.$$

We can now summarize as follows.

THEOREM 4.2. *If $\langle t_i \rangle$ forms a Poisson process with parameter $\omega$ and sequences $\langle t_i \rangle$ and $\langle V_i \rangle$ are independent, then the locations of vehicles on the highway at time $t = 0$, namely $\langle x_i \rangle$, form a Poisson process with parameter $\omega \int_0^\infty (1/v)\, dG(v)$.*

THEOREM 4.3. *If $\langle x_i \rangle$ forms a Poisson process with parameter $\lambda^*$ and sequences $\langle x_i \rangle$ and $\langle V_i \rangle$ are independent and $\langle x_i^+ \rangle$ denotes the positions at which the car $K(v_0)$ overtakes slower cars and $\langle x_i^- \rangle$ denotes the positions at which car $K(v_0)$ is overtaken by faster cars, then the two sequences $\langle x_i^+ \rangle$ and $\langle x_i^- \rangle$ form two independent (homogeneous) Poisson processes, with parameters*

$$(4.16)\qquad \lambda^*_+(v_0) = \lambda^* \int_0^{v_0} (v_0 - v)\, dG(v) \qquad \lambda^*_-(v_0) = \lambda^* \int_{v_0}^{\infty} (v - v_0)\, dG(v).$$

This result is analogous to the Rényi result which we developed as Theorem 4.1 except that the counting of overtakings is accomplished on the spatial axis rather than on the time axis. The next theorem provides results analogous to those in Theorem 4.2.

THEOREM 4.4. *If $\langle x_i \rangle$ forms a Poisson process with parameter $\lambda^*$ and sequences $\langle x_i \rangle$ and $\langle V_i \rangle$ are independent and the $\langle V_i \rangle$ are i.i.d. random variables with common distribution $G(v) = Pr\{V \leqq v\}$, then the corresponding $\langle t_i \rangle$ arrival times at position $x = 0$ form a Poisson process with parameter $\lambda^* E(V)$, where $E(V) = \int_0^\infty v\, dG(v)$.*

PROOF. The proof is again based on the binomial mixing as presented in property (B) and hence details are omitted.

## 5. Concluding remarks

REMARK 5.1. On the basis of the work in the previous sections, it appears that we can view the main structural property for a nonhomogeneous Poisson field of random lines $\mathscr{L}$ in the following way. The point process obtained by the intersections of lines in the field $\mathscr{L}$ with any fixed line $(p_0, \theta_0)$ forms a Poisson process subject to the existence of the integral $\int_0^\infty h(v)\, dG(v)$ for some suitable $h(v)$, say $1/v$, $v(1 + v^2)^{-1/2}$, $(1 + v^2)^{-1/2}$, and others.

REMARK 5.2. In light of the statement in Theorem 3.2, we can offer the more general result below for which the proof is immediate and hence is omitted.

THEOREM 5.1. *Let $\Theta_1, \cdots, \Theta_m$ be $m$ disjoint intervals on $\theta$ and let $P_1, \cdots, P_m$ be $m$ intervals on $p$. Recall that $\mathscr{L}$ is the nonhomogeneous Poisson field defined previously, then the random variables $N(P_i, \Theta_i)$, $i = 1, 2, \cdots, m$, where $N(P_i, \Theta_i) = \{$no. of $(p, \theta) \in \mathscr{L}$ such that $p \in P_i, \theta \in \Theta_i\}$, $i = 1, 2, \cdots, m$, are $m$ independent Poisson random variables. Consequently, the lines $(p, \theta)$ are points of a two dimensional nonhomogeneous Poisson process with parameter $\lambda(\Theta)$ that depends on $\theta$.*

Consider the strips in the $(p, \theta)$ plane where $0 \leqq \theta < \frac{1}{2}\pi$ and $-\infty < p < \infty$; see Figure 2. Thus, the number of $p$ in an interval of length $I$ on the $p$ axis whose $\theta$ are in the set $\Theta$ has a nonhomogeneous Poisson distribution with mean

$$(5.1)\qquad \lambda(\Theta) = \lambda I \int_\Theta dF,$$

where $F$ is the c.d.f. on the random variable $\theta$.

It is clear, for the homogeneous Poisson field of random lines where $F$ is the uniform distribution, that $\int_\Theta dF$ equals the length of the interval measure for $\theta$ divided by $\frac{1}{2}\pi$. Hence, the parameter

$$(5.2)\qquad \lambda I \int_\Theta dF = \frac{2}{\pi} \lambda I \text{ (length of } \Theta),$$

and thus it depends only on the length of the set $\Theta$ and the length of $I$ on the $p$ axis. Thus, Theorem 5.1 holds for homogeneous Poisson fields of random lines and in this way it adds to Miles' results.

All results obtained in this paper should be capable of extension to other nonhomogeneous Poisson fields, say, where $\lambda$ is the function of $p$, $\lambda = \lambda(p)$, or where $\lambda = \lambda(t, x)$.

REMARK 5.3. The results announced by Miles in [7] and [8] also fall out immediately from our development because there the orientations $\alpha_i$ are independent and uniformly, distributed, $0 \leqq \alpha_i < \pi$. Then the following result is immediate: the points of intersection of the random lines $\mathscr{A}$ and an arbitrary line $(p_0, \theta_0)$ form a Poisson process with parameter $2\lambda/\pi$.

REMARK 5.4. Based on the results stated in Theorem 3.3 (i) and Theorem 3.5, one might expect to get the following identity

$$\lambda_\tau = \lambda_\tau \int_0^\infty \frac{(1 + v^2)^{1/2}}{v} \, dG(v) \int_0^\infty v(1 + v^2)^{-1/2} \, dG(v). \tag{5.3}$$

But the identity is true if and only if the field $\mathscr{L}$ consists of parallel lines alone. This reduces the field of random lines $\mathscr{L}$ to the case initially studied by Goudsmit [5], who employed it as a first attempt to study random lines in the plane in connection with examining the randomness of tracks left in a cloud chamber by a particle.

REMARK 5.5. The structure and properties of random lines in the plane that are developed in this paper make it possible to review and extend results in still other applications. In a paper reporting on the pattern in a planar region of one species of vegetation with respect to another, Pielou [9] defined a random pattern as one in which the alternation between species along any line transect is Markovian. In a subsequent paper, Bartlett [1] indicated that she did not establish the existence of a two state planar process that could produce this Markovian property. Switzer [11] then demonstrated the existence of a finite state random process in the plane, namely, the homogeneous Poisson field or random lines with the property that alternation among states along any straight line is Markovian. In this paper, a whole class of finite state random processes in the plane that accomplishes this is presented by our results for nonhomogeneous Poisson fields of random lines.

## REFERENCES


[1] M. S. BARTLETT, "A note on a spatial pattern," *Biometrics*, Vol. 20 (1964), pp. 891–892.

[2] L. BREIMAN, "The Poisson tendency in traffic distributions," *Ann. Math. Statist.*, Vol. 34 (1963), pp. 308–311.

[3] M. BROWN, "Some results on a traffic model of Rényi," *J. Appl. Prob.*, Vol. 6 (1969), pp. 293–300.

[4] ———, "An $M/G/\infty$ estimation problem," *Ann. Math. Statist.*, Vol. 41 (1970), pp. 651–654.

[5] S. A. GOUDSMIT, "Random distribution of lines in a plane," *Rev. Modern Phys.* Vol. 17 (1945), pp. 321–322.

[6] J. F. C. KINGMAN, "Markov population processes," *J. Appl. Prob.*, Vol. 6 (1969), pp. 1–18.
[7] R. E. MILES, "Random polygons determined by random lines in a plane," *Proc. Nat. Acad. Sci. U.S.A.*, Vol. 52 1964), pp. 901–907.
[8] ———, "Random polygons determined by random lines in a plane, II," *Proc. Nat. Acad. Sci. U.S.A.*, Vol. 52 (1964), pp. 1157–1160.
[9] E. C. PIELOU, "The spatial pattern of two-phase patchworks of vegetation," *Biometrics*, Vol. 20 (1964), pp. 156–167.
[10] A. RÉNYI, "On two mathematical models of the traffic on a divided highway," *J. Appl. Prob.*, Vol. 1 (1964), pp. 311–320.
[11] P. SWITZER, "A random set process in the plane with a Markovian property," *Ann. Math. Statist.*, Vol. 36 (1965), pp. 1859–1863.
[12] P. C. C. WANG, "A characterization of the Poisson distribution based on random splitting and random expanding," Stanford University Technical Report No. 158, (NR 042–067), 1970.
[13] G. WEISS and R. HERMAN, "Statistical properties of low-density traffic," *Quart. Appl. Math.*, Vol. 20 (1962), pp. 121–130.

# IV
# Martingale Representation

# Editor's Comments on Papers 13 and 14

**13 Boel, Varaiya, and Wong:** *Martingales on Jump Processes: I. Representation Results*

**14 Boel, Varaiya, and Wong:** *Martingales on Jump Processes: II. Applications*

These two papers represent recently obtained results of broad applicability and significance. They were available only in technical-report form at the time of this writing and will soon appear in the journal literature. Both have been submitted to the *SIAM Journal on Control.*

Both papers are integral parts of a single work that essentially unifies and extends most of the previously considered models for point and jump processes. The basic description of these processes is in terms of stochastic integrals over martingales. The first (Paper 13) derives the representation results, and the second (Paper 14) applies these results to the problem of estimation, detection, and filtering in communications and control systems first considered by Bar-David, Rubin, and Snyder in the first five papers of this volume. It is expected that this work, together with other related contemporary work [1–3], will generate further advances in the application of the martingale models in engineering problems.

## References


1. P. Varaiya, The martingale theory of jump processes, *Proc. IEEE Decision Contr. Conf.*, pp. 48–57, (Dec. 1973).
2. A. Segall, A martingale approach to modeling, estimation and detection of jump processes, *Tech. Rep. 7050-21,* ISL, Stanford University, Stanford, Calif., Aug. 1973.
3. T. Kailath and A. Segall, A further note on innovations, martingales, and nonlinear estimation, *Proc. IEEE Decision Contr. Conf.,* pp. 616–620 (Dec. 1973).

# 13

Reprinted from *Martingales on Jump Processes: I. Representation Results* Mem. ERL-M407, Electronics Research Laboratory, University of California, Berkeley, 1973, pp. 1–44

# Martingales on Jump Processes: I. Representation Results

R. BOEL, P. VARAIYA, and E. WONG

Department of Electrical Engineering and
Computer Sciences and the Electronics
Research Laboratory
University of California, Berkeley

Abstract

The paper is a contribution to the theory of martingales of processes whose sample paths are piecewise constant and have finitely many discontinuties in a finite time interval. The assumption is made that the jump times of the underlying process are totally inaccessible and necessary and sufficient conditions are given for this to be true. It turns out that all martingales are then discontinuous, and can be represented as stochastic integrals of certain basic martingales. This representation theorem is used in a companion paper to study various practical problems in communication and control. The results in the two papers constitute a sweeping generalization of recent work on Poisson processes.

Research sponsored by the U.S. Army Research Office - Durham, Contract DAHC 04-67-C-0046 and the National Science Foundation Grant GK-10656X3.

The authors are very grateful to J. M. C. Clark, M. H. A. Davis and J. H. Van Schuppen for many helpful suggestions and discussions.

## I. Introduction and Summary

The theory of martingales has proved to be successful as a framework for formulating and analyzing many issues in stochastic control, and in detection and filtering problems [2,4,5,10,11,12,32,33,34]. Three sets of results in the abstract or general theory of martingales seem to be the most useful ones in these applications. The first set consists of the optional sampling theorem and the classical martingale inequalities [17]. The second set consists of the locus of results culminating in the decomposition theorem for supermartingales [24]. The third set includes the calculus of stochastic integrals [16,22] and the differentiation formula and its application to the so-called "exponentiation formula" [15].

In applications one is concerned with martingales which are functionals of a basic underlying process such as a Wiener or Poisson porcess, and in order to use the abstract theory one needs to know how to represent these martingales usefully and explicitly in terms of the underlying process. Thus the "martingale representation theorems" serve as a bridge linking the abstract theory and the concrete applications. Their role is quite analogous to that of matrix representations of linear operators which serve as the instrument with which one can apply the abstract theory of linear algebra.

The most familiar of all the basic processes which can arise in practice is the Wiener process. It is known that every martingale of a Wiener process can be represented as a stochastic integral of the Wiener process [6,22]. This fundamental representation theorem, together with the exponentiation formula, has been used to derive solutions of stochastic differential equations [2,19,20], to obtain recursive equations for filters [5,21,30,31] and the likelihood ratios for some detection problems [10,18], to mention just a few applications. These very results combined with the decomposition theorem for supermartingales form the foundation of an approach to one family of stochastic optimal control problems [12]. It turns out that every martingale of a Wiener process has continuous sample paths. This is fortunate because it implies that the martingale is locally square integrable, and hence most of the questions about martingales can be posed within the Hilbert space structure of the space of square integrable random variables.

However, for many processes, e.g. Poisson process, one can have martingales which are not locally square integrable. As Meyer and his co-workers have pointed out [16,26] the $L^2$ structure is no longer appropriate and one needs to be more careful in defining stochastic integrals and in obtaining the differentiation formula. Indeed the current theory of stochastic integration with respect to such martingales is still not completely satisfactory.

This paper is a contribution to the abstract theory and to its applications for the relatively simple case where the sample functions of the underlying process are step functions which have only a finite number of jumps in every finite time interval. In some ways this is the polar opposite of the Wiener process case since all the martingales are discontinuous, that is, all the continuous martingales have constant sample paths. The most important special cases covered by this paper include the Poisson process, Markov chains and extensions of these, such as processes arising in queueing theory. To some extent the results for some of these special cases are also covered in [4,5,10,11,29,30,31]

The next section gives a precise definition of the underlying process and exhibits some of the important properties of the generated σ-fields. Conditions are derived which guarantee that the jump times of the process are totally inaccessible stopping times. These preliminary results are used in Section 3 to show first that there are no non-constant continuous martingales and then to obtain an integral representation of all martingales. A particular example, which includes most of the special cases mentioned above, is presented in Section 4. Applications of the results are given in the companion paper [3].

## II. The Basic Process and Its Stopping Times

Let $(Z,\mathcal{Z})$ be a Blackwell space, that is a measurable space such that $\mathcal{Z}$ is a separable σ-field and every measurable function $f: Z \to R$ maps Z onto an analytic subset of R (see [24, p. 61 ]). Let $\Omega$ be a family of functions on $R_+ = [0,\infty)$ with values in Z, such that each $\omega \in \Omega$ is a step function with only a finite number of jumps in every finite interval, and such that for all $\omega \in \Omega$, $t \in R_+$, $\omega(t) = \omega(t+\varepsilon)$ for all $\varepsilon$ less than some sufficiently small $\varepsilon_0 > 0$. If Z is also a topological space, then each function ω is right-continuous and has left-hand limits. Let $x_t$ be the evaluation process on $\Omega$ i.e. $x_t(\omega) = \omega(t)$, $t \in R_+$. Let $\mathcal{F}_t$ be the σ-field on $\Omega$ generated by sets of the form $\{x_s \in B\}$, $B \in \mathcal{Z}$, $s \leq t$. Let $\mathcal{F} = \bigvee_{t \in R_+} \mathcal{F}_t$.[1]

Because the positive rationals are dense in $R_+$, it is clear that $\mathcal{F}$ can also be written as $\bigvee_n \sigma(x_{r_n})$ where $\sigma(x_{r_n})$ is the σ-field generated

[1] If $A_\alpha$ is a family of subsets then $\bigvee_\alpha A_\alpha$ denotes the smallest σ-field containing all the $A_\alpha$.

by the function $x_{r_n}$ and $r_n$ is rational. Hence the separability of $\mathcal{Z}$ implies the separability of $\mathcal{F}$. Moreover, as will be shown, every real-valued $\mathcal{F}$-measurable function on $\Omega$ will map $\Omega$ onto an analytic subset, hence $(\Omega,\mathcal{F})$ is a Blackwell space. The assertion follows from considering approximations for any measurable $f: \Omega \to R$ of the form $f^n = g^n \cdot h^n \cdot i$, where $i: (\Omega,\mathcal{F}) \to (Z^{\mathbb{N}}, \mathcal{Z}^{\mathbb{N}})$ is the natural isomorphism ($\mathbb{N}$ is the set of natural numbers), and $h^n: (Z^{\mathbb{N}}, \mathcal{Z}^{\mathbb{N}}) \to (R^{\mathbb{N}}, \mathcal{B}^{\mathbb{N}})$ ($\mathcal{B}$ is the Borel field on R) consists of measurable components $h_1^n, h_2^n, \ldots$ and $h^n(z_1,z_2,\ldots) = (h_1^n(z_1), h_2^n(z_2),\ldots)$, and finally $g^n$ is a measurable mapping from $(R^{\mathbb{N}},\mathcal{B}^{\mathbb{N}})$ into $(R,\mathcal{B})$. Since the Cartesian product of analytic sets is analytic (see [1]), the image of $Z^{\mathbb{N}}$ in $R^{\mathbb{N}}$ under $h^n$ is an analytic set which is in turn mapped into an analytic subset of R by $g^n$. Since analytic sets form a class closed under countable unions and intersections, this limiting procedure shows that every measurable function $f: \Omega \to R$ maps $\Omega$ onto an analytic set. Since $(\Omega,\mathcal{F})$ is a Blackwell space it follows from [24 , II-T16] that $(\Omega,\mathcal{F})$ is isomorphic to $(A,\mathcal{B}(A))$ where A is an analytic subset of R. Hence the results of [28 ] can be applied without assuming a topological structure on Z itself.

A Z-valued or $R \cup \{\infty\}$-valued function f on $\Omega$ is a <u>random variable</u> (r.v.) if $f^{-1}(B) \in \mathcal{F}$ whenever $B \in \mathcal{Z}$ or whenever B is a Borel subset of $R \cup \{\infty\}$. Unless otherwise stated a r.v. is $R \cup \{\infty\}$-valued. A non-negative r.v. T is said to be a <u>stopping time</u> (s.t.) if for every $t \in R_+$, $\{T \leq t\} \in \mathcal{F}_t$. If T is a s.t. then $\mathcal{F}_T$ consists of those sets $A \in \mathcal{F}$ for which $A \cap \{T \leq t\} \in \mathcal{F}_t$ for each $t \in R_+$, whereas $\mathcal{F}_{T-}$ is the $\sigma$-field generated by $\mathcal{F}_0$ and sets of the form $A \cap \{t < T\}$ where $A \in \mathcal{F}_t$, and finally $\mathcal{F}_{T+} = \bigcap_{n>0} \mathcal{F}_{T+\frac{1}{n}}$.

Define inductively the functions $T_n$:

$$T_0 \equiv 0, \quad T_{n+1}(\omega) = \inf\{t \mid t \geq T_n(\omega) \text{ and } x_t(\omega) \neq x_{T_n(\omega)}(\omega)\},$$

where the infimum over an empty set is taken to be $+\infty$. The next few results characterize the σ-field $\mathcal{F}_t$ and demonstrate that the $T_n$ are indeed s.t.s. The key results, Corollary 2.2 and Proposition 2.3, which are the only ones used subsequently, can in fact be proven from first principles assuming only the separability of $\mathcal{Z}$, but it is much more intuitive and easier to rely on the results of [7] and [28].

Let $H: \Omega \to [0,\infty]$ be any function. Then H defines three equivalence relations on $\Omega$ as follows:

$$\omega \overset{H}{\sim} \omega' \iff H(\omega) = H(\omega') \text{ and } x_t(\omega) = x_t(\omega') \text{ for } t \leq H(\omega).$$

$$\omega \overset{H+}{\sim} \omega' \iff H(\omega) = H(\omega') \text{ and there is } \varepsilon > 0 \text{ such that } x_t(\omega) = x_t(\omega') \text{ for } t \leq H(\omega) + \varepsilon$$

$$\omega \overset{H-}{\sim} \omega' \iff H(\omega) = H(\omega') \text{ and } x_t(\omega) = x_t(\omega') \text{ for } t < H(\omega).$$

A set $A \subset \Omega$ is said to be <u>saturated for H</u>, respectively $H_+$, $H_-$, if $\omega \in A$, and $\omega \overset{H}{\sim} \omega'$, respectively $\omega \overset{H}{\sim}{+}\, \omega'$, $\omega \overset{H}{\sim}{-}\, \omega'$, implies $\omega' \in A$. Let $\mathcal{S}_H$, $\mathcal{S}_{H_+}$, $\mathcal{S}_{H_-}$ denote the family of subsets of $\Omega$ which are saturated for H, $H_+$, $H_-$ respectively.

<u>Proposition 2.1</u> $\mathcal{F}_t = \mathcal{S}_t \cap \mathcal{F}$, where $\mathcal{S}_t = \mathcal{S}_H$ for $H \equiv t$.

<u>Proof</u> Follows from [28, proposition 1]. ⌑

Corollary 2.1 A non-negative r.v. T is a s.t. if and only if $\{T \leq t\} \in \mathcal{G}_t$ for all $t \in R_+$.

Corollary 2.2 $T_n$ is a s.t. for all n.

Proof $T_n$ is obviously a non-negative r.v. and $\{T_n \leq t\} \in \mathcal{G}_t$ by definition. ¤

Proposition 2.2 Let T be a s.t. then

$$\mathcal{F}_T = \mathcal{G}_T \cap \mathcal{F}, \quad \mathcal{F}_{T+} = \mathcal{G}_{T+} \cap \mathcal{F}, \quad \mathcal{F}_{T-} = \mathcal{G}_{T-} \cap \mathcal{F}.$$

Proof This follows from [28 , Propositions 1, 2]. ¤

For a s.t. T, $\mathcal{F}_\infty(x_{t\wedge T})$ denotes the σ-field generated by the Z-valued r.v.s. $X_{t\wedge T}$, $t \in R_+$. (If S, T are r.v.s. then $S \wedge T = \{\min S, T\}$,)

Proposition 2.3 Let T be a s.t. then $\mathcal{F}_T = \mathcal{F}_\infty(x_{t\wedge T})$.

Proof Since $\mathcal{F}_\infty(x_{t\wedge T})$ and $\mathcal{F}_T = \mathcal{G}_T \cap \mathcal{F}$ are sub-σ-fields of $\mathcal{F}$ they are separable. Hence the spaces $(\Omega, \mathcal{F}_\infty(x_{t\wedge T}))$ and $(\Omega, \mathcal{F}_T)$ are Blackwell spaces by [1, Corollary 3]. They also have the same atoms, namely, $\bigcap_n \{x_{r_n \wedge T} \in B_n\}$ where $r_n$ is a rational and $B_n$ an atom of Z. The result then follows from [1, Corollary 1] and Proposition 2.2. ¤

Corollary 2.3 $\mathcal{F}_{T_n} = \sigma(x_{T_i}, T_i;\ 0 \leq i \leq n)$.

Proof Follows from Proposition 2.3 since

$$\mathcal{F}_\infty(x_{t\wedge T_n}) = \sigma(x_{T_i \wedge T_n}, T_i \wedge T_n;\ 0 \leq i \leq \infty)$$

$$= \sigma(x_{T_i}, T_i;\ 0 \leq i \leq n)$$ ¤

Corollary 2.4 $\mathcal{F}_t = \sigma(x_{T_i \wedge t}, T_i \wedge t, 0 \le i < \infty)$

Corollary 2.5 Let T be a s.t. then $\mathcal{F}_{T_+} = \mathcal{F}_T$

Proof Since the sample functions are piecewise constant and $\omega(t) = \omega(t+)$ it follows that $\mathcal{G}_T = \mathcal{G}_{T_+}$ and then the result follows from Proposition 2.2. ⌑

Proposition 2.4 $\mathcal{F}_{T_{n-}} = \sigma(x_{T_i}, T_{i+1}, 0 \le i \le n-1)$

Proof Similar to the proof of Proposition 2.3, with both σ-fields having the atoms $\{x_{T_i} \in A_i, T_{+1} \in B_i ; 0 \le i \le n-1\}$ where $A_i$ is an atom of Z and $B_i$ is an atom of R.

Proposition 2.5 Let $n \ge 1$, and $\delta > 0$. Let $T = (T_{n-1} + \delta) \wedge T_n$, and let $A \in \mathcal{F}_T$. Then there exists $A^0 \in \mathcal{F}_{T_{n-1}}$ such that $A \cap \{T < T_n\} =$ $= A^0 \cap \{T < T_n\}$.

Proof By Proposition 2.3 $\mathcal{F}_T = \mathcal{F}_\infty(x_{t\wedge T})$ and it is easy to see that the latter coincides with the σ-field generated by the r.v.s. $\{x_{T_i \wedge T}, T_i \wedge T; i = 0,1,2,\ldots\}$. Hence there exists a function g, measurable in its arguments such that

$$I_A(\omega) = g(x_{T_0 \wedge T}(\omega), T_0 \wedge T(\omega), \ldots, x_{T_{n-1} \wedge T}(\omega), T_{n-1} \wedge T(\omega), x_{T_n \wedge T}(\omega), T_n \wedge T(\omega), \ldots)$$

$$= g(x_{T_0}(\omega), T_0(\omega), \ldots, x_{T_{n-1}}(\omega), T_{n-1}(\omega), x_{T_n \wedge T}(\omega), T_n \wedge T(\omega), \ldots).$$

Define the measurable function $g^0$ by

$$g^{o}(x_0,t_0,\ldots,x_{n-1},y_{n-1}) = g(x_0,t_0,\ldots,x_{n-1},t_{n-1},x_{n-1},t_{n-1}+\delta,\ x_{n-1},$$
$$t_{n-1}+\delta,\ \ldots.).$$

Now if $T_{n-1} \leq T < T_n$, then $x_{T_{n+k}\wedge T}(\omega) = x_{T_{n-1}}(\omega)$ and

$T_{n+k}\wedge T(\omega) = T_{n-1}(\omega) + \delta$ for all $k \geq 0$. Therefore,

$$I_A(\omega)\ I_{\{T < T_n\}}(\omega) = g^{o}(x_{T_0}(\omega),\ T_0(\omega),\ \ldots,\ x_{T_{n-1}}(\omega),\ T_{n-1}(\omega))\ I_{\{T < T_n\}}(\omega),$$

So that the set $A^{o} = \{\omega | g^{o}(x_{T_0}(\omega),\ \ldots,\ T_{n-1}(\omega)) = 1\}$ satisfies the assertion ◻

Lemma 2.1 Let $n \geq 1$, and let $S$ be a s.t. then there exists a r.v.f, measurable with respect to $\mathcal{F}_{T_{n-1}}$ such that $S\ I_{\{S < T_n\}} = f\ I_{\{S < T_n\}}$.

Proof $S\ I_{\{S < T_n\}} = S\ I_{\{S < T_{n-1}\}} + S\ I_{\{T_{n-1} \leq S < T_n\}}$, and $S\ I_{\{S < T_{n-1}\}}$, $I_{\{S < T_{n-1}\}}$ are $\mathcal{F}_{T_{n-1}}$-measurable so that by replacing $S$ by $S \vee T_{n-1}$ if necessary, one can assume that $S \geq T_{n-1}$. Let $\Gamma = \{S < T_n\}$. Then $\Gamma = \bigcup_m \Gamma_m$ where

$$\Gamma_m = \bigcup_k \{S \leq T_{n-1} + k2^{-m}\} \cap \{T_{n-1} + k2^{-m} < T_n\}$$

Fix $\delta = 2^{-m}$. By Proposition 2.5 there exist sets $A_k \in \mathcal{F}_{T_{n-1}}$ such that

$$\{S \leq T_{n-1} + k\delta\} \cap \{T_{n-1} + k\delta < T_n\} = A_k \cap \{T_{n-1} + k\delta < T_n\},\ k \geq 1.$$

Define sets $B_k$ by

$$B_1 = A_1 \text{ and } B_k = \{\omega \in A_k | \omega \notin A_i \text{ for } i < k\} \text{ for } k > 1,$$

and then define the function $f_m: \Omega \to [0,\infty]$ by

$$f_m(\omega) = T_{n-1} + k\delta \text{ if } \omega \in B_k \text{ and } f_m(\omega) = T_{n-1}(\omega) \text{ if } \omega \notin \bigcup_k B_k.$$

Certainly $f_m$ is $\mathcal{F}_{T_{n-1}}$-measurable. Also

$$f_m(\omega) - \delta \leq S(\omega) \leq f_m(\omega) < T_n(\omega) \text{ for } \omega \in \Gamma_m. \tag{2.1}$$

To see this note first that if $\omega \in A_1 \cup \{T_{n-1} + \delta < T_n\}$ then clearly $T_{n-1}(\omega) = f_m(\omega) -\delta \leq S(\omega) < f_m(\omega) < T_n(\omega)$. Next, as induction hypothesis, suppose that the inequalities in (2.1) hold for

$\omega \in \bigcup_{k=1}^{N} A_k \cap \{T_{n-1} + k\delta < T_n\}$, and let

$$\omega \in A_{N+1} \cap \{T_{n-1} + (N+1)\delta < T_n\},\ \omega \notin \bigcup_{k=1}^{N} A_k \cap \{T_{n-1} + k\delta < T_n\}. \tag{2.2}$$

Let $k \leq N + 1$ be the smallest integer such that $\omega \in B_k$. Suppose $k \leq N$. Then, since $B_k \subset A_k$, and since from (2.2) $T_n > T_{n-1} + k\delta$, it follows that $\omega \in A_k \cap \{T_{n-1} + k\delta < T_n\}$ which contradicts the second condition of (2.2). Hence $\omega \in B_{N+1}$ and so $T_{n-1}(\omega) + N\delta \leq S(\omega) \leq T_{n-1}(\omega) + (N+1)\delta = f_m(\omega) < T_n(\omega)$. Therefore (2.1) holds by induction. Finally, define the $\mathcal{F}_{T_{n-1}}$-measurable function f by $f(\omega) = \liminf_m f_m(\omega)$. The obvious inclusion $\Gamma_m \subset \Gamma_{m+1}$ implies that if $\omega \in \Gamma_m$ then $f_{m+k}(\omega) - 2^{-(m+k)} \leq S(\omega) \leq f_{m+k}(\omega)$ for all $k \geq 0$. Hence $f(\omega) = S(\omega)$ and the assertion is proved. ◻

To proceed further it is convenient to introduce a probability measure on $(\Omega, \mathcal{F})$[2]. Throughout this paper let P denote a fixed

[2] It may be of interest to note that Lemmas 2.2, 2.3 and 2.4 below can be proven without imposing a probability measure P by using the algebraic definition of a predictable s.t. of [28]. Then a predictable s.t. in the sense used here is simply a non-negative r.v. which is a.s. P equal to a predictable s.t. in the sense of [28].

probability measure on $(\Omega, \mathcal{F})$. Recall the following important classification of stopping times [25].

Let T be a s.t. T is said to be totally inaccessible if $T > 0$ a.s. and if for every increasing sequence of s.t.s. $S_1 \leq S_2 \leq \ldots,$

$$P\{S_k(\omega) < T(\omega) \text{ for all } k \text{ and } \lim_{k\to\infty} S_k(\omega) = T(\omega) < \infty\} = 0;$$

whereas T is said to be predictable if there exists an increasing sequence of s.t.s $S_1 \leq S_2 \leq \ldots$ such that

$$P\{T = 0, \text{ or } S_k < T \text{ for all } k \text{ and } \lim_{k\to\infty} S_k = T\} = 1.$$

The next three lemmas relate this classification to the properties of the jump times $T_n$ of the process x.

Lemma 2.2 Let T be a totally inaccessible s.t. Then

$$T\, I_{\{T < \infty\}} = [\sum_{n=1}^{\infty} T_n\, I_{\{T = T_n\}}]\, I_{\{T < \infty\}} \text{ a.s.}$$

Proof The equality above holds if and only if $P\{T_{n-1} < T < T_n\} = 0$ for each $n \geq 1$. Let n be fixed. By Lemma 2.1 there exists a $\mathcal{F}_{T_{n-1}}$-measurable function f such that $f(\omega) = T(\omega)$ for $\omega \in \{T_{n-1} < T < T_n\}$. Let $S_k = T_{n-1} \vee (f - \frac{1}{k})$. Then $S_k \geq T_{n-1}$ and $S_k$ is $\mathcal{F}_{T_{n-1}}$-measurable so that it is a s.t. Also $S_k$ is increasing and clearly

$$\{T_{n-1} < T < T_n\} \subset \{S_k < T \text{ for all } k \text{ and } \lim_{k\to\infty} S_k = T < \infty\}.$$

Since T is totally inaccessible, the set on the right has probability measure zero. The assertion is proved. ◻

Lemma 2.3 Let T be a s.t. such that for all $n \geq 1$, $P\{T = T_n < \infty\} = 0$. Then T is predictable.

Proof Let h be a function measurable in its arguments and taking values in the set $\{0,1\}$ such that the process $I_{T \leq t}$ has the representation

$$I_{T \leq t} = h(t, x_{T_0 \wedge t}, T_0 \wedge t, \ldots., x_{T_n \wedge t}, T_n \wedge t, \ldots.).$$

By modifying h if necessary it can be assumed that

$$h(t,\xi) = \max_{s \leq t} h(s,\xi).$$

Because of this property the r.v. $T_\varepsilon$ defined by

$$T_\varepsilon(\omega) = \inf\{t | h(t+\varepsilon, x_{T_0 \wedge t}, T_0 \wedge t, \ldots\ldots) = 1\}$$

in a s.t., and it is immediate that for $\varepsilon > 0$

$$T_\varepsilon(\omega) < T(\omega) \text{ for } \omega \in \{0 < T < \infty\}.$$

Furthermore $T_\varepsilon \leq T_{\varepsilon'}$ if $\varepsilon' \leq \varepsilon$. Define then s.t.s $S_k$ by $S_k = T_{\frac{1}{k}} \wedge k$.

It will now be shown that

$$\lim_{k \to \infty} S_k(\omega) = T(\omega) \text{ for } \omega \in \bigcup_{n=1}^{\infty} \{T_{n-1} < T < T_n\}.$$

Let $\omega \in \{T_{n-1} < T < T_n\}$. Then

$$h(t, x_{T_0 \wedge t}(\omega), T_0 \wedge t(\omega), \ldots, x_{T_n \wedge t}(\omega), T_n \wedge t(\omega) \ldots) = \begin{cases} 0 \text{ for } T_{n-1}(\omega) < t < T(\omega) \\ 1 \text{ for } t \geq T(\omega) \end{cases}$$

so that

$$h(t + \tfrac{1}{k}, x_{T_0 \wedge t}(\omega), T_0 \wedge t(\omega), \ldots.) = \begin{cases} 0 \text{ for } T_{n-1}(\omega) < t + \frac{1}{k} < T(\omega) \text{ or } T_{n-1}(\omega) < t < T(\omega) \\ 1 \text{ for } t \geq T(\omega) \end{cases}$$

Hence $T_{\frac{1}{k}}(\omega) = T(\omega) - \frac{1}{k}$ for $\frac{1}{k} < T(\omega) - T_{n-1}(\omega)$. It follows that $S_k(\omega)$ converges to $T(\omega)$ and the assertion follows. ¤

Lemma 2.4 $T_n$ is totally inaccessible if and only if for every $\mathcal{F}_{T_{n-1}}$-measurable function f, $P\{T_n = f < \infty\} = 0$.

Proof Suppose $P\{T_n = f < \infty\} > 0$. Let $S_k = T_{n-1} \vee (f - \frac{1}{k})$. Then $S_k$ is an increasing sequence of s.t.s and

$$\{T_n = f < \infty\} \subset \{S_k < T \text{ for all } k \text{ and } \lim_{k\to\infty} S_k = T < \infty\}$$

so that $T_n$ cannot be totally inaccessible thereby proving necessity. To prove sufficiency suppose that $T_n$ is not totally inaccessible so that there is an increasing sequence of s.t.s $S_k$ such that

$$P\{\Gamma\} = P\{S_k < T_n \text{ for all } k \text{ and } \lim_{k\to\infty} S_k = T_n < \infty\} > 0. \tag{2.3}$$

By Lemma 2.1 there exist functions $f_k$, measurable with respect to $\mathcal{F}_{T_{n-1}}$, such that $S_k(\omega) = f_k(\omega)$ for $\omega \in \{S_k < T_n\}$. Let $f = \liminf f_k$. Then from (2.3) it follows that $f(\omega) = T_n(\omega)$ for $\omega \in \Gamma$ so that $P\{f = T_n < \infty\} > 0$ and sufficiency is proved. ¤

From the lemma above the following intuitive sufficient condition follows immediately.

Theorem 2.1 Let $F(t_n | x_0, t_0, \ldots, x_{n-1}, t_{n-1})$ be the conditional probability distribution of $T_n$ given $x_{T_0}, T_0, \ldots, x_{T_{n-1}}, T_{n-1}$. Suppose that F is continuous in $t_n$ for all values of $(x_0, t_0, \ldots, x_{n-1}, t_{n-1})$. Then $T_n$ is totally inaccessible.[3]

[3] If Z is a Borel subset of $\mathcal{R}^p$ and $\mathcal{Z}$ contains all Borel subsets of Z then the conditional probability F exists by [23, p.361].

As an application of Theorem 2.1 note that if $x_t$ is a Poisson process, then $F(t_n|x_0,t_0,\ldots,x_{n-1},t_{n-1}) = (1 - \exp - (t_n-t_{n-1})) I_{t_n \geq t_{n-1}}$ is continuous. Hence the jump times of a Poisson process are totally inaccessible.

## III. The Martingale Representation Theorem

It will be necessary from now on to complete the σ-fields $\mathcal{F}_t$ and $\mathcal{F}$ with respect to the measure P. An additional condition is also imposed.

Assumptions (i) The σ-fields $\mathcal{F}_t$, $\mathcal{F}$ are augmented so as to be complete with respect to P. (ii) The stopping times $T_n$ are totally inaccessible for $n \geq 1$.

Note that after completion of the space $(\Omega,\mathcal{F})$ it ceases to be a Blackwell space. But, of course, the results of Section II continue to hold if the relevant equalities are interpreted as being true almost surely P.

The family $\mathcal{F}_t$ is said to be free of times of discontinuity if for every increasing sequence of s.t.s $S_k$, $\mathcal{F}_{\lim S_k} = \bigvee_k \mathcal{F}_{S_k}$.

Proposition 3.1 The family $\mathcal{F}_t$ is free of times of discontinuity.

Proof By Lemma 2.2 and Assumption (ii) a s.t. T is totally inaccessible if and only if its graph[4] $[T]$ is contained in the union $\bigcup_n [T_n]$ of the graphs of $T_n$, whereas by Lemma 2.3 T is predictable if $[T] \cap \bigcup_n [T_n] = \phi$. The assertion follows from [14,III-T51,p. 62]. ¤

It will be useful to recall some definitions at this time. This will

[4] $[T] = \{(\omega,T(\omega))|\omega \in \Omega\} \subset \Omega \times [0,\infty]$.

be followed by some remarks and a reproduction of some known results which will be used in the discussion to follow.

A process $y_t$ is said to be <u>adapted</u> (to the family $\mathcal{F}_t$) if $y_t$ is $\mathcal{F}_t$-measurable for all t. Two processes $y_t$ and $y'_t$ are said to be <u>indistinguishable</u>, and are written $y_t \equiv y'_t$, if for almost all $\omega$ $y_t(\omega) = y'_t(\omega)$ for all $t \in R_+$.

Let $m_t$ be a martingale with respect to $(\Omega, \mathcal{F}_t, P)$. It is said to be <u>uniformly integrable</u> (u.i.), and one writes $m_t \in \mathcal{M}^1$, if $\{m_t | t \in R_+\}$ is a u.i. set of r.v.s. It is said to be <u>square integrable</u> (s.i.), and one writes $m_t \in \mathcal{M}^2$, if $\sup\{Em_t^2 | t \in R_+\} < \infty$.

Let $m_t$ be a process. It is said to be a <u>locally integrable martingale</u> [locally square integrable martingale], and one writes $m_t \in \mathcal{M}^1_{loc}$ [$m_t \in \mathcal{M}^2_{loc}$], if there is an increasing sequence of s.t.s $S_k$ with $S_k \to \infty$ a.s. such that for each k $m_{t\wedge S_k} I_{\{S_k > 0\}} \in \mathcal{M}^1$ [$m_{t\wedge S_k} I_{\{S_k > 0\}} \in \mathcal{M}^2$].

An adapted process $a_t$ is said to be an <u>increasing process</u> if $a_0 = 0$ and if its sample paths are non-decreasing and right continuous. It is said to be <u>integrable</u>, and one writes $a_t \in \mathcal{A}^+$ if $\sup\{Ea_t | t \in R_+\} < \infty$. $\mathcal{A}^+_{loc}$ is defined in a manner analogous to the previous definition. Finally let $\mathcal{A} = \mathcal{A}^+ - \mathcal{A}^+ = \{a_t - a'_t | a_t \in \mathcal{A}^+, a'_t \in \mathcal{A}^+\}$ and $\mathcal{A}_{loc} = \mathcal{A}^+_{loc} - \mathcal{A}^+_{loc}$.

It will be assumed throughout that all the local martingales have sample paths which are right-continuous and have left-hand limits. It is known that since the $\sigma$-fields $\mathcal{F}_t$ are complete and since by Corollary 2.5 $\mathcal{F}_{t+} = \mathcal{F}_t$ for all $t \in R_+$ therefore one can always choose a modification of a local martingale so that its sample paths have the above mentioned property [see 24, VI-T4]. Two modifications with this property are indistinguishable.

It can be immediately verified that $\mathcal{M}^2 \subset \mathcal{M}^1$ and so $\mathcal{M}^2_{loc} \subset \mathcal{M}^1_{loc}$, and if $m_t \in \mathcal{M}^1$ has continuous sample paths then $m_t \in \mathcal{M}^2_{loc}$. However if the sample paths of $m_t \in \mathcal{M}^1$ are not continuous then $m_t$ may not belong to $\mathcal{M}^2_{loc}$. Thus in dealing with discontinuous martingales one may be unable to use the Hilbert space structure of square integrable r.v.s.

The next result follows from Proposition 3.1 and [22, Theorem 1.1].

Theorem 3.1 Let $m_t$ and $m'_t$ be in $\mathcal{M}^2_{loc}$. Then there exists a unique[5], continuous process $\langle m,m'\rangle_t \in \mathcal{A}$ such that $m_t m'_t - \langle m,m'\rangle_t \in \mathcal{M}^1_{loc}$.

Definition 3.1 Let $B \in \mathcal{Z}$. Let

$$P(B,t) = \sum_{s\leq t} I_{\{x_{s-} \neq x_s\}} I_{\{x_s \in B\}}$$

be the number of jumps of x which occur prior to t and which end in the set B.

Proposition 3.2 There is a unique continuous process $\tilde{P}(B,t) \in \mathcal{A}^+_{loc}$ such that the process $Q(B,t) = P(B,t) - \tilde{P}(B,t)$ is in $\mathcal{M}^2_{loc}$.

Proof Let $P_n(B,t) = P(B,t\wedge T_n)$. Then $P_n(B,t) \leq n$ so that it is square integrable. Furthermore the jumps of $P_n(B,t)$ occur at the s.t.s $T_n$, $1 \leq i \leq n$, and these s.t.s are totally inaccessible by assumption. It follows from [24, VIII-T31, p. 210] that there is a unique, continuous, integrable, increasing process $\tilde{P}_n(B,t)$ such that

[5]Throughout "unique" means unique up to modification.

$Q_n(B,t) = P_n(B,t) - \tilde{P}_n(B,t) \in \mathcal{M}^2$. From this last relation and the uniqueness of $\tilde{P}_n$ one can conclude that $\tilde{P}_{n+1}(B,t\wedge T_n) \equiv \tilde{P}_n(B,t)$, $Q_{n+1}(B,t\wedge T_n) \equiv Q_n(B,t)$. Hence the processes $\tilde{P},Q$ defined by

$$\tilde{P}(B,t\wedge T_n) \equiv \tilde{P}_n(B,t), \quad Q(B,t\wedge T_n) \equiv Q_n(B,t)$$

satisfy the assertion ◻

Two processes $m_t$, $m_t'$ in $\mathcal{M}^2_{loc}$ are said to be <u>orthogonal</u> if $m_t m_t' \in \mathcal{M}^1_{loc}$ or equivalently if $\langle m,m' \rangle_t \equiv 0$.

<u>Lemma 3.1</u> Let $B_i \in \mathcal{Z}$, $i = 1, 2$. Then $Q(B_1,t)\, Q(B_2,t) - \tilde{P}(B_1 \cap B_2,t) \in \mathcal{M}^1_{loc}$ i.e., $\langle Q(B_1,\cdot), Q(B_2,\cdot) \rangle_t \equiv \tilde{P}(B_1 \cap B_2,t)$. In particular $Q(B_1,t)$ and $Q(B_2,t)$ are orthogonal if $B_1 \cap B_2 = \phi$.

<u>Proof</u> $Q(B_1,t\wedge T_n) = Q(B_1 \cap B_2,t\wedge T_n) + Q(B_1 - B_2,t\wedge T_n)$ and $Q(B_2,t\wedge T_n) = Q(B_1 \cap B_2,t\wedge T_n) + Q(B_2 - B_1,t\wedge T_n)$ where $B - B' = \{z | z \in B,\ z \notin B'\}$. The s.i. martingales $Q(B_1 \cap B_2,t\wedge T_n)$, $Q(B_1 - B_2,t\wedge T_n)$ and $Q(B_2 - B_1,t\wedge T_n)$ have no discontinuities in common so that they are pairwise orthogonal by [24, VIII-T31, p. 210]. The assertion follows then if one can show that for any $B \in \mathcal{Z}$

$$Q^2(B,t\ T_n) - \tilde{P}(B,t\ T_n) \in \mathcal{M}^1. \tag{3.1}$$

Let $Q(t) = Q(B,t\wedge T_n)$, $P(t) = P(B,t\wedge T_n)$ and $\tilde{P}(t) = \tilde{P}(B,t\wedge T_n)$. Let $\varepsilon > 0$ and $s < t$ be arbitrary. Let $S_0 \leq S_1 \leq S_2 \leq \ldots$ be a sequence of s.t.s such that $S_0 \equiv s$, $\lim_{k\to\infty} S_k = t$ a.s. and such that $0 \leq \tilde{P}(S_k) - \tilde{P}(S_{k-1}) \leq \varepsilon$ a.s. Such a sequence exists since $\tilde{P}$ is continuous. Then

$$\sum_{k=1}^{\infty} (Q(S_k) - Q(S_{k-1}))^2 = \sum_{k=1}^{\infty} (P(S_k) - P(S_{k-1}) - \tilde{P}(S_k) + \tilde{P}(S_{k-1}))^2$$

$$= \sum_{k=1}^{\infty} (P(S_k) - P(S_{k-1}))^2 - 2\sum_{k=1}^{\infty} (P(S_k) - P(S_{k-1}))(\tilde{P}(S_k) - \tilde{P}(S_{k-1})) +$$

$$\sum_{k=1}^{\infty} (\tilde{P}(S_k) - \tilde{P}(S_{k-1}))^2.$$

The first term in the last expression is equal to $P(t) - P(s)$ so that

$$|E\{\sum_{k=1}^{\infty} (Q(S_k) - Q(S_{k-1}))^2 - (P(t) - P(s)) | \mathcal{F}_s\}|$$

$$\leq 2\varepsilon\ E\{P(t) - P(s) | \mathcal{F}_s\} + \varepsilon\ E\{\tilde{P}(t) - \tilde{P}(s) | \mathcal{F}_s\}.$$

Since $\varepsilon > 0$ is arbitrary it follows that

$$E\sum_{k=1}^{\infty} (Q(S_k) - Q(S_{k-1}))^2 - P(t) - P(s)) | \mathcal{F}_s\} = 0 \qquad (3.2)$$

Now $Q_t \in \mathcal{M}^2$ so that $E\{(Q(S_k) - Q(S_{k-1}))^2 | \mathcal{F}_s\} = E\{Q^2(S_k) - Q^2(S_{k-1}) | \mathcal{F}_s\}$.
Also
$P_t - \tilde{P}_t \in \mathcal{M}^1$ so that $E\{P(t) - P(s) | \mathcal{F}_s\} = E\{\tilde{P}(t) - \tilde{P}(s) | \mathcal{F}_s\}$.
Substituting these relations in (3.2) one obtains

$$E\{\sum_{k=1}^{\infty} (Q^2(S_k) - Q^2(S_{k-1})) - (\tilde{P}(t) - \tilde{P}(s)) | \mathcal{F}_s\} = E\{Q^2(t) - Q^2(s)$$

$$- (\tilde{P}(t) - \tilde{P}(s)) | \mathcal{F}_s\} = 0.$$

which is the same as (3.1). ◻

For fixed t $Q(B,t)$, $P(B,t)$ and $\tilde{P}(B,t)$ can be regarded as set functions on $\mathcal{Z}$. In order to define stochastic integrals and Lebesgue-Stieltjes integrals with respect to these set functions it is necessary to show that they are countably additive.

Lemma 3.2 Let $B_k$, $k \geq 1$, be a decreasing sequence in $\mathcal{Z}$ such that $\bigcap_k B_k = \phi$. Then for almost all $\omega \in \Omega$, $Q(B_k,t) \to 0$, $P(B_k,t) \to 0$, $\tilde{P}(B_k,t) \to 0$ for all $t \in R_+$ as $k \to \infty$. Furthermore for all $t \in R_+$ and $n \geq 0$. $E\, Q^2(B_k, t\wedge T_n) \to 0$ as $k \to \infty$.

Proof Fix $t \in R_+$. The non-negative r.v.s $P(B_k,t)$ and $\tilde{P}(B_k,t)$ decrease as k increases so that they converge to some r.v.s $P(t)$ and $\tilde{P}(t)$ respectively. Hence $Q(B_k,t) = P(B_k,t) - \tilde{P}(B_k,t)$ converges to $Q(t) = P(t) - \tilde{P}(t)$. From the definition of $P(B_k,t)$ it is clear that $P(t) = 0$ a.s. and from Lemma 3.1 it follows that $Q_t \in \mathcal{M}^2_{loc}$. Thus $Q(t) = -\tilde{P}(t) \in \mathcal{M}^2_{loc}$. But $\tilde{P}(t)$ is an increasing process and $\tilde{P}(0) = 0$ so that this is possible only if $Q(t) = -\tilde{P}(t) = 0$ a.s. Thus $P(t) = \tilde{P}(t) = Q(t) = 0$ for $\omega$ not belonging to a null set $N \in \mathcal{F}$. The monotonicity of the sample functions of $P$, $\tilde{P}$ implies that $P(s) = \tilde{P}(s) = 0$, hence $Q(s) = 0$ for $\omega \notin N$ and $s \leq t$. To prove the remaining assertion it is enough to note that by Lemma 3.1 and by what has just been shown

$E\, Q^2(B_k, t\wedge T_n) = E\, \tilde{P}(B_k, t\wedge T_n) \to 0$ as $k \to \infty$. ◻

The following definition relates to the different classes of integrands for which a satisfactory theory of integration is available.

Let $\mathcal{H}$ denote the set of all processes $h(t) = h(\omega,t)$ of the form

$$h(t) = h_0\, I_{(t_0,t_1]} + h_1\, I_{(t_1,t_2]} + \ldots + h_k\, I_{(t_k,t_{k+1}]}$$

where $h_i$ is a bounded r.v. measurable with respect to $\mathcal{F}_{t_i}$ and $0 \leq t_0 \leq \ldots \leq t_{k+1} < \infty$. Let $\mathcal{P}_0$ denote the set of all functions $f(z,t) = f(z,\omega,t)$ of the form

$$f(z,\omega,t) = \sum_{i=0}^{k} \phi_i(z)\, h_i(\omega,t)$$

where $\phi_i$ is a bounded function measurable with respect to $\mathcal{Z}$ and $h_i \in \mathcal{H}$.

Definition 3.2 A function $f(z,t) = f(z,\omega,t)$ is said to be predictable if there exists a sequence $f_k$ in $\mathcal{P}_0$ such that

$$\lim_{k\to\infty} f_k(z,\omega,t) = f(z,\omega,t) \text{ for all } (z,\omega,t) \in \mathcal{Z} \times \Omega \times R_+.$$

Let $\mathcal{P}$ denote the set of all predictable functions and let $\mathcal{F}^P$ be the sub-$\sigma$-field of $\mathcal{Z} \otimes \mathcal{F} \otimes \mathcal{B}$ generated by $\mathcal{P}$.

If $f(z,t) = f(z,\omega,t)$ is measurable with respect to $\mathcal{Z} \otimes \mathcal{F} \otimes \mathcal{B}$ and if for all fixed $(z,\omega)$ $f(z,\omega,t)$ is left-continuous in t then $f \in \mathcal{P}$.

Definition 3.3 $L^2(\tilde{P}) = \{f \in \mathcal{P} \mid (\|f\|_{\tilde{2}})^2 = E \int_Z \int_{R^+} f^2(z,t)\, \tilde{P}(dz,dt) < \infty\}$.

$L^1(\tilde{P}) = \{f \in \mathcal{P} \mid \|f\|_{\tilde{1}} = E \int_Z \int_{R^+} |f(z,t)|\, \tilde{P}(dz,dt) < \infty\}$. Similarly $L^1(P) = \{f \in \mathcal{P} \mid \|f\|_1 = E \int_Z \int_{R^+} |f(z,t)|\, P(dz,dt) < \infty\}$. $L^2_{loc}(\tilde{P})$ is the set of all $f \in \mathcal{P}$ for which there exists a sequence of s.t.s $S_k \uparrow \infty$ a.s. such that $f\, I_{t \leq S_k} \in L^2(\tilde{P})$ for all k. $L^1_{loc}(\tilde{P})$ and $L^1_{loc}(P)$ are defined in an analogous manner. The integrals in this definition are to be interpreted as Lebesgue-Stieltjes integrals. Finally let $L^1(Q) = L^1(P) \cap L^1(\tilde{P})$, $L^1_{loc}(Q) = L^1_{loc}(P) \cap L^1_{loc}(\tilde{P})$. If $f(z,t) \in L^1(Q)$ then the integral

$\int_Z\int_{R^+} f(z,t)\, P(dz,dt) - \int_Z\int_{R^+} f(z,t)\, \tilde{P}(dz,dt)$ is denoted $\int_Z\int_{R^+} f(z,t)$ $Q(dz,dt)$.

<u>Lemma 3.3</u> To each $f \in L^2(\tilde{P})$ there corresponds a unique process $(foQ)_t \in \mathcal{M}^2$, called the <u>stochastic integral of f with respect to Q</u> with the following properties:

(i) if $f(z,\omega,t) = I_B(z)\, I_A(\omega)\, I_{(t_0,t_1]}(t) \in L^2(\tilde{P})$ where $B \in \mathcal{Z}$ and $A \in \mathcal{F}_{t_0}$, then

$$(foQ)_t = \begin{cases} I_A(\omega)\,[Q(B,t\wedge t_1) - Q(B,t\wedge t_0)] \text{ for } t > t_0 \\ 0 \text{ for } t \leq t_0. \end{cases}$$

(ii) if f, g are in $L^2(\tilde{P})$ and $\alpha$, $\beta$ are in R, then

$$(\alpha f + \beta g) \circ Q \equiv \alpha(foQ) + \beta(goQ).$$

Furthermore the stochastic integral satisfies the following relations

$$\langle foQ, goQ\rangle_t = \int_Z\int_{R^+} f(z,s)\, g(z,s)\, I_{(0,t]}(s)\, \tilde{P}(dz,ds), \tag{3.3}$$

and in particular

$$E(foQ)_\infty^2 = (\|f\|_2^{\sim})^2. \tag{3.4}$$

<u>Proof</u> The proof follows quite closely that of [22, Proposition 5.1].

Let $f^j = \sum_{i=0}^{k} \alpha_i^j\, I_{B_i^j}(z)\, I_{A_i^j}(\omega)\, I_{(t_i,t_{i+1}]}(t)$, j = 1, 2, be <u>simple</u> functions in $L^2(\tilde{P})$ with $B_i^j \in \mathcal{Z}$, $A_i^j \in \mathcal{F}_{t_i}$ and $0 = t_0 < t_1 < \ldots < t_{k+1} < \infty$. Then from (i), (ii) and Lemma 3.1 it can be verified directly that

$$(f^1 oQ)_t (f^2 oQ)_t - \int_Z \int_{R^+} f^1(z,s)\, f^2(z,s)\, I_{(0,t]}(s)\, \tilde{P}(dz,ds) \in \mathcal{M}^1$$

so that (3.3) and (3.4) hold for all simple functions in $L^2(\tilde{P})$. Since such simple functions are dense in $L^2(\tilde{P})$ (3.4) implies that there is a unique extension of the map $f \to (foQ)$ to all of $L^2(\tilde{P})$. Evidently (3.3) and (3.4) will hold for the extension. ¤

Lemma 3.4 Let $m_t \in \mathcal{M}^2$ have continuous sample paths. Then $m_t \equiv m_0$.

Proof By replacing the martingale $m_t$ by $m_t - m_0$ it can be assumed that $m_0 = 0$. It will be shown that $m_t \equiv 0$. Suppose $m_{T_{n-1}} = 0$ for some $n \geq 1$ so that in fact $m_{t\wedge T_{n-1}} = E\{m_{T_{n-1}} | \mathcal{F}_{t\wedge T_{n-1}}\} = 0$ for all t, and consider the continuous martingale $\mu_t = m_{t\wedge T_n}$. By Corollary 2.2 there exists a function h, measurable in its arguments, such that $\mu_t \equiv h(t, x_{T_0\wedge t}, T_0\wedge t, \ldots, x_{T_n\wedge t}, T_n\wedge t)$. The process $\mu'_t = h(t, x_{T_0\wedge t}, \ldots, x_{T_{n-1}\wedge t}, T_{n-1}\wedge t, x_{T_{n-1}\wedge t}, t)$ is then measurable with respect to $\mathcal{F}_{T_{n-1}}$. Since $x_{T_n\wedge t} = x_{T_{n-1}\wedge t}$ and $t = T_n\wedge t$ for $t < T_n$ it follows that $\mu_t = \mu'_t$ for $t < T_n$ and so by continuity of $\mu_t$, $\mu_t = \mu'_t$ for $t \leq T_n$. For $\alpha \in R_+$ define $S_\alpha$ by

$$S_\alpha(\omega) = \sup\{s \leq \alpha \mid \mu'_s(\omega) \geq 0\}.$$

Then since $\mu'_s = \mu_s = 0$ for $s \leq T_{n-1}$ it follows that $S_\alpha \geq T_{n-1}$ and since $S_\alpha$ is measurable with respect to $\mathcal{F}_{T_{n-1}}$ therefore $S_\alpha$ is a s.t. for every $\alpha$. Now let

$$T_\alpha(\omega) = \sup\{s \leq \alpha\wedge T_n(\omega) \mid \mu'_s(\omega) \geq 0\}.$$

It will be shown that $T_\alpha$ is a s.t. Fix t: If $\alpha \leq t$ then $\{T_\alpha \leq t\} = \Omega \in \mathcal{F}_t$ since $T_\alpha \leq \alpha$. Suppose then that $\alpha > t$. Now

$$\{T_\alpha \leq t\} = (\{T_\alpha \leq t\} \cap \{T_n \leq t\}) \cup (\{T_\alpha \leq t\} \cap \{T_n > t\}). \tag{3.5}$$

Since $T_\alpha \leq T_n$ therefore $\{T_n \leq t\} \subset \{T_\alpha \leq t\}$ so that the first set on the right in (3.5) is equal to $\{T_n \leq t\}$ which is in $\mathcal{F}_t$ since $T_n$ is a s.t. It will be shown now that

$$\{T_\alpha \leq t\} \cap \{T_n > t\} = \{S_\alpha \leq t\} \cap \{T_n > t\} \tag{3.6}$$

Since $S_\alpha \geq T_\alpha$ the set on the right is at least as large as the one on the left. Suppose $\omega \in \{S_\alpha \leq t\} \cap \{T_n > t\}$. Then $\mu'_s(\omega) < 0$ for $s \in [t,\alpha]$ and $t < T_n(\omega)$ so that $T_\alpha(\omega) \leq t$ which proves (3.6).

Thus $\{T_\alpha | \alpha \in R_+\}$ is a family of s.t.s. and furthermore the sample paths $T_\alpha(\omega)$ are non-decreasing functions of $\alpha$. By the Optional Sampling Theorem [17, Theorem 11.8, p. 376] the process $\eta_\alpha(\omega) = \mu_{T_\alpha(\omega)}(\omega)$, $\alpha \in R_+$, is a martingale. But $\eta_0 = 0$ and $\eta_\alpha \geqq 0$ so that one must have $\eta_\alpha \equiv 0$. In turn this can happen only if $\mu_t \leqq 0$ which together with $\mu_0 = 0$ implies $\mu_t \equiv 0$. The lemma is proved. ◻

<u>Theorem 3.2</u> Let $m_t \in \mathcal{M}^1_{loc}$ have continuous sample paths. Then $m_t \equiv m_0$.

<u>Proof</u> The s.t.s. $S_k(\omega) = \inf\{t \mid |m_t(\omega)| > k\}$ converge to $\infty$ and $m_{t\wedge S_k} I_{\{S_k > 0\}} \in \mathcal{M}_2$ so that by Lemma 3.4 $m_{t\wedge S_k} \equiv m_0$.

Thus there are no non-trivial continuous martingales. On the other hand if $m_t$ is a martingale then its discontinuities occur at the jump times $T_n$ of the process $x_t$ as shown below.

Lemma 3.5 Let S be a predictable s.t. and let $m_t \in \mathcal{M}^2$. Then $\Delta m_S = m_S - m_{S-} = 0$ a.s.

Proof By [24,VIII-T29, p. 209] the process $\Delta m_S I_{t \geq s}$ is a martingale. By [25, Prop. 7, p. 159] $E\{\Delta M_S | \mathcal{F}_{S-}\} = 0$ a.s. But by Proposition 3.1 and [14, III-T51, p. 62] $\mathcal{F}_{S-} = \mathcal{F}_S$ so that $\Delta M_S = 0$ a.s. ⊓

The next result gives the first martingale representation theorem. It should be compared with [22, Thm. 4.2 and Prop. 5.2].

Theorem 3.3 Let $m_t \in \mathcal{M}^2$. Then $m_t - m_0 \in \{f o Q | f \in L^2(\tilde{P})\}$.

Proof It can be assumed without losing generality that $m_0 = 0$. The space $\mathcal{M}_0^2 = \{m_t \in \mathcal{M}^2 | m_0 = 0\}$ is a Hilbert space under the norm $\|m\|^2 = E\, m_\infty^2$ by [16, Thm. 1], and by Lemma 3.3 the set $\mathcal{N} = \{f o Q | f \in L^2(\tilde{P})\}$ is a closed linear subspace of $\mathcal{M}_0^2$. Furthermore $\mathcal{N}$ is closed under stopping i.e., if $(f o Q)_t \in \mathcal{N}$ and T is a s.t. then $(f o Q)_{t \wedge T} \in \mathcal{N}$. This is clear because $(f o Q)_{t \wedge T} = (f_T o Q)_t$ where $f_T(t) = f_t\, I_{\{t \leq T\}}$. Thus by [27, Thm. 2 and the remark following Definition 4] the theorem is proved if it can be shown that $m_t \equiv 0$ when it is orthogonal to $f o Q$ for every $f \in L^2(\tilde{P})$. By [16, Thm. 4] $m_t$ can be decomposed uniquely as

$$m_t = m_t^c + m_t^d$$

where $m_t^c \in \mathcal{M}_0^2$ is continuous and $m_t^d \in \mathcal{M}_0^2$ is orthogonal to every continuous martingale. By Theorem 3.2 $m_t^c \equiv 0$. By Lemmas 2.2 and 3.5 the discontinuities of $m_t^d$ occur during the stopping times $T_n, n \geq 1$. Therefore, by [16, Thm. 4] again, $m_t = m_t^d$ can be further decomposed as

$$m_t = \sum_{n=1}^{\infty} (M_n I_{t \geq T_n} - a_n(t)) = \sum_{n=1}^{\infty} \mu_{nt} \text{ say,}$$

where $M_n = \Delta m_{T_n} = m_{T_n} - m_{T_n -}$, $a_n(t) \in \mathcal{A}$ has continuous sample paths, and $\mu_{nt} \in \mathcal{M}_0^2$. Furthermore the martingale $\mu_{nt}$ is orthogonal to every martingale which has no discontinuities at $T_n$.

To prove that $m_t \equiv 0$ it suffices to show that $M_n = 0$ for each n. Fix n and suppose that $P\{M_n \neq 0\} > 0$. Since $M_n$ is measurable with respect to $\mathcal{F}_{T_n}$ therefore by Corollary 2.2 there must exist sets $A \in \mathcal{F}_{T_{n-1}}$, $B \in \mathcal{Z}$, and $C \in \mathcal{B}[0,\infty)$ such that

$$E\{M_n(\omega) I_A(\omega) I_{\{x_{T_n} \in B\}} I_{\{T_n \in C\}}\} \neq 0. \tag{3.6}$$

Consider the function $f(z,\omega,t)$ defined by

$$f(z,\omega,t) = I_B(z) I_A(\omega) I_C(t) I_{\{T_{n-1} < t \leq t_n\}}$$

The function $g(z,\omega,t) = I_B(z) I_A(\omega) I_{\{T_{n-1} < t \leq T_n\}}$ has left-continuous paths for fixed $(z,\omega)$ and for each fixed $z$, $t$ the set $\{I_A(\omega) I_{\{T_{n-1} < t \leq T_n\}} = 1\} = A \cap \{T_{n-1} < t\} \cap \{t \leq T_n\} \in \mathcal{F}_t$ since $A \in \mathcal{F}_{T_{n-1}}$. Therefore $g(z,t)$ is adapted, so that $g \in \mathcal{P}$ and hence $f = g I_C(t)$ is also predictable. Also $|f| \leq 1$ and $f(z,t) = 0$ for $t > T_n$ so that $f \in L^2(\tilde{P}) \cap L^1(\tilde{P}) \cap L(P)$. Therefore by Lemma 3.6 below it follows that

$$\eta_t = (f \circ Q)_t = \int_Z \int_{R^+} f(z,s) I_{(0,t]}(s) P(dz,ds) - \int_Z \int_{R^+} f(z,s) I_{(0,t]}(s) \tilde{P}(dz,ds)$$

$$= I_A(\omega) I_{\{x_{T_n} \in B\}} I_{\{T_n \in C\}} I_{\{t \geq T_n\}} - a(t)$$

where a(t) is a continuous process. Thus the discontinuities of $(f\circ Q)_t$ occur at $T_n$. Since $m_t$ is orthogonal to $\eta_t$ therefore

$$0 \equiv \langle m,\eta\rangle_t = \sum_{k\neq n} \langle \mu_k,\eta\rangle_t + \langle \mu_n,\eta\rangle_t$$

Also $\langle \mu_k,\eta\rangle_t \equiv 0$ for $k \neq n$, hence $\langle \mu_n,\eta\rangle_t \equiv 0$ so that $\mu_n\cdot\eta \in \mathcal{M}^1$. By the Corollary in [16, p. 106] and the Definition in [16, p. 87] it follows that $\Delta\mu_{nT_n}\cdot\Delta\eta_{T_n}\cdot I_{t\geq T_n}$ is a martingale so that

$$E\{M_n(\omega)\, I_A(\omega)\, I_{\{x_{T_n} \in B\}}\, I_{\{T_n \in C\}} = 0$$

which contradicts (3.6). The theorem has been proved. ¤

Lemma 3.3 provides an obvious extension of the definition of the stochastic integral $(f\circ Q)_t$ to $f \in L^2_{loc}(\tilde{P})$ and so Theorem 3.3 extends in the following manner.

<u>Corollary 3.1</u> $\{m_t - m_o | m_t \in \mathcal{M}^2_{loc}\} = \{(f\circ Q)_t | f \in L^2_{loc}(\tilde{P})\}$.

To obtain the representation for martingales in $\mathcal{M}^1_{loc}$ two preliminary results are needed.

<u>Lemma 3.6</u> i) Let $f \in \mathcal{P}$. Then $f \in L^1(P)$ if and only if $f \in L^1(\tilde{P})$. In fact $\|f\|_1 = \|f\|^{\sim}_1$. In particular $L^1(P) = L^1(\tilde{P}) = L^1(Q)$.

ii) Let $f \in L^2(\tilde{P})$. Then $f \in L^1(\tilde{P})$ and

$$(foQ)_t = \int_Z \int_{R^+} f(z,s)\ I_{(0,t]}(s)\ Q(dz,ds) \tag{3.7}$$ [6]

iii) If $f \in L^1(\tilde{P})$ then

$$m_t = \int_Z \int_{R^+} f(z,s)\ I_{(0,t]}(s)\ Q(dz,ds) \in \mathcal{M}^1 \cap \mathcal{A}.$$

Proof By an argument which is almost identical to the proof of [16,Prop. 3] it can be shown that (3.7) holds for $f \in L^2(\tilde{P}) \cap L^1(\tilde{P}) \cap L^1(P)$.

Since $L^2(\tilde{P}) \subset L^1(\tilde{P})$ the second assertion will then follow from the first one. Now let $\Phi$ consist of all bounded functions $f(z,t) \in \mathcal{P}$ such that $f(z,t) \equiv 0$ for $t \geq T_n$ for some $n < \infty$. Then certainly $\Phi \subset L^2(\tilde{P}) \cap L^1(\tilde{P}) \cap L^1(P)$. So $(|f| oQ)_t \in \mathcal{M}_2$ for $f \in \Phi$ and in particular by (3.7)

$$0 = E(|f| oQ)_\infty = \|f\|_1 - \|f\|_1^{\sim}.$$

Then the identity map, restricted to $\Phi$, from $L^1(P)$ to $L^1(\tilde{P})$ preserves norms. Since $\Phi$ is dense in $L^1(P)$ and $L^1(\tilde{P})$ the first assertion follows. To prove the last assertion let $f_k$, $k \geq 1$ be a sequence in $L^2(\tilde{P})$ such that $\|f - f_k\|_1$ converges to zero. Then $m_{kt} = (f_k oQ)_t \in \mathcal{M}^2$ and by (3.7) $E|m_{kt} - m_t| \leq 2\|f - f_k\|_1$ converges to zero uniformly in t

[6] It may be worth repeating, to clarify the content of (3.7), that the integral on the right in (3.7) is a Lebesgue-Stieltjes integral whereas that on the left is the stochastic integral as defined in Lemma 3.3.

so that $m_t \in \mathcal{M}^1$. ⌑

Proposition 3.3 Let M be a $\mathcal{F}_{T_n}$-measurable r.v. for some $n \geq 1$. Suppose $E|M| < \infty$. Then there is a unique $f(z,t) \in L^1(\tilde{P})$ such that

$$M\, I_{t \geq T_n} = \int_Z \int_{R^+} f(z,s)\, I_{(0,t]}(s)\, P(dz,ds). \tag{3.8}$$

Furthermore $f(z,s) = 0$ for $s \leq T_{n-1}$ and $s > T_n$, and

$$E|M\, I_{\{T_n < \infty\}}| = \|f\|_1. \tag{3.9}$$

Proof Since $M\, I_{t \geq T_n} = M\, I_{\{T_n < \infty\}} I_{\{t \geq T_n\}}$ it can be assumed that $M = M\, I_{\{T_n < \infty\}}$. By Corollary 2.2 there exist r.v.s $M^k$ of the form

$$M^k(\omega) = \sum_i \alpha_i\, I_{\{x_{T_n} \in B_i\}} I_{A_i}(\omega)\, I_{\{T_n \in C_i\}}$$

where $\alpha_i \in R$, $B_i \in \mathcal{Z}$, $A_i \in \mathcal{F}_{T_{n-1}}$ and $C_i \in \mathcal{B}[0,\infty)$, such that $E|M - M^k| \to 0$. If $f^k$ is defined by

$$f^k(z,\omega,t) = \sum_i \alpha_i\, I_{B_i}(z)\, I_{A_i}(\omega)\, I_{C_i}(t)\, I_{\{T_{n-1} < t \leq T_n\}}$$

then it is clear that (3.8) and (3.9) hold for $M^k$ and $f^k$. The assertion now follows by taking limits. ⌑

Lemma 3.7 Let $m_t \in \mathcal{M}^1 \cap \mathcal{A}$. Then there exists $f \in L^1(\tilde{P})$ such that

$$m_t - m_o = \int_Z \int_{R^+} f(z,s)\, I_{(o,t]}(s)\, Q(dz,ds) \tag{3.10}$$

and
$$E \int_0^\infty |dm_t| = 2\|f\|_1 \tag{3.11}$$

<u>Proof</u> $m_t$ has the representation

$$m_t - m_o = \sum_{n=1}^{\infty} (M_n I_{t \geq T_n} - a_n(t)) = \sum_{n=1}^{\infty} \mu_{nt}$$

where $M_n = \Delta m_{T_n}$, $a_n(t) \in \mathcal{A}$ is continuous, and $\mu_{nt} \in \mathcal{M}$. Since $m_t \in \mathcal{A}$

$$\infty > E \int_0^\infty |dm_t| > \sum_{n=1}^{\infty} E|M_n|,$$

so that by Proposition 3.3 there exist functions $f_n(z,t) \in L^1(\tilde{P})$ which vanish outside of $\{T_{n-1} \leq t \leq T_n\}$ such that $E|M_n| = \|f_n\|_1$ and

$$M_n I_{t \geq T_n} = \int_Z \int_{R^+} f_n(z,s)\, I_{(0,t]}(s)\, P(dz,ds)$$

By Lemma 3.6

$$\eta_n(t) = a_n(t) - \int_Z \int_{R^+} f_n(z,s)\, I_{(0,t]}(s)\, \tilde{P}(dz,ds) \in \mathcal{M}^1$$

But $\eta_n(t)$ is continuous so that $\eta_n(t) \equiv 0$ by Theorem 3.2. Therefore

(3.10) holds for $f(z,t) = \sum_{n=1}^{\infty} f_n(z,t)$ and (3.11) follows from Lemma 3.6 and the fact that $f_k(z,t)\, f_n(z,t) \equiv 0$ for $k \neq n$

Theorem 3.4 $m_t \in \mathcal{M}^1_{loc}$ if and only if there exists $f \in L^1(\tilde{P})$ such that

$$m_t - m_o \equiv \int_Z \int_{R^+} f(z,s)\, I_{(0,t]}(s)\, Q(dz,ds) \tag{3.12}$$

Proof The sufficiency follows readily from Lemma 3.6 (iii). To prove the necessity one starts by noting that by [16, Lemma 3 and Proposition 4] there exists an increasing sequence of s.t.s $S_k$ converging to $\infty$ such that for each k $m_{t\, S_k} - m_o$ has a decomposition

$$m_{t\wedge S_k} - m_o = \mu^k_t + \eta^k_t$$

where $\mu^k_t \in \mathcal{M}^2_0$ and $\eta^k_t \in \mathcal{M}^1_0 \cap \mathcal{A}$. By Lemmas 3.6 (ii) and 3.7 there exists $f^k \in L^1(\tilde{P})$ such that

$$m_{t\wedge S_k} - m_o = \int_Z \int_{R^+} f^k(z,s)\, I_{(0,\infty]}(s)\, Q(dz,ds).$$

It is clear that $f^k(z,t) = f^{k+1}(z,t)$ for $t \leq S_k$. Thus (3.12) holds for $f \in L^1_{loc}(\tilde{P})$ defined by $f(z,t) = f^k(z,t)$ for $t \leq S_k$. ¤

The results above give a characterization of the classes $\mathcal{M}^2$, $\mathcal{M}^2_{loc}$, $\mathcal{M}^1 \cap \mathcal{A}$ and $\mathcal{M}^1_{loc}$. It seems much more difficult to obtain a useful characterization of the class $\mathcal{M}^1$.

The (local) martingales with respect to $(\Omega, \mathcal{F}_t, P)$ have been represented as sums or integrals of the 'basic' martingales $Q(B,t)$. The latter are associated in a one-to-one manner with the counting processes $P(B,t)$ which count those jumps of the underlying process $x_t$ which <u>end</u> in the set B. Thus jumps are distinguished by their final values. Now it is also possible to distinguish jumps by their values. The corresponding counting processes will be of the form $p(A,t)$ which counts those jumps of the $x_t$ process which have values in the set A. The martingales $q(A,t)$ associated with the $p(A,t)$ also form a 'basis' for the set of all martingales on $(\Omega, \mathcal{F}_t, P)$ as will be shown below. The alternative representation obtained with this basis can sometimes be more useful since the description of the $x_t$ process is, in practice, often given in terms of a statistical characterization of the jumps of $x_t$.

For simplicity of notation it will be assumed in the remainder of this section that the $x_t$ process starts at time 0 in a fixed state i.e., $x_0(\omega) = x_0(\omega')$ for all $\omega$, $\omega'$ in $\Omega$[7]. Next it is assumed that there is given a set $\Sigma$ of transformations $\sigma: Z \to Z$ with the following properties:

i) $\Sigma$ contains the jumps of the $x_t$ process i.e., if $x_{s-}(\omega) \neq x_s(\omega)$ for some $s \in R_+$, $\omega \in \Omega$ then there is a <u>unique</u> $\sigma \in \Sigma$ such that $\sigma(x_{s-}(\omega)) = x_s(\omega)$,

ii) $\Sigma$ contains a distinguished element $\sigma_0$ corresponding to the identity transformation i.e., $\sigma_0(z) = z$ for all $z \in Z$.

To each sample function $\omega \in \Omega$ of the $x_t$ process is associated a function $\gamma(\omega): R_+ \to \Sigma$ defined as follows:

---

[7]It should be noted however that the results below continue to hold in the absence of this simplification.

$$\gamma_t(\omega) = \sigma_0 \text{ if } t = 0 \text{ or if } x_t(\omega) = x_{t-}(\omega)$$
$$= \sigma \quad \text{if } x_t(\omega) \neq x_{t-}(\omega)$$

where $\sigma \in \Sigma$ is the unique element for which $\sigma(x_{t-}(\omega)) = x_t(\omega)$.

Remark i) Given a sample path $x_s(\omega)$, $0 \leq s \leq t$, there corresponds in a one-to-one manner a sample path $\gamma_s(\omega)$, $0 \leq s \leq t$.

ii) The functions $\gamma(\omega)$ are not right continuous. However if $\gamma_t(\omega) = \sigma_0$ then $\gamma_{t-}(\omega) = \sigma_0$. This observation will be used later in an example.

The following 'regularity' assumption appears to be necessary. In practice it is readily verifiable.

Assumption. There is a $\sigma$-field $\Xi$ on $\Sigma$ such that $\mathcal{F}'_t$ coincides with the $\sigma$-field generated by subsets of the form $\{\omega | \gamma_s(\omega) \in A\}$ where $s \leq t$ and $A \in \Xi$.

With the assumptions above it is clear that the processes $x_t$ and $\gamma_t$ are equivalent alternative descriptions of the same process. In particular they generate the same $\sigma$-fields, so that the two processes have the same martingales. The representation theorems derived earlier for the $x_t$ process can be applied to the $\gamma_t$ process but there is a minor point to be cleared up. Recall that it was assumed that the $x_t$ process was right-continuous whereas $\gamma_t$ is not. However the assumption of right-continuity was used only to establish the right-continuity of the family $\mathcal{F}'_t$. This continues to hold of course since $\gamma_t$ and $x_t$ generate the same $\sigma$-fields $\mathcal{F}'_t$. Hence one can apply the representation theorems.

Definition 3.4 Let $A \in \Xi$. Let

$$p(A,t) = \sum_{s\leq t} I_{\{\gamma_{s-} \neq \gamma_s\}} I_{\{\gamma_s \in A\}} = \sum_{s\leq t} I_{\{x_{s-} \neq x_s\}} I_{\{\gamma_s \in A\}}$$

be the number of jumps of the $x_t$ process with 'values' in A and which occur prior to t.

By Proposition 3.2 there is a unique continuous process $\tilde{p}(A,t) \in \mathcal{A}^+_{loc}$ such that the process $q(A,t) = p(A,t) - \tilde{p}(A,t)$ is in $\mathcal{M}^2_{loc}$. In analogy with Definitions 3.2 and 3.3 one can define the subsets of $\mathcal{P}_\Sigma$ : $L^2(\tilde{p})$, $L^2_{loc}(\tilde{p})$, $L^1(\tilde{p})$, $L^1(p)$ etc.[8] Lemma 3.3 describes the stochastic integrals (foq) for $f \in L^2(\tilde{p})$. An application of Theorem 3.3, Corollary 3.1, Lemma 3.7 and Theorem 3.4 yields the following representation theorem.

Theorem 3.5 i) $m_t \in \mathcal{M}^2(\mathcal{M}^2_{loc})$ if and only if $m_t - m_0 = (foq)_t$ for some $f \in L^2(\tilde{p})$ $(L^2_{loc}(\tilde{p}))$.

ii) $m_t \in \mathcal{M}^1 \cap \mathcal{A}$ $(\mathcal{M}^1_{loc})$ if and only if $m_t - m_0 = \int_\Sigma \int_{R^+} f(\sigma,s)\, I_{(0,t]}(s)\, q(d\sigma,ds)$ for some $f \in L^1(\tilde{p})$ $(L^1_{loc}(\tilde{p}))$.

## IV An example

This section consists of a simple example showing how Theorem 3.5 can be applied. The example will be further elaborated in [3].

Let Z be countable and let $\mathcal{Z}$ consist of all subsets of Z. Let $x_t$ be a process with values in Z and satisfying the assumptions listed at the beginning of Section III. Suppose that from each state z the process $x_t$

---

8 $\mathcal{P}_\Sigma$ is the set of predictable functions of $(\sigma,\omega,t) \in \Sigma \times \Omega \times R_+$ defined in analogy with Definition 3.2.

can jump to one of n states. In terms of a state-transition diagram (see Figure 1) there are n transitions or links emanating from each state or node. Label these transitions by the symbols $\sigma_1, \ldots, \sigma_n$. Let $\Sigma = \{\sigma_0,\ldots,\sigma_n\}$. Thus each $\sigma \in \Sigma$ corresponds to a transformation in Z, $\sigma_0$ is the identity transformation. Let $\Xi$ be the set of all subsets of $\Sigma$. The $x_t$ process defines the process of transitions, $\gamma_t$. Evidently $\Sigma$, $\Xi$ satisfy the assumptions made above.

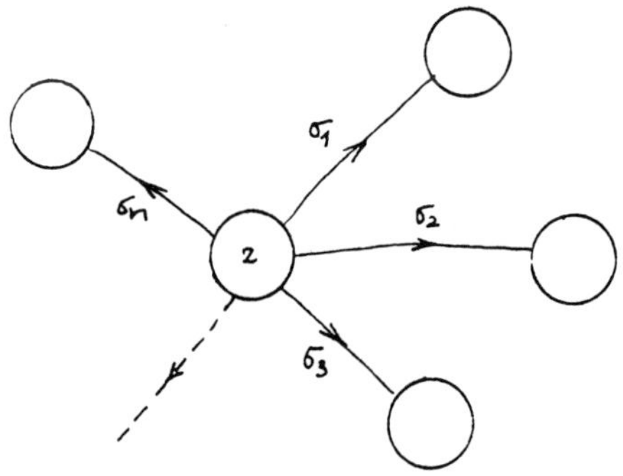


Figure 1: State-transition diagram for example.

Let $p_i(t) = p(\{\sigma_i\},t)$, $\tilde{p}_i(t) = \tilde{p}_i(\{\sigma_i\},t)$ and $q_i(t) = q_i(\{\sigma_i\},t)$, $0 \le i \le n$. From a remark made in the last section $I_{\{x_{s-} \neq x_s\}} \cdot I_{\{\gamma_s = \sigma\}} \equiv 0$. Hence $p_0(t) \equiv 0$ and so $q_0(t) \equiv 0$. Theorem 3.5 simplifies to the following. Here the predictable integrands are functions of $(\omega,t)$ only.

<u>Theorem 4.1</u> i) $m_t \in \mathcal{M}^2(\mathcal{M}^2_{loc})$ if and only if $m_t - m_0 \equiv \sum_{i=1} (f_i o q_i)_t$ for some $f_i \in L^2(\tilde{p}_i)(L^2_{loc}(\tilde{p}_i))$, $1 \le i \le n$.

ii) $m_t \in \mathcal{M}^1 \cap \mathcal{A}\ (\mathcal{M}^1_{loc})$ if and only if $m_t - m_0$

$$= \sum_{i=1}^{n} \int_{(0,t]} f_i(s)\, q_i(ds) \text{ for some } f_i \in L^1(\tilde{p}_i)(L^1_{loc}(\tilde{p}_i)),\ 1 \le i \le n.$$

Example Let $x_t$ be a process taking values in a countable state space and of the type described immediately above. From each state the process can make n transitious $\sigma_1, \ldots, \sigma_n$ as sketched in Figure 1. Let $p_i(t)$, $\tilde{p}_i(t)$, $q_i(t)$ be as in Theorem 3.6.

Let $\lambda(t)$, $\rho_1(t), \ldots, \rho_n(t)$ be non-negative predictable processes such that

$$\sum_{i=1}^{n} \rho_i(t) \equiv 1 \tag{4.1}$$

$$p_i(t \wedge T_k) - \int_0^{t \wedge T_k} \rho_i(s)\lambda(s)\, ds \in \mathcal{M}^1, \; k = 1, 2, \ldots, n \tag{4.2}$$

Then the processes $\lambda(t)$, $\rho_i(t)$ have the following interpretation: since from (4.1) and (4.2)

$$\left( \sum_{i=1}^{n} p_i(t \wedge T_k) - \int_0^{t \wedge T_k} \lambda(s)\, ds \right) \in \mathcal{M}^1 \tag{4.3}$$

and since $\sum_{i=1}^{n} p_i(t)$ is just the total number of jumps of the process occuring prior to t, therefore the probability that the process $x_t$ makes a transition in the time interval $[t, t+h]$, conditioned on the past $\mathcal{F}_t$ of the process, is equal to $\lambda(t)h + o(h)$. Similarly $\rho_i(t)$ is the probability that the process makes a transition represented by $\sigma_i$, conditioned on $\mathcal{F}_t$ and conditioned on the fact that a transition does occur at t.

Now since the process represented by the indefinite integral in

(4.2) has continuous sample paths it follows quite readily (see e.g. [25, p. 153]) that the jump times of the process are totally inaccessible. Hence from Theorem 4.1 it can be concluded that every $m_t \in \mathcal{M}^1_{loc}$ has a representation

$$m_t - m_o = \sum_{i=1}^{n} [\int_0^t f_i(s)\, d\, p_i(s) - \int_0^t f_i(s)\, \rho_i(s)\, \lambda(s)\, ds] \tag{4.4}$$

for some predictable processes $f_i \in L^1_{loc}\,(\rho_i\lambda)$ i.e., for which

$$\int_0^t f_i(s)\, \rho_i(s)\lambda(s)\, ds < \infty \text{ a.s. for all } t \in R_+.$$

This result indicates how one can immediately write down the representation results if the process $x_t$ is described in terms of the 'rate' processes $\lambda$ and the 'transition' probabilities $\rho_i$. It should be kept in mind, however, that it has <u>not</u> been proven that given processes $\lambda(t)$ and $\rho_i(t)$ there exists a process $x_t$ for which (4.2) holds. This question of existence will be pursued in [3]. The next remark relates to the representation (4.4), which asserts that the n local martingales in (4.2) indeed from a "basis" for the space of all local martingales $\mathcal{M}^1_{loc}$. The question is whether n is the minimum number of martingales in every basis of $\mathcal{M}^1_{loc}$. For the case where $x_t$ is a Gaussian process the minimum number of martingales has been called the "multiplicity" of the process by Cramer [8 ,9]. It turns out that this notion of multiplicity extends in a very natural way to arbitrary processes [13]. From the results of [13] the following sufficient condition can be obtained: Suppose that the processes $\rho_i(s)\lambda(s)$ satisfy

$$\rho_i(s)\ \lambda(s) > 0 \Leftrightarrow \rho_j(s)\ \lambda(s) > 0 \quad \text{all } i,j.$$

Then n is the minimum number of martingales in a representation of $\mathcal{M}^1_{loc}$.

Finally, specialize the example still further and assume that $x_t$ is a counting process i.e., $x_o = 0$, $x_t$ takes integer values and has unit positive jumps. Then $x_t$ is a direct extension of a Poisson process. The state-transition diagram then simplifies to that of Figure 2 and since n = 1 in (4.1), (4.2) and (4.4) therefore $\rho_1(t) \equiv 1$ and can be omitted. Also $p_1(t) \equiv x_1(t)$ and so the representation (4.4) simplifies to (4.5). Every $m_t \in \mathcal{M}^1_{loc}$ can be written as

$$m_t - m_o = \int_0^t f(s)\ dx_s - \int_0^t f(s)\ \lambda(s)\ ds \qquad (4.5)$$

where f is a predictable function such that

$$\int_0^t f(s)\ \lambda(s)\ ds < \infty \text{ a.s. for all } t \in R_+.$$

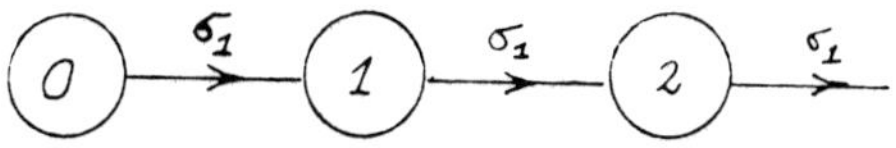


Figure 2. Transition diagram for counting process.

This representation result has been obtained by very different techniques from several authors [4, 5, 11, 12]. However even here the cited references prove (4.5) for the special case where the probability law of the $x_t$ process is mutually absolutely continuous with respect to the probability law of a standard Poisson process. Hence even for this special case (4.5) is a strict generalization of the available results.

Appendix: The increasing processes $\tilde{P}(A,t)$ and the Lévy system.

This section attempts to give an intuitive interpretation of the increasing processes $\tilde{P}(B,t)$ and shows the connection with the Lévy system for Hunt processes.

Begin with the observation that for all $B \in \mathcal{Z}$ the measure $P(B,t)$ is absolutely continuous with respect to the measure $\tilde{P}(Z,t)$ i.e., there exists a predictable function $(\omega,t) \to n(B,\omega,t)$ such that

$$\tilde{P}(B,t) = \int_0^t n(B,\omega,s)\, P(Z,ds) \tag{A-1}$$

To see this it is enough to demonstrate that for all predictable functions $\phi(\omega,s) = \phi^2(\omega,s)$ (i.e., all indicator functions)

$$E\int_0^\infty \phi(\omega,s)\, \tilde{P}(Z,ds) = 0 \tag{A-2}$$

implies

$$E\int_0^\infty \phi(\omega,s)\, \tilde{P}(B,ds) = 0 \tag{A-3}$$

Suppose (A-2) holds, then

$$\left\langle \int_0^t \phi(s)\, dQ(Z,s), \int_0^t \phi(s)\, dQ(Z,s) \right\rangle \equiv \int_0^t \phi^2(s)\, \tilde{P}(Z,ds) \equiv 0,$$

and so

$$0 \equiv \langle \int_0^t \phi(s)\, dQ(B,s), \int_0^t \phi(s)\, dQ(Z,s) \rangle$$

$$= \int_0^t \phi^2(s)\, \tilde{P}(B \cap Z, ds) \qquad \text{by Lemma 3.1}$$

$$= \int_0^t \phi^2(s)\, \tilde{P}(B, ds)$$

which proves (A-3).

In exactly the same way as Lemma 3.2 was proved it can be shown that the $n(B,\omega,s)$ considered as a set function in $\mathcal{Z}$ is countably additive in the sense that if $B_1, B_2, \ldots$ is a disjoint sequence of sets in $\mathcal{Z}$ then

$$\tilde{P}(\bigcup_i B_i, t) \equiv \sum_i \int_0^t n(B_i,s)\, \tilde{P}(Z,ds)$$

Hence if one sets $\tilde{P}(Z,t) \equiv \Lambda(t) \in \mathcal{A}^+_{loc}$, then the system $\{n(B,t,\omega), \Lambda(t)\}$ is analogous to a Lévy system for Hunt processes (see [22]), and has a similar interpretation : the probability of $x_t$ having a jump in $[t,t + dt)$ is $d\Lambda(t) + o(dt)$, while $n(A,t,\omega)$ is the chance that $x_t \in A$ given $\mathcal{F}_t$ and given that a jump occurs at t.

## References

[1] D. Blackwell: "On a class of probability spaces," Third Symposium on Math. Stat. and Prob., vol. II, Univ. of Calif. Press, Calif., 1-6 (1956).

[2] V. Beneš, "Existence of optimal stochastic control laws," SIAM J. Control 9, 446-475 (1971).

[3] R. Boel, P. Varaiya and E. Wong, "Martingales on Jump Processes Part II: Applications," in preparation.

[4] P. Brémaud, "A martingale approach to point processes," Electronics Res. Lab., Univ. of Calif., Berkeley, Memo #M-345 (August 1972).

[5] P. Brémaud, "Filtering for point processes," preprint, submitted to Information and Control, June 1973.

[6] J. M. C. Clark, "The representation of functionals of Brownian motion by stochastic integrals," Ann. Math. Statist. 41, 1285-1295 (1970).

[7] P. Courrège and P. Priouret, "Temps d'arrét d'une fonction aléatoire, théorèmes de décomposition," Publ. Inst. Stat. Univ. Paris 14, 242-274 (1965).

[8] H. Cramer, "Stochastic Processes as Curves in Hilbert Space," Theory of Prob. Appl. 9, 195-204, (1964)

[9] H. Cramer, "A Contribution to the Multiplicity Theory of Stochastic Processes," Fifth Symposium on Math. Stat. and Prob., Vol. II, Univ. of Calif. Press, Calif., 215-221 (1967).

[10] M. H. A. Davis, "Detection of signals with point process observations," Dept. of Computing and Control, Imperial College, London, May 1973.

[11] M. H. A. Davis, "Nonlinear filtering with point process observations," preprint (1972).

[12] M. H. A. Davis and P. Varaiya, "Dynamic Programming Conditions for partially observable stochastic systems," SIAM J. Control, 11(2), 226-261 (1973).

[13] M. H. A. Davis and P. Varaiya, "The Multiplicity of an Increasing Family of σ-fields," Electronics Res. Lab., Univ. of Calif., Berkeley, Calif., Memo #402, (August 1973).

[14] C. Dellacherie, Capacités et processus stochastiques, Berlin: Springer-Verlag, 1972.

[15] C. Doléans-Dade, "Quelques applications de la formule de changement de variables pour les semimartingales," Z. Wahrscheinlichkeits theorie verw. Greb 16, pp. 181-194, (1970).

[16] C. Doléans-Dade and P. A. Meyer, "Intégrales stochastiques par rapport aux martingales locales," in Séminaire de Probabilités: IV, Lecture notes in Mathematics, Berlin: Springer-Verlag, p. 77-107, (1970).

[17] J. L. Doob, Stochastic Processes, New York: Wiley (1953).

[18] T. Duncan, "Evaluation of likelihood functions," Information and Control 13, 62-74, (1968).

[19] T. E. Duncan and P. Varaiya, "On the solutions of a stochastic control system," SIAM J. Control 9, 354-371, (1971).

[20] Girsanov, "On transforming a certain class of stochastic processes by absolutely continuous subtitution of measures," Theory of Prob. and Appl. 5, 285-301, (1960).

[21] T. Kailath and M. Zakai, "Absolute continuity and Radon-Nikodym derivatives for certain measures relative to Wiener measure," Ann. Math. Statist. 42, 130-140 (1971).

[22] H. Kunita and S. Watanabe, "On square integrable martingales," Nagoya Math. J. 30, 209-245, (August 1967).

[23] M. Loève, Probability theory, 2nd edition, New York: Van Nostrand (1960).

[24] P. A. Meyer, Probabilités et potentiel, Paris: Hermann, (1966); (English translation: Probability and Potentials, Waltham, Mass: Blaisdell (1966)).

[25] P. A. Meyer, "Guide détailé de la théorie 'générale' des processus," in Séminaire de Probabilité, II, Lecture Notes in Mathematics Vol. 51, Berlin: Springer-Verlag, 140-165, (1968).

[26] P. A. Meyer, "Non-square integrable martingales etc.," in Lecture Notes in Mathematics, No. 190, Berlin: Springer-Verlag, 38-43 (1971).

[27] P. A. Meyer, "Square integrable martingales, a survey," in Lecture Notes in Mathematics, No. 190, Berlin: Springer Verlag, 32-37 (1971).

[28] P. A. Meyer:"Temps d'arret algebriquement prévisibles," Séminaire de Probabilités VI, Lecture Notes in Mathematics, No. 258, Berlin: Springer-Verlag, 158-163 (1972).

[29] D. L. Snyder, "A representation theorem for observed jump processes," Proc. IEEE Conf. on Decision and Control, New Orleans, Louisiana, p. 218, (Dec. 13-15, 1972).

[30] D. L. Snyder, "Information Processing for Observed Jump Processes," Information and Control 22 (1), 69-78, (1973).

[31] D. L. Snyder, "Statistical Analysis of Dynamic Tracer Data," IEEE Trans. on Biomedical Engr. BME-20(1), 11-20, (1973).

[32] J. H. Van Schuppen and E. Wong, "Transformations of Local Martingales under a Change of Law," Electronics Res. Lab., Univ. of Calif., Berkeley, Memo #M-385 (May 18, 1973).

[33] E. Wong "Martingale Theory and Applications to Stochastic Problems in Dynamical Systems," Publication 72/19, Imperial College, Dept. of Computing and Control, (June 1972).

[34] E. Wong, "Recent Progress in Stochastic Processes - A Survey," IEEE Trans Info. Theory IT-19(3), 263-275 (May 1973).

# 14

Reprinted from *Martingales on Jump Processes: II. Applications* Mem. ERL-M409, Electronics Research Laboratory, University of California, Berkeley, 1973, pp. 1–73

# Martingales on Jump Processes: II. Applications

R. BOEL, P. VARAIYA, and E. WONG

Department of Electrical Engineering and
Computer Sciences and the Electronics
Research Laboratory
University of California, Berkeley

Research sponsored by the National Science Foundation, Grant GK-10656x3 and the Army Research Office-Durham, Contract DAHC04-67-C-0046. Boel also supported by an ESRO-NASA International Fellowship.

## 1. Introduction and Summary

This paper is concerned with applying the theory of martingales of jump processes to various problems arising in communication and control. It parallels the approaches which have been recently discovered in dealing with similar problems where the underlying stochastic process is Brownian motion. Indeed these approaches have recently been extended, starting with the work of Snyder [14,16,30] and Brémaud [61,28], to the case of the Poisson process and its transformations. The paper can then be regarded as a sweeping generalization to this recent work.

The paper can also be considered as an illustration of an abstract view and a set of instructions which must be followed to obtain certain concrete results in the areas of communication and control. It is hoped that this 'tutorial' function will also be served.

Two results from the abstract theory of martingales form the basis of this abstract view. The first consists of the differentiation rule and the associated stochastic calculus for martingales and semi-martingales [1], and its application to the so-called 'exponentiation' formula [2]. The second result consists of the earlier Doob-Meyer decomposition theorem for supermartingales [3]. In order to follow the abstract view, one also needs a third set of results, the so-called 'martingale representation' theorems for specific processes. These results form a bridge between the abstract theory and the concrete applications. The representation results used here have been obtained in [4], hence the paper can also be viewed as a continuation of that work.

The paper is organized in the following manner. In the next section are presented many definitions, notations and results from [1, 2, 3, 4] which will be used in the succeeding development. These preliminaries are certainly longer than can be considered proper, and are justified partly to serve the tutorial function, partly because there is no consensus of usage in the literature, and lastly because some of the published literature contains errors and inaccurate or misleading statements which can be exposed only within a carefully and completely developed context.

Section 3 is concerned with showing the 'global' existence of jump processes over a finite or infinite interval which satisfy certain local descriptions. Existence of such processes is obtained by transforming the laws of 'known' processes by an absolutely continuous transformation. We also present a wide class of point processes which can be so transformed to yield solutions to prespecified local descriptions. Sufficient conditions are derived which guarantee when this technique is applicable. The question of uniqueness of the solutions is settled for a wide class of local descriptions.

Section 4 deals with a specific problem in communication theory, namely the calculation of the likelihood ratio of a process which may be governed by one of two absolutely continuous probability laws. The techniques for Sections 3 and 4 are the same. Section 5 is concerned with estimating certain random variables or processes which are statistically related to an observed process. The emphasis here is on obtaining 'recursive' filters. As special cases one obtains a 'closed form' solution for some of the situations where the estimated process is Markovian. Applications to optimal control will be made in a future paper.

Throughout, there has been an attempt to link up the results with those which have already appeared in the literature in as precise a manner as limitations of space permit. Any omissions are due to oversight of the authors.

## 2. Preliminaries and Formulations

This section describes most of the results from the literature which are necessary to the sequel. §2.1 is definitional in nature. §2.2 - §2.7 are taken mainly from [1], §2.8 is taken from [2], the remainder is from [4].

2.1 Processes. Throughout $\Omega$ is a fixed space, the sample space. The time interval of interest is $R_+ = [0,\infty)$ unless specified otherwise. For each t let $\mathcal{F}_t$ be a $\sigma$-field of subsets of $\Omega$. It will always be assumed that the family $\mathcal{F}_t$, $t \in R_+$, is increasing i.e., $\mathcal{F}_s \subset \mathcal{F}_t$ for $s \leq t$ and right-continuous i.e., $\mathcal{F}_t = \bigcap_{s>t} \mathcal{F}_s$. Let $\mathcal{F} = \bigvee_t \mathcal{F}_t$ be the smallest $\sigma$-field containing all the $\mathcal{F}_t$. Let P be a probability measure on $(\Omega,\mathcal{F})$. Thus one has a family of probability spaces $(\Omega,\mathcal{F}_t, P)$. It will always be assumed that probability spaces are complete.

Let $(Z,\mathcal{Z})$ be a measurable space. Let $x: \Omega \times R_+ \to Z$ be a function such that $\{\omega | x_t(\omega) \in B\} \in \mathcal{F}_t$ for all $B \in \mathcal{Z}$, $t \in R_+$. Then $(x_t,\mathcal{F}_t, P)$ is a (stochastic) process. Thus every process has attached to it a family $(\Omega, \mathcal{F}_t, P)$, $t \in R_+$, of probability spaces. The same function x defines a different process if either the family $\mathcal{F}_t$ or the measure P is changed. When the context makes it clear we write $(x_t,\mathcal{F}_t)$ or $(x_t, P)$ or $x_t$ instead of $(x_t,\mathcal{F}_t, P)$. If $(x_t,\mathcal{F}_t,P)$ is a process, then so is $(x_t,\mathcal{F}^x_t, P)$ where $\mathcal{F}^x_t$ is the sub-$\sigma$-field of $\mathcal{F}_t$ generated by $x_s$, $s \leq t$ and P is the restriction to $\mathcal{F}^x = \bigvee_t \mathcal{F}^x_t$. Two processes $(x_t,\mathcal{F}_t,P)$ and $(y_t,\mathcal{F}_t,P)$ are said to be equivalent or versions of one another if

$x_t = y_t$ a.s. P for each t, the set $\{x_t \neq y_t\}$ may vary with t. They are said to be <u>modifications</u> if there is a set N with P(N) = 0 such that for $\omega \notin N, x_t(\omega) = y_t(\omega)$ for all t. Given $(\Omega, \mathcal{F}, P)$, a <u>random variable</u>, or <u>r.v.</u>, with values in $(Z, \mathcal{Z})$ is a $\mathcal{F}$-measurable map from $\Omega$ into Z. Unless explicitly stated otherwise all r.v.s and processes take values in $(R \cup \{\infty\}, B)$ where B is the Borel field.

2.2 <u>Stopping Times</u>. Consider a family $(\Omega, \mathcal{F}_t, P)$. A non-negative r.v. T is a <u>stopping time</u>, s.t., of the family, if

$$\{T \leq t\} \in \mathcal{F}_t \qquad \text{for all } t.$$

The s.t. T is said to be <u>predictable</u> if there exists an increasing sequence of s.t.s $S_1 \leq S_2 \leq \ldots$ such that

$$P\{T = 0 \text{ or } S_k < T \text{ for all } k \text{ and } \lim_{k\to\infty} S_k = T\} = 1$$

The s.t. T is said to be <u>totally incaccessible</u> if $T > 0$ a.s. and if for every increasing sequence of s.t.s $S_1 \leq S_2 \leq \ldots$

$$P\{S_k < T \text{ for all } k \text{ and } \lim_{k\to\infty} S_k = T < \infty\} = 0.$$

2.3 <u>Martingales and Increasing Processes</u>. A process $(m_t, \mathcal{F}_t, P)$ is said to be a (uniformly integrable) <u>martingale</u> if the collection $\{m_t | t \in R_+\}$ of r.v.s is uniformly integrable, and if $E(m_t|\mathcal{F}_s) = m_s$ a.s. for $s \leq t$. The collection of all such martingales, for which $m_0 = 0$, is denoted $\mathcal{M}^1 = \mathcal{M}^1(\mathcal{F}_t, P)$. $(m_t, \mathcal{F}_t, P)$ is said to be a <u>local martingale</u> if there is an increasing sequence of s.t.s $S_k$, with $S_k \to \infty$ a.s. such that

$$(m_{t\wedge S_k} I_{\{S_k > 0\}}, \mathcal{F}_t, P) \in \mathcal{M}^1 \text{ for each } k.$$

The collection is denoted $\mathcal{M}^1_{loc}(\mathcal{F}_t,P)$. $(m_t,\mathcal{F}_t,P)$ is a <u>square integrable martingale</u> if $m_t \in \mathcal{M}^1$ and if $\sup_t Em_t^2 < \infty$. The collection is denoted $\mathcal{M}^2(\mathcal{F}_t,P)$ and the class of locally square integrable martingales $\mathcal{M}^2_{loc}(\mathcal{F}_t,P)$ is defined analogously. It is obvious that $\mathcal{M}^2_{loc} \subset \mathcal{M}^1_{loc}$.

Each $m_t \in \mathcal{M}^1_{loc}$ has a version whose sample paths are right-continuous and have left-hand limits. Clearly such a version is unique, i.e., unique modulo modification. It will always be assumed that local martingales have sample paths with this continuity property.

A process $(a_t,\mathcal{F}_t,P)$ is said to be <u>increasing</u> if $a_0 = 0$ a.s. and if its sample paths are non-decreasing. The collection is denoted $\mathcal{A}^+_0(\mathcal{F}_t,P)$. $\mathcal{A}_0 = \mathcal{A}^+_0 - \mathcal{A}^+_0 = \{a_t - a'_t \mid a_t \in \mathcal{A}^+_0,\ a'_t \in \mathcal{A}^+_0\}$.

$\mathcal{A}^+ = \{a_t \in \mathcal{A}^+_0 \mid \sup_t E\, a_t < \infty\}$, $\mathcal{A} = \mathcal{A}^+ - \mathcal{A}^+$. Members of $\mathcal{A}^+(\mathcal{A})$ are said to be <u>integrable</u> (or have <u>integrable variation</u>). $a_t \in \mathcal{A}^+_0$ is said to be locally integrable if there is an increasing sequence of s.t.s $S_k \to \infty$ a.s. such that

$$a_{t\wedge S_k} \in \mathcal{A}^+ \quad \text{for all } k.$$

$$\mathcal{A}_{loc} = \mathcal{A}^+_{loc} - \mathcal{A}^+_{loc}.$$

<u>Semi-martingales</u>. A process $(s_t,\mathcal{F}_t,P)$ is a <u>semi-martingale</u>, respectively <u>local semi-martingale</u>, if it can be expressed as $s_t = s_0 + m_t + a_t$ where $m_t \in \mathcal{M}^1(\mathcal{F}_t,P)$ and $a_t \in \mathcal{A}(\mathcal{F}_t,P)$, respectively $m_t \in \mathcal{M}^1_{loc}(\mathcal{F}_t,P)$ and $a_t \in \mathcal{A}_0(\mathcal{F}_t,P)$. The families are respectively denoted $\mathcal{S}(\mathcal{F}_t,P)$ and $\mathcal{S}_{loc}(\mathcal{F}_t,P)$.

2.4 __Predictable Processes.__ The family of all processes $(y_t, \mathcal{F}_t, P)$ which have left-continuous sample paths generates a $\sigma$-field $\mathcal{P} = \mathcal{P}(\mathcal{F}_t) \subset \mathcal{F} \otimes \mathcal{B}$ with respect to which the functions $(\omega, t) \mapsto y_t(\omega)$ are measurable. $\mathcal{P}$ is called the __predictable__ $\sigma$-field, and every process $(y_t, \mathcal{F}_t, P)$ which is $\mathcal{P}$-measurable is called a __predictable process.__ Note that if $\mathcal{F}_t \subset \mathcal{G}_t$, then $\mathcal{P}(\mathcal{F}_t) \subset \mathcal{P}(\mathcal{G}_t)$.

For $(a_t, \mathcal{F}_t, P) \in \mathcal{A}_0$,

$$L^P(a_t) = \{y_t \mid (y_t, \mathcal{F}_t, P) \text{ is predictable and } E\int_0^\infty |y_t|^P |da_t| < \infty\}.$$

$$L^P_{loc}(a_t) = \{y_t \mid \text{there is a sequence of s.t.s } S_k \to \infty \text{ such that}$$

$$y_t I_{\{t \leq S_k\}} \in L^P(a_t)\} \quad \text{for each } k .$$

The integrals above are Stieltjes integrals.

2.5 __Quadratic Variation__ Two martingales $m_t$, $n_t$ in $\mathcal{M}^1_{loc}$ are __orthogonal__ if their product, $m_t n_t \in \mathcal{M}^1_{loc}$. $m_t \in \mathcal{M}^1_{loc}$ is __continuous__ if its sample paths are continuous; it is said to be __discontinuous__ if it is orthogonal to every continuous martingale. Every $m_t \in \mathcal{M}^1_{loc}$ has a unique __decomposition,__

$$m_t = m^c_t + m^d_t$$

such that $m^c_t$ is continuous and $m^d_t$ is discontinuous. Clearly if $m_t \in \mathcal{M}^1_{loc}$ is continuous then it is in $\mathcal{M}^2_{loc}$. To every path $m_t$, $n_t$ in $\mathcal{M}^2_{loc}$ is associated a unique predictable process, denoted $\langle m,n \rangle_t$ or $(\langle m_t, n_t \rangle, \mathcal{F}_t, P)$ such that $\langle m,n \rangle_t \in \mathcal{A}^+_{loc}$, and

$$(m_t n_t - \langle m,n\rangle_t) \in \mathcal{M}^1_{loc}(\mathcal{F}_t, P).$$

$\langle m,n\rangle_t$ is called the predictable quadratic covariation of $m_t, n_t$. For $m_t \in \mathcal{M}^2_{loc}$, $\langle m\rangle_t = \langle m,m\rangle_t$ is the predictable quadratic variation of $m_t$. Note that generally $\langle m,n\rangle$ depends crucially upon the family $(\mathcal{F}_t, P)$.

If $m_t$, $n_t$ in $\mathcal{M}^1_{loc}$ have the decompositions $m_t = m^c_t + m^d_t$, $n_t = n^c_t + n^d_t$, then the process

$$[m,n]_t = [m_t, n_t] = \langle m^c, n^c\rangle_t + \sum_{s\leq t} \Delta m'_s \, \Delta n_s,$$

where $\Delta m_s = m_s - m_{s-}$, $\Delta n_s = n_s - n_{s-}$, is called the quadratic covariation of $m_t$, $n_t$ and $[m_t] = [m_t, m_t]$ is the quadratic variation of $m_t$. It turns out that

$$m_t n_t - [m,n]_t \in \mathcal{M}^1_{loc}$$

so that if, furthermore, $m_t$, $n_t$ are in $\mathcal{M}^2_{loc}$ then

$$[m,n]_t - \langle m,n\rangle_t \in \mathcal{M}^1_{loc}.$$

2.6 Stochastic Integration If $m_t \in \mathcal{M}^2_{loc}(\mathcal{F}_t, P)$ and $\phi_t \in L^2_{loc}(\langle m\rangle_t)$ then $\phi_t \in L^1_{loc}(\langle m,n\rangle_t)$ for all $n_t \in \mathcal{M}^2_{loc}(\mathcal{F}_t, P)$ and there is a unique process, denoted $(\phi \circ m)_t \in \mathcal{M}^2_{loc}(\mathcal{F}_t, P)$ which satisfies

$$\langle \phi \circ m, n\rangle_t = \int_0^t \phi_s \, d\langle m,n\rangle_s \text{ for all } n_t \in \mathcal{M}^2_{loc}. \tag{2.1}$$

The integral on the right is a Stieltjes integral. If $m_t \notin \mathcal{M}^2_{loc}$ then one cannot define a stochastic integral in this way. Two other possibilities are open.

If $m_t = m_t^c + m_t^d \in \mathcal{M}^1_{loc}(\mathcal{F}_t, P)$ if $m_t^d \in \mathcal{A}_{loc}(\mathcal{F}_t, P)$[1] and if $\phi_t \in L^2_{loc}(\langle m^c \rangle_t) \cap L^1_{loc}(m_t^d)$, then the process

$$(\phi \circ m)_t = (\phi \circ m^c)_t + \int_0^t \phi_s \, dm_s^d \in \mathcal{M}^1_{loc}(\mathcal{F}_t, P) \tag{2.2}$$

where $(\phi \circ m^c)_t$ is defined as in (2.1) whereas the second integral is a Stieltjes integral.

Finally if $m_t \in \mathcal{M}^1_{loc}$ and if $(\phi_t, \mathcal{F}_t, P)$ is a <u>locally bounded</u>[2] predictable process, then there exists a unique process $(\phi \circ m)_t \in \mathcal{M}^1_{loc}$ which satisfies

$$[\phi \circ m, n]_t = \int_0^t \phi_s \, d[m,n]_s \quad \text{for all } n \in \mathcal{M}^1_{loc}. \tag{2.3}$$

The integral on the right is not in general a Stieltjes integral unless $[m,n]_t \in \mathcal{A}_{loc}$. The precise interpretation of this integral is not given here since it is seldom used below. For details see [1].

The process $(\phi \circ m)_t$ is called the <u>stochastic integral of $\phi$ with respect to m.</u> Note that if $(\phi \circ m)$ makes sense according to more than one of the three possibilities (2.1), (2.2) or (2.3) then the resulting stochastic integrals coincide.

2.7 <u>Differentiation formula</u>. Let $s_t = s_0 + m_t + a_t \in \mathcal{S}_{loc}(\mathcal{F}_t, P)$. The decomposition is <u>not</u> unique. If $s_t = s_0 + m_t' + a_t'$ is another

---

[1] This is a non trivial restriction on $m_t^d$. It holds for the discontinuous martingales to be introduced in §2.9 below.

[2] $\phi_t$ is locally bounded if there is an increasing sequence of s.t.s $S_k \to \infty$ such that the process $\phi_{t \wedge S_k} I_{\{S_k > 0\}}$ is bounded for all k. Note that if $\phi_t$ is a right-continuous process, having left-hand limits, then the process $\psi_t = \phi_{t-}$ is locally bounded.

decomposition then the continuous parts $m_t^c$, $m'^c_t$ of the local martingale are modifications. This unique continuous local martingale is denoted $s_t^c$.

Let $s_t = (s_t^1, .., s_t^n)$ be a process with values in $R^n$ such that $s_t^i \in \mathcal{S}_{loc}(\mathcal{F}_t, P)$ i=1, ...,n. Let F: $R^n \to R$ be a twice continuously differentiable function. Then the following differentiation formula holds.

$$F(s_t)=F(s_0) + \int_0^t \sum_{i=1}^n \frac{\partial F}{\partial x_i} (s_{\tau-})\, ds_\tau^i + \frac{1}{2}\int_0^t \sum_{i,j=1}^n \frac{\partial^2 F}{\partial x_i\, \partial x_j} (s_{\tau-}) d\langle s^{ic}, s^{jc}\rangle_\tau$$

$$+ \sum_{\tau \leq t} [F(s_\tau)-F(s_{\tau-})- \sum_{i=1}^n \frac{\partial F}{\partial x_i} (s_{\tau-})\, (s_\tau^i - s_{\tau-}^i)].$$

As a special case one obtains the very useful 'product' rule. Suppose $m_t$ and $n_t$ are in $\mathcal{M}^1_{loc}$. Then (since $m_0 = n_0 = 0$), and recalling the definition of $[m,n]_t$

$$m_t n_t = \int_0^t m_{s-}\, dn_s + \int_0^t n_{s-}\, dm_s + [m,n]_t$$

2.8 <u>The Exponentiation Formula</u>: Let $s_t \in \mathcal{S}_{loc}(\mathcal{F}_t, P)$ with $s_o = 0$. Then there is a unique process $y_t \in \mathcal{S}_{loc}(\mathcal{F}_t, P)$ which satisfies the equation

$$y_t = y_o + \int_0^t y_{\tau-}\, ds_\tau \qquad , \qquad t \geq 0,$$

for a pre-specified $y_o$, and $y_t$ is given explicitly by

$$y_t = y_o \exp(s_t - \frac{1}{2}\langle s^c, s^c\rangle_t) \cdot \prod_{\tau \leq t} (1+\Delta s_\tau)e^{-\Delta s_\tau}$$

where the second term converges a.s.. $y_t$ is called the <u>exponential of</u> $s_t$ and is sometimes denoted $y_t = \mathcal{E}(s_t)$. Evidently $\mathcal{E}(s_t) \geq 0$ a.s. if $y_o \geq 0$ a.s., and if $1 + \Delta s \geq 0$ a.s. If, in addition, $m_o \geq 0$ and $m_t - m_o \in \mathcal{M}^1_{loc}(\mathcal{F}_t, P)$ then $(\mathcal{E}(m_t), \mathcal{F}_t, P)$ is a supermartingale i.e.

$$E(\mathcal{E}(m_t) | \mathcal{F}_s) \leq \mathcal{E}(m_s) \quad s \leq t,$$

and so in particular

$$E(\mathcal{E}(m_t)) \leq E(m_o), \ t \geq 0.$$

Finally if $m_t \in \mathcal{M}^1$ is bounded then $\mathcal{E}(m_t)$ is a martingale.

2.9 <u>The fundamental jump process</u> Let $(\Omega, \mathcal{F}_t, P)$ be a family of spaces and let $(x_t, \mathcal{F}_t, P)$ be a process with values in $(Z, \mathcal{Z})$ such that all the sample paths of x are piecewise constant and have only a finite number of discontinuities in every finite interval, and such that the sample paths are right-continuous i.e., for all $\omega$, t there is $\varepsilon_o > 0$ such that $x_t(\omega) = x_{t+\varepsilon}(\omega)$ for $0 \leq \varepsilon \leq \varepsilon_0$. Let $T_n$, n=0,1... denote the <u>jump times</u> of the process, defined inductively by $T_0 \equiv 0$ and

$$T_{n+1}(\omega) = \begin{cases} \inf\{t | t > T_n(\omega), x_t(\omega) \neq x_{T_n}(\omega)\} & , n \geq 0 \\ \infty \text{ if the set above is empty} \end{cases}$$

$(x_t, \mathcal{F}_t, P)$ is a <u>fundamental jump process</u>, or a fundamental process, f.p., with values in $(Z, \mathcal{Z})$, if in addition,

(i) $(Z, \mathcal{Z})$ is a Blackwell space, and then it turns out that the jump times are s.t.s, and

(ii) The s.t.s $T_n$ are totally inaccessible.

Evidently if $(x_t, \mathcal{F}_t, P)$ is a f.p., so is $(x_t, \mathcal{F}^x_t, P)$ where $\mathcal{F}^x_t$ is the sub-$\sigma$-field of $\mathcal{F}_t$ generated by $x_s$, $s \leq t$. For each $B \in \mathcal{Z}$ let

$$P(B,t) = \sum_{s \leq t} I_{\{x_{s-} \neq x_s\}} I_{\{x_s \in B\}}$$

be the number of jumps of x which occur prior to t and which end in the set B.

Associated with P(B,t) are two unique increasing continuous processes $\tilde{P}(B,t) \in \mathcal{A}^+_{loc}(\mathcal{F}_t, P)$ and $\tilde{P}^x(B,t) \in \mathcal{A}^+_{loc}(\mathcal{F}^x_t, P)$ such that

$$Q(B,t) = P(B,t) - \tilde{P}(B,t) \in \mathcal{M}^2_{loc}(\mathcal{F}_t, P)$$

and $Q^x(B,t) = P(B,t) - \tilde{P}^x(B,t) \in \mathcal{M}^2_{loc}(\mathcal{F}^x_t, P)$.

Furthermore,

$$\langle Q(B_1,t), Q(B_2,t) \rangle = \tilde{P}(B_1 \cap B_2, t),$$

and $\langle Q^x(B_1,t), Q^x(B_2,t) \rangle = \tilde{P}^x(B_1 \cap B_2, t)$

Finally, the functions $P$, $\tilde{P}$, $\tilde{P}^x$, $Q$, $Q^x$ considered as random set functions on $\mathcal{Z}$ are countably additive.

Note: The condition that the $T_n$ are totally inaccessible is equivalent to the assertion that the $\tilde{P}(B,t)$ are continuous. See [4] for alternative conditions.

A real-valued function $f(z,t) = f(z,\omega,t)$ is said to be predictable, and one writes $f \in \mathcal{P}(\mathcal{F}_t)$, if it is measurable with respect to $\mathcal{Z} \otimes \mathcal{F} \otimes \mathcal{B}$ and if for each fixed $z$, $f(z,\cdot,\cdot)$ is predictable in the sense of §2.4 above. The family $\mathcal{P}(\mathcal{F}_t^x)$ is defined similarly. If $f \in \mathcal{P}(\mathcal{F}_t)$, respectively $\mathcal{P}(\mathcal{F}_t^x)$, we call f a $\mathcal{F}_t$-predictable, respectively $\mathcal{F}_t^x$-predictable, process. The following classes of predictable functions are used in the martingale representation results.

$$L^2(\tilde{P}^x) = \{f \in \mathcal{P}(\mathcal{F}_t^x) \mid (\|f\|_2^{\sim})^2 = E \int_Z \int_{R_+} f^2(z,t)\, \tilde{P}^x(dz,dt) < \infty\}$$

$$L^1(\tilde{P}^x) = \{f \in \mathcal{P}(\mathcal{F}_t^x) \mid \|f\|_1^{\sim} = E \int_Z \int_{R_+} |f(z,t)|\, \tilde{P}^x(dz,dt) < \infty\}$$

$$L^1(P) = \{f \in \mathcal{P}(\mathcal{F}_t^x) \mid \|f\|_1 = E \int_Z \int_{R_+} |f(z,t)|\, P(dz,dt) < \infty\}$$

$$L^1(Q^x) = L^1(P) \cap L^1(\tilde{P}^x)$$

It turns out that $\|f\|_1 = \|f\|_1^{\sim}$, hence $L^1(\tilde{P}^x) = L^1(P) = L^1(Q^x)$.

$$L^2_{loc}(\tilde{P}^x) = \{f \in \mathcal{P}(\mathcal{F}_t^x) \mid \text{there exists a sequence of s.t.s } S_k \to \infty \text{ such that } f(z,t)\, I_{\{t \le S_k\}} \in L^2(\tilde{P}^x) \text{ for each } k\}$$

The classes $L^1_{loc}(P)$ etc. are defined in a similar manner. Evidently,

$$L^1_{loc}(Q^x) = L^1_{loc}(P) = L^1_{loc}(\tilde{P}^x)$$

Let $f(z,\omega,t)$ be a function which is measurable with respect to $\mathcal{Z} \otimes \mathcal{F}^x \otimes \mathcal{B}$ such that $f(z,\cdot,t)$ is $\mathcal{F}_t^x$-measurable for fixed z and such that $E\int_Z\int_{R_+} |f(z,t)|\tilde{P}^x(dz,dt) < \infty$. Then there exists a $\mathcal{F}_t^x$-predictable function $\hat{f}$ such that $E\int_Z\int_{R_+} |f - \hat{f}|\tilde{P}^x(dz,dt) = 0$. This result follows easily from [22, VT23]. The result will be used in §4, §5 in the following context: Let $f \in \mathcal{P}(\mathcal{F}_t)$ and let $\hat{f}(z,t) = E(f(z,t)|\mathcal{F}_t^x)$; it can then be assumed without loss of generality that $\hat{f}$ is $\mathcal{F}_t^x$-predictable.

2.10 <u>Representation of $\mathcal{M}^2(\mathcal{F}_t^x)$</u>. For each $f \in L^2(Q^x)$ there exists a unique process $(foQ^x)_t \in \mathcal{M}^2(\mathcal{F}_t^x)$ such that for all $g \in L^2(Q^x)$, $\alpha$ and $\beta$ in R

$$(\alpha f + \beta g)\, oQ^x \equiv \alpha(foQ^x) + \beta(goQ^x),$$

$$\langle foQ^x, goQ^x\rangle_t = \int_Z\int_0^t f(z,s)\, g(z,s)\, \tilde{P}^x(dz,ds)$$

Conversely if $m_t \in \mathcal{M}^2(\mathcal{F}_t^x)$ then there exists $f \in L^2(Q^x)$ such that

$$m_t = (foQ^x)_t.$$

Similarly, $m_t \in \mathcal{M}^2_{loc}(\mathcal{F}_t^x)$ if and only if there exists $f \in L^2_{loc}(Q^x)$ such that

$$m_t = (foQ^x)_t.$$

2.11 <u>Representation of $\mathcal{M}^1_{loc}(\mathcal{F}_t^x)$</u>. If $f \in L^1(P^x)$ then $(foQ^x)_t \in \mathcal{M}^1(\mathcal{F}_t^x) \cap \mathcal{A}$ where

$$(foQ^x)_t = \iint_{Z\,0}^{t} f(z,s)\, Q^x(dz,ds) = \iint_{Z\,0}^{t} f(z,s)\, P(dz,ds) - \iint_{Z\,0}^{t} f(z,s)\, \tilde{P}^x(dz,ds),$$

the integrals on the right being Stieltjes integrals. Conversely if $m_t \in \mathcal{M}^1(\mathcal{F}_t^x) \cap \mathcal{A}$ then there is $f \in L^1(\tilde{P}^x)$ such that

$$m_t = (foQ^x)_t .$$

Finally, $m_t \in \mathcal{M}^1_{loc}(\mathcal{F}_t^x)$ if and only if there is $f \in L^1_{loc}(\tilde{P}^x)$ such that

$$m_t = (foQ^x)_t = \int_Z \int_0^t f(z,s)[P(dz,ds) - \tilde{P}^x(dz,ds)].$$

Remark 2.1 1. If $m_t \in \mathcal{M}^1_{loc}(\mathcal{F}_t^x)$ has continuous sample paths then $m_t \equiv 0$.

2. If more than one representation above applies then the representations coincide.

2.12 Local description of a fundamental process. Let $(x_t, \mathcal{F}_t, P)$ be a fundamental process with values in $(Z, \mathcal{Z})$, and consider the increasing processes $\tilde{P}(B,t)$ and $\tilde{P}^x(B,t)$. Let $\Lambda(t) = \tilde{P}(Z,t)$, $\Lambda^x(t) = \tilde{P}^x(Z,t)$. The countable additivity of these functions with respect to $B \in \mathcal{Z}$ implies that there exist predictable processes $n(B,t)$ and $n^x(B,t)$ such that for all $B \in \mathcal{Z}$,

$$\tilde{P}(B,t) = \int_0^t n(B,s)\, \Lambda(ds)$$

$$\tilde{P}^x(B,t) = \int_0^t n^x(B,s)\, \Lambda^x(ds) .$$

Evidently it can be assumed that $n(Z,s) = n^x(Z,s) \equiv 1$. The system

$\{n(B,t),\ \Lambda(t)\}$ or $\{n(dz,t),\ \Lambda(dt)\}$ is analogous to a Lévy system for a Hunt process [5]. The system $\{n(dz,t),\ \Lambda(dt)\}$ will be called an <u>extrinsic local description</u> of x, whereas $\{n^x(dz,t),\ \Lambda^x(dt)\}$ is called the <u>intrinsic local description</u> of x, because of the following interpretation: the probability that x has a jump in [t,t+dt] given $\mathcal{F}_t$, (respectively $\mathcal{F}_t^x$) is $\Lambda(dt) + o(dt)$ (respectively $\Lambda^x(dt) + o(dt)$), while $n(B,t)$, (respectively $n^x(B,t)$) is the probability that $x_t \in B$ given $\mathcal{F}_t(\mathcal{F}_t^x)$ and given that a jump occurs at t. For future reference we note the following trivial but important fact.

<u>Fact</u>: Let $\{n(B,t),\ \Lambda(t)\}$ and $\{n^x(B,t),\ \Lambda^x(t)\}$ be extrinsic and intrinsic local descriptions. Then for all $B \in \mathcal{Z}$, and $t \in R_+$

$$E\left\{\int_0^t n(B,s)\ \Lambda(ds) \,\middle|\, \mathcal{F}_t^x\right\} = \int_0^t n^x(B,s)\ \Lambda^x(ds) \text{ a.s.} \tag{2.4}$$

2.12 <u>Fundamental Example</u>. The results in the succeeding sections will be specialized to the following example which covers many practical cases such as Poisson, counting, birth and death, and queueing processes.

Let $(x_t, \mathcal{F}_t, P)$ be a fundamental process with values in $(Z, \mathcal{Z})$. Suppose that from each $z \in Z$ the process can make at most n transitions where n is a fixed finite number. Thus the transitions can be represented by a 'state-transition' diagram of Figure 1, where the transitions are labeled $\sigma_1, \ldots, \sigma_n$. Define the counting processes $p_i(t)$, $1 \le i \le n$,

$p_i(t)$ = number of transitions of type i made by the process $x_t$ prior to t.

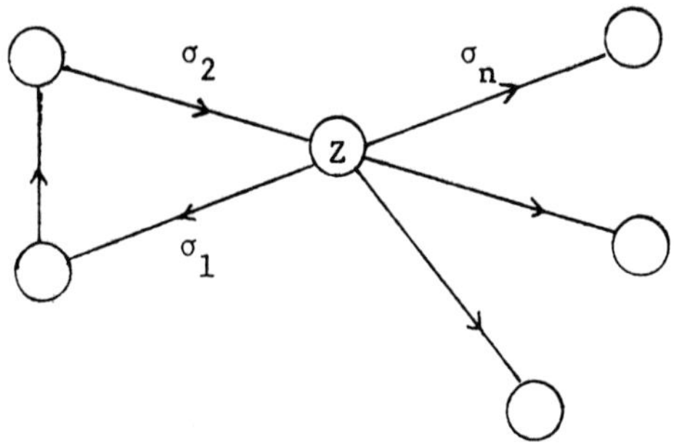


Fig. 1. State-transition Diagram for Fundamental Example

Then there exist increasing processes $\tilde{p}_i^x(t)$ and $\tilde{p}_i(t)$ such that

$$q_i(t) = p_i(t) - \tilde{p}_i(t) \in \mathcal{M}^2_{loc}(\mathcal{F}_t, P)$$

$$q_i^x(t) = p_i(t) - \tilde{p}_i^x(t) \in \mathcal{M}^2_{loc}(\mathcal{F}_t^x, P)$$

Furthermore,

$m_t \in \mathcal{M}^2(\mathcal{F}_t^x, P)$, respectively $\mathcal{M}^2_{loc}(\mathcal{F}_t^x, P)$, if and only if there exist $f_i \in L^2(\tilde{p}_i^x)$, respectively $L^2_{loc}(\tilde{p}_i^x)$, such that

$$m_t = \sum_{i=1}^{n} (f_i o q_i^x)_t; \tag{2.5}$$

and $m_t \in \mathcal{M}^1(\mathcal{F}_t^x, P) \cap \mathcal{A}$, respectively $\mathcal{M}^1_{loc}(\mathcal{F}_t^x, P)$, if and only if there exist $f_i \in L^1(\tilde{p}_i^x)$, respectively $L^1_{loc}(\tilde{p}_i^x)$, such that

$$m_t = \sum_{i=1}^{n} (f_i o q_i^x)_t, \tag{2.6}$$

where the integral is a Stieltjes integral.

We call $(\tilde{p}_1, \ldots, \tilde{p}_n)$, respectively $(\tilde{p}_1^x, \ldots \tilde{p}_n^x)$, the extrinsic, respectively intrinsic, local descriptions.

<u>Remark 2.2</u> If $(x_t, \mathcal{F}_t, P)$ is a counting process[3] then Fig. 1 simplifies to Figure 2 and there is only one transition. Hence in this case $n = 1$ in (2.5) and (2.6).

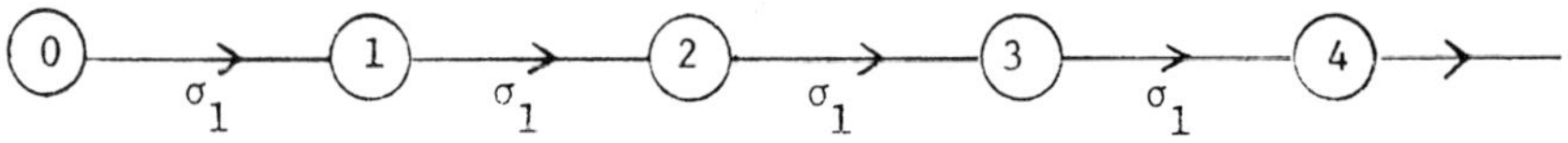


Fig. 2. State-transition diagram for counting processes.

For this special case Brémaud [5] has obtained the representation for $\mathcal{M}^2_{loc}(\mathcal{F}^x_t)$, whereas Davis [7] has extended it to the class $\mathcal{M}^1_{loc}(\mathcal{F}^x_t)$. However both these results were obtained only for the case where the law of $(x_t, \mathcal{F}^x_t, P)$ is mutually absolutely continuous with respect to the law for a standard Poisson process (see §3).

## 3. Solutions to Specified Local Descriptions by Change of Law

In §3.1 we present a very useful technique for transforming one fundamental process $(x_t, \mathcal{F}_t, P)$ with a l.d. $(n, \Lambda)$ to another process with a different prespecified l.d. The questions of uniqueness of the solution is discussed in §3.2. §3.3 consists of some sufficient conditions which guarantee that the technique is applicable. Finally §3.4 presents a class of processes which can be transformed into other processes with this technique.

Let $(x_t, \mathcal{F}^x_t, P)$ be a fundamental process with values in $(Z, \mathcal{Z})$ and with intrinsic local description (l.d.) $(n^x(dz,t), \Lambda^x(dt))$ so that

[3] A counting process is an integer-valued process which starts at 0 and has unit jumps.

$$\tilde{p}^x(B,t) = \int_B \int_0^t n^x(dz,s)\, \Lambda^x(ds), \quad t \in R_+$$

Since we will be only dealing with the 'intrinsic' σ-field $\mathcal{F}_t^x$ in this section, the superscript x will be omitted here. Hence $\mathcal{F}_t = \mathcal{F}_t^x$, $\tilde{P} = \tilde{P}^x$ etc.

## 3.1 The Transformation Technique

Let $P_1$ be another probability measure on $(\Omega, \mathcal{F})$ and suppose that

$$P_1 << P,$$

i.e., $P_1$ is absolutely continuous with respect to P. It is evident that the same function $x_t(\omega)$ defines another fundamental process $(x_t, \mathcal{F}_t, P_1)$ with a possibly different l.d. $(n_1(B,t), \Lambda_1(t))$ say. We are going to determine the relationship between the two descriptions.

Let $L = \frac{dP_1}{dP}$ be the Radon-Nikodym derivative. The r.v. $L \geq 0$ and $E(L)$[4] $= 1$. Let $L_t = E(L|\mathcal{F}_t)$. Then $(L_t, \mathcal{F}_t, P)$ is a uniformly integrable martingale, $\lim_{t\to\infty} L_t = L$ a.s. and in $L^1$ by ([3], remark after VI. T6).

<u>Proposition 3.1</u> i) If $L > 0$ a.s. P then for almost all $\omega$, $L_{t-}(\omega) > 0$ and $L_t(\omega) > 0$ for all t.

ii) Let

$$T(\omega) = \inf \{t | L_{t-}(\omega) = 0 \text{ or } L_t(\omega) = 0\} \tag{3.1}$$

Then for almost all $\omega$, $L_t(\omega) = 0$ for $t \geq T(\omega)$.

<u>Proof</u> i) Clearly $L > 0$ a.s. implies $L_t > 0$ a.s. and then the second part of the assertion follows from (ii), and the latter follows from [3,VI. T15]. ◻

---

[4] E, $E_1$, denotes expectation with respect to P, $P_1$.

<u>Remarks 3.1</u> **(i) If $L > 0$ a.s. P, then in fact $P << P_1$ i.e. the two** measures are mutually absolutely continuous.

(ii) It is easy to give examples such that $L_t > 0$ for all t but $P(L=0) > 0$.

For $\varepsilon > 0$ let

$$T_\varepsilon(\omega) = \inf\{t \mid L_{t-}(\omega) \leq \varepsilon\} \tag{3.2}$$

<u>Proposition 3.2</u> $T_\varepsilon$ is a s.t. for all $\varepsilon$ and

$$\lim_{\varepsilon \to 0} T_\varepsilon(\omega) = T(\omega) \text{ a.s. } P$$

<u>Proof</u> The fact that $T_\varepsilon$ is a s.t. follows from the fact that the process $L_{t-}$ is left-continuous and from [3, IV. T52]. Now $T_\varepsilon$ is clearly non-decreasing with $\varepsilon$. Let

$$T_0(\omega) = \lim_{\varepsilon \to 0} T_\varepsilon(\omega)$$

Suppose $T(\omega) = \infty$ and <u>per contra</u> $T_0(\omega) < \infty$. Then there exists a sequence $t_i$ increasing to $t_0 < \infty$ such that $L_{t_i-}(\omega) \to 0$. By left-continuity $L_{t_0-}(\omega) = 0$ and so $T(\omega) \leq t_0$. Next suppose $T(\omega) < \infty$. By Proposition 3.1, for almost all such $\omega$ $T_0(\omega) \leq T(\omega)$. If $T_0(\omega) < T(\omega)$ then a repetition of the previous argument will end in a contradiction. Once again $T_0(\omega) = T(\omega)$. ◻

For $\varepsilon > 0$ let

$$L_t^\varepsilon(\omega) = L_{t \wedge T_\varepsilon}(\omega), \ t \in R_+.$$

Then $L_t^\varepsilon - L_0 \in \mathcal{M}^1(P)$ and $L_t^\varepsilon \geq \varepsilon$ for all t. By §2.11 there is a predictable function $f^\varepsilon(z,t) \in L^1_{loc}(P)$ such that

$$L_t^\varepsilon = 1 + \int_Z \int_0^t f^\varepsilon(z,s)\, Q(dz,ds) = \int_Z \int_0^t f^\varepsilon(z,s)[P(dz,ds) - \tilde{P}(dz,ds)] \quad (3.3)$$[5]

Since $\frac{1}{L_{t-}^\varepsilon} \leq \frac{1}{\varepsilon}$, therefore the process

$$\phi^\varepsilon(z,s) = \frac{f^\varepsilon(z,s)}{L_{s-}^\varepsilon} \in L^1_{loc}(\tilde{P}),$$

and hence

$$m^\varepsilon(t) = \int_Z \int_0^t \phi^\varepsilon(z,s)\, Q(dz,ds) \in \mathcal{M}^1(\mathcal{F}_t, P) \quad (3.4)$$

which upon substitution into (3.3) gives

$$L_t^\varepsilon = 1 + \int_0^t L_{s-}^\varepsilon\, dm_s^\varepsilon$$

By the Exponentiation formula of §2.8

$$L_t^\varepsilon = \mathcal{E}(m_t^\varepsilon) = \exp(m_t^\varepsilon - \frac{1}{2}\langle m^{\varepsilon,c}, m^{\varepsilon,c}\rangle_t) \prod_{s \leq t} (1+\Delta m_s^\varepsilon) e^{-\Delta m_s^\varepsilon} \quad (3.5)$$

By the Remark in §2.11, $m^{\varepsilon,c} \equiv 0$, hence (3.5) simplifies to

$$L_t^\varepsilon = \exp(m_t^\varepsilon) \prod_{s \leq t} (1+\Delta m_s^\varepsilon) e^{-\Delta m_s^\varepsilon} \quad (3.6)$$

Rewriting (3.4) as

---

[5] Here it is being assumed that $L_0 \equiv 1$ which is indeed the case if $\mathcal{F}_0$ is trivial. Otherwise, in the sequel, replace the martingale $L_t$ by $\frac{L_t}{L_0}$.

$$m^{\varepsilon}(t) = \int_Z \int_0^t \phi^{\varepsilon}(z,s)\, P(dz,ds) - \int_Z \int_0^t \phi^{\varepsilon}(z,s)\, \tilde{P}(dz,ds) \tag{3.7}$$

and acknowledging that the second integral has continuous sample paths (since $\tilde{P}$ is continuous) it follows that for almost all $\omega$

$$\Delta m_s^{\varepsilon}(\omega) = m_s^{\varepsilon}(\omega) - m_{s-}^{\varepsilon}(\omega) = \int_Z \phi^{\varepsilon}(z,s)(\omega)[P(dz,s)(\omega) - P(dz,s-)(\omega)] \tag{3.8}$$

Also since $P(B,s)(\omega) - P(B,s-)(\omega)$ equals 1 or 0 depending upon whether or not $x_{s-}(\omega) \neq x_s(\omega)$ and $x_s(\omega) \in B$, therefore the term $(1+\Delta m_s^{\varepsilon})$ in (3.6) can be written as

$$(1+\Delta m_s^{\varepsilon})(\omega) = \int_Z (1+\phi^{\varepsilon}(z,s)(\omega))[P(dz,s)(\omega) - P(dz,s-)(\omega)] \tag{3.9}$$

From (3.8), (3.9) it follows respectively that

$$\sum_{s\leq t} \Delta m_s^{\varepsilon}(\omega) = \sum_{\substack{s\leq t \\ x_{s-}\neq x_s}} \phi^{\varepsilon}(x_s(\omega),s),$$

$$\prod_{s\leq t} (1+\Delta m_s^{\varepsilon}(\omega)) = \prod_{\substack{s\leq t \\ x_{s-}\neq x_s}} (1+\phi^{\varepsilon}(x_s(\omega),s))$$

which upon substitution, together with (3.7), into (3.6), yields after some cancellation the first interesting result

$$L_t^{\varepsilon} = \prod_{\substack{s\leq t \\ x_{s-}\neq x_s}} [1+\phi^{\varepsilon}(x_s,s)] \exp\left(-\int_Z \int_0^t \phi^{\varepsilon}(z,s)\tilde{P}(dz,ds)\right) \tag{3.10}$$

Finally let $\varepsilon_k > 0$, k=1,2,... be a sequence decreasing to 0, let $S_0 = 0$, $S_k = T_{\varepsilon_k}$, k=1,2,..., and let

$$\phi(z,s) = \sum_{k=1}^{\infty} \phi^{\varepsilon_k}(z,s)\, I_{\{S_{k-1} < s \leq S_k\}}$$

$\phi$ is predictable since $\phi^{\varepsilon_k}$ is predictable and $I_{\{S_{k-1} < s \leq S_k\}}$ is left-continuous. Since by definition $L_t^{\varepsilon} = L_{t \wedge T_\varepsilon}^{\varepsilon'}$ for $\varepsilon' < \varepsilon$ we have proved the following result.

<u>Theorem 3.1</u> Let $P_1 \ll P$, and let $L_t = E(\frac{dP_1}{dP} | \mathcal{F}_t^x)$. Let

$$T = \inf\{t | L_{t-} = 0 \text{ or } L_t = 0\}$$

Then there exists a predictable function $\phi(z,s)$ and an increasing sequence $S_k$ of s.t.s converging to T such that

$$\phi_k(z,s) = \phi(z,s)\, I_{\{s \leq S_k\}} \in L^1_{loc}(\tilde{P})$$

and

$$L_{t \wedge S_k} = \prod_{\substack{s<t \\ x_{s-} \neq x_s}} [1+\phi_k(x_s,s)] \exp[-\int_Z \int_0^t \phi_k(z,s)\, \tilde{P}(dz,ds)] \tag{3.11}$$

The product on the right converges a.s. whereas the integral is a Stieltjes integral.

<u>Remarks 3.2</u> (i) If $L = \frac{dP_1}{dP} > 0$ a.s. then $T = \infty$ a.s. so that the result above implies that $\phi \in L^1_{loc}(\tilde{P})$. However if this is not the case then it

is not true that in general $\phi \in L^1_{loc}$. Some additional properties of $\phi$ are given in Theorem 3.2 below. Nevertheless, very loosely speaking, one can interpret (3.11) as

$$L_t = \prod_{\substack{s \leq t \\ x_{s-} \neq x_s}} [1+\phi(x_s,s)] \exp[-\int_Z\int_0^t \phi(z,s) \quad \tilde{P}(dz,ds)], \text{ for } t < T \tag{3.12}$$

Indeed some such loose interpretation is the only way in which the results of [6, 23] can be construed as correct.

(ii) The characterization (3.11) has been derived earlier [23, 24] for the case where $(x_t, \mathcal{F}_t, P)$ is a Brownian motion. The techniques for the proof are identical except that in deriving (3.4) one observes that every martingale on a Brownian motion sample space is a stochastic integral of the Brownian motion (see [5]), and that all martingales are continuous so that (3.5) simplifies to

$$L_t^\varepsilon = \exp(m_t^\varepsilon - \frac{1}{2}\langle m^{\varepsilon,c}, m^{\varepsilon,c}\rangle_t)$$

(iii) For the fundamental example the representation (3.11) becomes, using §2.12,

$$L_{t\wedge S_k} = \prod_{i=1}^{n} \{ \prod_{\substack{s \leq t \\ (x_{s-},x_s)\in\sigma_i}} [1+\phi_k^i(s)] \exp[-\int_0^t \phi_k^i(s)\tilde{p}_i^x(ds)]\}$$

for some predictable $\phi^i(s)$, $1 \leq i \leq n$, such that $\phi_k^i \in L^1_{loc}(\tilde{p}_i^x)$. Here the notation $(x_{s-},x_s) \in \sigma_i$ means that x makes a transition of type i at time s.

If $(x_t, \mathcal{F}_t^x, P)$ is a Poisson process then in the above n=1 and as is well-known $\tilde{p}_1^x(ds) \equiv ds$. For this case the result was first obtained by Brémaud [6] with the loose interpretation of (3.12), and for the case L > 0 a.s., by Van Schuppen, [24], and by Davis [7] who proves in addition that then $\phi \in L^1_{loc}$. Brémaud [6] also obtains this representation for the case where the example is a Markov chain.

We proceed to obtain the relations between the local descriptions. The next result seems well-known.

<u>Lemma 3.1</u> $m_t \in \mathcal{M}^1_{loc}(\mathcal{F}_t, P_1)$ if and only if $m_t L_t \in \mathcal{M}^1_{loc}(\mathcal{F}_t, P)$

<u>Proof</u> Let $S_k \to \infty$ be a sequence of s.t.s such that for each k

$$m_{t\wedge S_k} L_{t\wedge S_k} I_{\{S_k > 0\}} \in \mathcal{M}^1(P) \tag{3.13}$$

First of all

$$\begin{aligned} E_1 |m_{t\wedge S_k} I_{\{S_k > 0\}}| &= E\, L |m_{t\wedge S_k} I_{\{S_k > 0\}}| \\ &= E\, L_{t\wedge S_k} |m_{t\wedge S_k} I_{\{S_k > 0\}}| \text{ by (3.13)} \\ &< \infty \end{aligned}$$

Next for $s \leq t$

$$E_1(m_{t\wedge S_k} I_{\{S_k > 0\}} | \mathcal{F}_s) = \frac{E(m_{t\wedge S_k} L_{t\wedge S_k} I_{\{S_k > 0\}} | \mathcal{F}_s)}{E(L_{t\wedge S_k} | \mathcal{F}_s)}$$

From (3.13) and the fact that $L_t \in \mathcal{M}^1(P)$ the right-hand side simplifies to

$$\frac{m_{s\wedge S_k} \, L_{s\wedge S_k} \, I_{\{S_k > 0\}}}{L_{s\wedge S_k}} = m_{s\wedge S_k} \, I_{\{S_k > 0\}}$$

which proves the "if" part of the assertion.

Conversely suppose that

$$m_{t\wedge S_k} \, I_{\{S_k > 0\}} \in \mathcal{M}^1(P_1) \tag{3.14}$$

It will be shown that for $s \leq t$

$$E(L_{t\wedge S_k} \, m_{t\wedge S_k} \, I_{\{S_k > 0\}} | \mathcal{F}_s) = L_{s\wedge S_k} \, m_{s\wedge S_k} \, I_{\{S_k > 0\}} \text{ a.s. } P \tag{3.15}$$

So let $A \in \mathcal{F}_s$. Then

$$E(I_A L_{t\wedge S_k} \, m_{t\wedge S_k} \, I_{\{S_k > 0\}}) = E_1(I_A \, m_{t\wedge S_k} \, I_{\{S_k > 0\}})$$

$$= E_1(I_A \, m_{s\wedge S_k} \, I_{\{S_k > 0\}}) \text{ by (3.14)}$$

$$= E(L_{s\wedge S_k} \, I_A \, m_{s\wedge S_k} \, I_{\{S_k > 0\}})$$

which proves (3.15). ◻

<u>Theorem 3.2</u> Let $(x_t, \mathcal{F}_t, P)$ be a fundamental process with values in $(Z, \mathcal{Z})$ and with (intrinsic) l.d. $(n(dz,t), \Lambda(dt))$. Let $P_1 \ll P$ and let $L_t = E(\frac{dP_1}{dP} | \mathcal{F}_t)$ have the representation (3.11). Then $(x_t, \mathcal{F}_t, P_1)$ has

1.d. $(n_1(dz,t),\ \Lambda_1(dt))$ where

$$\Lambda_1(t) = \Lambda(dt) \text{ and } n_1(dz,t) = (1+\phi(z,t))\ n(dz,t) \tag{3.16}$$

Furthermore, it can be assumed that

$$(1+\phi) \geq 0 \text{ and } (1+\phi) \in L^1_{loc}(\tilde{P}) \text{ with respect to probability measure } P_1. \tag{3.17}$$

<u>Proof</u> By §2.9 there exist continuous increasing processes $\tilde{P}_1(B,t) \in \mathcal{A}^+_{loc}(P_1)$ such that

$$Q_1(B,t) = P(B,t) - \tilde{P}_1(B,t) \in \mathcal{M}^2_{loc}(P_1) \tag{3.18}$$

Hence to show (3.16) it is equivalent to prove that

$$\tilde{P}_1(B,t) = \int_B \int_0^t (1+\phi(z,s))\ \tilde{P}(dz,ds) \tag{3.19}$$

Let $S_i$, $\phi_i$ be as in Theorem 3.1, and let

$$Q_1^i(B,t) = Q_1(B,t\wedge S_i) = P(B,t\wedge S_i) - \tilde{P}_1(B,t\wedge S_i), \tag{3.20}$$

$$m_t = P(B,t\wedge S_i) - \int_B \int_0^t (1+\phi_i(z,s))\ \tilde{P}(dz,ds) \tag{3.21}$$

It will be shown first that $m_t \in \mathcal{M}^1_{loc}(P_1)$. By Lemma 3.1 it is enough to show that

$$L_t m_t \in \mathcal{M}^1_{loc}(P).$$

Since $\phi_i \in L^1_{loc}(P)$ therefore $m_t$ is in $\mathcal{S}_{loc}(P)$, also $L_t \in \mathcal{M}^1(P) \subset \mathcal{S}_{loc}(P)$.

Hence one can apply the differential formula of §2.7 to obtain

$$L_t m_t = \int_0^t m_{s-}\, dL_s + \int_0^t L_{s-}\, dm_s + \sum_{s\le t} [\Delta(m_s L_s) - m_{s-}\Delta L_s - L_{s-}\Delta m_s] \tag{3.22}$$

From (3.21)

$$\int_0^t L_{s-} dm_s = \int_0^{t\wedge S_i} L_{s-} P(B,ds) - \int_B \int_0^{t\wedge S_i} L_{s-}(1+\phi)\, \tilde{P}(dz,ds),$$

and since $\Delta(m_s L_s) = (m_{s-}+\Delta m_s)(L_{s-}+\Delta L_s) - m_{s-}L_{s-} = m_{s-}\Delta L_s + L_{s-}\Delta m_s + \Delta L_s \Delta m_s$, therefore the last term in (3.22) equals

$$\sum_{s\le t} \Delta L_s\, \Delta m_s = \int_B \int_0^{t\wedge S_i} L_{s-}\phi(z,s)\, P(dz,ds)$$

from (3.11) and (3.21). Substituting these relations back into (3.22) gives

$$L_t m_t = \int_0^t m_{s-} dL_s + \int_B \int_0^{t\wedge S_i} L_{s-}(1+\phi) P(dz,ds) - \int_B \int_0^{t\wedge S_i} L_{s-}(1+\phi)\tilde{P}(dz,ds)$$

$$= \int_0^t m_{s-} dL_s + \int_B \int_0^{t\wedge S_i} L_{s-}(1+\phi) Q(dz,ds)$$

which is clearly in $\mathcal{M}^1_{loc}(P)$. Hence $m_t \in \mathcal{M}^1_{loc}(P_1)$. Since $Q^i_1(B,t) \in \mathcal{M}^1_{loc}(P)$, subtracting (3.21) from (3.20) implies that

$$\tilde{P}_1(B,t\wedge S_i) - \int_B\int_0^{t\wedge S_i} (1+\phi(z,s))\ \tilde{P}(dz,ds) \in \mathcal{M}^1_{loc}(P_1)$$

But this process has continuous sample paths, hence it must vanish i.e., for almost all $\omega$ ($P_1$ measure)

$$\tilde{P}_1(B,t\wedge S_i) = \int_B\int_0^{t\wedge S_i} (1+\phi(z,s))\ \tilde{P}(dz,ds) \text{ for all } t.$$

which proves (3.19) and thereby (3.16). The assertion contained in (3.17) follows from the fact that $\tilde{P}_1$ has increasing sample paths and is in $\mathcal{A}^+_{loc}(P_1)$. ◻

Remark 3.3 (i) It has been shown that $\phi \in L^1_{loc}(\tilde{P})$ in the probability space $(\Omega,\mathcal{F},P_1)$ and not in $(\Omega,\mathcal{F},P)$.

(ii) The transformation of l.d. for the case where $(x_t,P)$ and $(x_t,P_1)$ are both Hunt processes has been obtained in [5]. For this case the local description is called a Lévy system.

(iii) For the case of the fundamental example with l.d. $(\tilde{p}_1,\ldots,\tilde{p}_n)$ under P, the l.d. under $P_1$ is $((1+\phi^1)\tilde{p}_1,\ldots,(1+\phi^n)\tilde{p}_n)$ where the $\phi^i$ are as in Remark 3.2 (iii).

Theorems 3.1, 3.2 allow us to obtain in certain cases processes which have certain specified l.d. from known processes with other descriptions. Put differently, we have a 'synthesis' procedure for obtaining 'global' solutions for a class of l.d.s. This is summarized in the following theorem, whose proof is now immediate.

Theorem 3.3 (Existence of solutions to local descritpions). Let $(x_t, \mathcal{F}_t, P)$ be a fundamental process with values in $(Z, \mathcal{Z})$ and with intrinsic l.d. $(n(dz,t), \Lambda(dt))$. Let $\phi(z,s)$ be a predictable function such that

$$\phi(z,s) \in L^1_{loc}(\tilde{P}) \tag{3.23}$$

and

$$\int_\Omega L_\infty dP = 1 \tag{3.24}$$

where

$$L_t = \prod_{\substack{s\leq t \\ x_{s-}\neq x_s}} [1+\phi(x_s,s)] \exp[ - \int_Z\int_0^t \phi(z,s)\ \tilde{P}(dz,ds)]. \tag{3.25}$$

Then $(x_t, \mathcal{F}_t, P_1)$ is a fundamental process with l.d. $(n_1(dz,t), \Lambda(dt))$ where

$$n_1(dz,t) = (1+\phi(z,t))\ n(dz,t)$$

and where the probability measure $P_1$ is given by

$$dP_1 = L_\infty dP$$

Remark 3.4 (i) This result is extremely useful in practice since given an arbitrary l.d. there is no way to determine whether or not there exists a process with such a description. On the other hand from the viewpoint of dynamical processes a l.d. is much more natural and useful.

(ii) For the case of Brownian motion the result corresponding to the above was first obtained by Girsanov [9], and the technique was soon adopted in stochastic control problems [10, 11, 12, 13].

(iii) Brémaud [6] was the first to use this result, for the special case where $(x_t, \mathcal{F}_t, P)$ is a Poisson process, to obtain existence of several "self-exciting" counting processes $(x_t, \mathcal{F}_t, P_1)$. Snyder [14] and Rubin [15] introduce several jump processes through their l.d. However they do not discuss whether or not there indeed exist processes with these descriptions. The result above can be used to solve this problem.

(iv) The condition (3.24) is a non-trivial restriction. For the Brownian motion case some sufficient conditions on the local description have been derived which guarantee (3.24). See [10, 11]. For our case similar conditions are given below in §3.3.

(v) Theorem 3.3 does not address itself to the question of uniqueness of the solution. This question is discussed next.

### 3.2 Uniqueness of Solutions with Specified l.d.

To discuss uniqueness of laws of solutions it is convenient to assume that $\Omega$ is the space of sample functions and that the process $x_t$ on $\Omega$ is merely the 'evaluation' process i.e., $x_t(\omega) = \omega_t$. The probability on $\Omega$ is then the law of the process. We will be dealing with two such processes, $x_t$ and $y_t$ with the same set of sample functions but with different laws. Hence we must have two different probability spaces $(\Omega^x, \mathcal{F}^x_t, P^x)$ and $(\Omega^y, \mathcal{F}^y_t, P^y)$ where $(\Omega^x, \mathcal{F}^x_t)$ and $(\Omega^y, \mathcal{F}^y_t)$ are copies of the same family $(\Omega, \mathcal{F}_t)$. In particular, then, x and y are identical functions on $\Omega \times [0,1]$.

Since we are unable to obtain any interesting results for the infinite time interval, therefore in Theorem 3.4 and Corollary 3.1, $t \in [0,1]$.

Definition 3.1 An (intrinsic) l.d $(n,\Lambda)$ is said to have unique solutions if all fundamental processes $(x_t, \mathcal{F}_t, P)$ with l.d. $(n,\Lambda)$ have the same law.

Theorem 3.4 Let $x_t$, $y_t$, $0 \leq t \leq 1$ be fundamental processes with values in $(Z,\mathcal{Z})$, and on the (sample function) spaces $(\Omega^x, \mathcal{F}^x_t, P^x)$, $(\Omega^y, \mathcal{F}^y_t, P^y)$ respectively. Let $(n,\Lambda)$ be the l.d. of x and $((1+\phi)n,\Lambda)$ the l.d. of y for some predictable function $\phi$.

Suppose that $(n,\Lambda)$ has unique solutions, and suppose that for each $\varepsilon > 0$ there exist $Z_\varepsilon \in \mathcal{Z}$ and $k_\varepsilon < \infty$ such that

(i) $P^x(B_\varepsilon) \geqq 1 - \varepsilon$

where $B_\varepsilon = \{\omega | x_t(\omega) \in Z_\varepsilon \text{ for } 0 \leq t \leq 1\}$,

(ii) $$\int_Z\int_0^1 \left|\frac{\phi(z,\omega,s)}{1+\phi(z,\omega,s)}\right| (P^y(dz,ds) + \tilde{P}^y(dz,ds)) \leq k_\varepsilon \quad \text{for } \omega \in B_\varepsilon$$

where these are Stieltjes integrals.

Then

$$\int_\Omega \ell_1(\omega)\, P^y(d\omega) = 1 \text{ and } dP^x = \ell_1 dP^y$$

where

$$\ell_t = \mathcal{E}((\psi o Q^y)_t), \text{ and } \psi = -\frac{\phi}{1+\phi}$$

Proof The process $(m_t, \mathcal{F}^y_t, P^y)$,

$$m_t = \int_Z\int_0^t \psi(z,s)\, Q^y(dz,ds) = \int_Z\int_0^t \psi(z,s)\, [P^y(dz,ds) - \tilde{P}^y(dz,ds)]$$

is, by (i) and (ii), well-defined as a Stieltjes integral. Hence $m_t \in \mathcal{A}_0(\mathcal{F}_t^y, P^y)$ so that it is in $\mathcal{S}_{loc}(P^y)$. Therefore by §2.9 there is a unique process $(\ell_t, \mathcal{F}_t^y, P^y)$ where

$$\ell_t = \mathcal{E}(m_t).$$

Let $\varepsilon_n > 0$ be a decreasing sequence converging to 0. Define the predictable functions

$$\psi^n(z,\omega,s) = \begin{cases} \psi(z,\omega,s) \text{ if } z \in Z_{\varepsilon_n} \\ 0 \qquad \text{otherwise} \end{cases}$$

Because of (ii), the process $(m_t^n, \mathcal{F}_t^y, P^y)$ where

$$m_t^n = \int_Z\int_0^t \psi^n(z,s)\, Q^y(dz,ds)$$

is a bounded martingale. Hence by §2.9 the process $(\ell_t^n, \mathcal{F}_t^y, P^y)$ is a martingale, where

$$\ell_t^n = \mathcal{E}(m_t^n)$$

Furthermore from the definition of $\psi^n$

$$\ell_t^n(\omega) = \ell_t(\omega) \qquad \text{for all } t \text{ and } \omega \in B_{\varepsilon_n} \tag{3.26}$$

By Theorem 3.3 the fundamental process $(y_t, \mathcal{F}_t^y, P^n)$ where

$$\frac{dP^n}{dP^y} = \ell_1^n \tag{3.27}$$

has a l.d. $((1+\psi^n)(1+\phi)n,\ \Lambda)$, and by the definition of $\psi^n$ and $\psi$

$$(1+\psi^n)(1+\phi)(z,\omega,t) = 1 \quad \text{for all } t,\ \omega \in B_{\varepsilon_n} \text{ and } z \in Z_{\varepsilon_n}$$

Since $(n,\Lambda)$ has unique solutions, it follows that

$$\int_{B_{\varepsilon_n}} P^n(d\omega) = \int_{B_{\varepsilon_n}} P^x(d\omega)$$

$$\geq 1 - \varepsilon \qquad \text{by (i)}$$

From (3.26), (3.27) this implies

$$\int_{B_{\varepsilon_n}} \ell_1(\omega)\ P^y(d\omega) \geq 1 - \varepsilon$$

and since $\varepsilon > 0$ is arbitrary the assertion follows. ◻

Note: We must have $P^x(B,t)(\omega) = P^y(B,t)(\omega)$ and $\tilde{P}^y(dz,t)(\omega) = [1+\phi(z,t)] \times n(dz,t)\ \Lambda(t)$.

Corollary 3.1 (uniqueness) Let $(x_t, \mathcal{F}_t, P)$ be a fundamental process with values in $(Z, \mathcal{Z})$ and with l.d. $(n,\Lambda)$ which has unique solutions. Let $\phi$ be a predictable function such that

$$\phi(z,s) \in L^1_{loc}(\tilde{P}^x),\quad E[\mathcal{E}((\phi o Q^x)_1)] = 1$$

Suppose that $\phi$ satisfies (i) and (ii) of Theorem 3.4. Then the l.d. $((1+\phi)n,\ \Lambda))$ has unique solutions

Proof By Theorem 3.3 and the hypothesis there is a solution $(y_t, \mathcal{F}_t^y, P_1)$ with l.d. $((1+\phi)n, \Lambda)$ where $dP_1 = \mathcal{E}((\phi o Q^x)_1) dP$.

Suppose $(y_t, \mathcal{F}_t^y, P_2)$ is another solution with l.d. $((1+\phi)n, \Lambda)$. By Theorem 3.4

$$dP = \ell_1 \, dP_1 = \ell_2 \, dP_2$$

and since $dP_i = L_1 dP$ it follows that $\ell_i > 0$ a.s. $P_i$, $i=1,2$. Evidently then $P_2 = P_1$. ⌑

Remark 3.5 (i) Theorem 3.4 is inspired by [9,Lemma 7] and the development there suggests how the result can be generalized.

(ii) Condition (i) and (ii) of Theorem 3.4 are usually easy to verify in practice. Consider a special case of the fundamental example where $(x_t, \mathcal{F}_t^x, P^x)$ is a Poisson process with rate 1. Then Z is the space of integers and $y_t$ is then a counting process with local 'intensity' rate $1 + \phi(\omega,t)$. Suppose $\phi(\omega,t)$ is expressed explicitly as a function of the past of x i.e., $\phi(\omega,t) = f(x_{[0,t]}(\omega),t)$. Then the conditions (i) and (ii) are satisfied if, for instance, there is an increasing function $f_0$ such that

$$|f(x_{[0,t]},t)| + \frac{1}{|1+f(x_{[0,t]},t)|} \le f_0(N) \text{ when } |x_t| \le N.$$

For a similar condition in the Brownian motion case see [11]

(iii) Corollary 3.1 extends in an obvious way to the time interval $R_+$. However Theorem 3.4 does not.

### 3.3 Sufficient Conditions

Let $(x_t, \mathcal{F}_t, P)$ be a fundamental process with values in $(Z, \mathcal{Z})$ and with intrinsic description $(n(dz,t), \Lambda(dt))$. Let $\phi(z,t) \in L^1_{loc}(\tilde{P})$ and define the process $L_t$, $t \in [0,1]$ by

$$L_t = \prod_{\substack{s \leq t \\ x_{s-} \neq x_s}} [1+\phi(x_s,s)] \exp[-\int_Z \int_0^t \phi(z,s)\, \tilde{P}(dz,ds)] \tag{3.28}$$

then $L_t$ also satisfies

$$dL_t = L_{t-} dm_t, \tag{3.29}$$

where,

$$m_t = (\phi o Q)_t \tag{3.30}$$

We assume that $1 + \phi(z,t) \geqq 0$, then $L_t \geq 0$, $L_t$ is a supermartingale and

$$E(L_1) \leqq 1$$

The three results below state conditions on $\phi$ which guarantee

$$E(L_1) = 1$$

The following assumption is made throughout this subsection.

Assumption 3.1 There exists an increasing function $\mu$: $R_+ \to R_+$ such that

$$\tilde{P}(Z,t) \leq \mu(t) \text{ a.s.} \tag{3.31}$$

(Note that this implies $\tilde{P}(B,t) \leq \mu(t)$ for all $B \in \mathcal{Z}$).

Proposition 3.2 Suppose that for some $K < \infty$

$$|\phi| \leq K \tag{3.32}$$

Then $E(L_1) = 1$.

Proof From (3.28), (3.31) and (3.32)

$$L_t \leq (K+1) \exp K\mu(t)$$

Hence

$$|L_{t-}\ \phi(z,t)|^2 \leq K^2(K+1)^2 \exp 2K\ \mu(t),$$

so that

$$E\int_Z\int_0^1 |L_{t-}\phi(z,t)|^2\ \tilde{P}(dz,dt) \leq E\int_0^1 K^2(K+1)^2 \exp 2K\mu(t)\ \mu(dt) < \infty,$$

which implies that

$$L_{t-}\ \phi(z,t) \in L^2(\tilde{P})$$

By §2.10, $L_t$ is a square-integrable martingale, and in particular

$E(L_1) = E(L_0) = 1$ ⌑

Proposition 3.3 Suppose that for some $K < \infty$

$$\int_Z\int_0^1 (1+\phi(z,t))\ [\ell n(1+\phi(z,t))]^2\ \tilde{P}(dz,dt) \leq K \text{ a.s.} \tag{3.33}$$

Then $E(L_1) = 1$

<u>Proof</u> Define the function $\phi^n$ so that

$$\phi^n(z,\omega,t) = \begin{cases} \phi(z,\omega,t) & \text{if } \frac{1}{n} < 1 + \phi(z,\omega,t) < n \\ 0 & \text{otherwise} \end{cases}$$

and let $L_t^n$ be obtained from (3.28) by replacing $\phi$ with $\phi^n$. By Proposition 3.2 $E(L_1^n) = 1$ and it is clear that $L_1^n$ converges to $L_1$ in probability. Hence by [3, II. T21] $E(L_1) = 1$ if and only if the set of r.v.s $\{L_1^n | n=1,2,\ldots\}$ is uniformly integrable. Define the probability measures $P_n$ by

$$\frac{dP_n}{dP}(\omega) = L_1^n(\omega).$$

By Theorem 3.3 $(x_t, \mathcal{F}_t, P_n)$, $t \in [0,1]$, is a fundamental process with l.d. $((1+\phi^n)n, \Lambda)$ and so the corresponding martingales are given by

$$Q_n(B,t) = P(B,t) - \tilde{P}_n(B,t) = P(B,t) - \int_B \int_0^t (1+\phi^n(z,s))\, \tilde{P}(dz,ds)$$

Because $\phi^n$ is bounded and because of (3.31), $Q_n \in \mathcal{M}^2(P_n)$. For later reference define $\xi_t^n \in \mathcal{M}^2(P_n)$ by

$$\xi_t^n = (\ell n(1+\phi^n)\ oQ_n)_t,$$

and note that

$$\langle \xi^n, \xi^n \rangle_t = \int_Z \int_0^t [\ell n(1+\phi^n)]^2 (1+\phi^n)\, \tilde{P}(dz,ds) \tag{3.34}$$

We are ready to show that $\{L_1^n\}$ is a uniformly integrable family. Fix $M < \infty$. Firstly,

$$\int_{\{L_1^n > M\}} L_1^n(\omega)\ P(d\omega) = P_n\{L_1^n > M\}$$

Next, $\{L_1^n > M\}$

$$= \{\exp\left[\int_Z\int_0^1 \ell n(1+\phi^n)P(dz,ds)\right]\times\exp\left[-\int_Z\int_0^1 \phi^n\tilde{P}(dz,ds)\right] > M\} \text{ from (3.28)}$$

$$= \{\exp\left[\int_Z\int_0^1 \ell n(1+\phi^n)[P(dz,ds) - (1+\phi^n)\ \tilde{P}(dz,ds)]\right]\times\exp\left[\int_Z\int_0^1 [(1+\phi^n)\times \ell n(1+\phi^n) - \phi^n]\ \tilde{P}(dz,ds)\right] > M\}$$

$$\subset \{\int_Z\int_0^1 \ell n(1+\phi^n)\ [P(dz,ds) - (1+\phi^n)\ \tilde{P}(dz,ds)] > \frac{1}{2}\ \ell n\ M\}$$

$$\cup \{\int_Z\int_0^1 [(1+\phi^n)\ \ell n(1+\phi^n) - \phi^n]\ \tilde{P}(dz,ds) > \frac{1}{2}\ \ell n\ M\}$$

$= F_1 \cup F_2$ say.

So

$$P_n\{L_1^m > M\} \leq P_n(F_1) + P_n(F_2)$$

From (3.33) it is immediate that $P_n(F_2) = 0$ for all sufficiently large M. On the other hand $F_2 = \{\xi^n > \frac{1}{2}\ \ell n\ M\}$ so by the Chebychev inequality,

$$P_n(F_2) \le \frac{4}{(\ell n M)^2} \int_\Omega \langle \xi^n, \xi^n \rangle_1 \, dP_n$$

$$\le \frac{4}{(\ell n M)^2} K \qquad \text{by (3.34), (3.33)}$$

It follows that for all $n, P_n \{L_1^n > M\} \to 0$ as $M \to \infty$, i.e. $\{L^n\}$ is uniformly integrable ⌑

For the next proposition express $\tilde{P}(dz,ds) = n(dz,s)\, \tilde{P}(Z,ds)$ (see §2.11)

Proposition 3.4 Suppose that there exist $\alpha > 1$ and $K$, $K'$ finite such that

$$\int_Z (1+\phi(z,t))^\alpha n(dz,t) \le K + K'[P(Z,t) + \tilde{P}(Z,t)] \text{ a.s.} \tag{3.35}$$

and suppose that for all $0 < M < \infty$

$$E \exp[M\, P(Z,1)] < \infty \tag{3.36}$$

Then for $1 < \gamma \le \alpha^{\frac{1}{2}}$,

$$\sup_{t \in [0,1]} E\, L_t^\gamma < \infty, \tag{3.37}$$

in particular $E\, L_1 = 1$.

Proof If (3.37) is satisfied then by [8,II.T22] the family is $\{L_t;\ 0 \le t \le 1\}$ is uniformly integrable and so by [8,VI.T6] $L_t$ is a uniformly integrable martingale, hence $E(L_1) = 1$.

For $\alpha^{\frac{1}{2}} \geq \gamma > 1$ define

$$f_t(\gamma) = \exp[\gamma \int_Z \int_0^t \ell n(1+\phi)\ Q(dz,ds) + \int_Z \int_0^t [\gamma\ \ell n(1+\phi) + \frac{1}{\gamma} - \frac{(1+\phi)^{\gamma^2}}{\gamma}]\ \tilde{P}(dz,ds)],$$

$$g_t(\gamma) = \exp[\int_Z \int_0^t [-\gamma\phi - \frac{1}{\gamma} + \frac{(1+\phi)^{\gamma^2}}{\gamma}]\ \tilde{P}(dz,ds)$$

First of all

$$f_t(\gamma)\ g_t(\gamma) = \exp[\gamma \int_Z \int_0^t \ell n(1+\phi) Q(dz,ds) - \int_Z \int_0^t \gamma(\phi - \ell n(1+\phi))\ \tilde{P}(dz,ds)]$$

$$= L_t^{\gamma} \quad \text{by } (3.28)$$

Next it can be checked by substitution in (3.28) that $[f_t(\gamma)]^{\gamma}$ is obtained from (3.28) by replacing $(1+\phi)$ with $(1+\phi)^{\gamma^2}$. Hence if $\gamma^2 < 2$ so that $(1+\phi)^{\gamma^2} \in L^1_{loc}(\tilde{P})$, then we must have

$$E[f_t(\gamma)]^{\gamma} \leq 1 \text{ for all } t$$

Now by Hölder's inequality

$$E\ L_t^{\gamma} \leq (E[f_t(\gamma)]^{\gamma})^{\frac{1}{\gamma}}\ (E[g_t(\gamma)]^{\frac{\gamma}{\gamma-1}})^{\frac{\gamma-1}{\gamma}}$$

so that

$$E\, L_t^\gamma \le \left(E[g_t(\gamma)]^{\frac{\gamma}{\gamma-1}}\right)^{\frac{\gamma-1}{\gamma}}$$

Next,

$$[g_t(\gamma)]^{\frac{\gamma}{\gamma-1}} \le \exp \int_Z\int_0^t [\gamma - \frac{1}{\gamma} + \frac{(1+\phi)^{\gamma^2}}{\gamma}]\, \tilde{P}(dz,ds)$$

since $1+\phi \ge 0$ implies $-\gamma\phi \le \gamma$

$$\le \exp[\frac{\gamma^2-1}{\gamma}\, \mu(t) + \int_0^t \{K + K'(P(Z,s) + \tilde{P}(Z,s))\}\, \tilde{P}(Z,ds)]$$

from (3.31), (3.35)

$$\le \exp[(\frac{\gamma^2-1}{\gamma} + K + \frac{K'}{2}\, \mu(t) + K'\, P(Z,t))\, \mu(t)] \text{ from (3.31)}$$

$$\le \exp \beta \exp K'\, \mu(1)\, P(Z,1) \text{ for some constant } \beta$$

Hence

$$E\, L_t^\gamma \le (\exp \beta)\, E[\exp K'\, \mu(1)\, P(Z,1)]$$

and the result follows from (3.36). ⌑

Remark 3.6 (i) Suppose $(x_t, \mathcal{F}_t, P)$ is as in the fundamental example with corresponding increasing processes $\tilde{p}_1(t), \ldots, \tilde{p}_n(t)$. Then Assumption 3.1 translates into the following: there exists an increasing function $\Lambda: R_+ \to R_+$ such that

$$\sum_{i=1}^n \tilde{P}_i(t) \le \Lambda(t) \text{ a.s.}$$

Similarly (3.35), (3.36) become: there exist $\alpha > 1$ and $K, K'$ such that

$$\sum_{i=1}^{n} (1+\phi_i(t))^{\alpha} \leq K + K' \sum_{i=1}^{n} (p_i(t) + \tilde{p}_i(t)) \quad . \tag{3.38}$$

(ii) Now suppose that $(x_t, \mathcal{A}_t, P)$ is a standard Poisson process. Then (3.38) becomes

$$(1+\phi(t))^{\alpha} \leq K + K'(x(t)+t) \quad .$$

Suppose that $\phi(t) = c(x(t-))^{\alpha}$ for some $\alpha < 1$. According to Feller [27, p.452] a counting process $x_t$ with rate $[1+\phi(t)]$ has infinitely many jumps in a finite interval, so that it <u>cannot</u> be a fundamental process. Thus Proposition 3.4 is false if $\alpha < 1$. We have been unable to resolve the case of "linear" growth, i.e., $\alpha = 1$.

<u>Remark 3.7</u> Propositions 3.2, 3.3, 3.4 are inspired by corresponding results in [6], [24], [28] respectively.

## 3.4 A Class of Poisson-measure Processes

In order to apply the transformation technique presented earlier one must begin with a fundamental process (with a known l.d.) whose existence is guaranteed. In this section we present a large class of such processes for which the increasing processes $\tilde{P}(B,t)$ are deterministic.

Let $(Z,\mathcal{Z})$ be any Blackwell space and let $\mu$ be any positive measure on the space $(Z \times R_+, \mathcal{Z} \otimes \mathcal{B})$ where $\mathcal{B}$ is the Borel field on $R_+$. Suppose that for all $t < \infty$, $\mu(Z \times [0,t]) < \infty$.

Let $\Omega'$ be the space of all (non-negative) integer-valued measures N on $(Z \times R_+, \mathcal{Z} \otimes \mathcal{B})$. For each $T \in R_+$ let $\mathcal{F}'_T$ be the family of all subsets of $\Omega'$ of the form

$$\{N \in \Omega' \mid N(C) \in K\}$$

where $C \in \mathcal{Z} \otimes \mathcal{B}[0,T]$ and $K \subset I_+$, the set of non-negative integers. Evidently $\mathcal{F}'_T$ is a $\sigma$-algebra on $\Omega'$. Let

$$\mathcal{F}' = \bigvee_T \mathcal{F}'_T \quad .$$

Now, for each $T$ define the set function $P'_T$ on $(\Omega', \mathcal{F}'_T)$ by

$$P'_T(N(C) \in K) = \sum_{k \in K} \frac{\mu(C)^k}{k!} e^{-\mu(C)} \quad .$$

Note that $\mu(C) < \infty$ since $C \subset Z \times [0,T]$. By [31] $P'_T$ defines a probability measure on $(\Omega', \mathcal{F}'_T)$. Furthermore if $C_1$, $C_2$ are in $Z \times [0,T]$ and $C_1 \cap C_2 = \emptyset$, then the two random variables defined by

$$N \mapsto N(C_1) \ , \quad N \mapsto N(C_2) \ , \quad N \in \Omega'$$

are independent. Finally the random variable $N \mapsto N(C)$ has a Poisson distribution. For $A \in \mathcal{Z}$, consider the counting process $P'(A,t)$, $t \in R_+$ defined on the family $(\Omega', \mathcal{F}'_{t \wedge T}, P'_T)$, by

$$P'(A,t)(N) = N(A \times [0, t \wedge T]) \quad .$$

Evidently $E(P'(A,t)) = \mu(A \times [0,t \wedge T])$, and if $A_1 \cap A_2 = \emptyset$ then $P'(A_1,t)$ and $P'(A_2,t)$ are independent processes.

Next by Moyal [32], there exists a jump process $x_t$, $t \in R_+$, with values in $(Z,\mathcal{Z})$, defined on a family $(\Omega,\mathcal{F}_t^x,P_T)$ such that i) $(\Omega,\mathcal{F}_t^x,P_T)$ is isomorphic to $(\Omega',\mathcal{F}'_{t\wedge T},P'_T)$ and ii) the counting processes $P^x(A,t)$ corresponding to $x_t$ are "isomorphic" to the processes $P'(A,t)$ constructed above. Furthermore

$$\tilde{P}^x(A,t) = \mu(A\times[0,t\wedge T]) \quad .$$

To finish the construction we merely note that if $S < T$ then the probability measure $P_S$ on $(\Omega,\mathcal{F}_S^x)$ coincides with the restriction of $P_T$ (defined on $\mathcal{F}_T^x$) to $\mathcal{F}_S^x$. By the Kolmogorov consistency theorem therefore, there exists a probability measure $P$ on $(\Omega,\mathcal{F}_\infty^x)$ such that

$$\tilde{P}^x(A,t) = \mu(A\times[0,t]) \ , \quad A \in \mathcal{Z}, \quad t \in R_+ \quad . \tag{3.39}$$

However the process $x_t$ may <u>not</u> be a fundamental process. To guarantee this we must be sure that the jump times are totally inaccessible. As mentioned in §2.9 this is equivalent to the requirement that $\tilde{P}^x(A,t)$ have continuous sample paths, and hence, from (3.39), to the requirement that $\mu(A\times[0,t])$ be continuous in $t$ for each fixed $A$. We summarize the main conclusions as follows.

<u>Theorem 3.5</u> Let $(Z,\mathcal{Z})$ be a Blackwell space and let $\mu$ be any non-negative measure on $(Z\times R_+,\mathcal{Z}\otimes\mathcal{B})$ such that

(i) $\mu(Z\times[0,t]) < \infty$ for all $t \in R_+$,

(ii) $\mu(A\times[0,t])$ is continuous in $t$ for all $A \in \mathcal{Z}$.

Then there exists a fundamental process $x_t$ on a family $(\Omega,\mathcal{F}_t^x,P)$ with values in $(Z,\mathcal{Z})$ such that

$$\tilde{P}^x(A,t) = \mu(A\times[0,t]) \ , \quad A \in \mathcal{Z}, \quad t \in R_+ \quad .$$

Remark 3.8 (i) The $x_t$ process has independent increments in the sense that the $P(A,t)$ have independent increments. If $x_t$ were vector-valued this would indeed imply that $x_t$ has independent increments in the usual sense.

(ii) The most useful version of this result would be when $\mu$ is a product measure $\mu(dz,ds) = n(dz)\,\Lambda(ds)$ where $n$ is a finite measure on $(Z,\mathcal{Z})$ and $\Lambda(t)$ is a continuous increasing function on $R_+$, in which case $(n, \Lambda)$ would be a Lévy system.

## 4. Detection

The prototypical detection problem in communication theory is the following. We observe a sample $x_t(\omega)$, $0 \leq t < \infty$ of a stochastic process. The process is known to be governed by one of two laws $P$ or $P_1$. Based upon the observed sample one has to decide which of the two hypotheses, $P$ or $P_1$, is true. The term "detection" arises from a particular instance of this hypothesis testing model, namely, when the process $x$ has the representation

$$\begin{aligned} dx_t &= \text{white noise} \quad &, \text{ under } P \\ dx_t &= \text{white noise} + s_t \quad &, \text{ under } P_1 \end{aligned} \tag{4.1}$$

where $s_t$ is called the "signal". Thus deciding which hypothesis is true is, for the example, equivalent to "detecting" whether the signal is present (hypothesis $P_1$) or absent (hypothesis $P$).

Very recently this problem has been considered for the case where $x_t$ is a counting process under $P_1$ and a Poisson process under $P$ [6,7,15, 16,17]. The case where $x_t$ is a Markov chain under $P$ has also been discussed [6]. We generalize these results by considering problems where $x_t$ is a fundamental process.

A well-established procedure for judging which hypothesis is true consists in first calculating the "likelihood" ratio $\frac{dP_1}{dP}(x(\omega))$ and then in accepting $P_1$ if $\frac{dP_1}{dP} > \alpha$ and rejecting $P_1$ otherwise. The selection of the "threshold" $\alpha$ is discussed in [18]. The procedure is often called the "threshold detector".

Evidently for this procedure to be meaningful one must assume $P_1 << P$. Also to obtain results of practical value one must specify precisely how the "signal" affects the observation, as for instance in (4.1) where it is assumed to be additive. We proceed to the mathematical model.

Let $(\Omega, \mathcal{F}_t)$, $t \in R_+$, be a family of spaces and $P$, $P_1$ two probabilities on $(\Omega, \mathcal{F})$. The observed process is a family of measurable functions $x_t: (\Omega, \mathcal{F}_t) \to (Z, \mathcal{Z})$ such that $(x_t, \mathcal{F}_t, P)$ and $(x_t, \mathcal{F}_t, P_1)$ are both fundamental processes. The processes $P$, $\tilde{P}$, $Q$ and $\tilde{P}^x$, $Q^x$ are the extrinsic and intrinsic (i.e., relative to $\mathcal{F}_t^x$) processes corresponding to $(x_t, P)$. Similarly $P_1$, $\tilde{P}_1$, $\tilde{P}_1^x$ etc. correspond to $(x_t, P_1)$. The extrinsic and intrinsic l.d.'s are $(n, \Lambda)$, $(n^x, \Lambda^x)$ for $(x_t, P)$ and $(n_1, \Lambda_1)$, $(n_1^x, \Lambda_1^x)$ for $(x_t, P_1)$.

We now give the model corresponding to the "signal plus noise" model of (4.1).

<u>Assumption 4.1</u> There exist $\mathcal{F}_t^x$-predictable processes $\mu(B, \omega, t)$, $B \in \mathcal{Z}$, and $\mathcal{F}_t$- predictable processes $g(z, \omega, s)$ and $g_1(z, \omega, s)$ such that $E|g(z,s)| < \infty$ and $E_1|g_1(z,s)| < \infty$ for all $z$, $s$, and

$$\tilde{P}(B,t) = n(B,t)\Lambda(t) = \int_B \int_0^t g(z,\omega,s)\mu(dz,\omega,ds)$$

$$\tilde{P}_1(B,t) = n_1(B,t)\Lambda_1(t) = \int_B \int_0^t g_1(z,\omega,s)\mu(dz,\omega,ds)$$

where the integrals are Stieltjes integrals.

<u>Interpretation:</u> In communication theory terms we can say that the "jump rates" $P(B,t)$ are "modulated" by the signal through the functions $g$, $g_1$.

<u>Definition 4.1</u> Let $E(g(z,t)|\mathcal{F}_t^x) = \hat{g}(z,t)$ and $E_1(g_1(z,t)|\mathcal{F}_t^x) = \hat{g}_1(z,t)$.

<u>Proposition 4.1</u>
$$\tilde{P}^x(B,t) = \int_B \int_0^t \hat{g}(z,s)\mu(dz,ds) \quad \text{a.s.}$$

$$\tilde{P}_1^x(B,t) = \int_B \int_0^t \hat{g}_1(z,s)\mu(dz,ds) \quad \text{a.s.}$$

<u>Proof</u> It is enough to prove the first assertion since the proof for the second is identical. Fix $B \in \mathcal{Z}$. We know that

$$Q(B,t) = P(B,t) - \int_B \int_0^t g(z,s)\mu(dz,ds) \quad \in \mathcal{M}^2_{loc}(\mathcal{F}_t, P) \tag{4.2}$$

$$Q^x(B,t) = P(B,t) - \tilde{P}^x(B,t) \quad \in \mathcal{M}^2_{loc}(\mathcal{F}^x_t, P) \quad . \tag{4.3}$$

Let $T_n$, $n = 0,1,\ldots$ be the jump times of $x_t$. The $T_n$ are stopping times for the family $(\mathcal{F}_t)$ as well as for $(\mathcal{F}^x_t)$. Furthermore $E|P(B,t\wedge T_n)| \le n$. Hence $E|Q(B,t\wedge T_n)| < \infty$, and we can define a process $(\hat{Q}(B,t), \mathcal{F}^x_t, P)$ such that

$$\hat{Q}(B,t\wedge T_n) = E(Q(B,t\wedge T_n) | \mathcal{F}^x_t)$$

and it is trivial that $\hat{Q}(B,t\wedge T_n) \in \mathcal{M}^1(\mathcal{F}^x_t, P)$. Now $P(B,t)$ and $\mu(z,t)$ are $\mathcal{F}^x_t$-measurable, hence

$$\hat{Q}(B,t\wedge T_n) = P(B,t\wedge T_n) - \int_B \int_0^{t\wedge T_n} E(g(z,s) | \mathcal{F}^x_t)\mu(dz,ds) \quad .$$

Subtracting this from (4.3) implies that

$$\tilde{P}^x(B,t\wedge T_n) - \int_B \int_0^{t\wedge T_n} E(g(z,s) | \mathcal{F}^x_t)\mu(dz,ds) \quad \in \mathcal{M}^1(\mathcal{F}^x_t, P) \quad .$$

On the other hand it can be directly verified that

$$\int_B \int_0^{t\wedge T_n} [E(g(z,s) | \mathcal{F}^x_t) - \hat{g}(z,s)]\mu(dz,ds) \quad \in \mathcal{M}^1(\mathcal{F}^x_t, P) \quad .$$

Therefore

$$\tilde{P}^x(B,t\wedge T_n) - \int_B\int_0^{t\wedge T_n} \hat{g}(z,s)\mu(dz,ds) \in \mathcal{M}^1(\mathcal{F}_t^x,P) \quad .$$

But this is a continuous process. Hence it must vanish, i.e.,

$$\tilde{P}^x(B,t) = \int_B\int_0^t \hat{g}(z,s)\mu(dz,ds) \quad . \qquad ¤$$

Remark 4.1 The processes $(\hat{Q}(B,t),\mathcal{F}_t^x,P)$ are called the innovations processes of the process $(x_t,\mathcal{F}_t,P)$, in analogy with the Brownian motion case [21]. These processes will be used in the next section.

Theorem 4.1 Suppose that $P_1 << P$. Let $L_t = E(\frac{dP_1}{dP}\Big|\mathcal{F}_t^x)$ be the likelihood ratio and let

$$T = \inf\{t\,|\,L_t = 0 \text{ or } L_{t-} = 0\} \quad .$$

Then there is a sequence of $\mathcal{F}_t^x$ s.t.'s $S_k \uparrow T$ a.s. $P$ such that

$$\frac{\hat{g}_1(z,s)}{\hat{g}(z,s)} I_{\{s\leq S_k\}} \in L^1_{loc}(\tilde{P}^x)$$

and

$$L_{t\wedge S_k} = \prod_{\substack{s\leq t\wedge S_k \\ x_{s-}\neq x_s}} [\frac{\hat{g}_1(x_s,s)}{\hat{g}(x_s,s)}]\exp[-\int_Z\int_0^{t\wedge S_k} (\frac{\hat{g}_1(z,s)}{\hat{g}(z,s)} - 1)\hat{g}(z,s)\mu(dz,ds)] \text{ . (4.4)}$$

Proof By Theorem 3.1 there exists s.t.'s $S_k \uparrow T$ and an $\mathcal{F}_t^x$-predictable function $\phi$ such that $L_{t\wedge S_k}$ is given by (3.11), and by Theorem 3.2 the intrinsic l.d. of $(x_t,P_1)$ is $((1+\phi)n^x,\Lambda^x)$ where $(n^x,\Lambda^x)$ is the intrinsic l.d. of $(x_t,P)$; so from Proposition 4.1 we can conclude that

$$(1+\phi(z,s))n^x(dz,s)\Lambda^x(ds) = (1+\phi(z,s))\hat{g}(z,s)\mu(dz,ds)$$

$$= \hat{g}_1(z,s)\mu(dz,ds) = n_1^x(dz,s)\Lambda_1^x(ds) \quad .$$

Therefore

$$1+\phi(z,s) = \frac{\hat{g}_1(z,s)}{\hat{g}(z,s)}$$

which upon substitution into (3.11) yields (4.4). ◻

Corollary 4.1 Suppose in the above that $x_t$ is as in the fundamental example of §2.12. Suppose there exists a $\mathcal{F}_t^x$-predictable process $\mu(t)$, and $\mathcal{F}_t$-predictable processes $\lambda^i(t)$, $\lambda_1^i(t)$, $1 \le i \le n$, such that

$$\tilde{p}_i(t) = \int_0^t \lambda^i(s)\mu(ds) \, , \qquad \tilde{p}_{i,1}(t) = \int_0^t \lambda_1^i(s)\mu(ds) \, , \qquad 1 \le i \le n \quad .$$

Then the formula (4.4) changes to

$$L_{t\wedge S_k} = \prod_{i=1}^{n} \{ \prod_{\substack{s \le t\wedge S_k \\ (x_{s-},x_s) \in \sigma_i}} [\frac{\hat{\lambda}_1^i(s)}{\hat{\lambda}^i(s)}] \times \exp[-\int_0^{t\wedge S_k} (\frac{\hat{\lambda}_1^i(s)}{\hat{\lambda}^i(s)} - 1)\hat{\lambda}^i(s)\mu(ds)]\} \, . \tag{4.5}$$

Proof Follows from Theorem 4.1 and Remark 3.2(iii). ◻

Remark 4.2 (i) Very special cases of (4.5) have appeared in the recent literature. Suppose in Corollary 4.1 that $(x_t, \mathcal{F}_t^x, P)$ is a Poisson process with rate $\lambda_o$. Then in (4.5) $n = 1$, $\hat{\lambda}(s) \equiv \lambda_o$, $\mu(ds) \equiv ds$ and (4.5) becomes

$$L_{t\wedge S_k} = \left[ \prod_{\substack{s \le t\wedge S_k \\ x_{s-} \ne x_s}} \frac{\hat{\lambda}_1(s)}{\lambda_o} \right] \exp[-\int_0^{t\wedge S_k} (\hat{\lambda}_1(s)-\lambda_o)ds] \quad . \tag{4.6}$$

This version together with the comment in footnote 5 yields the result in [16, p.95]. Actually in [16] some strong unnecessary assumptions are also imposed. (4.6) has also been derived in [6] and [7]. Formula (4.5) for the case $n = 1$ and $\mu(ds) \equiv ds$ appears in [15], although the derivation is not satisfactory, and various additional assumptions, some of them unverifiable, were made there.

(ii) In [6] we can also find (4.5) for the special case where $(x_t, \mathcal{F}_t^x, P)$ is a Markov chain, in which case the $\hat{\lambda}^i$ can be interpreted in terms of various transition probabilities as suggested in §2.11, §2.12.

We apply formulas (4.5) and (4.6) to calculate the mutual information between two fundamental processes. Let $x_t$ and $x'_t$ be two such processes on $(\Omega, \mathcal{F}_t, P)$ with values in $(Z, \mathcal{Z})$ and $(Z', \mathcal{Z}')$ respectively. Let $\mu(dz,ds)$ and $\mu'(dz',ds)$ be $\mathcal{F}_t^x$- and $\mathcal{F}_t^{x'}$-predictable processes and $g(z,s)$, $g'(z',s)$ be two $\mathcal{F}_t$-predictable processes with finite expectation such that

$$n(dz,s)\Lambda(ds) = g(z,s)\mu(dz,ds)$$

$$n'(dz',s)\Lambda'(ds) = g'(z',s)\mu'(dz',ds) \quad .$$

Let $P_x$, $P_{x'}$ denote the restrictions of $P$ to $\mathcal{F}^x$ and $\mathcal{F}^{x'}$ respectively. Assume that $\mathcal{F}_t = \mathcal{F}_t^x \otimes \mathcal{F}_t^{x'}$, the product $\sigma$-algebra and let $P_{xx'} = P_x \otimes P_{x'}$ denote the product measure on $\mathcal{F} = \mathcal{F}^x \otimes \mathcal{F}^{x'}$. It is trivial that $P << P_{xx'}$. Assume further that $P_{xx'} << P$. The mutual information between $x$, $x'$ is the quantity

$$I(x,x') = E(\ell n \frac{dP}{dP_{xx'}}) \quad .$$

Let

$$\hat{g}(z,t) = E(g(z,t)|\mathcal{F}_t^x) ,$$

$$\hat{g}'(z',t) = E(g'(z',t)|\mathcal{F}_t^{x'}) .$$

By Remark 3.2(i),

$$\frac{g}{\hat{g}} \in L^1_{loc}(\tilde{P}) , \qquad \frac{g'}{\hat{g}'} \in L^1_{loc}(\tilde{P}') .$$

Assume further that

$$\ln(\frac{g}{\hat{g}}) \in L^1(\tilde{P}) , \qquad \ln(\frac{g'}{\hat{g}'}) \in L^1(\tilde{P}') .$$

Then by Theorem 4.1,

$$\frac{dP}{dP_{xx'}} = \{ \prod_{x_{s-} \neq x_s} [\frac{g(x_s,s)}{\hat{g}(x_s,s)}] \exp[-\int_Z\int_0^\infty (\frac{g(z,s)}{\hat{g}(z,s)} - 1)\hat{g}(z,s)\mu(dz,ds)]\} \cdot$$

$$\times \{ \prod_{x'_{s-} \neq x'_s} [\frac{g'(x'_s,s)}{\hat{g}'(x'_s,s)}] \exp[-\int_{Z'}\int_0^\infty (\frac{g'(z',s)}{\hat{g}'(z',s)} - 1)\hat{g}'(z,s)\mu'(dz',ds)]\}$$

so that

$$\ln\frac{dP}{dP_{xx'}} = \sum_{x_{s-} \neq x_s} \ln(\frac{g(x_s,s)}{\hat{g}(x_s,s)}) - \int_Z\int_0^\infty (\frac{g(z,s)}{\hat{g}(z,s)} - 1)\hat{g}(z,s)\mu(dz,ds)$$

$$+ \sum_{x'_s \neq x_s} \ln(\frac{g'(x'_s,s)}{\hat{g}'(x'_s,s)}) - \int_{Z'}\int_0^\infty (\frac{g'(z',s)}{\hat{g}'(z',s)} - 1)\hat{g}'(dz',ds)\mu'(dz',ds) . \tag{4.7}$$

Since $\ln(\frac{g}{\hat{g}}) \in L^1(\tilde{P})$ therefore

$$\sum_{x_{s-} \neq x_s} \ln(\frac{g(x_s,s)}{\hat{g}(x_s,s)}) - \int_Z\int_0^\infty \ln(\frac{g(z,s)}{\hat{g}(z,s)})g(z,s)\mu(dz,ds)$$

$$= \int_Z\int_0^\infty \ln(\frac{g(z,s)}{\hat{g}(z,s)})[P(dz,ds) - \tilde{P}(dz,ds)] \quad \in \quad \mathcal{M}^1(\mathcal{F}_t,P)$$

so that

$$E[\sum_{x_{s-}\neq x_s} \ell n(\frac{g(x_s,s)}{\hat{g}(x_s,s)})] = E\int_Z\int_0^\infty \ell n(\frac{g(z,s)}{\hat{g}(z,s)})g(z,s)\mu(dz,ds) \quad .$$

Similarly

$$E[\sum_{x'_{s-}\neq x_s} \ell n(\frac{g'(x'_s,s)}{\hat{g}'(x'_s,s)})] = E\int_{Z'}\int_0^\infty \ell n(\frac{g'(z',s)}{\hat{g}'(z',s)})g'(z',s)\mu'(dz',ds) \quad .$$

Taking expectations in (4.7) and substituting these relations gives the following result.

<u>Theorem 4.2</u> Suppose $P_{xx'} << P$ and $\ell n(g/\hat{g}) \in L^1(\tilde{P})$, $\ell n(g'/\hat{g}') \in L^1(\tilde{P})$. Then

$$I(x,x') = E[\int_Z\int_0^\infty (\ell n\,\frac{g(z,s)}{\hat{g}(z,s)} + \frac{\hat{g}(z,s)}{g(z,s)} - 1)g(z,s)\mu(dz,ds)$$

$$+ \int_{Z'}\int_0^\infty (\ell n\,\frac{g'(z',s)}{\hat{g}'(z',s)} + \frac{\hat{g}'(z',s)}{g'(z',s)} - 1)g'(z',s)\mu'(dz',ds)] \qquad (4.8)$$

<u>Remark 4.3</u>. This result for the case where x, x' are both counting processes has appeared in [6].

## 5. Filtering

A popular model for estimation and filtering problems in communication and control is where the observed process, $x_t$, depends upon the "signal" or "state" process, $y_t$, according to

$$dy_t = g(y_t)dt + dB_1(t)$$
$$dx_t = f(x_t, y_t)dt + dB_2(t)$$

where $B_1$, $B_2$ are Brownian motions. The problem is to determine $E(y_t | \mathcal{F}_t^x)$. Note that in the above $y_t$ is a semi-martingale.

We begin this section by examining this situation when $(x_t, \mathcal{F}_t, P)$ is a fundamental process with values in $(Z, \mathcal{Z})$. We need a preliminary fact.

Lemma 5.1 Let $(m_t, \mathcal{F}_t, P) \in \mathcal{M}^2(\mathcal{F}_t, P)$. Then there exists an $\mathcal{F}_t$-predictable process $h(z,t)$ such that

$$E \int_Z \int_0^\infty |h(z,t)|^2 \tilde{P}(dz,dt) < \infty \tag{5.1}$$

and

$$\langle m_t, Q(B,t)\rangle = \int_B \int_0^t h(z,s)\tilde{P}(dz,ds) \quad \text{for all } B \in \mathcal{Z} . \tag{5.2}$$

Proof. The set, say $L$, of all processes $(h\circ Q)_t$ where $h$ is any predictable process satisfying (5.1) is easily shown to be a stable subspace of $\mathcal{M}^2(\mathcal{F}_t, P)$ (see [19] for a definition of a stable subspace). Therefore by [19], there exists a unique decomposition of $m_t$, $m_t = n_t + \ell_t$, with $\ell_t \in L$ and $\langle n_t, \ell_t'\rangle \equiv 0$ for all $\ell_t' \in L$. Let $\ell_t = (h\circ Q)_t$ and the assertion follows. ⌑

Assumption 5.1 There exist $\mathcal{F}_t^x$-predictable processes $\mu(B,t)$, $B \in \mathcal{Z}$ and an $\mathcal{F}_t$-predictable process $g(z,t)$ such that

$$\tilde{P}(B,t) = \int_B\int_0^t g(z,s)\mu(dz,ds) \quad . \tag{5.3}$$

Notation: In the following for any process $(f_t, \mathcal{F}_t, P)$, $\hat{f}_t = E(f_t | \mathcal{F}_t^x)$

Theorem 5.1 Let $(x_t, \mathcal{F}_t, P)$ be a fundamental process satisfying Assumption 5.1. Let $(y_t, \mathcal{F}_t, P) \in \mathcal{S}(\mathcal{F}_t)$ have the representation

$$y_t = y_o + a_t + m_t \tag{5.4}$$

with $a_t \in A(\mathcal{F}_t)$, $m_t \in \mathcal{M}^2(\mathcal{F}_t)$. Then $\hat{y}_t$ satisfies the filtering equation

$$\hat{y}_t = \hat{y}_o + \eta_t + \int_Z\int_0^t k(z,s)Q^x(dz,ds)$$

where $\eta_t \in A(\mathcal{F}_t^x)$, $Q^x(B,t) = P(B,t) - \int_B\int_0^t \hat{g}(z,s)\mu(dz,ds)$, and

where the $\mathcal{F}_t^x$-predictable process $k$ satisfies

$$k(z,s) = \frac{\widehat{[(y_{s-} - \hat{y}_{s-} + h(z,s)]g(z,s)}}{\hat{g}(z,s)}$$

and $h, g$ are as in (5.2), (5.3) respectively.

Proof Let $\mu_t = E(m_t | \mathcal{F}_t^x)$. Clearly $\mu_t \in \mathcal{M}^2(\mathcal{F}_t^x)$. Now write $a_t = a_t^+ - a_t^-$ where $a_t^+, a_t^- \in A_+(\mathcal{F}_t, P)$. It is easy to verify that the $\mathcal{F}_t^x$-measurable processes $\alpha_t^+ = E(a_t^+ | \mathcal{F}_t^x)$, $\alpha_t^- = E(a_t^- | \mathcal{F}_t^x)$ are submartingales. By the Doob-Meyer decomposition theorem [3], there exist martingales $\xi_t^+, \xi_t^-$ in $\mathcal{M}^1(\mathcal{F}_t^x)$

and $\mathcal{F}_t^x$-predictable increasing processes $\eta_t^+, \eta_t^-$ in $A_+(\mathcal{F}_t^x)$ such that

$$\alpha_t^+ = \xi_t^+ + \eta_t^+ , \qquad \alpha_t^- = \xi_t^- + \eta_t^- .$$

Hence

$$\begin{aligned} \hat{y}_t &= \hat{y}_o + \alpha_t^+ - \alpha_t^- + \hat{m}_t \\ &= \hat{y}_o + (\eta_t^+ - \eta_t^-) + (\xi_t^+ - \xi_+^- + \mu_t) \\ &= \hat{y}_o + \eta_t + \xi_t , \quad \text{say} \end{aligned} \tag{5.5}$$

where $\eta_t \in A(\mathcal{F}_t^x)$, $\xi_t \in \mathcal{M}^1(\mathcal{F}_t^x)$. By §2.11 there exists a $\mathcal{F}_t^x$-predictable process $k(z,s) \in L_{loc}^1(\tilde{P}^x)$ such that

$$\xi_t = \int_Z \int_0^t k(z,s) Q^x(dz,ds) \quad . \tag{5.6}$$

It remains to evaluate $k$. By the differentiation formula of §2.7

$$y_t P(B,t) = \int_0^t y_{s-} P(B,ds) + \int_0^t P(B,s-) dy_s + [m_t, Q(B,t)] \quad .$$

Since $P(B,t) - \tilde{P}(B,t)$ and $[m_t,Q(B,t)] - \langle m_t,Q(B,t)\rangle$ are in $\mathcal{M}_{loc}^1(\mathcal{F}_t)$, therefore, from the above, for some $\gamma_t, \gamma_t' \in \mathcal{M}_{loc}^1(\mathcal{F}_t)$

$$\begin{aligned} y_t P(B,t) &= \int_0^t y_{s-} \tilde{P}(B,ds) + \int_0^t P(B,s-) dy_s + \langle m_t, Q(B,t)\rangle + \gamma_t \\ &= \int_B \int_0^t (y_{s-} + h(z,s)) g(z,s) \mu(dz,ds) + \int_0^t P(B,s-) da_s + \gamma_t' \end{aligned} \tag{5.7}$$

using (5.2), (5.3) and (5.4).

Now apply the differential rule to $\hat{y}_t P(B,t)$ to obtain

$$\hat{y}_t P(B,t) = \int_0^t \hat{y}_{s-} P(B,ds) + \int_0^t P(B,s-)d\hat{y}_s + [\xi_t, Q^x(B,t)] \quad .$$

Recalling that $P(B,t) - \tilde{P}^x(B,t)$ and $[\xi_t, Q^x(B,t)] - \langle \xi_t, Q^x(B,t)\rangle$ are in $\mathcal{M}^1_{loc}(\mathcal{F}^x_t)$, the relation above implies that for some $\delta_t$, $\delta'_t \in \mathcal{M}^1_{loc}(\mathcal{F}^x_t)$,

$$\begin{aligned}\hat{y}_t P(B,t) &= \int_0^t \hat{y}_{s-} \tilde{P}^x(B,ds) + \int_0^t P(B,s-)d\hat{y}_s + \langle \xi_t, Q^x(B,t)\rangle + \delta_t \\ &= \int_B\int_0^t (\hat{y}_{s-} + k(z,s))\hat{g}(z,s)\mu(dz,ds) + \int_0^t P(B,s-)d\eta_s + \delta'_t \quad ,\end{aligned} \tag{5.8}$$

using Proposition 4.1, (5.5), (5.6).

Next we make the following observations, which can be verified directly from the martingale definition.

$$\widehat{\left(\int_B\int_0^t (y_{s-}+h(z,s))g(z,s)\mu(dz,ds)\right)} - \int_B\int_0^t [\widehat{(y_{s-}+h(z,s))g(z,s)}]\mu(dz,ds) \in \mathcal{M}^1_{loc}(\mathcal{F}^x_t)$$

$$\widehat{\left(\int_0^t P(B,s-)da_s\right)} - \int_0^t P(B,s-)d\eta_s \in \mathcal{M}^1_{loc}(\mathcal{F}^x_t) \quad .$$

Using these facts and the fact that $\widehat{(y_t P(B,t))} = \hat{y}_t P(B,t)$ we conclude from (5.7), (5.8) that

$$\int_B\int_0^t \{(\hat{y}_{s-}+k(z,s))\hat{g}(z,s) - [\widehat{(y_{s-}+h(z,s))g(z,s)}]\}\mu(dz,ds) \in \mathcal{M}^1_{loc}(\mathcal{F}^x_t)$$

and since this process is continuous, it must vanish identically, so that we may assume

$$k(z,s) = \frac{[\widehat{(y_{s-} + h(z,s))g(z,s)}]}{\hat{g}(z,s)} - \hat{y}_{s-}$$

$$= \frac{[\widehat{(y_{s-} - \hat{y}_{s-} + h(z,s))g(z,s)}]}{\hat{g}(z,s)} \quad . \qquad \square$$

Corollary 5.1 Suppose in the above that $x_t$ is as in the fundamental example of §2.12 and that there exists an $\mathcal{F}_t^x$-predictable process $\mu(t)$ and $\mathcal{F}_t$-predictable processes $\lambda_t^i$ such that

$$\tilde{p}_i(t) = \int_0^t \lambda^i(s)\mu(ds)$$

and let $\langle m_t, q_i(t)\rangle = \int_0^t h_i(s)\tilde{p}_i(ds)$ for some $\mathcal{F}_t$-predictable processes $h_i$. Then

$$\hat{y}_t = \hat{y}_o + \eta_t + \sum_{i=1}^{n} \int_0^t k_i(s)q_i^x(ds)$$

with

$$k_i(t) = \frac{[\widehat{(y_{t-} - \hat{y}_{t-} + h_i(t))\lambda^i(t)}]}{\hat{\lambda}^i(t)} \quad , \qquad 1 \leq i \leq n$$

and

$$q_i^x(t) = p_i(t) - \int_0^t \hat{\lambda}^i(s)ds \quad .$$

Remark 5.1 (i) Suppose in (5.4) that $a_t$ is given as

$$a_t = \int_0^t \beta_s ds$$

for some predictable process $\beta_t$ in $L^1(\mathcal{F}_t)$. Since $\hat{a}_t - \int_0^t \hat{\beta}_s ds$ is in $\mathcal{M}^1(\mathcal{F}_t^x)$ it follows that in the representation for $\hat{y}_t$ we have the further specification

$$\eta_t = \int_0^t \hat{\beta}_s ds \quad .$$

(ii) Corollary 5.1 has appeared in the literature for the case where $(x_t, \mathcal{F}_t, P)$ is a counting process, i.e., $n = 1$. Even here some additional conditions have been imposed on the $y_t$ process (such as e.g. $y_t$ is Markov [6,16]) or on the $x_t$ process (such as e.g. $(x_t, \mathcal{F}_t^x, P)$ is obtained from a Poisson process by an absolutely continuous change of measure [6,20]).

(iii) Theorem 5.1 has been inspired largely by the procedures of [21], where the underlying process is Brownian motion. See also [24] for the Brownian motion case.

(iv) While Theorem 5.1 has some value in terms of clarifying the issues involved in obtaining the filtering equations it is of little practical importance since these equations do not lead to a realization by a dynamical system. This is so because the filtering equations contain the terms $\eta_t$, $k_t$ and $\hat{g}_t$ which are <u>not</u> computable in terms of $\hat{y}_t$ and $x_t$. In other words, the filtering equation is not recursive. This difficulty persists even when one imposes additional conditions such as $y_t$ is Markov. In the remainder of this section we seek to determine conditions under which the filter is recursive.

We impose conditions on the dependence between the "signal" or "state" process $y_t$ and the "observation" process $x_t$ which are considerably stronger than those of Assumption 5.1. For the remainder of this section the following assumption holds.

<u>Assumption 5.2</u> $(\Omega, \mathcal{F}_t)$, $t \in R_+$, is a family of spaces and $P$, $P_1$ are two probability measures on $(\Omega, \mathcal{F})$. $x_t$ and $y_t$ are measurable functions on $(\Omega, \mathcal{F}_t)$ with values in $(Z, \mathcal{Z})$ and $(Y, \mathcal{Y})$ respectively. The following properties are satisfied.

(i) $Z$ is a Borel subset of $R^n$, $\mathcal{Z}$ is the Borel field. (The most important practical cases are $Z = R^n$ and $Z$ is the space of all $z \in R^n$ with integer components.) $Y$ is a locally compact Hausdorff space, $\mathcal{Y}$ is the Borel field. $\mathcal{F}_t = \mathcal{F}_t^x \vee \mathcal{F}_t^y$.

(ii) Under the measure $P$

(a) $(x_t, \mathcal{F}_t, P)$ is a fundamental process with <u>independent increments</u>, i.e., $x_t - x_s$ is independent of $\mathcal{F}_s$ (under $P$), for $s \le t$,

(b) $(y_t, \mathcal{F}_t, P)$ is a <u>Markov</u> process whose sample paths are right-continuous and have left-limits, and the jump times of $y$ are totally inaccessible,

(c) the processes $x_t$ and $y_t$ are <u>independent</u>, i.e., $\mathcal{F}^x$ and $\mathcal{F}^y$ are independent.

(iii) $P_1 << P$, there exists an $\mathcal{F}_t$-predictable process $f \in L^1_{loc}(\tilde{P})$ with a representation

$$f(z,\omega,t) = \phi(z, y_{t-}(\omega), \omega, t) \quad ,$$

where $\phi(\cdot, y, \cdot, \cdot)$ is $\mathcal{F}_t^x$-predictable for fixed $y \in Y$, and there also exist $\mathcal{F}_t^x$-predictable processes $\mu(B,t)$ for $B \in \mathcal{Z}$ such that $E(|f(z,t)|) + E_1(|f(z,t)|) < \infty$ for all $z$, $t$ and

$$L_t = E\left(\frac{dP_1}{dP} \Big| \mathcal{F}_t\right) = \prod_{\substack{s < t \\ x_{s-} \neq x_s}} [1 + \phi(x_s, y_{s-}, s)] \exp\left[-\int_Z \int_0^t \phi(z, y_{s-}, s) \mu(dz, ds)\right] \quad .$$

Note that we must have $1 + \phi \geqq 0$.

Let $Q$, $\tilde{P}$ and $Q^x$, $\tilde{P}^x$ be the processes associated with $(x_t, \mathcal{F}_t, P)$ and $(x_t, \mathcal{F}_t^x, P)$. Similarly let $Q_1$, $\tilde{P}_1$, $Q_1^x$, $\tilde{P}_1^x$ be the processes corresponding with $(x_t, \mathcal{F}_t, P_1)$ and $(x_t, \mathcal{F}_t^x, P_1)$ respectively. From Assumption 4.2 and Proposition 4.1 it is immediate that

$$\tilde{P}(B,t) = \tilde{P}^x(B,t) = \mu(B,t)$$

$$\tilde{P}_1(B,t) = \int_B \int_0^t (1+f(z,s))\mu(dz,ds)$$

$$\tilde{P}_1^x(B,t) = \int_B \int_0^t (1+\hat{f}(z,s))\mu(dz,ds)$$

where $\hat{f}(z,t) = E_1(f(z,t) \mid \mathcal{F}_t^x)$.

For any $t$ let $\mathcal{F}_{t-} = \bigvee_{s<t} \mathcal{F}_s$, $\mathcal{F}_{t-}^x = \bigvee_{s<t} \mathcal{F}_s^x$, $\mathcal{F}_{t-}^y = \bigvee_{s<t} \mathcal{F}_s^y$.

<u>Proposition 5.1</u> For $t \in R_+$, $\mathcal{F}_{t-}^x = \mathcal{F}_t^x$, $\mathcal{F}_{t-}^y = \mathcal{F}_t^y$, $\mathcal{F}_{t-} = \mathcal{F}_t$.

<u>Proof</u> The jump times of $x$ and $y$ are totally inaccessible, hence by [4, Prop. 3.1 and 22, III.D38] $\mathcal{F}_{t-}^x = \mathcal{F}_t^x$ and $\mathcal{F}_{t-}^y = \mathcal{F}_t^y$. The last assertion follows because $\mathcal{F}_{t-} = \mathcal{F}_{t-}^x \vee \mathcal{F}_{t-}^y$ and $\mathcal{F}_t = \mathcal{F}_t^x \vee \mathcal{F}_t^y$. ¤

<u>Proposition 5.2</u> $L_{t-} = L_t$ a.s. P.

<u>Proof</u> Follows from [22, VT10] using a stopping time argument. ¤

<u>Proposition 5.3</u> $y_t = y_{t-}$ a.s. P.

<u>Proof</u> $\text{Prob}\{y_t \neq y_{t-}\} = \text{Prob}\{t \text{ is a jump time}\}$. However, since the jump times are totally inaccessible, this probability must be zero. ¤

For a real-valued function $g$ on $Y$ we are interested in determining a (recursive) expression for the process $E_1(g(y_t)|\mathcal{F}_t^x)$. Now

$$E_1(g(y_t)|\mathcal{F}_t^x) = \frac{E(g(y_t)L_t|\mathcal{F}_t^x)}{E(L_t|\mathcal{F}_t^x)} \quad . \tag{5.9}$$

It turns out that the numerator of the expression in the right is much better behaved than the ratio, and, furthermore, the denominator does not depend on $g$. Hence we will seek to determine instead an expression for $E(g(y_t)L_t|\mathcal{F}_t^x)$.

Definition 5.1 Let $G$ be the family of all bounded, measurable, real-valued functions $g$ on $Y$. For $g \in G$ and $t \in R_+$ let

$$\pi_t(g) = E(g(y_t)L_t|\mathcal{F}_t^x) \quad . \tag{5.10}$$

Proposition 5.4 $E(L_t|\mathcal{F}_t^y) = 1$ a.s.

Proof Immediate from the assumptions that $\mathcal{F}^x$, $\mathcal{F}^y$ are independent under $P$ and $\mu(B,t)$ is $\mathcal{F}_t^x$-measurable. ¤

Now fix $g \in G$. Since $L_t$ satisfies

$$L_t = 1 + \int_0^t L_{s-} d(\phi \circ Q)_s \quad ,$$

substitution into (5.10) gives

$$\pi_t(g) = E(g(y_t)|\mathcal{F}_t^x) + E[\int_0^t g(y_t)L_{s-} d(\phi\circ Q)_s|\mathcal{F}_t^x]$$

$$= E(g(y_t)|\mathcal{F}_t^x) + \int_Z\int_0^t E[g(y_t)L_{s-}\phi(z,y_{s-},s)|\mathcal{F}_t^x]Q(dz,ds) \quad . \tag{5.11}$$

Since $\mathcal{F}^x$ and $\mathcal{F}^y$ are independent under P,

$$E(g(y_t) \mid \mathcal{F}^x_t) = Eg(y_t) \quad . \tag{5.12}$$

Also

$$\begin{aligned}
&E[g(y_t)L_{s-}\phi(z,y_{s-},s) \mid \mathcal{F}^x_t] \\
&= E[g(y_t)L_s\phi(z,y_s,s) \mid \mathcal{F}^x_t] && \text{by Propositions 5.2, 5.3} \\
&= E[E\{g(y_t)L_s\phi(z,y_s,s) \mid \mathcal{F}^x_t \vee \mathcal{F}^y_s\} \mid \mathcal{F}^x_t] \\
&= E[L_s\phi(z,y_s,s)E(g(y_t) \mid \mathcal{F}^x_t \vee \mathcal{F}^y_s) \mid \mathcal{F}^x_t] \\
&= E[L_s\phi(z,y_s,s)E(g(y_t) \mid \mathcal{F}^y_s) \mid \mathcal{F}^x_t] && \text{by independence of } \mathcal{F}^x, \mathcal{F}^y \\
&= E[L_s\phi(z,y_s,s)E(g(y_t) \mid y_s) \mid \mathcal{F}^x_t] && \text{since } y_t \text{ is Markov} \\
&= E[L_s\phi(z,y_s,s)H_{t,s}(g) \mid \mathcal{F}^x_s] && (5.13)
\end{aligned}$$

since x has independent increments and where

$$H_{t,s}(g) = E(g(y_t) \mid y_s) \quad .$$

Substitution of (5.12) and (5.13) into (5.11) gives

$$\pi_t(g) = Eg(y_t) + \int_Z\int_0^t \pi_s(\phi(z,\cdot,s)H_{t,s}(g))Q(dz,ds) \quad .$$

Note that the integrand in the above expression is a predictable process, for each fixed t, as explained at the end of §2.9.

We summarize the above.

<u>Theorem 5.2</u> Under Assumption (5.2) the process $\pi_t(g)$ satisfies

$$\pi_t(g) = Eg(y_t) + \int_Z\int_0^t \pi_s(\phi(z,\cdot,s)H_{t,s}(g))Q(dz,ds) \tag{5.14}$$

where

$$H_{t,s}(g) = E(g(y_t) \mid \mathcal{Y}_s) \quad , \tag{5.15}$$

and

$$Q(B,t) = P(B,t) - \tilde{P}(B,t) \quad . \tag{5.16}$$

Remark 5.2 (i) Because of Proposition 5.4

$$Eg(y_t) = E_1 g(y_t) \qquad \text{and} \qquad H_{t,s}(g) = E_1(g(y_t) \mid \mathcal{Y}_s) \quad .$$

(ii) From (5.10), $\pi_t(1) = E(L_t \mid \mathcal{F}_t^x)$, where 1 denotes the function on Y which is identically equal to unity. Hence from (5.9),

$$E_1(g(y_t) \mid \mathcal{F}_t^x) = \frac{\pi_t(g)}{\pi_t(1)}$$

$$= \frac{Eg(y_t) + \int_Z\int_0^t \pi_s(\phi(z,\cdot,s)H_{t,s}(g))Q(dz,ds)}{1 + \int_Z\int_0^t \pi_s(\phi(z,\cdot,s))Q(dz,ds)}$$

from (5.14).

(iii) Suppose $(x_t, \mathcal{F}_t, P)$ is as in the fundamental example. Then (5.14) simplifies to

$$\pi_t(g) = Eg(y_t) + \sum_{i=1}^{n} \int_0^t \pi_s(\phi_i(\cdot,s)H_{t,s}(g))[p_i(ds) - \tilde{p}_i(ds)] \quad . \tag{5.17}$$

(iv) We now derive a more familiar-looking version of (5.14). For any set $A \in \mathcal{Y}$

$$\pi_t(I_A) = E(I_A L_t | \mathcal{F}_t^x) \quad .$$

If $P(y_t \in A) = P_1(y_t \in A) = 0$ then $\pi_t(I_A) = 0$ a.s. Hence there exists a measurable function $U_t: Y \to R$ such that

$$\pi_t(A) = \int_A U_t(y) P_t(dy) \tag{5.18}$$

where $P_t$ is the marginal distribution of $y_t$ under $P$ and $P_1$. Evidently if $h \in G$ then

$$\pi_t(h) = \int_Y h(y) U_t(y) P_t(dy) \quad .$$

Next let $P(A,t| y, s)$, $A \in \mathcal{Y}$, $s \leq t$, be the <u>transition kernel</u> of the Markov process $y$ so that

$$(H_{t,s}(g))(y) = \int_Y g(y') P(dy',t| y,s)$$

and let $P(A,s| y,t)$, $A \in \mathcal{Y}$, $t \geq s$, be the <u>backward kernel</u> so that for $h \in G$

$$E(h(y_s)| y_t) = \int_Y h(y') P(dy',s| y_t,t) \quad .$$

Substituting these relations into (5.14) leads to

$$\int_Y g(y') U_t(y') P_t(dy') = \int_Y g(y') P_t(dy')$$
$$+ \int_Z \int_0^t [\int_Y \{\phi(z,y,s) \int_Y g(y') P(dy',t|y,s)\} U_s(y) P_s(dy)]$$
$$\cdot \; Q(dz,ds)$$

$$= \int_Y g(y')P_t(dy') + \int_Y g(y')[\int_Z\int_0^t\{\int_Y \phi(z,y,s)U_s(y)P(dy,s|\ y',t)\}Q(dz,ds)]$$

$$\cdot P_t(dy') \quad .$$

Since $g \in G$ is arbitrary, the process $U_t(y)$ evolves according to

$$U_t(y) = 1 + \int_Z\int_0^t[\int_Y \phi(z,y',s)U_s(y')P(dy',s|\ y,t)]Q(dz,ds) \quad . \quad (5.19)$$

Remark 5.3 (i) For the case of the fundamental example (see (5.17)) the equation above simplifies to

$$U_t(y) = 1 + \sum_{i=1}^{n} \int_0^t\{\int_Y \phi_i(y',s)U_s(y')P(dy',s|y,t)\}[p_i(ds)-\tilde{p}_i(ds)] \ . \quad (5.20)$$

This equation has been derived in [28] for the special case where $(x_t,\mathcal{F}_t,P)$ is a counting process, so that $n = 1$, and with the additional condition that $\tilde{p}(ds) = ds$.

(ii) Equations (5.14) and (5.15) are <u>not</u> yet recursive since the functions $\phi(z,y,t)$, $\phi_i(y,t)$ are allowed to depend on the entire past $x_s$, $1 \leq s \leq t$. We will see later how under additional conditions these equations become truly recursive.

(iii) Notice that unlike the representation for $\hat{y}_t$ obtained in Theorem 5.1, those for $\pi_t$ in (5.14) and $U_t$ in (5.19) are not semimartingales because the integrands depend upon $t$. This dependency can be eliminated by some additional assumptions as follows.

For the remainder of this section the following holds in addition to Assumption 5.2.

**Assumption 5.3** The operators $H_{t,s}$ of (5.15) have the following properties:

(i) $\lim_{s \uparrow t} H_{t,s} = I$, the identity operator on $G$, (5.21)

(ii) there exist operators $A_t$, $t \geq 0$ on $G$ such that

$$\lim_{\varepsilon \downarrow 0} \frac{1}{\varepsilon}(H_{t+\varepsilon,s} - H_{t,s})(g) = H_{t,s}A_t(g) \quad . \tag{5.22}$$

We do not elaborate on the precise theoretical status of the operators $A_t$ (i.e., the precise definitions of their domain, range, etc.), since it would take us too far afield and since this topic is well-covered in the semigroup theory of Markov processes (see e.g. [29]). We merely note that (i) is a continuity assumption, (ii) is a differentiability assumption. The operators $A_t$ are often referred to as the infinitesimal generator, especially when $y$ is a Hunt process. If $y$ is a k-dimensional diffusion, for example, then $A_t$ is just a (partial) differential operator of the form

$$\frac{1}{2}\sum_{i,j=1}^{k} \sigma_{ij}(y,t)\frac{\partial^2}{\partial y_i \partial y_j} + \sum_{i=1}^{k} m_i(y,t)\frac{\partial}{\partial y_i} \quad .$$

We now develop the simplifications induced by (5.21), (5.22) in (5.14). First of all, recalling that $P_0(dy)$ is the probability distribution of $y_0$ and that $y$ is Markov, we get

$$Eg(y_t) = \int_Y (H_{t,0}(g))(y)P_0(dy) = E(H_{t,0}(g)(y_0)) \quad .$$

This, together with (5.22), implies that

$$E(g(y_{t+\varepsilon}) - g(y_t)) = \int_Y (H_{t+\varepsilon,0} - H_{t,0})(g)(y)P_0(dy)$$

$$\cong \varepsilon \int_Y (H_{t,0}A_t(g))(y)P_0(dy) = \varepsilon E[(A_t(g))(y_t)] \quad .$$

Substituting this into (5.14), and using (5.21) and (5.22), leads us to

$$(\pi_{t+\varepsilon}-\pi_t)(g) \cong \varepsilon E(A_t(g)) + \varepsilon\int_Z \pi_t(\phi g)Q(dz,dt) + \varepsilon\int_Z\int_0^t \pi_s(\phi H_{t,s}A_t(g))Q(dz,ds)$$

$$= \varepsilon\int_Z \pi_t(\phi g)Q(dz,dt) + \varepsilon\pi_t(A_t(g)) \quad .$$

Hence

$$\pi_t(g) = \pi_0(g) + \int_0^t \pi_s(A_s g)ds + \int_0^t\int_Z \pi_s(\phi(z,\cdot,s)g)Q(dz,ds) \quad . \tag{5.23}$$

<u>Theorem 5.3</u> Under the additional conditions of Assumption 5.3, the representations (5.14) and (5.17) simplify to (5.23), (5.24) respectively.

$$\pi_t(g) = \pi_0(g) + \int_0^t \pi_s(A_s g)ds + \sum_{i=1}^{n} \int_0^t \pi_s(\phi_i(\cdot,s)g)[p_i(ds)-\tilde{p}_i(ds)] \tag{5.24}$$

As an example illustrating (5.24) suppose that under $P$ $x_t$ and $y_t$ are independent standard Poisson processes. Then $Z = Y = I_+$, the set of non-negative integers. Also $n = 1$ in (5.24), $p(t) = x_t$ and $\tilde{p}(t) = t$. For $g: I_+ \to R$,

$$H_{t,s}(g)(y) = E(g(y_t) \mid y_s = y)$$

$$= \sum_{k=0}^{\infty} g(y+k)\frac{(t-s)^k}{k!}e^{-(t-s)} \quad ,$$

so that,

$$\frac{\partial}{\partial t}(H_{t,s}(g))(y) = \sum_{k=0}^{\infty} \frac{(t-s)^k}{k!}e^{-(t-s)}[g(y+k+1) - g(y+k)] \quad ,$$

and hence

$$(A_t g)(y) = (Ag)(y) = g(y+1) - g(y) \quad . \tag{5.25}$$

Consider the "indicator" functions $\delta_k : I_+ \to R$ where

$$\delta_k(y) = \begin{cases} 1 & \text{if} \quad y = k \\ 0 & \text{otherwise} \end{cases} .$$

By the linearity of $\pi_t$,

$$\pi_t(g) = \sum_{k=0}^{\infty} g(k)\pi_t(\delta_k) \quad ,$$

so that it is enough to determine the processes $\pi_t(\delta_k)$, $k = 0,1,2,\ldots$ . Substitution of $\delta_k$ for $g$ into (5.24) gives, using (5.25),

$$\begin{aligned} \pi_t(\delta_k) &= \pi_0(\delta_k) + \int_0^t [\pi_s(\delta_{k-1}) - \pi_s(\delta_k)]ds + \int_0^t \pi_s(\phi(\cdot,s)\delta_k)(dx_s - ds) \\ &= \pi_0(\delta_k) + \int_0^t [\pi_s(\delta_{k-1}) - \pi_s(\delta_k)]ds + \int_0^t \phi(k,s)\pi_s(\delta_k)(dx_s - ds) \end{aligned}$$

since $\phi(y,s)\delta_k(y) = \phi(k,s)\delta_k(y)$. Now

$$\pi_0(\delta_k) = E\delta_k(y_0) = \begin{cases} 1 & \text{if} \quad k = 0 \\ 0 & \text{if} \quad k > 0 \end{cases} ,$$

and $\delta_{-1} \equiv 0$, so that the expression above simplifies to

$$\pi_t(\delta_0) = 1 - \int_0^t \pi_s(\delta_0)ds + \int_0^t \phi(0,s)\pi_s(\delta_0)(dx_s - ds) \quad ,$$

$$\pi_t(\delta_k) = \int_0^t \pi_s(\delta_{k-1})ds - \int_0^t \pi_s(\delta_k)ds + \int_0^t \phi(k,s)\pi_s(\delta_k)(dx_s - ds) \quad , \qquad k \geq 1,$$

and these can be rewritten respectively as

$$e^t\pi_t(\delta_o) = 1 + \int_0^t \phi(0,s)e^s\pi_s(\delta_0)(dx_s - ds) \quad ,$$

$$e^t\pi_t(\delta_k) = \int_0^t e^s\pi_s(\delta_{k-1})ds + \int_0^t \phi(k,s)e^s\pi_s(\delta_k)(dx_s - ds) \quad , \quad k \geq 1 \ .$$

These linear integral equations can now be solved inductively to yield the explicit formulas

$$\pi_t(\delta_0) = e^{-t} \prod_{\substack{s<t \\ x_{s-} \neq x_s}} [1+\phi(0,s)]\exp[-\int_0^t \phi(0,s)ds] \quad , \tag{5.27}$$

$$\pi_t(\delta_k) = \int_0^t e^{-(t-s)}\pi_s(\delta_{k-1})\{\prod_{\substack{s<\tau\leq t \\ x_{\tau-}\neq x_\tau}} [1+\phi(k,\tau)]\exp[-\int_s^t \phi(k,\tau)d\tau]\}ds \ , \quad k \geq 1 \ . \tag{5.28}$$

Remark 5.4 The result just obtained illustrates the power of the formulation of Theorem 5.3 over the more usual formulations which involve obtaining a relation for the conditional density (e.g. [16]). We believe that equations (5.14), (5.20), and (5.23), (5.24) are much more useful since they are linear in the "unknown" linear operators $\pi_t$ whereas the evolution equations for the conditional density are nonlinear. Of course the latter can be easily derived from the former.

References

1. C. Doléans-Dade and P.A. Meyer, "Intégrales stochastiques par rapport aux martingales locales," in Séminaire de Probabilités:IV, Lecture Notes in Mathematics, Berlin and New York: Springer Verlag, 77-107 (1970).

2. C. Doléans-Dade, "Quelques applications de la formule de changement de variables pour les semimartingales," Z. Wahrscheinlichtstheorie verw. Geb. 16, 181-194 (1970).

3. P.A. Meyer, Probabilités et Potentiel, Paris: Hermann (1966) (English translation: Probability and Potential, Waltham, Mass: Blaisdell (1966)).

4. R. Boel, P. Varaiya and E. Wong, Martingales on Point Processes I: Representation Results, Electronics Research Lab, University of California, Berkeley, California, Memo #M-407 (September 1973).

5. H. Kunita and S. Watanabe, "On square integrable martingales," Nagoya Math. J. 30, 209-245 (August 1967).

6. P.M. Brémaud, A Martingale Approach to Point Processes, Electronics Research Lab, University of California, Berkeley, California, Memo # M-345 (August 1972).

7. M.H.A. Davis, Detection of signals with point process observation, Publication 73/8, Dept. of Computing and Control, Imperial College, London (May 1973).

8. T.T. Kadota and L.A. Shepp, "Conditions for absolute continuity between a certain pair of probability measures," Z. Wahrscheinlichts-theorie verw. Geb. 16 (3), 13-30 (1970).

9. I.V. Girsanov, "On transforming a certain class of stochastic processes by absolutely continuous substitution of measures," Theory of Prob. and Appl. 5, 285-301 (1960).

10. V. Beneš, "Existence of optimal stochastic control laws," SIAM J. Control 9, 446-475 (1971).

11. T.E. Duncan and P. Varaiya, "On the solutions of a stochastic control system," SIAM J. Control 9, 354-371 (1971).

12. M.H.A. Davis and P. Varaiya, "Dynamic Programming Conditions for Partially Observable Stochastic Systems," SIAM J. Control 11 (2), 226-261 (1973).

13. R. Rishel, "Weak solutions of a partial differential equation of Dynamic Programming," SIAM J. Control 9, 519-528 (1971).

14. D.L. Snyder, "Information processing for observed jump processes," Information and Control 22 (1), 69-78 (1973).

15. I. Rubin, "Regular point processes and their detection," IEEE Trans. Inform. Theory IT-18 (5), 547-557 (1972).

16. D.L. Snyder, "Filtering and detection for doubly stochastic Poisson processes," IEEE Trans. Inform. Theory IT-18 (1), 91-102 (1972).

17. O. Macchi and B.C. Picinbono, "Estimation and Detection of Weak Optical Signals," IEEE Trans. Inform. Theory IT-18 (5), 562-573 (1972).

18. E. Lehmann, Testing Statistical Hypotheses, New York: Wiley (1959).

19. P.A. Meyer, "Square integrable martingales, a survey," in Martingales: A report on a Meeting at Oberwolfach, Lecture Notes in Mathematics, No. 190, Berlin: Springer-Verlag (1970).

20. M.H.A. Davis, "Nonlinear Filtering with Point Process Observations," preprint.

21. M. Fujisaki, G. Kallianpur and H. Kunita, "Stochastic Differential Equations for the Nonlinear Filtering problem," Osaka J. Math. 9 (1), 19-40 (1972).

22. C. Dellacherie, Capacités et processus stochastiques, Berlin: Springer-Verlag (1972).

23. T.E. Duncan, "On the Absolute Continuity of Measures," Annals Math. Stat. 41 (1), 30-38 (1970).

24. J.H. Van Schuppen, Estimation Theory for Continuous Time Processes, a Martingale Approach, Electronics Research Lab, University of California, Berkeley, California, Memo #M-405 (September 1973).

25. J.L. Doob, Stochastic Processes, New York: Wiley (1953).

26. W. Feller, An Introduction to Probability Theory and Its Applications, v.I, New York: Wiley (1968).

27. T.E. Duncan and P. Varaiya, On the solutions of a stochastic control system II, Electronics Research Lab., Univ. of California, Berkeley, California, Memo #M406 (August 1973).

28. P. Brémaud, "Filtering for Point Processes," preprint (June 1973).

29. E.B. Dynkin, Markov Processes I, New York: Academic Press (1965).

30. D.L. Snyder, "Smoothing for Doubly Stochastic Poisson Processes," IEEE Trans. Inform. Theory IT-18 (5), 558-562 (1972).

31. A. Prékopa, "On stochastic set functions," Acta Mathematica Acad. Sc. Hungaricae 7 (2), 215-263 (1956).

32. J.E. Moyal, "The general theory of stochastic population processes," Acta Mathematica (Uppsala) 108, 1-31 (1962).

33. J.H. van Schuppen, "Filtering for Counting Processes, a Martingale Approach," Proc. 4th Symp. Nonlinear Estimation and Appl., San Diego, California (September 1973).

# Selected Bibliography


1. Bartlett M. S. (1966). *An Introduction to Stochastic Processes,* 2nd ed. Cambridge University Press, New York.
2. ______ (1966). The spectral analysis of point processes, *J. Roy. Statist. Soc.,* **B 25,** 264–296.
3. ______ (1967). Some remarks on the analysis of time-series, *Biometrika,* **54,** 25–38.
4. Bedard, G. (1966). Photon counting statistics of Gaussian light, *Phys. Rev.,* **151,** 1038–1039.
5. Blumenthal, S., Greenwood, J. A., and Herbach, L. (1971). Superimposed non-stationary renewal processes. *J. Appl. Prob.,* **8,** 184–192.
6. Clark, J. R., and Hoversten, E. (1970). Poisson process as a statistical model for photodetectors excited by Gaussian light, MIT Res. Lab. Electronics, *Quart. Progr. Rept.,* **98,** 95–101.
7. Cox, D. R. (1965). On the estimation of the intensity function of a stationary point process, *J. Roy. Statist. Soc.,* **B27,** 332–337.
8. ______ (1966). *The Statistical Analysis of Series of Events.* Methuen, London; Barnes and Noble, New York.
9. Gilles, D. C., and Lewis, P. A. W. (1967). The spectrum of intervals of a geometric branching Poisson process, *J. Appl. Prob.,* **4,** 201–205.
10. Hannan, E. J. (1970). *Multiple Time Series.* Wiley, New York.
11. Hellstrom, C. W. (1964). The distribution of photoelectric counts from partially polarized Gaussian light, *Proc. Phys. Soc.,* **83,** 777–782.
12. Karp, S., and Clark, J. R. (1970). Photon counting: a problem in classical noise theory. *IEEE Trans. Inform. Theory,* **IT-16,** 672–680.
13. Lampard, D. G. (1968). A stochastic process whose successive intervals between events from a first order Markov chain, *Int. J. Appl. Prob.,* **5,** 648–668.
14. Lewis, P. A. W. (1964). A branching Poisson process model for the analysis of computer failure patterns, *J. Roy. Statist. Soc.,* **B26,** 398–456.
15. ______ (1965). Some results on tests for Poisson processes, *Biometrika,* **52,** 67–77.
16. ______ (1969). Asymptotic properties and equilibrium conditions for branching Poisson processes, *J. Appl. Prob.,* **6,** 355–371.
17. Moore, G. P., Segundo, J. P., Perkel, D. H., and Levitan, H. (1970). Statistical signs of synaptic interaction in neurons, *Biophys. J.,* **10,** 867–900.
18. Snyder, D. L. (1971). Statistical analysis of dynamic tracer data, Proc. Workshop Processing Dynamic Tracer Data from Anger Scintillation Camera, Biomedical Computer Laboratory, Washington University, St. Louis.
19. Wold, H. (1948). On stationary point processes and Markov chains, *Skand. Aktuar. Tidskr.,* **31,** 229–240.
20. Breiman, L. (1963). The Poisson tendency in traffic distribution, *Ann. Math. Statist.,* **34,** 308–311.

21. Brown, M. (1970). A property of Poisson processes and its application to macroscopic equilibrium of particle systems, *Ann. Math. Statist.*, **41,** 1935–1941.
22. ______ (1971). Discrimination of Poisson processes, *Ann. Math. Statist.*, **42,** 773–776.
23. Kennedy, D. P. (1969). A functional limit theorem for *k*-dimensional renewal theory, *Tech. Rept. 9,* Stanford University, Stanford, Calif.
24. Belyaev, Y. K. (1969). Elements of the general theory of random streams, Appendix 2 of Russian ed. (MIR, Moscow) of Cramer and Leadbetter, *Stationary and Related Stochastic Processes,* Wiley-Interscience, 1967. (Translation: Dept. Statistics, Univ. North Carolina, Chapel Hill, N.C., Mimeo Ser. 703.)
25. Beutler, F. J., and Leneman, O. A. Z. (1966). The theory of stationary point processes, *Acta Math.*, **116,** 159–197.
26. Cramer, H., Leadbetter, M. R., and Serfling, R. J. (1971). On distribution function-moment relationships in a stationary point process, *S. Wahrscheinlichkeitstheorie Verw. Geb.*, **18,** 1–8.
27. Dobrushin, R. L. (1956). On Poisson laws for distributions of particles in space, *Ukrain. Mat.*, **A8,** 127–134.
28. Goldman, J. R. (1967). Stochastic point processes: limit theorems, *Ann. Math. Statist.*, **38,** 771–779.
29. Grigelionis, B. (1963). On the convergence of sums of random step processes to a Poisson process, *Teor. Veroyatnost. i Primenen.*, **8,** 189–194. (English translation in *Theory Prob. Appl.*, **8,** 177–182.)
30. Khinchin, A. Y. (1956b). On Poisson streams of random events, *Teor. Veroyatnost. i Primenen.*, **1,** 320–327. (English translation in *Theory Prob. Appl.*, **1,** 291–297.)
31. Lee, P. M. (1968). Some examples of infinitely divisible point processes, *Studia Sci. Math. Hung.*, **3,** 219–224.
32. McFadden, J. A. (1962). On the lengths of intervals in a stationary point process, *J. Roy Statist. Soc.*, **B24,** 364–382. Corrigenda, *J. Roy. Statist. Soc.*, **B25,** 500.
33. Neveu, J. (1968). Sur la structure des processus ponctuels stationnaires, *Compt. Rend. Acad. Sci. Paris,* **A267,** A561–A564.
34. Renyi, A. (1956). A characterization of Poisson processes, *Magyar Tud. Akad. Mat. Kutato Int. Közl.*, **1,** 519–527.
35. Bremaud, P. (1972). A martingale approach to point processes, *ERL Memo M345,* University of California, Berkeley, Calif., Aug.
36. ______ (1973). Filtrage d'un signal markovien modulant un processus ponctuel et les équations approchées, 4-ème Colloque sur le Traitement du Signal et ses Applications, Nice.
37. Clark, J. R. (1971). Estimation for Poisson processes with applications in optical communications, Ph.D. Thesis, MIT, Sept.
38. Davis, M. H. A. (1973). Detection of signals modulating the rate of a point process, IEEE Int. Symp. Inform. Theory, Ashkelon, Israel, June.
39. ______ (1973). Detection of signals with point process observations, *Publ. 73/8,* Dept. Computing and Control, Imperial College, London.
40. Papangelou, F. (1972). Integrability of expected increments of point processes and a related change of scale, *Trans. Amer. Math. Soc.*, **165,** Mar.
41. Reiffen, B., and Sherman, H. (1963). An optimum demodulator for Poisson processes: photon source detectors, *Proc. IEEE,* **51,** 1316–1320.
42. Van Schuppen, J. H., and Wong, E. (1973). Transformation of local martingales under a change of law, *Memo ERL-M385,* University of California, Berkeley, Calif., May.
43. Yashin, A. I. (1970). Filtering of jump processes, *Avtomat. i Telemeh.*, **5,** 52–58.

# Author Citation Index

# Subject Index